Reconstructing Democracy

Grassroots Black Politics in the Deep South after the Civil War

JUSTIN BEHREND

The University of Georgia Press   *Athens*

Paperback edition, 2017
© 2015 by the University of Georgia Press
Athens, Georgia 30602
www.ugapress.org
Set in Minion Pro by Graphic Composition, inc.

Most university of Georgia Press titles are
available from popular e-book vendors.

Printed digitally

The Library of Congress has cataloged the
hardcover edition of this book as follows:
Behrend, Justin, 1972–
Reconstructing democracy ; grassroots Black politics in
the deep South after the Civil War / Justin Behrend.
xi, 355 pages, 6 unnumbered pages of plates :
illustrations, map, portrait ; 24 cm
Includes bibliographical references and index.
ISBN-13: 978-0-8203-4033-3 (hardcover : alk. paper)
ISBN-10: 0-8203-4033-2 (hardcover : alk. paper)
1. African Americans—Mississippi—Natchez (District)—
Politics and government—19th century. 2. Freedmen—
Mississippi—Natchez (District)—History—19th century.
3. Reconstruction (U.S. history, 1865–1877)—Mississippi—
Natchez (District) Democracy—Mississippi—Natchez (District)—
History—19th century. 4. Natchez (Miss. : District)—
Politics and government—19th century. 5. Natchez (Miss. : District)—
Race relations—History—19th century. I. Title.
F349.N2 B34 2014
305.896'073076226—dc23
2014008626

Paperback ISBN 978-0-8203-5142-1

FOR MARIA, ZACHARY, AND MAYA

CONTENTS

ACKNOWLEDGMENTS

I owe a great deal of gratitude to a number of institutions and individuals who saw the value in this book and helped to see it to completion. Northwestern University, where this project began as a dissertation, provided essential funds for research and writing. A Faculty Grant from Mount Holyoke College, a Presidential Summer Fellowship from SUNY Geneseo, and additional grants from Geneseo's Research Council offered important resources to transform my dissertation into a book. I also wish to thank the librarians and archivists at the Northwestern University Library; the National Archives, Washington, D.C., and College Park; the Mississippi Department of Archives and History; the Hill Memorial Library at Louisiana State University; the Historic Natchez Foundation; the Moorland-Spingarn Research Center, Howard University; the Center for American History, University of Texas at Austin; the Rutherford B. Hayes Presidential Center; and Milne Library, SUNY Geneseo, who helped me to locate relevant primary sources. I especially wish to thank Anne Webster at the Mississippi Department of Archives and History and Mimi Miller at the Historic Natchez Foundation for making me feel at home in their respective archives.

Although I didn't know it at the time, the seeds for this project were first planted in Ron Davis's graduate seminar on the U.S. South at California State University, Northridge. He introduced me not only to Natchez but also to the problems and debates of southern history. It has been fourteen years since I was a student at CSUN, yet Ron has been a continual source of guidance and encouragement. At Northwestern I benefited immensely from great faculty and a supportive cohort of graduate students. Steven Hahn, Stephanie McCurry, Dylan Penningroth, Darlene Clark Hine, and Kate Masur not only guided my dissertation toward completion but also gave me cogent advice in developing this book. I couldn't have made it through the PhD program without friendship and support from Aaron Astor, David Brodnax, Katherine Burns-Howard, Debs Cane, Mike Crane, Greg Downs, Carole Emberton, Erik Gellman, Erik Mathison, Shuji Otsuka, Jarod Roll, Tobin Shearer, David Sellers Smith, Owen Stanwood, Rhiannon Stephens, Erik Taylor, and Dana Weiner.

Over the years, I've had the opportunity to test out my ideas at conferences and other forums. The criticism and advice that I received has been invaluable to this project and my own development as a scholar. I'd like to thank Aaron Astor, David Blight, Elsa Barkley Brown, Joan Cashin, Greg Downs, Walter Johnson, Anthony Kaye, Brian Kelly, Alison Parker, Susan O'Donovan, Jarod Roll, Andrew Slap, Frank Towers, Stephen Tuck, and Elizabeth Varon. In addition, Cathy Adams, Emilye Crosby, Kathy Mapes, Michael Oberg, and Helena Waddy provided important commentary on individual chapters and other components of the book. Most especially, I'd like to thank Steven Hahn, who has provided just the right amount of encouragement and counsel both in my scholarship and in my career. I couldn't have asked for a better mentor.

I've also had the good fortune to work with individuals who have made life in academia a rewarding experience. Lynda Morgan welcomed me with open arms at Mount Holyoke and has been a friend ever since. At Geneseo I had the luck to join a strong cadre of remarkable teacher-scholars in the History Department. Each has taught me important lessons about how to balance scholarship with teaching. My thanks to Cathy Adams, Bill Cook, Joe Cope, Emily Crosby, Bill Gohlman, Tze-ki Hon, Jordan Kleiman, Jennifer Lofkrantz, Kathy Mapes, Michael Oberg, Barb Rex-McKinney, Meg Stolee, David Tamarin, Helena Waddy, and Jim Williams. At Milne Library, Sue Ann Brainard and Corey Ha have cheered on my work and provided crucial support. I've also been lucky to work with some amazingly smart and talented students at Geneseo. I'd especially like to thank Katie Smart and Davis Parker for helping me collect newspaper articles. And I'd like to thank Cory Young for helping me set up this book's companion website of biographical data on black politicians.

I'm grateful to the talented folks at the University of Georgia Press. Derek Krissoff took a chance on this project and helped to shepherd it through its initial stages before he moved on to another press. Beth Snead filled in nicely and answered many questions from an inexperienced author. I'm also thankful to Mick Gusinde-Duffy and Jon Davies for their assistance. And I'm especially grateful to Susan O'Donovan and an anonymous reader for their incisive critiques.

Finally, this book could not have been finished without support from my family. My parents, Jean and Nelson Behrend, have never failed to show their love, and their timely assistance, especially during the lean years of graduate school, has been most welcome. I also wish to thank my in-laws, Michael and Patricia Simpson, for their unflinching encouragement. And thanks to my siblings and extended family, Hannah, Jeff, Micah, Georgia, Josh, Jen, Nate, Scot, and Toni, for all the fun on family trips and at biannual gatherings.

But it is to my immediate family that I owe my greatest debt of gratitude. Maya came along about the time when I began to turn attention to this book, and so she has been a marker of how long it has taken me to finish it. Fortunately, her gleeful smile has a way of helping me to remember more important things. Zachary is now ten years old and is just beginning to understand what I write about. I'm grateful for his many interruptions and for dragging me away from the computer to build Legos or play in the yard. Above all, it is Maria to whom I am most appreciative. She has shared this journey with me and still loves me for it. I couldn't have done it without her. And so it is with all my love and thanks that I dedicate this book to her and our children.

Reconstructing Democracy

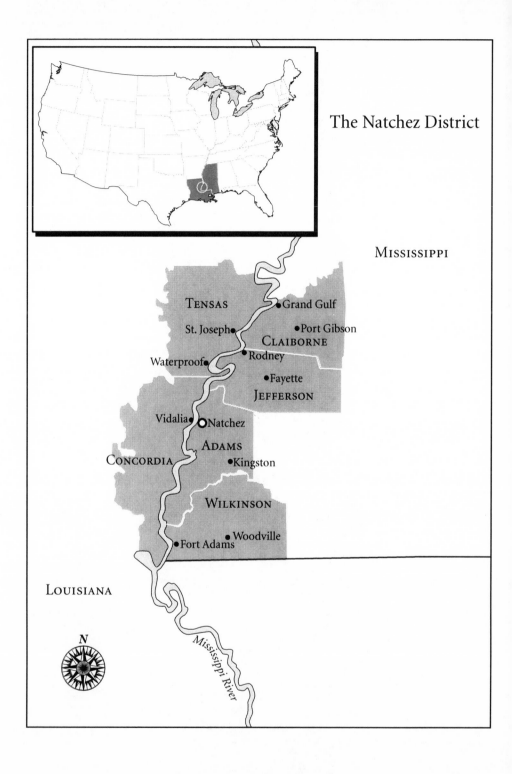

The Natchez District

MISSISSIPPI

TENSAS
•Grand Gulf
St. Joseph•
•Port Gibson
CLAIBORNE
Waterproof•
•Rodney
•Fayette
JEFFERSON
Vidalia• ○Natchez
ADAMS
CONCORDIA
•Kingston
WILKINSON
•Woodville
•Fort Adams
LOUISIANA
N
Mississippi River

"Wise in Time"

In the spring of 1874, journalist Edward King visited the vast cotton districts of the lower Mississippi River valley. He was on a tour of the "Great South" to see how the region had changed since the Civil War. When King landed at Natchez, he was smitten, like so many visitors, by the beauty of the small city on the bluffs. It was, he wrote, "a quiet, unostentatious, beautifully shaded town" with the "cheeriest of people." After surveying the social and economic life of the city, King took a ferry across the river to the small town of Vidalia, the seat of Concordia Parish. There he attended a parish jury meeting (equivalent to a county board of supervisors) and was struck by the fact that most of the members were black men. He was even more interested in "Mr. David Young, a coal black man" and a member of the Louisiana legislature.[1]

David Young was born into slavery in Kentucky on February 4, 1836. About fourteen years later, he ran away and escaped to the free state of Ohio before he was recaptured. As punishment, he was, in 1850, sold down the river to Natchez, Mississippi, then the second-largest slave market in the South. The teenage boy was then purchased by a Louisiana planter and moved to Concordia, eighteen years before he was to represent the parish as a legislator in the state House. It is unclear how the Civil War specifically affected Young or when he was emancipated. An 1875 profile in the *Weekly Louisianian* described him as a "natural leader and advocate of the newly obtained rights of his people." He was "a large and finely developed man, about six feet in hight [*sic*]" and "self-educated, of acute perception and vigorous intellect." Young became involved in Republican politics as early as 1868, but he also endeavored to become a landowner and a farm operator. By the time King met Young, the former slave owned multiple town properties and leased at least four plantations. In addition, he operated a grocery store, presided over a Baptist church on Third Street in Vidalia, was the editor and publisher of the *Concordia Eagle* newspaper, was the treasurer of the parish school board, and was in his sixth year as a state representative. There was, in short, no more influential figure in Concordia Parish in 1874 than David Young.[2]

The accomplishments of David Young illustrate the remarkable transformation that took place in the South after emancipation and the enfranchisement of black men. But Young's story—his rise to power as a self-made man—did not interest Edward King. Rather, King was captivated by an encounter between Young and several other black residents of Concordia Parish. Young was speaking to "a row of his fellow-citizens, who were seated upon a fence," trying to convince them to vote for his reform ticket in the upcoming election. "Brandishing his ballots," King wrote, "he warned the listeners to vote for honest representatives." But one of the men shot back, "I am going to vote to suit myself. Dave Young or any other man will not tell me anything about my vote." The comment was, on the one hand, rather unremarkable—little more than an expression of political independence. But on the other hand, the exchange was a rather extraordinary illumination of the political revolution that was remaking the South.[3]

The setting of this political discussion—a small town in the midst of vast cotton plantations—hardly brings to mind one of the places where democracy originated. We often think of democracy emerging from the Greek polis or an eighteenth-century European coffeehouse or a New England town hall, yet here in the Deep South was another display of democracy in the making. It was an open and public debate between citizens and an elected representative. And the substance of their discussion addressed competing philosophies of democratic governance. Young presciently warned that, in the words of Edward King, "northern sentiment was beginning to rebel against the misrule at the South." Speaking six months after the Panic of 1873 had begun to shutter businesses in northern cities and in the midst of a racist backlash against black politics in the South, Young could sense that advocates of Radical Reconstruction would soon be on the defensive. He argued that black voters "must be 'wise in time'" and select candidates not for their radical politics but for their commitment to "fair government." For David Young, voters needed to recognize the national implication of their selections and understand that events in Washington, D.C., were inextricably linked to life in Concordia Parish.[4]

But Young's constituents were unconvinced, in large part, because they held a different vision of democracy. For them and for many ordinary ex-slaves, what mattered most in selecting a representative was which candidate best embodied the values of their community. In Concordia, the county with the highest percentage of black people in the nation (at 93 percent), nearly all of whom had once been enslaved, those values were quite radical. Most constituents believed in free and public schools, in a progressive tax system that fell more heavily on the landed elite, in state support for economic development (particularly in railroad investment), in strong civil rights legislation, and in federal protection for voters. And so they were not concerned that the candidate who best embraced this social and political vision happened to be a white carpetbagger with a reputation for corruption.[5]

The election produced mixed results. David Young was elected to the state senate, yet the Democratic candidate for Congress, whom Young endorsed as part of a reform ticket, went down in defeat. We cannot know what would have happened if voters had followed Young's advice, but this one election likely would not have altered the fate of the Natchez District or interrupted the ultimate downfall of Reconstruction. The importance of Young's debate with his black neighbors lies not in the electoral verdict but in the social context that it reveals. The promise of democracy is that a public airing and a vigorous discussion between citizens and officials offers a better chance of solving difficult problems. And so the choice that these men made is less significant than the environment that they had created to make such a choice possible. They had to be "wise in time," not just in 1874 but also in the years before and after emancipation as they sought to transform a slave society into a democratic society and then later to withstand the backlash of white supremacist violence.

In general the political history of freedpeople has not received the attention that it deserves. A prior generation of scholarship focused on two distinct yet related fields of study: the transition from slave to free labor and the demise of Reconstruction. Although studies on the impact of capitalism on social relations and on party politics during the Civil War era did not necessarily intersect, they combined to create a narrative of oppression that spanned from slavery to segregation. By emphasizing the continuities in freedpeople's abject material status, they downplayed their political achievements. In recent years, historians have breathed new life into the field. Emancipation historians have demonstrated how freedpeople mobilized collectively to seek better terms of labor and how these mobilizations served as building blocks for ventures into the official arena of politics. Others have expanded the notion of the political and shown how households and kin networks contributed to freedpeople's growing political power during Reconstruction. And yet we still know comparatively little about how African Americans participated in the primary arena of public contestations—party and electoral politics. We also know little about why ordinary white men participated in elections, which only further compels a question: how was it possible that a group of mostly illiterate people with no prior experience in electoral politics, few economic resources, and insignificant social standing were able to create a sweeping political movement that transformed the South?[6]

Few consider the remarkable fact, for example, that virtually all black people identified with the Republican Party, leaving the impression that racial solidarity was an automatic corollary to emancipation and that black support for the Republican Party was inevitable. But black people had a choice. They were not predestined to become Republicans, nor was it at all likely in 1867 (or 1865) that former slaves would create a powerful political bloc and take control of political offices at all levels of government. To emphasize this choice, I highlight an alternative option—the forging of patron-client relationships with powerful whites. What needs explaining, then, is how most freedpeople in the American South rejected patron-client relations and instead made the conceptual leap of believing that protection and opportunity could arise from a broad-based community of poor people, linked with a distant and nebulous power in the nation's capital.

Beyond the political history of freedpeople after emancipation, the subject of democracy formation at the grassroots level has received little attention. To be sure, many works have explored the development of the party system and nineteenth-century voting patterns, yet in their quest to study average voters in average elections, political historians have found little room in their frameworks for African American politics. Indeed, many studies conclude their examination of the rise of American democracy with the Civil War. While the war did expose fundamental flaws in the nation's democracy, it also provided the seeds for the subsequent blooming of a new form of grassroots democracy, one that began with the experiences of black people under bondage. Not only have political historians avoided one of the most significant political struggles in American history but they have also left unasked seminal questions about how citizens develop a political consciousness and how and why ordinary people practiced politics.[7]

To explore the way that democracy takes root, I've endeavored to examine the political history of freedpeople. Emancipation offers a unique starting point from which to examine how political ideologies take root, how political movements are mobilized, how leaders are selected, and how politics becomes integrated into day-to-day practices. Democracy, most obviously, is the process by which the people vote and elect their leaders. But more fundamentally, democracy is a social system in which citizens participate in an ordered society and contribute openly to debates on public policy and social values. Given this, the major task of democratization was not necessarily the extension of suffrage rights but the creation of a democratic ethos that would enable voting to take place. Thus this book is not a typical political history. While voting and elections play a central role, they form a backdrop to the perceptions, experiences, and debates that ordinary freedpeople engaged in.[8]

The Natchez District is an ideal place to examine the rise and fall of democracy after the Civil War. Like all particular localities, the Natchez District was both distinctive and representative. It consisted of four Mississippi counties (Claiborne, Jefferson, Adams, and Wilkinson) and two Louisiana parishes (Tensas and Concordia) in the lower Mississippi River valley. Perhaps the most defining features of the district were the vast cotton plantations and the tens of thousands of black people who worked the fields as slaves and, later, as free farmers and laborers. That the Natchez District would become the preeminent center for cotton production in the world owed much to the geographical landscape. Bisecting the district was the Mississippi River. The overflow from the river's seasonal floods spread nutrient-rich silt across the Louisiana bottomlands, which attracted scores of planters, slaveholders, and fortune-seekers. But even on the Mississippi side, though spared from floods due to its elevation, the brown loam soil produced abundant returns. Large plantations extended out from the banks of the Mississippi River and thousands of slaves were imported into the region to coax the fibrous cotton boll from the ground. In 1860, 82 percent of the population was of African descent and in the plantation hinterlands blacks outnumbered whites ten to one. In other words, the Natchez District was a major slaveholding region and home to one of the greatest concentrations of black people in the South, comparable in many ways to the Mississippi Delta, the Louisiana sugar bowl, and the South Carolina and Georgia low country.[9]

At the center of this vast region of cotton plantations was the small city of Natchez. It was a major commercial hub for river transportation and the cotton economy and the largest urban area within one hundred miles. Although it had fewer than seven thousand residents in 1860, the city boasted the second-largest slave market in the South, a substantial river port, a commercial district that included a market square, numerous merchant stores, and even a few manufacturing shops. Wealthy planters lived in stately homes from which they supervised plantations throughout the district. Another feature that set Natchez apart from the surrounding countryside was the sizeable free black population—the largest in the state of Mississippi. Although vastly outnumbered by slaves, the two-hundred-plus free black residents would play a large role in the postemancipation era. Their wealth, educational attainments, and interpersonal relationships with white people gave them disproportionate influence in political and social struggles. Put briefly, Natchez, sitting along the most important waterway in the nation, dominated the social, economic, and political life of the region.[10]

Beyond its demography and geography, the Natchez District is an ideal place to study democracy because of the powerful coalition of white and black Republicans that emerged there during Reconstruction. As they gained partisan experience, African Americans moved into an assortment of political positions, ranging from constable, alderman, and circuit clerk to more influential posts such as mayor and state legislator. I've identified over four hundred black men who held political office or party leadership positions in these six counties, including ten different black men who served as sheriff—perhaps the most powerful local office in nineteenth-century America, since it was vested with taxing, judicial, and law-enforcement authority. National political figures such as Hiram Revels, the first black man to serve in the U.S. Senate, and John R. Lynch, a three-term, ex-slave congressman, hailed from the region. Additionally, the Natchez District was one of only four districts in the South to elect a black congressman after the end of Reconstruction. Because of the remarkable political success of former slaves in the Natchez District in unseating their former masters and establishing a grassroots democracy, this region offers an excellent place to analyze how freedpeople came together and took power.[11]

In addition, focusing on a district crisscrossed by governmental and geographic boundaries offers the opportunity to explore how political networks spread across borders and to identify how ordinary citizens conceived of and created allegiances and communities. Historians have evaluated urban-based politics and rural politics, but few studies address the relationship between rural and urban people in the process of political mobilization. Analyzing politics at the intersection of rural and urban spaces exposes the class and regional differences that inhibited community development. Yet this framework also illuminates the symbiotic connections between political operations based in towns and cities and the mass of voters in the countryside. Freedpeople may have lived in the countryside or in an urban neighborhood, yet their lives were not confined to their domestic spaces. It is imperative, then, to examine the fluidity between the rural and urban in order to fully understand the lives of these people.

The story of freedpeople creating a democracy might not seem particularly new or novel. After all, a democratic republic had been established in America nearly one hundred years before Reconstruction and the antecedents of democracy date back to the premodern and ancient world. But all too often our perception of democracy is limited to nation-states and elections. At its core, democracy is an expression of the people's sovereignty, yet time and again only certain people have been considered "the people" in terms of governance. The United States had a democratic government before the Civil War, and in the Natchez District elections took place at regular intervals. But as little as 5 percent of the population in the Natchez District elected governmental leaders, most of whom were slaveholders. The political system was more characteristic of an oligarchy than a democracy. By contrast, after emancipation former slaves created radical political structures that were truly grassroots and that incorporated the voices and interests of the laboring classes in unprecedented ways. Women and men, blacks and whites, field hands and planters all had a role in the expansive politics of Reconstruction. Likewise, in the institutions and organizations that arose after emancipation freedpeople practiced shared governance and broad participation. In a culture dominated by white supremacist thinking, this radically new democracy upended prevailing assumptions and gave people of color unprecedented opportunities for political engagement and advancement.[12]

Reconstructing Democracy is the story of how freedpeople in the Natchez District created a new, grassroots democracy. It argues that democracy can be at once transformative and precarious. Out of the ashes of the Confederacy—the most antidemocratic republic in modern history—freedpeople set up a political system rooted in egalitarian values, wherein local communities rather than powerful individuals held power and ordinary people exercised unprecedented influence in governance. The making of democracy was a complicated and contentious process, yet freedpeople rapidly created a surprisingly strong partisan framework that gave them a sense of belonging, purpose, and protection. By elevating ex-slaves to political offices, they upended prevailing racial, class, and gender hierarchies that had come to define southern life. Although this grassroots democracy rested on the exclusion of women from formal political power, it incorporated their voices and participation to a greater degree than ever before. Freedwomen took part in numerous partisan gatherings, and party leaders relied on their advocacy to ensure a solid Republican vote.[13]

The value of a political framework such as the one used in this study is that it can account for the internal struggles and divisions that lay at the heart of any democratic movement. Freedpeople were not of one mind, even if they did move in one direction. They had to learn to trust like-minded people beyond their neighborhoods. Their experiment in biracial, democratic rule could work only if they acted together. But they also had to trust outsiders, particularly white northerners. One of the paradoxes of democracy is that it demands solidarity and collective action from the very same people who are empowered as individuals by their elevated role. The tension between conformity and autonomy lends a degree of instability to the practice of democracy.[14]

Although long venerated as the preeminent political system, democracy has had many detractors. One of the greatest challenges that freedpeople faced was to convince local whites to trust their power and authority. Just a few short years after the Confederate nation came into being—founded on the principle that black slavery was a divinely sanctioned institution that made white civilization possible—black people asked Natchez District whites to recognize their legitimacy as elected officials. The fact that many former Confederates came to accept Republican governance demonstrates the unexpected success of freedpeople's democracy. But in this success lay its downfall. More than anything else, black people's embrace of the democratic ethos provoked a violent backlash in the Natchez District. Many whites could not brook former slaves following the logic of democracy in its diffusion of power among the landless and its incorporation of the voices of ordinary women and men in partisan politics. The white paramilitary groups and terrorists that overthrew Reconstruction were motivated not just by identity (race and party) but by the fact that a formerly enslaved and landless people had created a vibrant system of biracial governance with broad participation. Drawing attention to the particulars of local political history reveals the deep strain of antidemocratic practices that lies at the heart of the American experience.

Freedpeople's effort to establish the legitimacy of democratic rule is not merely a southern story; it is an American one. The struggle among ex-slaves in the Natchez District paralleled other struggles in nineteenth-century America among workers in industrializing cities. The quest to establish an ethos of diffused and shared power among the citizenry animated many violent clashes. It is a quest that remains both promising and elusive.[15]

This book is divided into three sections. Part 1, "Constructing Democracy," begins with the Civil War and the various moments of emancipation in order to understand how ex-slaves confronted a new world of freedom. The powers of the Confederacy and the Union gave slaves and free blacks a sense of the possibilities as well as the perils of living in an emancipated society. Once freed, they utilized social networks formed while under bondage in order to establish churches, schools, and labor associations that would become the foundation for a new democratic polity. This nascent civil society helps to account for the stunning electoral results of 1867 and 1868, when black voters swept away the existing hierarchical system of governance and established a new blueprint for an egalitarian-minded society.

Part 2, "Maintaining Democracy," examines the process by which Republicans created a new party system and filled offices with new people. By opening up the body politic to all residents and establishing practices that incorporated disparate voices, freedpeople created a political system that tended toward instability. Dissenters from within (such as moderate Republicans) and opponents from without (such as black Democrats) pressed at the boundaries of the body politic, forcing its members to contend with an array of factional challenges. Nevertheless, ordinary freedpeople consolidated their power and their elected leaders reshaped the social order by creating a public education system, lessening the tax burden on the laboring classes, establishing a more equitable judicial system, and opening public institutions and spaces to all people.

Because freedpeople's successful governance aimed at the needs of the majority, not the few, white Democrats resorted to terroristic violence as the only means to unseat their elected representatives. This is the subject of part 3, "Constricting Democracy." Taking advantage of a national mood that had soured on suffrage and civil rights, white supremacist Democrats drew the color line and attacked the heart of black politics, killing key leaders, driving families into the woods, and purging the electoral system of those dedicated to equality and the diffusion of power at the grass roots. Five of the six counties in the Natchez District succumbed to this electoral violence, but even in Adams County, where violence did not prevail, democracy was severely circumscribed. Although black and white Republicans continued to hold certain local offices and were free to vote, the influence of grassroots voices was narrowed as party brokers dispersed offices, sidestepping the vibrant neighborhood clubs that had once been the basis of democratic rule. By 1890, the year when state leaders began to legally drive black men from the electoral arena, democracy had fallen, replaced by a version of the oligarchic system that preceded emancipation and one that laid the foundation for Jim Crow rule.

To better understand the rise and fall of democracy, I have focused on a few key individuals. Their stories, interspersed throughout the book, help to anchor the revolutionary changes in the Civil War era to the lived experiences of those who helped to enact these transformations. David Young is one. Another is James Page, who, like Young, was born enslaved and who rivaled Young in ambition. Page audaciously purchased his own freedom at auction four years before the Civil War and later almost single-handedly created a school system for black children in Claiborne County. After a successful career as an officeholder, Page was cut down viciously by white liners. Agnes Fitzhugh also had a brief run-in with white supremacists, but it did not impede her efforts to establish mutual aid societies in Natchez or to guide her family into unparalleled involvement in local politics. Another pivotal but unheralded figure was David Singleton. He never held office, but his financial support of black Republicans was essential for the elevation of black radicals to positions of power in Adams County. Perhaps the biggest beneficiary of Singleton's support was John R. Lynch, an incredibly gifted politician who rose from slavery to become a congressman. Episodes from Lynch's amazing career are recounted in each of the chapters because in many ways he embodied the promise of democracy and few fought harder to retain its inclusive features.[16]

These particular individuals are merely the most well known of the tens of thousands of freedpeople who made democracy a reality after emancipation.

The stories of most of the ordinary men and women who attended political meetings and became Republicans have been lost to history. But in the fragments of many hundreds of individual lives we can begin to see more clearly the freedmen who risked their livelihoods to march in a political parade, as well as the freedwomen who stormed the polling places to ensure a solid Republican vote. We can begin to see more clearly how freedpeople acted "wise in time."

PART ONE

Constructing Democracy

ONE

Into the Arms of Strangers

On a warm summer day in 1863, a passing Union gunboat attracted the attention of a group of slaves working on a road along the Mississippi River in Concordia Parish, Louisiana. When the sailors called out and asked the slaves "to come on board," four young men dropped their tools and immediately "went off with the Yankees." Fanny E. Conner, in reporting the incident to her husband, seemed shaken by the audacity of their slaves and the casual manner in which they walked away from bondage. Those four young men, John, William, Bill, and the son of Tom Gaillaird, chose a propitious moment to make their escape. One week earlier, Vicksburg had fallen to General Ulysses S. Grant's forces, opening up the Mississippi River to federal control and severing the backbone of the Confederacy. Three days after the slaves ran off, a Union occupying force landed at the city of Natchez, opposite Concordia Parish. Recognizing the changes that were about to upend the social order of the Natchez District, Fanny Conner ruefully noted, "This is the first of ours who have left us." But they were not the last. Over the coming weeks and months, thousands of slaves ran away from bondage in a stream of humanity that effectively destroyed the institution of slavery in the lower Mississippi River valley.[1]

The timing of the four slaves' escape, as well as the seeming ease with which they discarded the bonds of slavery, raises questions about slaves' understanding of the Civil War, the federal government, and freedom. Was their escape spontaneous, or did they wait until Union victory had been assured at Vicksburg? Did they know that boarding that gunboat would effectively free them? What did they think freedom would mean? In all likelihood, John, William, Bill, and Tom Gaillaird's son did not know the Union sailors on the boat, they had not seen armies marching through their neighborhood, and although they probably had heard stories of distant battles and had seen Yankee gunboats pass by, they took a big risk in putting their trust in unknown persons and an unfamiliar entity (the Union military). In other words, they left a world of bondage where face-to-face contact governed power relationships and jumped into the arms of strangers.[2]

To understand the intellectual leap that the four enslaved men made when they boarded the Union gunboats, we need first to examine the scope of slave life. Slaves forged numerous relationships with locals and other enslaved people that militated against the dehumanization inherent in the institution of slavery, but meaningful connections rarely extended beyond a small geographic area or beyond networks of face-to-face contact. To be sure, in certain spaces, such as cities and black-dominated plantation districts, slave communities extended beyond neighborhoods and neighboring plantations, and yet even in those regions slaves lived in severely circumscribed worlds. Slaves often viewed power as residing within individuals and the exercise of power as subject to impulsive and fickle personalities, which left little space for collective organizing or for participation in broader communities.[3]

The Civil War gave slaves an opportunity to expand their relationships beyond the local. Taking advantage of the opportunities unleashed by war, they leveraged their family and kin networks, encounters in the market, and religious congregations to shed the burdens of slavery and begin to establish new relationships with family, neighbors, employers, and governmental authorities. In uprisings, rebellions, and other forms of resistance, African Americans contributed to their own emancipation and the construction of a new nation. During the Civil War, former slaves drew on their experience under bondage to force government officials to confront emancipation and to define the slaves' new freedom. And yet in looking to the slave past, historians have tended to focus on physical acts of resistance instead of the intellectual work of developing a political consciousness.[4]

In ways that we have yet to fully recognize, the war politicized life for slaves and free blacks. The introduction of outside entities (nation-states) and new peoples (northern soldiers and missionaries) permanently altered the neighborhoods of slaves and free people of color. The creation of the Confederacy ushered in a new form of power that at once demonstrated that slaveholder authority was not total and that local events could have national repercussions. Under Confederate rule, survival depended on public silence and neutrality for slaves, and for local whites, their racial identity and class standing proved to be less influential than they had anticipated. At the same time, Union intervention broadened the world of slaves, in that the actions of the armies in the east and events in Washington and Richmond took on new meaning for their day-to-day lives. Ordinary freedpeople joined the struggle at home, transforming everyday acts—from running away from a master to offering a meal to a Yankee solider—into a diffuse yet collective project to defeat the Confederate nation and the slavocracy that undergirded its power. Whether they chose to enlist in the army, work for wages on a distant plantation, or just stay at home in the quarters, freedpeople redrew the lines that had once bounded their world, and they laid the foundation for a grassroots democracy.[5]

Subterranean Communications Networks

At first it seemed that the Confederate nation would not have much impact on the day-to-day lives of slaves and free blacks. Slaveholders and local authorities worked vigilantly to restrict black access to the outside world by investing near-complete authority for a slave's life in the owner's hands and by prohibiting slave access to education and printed materials. An enslaved person's survival depended primarily on the whims and prerogatives of the owner, and so official political events diminished in importance, be they at the county, state, or national level. Free blacks could travel and receive an education, but their relative independence was curtailed by discriminatory legislation and white suspicion. During the presidential campaign of 1860, however, slaves and free blacks sensed that something was different about Abraham Lincoln and the Republicans. When the southern states seceded and formed the Confederate nation—expressly designed to protect the right to slave property—slaves' position in society changed dramatically. No longer were they merely a laboring class; now they were the reason for the Confederacy's existence. With this shift, slaves and free blacks struggled to break out of their confined world and make sense of the distant conflict between two massive armies.[6]

On the eve of the Civil War, locally based social networks provided a foundation from which slaves could engage the outside world. In Natchez, it was a community of draymen that spread news and gossip across the city as they carried out their trade. Draymen (also referred to as hackmen and carriage drivers) hauled cotton bales to the docks, moved imported goods from the riverboats up the bluff to merchant stores, and transported people and goods within the city and to the countryside and back. Many were slaves who hired themselves out, but some were free blacks. As an integral component of a regional transportation infrastructure, they were uniquely positioned to acquire and spread information throughout the city and to the countryside and back, placing them at the center of an undetected communication network.[7]

Eager to learn any information about the progress of the Union army, draymen passed along war news gleaned from newspapers and from overheard conversations among white people. "I used to read the papers," recalled George Carter about life during the Civil War. Freeborn and educated, Carter worked for his father, a prominent drayman, and alongside many other draymen. According to testimony before the Southern Claims Commission (scc), Carter testified that whenever he got hold of newspapers, he would seek out Richard Dorsey, "a man to be trusted in respect to keeping silent about what I would say to him." Dorsey, a slave drayman, in turn, talked with James K. Hyman ("I often talked to him during the war about the fighting"), Randall Pollard, Lydia Gaines, and at least four other black people. Hyman discussed the war with four additional draymen, besides Dorsey and Carter, and three other black residents. Pollard, an enslaved Baptist minister, spoke with four others who eventually filed claims before the SCC. All told, at least 260 individuals were connected — through political conversations about the war and freedom — to each other in an extensive network.[8]

In Claiborne County, at least fifty-one black people were similarly connected in a web of relations that extended from the streets of Port Gibson to farms in the countryside. At the center of this network was James Page, a leader with an uncommon flair for enterprise and ambition. Although enslaved, he purchased his own freedom for $3,000 by outbidding the slave owners at a public auction at the door of the county courthouse in 1857. Trained as a blacksmith, he prospered rapidly, even before the war. He employed four or five workers at his shop, which he claimed grossed $4,000 annually. In addition, he operated a hack business, owned a six-mule team and a six-horse team, and during the war, rented a two-hundred-acre farm. Page discussed the Civil War with at least sixteen business associates and friends, including John Byrd, a friend for twenty-five years. Byrd, born free, owned a sizeable farm, which was plundered by Gen. U. S. Grant's forces in 1863 as they made their way to the state capital in Jackson. Given James Page's friendships, contacts, and business acumen, it is not surprising that he would later become the leading black political figure in Claiborne County, holding, at different times, positions on the board of police and board of selectmen, as well as serving as sheriff and county treasurer.[9]

Port Gibson and Natchez were primary hubs in an extensive black communication network that extended out to the hinterlands through conduits such as carriage drivers and house slaves. Thomas Turner, a mail and messenger slave for Francis Surget, an elite Adams County planter, "used to come over to our place often," recalled George Braxton, himself a drayman and a slave of Gabriel Shields. Braxton relied on his friend to supply him with information, gleaned from stray comments and private conversations among white people. "He told me once during the war that the Union soldiers were going to gain the day[,] that he heard his mistress say as much, and that if they did we would be free," testified Braxton. William Smoot, owned by the same slaveholder as Turner, disclosed that he would tell his friend Abner Pierce and others of "the news that I heard the white people talking about" when he made deliveries to Pierce's master, Alfred V. Davis. Smoot's access to the conversations of elite planters led him to deduce "that we would not be slaves very long" and then to spread that news among his fellow slaves.[10] Collectively, the masters of these enslaved draymen owned 1,551 slaves on plantations in Adams County, Wilkinson County, Concordia Parish, and Madison Parish. Coupled with the fact that Smoot and Turner traveled to more than one plantation in the course of their labors, it is not difficult to imagine how word of war and freedom could spread to thousands of slaves across hundreds of miles in the densely populated plantation districts along the Mississippi River.[11]

As sectional tensions came to a head and political leaders began to mobilize for war, national politics began to have more of a day-to-day impact on life in the Natchez District. Richard Stamps, a free man of color who had purchased his and his wife's freedom before the war, was probably like many when he admitted, "At the beginning of the war or rebellion I knew but little about the Union cause, or the cause of the Confederates." Concerned about events and ideas that were swirling around his neighborhood in Port Gibson, Stamps made inquiries "among my friends" and "found out which was which." "From that time," he told the scc investigators, "my whole sympathy was with the Cause of the Union."[12]

The political implications of the subterranean communications network did not go unnoticed by the region's slaveholders and governmental authorities. Word of the war and the implications of the struggle seeped into the Natchez District despite the best efforts of masters to keep their slaves ignorant. But with the Mississippi River—the most important transportation artery in the nation—running through the middle of the district, it was nearly impossible to suppress news of the 1860 election, President Lincoln, and the Union army. Draymen and free blacks, in particular, came under intense scrutiny during Confederate rule, forcing black residents to be even more mindful of their everyday interactions.[13]

Just before the war began, Isaac Hughes, a free black hackman, recalled discussing the growing tensions with David Singleton, also a former slave. Singleton may have been the wealthiest black man in the district, and he had unusual knowledge of the North. As a personal body servant to Alfred V. Davis, one of the largest slaveholders in the South, Singleton earned significant sums of money "by waiting on" the Natchez nabobs and other wealthy whites at "balls and part[ies]." When he became free in 1854, he estimated that he had saved "seventeen to eighteen thousand dollars," an astounding (and improbable) sum for a black man in that era. Most important, he had enough money to purchase himself, his wife, and his children from bondage, as well as buy a new home in the North. He retained his business as a livestock dealer in Natchez, but Singleton moved his family to a village just outside of Cincinnati, "so that my children could be educated" in a free state. (In the late 1850s Cincinnati had three free schools for colored children, and black men could vote for the colored Board of Education.)[14]

Based on his experience in Ohio, Singleton explained to Isaac Hughes and other friends that the Union would be better for black people, even for free black men. He told Alex Carter, a black farmer, "that the colored men up North were treated right and that the people respected them up there." In conversation with Hughes, Singleton predicted that the South would start a war with the North, and "if the South did begin the war, it was for the purpose of keeping us slaves and to build a rich man[']s government to do as they pleased." Fearing such a prospect and taking into account comments from white folks that "if there would be a war they would force all free negroes to help them by making them cook for the army and doing other service for the army," Singleton left Natchez for Ohio a few days after the attack on Fort Sumter. His escape to the North demonstrates the growing concern among black people (slave and free) that distant events might soon have profound local implications.[15]

Confederate officials did not impress many free blacks into service as cooks, although they did impress some to build military fortifications. Confederate authorities impressed Adams County slaves to build fortifications at Port Hudson, Louisiana. More important, Confederate leaders did not allow black people to go on living as they had before the war. Just as runaways could not expect unquestioned assistance from people of similar race or class, slaves and free blacks had to be mindful during the war of what they said around other black people. Living under a cloud of suspicion prompted many to take stock of their friends and consider who could be trusted. "In these times a man had to be mighty shy as to who he trusted," explained one slave drayman. To emphasize the point, he repeated that there were only "some black people whom I could trust." Another slave said that he and his longtime friend would discuss the war only "in the presence of other colored men who were true." Plantation slaves had even more reason to be cautious with what they said and in whose company they said it because some slaves acted as surreptitious informants for their masters "in order to make it easy on themselves." In an environment of personal domination, where the master's word was treated as law, obstacles to racial, class, and community solidarity abounded.[16]

Personal friendships and close-knit neighborhoods, however, helped slaves and free blacks to make sense of the war. Richard Dorsey and James Hyman's friendship dated to the early 1850s, growing closer over time as they rode the streets of Natchez in their carts. When they talked about the war and the Union, they made sure that they were "always alone." Likewise, Hyman and Israel Jones, a hired slave carpenter, conversed only in private and in "whisper[s]" about how the Union army was "getting ahead." Hyman also "talked together very often" with William Jones, his neighbor and fellow drayman, "about the war." Richard Dorsey lived only four hundred yards from Jones, whom he considered "the best of friends," and they "talked frequently about the War." Similarly, in Claiborne County Richard Stamps, a free drayman, lived down the road from Henderson Moore, a free drayman and farmer and a friend for thirty years. "If I heard of a battle or he did, wherein the Union troops had been successful we were always seen to get together and have our own little rejoicing over it," recollected Stamps. He undoubtedly passed on this information to James Page, a friend since 1840, with whom Stamps met "3 or 4 times a week" to discuss "the war[,] its causes and progress." In spite of Confederate prohibitions restricting the gathering of black people in public, these black draymen passed information through an underground network linked by person-to-person contact.[17]

The fluidity of the information channels owed in part to the fact that this communications network not only drew on commercial contacts in public spaces but utilized family and kin connections to spread news far beyond individual neighborhoods. Washington Jefferson, a carriage driver, "had many conversations" with the entire Gideon Lucas family, including "ladies," in which they would discuss their "opinions" on the "Union troops." Likewise, Lewis Thompson, another slave carriage driver, discussed the prospect of Union soldiers landing in Natchez with John and Deborah Smith. Anthony Lewis, a slave in Claiborne County, met with his friends "during the night" and discussed how "the Yankees [were] fighting to free them." As a preacher, he quickly gained renown as "being in favor of the Union cause" among plantation slaves in the neighborhood. But as Lewis's reputation spread, word got back to local whites, at which point they dragged him into "the woods to shoot him or hang him." "He only escaped by disowning what they said he had talked of," explained his friend Clem Hardiman, a plantation slave.[18]

In these conversations, African Americans discussed the causes of the war, its implications for their future, and their conceptions of the Union. From the beginning, they believed that the war was about "keep[ing] the colored people in slavery" and suppressing black people in general. John Holdman spoke for many slaves when he announced his sympathy for "the Cause of the Union because . . . I thought that if the Union forces succeeded that I would receive my freedom." However, it was not at all clear in the early years of the war that the Union would win. Preparing for the worst, one freeborn man saved his money for a move to "Chilli [sic] in South America," just in case the Confederates won. But most believed that the North would defeat the South, hoping, as one black hackman put it, that "the Rebels would be whipped so bad that Gabriels trumpet would not resurrect them." Still others, particularly free blacks, sensed a larger meaning in the Civil War, viewing the Union army's effort as part of a greater project "destined to free our race." "The Cause," to their minds, had larger implications than simply the abolition of slavery. Union victory, James Page believed, "would be better for the Black people" because it would lead to equal treatment and an expansion of rights. George Carter hoped that with Confederate defeat "we could all speak out our minds freely." By framing the war as a struggle between slavery and freedom, African Americans in the Natchez District came to understand how their personal future was connected to the actions of armies hundreds of miles away. The local implications of this struggle, however, remained elusive as longtime residents and neighbors grappled with the intrusion of Confederate power.[19]

Rumors of Freedom and Confederate Repression

As much as slaves and free blacks tried to keep their true feelings to themselves during the Confederate occupation, "white people" reasoned, quite rightly, that black people "all desired the success of the Union forces," recalled one drayman. Putting it more bluntly, Levin Hooper, a black barber from Wilkinson County, boasted, "I would like to see the nigger that didn't want the Union to succeed." The problem that people of color faced was not in harboring sympathy for the Union; after all, slaves were rather adept at masking their true feelings, and most whites assumed that their sympathies lay with the North. Rather, they had to be especially mindful of how they acted and what they discussed in public. To an extent never before seen in the Natchez District, the war politicized everyday interactions among free blacks and slaves.[20]

In this highly charged atmosphere, rumors of impending freedom, outside agitators, and slave insurrections swirled around the Natchez District. Uncovering the "truth" in the rumors and tall tales is a near-impossible task; instead, the stories that circulated outside the channels of official discourse offer us a window into slaves' encounters with new forms of power, beyond their personal experience. Probing the rumors that gained a wide hearing reveals how slaves reconciled federal power, the promise of freedom, and the new authority of the Confederacy.[21]

Not long after the war broke out, Jefferson County slaveholders became suspicious of a network of slave carriage drivers, whom they accused of "forming plans about an insurrection" and spreading word "about Lincoln freeing the servants." Although "several Pistols and Knives" were uncovered in the subsequent investigation and a few slaves were questioned and jailed, conflicting testimony from the accused slaves failed to put to rest the rumors of murder and pillaging. Around the same time a planter in Tensas Parish, across the river from Jefferson County, uncovered a slave plot to join up with "Lincons [sic] troops" and slaughter the slave owners. "Being aware that the negros [sic] all knew of the war and what it was for," the planter hid underneath his house and overheard his slaves set the launch date for their revolt on "the 4th of July," choosing the celebration of national independence to coincide with their own "freeing." In response, Tensas Parish whites executed one slave and detained another. Similarly, Jefferson County slaveholders executed at least four slaves and whipped and jailed many more, but the punishments did little to dampen the aspirations of the region's slaves, or to calm the fears of whites.[22]

During the period of Confederate rule, a particularly powerful rumor of emancipation and black empowerment made the rounds among rural slaves in Adams County. Three former slaves who had lived in Natchez during the Civil War recalled to Works Progress Administration (WPA) interviewers many years later a story about Abraham Lincoln visiting the region's plantations.[23] Despite the seventy intervening years between the events alleged in the story and the recollections of them, there is good evidence to suggest that the story circulated in Natchez during the war, and not at a later time or in other locations. At the time of the WPA interviews, the three former slave men who recalled this story—Charlie Davenport, Bob Maynard, and J. T. Tims—lived in different states: Mississippi, Oklahoma, and Arkansas, respectively. The only time that these men lived in proximity to each other was in Natchez during the Civil War.[24]

In the story, Lincoln embraces emancipation only after personally observing the suffering of Adams County slaves. Bob Maynard insisted that Lincoln visited "our house" and that the soon-to-be president witnessed slaves receiving their meager rations on Saturday as well as slaves being "whipped and sold." Likewise, Charlie Davenport claimed to have encountered Lincoln personally. "Abe Lincoln what called hisse'f a rail-splitter come here to talk wid us," recalled Davenport, "I so' hear'd him" talking about "us bein' his black brothers."[25]

As the three retellings of the story make clear, Lincoln went undetected by the white community. J. T. Tims remembered that in "the story I heard them tell," Lincoln "had guards with him but they didn't see 'em." "De marster didn' know nothin' 'bout it, 'cause it was sorta secret-lak," explained Davenport. And Maynard gleefully noted, "Didn't nobody know who he was." The secrecy of Lincoln's visit may have served to embolden slaves, inspiring hope that even though they lived in the Deep South the most powerful man in the nation knew of their sufferings. The story also invested Lincoln with a spiritual power that lent credibility to his rumored authority to override the earthly powers of slave owners. Maynard considered Lincoln "next to de Lawd," attaching to the president a divine purpose that comports with Davenport's description of Lincoln as "a-rantin' an' a-preachin'" through the countryside.[26]

Maynard's description of Lincoln's visit to his master's house emphasized further how slaves appropriated the mythical power of the president to undermine slaveholder authority. As it "was a custom to take strangers in and put them up for one night or longer," Maynard explained, his owners invited Lincoln, whom they did not recognize, into their house and let him sleep "in old Mistress' bed." Lincoln further violated the inner sanctum of this slave owner by carving his name, "A. Lincoln," in the top end of the bedstead to prove that he had visited the house. Upon his return to the North, he wrote a letter to "old Master," explaining that "he was going to have to free his slaves." By surreptitiously taking the place of the master in the mistress's bed, Lincoln displaced the authority of the slaveholder to decide the fate of his slaves and appropriated the power as his own, thereby becoming their intercessor. The story invested power in slaves' daily struggles and conflated these struggles with the struggles of the nation. Rumors and tales like this may have given solace to slaves as they bided their time, waiting for physical and spiritual deliverance. For others, the message of common cause in uniting lowly slaves with the powerful armies of the North may have empowered slaves to challenge their master's authority. "It sho' riled de Niggers up an' lots of 'em run away," claimed Davenport.[27]

The Lincoln story reveals much about how slaves struggled with new forms of power beyond the reach of slaveholders. Living in circumscribed worlds, enslaved people likely could make little sense of the rumor that Lincoln would free the slaves, since a distant man could not possibly understand their plight. If Lincoln could see for himself the brutalities of enslavement, however, then he might be willing to act on that personal knowledge. Similarly, investing Lincoln with spiritual authority would help explain how one man could supersede the authority of masters. Akin to the way European peasants constructed the power of distant rulers through rumors, the Lincoln story offered slaves a means to delegitimize their enslavement by appealing to an outside authority with more power than local slaveholders. For a population conversant in the power of personal domination, investing one individual, President Lincoln, with the power to emancipate helped to reconcile the new power of the nation-state.[28]

As stories of Lincoln's visit to Natchez were passed from slave to slave and from plantation to plantation, it is very likely that whites picked up on some of them. The Lincoln story fit into existing narratives that planters and slaveholders used to explain slave unruliness. Above all, they feared that abolitionists and outside agitators would slip into the Natchez District to rile up the slaves, since in their estimation slaves could not possibly rise up on their own. In the planter mind, there was no one worse than the "black Republican" Lincoln to contaminate the master-slave relationship. The Jefferson County and Tensas Parish slave conspiracies, as well as another one in Adams County, each involved rumors of whites assisting slave rebels.[29]

In the early fall of 1861, Adams County slave owners uncovered what they believed to be a massive slave conspiracy: a plan to kill masters, rape white women, and set fire to the city of Natchez. A vigilance committee initially rounded up nearly two dozen slaves from the Second Creek neighborhood ten miles southeast of Natchez, brought them to a horse-racing track at the county fairgrounds just outside of the city, and subjected them to a quasi-judicial proceeding. Little is known about the proceedings of the committee, but cryptic notes taken by the Lemuel P. Conner, "President of the Vigilance Committee," have survived. The notes, which record only the answers to questions posed by the committee, emphasize the destructive and deviant intentions of the slave rebels, while remaining noticeably silent on the organizational details of the plot. The indeterminacy of the plans is yet another indication of how slaves struggled to understand the outside forces that were increasingly shaping life in the Natchez District.[30]

Analyzed another way, the Conner transcript reveals a slave neighborhood struggling to come to grips with the implications of war and trying to determine the intentions of President Lincoln. Instead of planning an imminent revolt, the slaves appeared to be waiting for the defeat of the Confederacy, and with defeat would come freedom for them and the opportunity for vengeful justice against their masters. The testimony refers to varying starting points for the revolt: "when Abolitionists come," "when the enemy took New Orleans," when Union forces landed in Natchez, and even "No time fixed." One observer of the inquisition, the planter William J. Minor, concluded in his diary that the slaves planned to "rise and kill their masters" and "take possession of the big house" after "the 'whipping' of the Southern people by the people of the North." Although the presumption was that Union forces would prevail, it was unclear to the slaves and the rest of southern society what would happen when "Capt. Lincoln was to set them free." The uncertainty of emancipation, Lincoln's plans, and the course of the war prompted local white leaders to interpret slave rumors as the makings of a massive slave insurrection. From this perspective, slaves' hopes for freedom were turned into a rebellious act. Wishing that the North would be victorious became a treasonous offense. Wanting to join up with the Union army was deemed revolutionary. And as we shall see, the slaves executed for the Second Creek conspiracy were only a portion of the black victims in a long Confederate campaign to stifle black underground networks and dissent.[31]

In testimony before the Southern Claims Commission, black witnesses rejected the vigilance committee's narrative that a rebellious plot was in the works. The lack of evidence of a conspiracy is not surprising, since most of the scc testimony came from urban black residents, not plantation slaves. Yet given the flow of information through the subterranean communication network, there should have been some indication of an insurrectionary plan if one had existed. Instead, witnesses frequently brought up the numerous executions of slaves. To a person, they charged that slaves were hanged for public expressions of Union sympathy, not for fomenting an insurrection.[32] And they tallied numbers far larger than those from planter sources. Although accounts differ as to the number executed—"some 25 or 30 people hung," "at least 50 or 60," "between 75 + 100 hung here," "a total of 209"—they collectively describe a concerted and widespread campaign during the years of Confederate occupation, 1861 to 1863, to stamp out black political discourse and assembly.[33]

Freedpeople blamed A. K. Farrar, the Confederate provost marshal at Natchez and an elite slaveholder, for the mass executions. "Farrar . . . did not think much of life," explained Richard Dorsey, the drayman; "there was a great many black people hung, and many of them were hung just as innocent as a baby, and a heap just on suspicion." At a time when the Confederacy was making increasing demands on white manpower, Farrar tried to forestall slave insubordination and slave runaways by drafting every white man with direct slave-management responsibilities (overseers and small planters) into a "police and patrol" unit. Farrar justified the committee's extralegal authority by noting that slaves were receiving, through newspapers and "oral communication[,] all intelligence respecting political disturbances," and he especially warned of "slaves" who came in "from the country with waggons" and congregated at Natchez stores. In addition, Farrar complained to the governor of Mississippi that "the negroes have such large liberties," owing to lax enforcement by some owners, and that slaves were "harbor[ing] runaways" and crisscrossing the countryside, stealing and killing stock. So to keep the edifice of slaveholder authority intact, Farrar brought hundreds of slaves and free blacks before the vigilance committee, jailed some, and killed dozens more, in what one contemporary called a "reign of terror." Quite against his intentions, however, these measures had the air of desperation and sent a signal to slaves and free blacks that there was some truth to the rumors that the imminent arrival of Lincoln's army would profoundly alter the political and social terrain of the district.[34]

In the context of rumors of armed slaves roaming throughout the hinterlands, northern agitators spreading stories of abolition, and Yankee armies closing in on the heart of the Deep South, public expressions of support for the Union cause or even acknowledgement of Union victories became tantamount to fostering a rebellion. Confederate authorities hung dozens of black men "at the fair grounds . . . as a warning to other colored people what they had to expect if they did not keep quiet," explained George Carter, a free black drayman. Every black person supported the Yankee forces, and "that is the reason so many were hung," reasoned one former slave. Other black men were accused of specifically colluding with the enemy, such as John Smith, a freeborn livery stable owner, who was detained by the vigilance committee because they said he gave "word to the Yankees." As was typical of the overblown proceedings, officials inflated tangential information to prove the existence of an extensive and well-planned conspiracy. Margaret Bush's enslaved husband was executed in 1862, she claimed, because "he could read and write." According to Laura S. Haviland, an abolitionist missionary who in 1864 investigated the fallout from the insurrectionary scare, "every thing that had occurred during a few years past . . . was magnified and construed as pointing toward a long settled purpose among the slaves to rise in insurrection."[35]

Encounters with Confederate authority introduced slaves and free blacks to a different form of power. Whereas before the war the authority of the master was preeminent, during the war Confederate military authorities undercut slave owners' prerogatives. Slaveholders Mary Dunbar and Joseph Reynolds, for instance, tried to bribe the committee for the release of their slaves, but to no avail. No longer did one person hold the preponderance of decision-making power over slave lives, and no longer would ownership suffice in determining the quality, extent, and limits of black lives. As the Union army drew closer, the cracks in white unity grew larger, exposing to slaves and free blacks the mortality of the slave regime and confirming the rumors that "Capt. Lincoln" was coming to whip the South and free the slaves.[36]

In an environment in which men and women were hanged "for talking too much," black people put a premium on relationships of trust. Since their lives depended on strict confidentiality, they forged strong networks of support that endured Confederate power and laid the groundwork for networks of solidarity that bolstered freedpeople's entry into the realm of formal politics. Far from stifling black people's aspirations for freedom, the hangings in Adams County and other forms of repression in the Natchez District emboldened these subjects of the Confederate nation to bide their time until the Yankees arrived. A slave drayman told his friend in the middle of the wave of hangings that "this thing could not continue," and he resolved "to make a full statement" once the Union troops arrived.[37]

Joining the Union Cause

J. T. Tims's parents had had enough. The plantation mistress had whipped young J. T. and his mother for no good reason, and when his father complained to their master, the slave owner grabbed the elder Tims's shoe hammer and beat him over the head with it. The next week the Tims family and a few others ran away from their plantation in Jefferson County, heading straight for the Mississippi River. Unable to secure passage on a federal gunboat because "the war was goin' on then," the runaways went "walking and wading" along the riverbank, evading hounds as they made their way to Natchez. It took the group a week to travel the twenty or so miles to Union lines and freedom. The Tims family was just one of thousands of slave families in the Natchez District that made the perilous decision to escape from bondage. With Union soldiers occupying

Natchez, Vicksburg, and other places, thousands of slaves flooded across the Union lines, turning army posts into "liberation zones."[38]

Union occupation introduced African Americans to a new world of freedom. In the urban outposts of federal occupation, newly freed slaves from across the Natchez District rubbed shoulders with thousands of other former slaves in the streets, in army barracks, and in contraband camps. For those who remained on plantations during the war, the rhythms of everyday life continued much as before, and yet, just like that of their urban counterparts, their world was expanded by the presence of Union military authorities. Thousands of freedmen joined the Union cause by enlisting in the army. Thousands of freedpeople worked for the U.S. military, labored on government-supervised farms, and devoted themselves in numerous small ways to advancing the cause, such as leading military officials to hidden Confederate cotton or giving a Yankee soldier a hot, home-cooked meal. Life in the cities and in the camps expanded freedpeople's horizons, offering them the possibility of seeing themselves as part of a broader community. These encounters with the Union gave freedpeople a sense that they were part of a much larger effort. Far from being cut adrift and floundering in a new world of emancipation, they recognized the stakes in the war and sided with a distant nation-state in opposition to the local white population that they knew best. Or, because they knew local white people so well, they joined up with the outsiders.

Only three days after taking the city of Natchez, Gen. Thomas E. G. Ransom complained that black people were "flock[ing] in by thousands." "On every road they came in crowds, mothers carrying their babes, with every size and age streaming along behind," remembered a white resident of Natchez. "The day of jubilee had come." The city surrendered without a fight, and with the white residents retreating to their homes, the black residents erupted in celebration. When Yankee soldiers told him that he was free, Abner Pierce said, "I fell on my knees and thanked God, and felt there after I had but two things to do—to be thankful to God and loyal to the Union." When Ben Lewis saw the blue-uniformed Yankees marching, he remembered that the slaves "jus' laughed an' laughed. Some of 'em even shouted out loud." Experiencing freedom for the first time, an elderly slave woman danced in the streets of Natchez "right lively" and grabbed "passing soldiers, hugging them, and making a tremendous ado over them."[39]

While slaves rejoiced in the streets of Natchez, their former owners contemplated a new and incomprehensible world in which some of the most mundane matters, like "how to get a breakfast," confounded even the most powerful of masters. Many a white family would bed down for the night and awaken to silence: "[A] deserted kitchen—no fire—no water all things cold and dark and dreary," wrote Annie Harper, a city resident. Their slaves had run away to Union lines in the night in a collective effort that made their escape swift and unde-tected. Slaveholders were awestruck by, on the one hand, the seeming spontane-ity of the slaves' escape and, on the other, their foreknowledge of Union soldiers' presence in the area. But slaves' "intuitive familiarity" with "the moment of deliverance," as one slaveholder derisively wrote, had little to do with happen-stance and more to do with established networks of communication and time-tested kin relationships. If it was the slaves' day of deliverance, for slaveholders "their waterloo had come."[40]

The existing social order cracked under pressure from rebellious slaves and Union forces. General Grant's forces swept through Claiborne County in May 1863, taking provisions from everyone in their path, white and black alike, and liberating the black inhabitants in the vicinity. At the battle of Port Gibson, Jack-son French—a free black drayman from Port Gibson—joined Grant's troops on his gray horse and led them to the retreating Confederate army. Only a few weeks before French had needed a white guardian, or a "nominal owner," to watch over his business and legal transactions, but now that he had allied him-self with the Union army, his standing in the neighborhood took on new mean-ing. After the capture of Vicksburg two months later, the inversion of social roles came full circle when he became the protector. Loyal white citizens, in-cluding his "nominal master," depended on French to lead them to Union lines and to escape the roving bands of rebel guerillas in the countryside.[41]

The impact of emancipation was also evident in the way Union occupation transformed public spaces and made public what had once been private. Across Natchez, painters whitewashed the numerous slave sale advertisements across the city, a small alteration to the physical landscape but a visible reminder of the revolutionary changes. Union soldiers camped near the bluff park on the west-ern edge of the city that overlooks the Mississippi River and opened the scenic spot to black people for the first time. More telling, Annie Harper, the white daughter of a Natchez merchant, lamented the fact that the enemy had infil-trated her house. "We were almost afraid to speak at home," she wrote, lest one of her black servants, whom Harper referred to as "spies," would overhear their "disrespectful" conversations and report back to the military authorities, who showed little hesitation in jailing white men and women of wealth and status. All the residents, no doubt, took notice when the Union army jailed a slave-holder for whipping one of his former slaves, emphasizing the new power of Lincoln's troops to restrain the master class.[42]

Under the protection of the U.S. government and with the establishment of a major military post, the city of Natchez buzzed with activity and commerce. The outpost also attracted outside aid from northern missionary societies, as well as entrepreneurs and capitalists hoping to turn a profit on the rich lowland fields abandoned by their Confederate owners. For the young and skilled, employment abounded. Future congressman John R. Lynch abandoned slave labor on a plantation in Concordia Parish and found employment in Natchez during the war as a dining room waiter at a boarding house, as a cook for a company of Illinois soldiers, and as a pantryman on a naval transport vessel. "Dealers in fruit, coffee, lemonade, and similar articles, could be found in abundance," reported a northern journalist. In addition, freedpeople in Natchez and other urban environs took up washing, "wood-sawing, house-cleaning, or any other kind of work requiring strength." Draymen took particular advantage of the military's presence, for there was no shortage of supplies that needed to be hauled from ship to shore and back again. Freed from the burden of giving a cut of their earnings to their master, former-slave draymen prospered as clients of the federal government. For even more lucrative—and dangerous—work, draymen took part in excursions into the plantation hinterlands to confiscate hidden Confederate cotton. If he could avoid rebel guerillas, a drayman could make twenty-five to fifty dollars per cotton bale, whereas before the war a successful drayman could expect to earn only fifteen dollars a month.[43]

For the slaves who made their way to Union lines there was no better way to demonstrate their new freedom than by joining the federal army. By donning Union-blue uniforms and swearing allegiance to the United States of America, black soldiers assumed the authority of the nation, forever altering the social dynamics of the region and transforming the war into a struggle for liberty and equality. Within six days of enlistment, new soldiers swore their "true allegiance to the United States of America" and pledged to obey the laws of the army. Not just in battle but also in drilling, in reconnoitering operations, and in the exercise of military weaponry, black soldiers were a visible reminder of the new world created by emancipation. One man asserted that his friend, a slave who joined the army, was "fighting for his freedom as well as his country." In addition, economic incentives, such as enlistment bounties, regular wages, and the promise of a pension, also played a role in the decision to volunteer for service.[44]

Black regiments—made up almost entirely of former plantation slaves—absorbed much of the male slave population that continued to stream into Natchez long after Union forces had secured the city. Within a few months, they had become the primary occupying force in the region, freeing up other Union forces to fight large Confederate armies in the east. Although no battles of significance took place in the district, black troops clashed with rebel guerillas in the plantation hinterlands, no doubt taking pleasure in chasing slaveholders and other Confederates through the bayous and backwoods and dislodging them from their seats of power. Operating from camps in Natchez, Vidalia, and Waterproof, black regiments had close contact with their families and other contraband refugees. Soldiers often served in the same company with men they had known before the war, such as their brothers and slaves from the same plantation. But camp life also offered opportunities for soldiers to forge contacts with people from across the district as they encountered recruits from outside their home neighborhoods and served at postings where they came in contact with different types of civilians.[45]

Women and men unfit for military service participated in the Union cause in other meaningful ways. Thousands of freedmen constructed "earthworks" around Natchez to guard against rebel attacks from the east. Women "waited on the sick" at military hospitals and "cooked and washed" for the U.S. soldiers. "I feels so sorry for a sick soldier, so far from their home," said one black woman who fed soldiers chicken, geese, and ducks from her own yard. "I feels happy for all I kin do for 'em." Women may not have been able to enlist, but they could impress upon eligible men the importance of joining the Union army. Amanda Jones, the wife of a prominent drayman in Natchez, pressured black men to join the army and "despised" those who did not. Some draymen participated in the Union effort by hauling commissary stores and giving soldiers transport free of charge. Richard Dorsey claimed that he "didn't want pay" for such work; rather, he was just "glad for the chance to do something." And Richard Stamps testified that he "never asked them for a Cent" for the food he fed Union soldiers, "except maybe a Chew-Tobacco to remember them by."[46]

Allegiance to the Union army proved to be a commonality that many newly freed people could share. Whether in contraband camps, in towns, or on plantations, they followed the operations of local black troops and national armies with keen interest. In the small town of Waterproof in Tensas Parish, a small detachment of black soldiers attracted great attention from black people on the neighboring plantations. Even though these troops came from another parish, local blacks "had a strong desire to go . . . see the soldiers" march in "military drills," noted a visiting northern reporter. But beyond their symbolic importance, the black troops at Waterproof protected the growing number of freed slaves who sought refuge behind Union lines from guerrilla raids and harassment. And, in turn, black civilians took great interest in the military operations of the local U.S. Colored Troops.[47]

After a skirmish with Confederate guerillas two miles outside of Natchez, a black regiment returned to camp victoriously and somberly. Having just learned of the Fort Pillow massacre, in which black soldiers were shot down after they had surrendered, the black soldiers stationed near Natchez fought ferociously, continuing to cut down the Confederate enemy over the objections of white officers who commanded them to halt the attack. The black soldiers yelled out, "They hear no cry for quarter at Fort Pillow" and fired into the retreating ranks of the rebels. But when this unit returned to their camp, their eventual compliance with the orders to stop the fight was met with scorn. The wife of one soldier who also had two sons in the company scolded the returning men for their restraint: "I don't care for that." Referring to rebel soldiers and Confederate sympathizers, she continued, "they need killin', *every one*." Although harsh and uncompromising, the sentiments of this newly freed woman, who had recently been liberated from an ardent secessionist, are suggestive of the importance that ordinary freedpeople invested in the military campaign to destroy the Confederacy.[48]

From large bases in Natchez and Vicksburg to small posts scattered along the river, these oases of freedom became the focal points of an expanding community of black people. Wearing Union blue or working for the army gave freedpeople a sense that they were part of a much larger endeavor. They shared a common objective in the defeat of the Confederacy and a common language in discussions about the Union that connected their local experience with an emerging loyalty to the nation.

The Capriciousness of Federal Power

Although joining the Union cause gave a sense of meaning and purpose to thousands of African Americans, their allegiance to the nation was not necessarily reciprocated. Freedpeople faced indifference and hostility from government officials and northerners. In particular, the free black elite and other well-off blacks found that the federal government was just as likely as Confederate authorities to use racial proscriptions to subordinate their interests. In the plantation hinterlands, former slaves confronted northern employers who could be every bit as exploitative as their former masters. Solidarity with the Union did not immediately translate into a shared political project that addressed the varying needs of freedpeople.

The joy of freedom that accompanied liberation was often tempered by the risks that escaping slaves faced in their flight. From distant plantations, slave families made perilous journeys, avoiding rebel pickets and dogs, going without food for days, traveling on swollen feet through swamps, trying to make it to the blue-coated men. Some did not make it. A Union officer testified that at least twenty slaves were "executed within thirty or forty miles of Natchez for trying to escape to our lines" in the summer of 1863. In one incident, a baby was shot dead in her mother's arms as they fled a "shower of bullets" from pursuing slave owners, and yet the mother held on to her child until she reached the Union lines because "she wanted her child to be buried 'free.'"[49]

The same mixture of joy and disappointment greeted many runaway slaves in Natchez when they found themselves shuffled off to contraband camps by military authorities. Before the war runaways had tended to be able-bodied young men, but families now dominated the ranks of those seeking refuge behind

Union lines. The army had uses for men and funneled them into regimental service or into labor groups, but six times as many women and children as men were taking up residence in occupied Natchez. Military authorities were ill-equipped to care for dependents, so they herded the slave refugees into contraband camps. The camps were located in Natchez Under-the-Hill, a seedy district below the city bluffs and far removed from the plush homes of the white elite. As a result, the camps had inadequate access to drinking water, and the refugees were forced to live in hastily constructed shelters.[50]

Nearly four thousand former slaves struggled to survive in the contraband camps. They quickly became breeding grounds for disease because the army failed to provide sufficient rations or even small plots of land for the majority to make their own living. By the fall of 1863, local white residents complained of the smell emanating from the assemblage of dilapidated structures in the overcrowded camps, and the medical director of freedmen confirmed the locals' suspicions when he condemned the sanitary condition of the camps. The cabins had inadequate ventilation and light, which, combined with overcrowding and meager rations, produced a deadly result. "There was not one house that I visited where death had not entered its portals," reported James E. Yeatman of the Western Sanitary Commission after an investigation. Approximately seventy-five freedpeople perished in a single day at the Natchez camp. Although sanitation and the distribution of rations did improve, in the first few months hundreds, perhaps thousands, of freedpeople died. Some were so disillusioned with the freedom that they found in the camps that they "returned to their masters."[51]

Although the military proved to be a boon for African Americans in Natchez by providing employment and enlistments, military regulations could also undercut freedpeople's efforts to establish independent households. On April 1, 1864, Dr. A. W. Kelly, the health officer at Natchez, ordered every black person "who is not employed by some *responsible white person*" and who did not live with his or her employer to be "removed to the contraband encampment." Dr. Kelly justified his health order as a preventive measure, arguing that "the large numbers of *idle* negroes which now throng the streets, lanes and alleys, and over-crowd every hovel" represented a dangerous threat to the health of the city. The population of Natchez had grown substantially since the start of the war, and the diseases that had ravaged the camps the previous summer and fall threatened to plague the city proper. But the order also originated in a military policy that limited freedpeople to working for "some white person" or exposed them to the risk of being "sent to the camps." The timing and context of Kelly's order suggests that his real target was black women, particularly servants. By designating black households—most of which were female-headed, since a good number of adult males were housed in military camps—as unsanitary, federal authorities in Natchez acceded to the prevailing gender and racial strictures that had governed the district before the war.[52]

Carrying out Dr. Kelly's order, U.S. soldiers marched through the streets of Natchez and drove over 250 people, mostly women and children, into the contraband camp. Little effort was made to determine the employment status of those herded out of the city, or even their living situation; rather, the white soldiers indiscriminately targeted black people. They rejected the protestations of gainfully employed blacks who asked for time to produce their certificates of employment, as well as those working for black employers, who by definition failed to meet the criteria of the health order. Taxpayers and renters met the same fate—all lumped into the same category of "idle negroes," including one fifty-year resident of the city who found herself driven "at the point of the bayonet to the camp." Women who were supported by their husbands were forced out of comfortable homes and into ramshackle barracks. But most contemptible, from the freedpeople's perspective, was Dr. Kelly's direct instructions to soldiers to visit "every school room." The soldiers rounded up the black children and sent them to the contraband camp without their parents' knowledge. The schoolchildren represented a cross-section of the black population: some were born free, some had their freedom purchased by their parents, but most were enslaved before federal occupation. As such, all classes of freedpeople joined in public denunciations of the health order and the military officials who authorized it.[53]

The political implications of the health order did not go unnoticed by the black population. Freedpeople interpreted the order as an attempt to force them back into the clutches of their former masters and as a direct assault on their freedom. Dr. Kelly had made no secret of his desire that the black *schools should be broken up*," nor was he, like other high-ranking officers stationed in Natchez, shy about consorting socially with former slaveholders. As the freedwomen trudged through the streets toward the camp, white citizens mocked their situation: "That's the way the Yankees treat you, is it? You'd better come back to us; we never treated you like that." Faced with the prospect of living in the dreaded contraband camp, "hundreds" of freedpeople "returned in despair to their former masters," which, as a result, weakened the newly established black schools, lamented an American Missionary Association (AMA) leader. Nearly "one third of the scholars" never returned to class. Those who resisted return to their former masters still faced the loss of employment and a life in camp where "sickness prevails . . . and death is fast putting an end to the sufferings of many of this long and still deeply oppressed people," wrote one AMA missionary. In the end, Dr. Kelly's health order did little to mitigate disease, but it did strike a blow at the emerging community of freedpeople.[54]

Yet even as Natchez's black residents were dispersed, the health order brought people together in unanticipated ways. Because the order targeted all black people, they joined together in support of a common cause that transcended differences in wealth, color, residency, age, and education. Freedpeople's protests took two forms: direct pressure from soldiers and appeals to influential northern white missionaries for intervention. A white officer in a black regiment reported that he heard his soldiers "swear desperately that they would have revenge" after they learned that white soldiers had shuffled off their wives and children to the contraband camp. The officer grew wary of the bitter complaints and, sensing indifference from his commanders in Natchez, appealed directly to the national office of the AMA, asking for immediate assistance. "I tremble," he pleaded, "as do many of the officers in the colored regiments," for fear that "blood equaling the day of vengeance on the island of Hayti" would be the result. In another regiment, fifteen black soldiers "deserted" in order to personally protect their wives and children, leading one observer to wonder if a general mutiny was approaching. Facing the prospect of an armed black insurrection, Kelly scaled back his deportment efforts and exempted the wives and children of black soldiers.[55]

Freedpeople also made their displeasure known to northern white missionaries working in the district. Outraged at the capricious actions of the military authorities, the local leaders of four missionary societies penned a letter of protest to Gen. J. M. Tuttle, commander of the U.S. forces in Natchez. They expected little from Tuttle since he had openly endorsed Dr. Kelly's order, but they hoped to excite northern public opinion by circulating the letter in northern newspapers, including the widely read *New York Tribune*.[56] Going a step further, the head of AMA operations in Natchez asked Rev. George Whipple, one of the national AMA leaders, to use his contacts in Washington, D.C., to present "in person" the complaints of the freedpeople "to the Secretary of War." Owing to pressure from the missionaries' contacts and an outraged northern public, Congress took up the matter and passed a resolution directing the Committee on the Conduct of the War to investigate the charges. The protest even reached the desk of President Lincoln. A month after Kelly issued the health order, he and Tuttle were relieved of duty, and Tuttle resigned from the army in June 1864. Having the officers responsible for the health order dismissed probably was of little consolation for those who lost their homes and those who were forced to return to their former masters. Nonetheless, by beating back the racist health order, freedwomen and freedmen got a taste of how their collective power, along with timely assistance from northern allies, could alter the policies of the federal government.[57]

The fallout from the health order also demonstrated to freedpeople the importance of having sympathetic local leaders. Not long after General Tuttle's departure, his replacement, Col. B. G. Farrar, moved against Confederate sympathizers in occupied Natchez. As the commander of a local black regiment, Farrar gained the confidence of the local black population, who believed that "we will now have justice done us," wrote a local correspondent to the *Christian Recorder*. Disturbed that local white churches still failed to recognize the authority of the U.S. government, as evidenced by their deliberate refusal to pray for President Lincoln, Colonel Farrar ordered every minister to offer prayers to "the Chief Magistrate of the United States." Most preachers complied with the order, but the bishop at St. Mary's Cathedral refused to obey, whereupon the colonel suspended the bishop's clerical authority and banished him to Vidalia, across the river. It was plain for all to see that federal power reached into even the most sacred spaces and that if harnessed properly this new form of power could serve the interests, large and small, of freedpeople.[58]

In Between State Power

In the hinterlands of the Natchez District, changes were less dramatic. Without the benefit of an occupying force, black people who remained on plantations found themselves in the midst of a guerilla war, where neutrality offered the best hope for survival. Not quite free nor still enslaved, these rural people carefully negotiated a world on the brink of chaos. Although still laboring much as they had under bondage, they redefined the terms of labor, whether working for a northern lessee or a former master, and they placed personal and family survival at the forefront of their aims. Nonetheless, the war offered new opportunities for plantation freedpeople.

From 1863 to 1865 thousands of slaves gathered their belongings and ran to freedom behind Union lines, but some did not leave their masters quietly. "All is anarchy and confusion here," protested a white overseer on a Concordia Parish plantation. "[E]verything's going to destruction and the negroes on the plantations [are] insubordinate. My life has been several times in Danger." The same overseer, Wilmer Shields, gave up on the hope of putting in the 1864 crop, facing as he was "negroes who will not work for love or money, but who steal every thing they can lay their hands on." When Union soldiers liberated one Claiborne County plantation, the newly freed slaves "laid hands on the farming utensils," taking the equipment and other plantation property for themselves. At a Tensas Parish plantation, former slaves carried off the furniture and other belongings from the planter's house before the mansion was burned to the ground. Just outside of Natchez, newly freed people sacked Carthage plantation soon after federal troops landed. Carthage was the property of Katherine S. Minor, a well-to-do planter with deep family connections to the elite slaveholders of the district. Her plantation, because of its close proximity to Union lines, offered aggrieved slaves an opportunity to exact some revenge, her purported allegiance to the Union notwithstanding. Giles Brooks, a former slave living at Carthage, witnessed black people, some who were former slaves of Mrs. Minor but others from surrounding plantations, descend on the plantation and kill the livestock. Gabriel Powers, another former Minor slave, testified that black people "helped them selves to the cattle, Hogs, sheep and corn" on the plantation, in part to supplement their meager government rations.[59]

Former slaves who remained on plantations often disapproved of the plundering because, once freed, they took ownership of the supplies and provisions. Gabe Emanuel did not welcome a foraging party of Union soldiers on his plantation in Claiborne County. After the soldiers had confiscated a hefty supply of cured meat, Emmanuel snuck into their encampment and stole back the meat. Frequent visits from U.S. soldiers prompted Emmanuel and his fellow ex-slaves to set fire to the bridge that led into the plantation in order to prevent Yankees from raiding their supplies again. Similarly, a plantation mistress lamented the fact that her white neighbors willingly hired out their wagons and teams to her former slaves so that the ex-slaves could sell the plantation provisions in town. More troubling than the loss of control over plantation products, though, was the ex-slaves' response to her protestations: "[T]hey say they have a right to do so," she complained.[60]

Outside the Union army encampments, on either side of the Mississippi River, neither Unionists nor Confederates, planters nor freedpeople had complete control. Slaveholders fleeing from the advancing Union army had abandoned dozens of plantations, and into this power vacuum stepped enterprising white northerners hoping to turn a quick profit on the famously rich cotton lands. Before the war, no other region in the South produced as much cotton or as many planter millionaires, leading one historian to conclude that "no place so clearly epitomized the enduring and triumphant nature of the reign of King Cotton" as the Natchez District. Anchored by posts at Natchez and Vicksburg, the military encouraged this flow of northern capital into the district in order to jump-start the region's economy and demonstrate that free labor could be more productive than slave labor. Under the authority of provost marshals, northerners leased plantations with the promise to pay ex-slaves in wages and provide them with rations and clothing. The military also entered the planting business, establishing government-run Home Farms that attempted to induce the most dependent freedpeople to work in the fields.[61]

From the outset, northern lessees confronted a depleted and reluctant workforce. Fleeing planters often took their ablest slaves with them to Texas, Georgia, or Alabama, leaving behind women, children, and the aged. As for the able-bodied workers who evaded their masters' flight, they were often the first to run away to Union lines and enlist in the army. Many of the limited pool of laborers rejected offers from lessees to return to plantations and work in the cotton fields, likening such prospects to a return to bondage. Still others preferred not to work and chose to rely on government rations in the camps. After an officer at the Home Farm explained that freedom meant that "they need not work unless they chose, and if they did work, they had a right to wages," the freedpeople exercised their freedom and "refused to work" the next morning. So to put in a crop, northern lessees had to provide enough incentives to keep their laborers from running off to other plantations or to military posts, and thus they had to "rely mainly upon the labor of women."[62]

In the midst of these tentative steps toward a free labor system, an extensive guerilla war raged on, undermining planter authority and subjecting rural freedpeople to random and vicious raids. After the fall of Vicksburg, the Confederate army moved east, but a few remnants of those forces combined with local white militias and continued to fight in the hinterlands of the Natchez District. Hiding out in the bayous on the Louisiana side of the river and in the hilly terrain on the Mississippi side, rebel raiders wreaked havoc on river steamboats and on whites and blacks in the countryside. One overseer complained that "all sides" were against him, since both "Federal gun boats and Confederates" had looted his plantation. Members of a rebel band, the "Jones Scout," plundered a plantation house in Tensas Parish and threatened to return and "carry off the Cotton." As much as white planters and overseers were subject to guerilla raids, black people were all the more vulnerable. Confederate deserters and "Jayhawkers" preyed on isolated black settlements on the edges of the district, stealing horses and kidnapping black people "for the purpose of selling them" in Georgia, recalled the wife of a Union general.[63]

Plantation security ultimately depended on proximity to a major military post. Laborers and lessees were the most vulnerable in Tensas Parish, located halfway between Natchez and Vicksburg on the Louisiana side of the river. One northern lessee narrowly escaped rebel raids on his Tensas plantation on two different occasions by fleeing to safety in Natchez. Guerillas plundered the plantations near St. Joseph and Waterproof to such an extent that by the summer of 1864 mostly old men and women, who lived in the "old plantation quarters," occupied the subdistrict. In Concordia Parish freedpeople had more protection due to the presence of a sizeable military contingent in Vidalia, the parish seat, which enabled 2,390 freedmen to work thirty-four plantations. Protected by local black troops, most of the laborers were the "original hands" who had worked the land under bondage. "This fact makes them work better and more contentedly," concluded Col. Samuel Thomas, the provost marshal of freedmen, "as they have a little community commonly known as 'fellow servants.'" Nonetheless, they were not immune to the guerilla war; in a one-week span, rebel raiders burned nine steam-cotton gins at the lower end of the parish.[64]

In spite of the chaos that infected the river plantations, freedpeople quickly adapted to the new labor system. "A planter must pay well and punctually, or he will not get laborers to do his work," remarked Colonel Thomas. Freedpeople moved throughout the district, seeking high wages and labor terms with the least restriction on their personal freedom. The laborers on one leased plantation in Tensas were indicative of a phenomenon that brought increasing numbers of rural and urban freedpeople into contact with one another. After one white northerner gave up on his planting venture, some of his black workers moved to Natchez "to live near their 'missus,'" while others relocated to "the Contraband Home at Davis's Bend, others to the negro quarters at Natchez, others to plantations near Vidalia, and a few returned to their former homes." Their actions underscore the fluidity of labor relations and demonstrate how even rural freedpeople saw whole new worlds open up before them. In the process of moving from plantation to plantation, rural freedpeople forged new relationships with one another and gained new understandings of power through encounters with guerillas, military officials, and northern whites.[65]

A New Political Consciousness

The flow of information and people from plantation to city and back again facilitated the spread of new ideas about freedom, politics, and community. Freedpeople tested this new world through encounters with employers, government officials, and other black people from varying backgrounds, but even after the defeat of the Confederacy the implications of federal power and the prospect of a new political community were still indistinct. One way to measure the indeterminacy of this period is to examine the Christmas Insurrectionary Scare of 1865 in light of freedpeople's evolving notions of power and the history of insurrectionary scares in the Natchez District.

A rumor of a massive, federal government–sponsored land redistribution plan began to spread throughout the South in the summer months of 1865. Government agents reported and ex-Confederates complained of an imminent uprising among rural blacks. The rumor reflected debates in Congress, particularly among Radical Republicans, over allotting forty-acre farms to freedpeople; however, President Andrew Johnson rejected the proposals in favor of a conciliatory policy toward the planter class, including amnesty and the return of confiscated property. Somewhat mollified by the backing of the federal government, planters nevertheless noticed increasing recalcitrance and hostility among a workforce unmoved by official pronouncements from the Johnson administration. One plantation mistress in Jefferson County grew alarmed when her friend reported that "the negroes are going about from place to place in rage; [and] will not work." Freedpeople in the Natchez District believed, claimed a Freedmen's Bureau official, that "the late President Lincoln" intended to "divide the lands of their former owners among them, giving to each family a small farm." Like peasants who appropriated a king's or tsar's authority to justify their claims on power, former slaves concluded that they had been "cheated out of their rights" by the unscrupulous inheritors of President Lincoln's power; they used that belief as a political wedge to demand redemptive justice across the land and, failing that, to extract concessions in their local struggles with planters and Freedmen's Bureau agents.[66]

Confirmation of the rumor's power was borne out in the white response. In Claiborne County planters met on subsequent Mondays in December 1865, first to organize "the military strength" of the county and then the following week to adopt "some system . . . to avoid trouble" concerning the "new experiment" in free labor. Adams County planters similarly colluded, offering freedmen only five-year contracts. They also attempted to limit black mobility by warning freedpeople who ventured into a different neighborhood seeking better terms that they would be shot if they ever returned to their original employer. At Laurel Hill plantation, Wilmer Shields complained one week before Christmas 1865 of the field hands "having arms" and of some even traveling as far away as Vicksburg to obtain muskets. Recent purchases of shotguns by freedmen in Jefferson County did not go unnoticed by local whites. In fact, it was a common sentiment among the local white population that "a large number of the negroes are possessed of arms and ammunition" and that only "immediate measures" would avert an insurrection.[67]

Planters backed up their lethal threats by organizing militia companies. Sixty-one men joined the "Volunteer Militia Company" of Claiborne County, heeding the Mississippi governor's general call to arms. Leading whites in Adams County organized a cavalry company and an infantry company of over one hundred men in order to "disarm all the negroes in the county." "There is more reason now than in 1860 to disarm free negroes," wrote Adams County attorney William T. Martin to Mississippi governor Benjamin Humphreys. "They [had] tens then, but thousands now." It was no coincidence that Martin, a former Confederate general who had founded a vigilance committee that investigated rumors of slave rebellion before the Civil War, was now organizing another militia to meet the Christmas Insurrectionary Scare of 1865. Even Martin admitted some justification for the rumors of insurrection by noting that former masters "are hostile to" freedpeople and kept some of them "in a state of actual slavery." Nevertheless, Martin was clearly frightened by the "bad humor" that he noticed among local blacks. "Many wholly refuse to work. and insist that they will have land of their own, & will never again work for white men," he wrote to the governor of Mississippi. Particularly worrisome were the thousands of "negro soldiers" in the area that "have learned a little of impromptu fortifications" and were armed with "guns & pistols." The military experience of former slaves and their presumed organizational abilities prompted Martin to make an unusual request: "Now is it possible to get a section of howitzers?" Asserting that armed blacks "could be put down by a few shells without loss of life on the part of the [white] citizens," Martin believed that the cannon "would have a happy effect" in Natchez, apparently to soothe the unnerved white population.[68]

Even as leading white residents grew more fearful, the urban black elite dismissed the rumors of insurrection and land redistribution as folly. One black observer alluded to the fact that rumors of revolt were not new in this region, seemingly referencing the murderous vigilance committees in the early days of Confederate control. "The old cry of 'Insurrection' has again been raised in this locality," the observer wrote in a letter to the *Christian Recorder*, noting that such talk had prompted military authorities to launch a "strict surveillance" on the "actions and movements of the colored people." Hoping to quell white paranoia, Maj. George D. Reynolds, the federal provost marshal in Natchez, met with "several leading colored men" about the rumors of an impending rebellion. They confirmed his suspicion that freedpeople were not planning an uprising; however, they warned Reynolds of an insurrection "by the whites." Black leaders, while dismissive of black insurrectionary talk, recognized the political implications of the rumors. "Give to the colored man his rights as an equal before the law," wrote the Natchez correspondent, "and I think that the Southern people will not be troubled with any more insurrectionary hallucinations."[69]

The rumors of insurrection and land redistribution fed into competing narratives about the repercussions of freedom and federal power. The editor of the *Natchez Democrat* was no doubt correct in assuming that "the idea of a division of lands" was harbored by "those farthest removed from the highways and centers of commerce." Rural freedpeople had less contact with federal officials than their urban counterparts, and they also lacked ready access to discourses on national power. The struggle to understand the implications of the rumors was expressed in a petition to the governor of Mississippi from Claiborne County freedpeople. "[W]e hav[e no s]uch thought now," the petition read; nevertheless, they were insistent in their demand for "our rights," just not "by murdering." In Wilkinson County the possibility of insurrection seemed to have a greater hold on the freedpeople because many believed that if they remained on the land of their former masters then "they were still slaves." Despite conflicting accounts and murky perceptions of state power, the rumors dramatically affected the Natchez District. "The circulation of rumors, like the ones referred to, among the blacks," protested the *Natchez Courier*, "has prevented the profitable cultivation of hundreds, if not thousands of plantations."[70]

The insurrectionary scare reflected the idea, common among slaves, that power resided in individuals, and thus only one man—President Lincoln—

could fulfill their desire for independent land proprietorships. On the other hand, the rumor of land redistribution went far beyond slaves' conception of power and illuminates freedpeople's emerging political consciousness in an emancipated world. The rumor claimed that the federal government was to divide the lands, referencing federal power, an amorphous entity to be sure, but one that was connected to local authorities and the military. Moreover, freedpeople considered themselves subjects of the nation-state, believing that the federal government owed them something for their years of suffering in bondage. The rapid spread of this rumor across the major plantation regions in the South reveals, as well, an extensive communication network that in the coming years would help freedpeople make sense of the changes wrought by Reconstruction and a free labor economy.[71]

Two insurrectionary scares framed the Civil War experience for African Americans in the Natchez District. Both panics fed off of white paranoia, and yet they both reflected the political insurgency of black people, even if a plot never materialized. Uncovering the roots of the insurrections reveals much about how emancipation transformed the lives of black people in the cities and in the countryside. In the so-called Adams County slave conspiracy, Confederate authority subverted the power of individual slave owners by punishing slaves without their compliance. It also centralized the examinations by bringing hundreds of slaves and free blacks to one location: the county fairgrounds. In the Christmas Insurrectionary Scare, planters no longer had the power to bring black people to the center of the district; instead, they had to go out and patrol the countryside, or worse, rely on U.S. military authorities for protection. Dozens of black people were executed under the Confederate regime, yet in the postwar insurrectionary scare no one was killed, although many were harassed. The earlier rebellion tapped into a generalized anxiety about the war, but it was a localized affair, whereas the postwar insurrection scare was regional in scope. Both panics relied on subterranean communication networks, but with the defeat of the Confederacy and, more important, the uprooting of black people during the war, African Americans added many new contact points, thereby allowing rumors of land redistribution to spread far and wide. And finally, in 1865 freedpeople protested their harassment at the hands of ex-Confederates to federal authorities, while just a few years before the mere mention of the Union or freedom could lead to an execution.[72]

The Civil War was a shared experience for African Americans in the Natchez District like none other. Whether free or slave, wealthy or poor, they suffered under varying forms of unfreedom, and they all shared the burdens of war. Hundreds were executed in the slave insurrectionary scare of 1861–63; even more perished in contraband camps or while trying to escape to Union lines.

Devastation and death were widespread. (The chief quartermaster charged with locating the graves of Union soldiers across the South found perhaps "forty thousand" dead Union bodies between Vicksburg and Natchez.)[73] For those black people who were lucky enough to survive, emancipation offered an opportunity to shape a new world in freedom.

The Civil War expanded freedpeople's notions of the world and their place in it. Formerly closed off from state power, African Americans felt the harsh hand of the nation-state in the form of Confederate repression, as well as the liberating potential offered by allegiance to the Union cause. The war split families and uprooted neighborhoods, yet in this fluid environment freedpeople could interact with an array of new people from different backgrounds and forge new connections. Freedpeople saw how the power of the federal government could improve their lives, yet they retained their skepticism toward outsiders. Misguided and punitive federal policies disabused freedpeople of any reflexive notion that the Union army was an unqualified ally; even so, they quickly discovered that its awesome power could be harnessed toward their ends. In daily encounters, ex-slaves gained a new sense of their place in the nation as well as their part in an emerging community of like-minded people. Draymen and other urban laborers, in particular, developed a web of connections among slaves and free blacks that, while tested under the Confederate reign of terror, survived the war years and became a foundation for a new political community.

Emancipated Communities

With the war over, the former Confederate states began to reorganize themselves to address the twin realities of defeat and slave emancipation. President Andrew Johnson's administration gave state leaders wide latitude in constructing a free society on their terms. The result was a set of new laws, known as the Black Codes, that created new categories based on race and labor in order to perpetuate the subordination of people of color. The intent was also to atomize black people, making them subject to white employers and white officials and thereby limiting their efforts to mobilize their own networks and communities. The laws were both backward and forward looking. In general, states, including Mississippi and Louisiana, sought to re-create the antebellum environment of individual domination in which whites retained supervisory authority over black people. But they also implicitly acknowledged the grassroots mobilizations taking place in the latter years of the war. Fearing the political implications of increasingly mobilized black communities, the laws restricted black people's opportunities to act collectively in public matters. Needless to say, the Black Codes represented a social vision that sharply diverged from the aspirations of freedpeople in the postemancipation South.[1]

Mississippi stood out among its southern peers not just because it was the first of the former Confederate states to revise its statutes in relation to the newly freed population but also because of the bluntness and severity of its Black Code. Concerned that emancipation would lead to labor instability, Mississippi legislators used the power of the state to enact strict controls on black workers and to limit black autonomy in public spaces. In order to keep freedpeople working on plantations and to ensure that only white men could be farmers or planters, a new law prevented freedpeople from renting or leasing land in rural areas. They were also forced to obtain licenses from local officials to verify employment and residence, and they had to renew these licenses on a semiannual basis or face charges of vagrancy. Civil officers were empowered to arrest employees who had absconded before the termination of their contracts and to punish any person who enticed a freed person away from lawful employment.[2]

Beyond labor issues, the laws set up a two-tiered system in which blacks were subjected to different restrictions than whites. On the one hand, black people could not possess firearms, absent consent from the local board of police, and they were burdened with extra taxes, such as a special poll tax for the care of "colored paupers." White people, on the other hand, were prohibited from selling liquor to freedpeople, unless those whites happened to be a freed person's "master, mistress, or employer," and they could not marry a black person. In the political arena, blacks could not vote or sit on juries, and they could not testify in court if both parties were white, although testimony would be admitted if one of the parties was also African American. Perhaps most stinging to freedpeople, the apprenticeship law gave "preference" to former masters when the courts had to determine a "suitable person" to care for a minor. Finally, this new legislation lumped—for the first time—all people of African descent into one subordinate category: "freedmen, free negroes, and mulattoes." Not only did free blacks lose their special distinction that accorded them more rights than slaves (though fewer rights than whites) but they also faced stiffer punishments than before.[3]

The Louisiana Code, while less harsh than Mississippi's, likewise circumscribed freedpeople's actions and gave planters considerable power to govern their employees. Mindful of the northern public's dissatisfaction with the Mississippi Black Code, Louisiana's laws avoided the use of explicit racial language, referring to black people as "laborers," not "freedmen, free negroes, and mulattoes." But there was little doubt among the legislators that the new laws were designed to ensure a stable supply of black laborers for the plantation economy. Louisiana's code went into much greater detail on labor regulations. It specified the number of hours per day and the number of days per week that farm laborers were permitted to work. It also detailed the punishments for sickness and idleness. Laborers were to be fined one dollar for disobedience and two dollars if they were absent "from home without" permission. Even the theft of "hogs, sheep, [and] poultry" was carefully proscribed. In short, the intent of the laws was to ensure that "[b]ad work shall not be allowed." In contrast with Mississippi's code, Louisiana's made no mention of marriage, speech, assembly, or other restrictions on public behavior, choosing instead to emphasize restrictions on workers' rights. Similarly, whereas Mississippi prohibited black people from owning guns, except for those who obtained a license from the board of police, Louisiana theoretically allowed for gun ownership but prohibited it on plantations without the express permission of the owner.[4]

For all of their draconian provisions, the Black Codes were less significant for the way they shaped the postwar social order than for their articulation of southern whites' vision of an emancipated society. The federal government stepped in to nullify some of the harsher aspects, such as when the Freedmen's Bureau struck down the prohibition on renting or leasing land. The Civil Rights Act of 1866 superseded the codes by empowering the bureau to bring action against state officials who enforced discriminatory legislation. But local blacks accurately recognized that the underlying assumptions in the codes represented a strident challenge to their emerging sense of what a free society should look like and how free people should live and work together. Referring to the white legislators who authored the codes, a correspondent to the *Christian Recorder* observed, "They well know that wealth is power, and they seem determined that [the freedman] shall not acquire either money or land." Merrimon Howard, an ex-slave and school organizer from Jefferson County, complained to the head of the Freedmen's Bureau that the new laws prevented "Loyal *Blacks*" from "de fend[ing] him self aganest the entrader er envader of his rights." It was "an over balance of credit to the [enemies] of the Country," he continued, when ex-Confederates walked the streets of Fayette "in uniform displade with gilt buttons armed to the teeth while Blaks is not to be seen with a gun er Pistol."[5]

More generally, the "Colored people" of Claiborne County, in a petition to the governor of Mississippi, complained of the "stringent Laws" that "will not treate us as free." In deferential terms, they denounced the prohibition on renting or leasing rural lands and the harsh vagrancy statutes. But the petitioners had a difficult time pressing their demands on the state. They recognized that they possessed latent power. What "if evry one of us Colord people were removed from the state of Mississippi," they asked. "[W]e the labrors hav inriched [the planters] and it is as much imposible for them to live with out us as it is for we to be removed from them." And yet they undercut their veiled threat to withhold their labor by admitting that they would "worke for our former Masters or eny Stranger that will treat us well and pay us what we earn." They admitted that "the worde freedom is sweet to us all and greate will be the day when we [are] assured of our freedom," but they seemed to be confounded about how to bring about that day of "gustice [justice]."[6]

The petitioners placed their hope in the "kinde [and] gust Masters" in December 1865, but within a couple years they had abandoned, both rhetorically and materially, their former masters in favor of a new political community. This chapter explores how freedpeople rejected the racist and exploitive social vision expressed in the Black Codes and how they began to form institutions and organizations that brought like-minded people together in a democratic fashion. They created new churches, benevolent associations, schools, and labor cooperatives. Their goal was not to build a democracy. But in the process of working with neighbors, forging connections to national organizations and governmental bodies, and establishing governing structures, they gained practical experience in developing the values and networks that would become essential to a grassroots democracy.[7]

Freedpeople did not wait for their status to be officially determined by the state; instead, they plunged ahead into the political vacuum that emerged in the wake of war to make a claim for their rights and their place in local society as well as in the nation. The radical nature of their claim is all the more significant when we take into account the ideal of legal personhood in nineteenth-century America, which ascribed citizenship to white, able-bodied men. Official emancipation would not come until December 1865, with the ratification of the Thirteenth Amendment, and it would be another two years before the nation recognized African Americans as citizens with the Fourteenth Amendment. In the meantime, black congregations and rural religious communities formed independent churches. Where once black education was forbidden, freedom schools sprouted across the landscape. And while many former slaves continued to labor in the cotton fields, they did so now in collective units of their own making and on their own terms. In other words, freedpeople jumped at the chance to forge connections with others from a similar background. Set free from the tyranny of individual domination, newly freed women and men sought comfort and protection in congregations, benevolent societies, educational associations, squads, and labor collectives. Their new freedom meant little if it could not be shared. And maintaining their freedom meant working together.[8]

This radical restructuring of the social order did not occur without complications, obstructions, or confusion. Local freedpeople were necessarily dependent on outside groups, such as missionary organizations, denominational bodies, and the federal government, for financial assistance and experienced leadership in the creation of institutions and associations. While this aid was indispensable, it also sowed the seeds of factional conflict as locals struggled with outside leaders for control of the new institutions. Meanwhile, ex-Confederates did not sit idly by as black people altered their place in society. White Southerners used legal and extralegal means to maintain their privileged position in society and in the economy. Although churches, schools, and informal labor organizations went a long way toward equalizing freedpeople's place in southern society, they could not, by themselves, overcome the constraints imposed by the landed and political elite. Only when those institutions combined and utilized black communication networks under the auspices of a formal political organization would a broad-based community be realized, and only then would freedpeople's collective strength be put to maximum use.

"The loyal man's God"

Although enslaved blacks and free people of color attended and were members of established churches in towns and cities prior to the Civil War, denominationally sanctioned black churches did not exist in the Natchez District. On plantations, slaves often attended services initiated by their master, but they also organized informal religious gatherings beyond the scrutiny of overseers and slaveholders. The challenge of emancipation, then, was to transform these dependent congregations into independent and public institutions. Churches offered freedpeople an opportunity to practice their faith as they saw fit, but freedpeople also used churches as spaces to share information, to convene with friends and family, and to share risks through mutual security. Moreover, churches were often the first black-owned buildings in a neighborhood, symbolizing African Americans' new newfound collective power and presence in public life.[9]

By now it has become commonplace to assert that black churches were the embodiment and foundation of the black community. Scholars often assume that the church was just a local community, in that it functioned as a center of religious and secular life, serving as a place to gather, communicate, and commiserate. But the church was more than a meetinghouse. Churches represented vital linkages to worlds beyond neighborhoods and farms. Black congregations joined up with national denominations, formed regional missionary associations, and joined in national dialogues on Christianity, emancipation, and politics. In these ways, black churches helped to establish democratic practices and to ground local freedpeople's religious affiliations in networks that extended beyond the Natchez District.[10]

Building off the legacy of religious life under slavery, freedpeople established dozens of churches varying in size, location, and theology in the postemancipation period. Accustomed to separate seating arrangements and segregated worship services, black congregants took the next logical step and established separate churches. Breaking away from white-dominated churches allowed freedpeople to become full members of a church body, and it gave them the opportunity to develop their distinctive approach to Christianity. Preeminent among the churches established by freedpeople were Baptist and African Methodist congregations, and it is these two denominations that dominated the religious landscape of the Natchez District.[11]

One of the first independent black churches to be organized after Union occupation was the Wall Street Baptist Church in Natchez. Before the war, slaves and free people of color constituted the vast majority of its members—499 black members in 1856 compared to 16 white members. This demographic imbalance did not sit well with the few whites who managed the church, so they built a separate building, known as the Rose Hill Church, to house the black worshipers. The black members, who had contributed most of the funds for the building's construction, gained informal control over the Rose Hill Church. The building was deeded to Harry Marshall, a free black drayman. Randall Pollard, a slave, became its first preacher. A few whites attended services to maintain authority and legalize the gatherings under denominational rules. Thus, Rose Hill was an adjunct of the Wall Street Baptist Church and not an independent black church. But after the Civil War broke out, the few white members at Wall Street abandoned the church, shutting its doors for two years until the arrival of federal troops. Union military chaplains revived the church and began conducting services for Union soldiers stationed at the post in Natchez, but local white Baptists refused to return to their church while it was under federal authority. "Our [white] citizens had so much of old man Jeff [Davis] in them," explained a few black members in a letter to the Freedmen's Bureau, "they would rather hear the Devil Preach then [*sic*] a Yankee."[12]

The doors of the church remained closed to black congregants until 1864, when Rev. E. G. Trask, a northern white missionary from the American Baptist Home Mission Society, opened the Wall Street Baptist Church to the black members under his authority as a denominational leader. Soon the church became a focal point of black assembly during the latter years of the Civil War. On Sundays, black citizens met for worship in the morning, and in the early evening Union soldiers gathered for prayer and exhortation. During the week, American Missionary Association (AMA) teachers schooled black children and adults, and female members organized and "sustained" a weekly women's-only prayer meeting at the church. Local leaders administered spiritual and social services much as they had before the war, except now they did so independent of local white supervision. Recognizing the importance of these grassroots church leaders, Reverend Trask validated their positions of influence by ordaining some of the female leaders as deaconesses and some of the black preachers, including Randall Pollard, as Baptist ministers.[13]

With the surrender of Confederate forces and the resumption of civil authority in 1865, however, the white members of the Wall Street Baptist Church demanded that their black counterparts vacate the property and return the church to their control. Not about to give up the building to members who had abandoned the church and the nation four years before, the black congregants held fast, asserting that they were the true inheritors of the church. They sent two church leaders, Reverend Pollard and Daniel Holley, a deacon and a blacksmith, to the North-Western Missionary Baptist Convention in St. Louis to seek official Baptist recognition for their congregation. In response, the convention recognized their authority to speak for the church and commissioned Rev. Dr. Jesse F. Boulden, a black minister from Chicago, to go to Natchez in early 1865 and lead the black congregation.[14]

Although they had quickly secured denominational legitimacy, legal authority was another matter. Over the next three years the black members of the Wall Street Baptist Church struggled to continue their mission of providing spiritual assistance and community support while fighting off white members' claims to the church and its property. It was an audacious claim—that legal status should be voided and ownership granted on the basis of loyalty—but not an unusual demand, since many farm laborers made similar claims in relation to plantation lands. Seeking authorization for their radical contention, Reverend Boulden and four deacons from the Wall Street Baptist Church appealed to President Andrew Johnson, Freedmen's Bureau Commissioner O. O. Howard, and Supreme Court Chief Justice Salmon P. Chase—the most powerful men in the nation, in their estimation. They based their claim on their understanding of federal policy toward abandoned lands. The white members lost their right to the church, they argued to Howard, when they deserted the property at the start of the war and when they refused to return to the church under the auspices of the Union military. "We are the only rightful owners of the said Wall St. property," they asserted, a property that they believed had "been abandoned by trators [sic]." To President Johnson, they maintained that they deserved at least partial title to the property because they had contributed to the general church fund and the construction of the church meetinghouse, including "one contribution" of "$500 to help build" the Wall Street Baptist Church. Boulden and the deacons knew that their quest to obtain legal title to the church would be difficult because there was little chance that the white members would sell them the church property or transfer it to their name. They pinned their hopes instead to the benevolence of distant yet powerful men.[15]

It was a wise move. Upon the recommendation of the Freedmen's Bureau agent in charge of the Natchez post, General Howard ordered the bureau to "retain possession" of the Wall Street Church for the use of the black members "until compelled to give it up by law." He dismissed the claim that the church could be legally classified as an abandoned property, but he recognized that the black members had, at the very least, a financial interest in the church and that this interest would be endangered if the white members resumed control. "Their rights on it," he ordered Samuel Thomas, the assistant commissioner for Mississippi, "must be guaranteed and protected." With the Freedmen Bureau's backing, the black members held onto the property for another year, but eventually the church was returned to the white church members who possessed legal title. Despite the loss, the black congregation, in those intervening years, established a thriving institution that would play a vital role in the development of a grassroots democracy.[16]

In the short run, the black Baptist congregation in Natchez struggled to regain its footing. Just prior to their expulsion from the Wall Street Church, Reverend Boulden was called to lead a church in Columbus, Mississippi, leaving the congregation leaderless and now churchless. They moved to the Rose Hill Church, but the building could not hold the congregation of nearly five hundred. Without a structure to call their own, the Wall Street Church members split, with some joining a church led by Reverend Trask that met "in an abandoned school house once used by northern teachers," while others stayed with Reverend Pollard, apparently at Rose Hill. The church remained divided until Rev. Henry P. Jacobs took over and built a church meetinghouse on Pine Street, "the first Negro Baptist church erected in Mississippi after freedom was declared," boasted a late nineteenth-century church historian. But Jacobs did more than build churches; he became one of the most powerful preacher-politicians in the Natchez District.[17]

Born a slave in Alabama, Henry P. Jacobs learned to read and write from "a crazy white man" whom he was charged with looking after. In 1856 he forged a pass for himself, his wife, his three children, and his brother-in-law, and they all escaped to Canada, taking his master's wagon and horses with them. Ordained a Baptist minister three years before the war, Jacobs settled with his family in Ypsilanti, Michigan, and then later moved to Natchez in 1866 to work as a missionary, where he quickly established himself as a religious leader and political organizer. In his capacity as church leader, Jacobs transformed the church (now named Pine Street Baptist Church) into a major congregation in Natchez and used the church as a springboard for benevolent aid in the city and missionary activities in the district. He established three statewide missionary organizations, including the First Baptist Antioch Association, which met at Rose Hill Church in December 1868. The Antioch Association formed a missionary board based in Natchez with the intention of establishing Baptist churches throughout the region. Both the missionary board and the church board served as stepping-stones for a few political leaders. Reverend Pollard, the elected moderator of the missionary board who had previously been the enslaved minister at Rose Hill, was appointed to the board of the state hospital in Natchez in 1869 and later served on the city's school board and as a Republican Party delegate. H. A. Smith, a Natchez policeman, also was a missionary board secretary and a partisan Republican leader, serving on the hospital and school boards in addition to the board of the poor farm. Another missionary board secretary, Rev. Jeremiah M. P. Williams, attained even higher office as a state senator from 1870 to 1875 and from 1878 to 1879. Similarly, Henry P. Jacobs served in the Mississippi House for two terms, was appointed the superintendent of the poor in Natchez, and remained a Republican leader throughout Reconstruction.[18]

In addition to his church-planting and partisan activities, Jacobs also organized a benevolent society, which he named after himself. The Jacobs Benevolent Society was organized in 1867, and the state granted it a charter four years later. Primarily designed as a mutual aid association to care for the sick and pay funeral expenses, the society also purchased homes for its members and pledged assistance in "the erection of colleges, academies and schoolhouses for the education of our children." Beyond practical goals, this society, like other black benevolent associations, provided a support structure and a sense of belonging to its members. Through regular meetings, rules of debate, and established leadership positions, the Jacobs Benevolent Society, like other mutual aid societies, formalized social networks and gave their members a measure of collective security. Often overlapping with church memberships, these societies were tangible manifestations of the collective efforts that freedpeople employed to bring stability to the uncertainties of a postslave society.[19]

Mutual aid associations provided members with a collective identity and safety net in times of crisis, but they did not always look inward. The Good Samaritans, one of the most prominent benevolent associations in Natchez, took pride in its respectful public image. In the midst of the first political campaign after black enfranchisement, the *Natchez Democrat* described the Good Samaritans as "excellent," in that the black members demonstrated "good deportment" and "good character and respectability." A couple of years later, in 1869, society members marched through the "principal" streets of Natchez to celebrate its third anniversary "with banners, music, etc., all the members being dressed in the regalia of the order," demonstrating their prominent place in the public sphere of Natchez.[20]

Although it was organized in 1866, antecedents of the Good Samaritan association dated back to antebellum times. The postemancipation association consisted of two branches totaling two hundred people: a female society called the Good Samaritan Daughters and a male branch that numbered ninety members. Each society pledged itself to "relieve want and destitution, nurse the sick, bury the dead, and to do good to all men." Like the Jacobs Benevolent Society, the Good Samaritans were affiliated with a local church, in this case the African Methodist Episcopal (AME) Church. Two of the officers were members of the AME Zion Chapel's board of trustees; however, denominational affiliation did not preclude organizing events with other societies and churches, especially for the female branches. The Good Samaritan Daughters held a "Grand Concert" at Rose Hill Baptist Church and joined with the Daughters of Zion, another benevolent society, in hosting an entertainment festival, which included singing by the Young Ladies Choir, a discussion, and a lecture given by an up-and-coming political leader, John R. Lynch. (Lynch, a former slave, was elected to Congress three years later at the age of twenty-six.)[21]

Equally dedicated to the uplift and support of its members, the Daughters of Zion had a stronger focus on institution building than its associational counterparts. The cofounder of the Daughters of Zion, Agnes Fitzhugh, was herself a prominent figure in black Natchez society. Born into slavery, she was freed in 1834 when her husband, Nelson, purchased his and Agnes's freedom, and after the Civil War she became "the leader of the women of the church in those early days," noted a local history from the early twentieth century. The Daughters held fairs and festivals in the city to raise funds for the "buying or building [of] a colored church," reported the *Christian Recorder*. Since they were barred from using public buildings, such as city hall or the Natchez Institute, for their fairs, the Daughters convened their gatherings at the homes of their members. One was held at the residence of Hannah Thompson, the treasurer of the Daughters, a cake baker and the mother of two schoolteachers. Over two days and three nights, they raised $900, a significant sum that was nearly a third of the monies needed for a down payment on a new church building.[22]

The leading women in the Daughters of Zion were also the leading members of the African Methodist Episcopal Church in Natchez. Three of the board members' husbands were incorporators of the church. Similar to the Baptists, the AME Church grew from modest beginnings in occupied Natchez to spread throughout the district. But whereas the black members of the Wall Street Baptist Church struggled to claim the mantle of the true Baptist church in Natchez, the new AME Church diverged from the Baptists in two ways: they made explicit their separation from white Methodists, and the congregation grew to see themselves as part of a nationwide community of black Christians.[23]

In a move replicated across the South in thousands of biracial churches, the black members of the local Methodist church split off from the white members. The reasons for the separation were readily apparent. White church leaders restricted black men from leadership positions and limited the influence of black congregants over church worship and policy. The Methodist Episcopal Church, South considered slavery a legitimate institution, and most of its white members sided with the Confederacy during the war. In addition, Methodist churches segregated their buildings, forcing black members into separate seating areas or galleries and offering special services for slaves. Thus the establishment of an independent and separate church seemed to be the next logical step after emancipation, a step that Rev. Page Tyler, a black AME missionary, formalized in March 1864. In these heady days, the new church in Natchez, known as Zion Chapel, grew under the protection afforded by the U.S. military. The members held revival meetings, and local ministers spoke to the black Fifth and the Fifty-Eighth Regiments. Rev. Tyler recognized the local leadership of this congregation, licensing "four brethren as local preachers, and one as an exhorter," noted Robert McCary, a free black barber of some wealth and prominence who also preached on occasion to black soldiers in the city.[24]

Building off of networks and experiences forged under slavery, local leaders quickly created vibrant church communities. Houston Reedy, born enslaved and a saddler by trade who hired himself out for fifty dollars a month, exemplified these early organizers. While still under bondage, he studied at night, "between midnight and day light," and acquired a rudimentary education. Freed by Union forces, Reedy became an ordained AME minister in September 1864. His leadership abilities attracted the attention of the head of AMA operations in Natchez, who thought Reedy would make a strong initial candidate for a program to train local black preachers. Reedy served for a short while in Natchez, but his skills and experience led him to establish other AME churches in the region: in Baton Rouge, Louisiana, and in Fort Adams in Wilkinson County, Mississippi.[25]

Reedy's missionary work illustrates the aggressive efforts of the AME Church to establish independent black churches from the remnants of the white-dominated Methodist Episcopal Church, South. The most prolific church organizer in the Natchez District was Rev. Abram H. Dixon. Like many former slaves, Dixon moved to an urban area after the war, in this case to Natchez. He joined the AME Church and was soon licensed as a local preacher. He went on to organize an AME Church in Fayette, Jefferson County, and to pastor churches in the towns of Port Gibson, Woodville, Washington, Grand Gulf, and Summit Station, as well as churches on the Grove and Ebeneezer plantations. By the spring of 1867, the AME Church in the Natchez District claimed nine satellite churches—Natchez, Pine Ridge, Hall's Place, Woodville, Sweet-Home, Vidalia, Rodney, Port Gibson, and Davis Bend—with a total of nearly one thousand church members, nine schools, 470 students, and church property valued at a little over $10,000. From its urban base in Natchez, the AME Church extended its reach to the plantation hinterlands by organizing churches in rural neighborhoods, a process that brought local black communities together in a common organizational framework.[26]

In the meantime, a succession of missionary-ministers headed Zion Chapel in Natchez, establishing its presence as one of the preeminent black institutions in the district. Between 1864 and 1868 five different ministers passed through the pulpit; however, the congregation and its lay leaders—the core of the church—sustained the church through these volatile times. With 350 members and two hundred students, Zion Chapel was the "central point" in a mission that extended from Natchez "in a circumference of sixty miles in every direction," boasted one minister.[27]

Like the Wall Street congregation, the AME members occupied a Methodist church building during the war, and like their Baptist counterparts, they were "turned out" by white members. So they purchased a church property from the Methodist Episcopal Church, South in 1866, but the building burned to the ground in a city fire two years later. Four years after the church's founding, members finally secured a permanent and lasting home when they purchased a church and lot from the Presbyterians. The white members of the Second Presbyterian Church, on the corner of Pine and Jefferson Streets, abandoned the church property after the occupation of the city by federal soldiers. Freedpeople then used the building as a church and school as early as 1866, and it was this building that became the home of Zion Chapel, where it remains to this day.[28]

Some of the most respected, well-connected, and financially independent black families joined the AME Church in Natchez. The seven original trustees included two draymen, a grocer, a carpenter, a plasterer, a jeweler, and a licensed local preacher. Other "colored men in business in Natchez" made the AME Church their home, including two blacksmiths and wagon makers, a brick mason, an undertaker, a gunsmith, and three cotton planters. Benjamin Dixon, born in Kentucky, operated a gun shop of some prominence in Natchez, was a founding member of the Natchez Good Samaritans, and later served as an officer in the Good Will Fire Company. He was "respected by white and colored people," even though he was a black man who had an accessible supply of "guns, pistols and every thing in his line." His son, A. B. Dixon, continued in the path of his father's community involvement by becoming the pastor of Zion Chapel in the early twentieth century. According to Thomas W. Stringer, the head of AME operations in Mississippi, the Natchez church boasted many families of "a considerable degree of refinement." On the cusp of Radical Reconstruction, the church had grown to a membership of seven or eight hundred, including members from "every branch of industry," and the religious community extended to "day-schools, Sabbath-schools and singing schools, together with their other benevolent enterprises." They were determined, concluded Stringer, "to be something more than the mudsills of society."[29]

The institutional structure of the AME Church and the involvement of wealthy families served to demonstrate the distance that black people had traveled in the wake of emancipation, but reminders of their precarious position in a society that rejected their citizenship were all too evident. Meeting for Sunday evening service in the summer of 1866 at a building on Madison Street, AME congregants sent up a cry that "powder had been put under the Church, and that it was about to be blown up," reported the local newspaper. A general stampede ensued, resulting in the death of a child and the injury of several other persons. Across town, congregants at a "negro Baptist Church" likewise believed the plausibility of a rumor that someone in the city planned to bomb the black churches. Three hundred members stormed out of church, fearing that their church was a target.[30]

Living in the midst of a free society but lacking specific protections, church members took some refuge in their networks of support within the local Natchez community, but increasingly black members looked to a national AME community for encouragement, common cause, and affinity. The vehicle for this broad-based community was the official organ of the AME Church—the *Christian Recorder*. Between 1863 and 1867, the *Christian Recorder* served as a vital point of contact for newly freed blacks across the South as they struggled to make sense of war, emancipation, and political empowerment. Each week the pages of the *Recorder* were peppered with correspondence from all corners of the nation, but particularly from members of emerging congregations and black regiments stationed in the South. Correspondents wrote of camp life, battles against Confederates, and the trials of working with northern whites, and they used the paper to reconnect with family they had been separated from by slavery.[31]

Church members and preachers from Natchez often wrote letters to the *Christian Recorder*. They described community life, solicited help, and added their voices to the political issues of the day. One letter writer from Natchez used the columns in the *Recorder* as a messenger board, asking the "brethren" for help in finding a permanent pastor. "Pardon my boldness," the letter began, "... but this is a voice speaking out of the darkness, and crying.... Truly we are in need. We have no regular pastor, as yet, in charge of our church." Various correspondents kept the readers of the newspaper appraised on the status of Zion Chapel, described prominent ministers who spoke at the church's pulpit as they passed through the region, and complained about conflicts with northern whites and government officials. In one particularly noteworthy letter, Catherine A. McCary called on black readers to set aside denominational and factional conflicts and to unite "as professed Christians, to banish slavery and sin." Nothing in the letter explicitly referenced Natchez; rather, McCary seems to have written the letter as an exhortation to a national black community to continue the good work of church building and to encourage "the members of our Church, and every society which has for its object the amelioration of the condition of our race, [to] cultivate a spirit of union." While spiritual in tone, the plea had an undeniable political message, in that it called for black solidarity at a time when southern state legislatures were debating the Black Codes.[32]

That such a political statement and encouraging message came from the pen of Catherine McCary was not so unusual considering her family background. Her parents were Nelson Fitzhugh (a trustee of Zion Chapel) and Agnes Fitzhugh (president of the Daughters of Zion). Six of Catherine's seven brothers would become partisan political leaders during Radical Reconstruction. Catherine herself was a teacher and married into the McCary family, another prominent and politically active free black family. Robert McCary owned and operated a well-respected barbershop in town that catered to elite whites. His sons, Robert Jr. and William, continued in their father's footsteps until emancipation opened new worlds to the McCary boys. Robert Jr. became a minister in the AME Church and went on to pastor a church in Indianapolis. William stayed in Natchez and entered politics, becoming one of the leading members of the local Republican Party and serving as city alderman, postmaster, county treasurer, tax collector, and sheriff.[33]

Catherine's father, Nelson Fitzhugh—a grocer, part-time preacher, and trustee of the AME Church—was the most prolific *Christian Recorder* correspondent from Natchez. He wrote letters to the newspaper to keep the national audience informed on local developments, and in a reciprocal relationship the editors promised to "keep a strict watch over the rebels in that district, and if they continue to oppress the freedmen, we will expose them to the world." At a time when blacks had minimal access to political or media outlets, the *Christian Recorder* served as a public sphere in which national leaders and local activists could exchange ideas and concerns. Indeed, it was one of the few black newspapers to circulate across the entire South during Reconstruction. And equally important, it allowed local people to shape national discussions on Reconstruction policy and the future of black politics.[34]

The melding of local and national networks is demonstrated further in an impassioned plea for suffrage written by P. Houston Murray, a black phrenologist and journalist from Pennsylvania. Writing from Natchez, he began his letter by documenting, in the few weeks following the end of the war, the "horror, violence and injustice, done to colored people." He mentioned conflicts and atrocities across the South, in Alabama, Mississippi, Virginia, Louisiana, and Tennessee, to drive home the point that freedpeople were unprotected and their loyalty to the Union was besmirched. At least under slavery, he maintained, the master's financial interest in his slaves gave them some measure of security, but now, freed, they felt the sting of "political nudity" and found themselves without access to the courts, the right to private property, or protection "against the virulence of the body politic of the state."[35]

Turning then to events in Natchez, Murray rebuked the military's efforts to return freedpeople to the employment of their former masters. "Has not the government armed the negro," he asked sarcastically, "and taught him to hate and kill his master, as he would a viper? Did they not know that the enmity between the master and slave would be doubly deepened, and that they could not live together in harmony again?" Epitomizing the sense of injustice felt in the hearts of freedpeople, Murray described how "a notorious rebel deserter" assaulted Agnes Fitzhugh in the streets of Natchez, yet the provost marshal of freedmen only fined the attacker fifteen dollars, of which ten dollars went to Fitzhugh as compensation for her beating. "I don't want money, but justice!" Fitzhugh protested and promptly deposited the money in the Lincoln Monument Fund. Murray concluded his litany of injustices by drawing attention to the small and unspoken ways that freedpeople were oppressed:

Colored people here are excessively taxed: for a pass or permit to work for six months, or less, they must pay $3, or more. For every little script of writing they pay from $1 to $5, and sometimes even more. Men and women pay a *poll tax* of two dollars. In many of the Freedmen's Schools, each scholar pays from $1.25 to $1.50

per month. In many other shameful ways their ignorance and helplessness are taken advantage of, even to a forcible violation of the virtue of their wives and daughters, by white guards and soldiers. I only say what I *see* and *know*, and what ten thousand injured black men in this valley will testify to, to day.[36]

The only solution to the plight of black people, Murray argued, was "*complete personal* enfranchisement" of men and the guarantee of "civil franchises which indemnify an American *soldier* and *citizen.*" By drawing on the plight of poor freedpeople as well as the troubles of more wealthy people of color, Murray crafted an inclusive argument in favor of unrestricted male suffrage. People of African descent confronted a shared struggle in the wake of war, but their suffering was not all equal. For Murray, suffrage promised to give men the means to protect their women. Murray's letter also engaged in and helped propel a national debate over the political rights of black people that, while discussed in the pages of national publications and in the halls of conventions and legislatures, emanated from the grassroots conflicts that freedpeople faced on a daily basis. No doubt influenced by Murray's impassioned appeal, the editor of the *Christian Recorder*, for the first time, called for the extension of suffrage to the "colored race."[37]

Political discussion and debate did not just grace the pages of the *Recorder*; they became a part of local church life. Murray argued that "the *press*, the *pulpit*, and all the deliberative bodies of the country" should be demanding universal male suffrage. Given the centrality of the AME Church to political mobilization, it was not surprising that church members integrated the political and the religious into a seamless discussion about how to better their lives in freedom. Reverend Pennington of Zion Chapel read to his congregation an order from Gen. O. O. Howard explaining that the Freedmen's Bureau would "continue to protect" freedmen's right to lease cotton lands, and at a related public meeting Pennington encouraged freedpeople to join the cotton economy and become independent producers. Zion Chapel housed some of the first organizational meetings of the Union League. Four AME trustees went on to hold political positions in the local Republican Party, and at least four AME ministers held political office in the Natchez District.[38]

These political discussions were not unique to African Methodists. Baptists, of course, blended the political and the religious, and they often did so in conversation and collaboration with AME Church members. J. S. Habersham, the minister at the Rose Hill Baptist Church, was also a correspondent to the *Christian Recorder*. In one letter written just as the Christmas Insurrectionary Scare was heating up, he described a visit from Elder Elisha Weaver, the editor of the *Recorder*. Recognizing the unique place that the *Recorder* held in black life, Habersham began by referring to the "Readers of the North, South, East and

West." He offered praise to "God, I mean, the loyal man's God" for breaking the shackles of slavery that had prevented "our friends and brothers in Christ Jesus" from meeting "face to face." While in Natchez, Reverend Weaver spoke at Rose Hill, Zion Chapel, and the Wall Street Baptist Church. Even though denominations often bickered over territorial disputes in missionary work, Weaver's presence at Natchez's black churches helped to bring together local black Christians in common cause, and it forged connections between northern and southern church communities.[39]

At the local level, the *Christian Recorder* circulated through the churches and byways of Natchez. As subscription agents, J. S. Habersham and Nelson Fitzhugh circulated the newspaper in the Baptist and AME communities, respectively. Fitzhugh personally placed the *Recorder* in the hands of local residents. In one letter he described how he gained three new subscribers: a young woman, a black deacon in the Wall Street Baptist Church, and an ex-Confederate. In addition, Fitzhugh employed his "little son" to sell copies of the newspaper on the streets of Natchez and then gave the unsold copies "to our poor colored friends in the country." Through individuals like Nelson Fitzhugh, the *Recorder* gained a widespread readership that helped circulate notions of black cooperation in the Natchez District; in addition, the paper created a space where black Christians from different churches and localities could enter into a dialogue about the condition of freedpeople in America.[40]

Not unlike the AME Church with its broad political mission, the Baptists envisioned their mission extending beyond the establishment of individual churches. It was their duty, they believed, to agitate for the rights of black people and to dissociate from any church, group, or individual that was "opposed to us having equal rights." According to resolutions agreed to at a missionary conference at Rose Hill Church in 1868, local Baptist churches, as well as "sister and neighboring churches," were admonished to "pray for the success of that great party known as the Republican Party." Recognizing the role of divine providence and the Republican Party in their emancipation, black Baptist leaders called on their fellow church members to work toward creating a nation where "the poor and oppressed of every land" would find refuge and assistance. By linking the political and spiritual aspects of freedom and equality, they extended their community from black Baptist churches to other black churches and the black community writ large, yet they also marked boundaries of exclusion. They called on black churches to treat "all parties that are opposed to us having equal rights before the law" with contempt and called for church members to "withhold their aid" from those unwilling to recognize equal rights. Eschewing an essentialist racial category for membership, local Baptists envisioned a Christian community in which equality and compassion for the lesser members of society would influence daily interactions.[41]

Zion Chapel and the Wall Street and Rose Hill Baptist Churches represented the largest and most influential churches in the Natchez District, in part due to their location in the federally protected city of Natchez and due to the wealth and varied membership of the church congregations. In contrast, establishing and sustaining a rural church proved to be a much more difficult enterprise. Whereas urban churches offered their members a measure of protection and affiliation beyond the purview of white society, rural churches had to be mindful of white landowners. Urban church leaders could openly debate political issues—a luxury few rural congregations could afford because they lacked public spaces and did not own church buildings.[42]

Although far less documentation exists on postemancipation rural black churches, they originated, like their urban counterparts, from congregations formed under bondage. In the rural town of Fort Adams in Wilkinson County, "surrounded by large cotton plantations," Houston Reedy established an AME church by attracting the black members from the local white Methodist church. Some of the older black church leaders, as slaves, had preached under the auspices of the white church for twenty-five years, yet they quickly joined the new AME congregation, accepting ordination and devoting themselves to "the elevation of their people," noted a *Recorder* correspondent. Most rural and small-town churches drew on indigenous leaders. Rev. John H. Allen, born a slave in Virginia, joined the Methodist Episcopal Church, South four years after being sold and transported to Natchez in 1839. Although a licensed Methodist preacher, he joined the AME denomination after the war and pastored churches in Kingston, Pine Ridge, and Woodville. Of similar origins, at least seventy-seven black preachers and forty-two black churches were established in Tensas and Concordia Parishes between 1865 and 1880.[43]

While church congregations were ubiquitous across the postemancipation rural landscape, church buildings were an uncommon sight. After an inspection tour of the Louisiana river parishes, a Freedmen's Bureau official reported that freedpeople "have their regular days of worship," but they had "very few, if any churches outside the principal Cities." "Their meetings," he continued, "are generally held under the canopy of Heaven, and even here they are often disturbed by ruffians." Although "the enmity of whites" had brought "great trials and sufferings," he continued, "they never forget to thank God for their freedom, and all other privileges they now enjoy." In time, as freedpeople developed the tactics of collective labor negotiation, they pressed planters to provide churches for neighborhood communities, in return for agreeing to yearlong labor contracts. The AME church at Clift Mission, just outside of Natchez, was typical of many rural church communities in that planters set aside land and sometimes contributed a building for worship.[44]

In those communities fortunate enough to possess a house of worship, the physical structure was the sole collective space where black people could share their burdens to a sympathetic audience, seek spiritual sustenance, and express their hopes, visions, and celebrations. Edward Henderson, a Freedmen's Bureau agent in Tensas Parish, noted, in the course of his plantation inspections, that most freedpeople visited "the various houses dedicated to God" and that "they seem[ed] to enjoy the comfort of divine worship." Whitelaw Reid, a white northern journalist, visited one black church on a Concordia Parish plantation in April 1866 and recorded its humble origins and collective aspirations. Situated at the center of the quarters, the church had been converted from a typical slave double cabin by knocking out the middle divider. Under the darkened rafters a few benches served as pews, and on the weatherboarding that covered the walls the congregants had tacked on pictures. Near the pulpit hung an "enlarged copy of Brady's well-known photograph of Mr. Lincoln, with 'Tad' standing at his knee," and nearby a picture of General Grant graced the rough-hewn wall. While it could be argued that the pictures suggest a religious iconography, a more plausible explanation for their prominent display is that the images of Lincoln and Grant communicated to members and visitors alike the congregation's shared allegiance with the Union, and they served to connect their small church community to two of the most powerful men in the nation. In sum, the pictures identified the politics of the members and symbolized the independence of the community from local domination.[45]

Black churches melded politics and religion in a way that was uncommon in white churches. Dispensing political opinions from the pulpit was not unusual, yet few white churches institutionalized their political affiliations, and white ministers were far less likely to seek elective offices. Black churches served political purposes by connecting people across a region into a centralized unit, as well as by explicitly encouraging the development of a democratic ethos in their institutional structures. Although class and gender differences pervaded these denominational bodies, men and women were able to forge new connections between rural and urban communities and to participate in an expanding conversation on the meaning of emancipation by offering a sphere for political dialogue and a space where women could participate in public matters. Black churches also gave shape to local communities by providing an opportunity for communal worship and by providing members with a collective identity that transcended local constraints based on race and place.

"Schools all thrugh the county"

Schools, like churches, sprang up from the grass roots in black neighborhoods and, to some extent, relied on affiliation with church congregations. But schools depended to a far greater degree than churches on assistance from outside organizations for their development. Lacking school buildings, supplies, and, most of all, teachers, freedpeople looked to missionary associations and the Freedmen's Bureau to provide financial and material support for the establishment of individual schools. Reliance on outside groups generated internal conflicts, however, as missionary leaders and government agents clashed with local black leaders and communities over the control of schools and curricula. Moreover, local white communities rarely greeted the establishment of black schools with approval or support. Especially in the rural hinterlands, black families and plantation communities faced considerable obstacles in creating schools. They persevered nonetheless. Learning to read and write gave freedpeople an advantage in the practical matters of work and commerce; however, they valued it more for the new worlds of information and knowledge it opened up to them, independent of whites and the rumor mill. In the struggle to establish schools, freedpeople gained practical experience in institution building and in forging the neighborhood and national connections that would become essential to gaining political power.[46]

When AMA missionaries arrived in Natchez in the fall of 1863, they encountered a strong desire among the freedpeople for learning, but they did not initially see any schools, teachers, or supplies. They assumed that the region was educationally barren, when in fact at least four black schools were already in operation. Jackson Habersham, the subscription agent for the *Christian Recorder* and a member of Rose Hill Baptist Church, rented a house and taught a room full of students. Catherine McCary, daughter of Agnes and Nelson Fitzhugh, taught at a school for the children of free blacks that she probably inherited from her father-in-law. Josephine C. Nicks, described by an AMA agent as "well educated," taught "a sort of select school," suggesting that her students were probably children of the free black elite. The fourth school, operated by Lily Ann Granderson, was quite rare in the annals of the antebellum South—a secret night school for slaves taught by a slave.[47]

Born into slavery in Virginia in 1816, Lily Ann Granderson was of mixed parentage. Her mother was enslaved at age three after Lily Ann's grandmother, a freeborn woman of Indian descent, died. On her father's side, Granderson traced her lineage to the First Families of Virginia, an exclusive group of elite whites descended from the first colonial settlers. At some point in her childhood Lily Ann was moved to Kentucky. There she worked as a house slave and grew to know her master's family quite well, so well that her master's children taught her how to read and write. But whatever stability she knew in Kentucky was ruptured when her master died and, in the subsequent settling of the estate, she was sold down the river to a Mississippi slaveholder. Compounding the shock of moving to the Deep South was the fact that she now had to work as a field hand on a cotton plantation. "O, how I longed to die!" she told a friend, "and sometimes I thought I would die from such cruel whippings upon my bared body." Under these conditions it did not take long for Granderson's health to deteriorate, but after much pleading, her master agreed to her request for a transfer to the kitchen, for part-time work.[48]

Moving from the fields to her master's house in Natchez gave Granderson the opportunity to establish a night school for slaves. Beginning at eleven or twelve o'clock at night, slaves would sneak into a secluded room off of a back alley. All the doors and windows were shut tight, and the enslaved students used pitch-pine splinters to illuminate their reading materials and writing instruments. These precautions were necessary since state law forbade slave education, and masters feared—with good reason—that a basic education could expose slaves to abolitionism or means of escape from slavery. In confirmation of their fears, Granderson claimed that many of her students wrote their own passes and headed for Canada. Since these slaves were never heard from again, she surmised that they had successfully escaped.[49]

For about seven years this little slave school operated under the noses of Natchez authorities. Granderson took on twelve students at a time, and after they had learned to read and write, she graduated them and accepted another twelve under her charge. All told, hundreds of slaves passed through her classroom. But word of the school's existence eventually leaked out. Worried that her former students would be punished, Granderson was surprised to learn that the local authorities, for unknown reasons, decided not prosecute her or them. Emboldened by the positive turn of events, she opened a Sabbath school along with her midnight school. In 1863 when federal soldiers and northern missionaries arrived in Natchez, they found an experienced slave teacher and quite a few literate slaves. Once freed, Granderson continued her educational work and also branched out into religious service as an ordained deaconess at the Pine Street Baptist Church and a trustee of the Jacobs Benevolent Society. (Her son, David C. Granderson, later became the pastor of Pine Street Baptist Church and was nominally affiliated with Republican political organizations in the 1870s and 1880s.)[50]

The already-established black schools had secured rooms for their classes, but finding other suitable rooms and buildings for schools proved to be a continual challenge for AMA missionaries and teachers. The first AMA school commenced beneath a large magnolia tree, but so eager were freedpeople for education that "at least 1000 persons" assembled underneath its broad limbs, reported the superintendent of the Freedmen's Camp in Vidalia, Louisiana. Other creative places used for schoolrooms included the upper floor of "an [fire] engine house" and a temperance hall, but most classes for children were held in churches, particularly at the Wall Street Baptist Church and the Rose Hill Baptist Church. Despite these inauspicious beginnings, the AMA had organized six hundred students into regular classes less than two months after the first teachers arrived in 1864, and within a short time six day schools and three night schools were in operation, led by "twenty-seven teachers and missionaries."[51]

Founded as an antislavery organization, the AMA became a leading provider of education and poor relief to freedpeople during the Civil War and Reconstruction. Believing that a Christian education would weaken race prejudice and transform ex-slaves into virtuous citizens, the AMA tapped into northern philanthropic networks and sent dozens of teachers to the former Confederate states to establish some of the first schools for former slaves. The first schoolhouses were rudimentary and the teachers rarely received full compensation for their work, yet the schools seldom lacked for eager students. It came as little surprise, then, that local freedpeople readily accepted AMA teachers and missionaries into their communities, given the indispensable services that they provided.[52]

Despite freedpeople's strong desire to learn, the AMA struggled to keep its schools open over the next four years. With the children of the black elite attending their own private schools, it fell on the AMA—in conjunction with the Freedmen's Bureau—to provide classes for the thousands of poor black families in the Natchez District. The superintendent of freedmen's schools tried to avoid charging tuition, but in late 1866 the schools were forced to charge students one dollar a month in tuition, a substantial sum for laboring families. Few farm laborers received their promised wages at the end of the contract year, owing to a very low cotton yield in 1866, and, as a result, schools suffered. The school at Rose Hill Church opened in the fall after the cotton-picking season, but attendance had fallen by over 80 percent from the previous spring. The same was true at a school in Vidalia. After another failed crop in 1867, the prospects for schooling looked no better. Seven schools enrolling over 450 students operated under the authority of the AMA, but by 1868 the scope of AMA operations had dwindled to four schools, employing six teachers and enrolling fewer than 300 students. And while there still was a great demand for more teachers and supplies, the existing teachers begged for the most basic necessities for their students. "The schoolrooms are so open, and many of the children so poorly dressed, they do not attend when it is so cold," wrote Hattie E. Stryker, an AMA teacher, "but some will come ragged and barefooted[;] when it is so cold we need our thick winter clothing."[53]

Although the education of children was a primary goal of black parents and the AMA, a number of schools were established for adults. A night school with thirty men and women met at the military hospital. The AMA set up an "industrial school" for freedwomen and a "free night school," presumably for working adults. Housed on the second floor of a building that was also occupied by a school for children and a Freedmen's Store, which sold low-cost clothing, the industrial school taught fifty "poor women" how to sew, make garments, and repair tattered clothing. Schools for black soldiers, however, offered adult men the best opportunity for a formal education. The regimental school at the barracks of the Sixth Colored Heavy Artillery was typical. Classes were held in the morning and evening to accommodate drilling and other military routines and, within four months, all but two of the sixty-one soldier-students could read and spell.[54]

Most working adults, however, found it difficult to find the time and tuition for school; thus most cobbled together various experiences in and outside of the classroom to get a basic education. A good example is John R. Lynch. The future congressman was nineteen when he began night school, where he learned basic grammar, spelling, and writing, but the school closed after four months. Fortunately, his place of work, a photography shop, shared an alley with a white public school. Perched in the back room of the shop, Lynch would listen to the teacher reciting lessons for hours on end. During other free moments at the shop, he read privately. He was "especially interested," he recalled many years later, in newspapers and magazines that reported on President Andrew Johnson's impeachment. He also took a keen interest in a book of parliamentary law, going even so far as to consult frequently with the most prominent white attorney in Natchez on his budding legal interests. Lynch's education undoubtedly assisted his meteoric rise in politics, including stints as justice of the peace, speaker of the Mississippi House of Representatives, and three terms in Congress.[55]

Lynch would prove to be adept at bringing together various factions and communities in the Natchez District, divisions that were all too apparent in the fraught period between emancipation and black male enfranchisement. In the difficult task of creating schools, class and regional divisions boiled to the surface. As was typical of northern white benevolence, AMA leaders had a firm idea about how to uplift former slaves, and they were ill inclined to accommodate freedpeople's vision of freedom, education, and citizenship.[56]

These competing visions came into conflict when three northern black teachers moved to Natchez in 1865. In an attempt to mollify local white residents who were critical of black education, S. G. Wright, the head of AMA operations in Natchez, told the new black teachers that "he could not treat them *here* as he would in *Oberlin*" and that he would not permit black and white teachers to live together for fear that whites "would mob the house." Educated at Oberlin College in Ohio—a school famous for its abolitionist principles and its admittance of black and female students—these women were well acquainted with the AMA and the cause of progressive reform. Blanche Harris, for example, had taught at one of the first AMA schools for freedpeople in Norfolk, Virginia, and as a result, she and the other black teachers did not expect discriminatory treatment from their missionary friends. Given that Wright had hired local black teachers to work for the AMA and he had boarded white teachers with black families, his decision to keep these new black teachers at a distance seemed hypocritical. The women felt slighted further when Wright refused to let them sit at the same table with other white teachers, and also when white AMA teachers did not extend to them an invitation to a weekly prayer meeting. Feeling "forsaken," they sought refuge with local blacks, for whom accounts of missionary discrimination and condescension were not unusual. "The excellent young ladies . . . from Oberlin," remarked Nelson Fitzhugh, the AME Church leader, "are much respected as teachers in our community."[57]

Local black leaders also clashed with the AMA over the use of buildings and filling leadership roles, but the source of the conflict concerned the control and direction of the emerging freed community. AMA leaders quarreled with the black leaders of the Wall Street Baptist Church over the use of their gallery. The AMA wanted to use it for desperately needed classroom space, but church leaders claimed that a gallery "was not a proper place to have a school." Responding to this slight, the local superintendent of AMA schools expressed his suspicions that more was at issue than the use of a gallery: they "are determin[ed] to have the rule in regard to teachers and preachers and their favorite is Black." What the AMA viewed as ungratefulness, local church leaders considered part of a larger effort to establish a viable and independent local institution. And although they were grateful for AMA assistance, they rejected the northern organization's patronizing sentiment. A white minister passed over in favor of a black preacher remarked that the freedpeople had "an utter unappreciation of what was being done for them." Going further, S. G. Wright thought it "*exceedingly* unwise + *dangerous*" to tell freedpeople that they "will soon become citizens" with the same rights as white people, especially when AMA teachers had not yet instructed ex-slaves on the responsibilities of citizenship. To the dismay of the white AMA leaders, freedpeople rejected the idea that they needed to be "qualified" in order to receive basic civil and political rights. Instead, they looked for leadership among those who affirmed their expectation of imminent citizenship, and they applauded those who called for "colored soldiers . . . to defend *their* rights . . . with the bayonet."[58]

In the context of growing antagonism between local blacks—especially members of the black elite—and AMA leaders, the mistreatment of black teachers highlighted one of the larger struggles after emancipation. "We thought . . . that our greatest trouble would be to get along with the whites of the South," wrote Nelson Fitzhugh, but it turned out that relations with northern whites could be problematic as well. Describing the handling that the Oberlin teachers received, Fitzhugh accused S. G. Wright and the white AMA teachers—whom he called "a Northern copperhead preacher and his clique"—of a "cruel and wicked injustice." Reading Fitzhugh's inflammatory comments in the *Christian Recorder*,

J. P. Bardwell, an AMA agent, lashed out at the trustee of the AME Church, even though he later acknowledged that Wright had made a serious mistake in his effort "to propitiate the favor of Military officers" at the expense of black teachers. As a result, the Natchez black community lost confidence in Wright and the entire leadership of the AMA. "Our hold upon the colored population has been much weakened by this state of things," Bardwell acknowledged.[59]

From the black elite's perspective, there was little need to take direction from an outside organization, since they had established independent schools before the arrival of the AMA. By the end of 1865, six private, black-run schools were in operation, reflecting the growing wealth in the urban black community, as most of these children had "to pay tuition [to] attend these schools." But mandatory tuition was not the only feature separating independent black schools from missionary schools. The curriculum of the independent schools went beyond the basics of reading, writing, and arithmetic to include the arts, music, and dance. At May Day festivities, students from private black schools showed off their learning in public displays designed to demonstrate racial progress as well as class distinction. Catherine McCary, a longtime teacher and member of the Fitzhugh family, directed a May Day program that included a "mixture of music, declamation, dialogues and acting"—a far cry from the typical lessons found in the missionary schools. Students dressed up as the May queen, a fairy queen, and maids and performed for an audience composed mostly of parents and relatives. But McCary had a larger audience in mind than just the students' families. "Among the invited guests present, we noticed His Honor the Mayor, and Rev. Dr. Stratton [of the First Presbyterian Church], both of whom expressed a high appreciation of the excellent manner in which the whole festivities were conducted," observed the *Natchez Democrat*. At stake was not just a year's worth of learning but also the public image of African Americans. By aspiring to the standards of bourgeois cultural refinement, McCary (and her students) challenged prevailing assumptions of innate black inferiority and asserted freedpeople's right to participate in public culture.[60]

May Day programs were not the only large gatherings of freedpeople in the city. An assortment of black Sabbath schools from across the city came together for an emancipation celebration on New Year's Day 1865 that included "singing, prayer, recitations, Reading the Emancipation Proclamation, a declamation and oration, short speeches +c." The Wall Street Baptist Church hosted the morning exercises, and then the celebrants moved to the Methodist church for the afternoon program. Nearly six hundred black children crowded into the house of worship—the largest building in the city—along with hundreds of other family members and onlookers. Before perhaps the largest black audience to ever voluntarily assemble in Natchez, various black speakers gave testimony to the "past and present condition of the slaves," and the participants celebrated their liberation in song—songs that produced "an intense stillness in the house." While it could be argued, as one AMA official did, that Lincoln's proclamation created "a nation born in a day," the real work of nation building was made in moments like this, when different groups came together to celebrate a common experience and to gather momentum for the coming struggle over civil and political equality.[61]

Collective efforts such as these paved the way for an unprecedented project in the region—the construction of a public school building for black children. The local black community, in conjunction with the missionary societies and the Freedmen's Bureau, shared the costs of construction (including "gratis" lumber), despite the fact that the "richer portion of the colored people" held back their donations because they had lost confidence in the AMA leadership. The Union School opened its doors to nearly two hundred students on February 1, 1866. The school would later become a focal point for black and Republican political activism; its initial objective was also political, although narrower. It attracted the "most advanced pupils" from "the best classes" in the city in order to train a new cadre of black teachers to fill the earnest demands for education in the rural hinterland. "A large number of pupils in our school are now qualified to teach others," wrote one teacher at the Union School in the spring of 1866. "They will undoubtedly secure schools on plantations, as planters are frequently asking our Supt. to furnish them teachers; colored teachers . . . seem to have the preference."[62]

Freedpeople in the plantation districts, however, did not wait, nor could they wait, for the Union School graduates to establish their own schools. In contrast to Natchez, rural schools faced more public and violent opposition. Ex-Confederates ran a black teacher from Pennsylvania out of Concordia Parish, and in rural Adams County two female teachers were "driven back by the [white] citizens." In Jefferson County soon after the end of the war, hostile whites openly proclaimed their intention to "re-enslave" the black population in a condition similar to "serfdom or peonage," lamented one Freedmen's Bureau agent, and they thwarted the efforts of the bureau to establish two black schools in Fayette. Too poor to organize even a modest school, the freedpeople of Union Church, on the eastern edge of Jefferson County, unsuccessfully petitioned the Freedmen's Bureau to redirect funds allotted for rations toward the construction of a schoolhouse. Freedpeople in Rodney, a small town on the Mississippi River, were more successful; they assembled and pledged "to raise seventy eight dollars ($78.00) per month for school purposes." In response, local missionary societies supplied them with a teacher from the Northwestern Freedmen's Aid Commission. White townsfolk shunned the new teacher, yet the school persisted due to local freedpeople's willingness to assume the costs of running it.[63]

About sixteen miles inland from Rodney, in Fayette, the Jefferson County seat, local blacks overcame white opposition and eventually established the first independent black school in the county, a feat the Freedmen's Bureau and northern missionary societies could not achieve. The leader of this effort was Merrimon Howard, a former house slave and carriage driver who was freed in 1854 and later became the most powerful black politician in the county as a three-time elected sheriff. After failed attempts by the local Freedmen's Bureau to establish a school, Howard, who had acquired a rudimentary education, turned to the head of the Freedmen's Bureau, Gen. O. O. Howard, for assistance in the fall of 1865. Hoping that General Howard would "pay som attention to me," Merrimon Howard (no relation) argued that the freedpeople desperately needed schools and the means to protect their nascent community. But Howard wanted more than just money for teachers; he envisioned a democratic community that could shepherd a public school system. "[E]very Cullerd person of proper age should pay a small tax to ade the government in learing," he suggested. At a time when the state government limited black rights and passed off the care of poor blacks solely onto shoulders of black taxpayers, Howard declared, "we dont think the steat has any right to our suport." Instead, he called on the federal government to live up to its reciprocal obligations to its citizens. It was the freedpeople "who has ben the loyal people of the South," and now they ask, "whare is the protection to shelter us from the beting Storms that now threttens us with Destruction?" Especially for the rural "people in back + midel countrys," who felt the desperation of freedom keenly: "peneless and houseless + landless and in poverty[,] Despiesed by the world, hated by by [sic] the Country that gives us birth[,] denied of all our writs as a people." The bureau, however, rejected Howard's plea, claiming that it could not spare any extra officers for such a remote area, in which white residents ignored federal authority with impunity.[64]

Thus left to his own devices, Merrimon Howard led the effort to set up a separate school system for freedpeople. He worked out an arrangement with local white leaders to gain their "consint" and then gathered together "some of our best Colord men" to form a board of trustees, on which Howard served as president. The board set up a system of taxation to pay for a rented house and for a teacher, and Howard recruited Susan Foster, a black graduate of Oberlin College who was born in Port Gibson, Mississippi, to teach the black children of Fayette. In addition to her obvious qualifications, Foster gained the approval of the local white elite who had previously harassed white teachers sent to teach black children. Emboldened by the success of the first black school, with an initial class of twenty students, in Fayette, Howard looked to establish "schools all thrugh the county," but limited financial resources and the 1866 and 1867 crop failures further weakened the already precarious economic position of local freedpeople, preventing the establishment of other black schools. In the meantime, Howard continued to pressure the bureau and demand "the ade of the government."[65]

A few other rural black communities formed educational associations not unlike Howard's school in Jefferson County and brought teachers to their small locales, but even with strong support among local freedpeople, these rural schools struggled to maintain their independence. In Port Gibson, Claiborne County, the freedpeople formed a school association that included a six-member board of trustees. Leading the board was James Page, the ex-slave drayman and farmer whose political talents would be on full display during Radical Reconstruction when he would be elected sheriff and county treasurer. But obtaining a school property proved to be a substantial challenge for the small community of less than five hundred freed persons. The association purchased four acres of land for $2,000, which included two school buildings (one of which was also used as a church meetinghouse) that could accommodate nearly two hundred children. James Page covered the first payment of $1,000, which was nearly equal to half of his net worth. The remaining thousand dollars was to be paid a year later, on January 1, 1868, with funds raised by "the Freedmen in Port Gibson and vicinity."[66]

The best-laid plans of the community, however, were undone by the dismal 1867 crop. Many contracted laborers never received their promised wages and the poor yield reduced the income of town laborers and artisans who depended on the cotton economy. With the deadline looming for the second payment, the school association scrambled to find the funds to cover the remaining costs before they defaulted on the purchase agreement. Carrie Clark, a northern white teacher at the school who was affiliated with the American Freedman's Union Commission, begged her missionary sponsors and her wealthy father for help, but to no avail. Because the Port Gibson freedpeople could not make the payment, the land was sold at auction to the son of the former owner. But in a surprising move, the Freedmen's Bureau annulled the sale and transferred the title to James Page, preserving local black control until the school was incorporated into the state system in 1871. The travails of the Port Gibson school association highlight not only the difficulties in setting up schools outside of major urban centers but also the impediments in establishing black institutions without access to the official arena of politics. Only with Republican control of state and local governments would black schools receive regular governmental assistance and become a permanent presence in the public life of the Natchez District.[67]

Beyond the rural towns, freedpeople used the Freedmen's Bureau and labor negotiations as leverage to convince planters to build schoolhouses and employ teachers. Since the 1866 crop failed to pay anywhere near the wages promised in the labor contracts, freedpeople demanded concessions in terms of fewer restrictions on personal movement, shorter labor hours, cheaper plantation supplies, and the establishment of schools. Still other freedpeople packed up their belongings and moved to "points further north" where they hoped "to obtain their rights by law," noted one bureau official. Planters, faced with dismal yields and a labor shortage that forced them to compete with their neighbors for laborers, were not in a strong position to resist their workers' demands. "One of our negroes told me to day that *he* thought that the *whole* of *Saturday* and a school would keep nearly all," wrote Wilmer Shields, the overseer on William N. Mercer's Laurel Hill plantation. Unwilling to concede a day of work, Shields suggested to his boss that they set up a school. Many other planters across the Natchez District set up schools to placate freedpeople's demands. Once a few schools were in place, rural laborers came to expect education for their children as part of the conditions for their work. Said one Freedmen's Bureau agent in 1866, "I think the next year the hands will give a preference to places where they know there is a school."[68]

Schools sprouted up in the rural hinterlands, yet the chronic shortage of teachers and resources, persistent harassment from planters and overseers, and the harsh environment of rural life kept schools from establishing deep roots. Planting and harvesting season kept attendance numbers low, and the summer heat made classroom instruction arduous, limiting schooling to only a few months a year. In the winter months, porous schoolhouses kept teachers and students cold and damp. During the spring, the western bank of the Mississippi River often gave way to massive overflows that inundated plantation lands, forcing the suspension of planting operations and the discontinuation of schools. When not flooded, schools suffered from want of funds. In Concordia Parish, local freedpeople had great difficulty paying the school tax, so with the help of the Freedmen's Bureau, they formed a committee of three freedmen to create a sliding tuition scale based on ability to pay. Under the agreement, the freedmen's committee selected a teacher and negotiated payment based on the financial means of the community, while planters were obligated to provide "Books, Slates, and School rooms." In Tensas Parish, only one school was still operating near the end of the 1867 harvest. Despite a strong "disposition of the Parents to have their Children educated," noted one bureau report, "poverty . . . reigneth supreme" and "it was impossible to keep education among the Freed children afloat." With floods and failed crops, few families could afford schooling, and as a result only the schools in towns met with any degree of regularity.[69]

In most parts of the Natchez District, establishing local schools demanded a broad community effort. And although public school systems would eventually be created in Louisiana and Mississippi, freedpeople did not wait for the state or outside organizations to bring education to children and adults alike. The experience of establishing school boards, nominating leaders, selecting teachers, and assigning tuition fees provided freedpeople with practical experience in operating institutional bodies—experiences that they would draw on to run local governments during Reconstruction. Their intention was not to establish a democratic system of government, but the particular needs of schools—buildings, tuition, and teachers—forced men and women to pool their resources and work together. Stark divisions persisted, especially between rural and urban schools and between schools for the children of artisans and those for the children of field hands, but by pulling together in a collective endeavor and utilizing neighborhood and national networks, freedpeople forged a democratic ethos that emphasized mutual obligation and grassroots participation.

Squads and "ownership of the soil"

In the midst of efforts to create local churches and schools, freedpeople sought to reconfigure the terms of labor to better suit their collective aspirations. In the difficult and chaotic transition from slave labor to wage labor, freedpeople resisted arrangements that harked back to slavery, such as restrictions on leaving the plantation, a six-day workweek, and the enforcement of yearlong labor contracts. Generally, freedpeople preferred share-wage agreements, which offered them more control over their work and the product of their labors. Above all, they wanted to ensure the cohesiveness of their families and adjust their labor to the needs of the family and not the other way around. To do so, they gravitated toward the squad system, in which a small group of workers—often connected by kin relations—negotiated contracts and set the terms of labor in the fields. Many also aspired to own land, to further ensure the stability of their families and their economic standing, and a few were able to pool their resources and enter into planting arrangements.[70]

On the district's cotton plantations, planters and lessees sought to reinstitute a system of coerced labor. Forced by the Freedmen's Bureau to pay wages to laborers, planters quickly adapted to the new system and used contracts to dictate the movement and behavior of freedpeople. On some plantations, overseers distributed whole-day, half-day, or quarter-day tickets based on the number of hours worked, and then they capriciously withheld tickets for insubordination, unannounced visitors, or failure to return promptly to the fields after a trip to town. According to an 1868 labor contract on the York plantation in Adams County, the first instance of "insubordination or insolence" resulted in a fine, but the second offense led to "expulsion from the plantation and forfeiture" of the entire crop.[71]

Freedpeople resisted the imposition of strict social and labor controls by organizing themselves into informal groupings, often referred to as squads. A squad typically consisted of three to eight able-bodied laborers, although in plantation districts, as in the Natchez District, they tended to be larger. Clairmont plantation in Concordia Parish was typical in this regard. One thousand acres of improved land was divided into ten parcels, with a squad of ten laborers working each division. By most accounts, squads were self-selecting, in that neither planters nor the Freedmen's Bureau determined their size or membership. In larger groupings that included unrelated individuals, squads selected their own leaders, usually by democratic means, who then served as the lead negotiators with the planter over the terms of the contracts. "All the business transactions of the year, are conducted thro' these leaders," wrote one observer, "they becoming responsible for the rent, to the landowner, and often for a large bill of supplies to a merchant outside." In some cases, squad leaders negotiated a lease agreement rather than a labor contract, which gave the squad members greater freedom over the use of resources. The six squads that leased the Home Place plantation pooled their collective gains to construct a storehouse to protect plantation supplies. Democratic aspirations were also evident in the internal discipline of squads. According to one agreement, a two-thirds vote was required to dismiss without pay any member who was "lazy, insolent, or disobedient, or refuses to do full duty." On the Ellis Cliff plantation, the freedpeople, "by a majority," explained the overseer, "decided to take the money instead of a share in the crop, and the papers are now signed to that effect."[72]

As modest collective groups, squads gave freedpeople greater bargaining power when negotiating with planters and a greater voice when making complaints to Freedmen's Bureau agents. The laborers on the Russell plantation in Concordia Parish feared that they would not receive their wages, so they sent James Jackson, who may also have been a Baptist minister, to speak for them and to seek protection from the bureau. At the suggestion of a northern lessee that the laborers go to work at the blast of a horn, five freedmen marched to the office of the local bureau agent and ridiculed the planter's attempt to enforce a time-oriented mode of labor on rural people more familiar with a task-oriented system. "Haven't we been working ten hours a day all summer for a share of the crop," they protested, "and now you begin to keep our time!"[73]

Squads of soldiers and ex-soldiers were particularly successful in gaining additional leverage in labor negotiations. As disciplined and able-bodied men, they were highly sought after by the region's planters. Corporals and sergeants were offered higher wages in the hopes that they would bring "a certain number of men with them." "Scarcely an old planter got a negro unless by some bargain with the officers," reported Whitelaw Reid soon after the black regiments at Natchez were mustered out of service. Soldiers used their experience and status not just to negotiate more reasonable contracts but also to seek out better places of employment. "One of the colored regiments sent a delegation around to the several plantations to see how the hands were treated," testified Maj. Gen. Lorenzo Thomas, who had stayed in the region after the war to help his son acquire laborers for planting operations in Concordia Parish. The regiment then offered their services to those planters with good reputations for honest management.[74]

When negotiations broke down, freedpeople's collective organizing gave them the leverage to resist planter actions. The laborers on the Lakefield plantation in Concordia parish went on strike when their contracted wages were not paid on time. The local Freedmen's Bureau agent negotiated an end to the work stoppage by promising to confiscate the future cotton crop and give the first proceeds to the freedpeople. Similarly, another bureau agent intervened to end another "strike" after the field laborers became suspicious about the proprietor, who was not the man they had contracted with at the beginning of the year. According to Whitelaw Reid, a northern journalist who toured the South in the year following the war, strikes and work stoppages were a somewhat common threat on the Louisiana side of the Natchez District. At least a "dozen heavy planters" turned to the bureau to resolve disputes with mobilized freedpeople. As a result, planters, within a few years, had abandoned most attempts to control the behavior of their workers. After 1870 labor contracts specified only work-related matters, such as the amount of land to be cultivated and the division of cotton. In effect, the squad system proved to be a powerful tool for rural freedpeople to ameliorate the harsher aspects of field labor and the coercive legacy of slavery that controlled bodies and behavior.[75]

The features that made squads so pervasive—their basis in family networks, simple organizational structure, and mild limits on membership—helped around the edges but did not fundamentally alter power dynamics in the fields. From freedpeople's perspective, squads were a vast improvement over the gang labor system that was common under slavery, but freedpeople often needed a receptive Freedmen's Bureau agent to address grievances and to alter planter actions. Moreover, poverty and destitution cut against collective organization. After two succeeding years of crop shortages, hundreds, perhaps thousands, of freedpeople in Tensas and Concordia Parishes had little money to show for their labors. Most were without shelter since planters had evicted them from their homes at the conclusion of their contracts, leaving many to subsist "on fish exclusively," reported a bureau agent. Particularly hard hit were the elderly with broken bodies no longer suited for work in the fields. In one instance an aged ex-slave couple traveled twelve miles to Natchez in search of some clothing. They were "overcome with emotion" upon each receiving "a suit and a quilt," noted Rev. Palmer Litts, an AMA teacher and Freedmen's Bureau official. But even for adults of prime age and health, the exigencies of the cotton economy could be cruel.[76]

Perhaps it was not surprising, then, that some freedpeople endeavored to remove themselves from the cotton economy, or at least gain more control over their labor. Thousands moved to major towns and cities along the Mississippi

River. Others pulled up their stakes and lived off of the river. Soon after the end of the war, Col. Samuel Thomas estimated that five thousand black Mississippians cut wood for steamers along the river. At least one village of freedpeople exhibited a degree of order and "regularity" that surprised outside observers. Situated on the river near Natchez, related the *Natchez Democrat*, "not less than a thousand souls" lived in a community of small cabins, each with a small plot of land for growing vegetables. Perhaps these were the same people that northern journalist Edward King encountered seven years later, in 1874. Downriver from Vicksburg on the eastern bank of the Mississippi, he found several makeshift villages of freedpeople. The villagers cut wood and raised chickens, which they traded to captains on passing steamboats for "cornmeal, molasses, pork and whiskey."[77]

Living off the river afforded these people considerable autonomy, or "merry-makings," as King put it, yet others desired the independence that came from landownership. "What's de use of being free," complained an elderly ex-slave, ". . . if you don't own land enough to be buried in? Might just as well stay slave all yo' days." Of course, freedpeople desired land for many more reasons than just having a place to lay their bones. Merrimon Howard, the Jefferson County school organizer, swore that "the Country would be more prspous then ever before" if the federal government would sell land to black people. Others had a more radical view of landownership. Not unlike the deacons of the Wall Street Baptist Church, some viewed occupancy and cultivation as the primary determinant in considering title to the land. The freedpeople on Ballina plantation in Concordia Parish, wrote a bureau agent, "think their old masters should divide the land with them on which they were born and raised and consider their homes." Many others saved their meager proceeds, such as one freedman who had accumulated $400–500 in the hopes of purchasing "fo' or five acres ob land, dat I can build me a little house on and call my home." Similarly, Ben Thornton saved $300 from operating a single-mule dray in Natchez for five months in 1865, in order to purchase a small plot of land just outside the city, but he had to resort to begging his former master to intervene on his behalf. Thornton recognized that most white landowners were intent on preventing black people from owing land, expressed most notably in the Mississippi law that restricted blacks from renting or leasing farmland except in towns. But even though the Freedmen's Bureau nullified the law, there was powerful social pressure among whites to prevent land sales to freedpeople. In the lower Mississippi River valley, Whitelaw Reid learned, "the feeling against ownership of the soil by the negroes is so strong, that the man who should sell small tracts to them would be in actual personal danger."[78]

In the face of such stiff white opposition, only a handful of freedpeople were able to acquire land. One ingenious group from Concordia Parish turned to the

Freedmen's Bureau for assistance and purchased a cotton plantation. Between fifteen and twenty freedpeople pooled their resources, selected a leader, and approached the local bureau agent with their aspirations. The owner was not inclined to sell the land, according to bureau agent Capt. James T. Organ, because "of the state laws prohibiting it." So Captain Organ "purchased the place in my own name" in January 1866 on behalf of the freedpeople, who had organized themselves as William Shorter and Company. The place was Marengo plantation, 581 acres near Lake Concordia. William Shorter was likely a former slave and about forty-eight years old in 1866. He could read and write but his wife and three children could not, and he may have been a Baptist minister. After the first year's harvest, Shorter and Company purchased the land outright from Captain Organ.[79]

This black-owned plantation continued for some time, and although it operated much like all the white-owned plantations, the absence of labor strife made it unique. Whether it was because each laborer had a personal stake in the whole operation or because of their willingness to trust a black leader as opposed to a white overseer or planter, the freedpeople of Marengo trusted Shorter. According to Freedmen's Bureau rules in 1867, a planter had to pay his laborers before shipping cotton to market because many failed to set aside money for wages once they had sold the year's crop. Yet when a local bureau agent halted the Marengo shipment for violating the rule, some of the freedmen interceded, claiming that they believed Shorter's promise that he would pay them. Shorter's successful management of the Marengo plantation undoubtedly contributed to his election to the parish police jury (similar to a county board of supervisors) in 1868.[80]

The black landowners of Marengo plantation were the exception; a bit more common were small groups of freedpeople who leased portions of plantations, as groups did near Lake St. John and on the Franklin estate in Tensas Parish. The overseer at Laurel Hill plantation complained of the many "negro planters" who flooded him with lease applications for the coming year, even before the harvest was in. The opportunity to lease or purchase land, of course, often depended on the planter. Freedpeople, as part of their contract negotiations, requested that planters set aside an acre or two of land for planting cotton because it was the only local crop with sufficient cash and credit value for a field laborer to begin to establish economic independence. A northern journalist witnessed freedmen confronting a planter on the streets of Natchez, attempting to "wheedle or extort permission" to plant their own cotton. Planters, however, worried that freedpeople would steal cotton at picking time and claim it as their own. They also feared, according to one AMA agent, the competition from freedpeople who realized that "raising cotton for themselves is a more lucrative business than working by the month for others." Thus most planters refused to allow wage laborers to grow cotton for personal use, and some responded to the prospect of black landownership with violent threats. "In Mississippi, opposite Water-proof," explained an agent of the Hope Estate in Tensas Parish, "there's a minister collecting money to buy plantations in a white man's name, to be divided in little farms of ten and fifteen acres for the niggers. He couldn't do that thing in my parish: he'd soon be dangling from some tree."[81]

A few prominent black Natchezians, however, were able to crack the white barrier to black landownership. David Singleton, one of the wealthiest ex-slaves in the region, first purchased a plot of land six months after Gen. Robert E. Lee's surrender and then a year later entered cotton planting, producing eighty bales in 1866. Two years later, with William H. Lynch (the brother of John R. Lynch), Singleton contracted with thirteen freedmen to farm the Duck Pond plantation in Adams County. Both Singleton and Lynch were former slaves of Alfred V. Davis, the elite plantation owner. In another enterprise, William Holmes, trained as a blacksmith, collaborated with Robert W. Fitzhugh, a free-born carpenter who was also a member of the prominent free black Fitzhugh family. Holmes and Fitzhugh produced seventy-five cotton bales and planted one hundred acres of corn in 1866. Four years later Holmes plantation was valued at $12,000. Finally, the children of William Johnson—the well-known free black barber—leased plantations from white landowners and then contracted with freedpeople to work the land. The Johnsons likely used capital from the barbering business, run by Byron Johnson, to acquire the plantations, which were valued at $13,000 in 1870.[82]

In each of these examples, the acquisition of planting operations—most seem to be lease agreements—was a collaborative effort of family or friends, and it seemed to pave the way for future political activism. Singleton became a major donor to Republican officeholders; Lynch was elected to the Natchez board of aldermen, the county school board, and the state house of representatives; Fitzhugh was also an alderman and served as postmaster from 1876 to 1882; Byron Johnson was selected as an alternate delegate to an antiradical political convention in 1869. The planter class had good reason to worry about the effect that black landownership could have on their control of the region.[83]

A little over a year after the cessation of hostilities, the impact of emancipation had reached into the mundane activities of everyday life for freedpeople. "It affords us no little pleasure," exuded Nelson Fitzhugh, the ex-slave turned grocer and church organizer, "to see our children on the streets, about 9 o'clock, A. M., with books in their hands, on their way to school, in common with others." For Fitzhugh, who was born enslaved and had lived in Natchez as a free man for over three decades, the changes had come rapidly. "Schools have been established, churches have been organized," he continued, "and the way opened to our brethren from afar to come among us, both to preach and teach." Black teachers and preachers—the "brethren from afar"—had come to help establish new institutions for the newly emancipated, and in the process they helped to lay the foundations for a new democracy in the Natchez District.[84]

As schools and churches proliferated across the landscape, the connections between freedpeople of different localities and classes began to deepen. Emancipated communities offered freedpeople a sense of belonging. While families and kin networks formed the foundation of community, these relational affiliations, in and of themselves, were ill-equipped to protect former slaves in public contests or in relations with planters and employers. In contrast, membership in a church, participation in a school, or activism in a mutual aid association gave freedpeople more security and allowed many to step free from the influence of white patrons. Moreover, participation in denominational bodies, in educational associations, and in labor squads provided freedpeople with practical experience in governance and mobilization. This process was not complete, however, until freedpeople attained political rights and formed local Republican organizations. But the development of emancipated communities demonstrates the particular type of freedom that most freedpeople cherished—the freedom to join. In establishing churches, building schoolhouses, and forming collective labor associations, freedpeople showed that these shared endeavors were necessary to achieve their vision of a free society.

New Friends

Standing at the polls on Election Day in Claiborne County, Mississippi, an elderly freedman confronted a problem that many others faced when they voted for the first time: whom to trust? If he voted the Republican ticket, he faced ejection from his home. The planter whose land he worked had warned him, "I don't intend that any damned radical nigger shall live on my place." But if he voted the Democratic ticket, the ex-slave heard that he might be "violating some law of the Union" and the Union League would "punish him for so doing." Unsure whether to face unemployment or communal retribution, the old freedman sought out the advice of a Republican official, who assured him of the illegality of reprisals for voting. Moreover, the official added that he would "take particular pains" to send the planter to the penitentiary for turning the freedman off the land. Then the Republican official took out two tickets, a Republican ticket in one hand and a Democratic ticket in the other, and asked the elderly freedman to choose. "'I want to vote the republican ticket,'" declared the former slave, and then he "went right before his [former] master and put that ticket in the box."[1]

Thousands of freedmen cast similar ballots, and even if their former masters or current employers were not present to witness the event, the act of voting had a similarly ominous impact on social relationships and the future of the political order. Few instances of social upheaval have been as swift and profound as the transformation of slaves into voters. Not only did former bondsmen shed the lingering vestiges of slavery when they entered polling places, but their organizational sophistication, solidarity, and determination surprised their supporters and demoralized their detractors. Even as they became the most loyal bloc of voters for the Republican Party, they were not predestined to become Republicans.[2]

All too often, former slaves' embrace of the Republican Party is accepted uncritically. Most studies of this era focus on the politics of resistance—resistance to planters, government authorities, and white supremacists—or examine the political careers of black politicians. Few examine how and why southern black people identified with the Republican Party. It was not foreseeable at the time (nor in hindsight) that a group of people with no prior experience in electoral politics, who were mostly illiterate, with few economic resources or significant social standing would unite and create a sweeping political movement that would transform the South and the nation. Nor is it sufficient to assume that ex-slaves were of one mind and purpose. Some, particularly those with modest wealth in the towns and cities, chose to defer to former slaveholders, while others organized independent parties with conservative whites. That most freedpeople chose to forge new relationships with Republicans tells us less about racial identity than it does about their vision of community and democracy.

This chapter covers the electoral mobilizations of 1867 and 1868, as well as the remarkable mobilization of freedpeople to create a separatist land colony in Adams County. Occurring between the first two momentous election campaigns of Radical Reconstruction, the effort to establish a black colony highlights freedpeople's reservations about the potential for electoral politics to address their interests. Even as they were creating a powerful political movement, they faced destitution and poverty. Translating their newfound political power into tangible economic gains proved to be a frustrating endeavor. It was made all the more difficult when the plans for a colony floundered because, with its demise, the hopes for any form of substantial land redistribution came to an end.

But with access to the formal political sphere, freedpeople began to stitch together their local communities into a grassroots democracy. Freedpeople shared a common heritage, whether in bondage or in semifreedom, yet a common affliction or a common oppressor does not beget a singular purpose or united front. They were able to forge a powerful movement by sharing a common goal—pushing aside the planter class—and a social vision based on mutual support, egalitarian principles, and grassroots power. Partisan politics provided a structure for ordinary people to connect their ideas to institutions beyond their local networks and neighborhoods. To be sure, class and gender divisions remained entrenched, but in the electoral mobilization campaigns of 1867 and 1868, these differences declined somewhat. Freedpeople exploited their own distinct advantage—their population majority—and devoted their meager resources toward the mobilization of the entire community: women, men, and children from all classes. In a localized world where face-to-face contact governed social intercourse, economic transactions, and political relationships, freedpeople took the radical step of placing their trust in the collective expression of like-minded people and in the Republican Party—their new friends.

These transformed social relationships provided a context in which a new structure of governance could be grafted onto a society shaped by slavery. Thanks to the congressional Reconstruction Acts, the restrictive Black Codes were invalidated and freedpeople began to fashion a new political framework. The product of these efforts was realized in the radical state constitutions of 1868, but we should not forget how the electoral struggle in the campaigns of 1867 and 1868 laid the foundation for a new order, not only in terms of governance but also in the public life of ordinary people.

Old Friends

Even as freedpeople were creating churches, schools, and other social networks, some freedmen and freedwomen remained closely connected to powerful whites. While most freedpeople sought to limit their contact with white employers and the white elite, some individuals found it necessary to align themselves publicly with white leadership. Exploring a handful of these instances shows some of the limitations that freedpeople encountered in an emancipated society. Sometimes their "old friends," as the master class liked to think of themselves, were useful protectors at a time when federal officials could be fickle allies and before Republicans took over local and state governments. It should be remembered that maintaining ties with former slaveholders and ex-Confederates was also an option for freedpeople as they negotiated the transformations wrought by the Civil War.

Few better exemplified the benefits of fidelity to the old master class than David Singleton. A farmer and freedman of unusual wealth, Singleton called on some of the most powerful white men in the Natchez District when he ran into trouble with local authorities in April 1866. The circuit court in Natchez indicted Singleton for receiving stolen property, specifically two mules owned by a white cotton planter, valued at $150 apiece. The case attracted considerable attention because, as the local newspaper reported, Singleton was "very generally known in this community as one of the most intelligent and shrewd of his race, and one who has acquired a considerable amount of property by his bargaining." Additionally, this case fit into a pattern of black lawlessness that, at least in the eyes of local whites, had aroused "the just indignation of the people," leading many to hope that "the strong arm of the law" would be meted out. Singleton, fearing that his chances for a fair trial would be undone by a white jury, hired one of the most powerful attorneys in the city, William T. Martin—a former major general in the Confederate army, militia organizer, and prominent conservative politician. Martin's spirited defense led to a mistrial, but in the subsequent and lengthy retrial—in which thirty-seven witnesses were called to the stand—the jury convicted Singleton of larceny, and he was sentenced to three years in the state penitentiary.[3]

Martin attributed the conviction to two factors unrelated to the evidence at trial. Jurors in Adams County, he argued, were inclined "to convict negroes upon the slightest evidence," and the jury, composed mostly of white men of modest means, was prejudiced against Singleton for being "a favorite servant" of one of the wealthiest planters in the nation, Alfred V. Davis. Encouraging the speculation about favoritism, Davis, along with two other wealthy white men, posted a $500 bail bond for Singleton after his initial indictment. If the jury members were indeed jealous of Singleton's favored position before emancipation, their class and racial resentment would have only grown more bitter once they learned of Singleton's next move. He secured a $2,000 bond to appeal his conviction and then, through the assistance of Martin, enlisted the aid of eleven white men, each of whom wrote a letter to the governor of Mississippi, seeking executive clemency for the former slave. The petitioners—six planters, two attorneys, a physician, a merchant, and the minister of the Methodist church in Natchez—represented the elite of southern society. Most dabbled in politics and all had been slaveholders before the war, collectively owning 2,520 slaves in the Natchez District.[4]

To a person, these elite white men praised Singleton for his loyalty to his master, his trustworthiness as a bondsman, and his fidelity to the class of elite slaveholders. In their minds, Singleton represented the ideal black man. He was "trustworthy," "respectful and obedient," "faithful and well behaved," and "true when so many proved otherwise." Singleton's former master, Alfred V. Davis, confessed that he had entrusted him with "with large sums of money . . . to purchase slaves and stock," and he allowed Singleton to travel unaccompanied to the northern states and even on one occasion to Italy. Davis admitted that he "confided in his judgment, and integrity, as fully as if he had been white." Pleased with his faithful service, Davis had emancipated him, but "sometime afterwards," Singleton "voluntarily returned" and legally bound himself to his former master. Singleton could act more freely in his business of stock trading as the slave of a wealthy planter than as an independent freedman, since free blacks, especially those with modest wealth, attracted undue scrutiny from white authorities. (Upon his manumission in 1854, Singleton purchased the freedom of his wife and children and then moved his family to Mount Pleasant, Ohio. Once his family was secured in a free state and his children enrolled in a school, he returned to Natchez to continue his business interests.)[5]

For the master class, there was no greater act of devotion or subservience than to freely re-enslave oneself. And in Singleton they saw a future in which emancipation would not erode the power relationships that had come to define their lives. "At no time could he be induced to take part against the [white] people of the South," confidently proclaimed one correspondent. While so many other freedpeople had abandoned ties to their former masters by running away during the war or seeking new employers after emancipation, Singleton had remained dependent on the white elite, even at the risk of being labeled a "Reb Negro," and for that, argued the ex-slaveholders, he should be granted a pardon. Swayed by the master class's petitions, Governor Benjamin B. Humphreys pardoned him.[6]

In the midst of ongoing labor strife over the terms of control and authority in the fields, the white elite could take solace in a freedman who still looked to them for support and protection. This helps explain, in part, why white Democrats did not despair once the federal government granted black men the franchise, for they believed that David Singleton's "influence, which was great, over the other negroes" would ensure their class's continued dominance. Of course, the planter elite were completely wrong about the freedmen, and even more pointedly, they were wrong about Singleton. Far from being a tool of white Democrats, he became an active supporter of Republicans by putting up bond money for local black officeholders. Singleton was one of two sureties on ex-slave John R. Lynch's bond for justice of the peace in 1869, thus providing the seed money for a budding political career that would lead to substantial black Republican power in the region.[7]

David Singleton, not unlike many shrewd freed persons, hid his true feelings behind a mask of dependency. Although he appears to have retained his "old friends" with relative ease, others, such as Nelson Fitzhugh, could not sustain the duality in the new politics of emancipation. Over the years Fitzhugh had earned a reputation among local whites as a "proper man," distinguishing himself as "a bright mulatto lad, humble, submissive, quiet, unobtrusive." Manumitted in 1834, he educated himself, married, and continued to work for a number of merchant establishments in Natchez, earning recognition as "a useful member of society." Mentioned in connection with William Johnson and Robert McCary—well-known and esteemed free black barbers—Fitzhugh played the role of the deferential man of color. "He was seemingly a Confederate," explained the *Natchez Courier*, "seemingly attached to those who had nursed, nourished, cared for, protected, defended him, and promoted his interests. . . . [White people] had faith and trust in him. They relied on him. They believed him attached to them. They had every reason to believe so." But then someone informed the *Courier* of a letter that Fitzhugh had written to the *Christian Recorder*, the newspaper of the AME Church with a nationwide circulation. In the letter, Fitzhugh, a trustee of the Natchez AME Church, described the local newspaper as "poor, [and] contemptible." These words prompted the white editor of the *Courier* to lash out at Fitzhugh in a stinging editorial entitled "The Mask Off."[8]

By alienating his white friends, Fitzhugh was cast in an unenviable position, especially since his popularity among local black people was questionable. A few months before, Fitzhugh and a few others were attacked in the street by a mob of black men, but his white benefactors came to his aid, including the *Courier* editor. His white friends made sure that the attackers were convicted and sentenced, but now, feeling betrayed, the white community turned on Fitzhugh, describing him as a man "full of deceit and hypocrisy," "a systematic hypocrite," and "a Radical agent." Pouring further salt in his public wounds, the *Courier* reminded its readers, particularly freedpeople, that Fitzhugh "became a slave-holder and owner himself, and was a very hard task-master, as the proofs in this city will show." Indeed, he owned a seven-year-old girl in 1860. By serving as a local agent for a racially separatist organization and by publicly denouncing his white neighbors, Fitzhugh had committed an act of betrayal. "The whites of Natchez," the paper concluded, "have not cast off their old friends," and despite Fitzhugh's treachery, they remained committed to helping their former slaves.[9]

The editorial severely wounded Fitzhugh's public character and threatened his and his family's future in Natchez. Seeking to limit the damage and re-store the mask of dependency, Catherine McCary, Fitzhugh's daughter, wrote a pleading letter that agreed with the condemnations heaped on her father. She dismissed him in the pages of the *Courier* as "weak-minded and thoughtless" and begged the readers to overlook "my father's indiscretion, for he is old and childish." Describing herself as a "Southerner born and bred, and having im-bibed sentiments in harmony with those of the land of my nativity," McCary refuted the original *Christian Recorder* article that left the impression that she was "inimical to the Confederate cause." Her claims of allegiance to the Confed-eracy, in fact, may have been more than rhetorical posturing; her mother, Agnes Fitzhugh, was convicted by a federal military commission in 1864 for smuggling "Confederate gray cloth" across Union lines. Although the internal dynamics of the Fitzhugh family remain a mystery, Nelson's public humiliation, which his daughter perpetuated, must have burdened its members. Perhaps Cathe-rine's letter was an effort to cauterize the wound and enable her father to retain employment from white-owned establishments. Both Catherine's educational work and her mother's benevolent work for the AME Church were put at risk if powerful whites turned against the family.[10]

With time and after tens of thousands of freedmen had cast Republican votes, Nelson Fitzhugh and his family would be able to branch out from their "old friends" and openly express their opinions and political beliefs. Not unlike the dual loyalties that Nelson, Agnes, and Catherine displayed in the 1860s, their sons were not of one mind. Four of Nelson's eight sons held elective office as Republicans during Reconstruction, while John, a thirty-two-year-old porter, joined the Democrats, serving as a secretary for a black Democratic club.[11]

During the period after emancipation but before enfranchisement, culti-vating dependent relationships with white patrons and former masters gave freedpeople protection in uncertain times, but some also looked to the federal government, hoping that this distant power could act as a patron and protector. "A delegation of colored citizens" from Natchez considered the Freedmen's Bureau to be their "only protection," wrote the leading federal officer in Mississippi at about the same time that David Singleton was arrested for stealing mules. A bureau agent, after an inspection tour of the entire district, found that freedpeople looked to the bureau to provide "all needful support." Picking up on this sentiment, some officials attempted to step into the role as patrons. The assistant commissioner for Mississippi demanded that subcommissioners act as "*next friends*" to freedmen in court proceedings. Later, in an address to freedpeople, the same officer declared, "I am your lawful protector and advisor." Similarly, a local agent assured the freedpeople on one Concordia plantation that he "would protect them in their rights providing they did what was right."[12]

As essential as the bureau was to freedpeople's efforts to negotiate fair terms of labor and to provide security from hostile whites, the agency proved to be a difficult ally. The bureau did not have much of a role for ex-slaves in its organization, limiting the impact of local freedpeople on policy matters. Moreover, agents could not act as unambiguous advocates of freedpeople, since they were also charged with defending the contractual rights of employers. When one Claiborne County freedwoman complained that her employer withheld eight months' worth of wages, a bureau agent investigated the matter and, while agreeing with her claim, added that she actually owed her employer $8.50 for clothing, medicines, and other advances on her contract. Gaining nothing from the contract or the complaint, the freedwoman returned to the employ of her former master.[13]

The Union army offered another option, particularly for freedmen seeking public protection. Some former soldiers donned blue uniforms when they walked the streets to signal that they were attached to a powerful entity. In response, white citizens heaped abuse on black and white men in blue uniforms, cursing them as "'G–d D––d Yankee' [and] 'D––d nigger Yankee.'" When a drunken group of white policemen began attacking black men in blue uniforms with "Pistols and Clubs" one spring day, the locally stationed U.S. soldiers in Natchez defended the ex-soldiers by firing on the policemen, fatally wounding one police officer. Outraged at the death of a white policeman at the hands of a black soldier protecting black ex-soldiers, the *Natchez Courier* suggested that discharged troops who continued to wear the uniform ought to be arrested. After all, the paper continued, "[t]he uniform is all they have to go by." Without direct access to the levers of power, freedmen used symbolic gestures, such as wearing a blue uniform, to claim membership in a polity more powerful than local white authority. However, as much as freedpeople relied on the military power of the U.S. government to keep civil authorities and white employers in check, the federal government was not a reliable patron. Its distant center of authority and levels of bureaucracy complicated the efforts of freedpeople to use its immense power in their day-to-day struggles.[14]

These few examples are but a small window into the postwar struggle to find security and protection under a neo-Confederate regime. Most freedpeople rebuffed the entreaties of former masters, the so-called old friends, but not all. Some bided their time under masks of dependency, while others found solace and stability under the watchful eye of a white patron. And while the political mobilization of the Radical Reconstruction era broke open the possibilities for politics and policies, the varied responses of freedpeople to authority and patronage would persist.

Mobilizing for the First Vote

In the immediate years after emancipation, while freedpeople were building social institutions, transforming the terms of labor in the cotton economy, and expanding communication networks, they were also chipping away at the wall that separated people of color from the formal arena of politics. Before the war had come to an end, "secret societies" had formed in Adams County in which freedpeople discussed the "rights and privileges" of citizenship, and in emerging public arenas, black Natchezians were arguing for universal manhood suffrage. Beyond clandestine meetings and informal political discussions, there were few outlets for formal black political mobilization in the Natchez District. Not until the passage of the Military Reconstruction Acts in the spring of 1867 would freedpeople have an opportunity to fully engage in electoral politics much like their white neighbors.[15]

Incensed at the audacity of unrepentant former Confederates who were elected to fill congressional seats only a few months after the Confederate surrender and disturbed by the surge in violence manifested in riots in New Orleans and Memphis in 1866, Republican leaders in Congress grabbed the reins of power from President Johnson and enacted their own Reconstruction policy. They dissolved civil governance in ten of the eleven former Confederate states, placed Union army generals in charge, demanded that elections be opened to black men, and required that each state craft a new constitution that dispensed with the Black Codes and incorporated the principles of the Fourteenth Amendment. The revolutionary implications of this legislation gave pause to most Americans, and few had any idea what this radical template for political reform would mean in practice.[16]

Congressional legislation mandated universal manhood suffrage, but the work of organizing, mobilizing, registering, and voting was a decidedly local affair. To that end, the Union League provided invaluable instruction on the political issues of the day, the organization of political parties, and the rituals of partisanship. Originally formed to support the Lincoln administration, the Union League became the major conduit for promoting the Republican Party and black political mobilization in the South. Using funds provided by the Union Republican Congressional Committee, the league sponsored speakers and distributed political literature. Locally, Natchez became a center for league operations in the region. League activists, many of whom were former Union army officers, organized meetings, initiated new members, and began planning for the drafting of a new state constitution.[17]

Fittingly, black institutions hosted the first partisan gatherings of freedpeople in public. Not long after the passage of the first Reconstruction Act, "the freedmen of Natchez and vicinity" met in a political meeting at the AME Church. "Two or three black speakers" addressed a mixed-race audience of 413 men, in which they discussed the implications of the new military order and selected a committee of twelve freedmen to "meet and confer" with Mississippi's military commander. Over the next few weeks, freedpeople met at least once a week at different locations throughout the city: one week at the Union schoolhouse, another at the Rose Hill schoolhouse, and still another at an undisclosed spot that the snooping eyes of the white Democratic press could not determine. The institutional framework of black associational life was a godsend for Union League and Republican activists, particularly in urban areas, because it provided a space where political issues could be aired with minimal interference from employers and political opponents.[18]

Despite freedmen's lack of formal political experience, they immersed themselves in the procedures and rules that characterized nineteenth-century partisan meetings. The AME church meeting was "organized by the election of a colored chairman and secretary," and at the Rose Hill meeting, "not less than two hundred members (colored), were admitted to the [Union] League." Each member received a certificate of membership, signed by the league president, E. J. Castello—a former Union army officer from Missouri—and by the league secretary, Wilson Wood—a twenty-four-year-old literate freedman. (Wood was originally from Kentucky and would later become a storekeeper and a member of the "Governing Six," a group of black Republicans that controlled Natchez politics in the mid-1870s.) Arrayed before the new Union League inductees were symbols intended to represent the spiritual bond among those who valued union (the U.S. Constitution, the flag of the Union, and a sword), Christianity (an altar and the Holy Bible), free labor (a sickle, a shuttle, and other emblems of industry), and liberal political rights (the Declaration of Independence, a gavel, and a ballot box). In a highly ritualistic and gendered ceremony, freedmen were led arm in arm into a darkened room, where they pledged their fidelity to the U.S. government. Prospective members placed their "left hand on the national flag" and raised their right hand "toward heaven," while the existing members joined hands in a circle around the inductees. Within this sphere of fraternal affection, they swore to defend the United States against all enemies, to "do all in [their] power to elect true and reliable Union men," and to "protect, aid and defend all worthy members of the U. L." To add further assurance, they reaffirmed these oaths by placing their right hand on the Bible, the Declaration of Independence, and the Constitution. Finally, as a "band of brothers," they took the Freedman's Pledge: "To defend and perpetuate freedom and the Union I pledge my life, my fortune and sacred honor. So help me God."[19]

Membership in the Union League was unlike any other affiliation that freedmen had ever experienced. To be sure, black soldiers also pledged their loyalty to the U.S. government; however, membership in the league differed in that freedmen held leadership posts and black men participated as equals with white members. Additionally, the league drew its power from grassroots connections and linked local governance to national dominance, not the other way around, as with the military. Over the spring and summer of 1867, local chapters of the Union League educated freedpeople on the electoral process, and within a short time, leagues began to function like any other nineteenth-century political organization: selecting leaders, debating party platforms, nominating delegates, and incorporating the aspirations of their members into a political framework. In October a meeting of black Union Leaguers selected "two white men . . . and three negroes" to be sent to the Adams County Republican convention. One young photography assistant recalled that he attended club meetings on a weekly basis soon after the implementation of military Reconstruction and that he was soon speaking before the assembled members. Within a couple of years, this ambitious former slave, John R. Lynch, rose through the ranks of the local club and, aided by David Singleton, became the first black officeholder in the Natchez District, assuming the office of justice of the peace in 1869.[20]

The growing awareness of partisan processes and organizations was further enhanced at public meetings that began to sprout up across the landscape. In addition to gatherings at churches and schools, meetings were held on the Natchez bluff overlooking the Mississippi River, at the Union League Hall in Wilkinson County, on plantations throughout the district, and even at merchant stores in Concordia Parish. But the most common meeting place and the location most laden with symbolic importance was the county courthouse. Standing at the center of town, the courthouse was an imposing presence in the political life of rural communities, for within its walls politicians administered municipal and county governments and ordinary citizens adjudicated judicial disputes before magistrates. Moreover, the courthouse was a desirable meeting place for political parties—a public facility with ample space for gatherings and easily accessible. Often political meetings would be announced by ringing the courthouse bell, signaling to the entire town that a major event was about to take place.[21]

For freedpeople, however, meeting at the courthouse symbolized the revolutionary implications of emancipation and enfranchisement. When freedpeople met one summer night to listen to radical speeches at the Natchez courthouse, they met as citizens, not subjects. They came not as slaves waiting to be auctioned off but as free women and men in a democratic gathering. They came not as individuals seeking justice through the courts but as communities yearning to influence political events and to evaluate potential political leaders.[22]

While most freedpeople embraced the values and principles expressed at these meetings, they were leery of the northern-born leaders who had recently moved into the region. Union League activists insisted on bringing rural workers to urban centers, where they could more easily discuss the process of voter registration and how to prepare for the upcoming election. But some also hoped to profit from the freedmen. A number of ex-Union officers had set up merchant stores in Natchez, which they hoped rural freedpeople would patronize. According to one dismayed Freedmen's Bureau agent, who took a dim view of white Union League organizers, they circulated among plantation workers spreading "exciting messages, calculated to bring them to town at the expense of the crop," such as "come to the Freedmens Bureau and get your Money" and "come to the Freedmans Bureau and get [your] ticket, your justification, your protection in your freedom." As a result of high rates of black enlistment in the Union army during the war, quite a few households had a substantial military bounty owed to them, between $100 and $300. With wages on a cotton plantation averaging ten dollars a month, the bounty was worth one to two years' wages or equivalent to the value of about ten to thirty acres of cleared land. The federal government, however, was slow to pay out the bounties. John Washington, an ex-soldier from the Sixth Regiment, U.S. Colored Heavy Artillery, took out a loan from a northern man for thirty-five dollars to be charged against his bounty, but the interest on the loan was over 100 percent. Washington was not alone in being a victim of these scams. Nor were local Freedmen's Bureau agents acting as honest brokers when it came to cashing in military bounties. The agent who had criticized Union League organizers, E. E. Platt, charged black men three times the going rate to process soldier claims, and in at least two instances Platt charged widows between five and eight dollars to process the "pay and bounty due" to their husbands at their death. The unscrupulous behavior of some Union League organizers and bureau agents made it all the more difficult for freedpeople to place their trust in Republican leaders from the North.[23]

The registration of new voters began in May 1867, supervised by federal officials. Military officers, who often were also Freedmen's Bureau agents, set up offices in county seats and other substantial towns for freedmen to register, to inquire about their rights and citizenship duties, and to make complaints against the illegal practices of their employers. The handful of bureau agents stationed in the Natchez District had only limited means by which to educate the population on the new terms of Reconstruction, so they relied on the Union League's and freedpeople's vast communication network to spread word of the new laws. An agent in Tensas Parish reported that hundreds of freedmen had sought him out to confirm their rights and duties as citizens. Despite the logistical hurdles, the impact was immediately felt. "The negro men all went to Fayette to register their names so they can vote," confided Susan Sillers Darden, a Jefferson County diarist. "It is a disgrace to civilized people to have ignorant persons like negroes voting." As dispiriting as it was for the planter class to be placed on terms of equality with their former slaves, the meaning of registration had the opposite effect on black men. As one government official explained, "[R]egistration was their newly acquired badge of citizenship." On the first day of registration in Vidalia, four-fifths of those registered were black men, setting a pattern that would continue throughout the Reconstruction years of freedmen greatly outnumbering whites as voters.[24]

To drum up support for the voter registration campaign, Union League and Republican leaders planned a massive parade and celebration for the Fourth of July in downtown Natchez. From "an early hour," wrote an astonished reporter for the local paper, freedpeople from the surrounding countryside began to pour into the city. "The streets of the city, the roads leading from the country, the ferry-boat, and all avenues of approach" were inundated with "freedmen and freedwomen," perhaps as many as eight thousand—nearly double the existing number of black residents in the city of Natchez. At the park on the bluff that loomed over the Mississippi River and the extensive Louisiana bottomlands beyond, the procession formed and began to march up Main Street, through the heart of downtown Natchez. Twenty-five hundred freedmen, "nearly all decorated with ribbons, and many carrying flags" representing the local branches of the Union League as well as fraternal orders such as the Good Samaritans, advanced east through the city, passing merchant stores, banks, St. Mary Basilica, and other institutions that reflected white dominance. At the head of the marchers were both black and white marshals, testifying to the integration of white northerners and local black residents in a movement that disregarded racial differences. Thousands of freedpeople lined the sidewalks to watch the procession. As the parade made its way toward the outskirts of the city, marchers saluted American flags to signify their loyalty to the nation. The crowd then marched along Woodville Road about two miles to the picnic grounds on a nearby plantation.[25]

As the thousands of freedpeople rested their tired feet, shared a meal, and continued the day's celebration, they listened to an array of political speeches. The main speaker was John Mercer Langston, the renowned black political activist. Langston was born free in Virginia and educated at Oberlin College, held elective office in antebellum Ohio, recruited black soldiers during the war, and headed up the National Equal Rights League. In 1867 he traveled to the South as an educational inspector for the Freedmen's Bureau and as a Republican Party organizer. His address, one of two that he gave in Natchez to large audiences, was only briefly mentioned in the local paper's report on the day's events, but if it was anything like his other speeches from 1865 to 1867 Langston probably focused on the importance of suffrage, citizenship, and equality before the law. The paper did mention that "he told his hearers that they ought to have land," but Langston probably was not referring to land confiscation. For one thing, the Democratic paper complimented the speech for its "good sense and moderation," and for another, Langston typically emphasized "industrious, economical habits of life" in his addresses and called for a restructured tax system to facilitate black landownership, not redistribution. The content of Langston's speech and his very presence at the Fourth of July celebration testified to the growing strength and ambition of the Natchez District freedpeople. They had attracted one of the few nationally known black leaders to their gathering and had linked local mobilization efforts to the national project of Radical Reconstruction.[26]

Another indication of the broad impact that public parades had on freedpeople during the first summer of black partisan activity can be found in the experiences of Keziah Mably, a freedwoman. The day before the grand event, Mably took the afternoon off from her work on the Forest plantation in Concordia Parish to do "some washing for herself," so that "she might have clean clothing to wear, to the celebration that was to take place in Natchez, Miss. on . . . the 4th of July," reported a Freedmen's Bureau official. The next day, Mably crossed the Mississippi River, met her brother in Natchez, and took part in the festivities. Increasingly, these partisan gatherings served as a means for ordinary people to renew kin relationships and expand social networks. They offered an opportunity to celebrate and to dissociate oneself from the harsh labor and strict rules of the plantation. Participants also came away from these events with greater political knowledge and a greater sense of their involvement in a movement to radically change the prevailing structures of their society. The procession on the Fourth was likely the largest gathering of black people in the history of the Natchez District and perhaps one of the largest partisan gatherings ever attempted in the region.[27]

Celebrations and parades of this kind were essential to the work of mobilization, for they made politics a communal experience. By marching in a parade, black Union League members stepped forward from their secret meetings and gave public testimony to their political loyalties. For the parade watchers and picnic goers, public identification with a Republican event brought them closer into the political fold by similarly making a public statement about their political leanings. Even though Keziah Mably's primary motive in attending the Republican celebration may not have been partisan, grassroots activists, in attracting freedwomen like Mably, extended their political network into the interstices of everyday life. To be sure, there is little to suggest that Mably was opposed to the Republican Party, but her eager participation underscores the kind of political community that local activists hoped to nurture: a community of women, men, and children—not just voters.

The Natchez parade illustrates the social and communal reasons for freed-people's affiliation with the Republican Party. Freedpeople also were drawn to Republicanism for its positions and policy prescriptions. In preparation for a Republican convention in Mississippi, local clubs and leagues elected delegates and approved a series of resolutions. The Natchez District sent seven delegates, four white and three black, to the convention at Jackson in September 1867. While most of the resolutions called for support of the national Republican Party and its platform, the convention laid out a few core principles that reflected the aspirations of ordinary freedpeople. First, they dedicated themselves to giving a "free education to every child" and "the ballot to every man not disfranchised for crimes including treason." Next, they called for equal treatment in all civil and political rights. And finally, in an irresolute measure that probably reflected a compromise between the competing visions of Republican free labor ideology and black demands for land redistribution, the delegates pledged support for "honest industry."[28]

While these principles drew many freedpeople to the Republican Party, deteriorating conditions in the cotton fields and employer hostility to freedpeople's politics likewise propelled former slaves into the Republican camp. To start with, many freedpeople had not been paid from the previous year's crop. The 1866 cotton harvest was less than most expected, but some Freedmen's Bureau officials suspected that planters had fraudulently withheld wages from their workers. Then, in the late spring, the parishes of Tensas and Concordia were inundated with rising floodwaters. Freedpeople, reported one agent, were "driven from their homes," the schools were closed, and most planting operations were suspended. Between May and June 1867, the number of people in the Natchez area who needed supplemental food from the Freedmen's Bureau tripled.[29]

When the waters receded, the army worm appeared, destroying much of the cotton crop in Concordia Parish. The Concordia planters then kicked their laborers off the land and refused "to pay them for work done thus far," reported the *New Orleans Republican*. Another side effect of the summer flooding was the outbreak of cholera. In Tensas Parish alone, "about four hundred" freedpeople had died by summer's end, estimated a bureau agent. With the high probability of a poor crop in 1867, more planters began to expel freedpeople from their lands, claiming that they could not afford to pay them. Compounding the problem, commission merchants refused to send supplies to planters on credit, prompting the discharge of even more workers from their homes and employment.[30]

Another reason for the high discharge rates was the increasing political activity of workers. The accumulation of "frequent meetings where negroes are called to attend," a Natchez Freedmen's Bureau agent reported, had an aggregate effect that eroded the productivity of plantation labor: "In a great-majority of the instances of dissatisfaction the cause may be traced to the efforts made to call the negroes together for Political purposes." Those in the hinterlands disrupted work routines by making long journeys to county seats in order to register to vote. Henry Pickney, a youthful freedman from a plantation along the Tensas River in Concordia Parish, traveled at least eighteen miles to attend a political meeting in Natchez. In the area around Woodville, freedpeople frequently attended public meetings and "speakings of various kinds and at different places travelling the distance of from 2 to 25 miles." Buttressing these larger political meetings were "private club meetings," all of which "cause dissatisfaction on the part of their employer," reported a bureau agent. "Nearly every Saturday," noted one white resident of Woodville, "the town merchants are apprehensive . . . that political turmoils are about to be enacted."[31]

Indeed, as the election grew closer the line between political and labor disputes was difficult to discern. One agent complained that "a great many freedmen" were "being discharged . . . for frivolous offenses," a seeming recognition of overseers' practice of punishing political activity by highlighting minor labor infractions. Farm laborers at Freedmen's Bureau offices described situations in which freedpeople were discharged for leaving work to find food, of freedpeople being subjected to violent and abusive language, and of freedpeople talking back to overseers. In Wilkinson County the local agent made the most explicit link between discharges and local politics, noting that "[m]any Contracts have been annuled by planters since the Organization of the Union Republican Club." The contracts stipulated that freedpeople could venture off the plantations only for part of Saturday and all of Sunday, but "the Colored people have frequently left off their work when they liked it during week days to attend to meetings of the club." The planters retaliated by withholding rations, laying fines, and discharging dozens of workers.[32]

The combination of work interruptions related to voter registration and a damaged crop on top of the dismal returns from the previous year contributed to a transformed relationship between local whites and blacks and between laborers and employers. The stakes of the current political struggle were heightened for Tensas Parish residents when a group of freedpeople from Franklin

Parish to the west sought refuge in the river parish from marauding bands of disguised white men who had killed four men and wounded a man, woman, and child. But the impact of voter registration and the implementation of Radical Reconstruction policy was also registered in the ways that some freedpeople began to frame their labor struggles in political terms. After a Freedmen's Bureau agent inspected one Concordia Parish plantation, he asked the laborers "if they had anything to say." They replied that all they wanted "was justice, and the rights the Government allowed them."[33]

The increase in punishments and discharges in the late summer and early fall are a good indication of the growing number of Republican political meetings. In the middle of August in Port Gibson, the county seat of Claiborne County, approximately four thousand people gathered for a "political barbecue." The size of this gathering was immense, quadruple the number of residents of the small town. Freedpeople traveled from distant rural neighborhoods, some beginning their journey the day before, in order to enjoy the music and festivities, including the "feast of politics and flow of patriotism."[34]

Much like the Fourth of July procession in Natchez, the Port Gibson barbecue celebrated partisanship and the mobilization of freedpeople, but the harder work of preparing for the coming election took place in innumerable neighborhood meetings across the district. We have little knowledge of the internal dynamics of these meetings, whether rural or urban, but we can see their impact in the reports from Freedmen's Bureau officials who were charged with dispensing political information. Lt. George Haller, stationed in Wilkinson County, visited forty-seven plantations in August and September 1867 and found that most of the freedmen had already registered to vote. He also "conversed daily with freedmen who came from different parts of the Sub District" and found them to be "fully informed" on suffrage issues. Another federal officer ordered his agents in Adams County to "read at every Political Meeting held in this Sub District" information regarding registration and voting procedures. "By this means," he continued, "they have been better informed than a year travelling among the Plantations would have done." A Tensas Parish agent testified to the detailed political conversations occurring in the hinterlands when he related how a "great many of the freedmen" discussed with him "whom they should cast their vote for, who were the best men, and particularly to find out who would study their interest and advancement most."[35]

The spread of political information between the rural interiors and the population centers may also have been facilitated by the grassroots militias that materialized after the war. It is not clear how many there were or how many people were involved, but at least in Wilkinson County, they seemed to have a prominent presence. One planter recalled how hundreds of freedmen "had formed a perfect military organization" around the time that "many of them

[were] freshly discharged from the U. S. Army." This would place the origins of the militia in the spring and summer of 1866. "About nine or ten o'clock in the evening," wrote the planter in an unpublished autobiography,

> one would hear a heavily-loaded musket fired. In a very few minutes it would be answered from a point five or six miles distant. It would then be taken up by seemingly appointed stations at about this distance apart radiating in every direction. Within the course of an hour we could sit on our gallery, which was half a mile from the public road, and hear the measured tread of hundreds of men, and frequently the military orders: "Hep! Hep! Hep! Close up! double quick!" and many others that have been forgotten. . . . Finally the negroes became so bold that on Saturday afternoons they would take possession of open fields belonging to individual white men and throwing out picket lines around them[,] train and drill openly.

The planter, who estimated that at least fifteen hundred freedmen were members, despised the black militia, which undoubtedly colored his recollection of the events. While it is not clear how long this militia operated (some evidence suggests that it operated for at least a decade), the means by which the neighborhood groupings communicated with each other reveals a measure of interconnectedness that undoubtedly assisted electoral mobilization the following summer.[36]

At the conclusion of the registration period, the success of the Republican mobilization campaign became apparent to all, and it foretold the radical changes that were to come. Among nearly seventeen thousand registered voters in the Natchez District, 82 percent of the electorate was black. Where once white men had sole power to select elected officials and to shape public policy, now black people had an eleven-thousand-vote majority. The mobilization did not just produce a voting population that reflected the racial demographics of the region; it also was highly successful in registering most of the eligible male citizens, approximately 88 percent. Statewide, black registered voters outnumbered whites in Mississippi by twenty thousand and by thirty thousand in Louisiana. The political culture of the region would never be the same again.[37]

The success of the mobilization campaign, however, did not lay to rest the great concern among Republicans leaders about whom the freedmen would actually vote for. When Congress first began to debate the issue of universal manhood suffrage in the spring of 1866, a joint committee on Reconstruction asked Maj. Gen. Lorenzo Thomas to comment on the feasibility of extending suffrage rights to black men. Thomas, who had organized black regiments in the lower Mississippi River valley during the war and had since helped his son establish a plantation in Concordia Parish, expressed the common belief among white elites that new black voters would select white men from the "upper classes." Just as he believed that black laborers "want[ed] some one over them to direct them," he asserted that the same principle would hold in the political realm. A little over a year later, Alston Mygatt, who was the president of the Union League's central committee in Mississippi and far more radical in his politics than General Thomas, worried that the freedmen would vote for those representing the interests of the planter class. He begged Gen. O. O. Howard of the Freedmen's Bureau to quickly reconcile black soldiers' claims for military bounties. Mygatt explained that paying the bounties would bolster Republican credibility by providing promised and tangible aid, especially since the freedpeople in the river counties faced destitution. An infusion of cash, then, would enable freedmen to maintain their political independence by not making them so dependent on white employers and former slaveholders.[38]

To Mygatt's chagrin, the purse strings of the federal government were not unloosened, prompting local leaders to step up their efforts to convince newly registered voters to cast their lot with the political ideals of the Republicans and avoid the economic appeals from the planter class. In a speech to freedpeople in Fayette, Jefferson County, James Cessor, a freeborn saddler and carpenter, warned them not "to go to their old masters to get advice," if nothing else because "they are not in the right humor" after having lost the war and their slave property. Similarly, James Lynch, an AME minister and the leading black political organizer in Mississippi, worried that too many freedpeople would align with conservatives, thereby threatening the formation of a bloc of black voters that Republicans needed to authorize a constitutional convention. "You cannot imagine what unbounded influence one white man wields in a section where there is not counter influence," he wrote to Union League supporters in Ohio. But all was not lost; when freedpeople were "instructed in the least degree as regards the political situation," Lynch believed, "they quickly comprehend the whole."[39]

On the other side of the partisan divide, the planters were also assessing the registration process and wondering how military Reconstruction would unfold. Voter registration was already disrupting the economic and social rhythms of plantation life. Planters complained bitterly about their laborers leaving the fields to attend rallies or meetings. But some were confident that federal interference would have only a minimal impact on their livelihoods. According to one northerner who joined the ranks of planters in Concordia Parish, the idea that freedpeople would turn away from their "most reliable friend[s]," by which he meant southern white men, was incomprehensible. The freedmen "will cast their votes," he confidently asserted in the *Chicago Times*, "as the old residents of the State may dictate."[40]

The election in Louisiana took place without incident on September 27 and 28, 1867, just as the cotton harvest began. In their first vote, freedmen elected a slate of Republican candidates to transform the state government. Statewide,

75,083 voted for a constitutional convention, with 4,006 against. The spectacular success at the ballot box, however, was tempered by continued difficulties in the fields. The cotton crop that had seemed so imperiled in the summer turned out to be "much larger than was anticipated," wrote one Freedmen's Bureau agent, but when it came time to settle accounts for the year the workers were invariably left with little to nothing. Local bureau agents fought a rearguard battle by confiscating some property and cotton on a dozen or so plantations in order "to satisfy the claims of Freedmen." But overall most freedpeople found themselves driven off the plantations after the cotton-picking season ended. The one remaining school in Tensas Parish closed, like all the others, because "money throughout the Parish [was] so very scarce," and only two schoolhouses remained in operation in Concordia. Lacking shelter and rations, black workers faced imminent "destitution."[41]

The balance of the year was mixed. Nearly twenty-two hundred freedmen in Concordia Parish and over twenty-four hundred freedmen in Tensas had registered to vote, sending a shockwave through the American political system. But closer to home at least four hundred freedpeople in Tensas Parish had died as a result of cholera and other diseases, and the laborers in the Natchez District's Louisiana parishes had little to show for another year's worth of labor.[42]

The peaceful unfolding of the election in Louisiana may very well have shocked white Mississippians in the river counties out of their resigned approach to the Reconstruction process. Some former Confederates had initially cooperated with military Reconstruction and pledged to work toward racial harmony, which, in their view, could be achieved only through black deference. But by the fall of 1867 many white Mississippians had come to reject the cooperationist strategy, with some choosing to ignore the electoral campaign altogether, an approach known as "masterly inactivity," while others intensified their open opposition to black political mobilization.[43]

Soon after Louisiana voters sent a slate of Republican delegates to their constitutional convention, attacks on Union League officials and dire warnings about the future increased in frequency and in hostility of tone in the Natchez newspapers. White leaders castigated freedpeople for their political independence and affinity for Republican policies, but they were also aggrieved by freedpeople's willingness to pay attention to and join organizations run by outsiders. The newspapers cautioned freedmen to choose "intelligent men of their own color" rather than "strangers, who only stay here to manipulate Union Leagues, and use the colored people to make money and position for themselves." Targeted for particular scorn were the white Union League activists who had assumed the role of patrician to the freedpeople, or so their political opponents believed. Three white men led the Natchez Union Leagues—E. J. Castello, Frederick Parsons, and George St. Clair Hussey—none of whom were native to the region or had lived in Natchez for longer than a couple of years. Hoping to exploit divisions between the leadership and the rank and file that had surfaced over the payout of military bounties, the press vilified these Republican leaders as "scoundrels" and "unprincipled spoil-seekers," but scorn was also reserved for black outsiders, such as Henry P. Jacobs. Along with Castello and Parsons, Jacobs was a candidate to represent Adams County at the constitutional convention. A local paper excoriated him, calling Jacobs a "frothy negro preacher" because he lacked experience in "the science of jurisprudence" and because he had questionable ties to the local community, since his family resided in Michigan and he was originally from Alabama.[44]

The activities of radical outsiders troubled local whites because they were unknown quantities. The *Natchez Courier* asked, "What interest have they in the State or in the community, except that of self?" With no familial ties to the community and few economic interests there, these Union League organizers could not easily shake the charge that they were opportunists. Castello, for example, a former Union officer from St. Louis, had moved to the region to try his hand at planting in Tensas Parish in 1866. In a localized world in which face-to-face contact governed most political and economic transactions and where a person's character was not the sum of his actions but the product of his background, these outsiders represented a threat to the manner in which social relationships were conducted. Fred Parsons, an attorney, sent an autobiographical account of his life to the *Natchez Democrat*, hoping to dispel the vicious rumors about his character and to establish his good name in the community. The newspaper, however, refused to publish his account, noting, "We . . . are reminded of that trite old adage that 'a man may be known by the company he keeps.'" In other words, personal testimony was not enough to vouch for a man. In the absence of family or kin connections, the paper concluded that Parsons's "company" with radicals was enough to condemn him.[45]

As the election in Mississippi grew closer and the prospect of tens of thousands of freedmen voting for Republican candidates became a greater possibility, white conservatives shifted their focus to the new voters and laid out the broader risks in voting for radical change. "No white man will employ the negro who is striking at his political freedom," editorialized the *Natchez Courier*. The election, as understood by many whites, was about defining social relationships. The *Courier* continued, "No employment, no friendship, no kindly office, no hearth, no assistance will be given to you. When the cold day comes, the day of sickness, of want, of destitution, you cannot expect that the Southern people, whose disfranchisement is aimed at, whose lands are sought to be taken away, whose social position is to be destroyed, will hesitate one hour in turning you over to the tender mercies of the [radicals], and letting you feel that as you have sown, so must you reap." Put simply, a radical vote threatened to sever the last remaining thread of connection—no matter how ill-gotten or hierarchical—between southern whites and blacks. In voting for the slate of Republican candidates, freedmen put their work contracts, their homes, their rations, and whatever goodwill still existed between them and the planter class in jeopardy. "The negro marches to his inevitable doom," railed the *Courier*, because by voting with the Republicans, "he separates himself forever from the white race who will yet remain masters of the land."[46]

But these public and forceful appeals seemed also designed to sow seeds of division within the ranks of the newly organized leagues. By professing that they would be far more comfortable with local blacks seeking office than with outsiders, either white or black, the "old-line white citizens" hoped that the emerging Republican Party would eschew partisan experience and thereby increase the chances that it would implode. Speaking of Union League candidate E. J. Castello, the *Democrat* explained, "If we are called upon to choose between this man and any respectable colored gentleman to represent us in the convention, give us the latter, every time." Likewise, as much as conservative whites prized locality and nativity they also believed that local blacks were more susceptible to their paternalistic influences. Nevertheless, we should not completely discount their concern that leaders ungrounded in local families and neighborhoods made the entire community vulnerable to the personal interests of a few outsiders.[47]

The hoped-for rebellion against the Union League was realized late in the election season when a group of "bolters" organized a competing ticket in Natchez that emphasized moderation and some fidelity to the old planter class. The bolters denounced the outsider candidates who hailed from the North, calling one a "swindler" and another a "black sheep" and insinuating the sexual depravity of another by noting that he had contracted "loathsome diseases." They nominated E. Jeffords, a white lawyer born in Ohio who later became affiliated with the conservative National Union Republican Party, and two black men: Edmund Fletcher and Robert H. Wood. Fletcher was an illiterate waiter in Natchez who had previously been a house slave for Henry Chotard, a wealthy cotton planter. Robert H. Wood was born free in Mississippi and of mixed-race descent. His father, Robert W. Wood, was a white Natchez physician who had served as mayor of the city in the mid-1850s. After the war the younger Wood worked in a photography studio, where he met John R. Lynch, forging a decades-long friendship and political alliance. His local connections to friends, family, and community (he served as secretary of the Good Samaritans benevolent association) eventually propelled him into a twenty-five-year political career in which he held numerous offices, such as mayor and sheriff. In short, both Wood and Fletcher offered a sharp contrast to the Union League slate as locally born black men with close ties to the white elite.[48]

But the bolters were no match for the Union League–backed Republican candidates, who garnered 88 percent of the vote in an election in which virtually the entire white population sat out. In the rural precincts of Adams County, where blacks made up 90 percent of the population, nearly every vote cast came from freedmen, and in the county as a whole 99 percent of the 2,872 ballots were cast by men of color participating in the first political election of their lives. As in Louisiana, the "masterly inactivity" strategy failed spectacularly. Over 69,000 Mississippians voted in favor of calling a constitutional convention, with only 6,277 opposed.[49]

In the other Natchez District counties, Republican and Union League candidates easily won election as delegates to the constitutional convention. But of the newly elected delegates, only one was a locally born black person. Not surprisingly, this delegate, Charles W. Fitzhugh, was an AME minister and came from one of the most politically active families in the region. His parents, Agnes and Nelson Fitzhugh, were founders and leaders in the Natchez AME Church (Nelson had run into trouble when he criticized a Natchez newspaper one year before), and six of their sons became political leaders during Reconstruction.[50]

For most local freedmen, there were too many obstacles to higher political office so soon after emancipation. Most were illiterate and nearly all lacked experience working in governing bodies. It was no coincidence, then, that the three black delegates to the constitutional convention from the Natchez District were all ministers: Matthew T. Newsome from Claiborne County, Henry P. Jacobs, and Charles Fitzhugh. Although lacking in partisan experience, they had a few advantages, including literacy, a natural constituency in their church congregations, and a familiarity with denominational conventions. Reverend Jacobs, noted a late nineteenth-century church historian, "obtained a practical knowledge of the rules and regulations" governing church conventions before his arrival in Natchez—an experience that undoubtedly served him well at the constitutional convention. As one future black politician, James D. Cessor, admitted in 1867, "The colored man is harder to find than the white man, for there is not one in the country that is capable." Cessor, a literate saddler with about $1,500 worth of personal property, worried that if those inexperienced in the practice of law and policy making were "sent to the convention [and] they don't know how to put motions before the house, . . . they never will get nothing done." Cessor absented himself from consideration because of his lack of experience, but in time he, like many other neighborhood leaders, sought out positions that gave him experience in the art of politics. Cessor would later be elected marshal and alderman of the town of Rodney and serve four terms in the Mississippi House of Representatives.[51]

After a season of public meetings and political events, one federal agent in Wilkinson County suggested that political power on the ground had shifted noticeably. "The negroes are largely in the majority and conscious of their strength," he explained. "[T]hey will not submit to indignities or any infringement on their liberty." Of course, black people had outnumbered white residents for decades in the Natchez District, and although they were probably aware of their demographic majority, only with Republican mobilization did they have a mechanism by which to act in unison. Their white neighbors, in the wake of the election, also detected a change in their attitude toward the labor struggles and begged the U.S. Army to send more troops; otherwise, warned the Wilkinson County sheriff, the freedpeople "may involve the community in riot and bloodshed." The local bureau agent dismissed these fears that local blacks would foment a race war; while he acknowledged that "many of the negroes are not averse to the prospective disturbance," they would not strike the first blow.[52]

The growing white fears seemed to be confirmed when Dan Hoard, a forty-five-year-old farm laborer, rose before a Republican club meeting soon after the 1867 election and "denounced several white citizens by name, [including] some of the officials." In an incendiary call to action, he warned that "the time was at hand" and that freedpeople must arm themselves with guns or broadaxes so as to "be ready for bloody work" ahead. What made this meeting stand out was not just Hoard's inflamed rhetoric but that the details of the meeting were leaked to the public. "Two respectable white men" in attendance informed Henry S. Van Eaton, a conservative leader and local Democrat, of the content of Hoard's speech, and Van Eaton promptly relayed the information to the military governor of Mississippi. After an investigation, however, the Freedmen's Bureau concluded that Hoard's comments merited no action, and a violent clash never materialized. Speaking to his club, Hoard probably never intended his speech to be heard by non-Republicans. In one sense, the vitriolic speech suggests how club meetings offered politically engaged freedpeople opportunities to expend their frustrations safely, knowing that the club members were sworn to honor and protect each other. But Hoard's inflammatory speech also reveals the simmering tensions that were brought to the surface by political mobilization. Although violent conflict didn't break out in 1867, nine years later the "bloody work" that Hoard warned of commenced as black militias in Wilkinson County clashed with white paramilitary forces in a pitched battle that spelled the end of Reconstruction.[53]

Perhaps the heated rhetoric also stemmed from the economic disaster that freedpeople confronted in the midst of their political triumph. In Adams County those who had contracted for a share of the crop received "*nothing at all,*" reported a despondent bureau agent based in Natchez. "The consequence is that in ninety nine cases out of a hundred, the free people are in an absolute state of destitution, with starvation staring them in the face, as almost the entire population connected with the planting interest are out of employment."

In Claiborne County similar stories of planters defrauding freedpeople after the cotton harvest and violent threats against black men who voted Republican made their way to Freedmen's Bureau officials. The freedpeople, wrote the Natchez agent one month after the election, "are thoroughly disgusted, and most of them believe that they have been wronged." "The excitements occasioned by the recent election," he continued, had raised the expectations of the former slaves, but their hopes had been dashed by the dismal results in the cotton fields.[54]

"Black Power in the Soil"

The triumphant success of the electoral mobilization combined with the disappointing results of the new free-labor economy did little to assuage the unsettled state of affairs in the Natchez District. Freedpeople exercised their collective strength at the polling places, but the vote had no impact on the cotton crop and seemed to only embolden the planters who stiffed the laborers out of their contractual wages. In the midst of economic uncertainty and political success emerged one of the most remarkable social experiments in the history of the Natchez District. In the latter stages of the 1867 electoral campaign another kind of mobilization took place, one in which nearly one thousand freedpeople in Adams County attempted to form a land colony. In their efforts to separate from planter-dominated society, these freedpeople gave voice to the labor frustrations that electoral politics could not (or would not) address.

This was not the first time that a black colony has been proposed in the region. Col. S. M. Preston, of the Fifty-Eighth U.S. Colored Troops, devised a colonization scheme in 1866 whereby a soldier's monthly salary would be withheld in order to purchase twenty acres for each soldier and his family. Senior officials in the Freedmen's Bureau endorsed Preston's plan; however, the proposal attracted little interest from the people who stood to benefit most—the soldiers and their families. Preston was motivated less by freedpeople's desire for land and an independent living than by the fact that, as he said, black soldiers "squander all" of their salaries and would continue to do so until "some kind and firm hand interposes to cause it to be properly invested." Even with the prospect of land, homes, mills, and schools, the soldiers could not have been pleased by Preston's transparent paternalism. "I believe I have an unbounded influence over my men," he wrote, "and shall have no difficulty in controlling them in this enterprise for their welfare." Preston was never able to prove his boast, however, because the Vicksburg office of the bureau stalled the proposal, and within a few months the means to fund the colony evaporated when all the black regiments were mustered out of service. The lack of capital and credit prevented most freedmen's land associations from ever obtaining any land, but even if a black organization had the financial means, few whites were willing to sell them land. Still, in a postwar economy where long-established planters had difficulty obtaining credit from cotton factors or merchants, an infusion of cash could ease their distaste for black landownership.[55]

In contrast to Preston's plan, the attempt to establish a black colony during the 1867 election season attracted strong support from ordinary freedpeople. This one was directed by black men with the goal of creating, in the words of one supporter, a "neighborhood of our own." They formed an organization known as Jacobs, Williams, Wood & Company, which by January 1868 had 260 investors: 242 freedmen and 18 freedwomen. Membership consisted of sub-scribing at least ten dollars. Most probably subscribed with a military bounty of $100 to $300, which Congress had authorized for black military enlistment. The average freedman's pledge (about $100 to $150) was equivalent to the purchase price for ten acres of land. Since each member likely represented the head of a household, "the Colony" probably encompassed close to one thousand people when family and kin relations are taken into account.[56]

Most members (nearly eight in ten) resided in Natchez, and of these none appeared to belong to any of the elite black families. The desire for urban freed-people to move to the rural hinterlands might suggest disenchantment with urban life, especially among people who, in all likelihood, had been raised in the countryside. Then again, the quest for land and a farming enterprise re-flected long-held aspirations among freedpeople after emancipation. Even more indicative of the desire for separation and communal living, at least four mem-bers were already landowners, for whom a black land colony offered potentially more security and affinity that mere property holding.[57]

A seven-member board of directors governed Jacobs, Williams, Wood & Company. It is not clear how they were selected, but a few democratic mecha-nisms suggest that the organization reflected the aspirations of ordinary freed-people. The board held public meetings, and each shareholder had a vote at the company's business meetings. Henry P. Jacobs, the minister of Pine Street (formerly Wall Street) Baptist Church, headed up the board. While he was "elec-tioneering," as one planter put it, to be a delegate to the Mississippi constitu-tional convention, Jacobs was also visiting various plantations to assess their potential for a colony. "A few days before the election," wrote the planter who eventually agreed to sell his land, "I was called upon by H. P. Jacobs (col'd)." Jacobs explained that "he belonged to a company" intent on purchasing a plan-tation "for the purpose of colonizing it with Freedmen." Later, Jacobs informed the planter that "the company had held a meeting since he had seen me, and had resolved to purchase 5,000 acres."[58]

Identifying the other leaders of Jacobs, Williams, Wood & Company is more difficult. Four men and one woman named Williams appear on the subscribers' roll. Of the five, only Jerry Williams stands out as a possible organizer, because Jerry might have been Jeremiah M. P. Williams, who, like Jacobs, was a former slave and a Baptist minister and would later serve in the Mississippi legislature. Three men on the subscribers' list were named Wood, yet none of these men were of distinction or influence. Assuming that Jacobs, Williams, and Wood were members of the board, only one of the remaining four board members is possible to identify: George Hitchen, the company's secretary and treasurer. Hitchen, who was well educated and from Michigan, referred to himself as "the son of a Virginia slave holder" and was so light-skinned that he "pass[ed] for white." He came to Natchez in 1864 as a member of the Christian Commission and taught in black schools before joining the land company. Unlike Jacobs, and perhaps the other board members, Hitchen had received a formal education and was moderately well connected, as he had corresponded since 1858 with Senator Charles Sumner of Massachusetts, one of the most well-known Radical Republicans.[59]

The colonists were looking, of course, for a place to work, wrote Hitchen to Senator Sumner, but one where they "work[ed] for themselves, and for nobody else." Paramount in their minds was a desire to distance themselves from whites who heaped abuse on them. Writing to Gen. O. O. Howard, the commissioner of the Freedmen's Bureau, Hitchen lamented the plight of freedpeople who had been "fleeced . . . of all their years earnings" and subjected to invectives, such as "'Get out of this, you G–d D––d Son of a B––h' which, now is an every day occurance." All they wanted was to "form a little community among ourselves, where each man can sit down under his own Corn and Cotton stalk." They wanted to separate themselves from unruly and intrusive neighbors and yet remain close to the land and people they knew best. Rejecting a proposal to purchase a tract of land close to the state capital in Jackson, they emphatically declared that they wanted land "near Natchez." Most of the members had lived in the area before the war and considered it home, but there may also have been a strategic decision to stay relatively close to a major Mississippi city. Natchez offered freedpeople many options, including a Freedmen's Bureau post, a port, a commercial district, churches, schools, and other social and political institutions.[60]

"You know that ever since we were Free," Hitchen wrote in hyperbolic language not uncommon in his letters, "we have been calling for land, land, land, the everlasting cry has been 'Give me land or give me death,' or words to this effect." In the nineteenth century, landownership was equated with independence, and even though the 260 subscribers chose to purchase their land collectively, they did so with the intention, as specified in the company's constitution, that each member would one day own an individual plot of land outright. Some were so taken with the idea that they refused to contract for the coming year or even to "work for any one," wrote one planter, "believing they are to have a place of their own." "Having a thorough knowledge of all the country," the colonists set their sights on ten thousand acres of prime cotton land along the Homochitto River in the southeastern corner of Adams County. They could have paid considerably less for hilly and wooded land in other parts of the county, or they could have purchased public land, also at a much lower cost, in the eastern part of the state, even if it tended to be of poor quality. But their selection of a major cotton plantation suggests that they were interested in more than household production. Not only was the land particularly productive, it came with all the implements of a modern cotton plantation: a steam cotton gin, a corn mill, cotton presses, barns and stables, a steam sawmill, fourteen dwelling houses, and quarters containing 160 rooms. In addition, and not without importance for the freedpeople, a brick church and a schoolhouse were already in place. A few subscribers were so enamored with the land that they did not wait for the transfer of title and squatted on the plantation, with some even beginning to raise a crop before the purchase had been finalized.[61]

It was such a good deal that the freedpeople were willing to overlook the fact that the owner of the plantation, Alexander K. Farrar, was the man most responsible for the mass execution of rebellious slaves during the Civil War. The investors in the land colony were fully aware that they were dealing with the devil, so to speak. Hitchen informed Freedmen's Bureau commissioner O. O. Howard that Farrar "helped to Hang 88 of our People during the late Rebellion," and thus "we all fear him as much as we do the -- himself." Thomas Turner, a forty-seven-year-old ex-slave, was a colony subscriber and also filed an scc claim. In Turner's approved claim, his friend, George Braxton, testified that Farrar "was always looking for a chance to get a hold of some of us." Similarly, Alfred Doxey, another subscriber, testified for Deborah Smith's scc claim. Her husband, John Smith, was arrested by the vigilance committee headed by Farrar, and Smith was nearly executed for being an "abolitionist." The company favored a former Confederate, it seems, because Farrar's land was of better quality and he was a known quantity. By contrast, a white former Union officer, Capt. B. D. Whitney, offered to sell much cheaper land to the colony. It was an attractive offer from a more agreeable person, since Whitney had given "many speeches" at Union League meetings in Natchez. But because Whitney had abandoned "the regular Republican or colored Man's Ticket" in the recent election, they could not trust this recently arrived northerner. Hitchen called him a "Copperhead" and dismissed him as "a sort of a Democratic carcass, with a Republican coat on."[62]

Five years after the "reign of terror" and now flexing their political muscles after the election of 1867, perhaps freedpeople could look past Farrar's dubious past, but what could explain Farrar's interest in selling land to freedpeople? Although he was a prominent planter who had owned over three hundred slaves, he had never been particularly prosperous. The freedmen's offer would have enabled him to pay off large debts that dated back to the 1850s. Speaking for his entire family, Farrar, age fifty-two, explained, "We are all desirous of disposing of our lands, thereby enabling us to curtail the quantity, and situate ourselves all-together, and in a more profitable and suitable manner."[63]

Farrar also recognized that there were very few opportunities like this for "the freedman to sustain himself," a hint of altruism that provoked considerable enmity among his fellow planters. Farrar, like many of his fellow Adams County planters, opposed secession (he even voted against it as a representative at Mississippi's secession convention) but joined the Confederacy nevertheless. When his peers learned of his "unprecedented dereliction" of duty, nearly three hundred planters, Hitchen reported, gathered in Natchez to condemn "the terrible Calamity." Many feared that other "eligible localities throughout the country" would soon adopt the same idea. Unable to force Farrar to reconsider, the planters retaliated by turning colony members out of their homes upon learning that they planned to settle on "the A.K. Farrar Farm" for the next year.[64]

Because the proposed colony involved more than the purchase of one plantation, "the Politics of this County and State, would be completely transformed," or so thought George Hitchen. Only a couple of months after the first election in which freedmen voted, the prospect of economic independence along with a nascent political independence foreshadowed a radical restructuring of power relations. Sounding much like John Mercer Langston, Farrar argued that a "permanent, social, and industrial establishment" would be "a general benefit to the race, of incalculable value" to an ordinary freedman because it would "improve permanently his condition, without the presence and cooperation of the white race." If a few hundred freedpeople were able to establish an independent community, removed from white influence, they would be well positioned to spread radicalism throughout the rural hinterlands. Planters realized that "the Black Power in the Soil," to use Hitchen's evocative expression, represented a threat to their dominance over black workers. This potential makes its demise all the more tragic.[65]

The sticking point was the military bounties, which, according to federal law, could be redeemed only by former soldiers or their heirs. The vast majority of subscribers seemed to be veterans or widows of deceased soldiers, but the process of redeeming the bounties was rather protracted. The company tried to pay Farrar with their collected bounty claims, but they were worthless in his hands. Next, the board solicited the aid of General Howard and Senator Charles Sumner to plead with Congress to authorize a special amendment to the military bounty law exempting Farrar from the prohibition on receiving the claims. Short of that, they pleaded with the bureau to purchase the land outright and then transfer the title over to Jacobs, Williams, Wood & Company. Sumner seemed interested in the endeavor and met with Howard to press the issue. At first, Howard endorsed the colony and suggested a plan whereby the bounties would be transferred to the Treasury Department and settled quickly, and then a special agent would be sent to Natchez to purchase the land. But before the agent could be dispatched, an investigative report, commissioned by Howard, reached his desk. It painted a gloomy picture of the planned colony.[66]

Howard had sent Gen. F. D. Sewall to Natchez to interview the principal leaders of the proposed colony and determine the feasibility of the plan. Sewall concluded that while the proposal to use bounties was "very desirable," this particular venture was "impracticable," primarily because "the parties at the head of it, are not suitable or qualified to manage so large a scheme." Sewall criticized the board of directors for not considering other, cheaper tracts of land. More troubling, the board had no plan for the division of the land among the shareholders, no arrangements for subsisting until the first-year crops were harvested, nor any idea how they would raise money after the initial payment in bounties to resolve their debt. As for Hitchen, Sewall found him to be "perfectly irresponsible." While the board claimed that it had $36,000 in subscriptions, mostly from the bounties, its bank account held only $448. Other Freedmen's Bureau agents charged Hitchen with practicing "Voodooism," "selling whiskey to the Freedmen at exorbitant prices," and distributing counterfeit currency. H. P. Jacobs was castigated for selling free copies of "Homestead Act" pamphlets to freedmen. And both Jacobs and Hitchen were also criticized for running an unneeded and underpopulated school. It was true that Hitchen operated a grocery store where he likely sold liquor and made transactions in questionable currency. And Jacobs certainly had an interest in the Homestead Act, as he led a land company for freedmen. But beyond the leaders' foibles lay problems with the organization of the colony.[67]

The board did not appear prepared to deal with the complexities of managing the day-to-day operations. Farrar suggested that the proposed colony needed a more direct management structure to keep track of each subscription, the supplies needed, and the amount of labor output from each member, as well as provide for a settlement for those who chose to opt out of the association. Resentment at free riders and others not pulling their fair share plagued similar organizations. And, of course, the whole scheme was predicated on the idea that at some future date, each subscriber would accumulate enough funds to purchase an individual farm—a precarious prospect at best, considering the economic misfortunes in previous years and white hostility even before the project got off the ground.[68]

With Sewall's damning report in mind, Howard refused to approve the exchange of bounties for cash payment, and so the purchase of the Farrar land could not go forward. While Jacobs, Williams, Wood & Company failed to establish a land colony, the struggle to acquire land suggests that freedpeople wanted to live in a protected society, one in which black enterprise, communalism, and independence could be nurtured and sustained. But the obstacles to landownership and communal living were many. The prospects of land reform were never very promising, but after the failure of the colony the chances diminished considerably.

Disappointment with the failure of the land colony and lack of land reform was not limited to Adams County. Leading white citizens in Jefferson County, who were worried about the palpable frustration of black farm laborers, organized a large meeting in Fayette at the end of 1867. They advised "the negroes to go to work" and, "if they could not get wages, to work for their meat & bread." Then they turned the speaker's platform over to Merrimon Howard, the former slave who had successfully established the first black school in the county. Howard similarly implored black people to "make the best contract they could" and not wait for federal intervention. A large "class of freedpeople" in Claiborne County were equally unconvinced that the contract system held any promise for the coming growing season. Large numbers refused to enter into labor contracts because, lamented one bureau agent, they were "waiting for the new law to pass," which would provide "lands, teams and provisions" from the federal government. They held out for at least two months, adamantly refusing to reconsider their decision. The local bureau agent "found it impossible to convince some of them to the contrary."[69]

Broadening the Mobilization Campaign

By the spring planting, with little changed in the fields, attention returned to the political realm. The state constitutional conventions were at work restructuring the social and political framework for the region, and freedmen and freedwomen prepared for another season of labor and electoral strife.

Responding to the Republican Party's and Union League's initial success in the fall 1867 elections, Democrats looked to the important elections in 1868 with renewed interest. In April and June, respectively, Louisiana and Mississippi voters would go to the polls to ratify the state constitutions produced by the Republican-dominated conventions. As a consequence, every elective office and most appointed positions were thrown open to a whole new set of people. Then, in November, voters would return to the polls to elect congressmen and vote for president.[70]

In Louisiana Democrats were still demoralized from the fall campaign and barely put up much of fight in the April ratification election. The new constitution was easily ratified. In Tensas Parish black voters produced one of the most lopsided results in the state; 1,334 in favor and only 144 against. A few planters continued to discharge black workers for "attending political meetings," reported a bureau agent, but they seemed to have little impact on the election campaign. In Mississippi, by contrast, Democrats sensed an opportunity to turn back the tide of radicalism and began to organize in the towns to blunt black mobilization efforts.[71]

Freedpeople's growing militancy in the fields coupled with the effective Republican mobilization across the Natchez District led planters and Democrats to adjust their strategy and tactics. Not only were freedpeople setting aside their labor obligations to attend political meetings, they were following the advice of outsiders, such as Union League activists. White Democrats therefore mounted a concerted campaign to attract black voters by highlighting the benefits of paternalistic politics. They believed, even after the stunningly lopsided results of the 1867 election, that most or at least some freedpeople would accede to a system in which their subordination was perpetuated. Still, in their emphasis on locality and their discourse of "friendship," Democrats offered a stark challenge to the embryonic Republican community.

In the month before the June election, Mississippi Democrats in the Natchez District began an unprecedented campaign to entice and coerce black voters to join the Democratic Party. Turning away from their failed strategy of inactivity in the face of Republican mobilization, they now recognized the political standing of black male citizens. Just as the Republicans had done a year earlier, now Democrats were hosting mass meetings and appealing directly to the ex-slave population. On the Saturday two weeks before the election, Democrats in Adams County held two mass meetings on plantations and another at the village of Washington and capped off the day's events with an evening meeting at the Natchez courthouse. Most meetings, including barbecues, attracted some freedpeople; however, those freedpeople publicly allied with the Union League or with Republicans usually kept their distance. Of course, freedpeople never faced dismissal for attending a Democratic meeting.[72]

This was not the first time that conservatives had attempted to appeal to freedmen. Three weeks after Republicans met at the Natchez AME Church in April 1867, local white conservatives hosted their own meeting where they proclaimed their willingness to obey the provisions of military Reconstruction. Speaking to an audience of "about equal numbers of white and colored people," white Democratic leaders and at least two black men, Tony Jones and Burrell Foley, tried to allay the concerns of ordinary freedpeople and to convince them that local whites were their friends. Jones, a sixty-seven-year-old laborer, and Foley, a thirty-year-old freeborn carpenter, would both go on to become prominent in local Democratic politics. But in this initial phase of mobilization their impact was negligible.[73]

The overwhelming Republican victory in the 1867 elections convinced many white conservatives to drop the pretense of a "Union" party and organize under the Democratic Party. At the head of the white conservative movement was William T. Martin, an ex-Confederate general, the leader of the Adams County white militia, and the defense attorney for David Singleton, the wealthy freedman. Martin represented the Natchez District at the Union Party's national convention in 1866, which endorsed President Johnson's tentative plans for Reconstruction. Locally, Martin held office as president of the board of police, helped organize the Constitutional Union Party, and became the Democratic candidate for Congress in 1868. No matter the political label, Martin reflected the values of the planter class, which stood in opposition to the Union Leagues, Republicans, and black equality. Moreover, Martin and his white conservative allies were formidable opponents with extensive political experience, supported by a well-organized and well-funded partisan organization.[74]

The effectiveness of the Democrats' new friendship strategy was coupled with harsh labor reprisals against plantation workers aligned with Republicans. "Vote with these radicals," thundered one Claiborne County planter, "and you shall not live on my land; I will never let a radical nigger stay on my place." In addition to threats, planters were not shy about using extortion to increase the Democratic vote. Planters in Claiborne County often joined the sheriff as he made the rounds collecting taxes from black farm laborers. Few could afford the disproportionately high taxes—particularly the poll tax and taxes on guns and dogs, which often amounted to six to eight dollars—but before the sheriff confiscated a horse or other piece of household property in lieu of cash, the planter would step in and promise "that if he would vote the democratic ticket, he (the employer) would be responsible for the taxes."[75]

These retaliations were not unlike those from the previous summer, only more intensified. Some freedpeople were fined for violating their labor contracts, others were denied rations, and still others had their wages docked. Those discharged off the land lost their homes, access to schools, and their share of the crop. Godfrey Brown, a freedman, attended many political meetings, but when it came time to register for the 1868 vote, his overseer refused to grant him permission to travel into town. Another freedman was fined for leaving his plantation to "hear the political speeches" on a neighboring plantation. When he attended another meeting a few days later, he was turned off the land and denied "all interest in the crops." In a one-month period, at least eleven freedpeople filed formal complaints with the Freedmen's Bureau in Wilkinson County for politically motivated dismissals, such as those for attending a meeting, registering to vote, voting Republican, or, as happened to Sam Anderson, a farm laborer, for "refusing to vote the Democratic ticket." The threat of being discharged and losing half a year's crop had a noticeable effect on Republican meetings. E. J. Castello, the most prominent Union League organizer in the Natchez District, complained to the head of the league's state council in Mississippi that attendance was down at a recent meeting because "the rebels use [freedpeople's] going to Meetings as a pretext to discharge them and cheat them out of their Labour."[76]

Democrats balanced their coercive rhetoric and action with patronage appeals and calls for "friendship." On the eve of the June election, the *Natchez Democrat* spoke directly to the city's black laborers, who were often employed by white businessmen, declaring "FRIENDSHIP FOR OUR FRIENDS is the motto of merchants and all other white men in Natchez who have work for drays, hacks and wood-sawyers." "Friends," the newspaper wanted to make clear, voted with the Democrats, while "those who vote for the iniquitous [Republican] constitution are enemies." "If you have not the courage to vote the Democratic ticket, keep away from the polls," the piece continued, and then the blank registration ticket "will be a lasting card of recommendation to all white men who have employment to give." The Colored Democratic Club, one of the few black organizations to swim against the tide of Republicanism, asserted that Republicans were not "our true friends" but that southern whites were the "real true friends upon whom we can at all times rely for counsel and advice, and . . . for material aid" because they "have known us from infancy."[77]

Some former slaves embraced the rhetoric of "friendship," but determining who was a friend and who was an enemy was not always clear-cut and had much to do with one's circle of contacts. After moving to Natchez from a plantation in Concordia Parish, Thomas Burke, a young freedman, had difficulty discerning whom to trust during the heated electoral campaign. "I did not know who my friends were," he testified, and so he voted the Democratic ticket after his former master convinced him that "he would give me as much land as" the Republicans. Nor was Burke the only freedman seduced by the language of friendship. Because so many freedpeople were tempted by this rhetoric and the promise of material improvement, Republican activists, such as David Young, had to speak forcefully against it. Young, a thirty-one-year-old ex-slave, farm laborer, and rising star in the Concordia Parish Republican Party, made it a point in his public speaking in Natchez's Cotton Square to instruct freedpeople "to cut loose from the whites of the South" and to ignore their "protestations of friendship."[78]

In one sense, political appeals based on "friendship" represented an extension of the paternalistic relationship that white slaveholders believed had governed their interactions with slaves, but in the new politics of emancipation, "friendship" connoted an altogether different meaning. Democrats realized that freedpeople faced possible retribution from black Republicans for voting the Democratic ticket; thus the offer of employment was more than a financial inducement but also a way of offering protection. The motto "FRIENDSHIP FOR

OUR FRIENDS" also illustrates the profound shift in the social order now that black enfranchisement had become a reality. It suggested that there was room in the white political community for freedpeople, although this space was carefully circumscribed.[79]

Black Democrats traversed a liminal world in which their white "friends" did not treat them as equals and most freedpeople shunned them. The few who did publicly ally with the Democrats, however, received favored treatment from white Democratic leaders. Black Democrats shared the stage and made speeches at Democratic rallies. They marched in Democratic processions and formed their own race-specific political clubs. They were a small group who accepted racial subordination and defined themselves in opposition to the egalitarian-based Republican community. Their beliefs were best articulated by the Adams County Colored Democratic Club's resolutions, which dismissed the Union League and other Republican clubs as "secret political organizations" that "are dangerous in character" but saved the sharpest criticism for "carpet baggers." The problem with these white northerners was that they took the place of the local white leaders, "our true friends," as the leaders of blacks. Because these outsiders subverted what the club believed was the natural social order, they had in effect imperiled the "peace and harmony" in the community. For the men at the head of the Colored Democrats, decrying Republican organizers and urging freedpeople to submit to white rule made sense because deference to powerful whites had been good for them. Their president, Burrell Foley, a thirty-one-year-old freeborn carpenter, had two white men swear to his loyalty in his scc claim, which was quite unusual, as black claimants typically called on other blacks to certify their loyalty. Israel Jones, the club's vice president, was also a carpenter, an ex-slave whom the *Natchez Democrat* identified as a model black Democrat.[80]

Although it employed the language of "friendship" and offered freedpeople powerful allies among the white elite, the Democratic Party attracted only a small following among freedpeople. Its failure owes much to the organizational sophistication of grassroots Republican activists, but the party also failed to catch on because it relegated black Democrats to subordinate positions. In parades, Democratic leaders consigned "Colored Democrats" to marching on foot behind white Democrats, while whites rode on horseback or in carriages. Black Democrats could form their own clubs, but they had to be segregated, unlike the cross-racial Union Leagues and Republican clubs. Even though Democrats talked of "friendship," the platform of Mississippi's "Democratic White Men's Party" rejected the constitutionality of military Reconstruction and proclaimed white superiority—political positions that were antithetical to nearly all freedpeople.[81]

The planters' two-front campaign—stifling Republican mobilization efforts through economic coercion while persuading freedmen to join the Democrats—failed in both instances, but their campaign is instructive because it reveals how planters adapted to freedpeople's nascent yet formidable political movement. Planters realized that centralized contact points, such as plantation quarters, churches, and schools, drew together people who were dispersed across the countryside and provided space for information sharing and political learning that militated against the strictures of local planter power. They had learned from the 1867 campaign that freedpeople's power originated in local communities and kinship networks. The following spring many freedpeople were turned off the land in order to "intimidate and scatter them that they may not vote at the approaching elections," reported a bureau agent who grew wise to the planters' tactics. "I may say that it seems to be almost an organization to accomplish that result."[82]

Freedpeople matched planters' organized reprisals with collective responses of their own. Freedmen in Jefferson County sometimes stayed away from work for "a week at a time" to attend the political gatherings, and, more provocatively, some came armed to public assemblies. In Wilkinson County, as they had the year before, "at their preconcerted signals," recorded a white resident, "every man on the plantation is mounted and gone, those who have nothing to ride following in the rear." "Political meetings have been held daily in this Sub District," noted a bureau agent stationed in Adams County, and "in many cases *all the freed people men and women* left to attend such meetings, trusting that the planter could not discharge all of them at once without loss to themselves."[83]

The ubiquity of political meetings inflamed planters and worried local whites, not just because freedmen flocked to the gatherings but also because they attracted women, children, and families. Black women had attended political meetings almost from their inception, as with the 1867 meeting at the Natchez courthouse that included "a large attendance of negroes, including women and children" to hear a traveling organizer from the Union League speak on radical issues that, according to the *Natchez Democrat*, would have made "even the Arch Rad. [Thaddeus] Stevens" blush. And a year later at least 150 freedwomen attended a "grand mass meeting" on the Natchez bluff to listen to Republican nominees for the state ticket. But in 1868, planters began to recognize that politically active freedwomen were a central component of Republican mobilization. "The rebels," complained Union League organizer E. J. Castello, "are treating the Men and in many instances the Women in a Most Outrageous and inhumane Maner for the reason that they attend Meetings." Freedpeople deluged federal agents with complaints of planters "discharging men and women for attending public meetings." Eliza Roney, a freedwoman, was ejected from her home "for coming to town to attend a political meeting." Planters at first had mocked freedwomen who participated in political affairs. "If the radicals want to be successful in electing men to office," wrote one Concordia Parish planter in 1867, "let them put their whites on their ballots, and then expend their electioneering efforts among the negro women. The latter I can recommend as good politicians and true." The planter recognized an implicit threat from freedwomen, whom he considered to be "all-powerful to lead the colored man." A year later the joking had been set aside and planters targeted black women as they did men, an implicit recognition that freedpeople's sense of communal obligation and broad participation were having an impact on electoral mobilization.[84]

The patterns of opposition to blacks and Republicans in the Natchez District were replicated across Mississippi by Democratic leaders. To mobilize white voters, many of whom sat out the 1867 election, Democrats pointed to two proscriptive provisions in the proposed constitution that seemed intent on disenfranchising conservative whites. One clause banned former Confederate leaders from holding office until a future legislature removed the prohibition. The other was even more controversial and far-reaching. Every potential voter had to take an oath that included the phrase "that I admit the political and civil equality of all men; so help me God." For most white Mississippians, accepting the civic equality of black men was a step too far. Contrary to the intentions of the Republican delegates, the equality oath became a rallying cry for white opposition to the entire constitution.[85]

But in a state nearly equally divided between white and black voters, mobilizing whites would not ensure the defeat of the constitution. What was needed was a weak showing of black Republicans at the polls, and the Ku Klux Klan was designed to cause just that. The Klan, however, did not operate uniformly statewide. It was most likely to attack Republican activists and black leaders in counties with a proportionally equal number of white and black residents. Across the state, Klans wreaked their vengeance on smaller Union Leagues, resulting in a reduced Republican vote and defeat for the radical constitution. In the Natchez District, with its overwhelmingly black population, white residents were reluctant to organize Klans for fear of disrupting plantation labor and for fear of black reprisals. Betty Beaumont, a Wilkinson County merchant, spoke for many in the planter class when she chastised the Klan for "driving our best labor from our midst." "The colored element," she continued, "know that the white man can make nothing if they leave the plantations." But local blacks did not just flee; sometimes they stood up to the Klan. In Natchez the Klan posted handbills on street corners, "warning Union men to be aware of their vengeance," reported the *Natchez Democrat*. When a couple of Klansmen tried "to frighten" two black Union League members, "the colored men halted them in regular military style—forced them to uncover their faces and disclose their names, and chastised one of them so severely that he kept his bed for some days."[86]

The assertiveness of the black Union Leaguers was not an aberration. As more and more freedmen made a public declaration of allegiance to the Republican Party, there seemed to be more instances of freedpeople expressing their true feelings. During the first voter registration campaign in 1867, a Jefferson County resident was stunned when on a visit to Natchez her former slave confronted her on the streets and "cursed her for everything," wishing that the entire "family was in the hottest spot." After that election a group of Concordia Parish freedmen, selected to be jurors for the first time, marched to the courthouse, "all decked out in their best Sunday" dress, and boasted to white onlookers that "they had come to 'tend to de white folks.'"[87]

The newfound public confidence of freedpeople was on display in the aftermath of the defeat of the Republican constitution in Mississippi. Although Klan violence seemed to be decisive in turning the election to the Democrats and even though voters in the Natchez District gave large majorities to the Republican ticket, in the days immediately following the election many believed that black Democrats had tipped the results against the radical constitution. In Port Gibson the black Baptist church expelled "its Democratic members" after the election. In Natchez "seven or eight Radical negroes," one of whom (Peter Griffin) was an investor in the failed land colony, surrounded a black Democrat from Franklin County during a visit to Natchez, "abused and insulted [him], and threatened if he did not disown the Democratic conduct with which he was charged, they would mob him on the spot." In another example of retribution against black Democrats, "Radicals, black and white," assaulted Israel Jones, the vice president of the black Democratic club, "on several occasion[s]" for espousing "Conservative principles." They sought "to compel him into submission to the [Union] league" because he "influence[d] other colored men to follow his example." Republican attacks were so frequent that the Natchez Democrat had to remind its readers that "Democratic colored men must be protected in safety by the people to whom they have proved true."[88]

The political momentum seemed to be shifting away from the insurgent black Republicans. For the first time in eight years, white Democrats openly celebrated the Fourth of July with a parade. By contrast, the Republican parade was only one-twentieth the size of the previous year's massive procession. Adding further salt in the political wounds of their rivals, Democrats hosted a "Grand Democratic Ratification Procession" just two weeks later, celebrating the "coming downfall of Radicalism" and launching the fall campaign for the presidential ticket of Horatio Seymour and Francis Preston Blair. But this was too much of an affront for some residents. As the parade made its way through downtown Natchez, a group of "negro boys" and a few freedmen began to throw rocks at "the Seymour and Blair banner extended across the street," and later, as the beginning of the procession passed by the Commercial Bank, they pelted the

Democratic club officers' carriages with other "missiles." It was a rare outburst of black violence against whites.[89]

Perhaps in retaliation for the attack at the Democratic parade, or as just a further sign of the bitter partisan struggle, a group of Democrats kidnapped a white Republican and nearly lynched him. On the night of the Grand Democratic Procession, a group of white men disguised as "negroes" visited George Stewart, a white Mississippian, at his home in the village of Washington in rural Adams County. They forcibly removed Stewart from his home, dragged him into the woods, and tarred and feathered him. That he was a teacher of black children had little to do with the outrage, according to an investigation by the Freedmen's Bureau.[90] Instead, Stewart's marriage seemed to provoke a violent response, for the reason that Stewart's wife, also a teacher at the colored school, was "a lady of color." "He has been cohabitating notoriously with a negro woman," reported the *Democrat* in an attempt to justify the attack. But there was another reason for the outrage: "It is said Stewart is a violent Radical." He had recently "expressed himself very strong at a republican Meeting," and his attackers, according to Stewart, demanded that he reveal the Union League's "signs and passwords." Further evidence of the partisan nature of the attack comes from the identity of the chief assailant: William T. Hewett, a prominent conservative and the county attorney for Adams County. More than likely, Hewett was also one of the Democratic Club officers who were pelted with rocks at the Natchez parade. But it was not just white Democrats who were involved. The four white assailants, including Hewett, were transported to Stewart's home by William Cotton, a fifty-two-year-old drayman who was a publicly identified black Democrat and had been a featured speaker at the Democrats' Fourth of July celebration.[91]

Attacked by Democrats both white and black because of his political advocacy (as a teacher and speaker at club meetings) and for his marriage to a black woman, George Stewart, a native white Mississippian, epitomized the potential of Republicanism and grassroots mobilizations for transforming social relationships and destabilizing racial boundaries. In an environment in which racial and class hierarchies were under attack, political identification gained added saliency as locals used partisan allegiances to differentiate between friends and foes. On the surface, it made little sense for a black Democrat to attack a white radical for espousing political and social equality. In fact, the attack reveals how the 1867 and 1868 mobilizations unsettled existing social identities and led to a reconfiguration of freedpeople's relation to the body politic.

Although there were premonitions of violence during the fall campaign, they did not surface—at least not in Natchez. Even though Mississippi voters would not participate in the presidential election because the state had not yet been readmitted into the Union, a tense state of relations still persisted in the Natchez District. "Political feeling runs very high at present and controls everything, Civil offices and all," reported a bureau agent in Port Gibson at the end of August 1868. Similarly, an agent in Wilkinson County conveyed "an apprehension of a conflict, growing out of political gatherings and the heated canvass." In Louisiana the political situation was more worrying. The assistant commissioner for Louisiana warned Freedmen's Bureau headquarters in Washington of the violent tension seeping into the state, passing along reports that "arms have been shipped to the whites, and the lives of freedmen threatened." In Tensas Parish the warning was born out. A freedman was killed for "saying he intended to vote for Grant" about one week before the presidential election, one of thirteen freedmen in the parish murdered in 1868 for political reasons. A white engineer working in Tensas Parish confirmed these statistics when he noted to his parents, who lived in New England, that "Union men and women are still robbed, murdered and ravished, in the broad light of day and the rebellion still rages." The increasing violence spurred federal authorities to send a small contingent of soldiers to the parish seat in St. Joseph for the election.[92]

Except for the politically related murders in Tensas, the 1868 presidential election took place without much violence, intimidation, or fraud in the Natchez District. Freedpeople faced the same economic pressures from employers and planters that they confronted over the previous year and a half, but by now ordinary black voters anticipated these responses and through their sophisticated mobilization practices were able to deflect Democratic subterfuges. In both Tensas and Concordia Parishes, voters overwhelmingly cast their ballots for the Republican candidate and eventual winner, Ulysses S. Grant. But these votes were outliers in a state that voted 70 percent Democratic and in an election that was marred by extensive violence against freedpeople in most other parishes. Nevertheless, Grant's election, propelled by freedmen's votes in the South, signaled national support for the continuation of Reconstruction. More specifically, Grant's election preserved Mississippi's radical constitution. The new president pushed Congress to authorize a revote, but one with separate votes for the controversial proscriptive sections. The following year Mississippi voters overwhelmingly approved the new state constitution and set aside the disfranchising clauses.[93]

As was becoming clear to all sides, universal manhood suffrage had weakened the racial and class designations that had once structured southern society. Neither color nor previous condition of servitude was enough to categorize an individual in the new politics of emancipation. And the master class could no longer refer to black people in public as subordinate members of a broad paternalistic family. Rather, in an implicit recognition of the public shift toward equality, conservative leaders spoke in egalitarian terms, referring to former slaves as "friends" and indeed hoping that this formerly subject people would agree to an alliance of equals, at least rhetorically. But Republicans were also endeavoring to forge new relationships. They too envisioned their political community as one of like-minded friends, drawn together on the basis of shared values and assumptions. Ulysses Grant and Schuyler Colfax "are your friends," stated a Republican pamphlet distributed to black voters, adding that they would continue the work of reconstructing "the former slave States on the basis of equal laws, education and liberty." For the ordinary freedperson, never before had political leaders and powerful whites extended the hand of friendship in such a public way.[94]

The Military Reconstruction Acts gave local freedpeople an opening to refashion the social order to their liking. They took advantage of this opportunity by using their existing church, school, and labor communities to expand and enrich a regional political community of like-minded people. They emphatically rejected the paternalistic politics of the planter class and the Democratic Party. Instead they put their trust not just in a partisan organization (the Republican Party) but in themselves. Through local networks and institutions freedpeople reached beyond their neighborhoods to participate in a new democracy, a democracy based on a few fundamental principles: educational opportunity, black suffrage, equal access to public spaces, and shared governance. These ideas motivated freedmen and freedwomen to congregate in mass celebrations, to march to the ballot box, and to attend political meetings, even at the risk of dismissal and ejection from their homes. Additionally, conflicts with employers and political opponents helped to draw community boundaries. When freedpeople lashed out at black Democrats in the streets of Natchez, they gave public expression to the community's ideals and aspirations just as surely as they did in public meetings. While land reform proved to be elusive, the returns from the 1868 cotton crop soothed somewhat the tension in the fields. Nearly twice as many bales were shipped to New Orleans as had been in the previous year. With some tangible earnings from the year's labor, freedpeople could reflect more on the fact that they had fundamentally altered the political order of the region through their effective voter mobilization and had enshrined this new order in radical state constitutions.[95]

PART TWO

Maintaining Democracy

FOUR

"A New Machinery of Government"

In June 1872 a Grand Railroad Barbecue was held at the Bend, a neighborhood along a hairpin curve of the Mississippi River about three miles southwest of the small town of Rodney, Mississippi. The event featured some of the most influential politicians and businessmen from Jefferson and Adams Counties. They were there to give speeches to convince local voters that they should adopt a railroad bond that would finance construction of a railroad trunk line through the Natchez District. "There was plenty to eat, [and] a good crowd to eat it," reported one participant. But beyond the specific reasons for the gathering, what stood out about those assembled at the speaker's platform was the varied backgrounds of the leading men. They included Republicans and Democrats, black and white officeholders, northerners and southerners, ex-slaves and ex-slaveholders. Representing Adams County were Gen. William T. Martin (a former Confederate general, attorney, Democratic politician, and ex-slave owner), Henry P. Jacobs (a Republican state legislator and Baptist minister who successfully escaped from slavery in the mid-1850s), and E. J. Castello (the Natchez postmaster, a Union League organizer, a delegate to the 1868 constitutional convention, and a former Union army officer from St. Louis). From Jefferson County were Merrimon Howard (the Republican sheriff and tax collector who was born enslaved but freed in 1854), Dr. Robert E. Richardson (a white planter and physician who had owned twenty slaves in 1860), and Henry B. McClure (a Republican state senator who was born in England).[1]

These men from disparate backgrounds and with different perspectives were united in a common purpose—working together to advance the economic interests of the region. Summing up the bipartisan and biracial gathering, Martin reported that the meeting was "very good." It was a judgment that signified how much Reconstruction had upended social norms and power relations in the seven years since slavery was abolished.[2]

In that moment, at the Grand Railroad Barbecue, the black politicians had achieved a long-sought-after goal—they were perceived as legitimate power brokers. One of the great challenges for black Republicans was to establish the credibility of their power, especially in the eyes of the southern white population. The federal government's dissolution of state and local governments under the Military Reconstruction Acts, followed by its expansion of the franchise to include black men, sowed deep distrust among southern whites. With the electoral campaigns of 1867 and 1868, it became clear that freedpeople would vote for their own interests and for their party, but how would they govern? Could Republican officeholders gain the consent of the governed? Would southern whites abide by laws and listen to officials put in place by black votes, or would consent come only through the force of arms? Ordinary freedpeople had fewer concerns about the legitimacy of their elected officials, but they did worry about how effectively these officials would govern. Would they boldly transform southern governance, or would they shrink back from white opposition? Would their inexperience doom their effectiveness, or would their fresh approach to lawmaking lead to innovative policies? These were questions that loomed large as Republicans crafted new state constitutions and as new officeholders took power in the spring and summer of 1868.

Historians have devoted more attention to how black men became officeholders than what they did with their new power. Because so few studies have waded into the complicated terrain of legislative history (especially at the state and municipal levels), a perception persists that Republican officeholders in the Deep South were abject failures as representatives of freedpeople and that their only success owed to their moderation. That black Republicans had moderate tendencies would have been news to white Democrats. Rather, elected black officials invariably endorsed numerous radical policies that accurately reflected their constituents' views. And they implemented much of their radical agenda. Where they seem to have fallen short, particularly in hindsight, is in the realm of agricultural reform and their inability to stem the poverty of ex-slave farm laborers. While a few black legislators tried to facilitate black landownership, most believed that economic development through railroad construction would help to solve the problem of debt and tenancy. Their response to agricultural poverty, in other words, was mediated by what was possible at the time and their distinct vision for the future. Land redistribution proved to be politically impossible, but many thought that railroad development could be the harbinger of broad prosperity.[3]

Local freedpeople voted for and supported the Republican Party not merely for its previous advocacy of emancipation and Reconstruction but also because of its support for specific policies that had the potential to improve the quality of their lives. Perhaps the greatest achievement of Reconstruction, and one of the most pressing grassroots demands, was the creation of free public schools. In the span of a few years, dozens of school buildings were constructed across a largely rural landscape, hundreds of teachers were hired, and thousands of children began attending classes. Not only did this meet the needs of freedpeople who clamored for an educational system, but it exemplified their broad democratic vision in which the community, through taxation, was obligated to help certain individuals for the betterment of the whole.

Economic policies were far less successful, yet the debate over reform testified to the resilience of grassroots democracy. What is interesting about the numerous railroad campaigns, most of which failed, is the bipartisan and biracial character of these policies. In other states and regions during the early 1870s, violent extremists joined with Democrats to oust Republican officials from power, but in the Natchez District there was no violent spasm of Ku Klux Klan terrorism. Rather, Democrats and Republicans found some common ground. The debate over railroad construction and funding also reveals that local interests often conflicted with regional interests, creating a situation in which race and partisan issues were not determinative in the fight over economic development. It also demonstrates the difficulty of implementing substantive public policy, for while one rail link was constructed, the railroad only tempered the postwar economic decline of the region.

As a result of war and Reconstruction, "a new machinery of government" had been created, declared State Senator Jeremiah M. P. Williams, a forty-year-old Baptist minister and former slave. And with the establishment of a democratic form of government and the extension of political rights, black people expected their elected leaders to turn the wheels of government in their favor. Although black Republicans dominated county and municipal offices in the Natchez District and had significant influence in state legislatures during Reconstruction, considerable obstacles confronted politicians attempting to translate freedpeople's aspirations into public policy. They faced stiff opposition from white Democrats, who despite their weakness in local politics still wielded considerable social and economic power. How Democrats would exercise their informal power was one of the most important questions in the Reconstruction years. The challenge for Republican officeholders, then, was to balance the interests of their grassroots constituents with what was politically possible in a society still reeling from war and emancipation. To a large extent, black Republicans in the Natchez District accomplished an extraordinary feat: they implemented public policies that addressed many of the concerns of freedpeople while also developing a biracial politics that accommodated some of the concerns of the indigenous white elite.[4]

Radical Constitutions

When the constitutional delegates met in their respective state capitol buildings after the historic election of 1867, they faced the daunting challenge of crafting a governmental framework that would incorporate formerly enslaved people. They also needed to address two potentially conflicting tasks: establishing a more equitable society and doing it in such a way that a majority would accept the results. What Republicans were up against was not just partisan opposition but outrage from large segments of the southern white population, who denounced the integration of ex-slaves into the body politic.

As the Mississippi constitutional convention was meeting, the state's Democratic Party channeled these sentiments into a series of resolutions that highlighted white opposition to military Reconstruction. They denounced the audacity of Republicans in Congress, in that they would "place the white men of the Southern States under the governmental control of their late slaves and degrade the Caucasian race as the inferiors of the African negro." To do so was "a crime against the civilization of the age" because black people were "destitute alike [in] the moral and intellectual qualifications required of electors in all civilized communities." Democrats further worried that the large majority of Republican delegates were "wickedly conspiring to disfranchise and degrade the [white] people, to rob them alike of their liberty and property, to destroy their social and political status, and finally place them under the yoke of a negro government." In other words, Democrats rejected the notion that Republican delegates and the black voters who elected them held legitimate power. Their outrage ran far deeper than partisan politics because Republicans took aim at white privilege.[5]

The Republican delegates from the Natchez District represented a sharp break in the political history of the region, yet not all the delegates were radical and in fact they were drawn from the varied factions of the Republican Party. The nine delegates from the four Mississippi counties included three black radicals, five white radicals, and one white moderate—their numbers and wide-ranging experiences gave them inordinate influence at the convention. The most influential among the delegation were E. J. Castello (an ex-Union captain from Missouri representing Adams County), Abel Alderson (a white attorney from Jefferson County who was born in Maryland but moved to Mississippi as an adult about ten years before the Civil War), W. H. Gibbs (a white Illinoisan and former Union colonel representing Wilkinson County), and Henry P. Jacobs (a Baptist minister from Adams County who was born enslaved in Alabama but escaped to Canada in 1856).[6]

By contrast, the four delegates representing the two Louisiana parishes of the district had much less influence. Political power in Louisiana was centered in New Orleans, and delegates from the great city dominated the convention. The size and politics of the delegates from Concordia and Tensas Parishes ensured that they would play only a marginal role in the crafting of a new constitution. They were all white planters and northern-born. Three of four were former Union army officers. Moreover, the Tensas delegates, unlike any of the other delegates from the district, voted with the conservative faction at their convention. These delegates from the Natchez District were decidedly unrepresentative of their rural, ex-slave constituency. The lack of a substantial Union League presence, combined with fewer black people of wealth and weaker connections to national religious institutions, made it more difficult for local black leaders to win elective office so soon after enfranchisement.[7]

While it is always precarious to draw too many conclusions about a voting population from the representatives that were sent to constitutional conventions or legislative halls, a close analysis of the delegates at the constitutional conventions is revealing. The Mississippi delegates represented many of the Republican constituencies in the Natchez District (ex-slaves, freeborn blacks, local white Unionists, and white northerners). Through their votes as well as the motions that they submitted we can see how they tried to fulfill the interests of ex-slaves while working toward a constitutional framework that would meet the needs of the state's other interests. The tension over policy priorities was in evidence early in how the delegates shaped the body politic. Great time and effort were put into limiting the power of former secessionists and the Confederate leadership, but suffrage restrictions had to be balanced with measures to ensure that poor black men would be able to vote.

The federal Reconstruction Acts had provided a template for incorporating black men into the body politic as voters, but there was less consensus on the status of former Confederates. E. J. Castello, the carpetbagger from Natchez, established his radical credentials by offering an extensive motion on suffrage rights. He suggested that only those who were Unionist during the war should be able to vote or hold office. Castello further envisioned a strict loyalty oath for voters and officeholders that affirmed their past Unionism and their future fidelity to racial equality. The suggested oath read, in part, "I have always been truly and loyally on the side of the United States; . . . I accept the civil and political equality of all men, and agree not to attempt to deprive any person or persons on account of race or color, or previous condition, of any political, religious or civil rights, privileges or immunities enjoyed by any other class of men." While these strict measures were softened over the course of the convention, they reveal the concern among Republicans over how to create an electorate composed of Unionists and former Confederates, one of ex-slaves and ex-masters. Castello's solution was to prevent the treasonous side from participating, but that position flew in the face of arguments advanced by black activists that suffrage was an inherent right of all male citizens in the United States.[8]

Castello's attempt to purge the electorate of Confederate sympathizers set the tone for the framing of the constitution's suffrage provisions. The final document very nearly prevented all former Confederates from holding political office. Those disfranchised under Congress's Reconstruction Acts and those who had signed or voted for the ordinance of secession were not eligible for any "office of profit or trust, civil or military, in the State." Additionally, any person who "gave voluntary aid, countenance, counsel, or encouragement to persons" fighting the United States was excluded from office, but not, strangely, "the private [Confederate] soldier." Confederate sympathizers could redeem themselves, however, by publicly supporting the Reconstruction process then underway. No matter one's loyalty during the war, every potential voter was required to swear to "the civil and political equality of all men," a more contentious feature, as the previous chapter indicated. Perhaps foreshadowing the divisiveness that the voting restrictions were to provoke, the Natchez District delegation divided on the vote to adopt the franchise provisions, with only Castello and the three black delegates voting in favor. Louisiana also mandated an oath attesting to racial equality, but because it was limited to legislators and other officeholders it did not garner nearly as much outrage as Mississippi's.[9]

Limiting Confederate participation in the new body politic was only half the battle; delegates also needed to ensure that the newly enfranchised would continue to vote freely and fairly. Mississippi delegates added a provision to the bill of rights that banned educational and property qualifications for voting and similarly banned property qualifications for jury service and office holding. Natchez District delegates unanimously voted in favor of these provisions to ensure an expanded electorate. But there was a more pressing matter for delegates in regard to the electorate. Tens of thousands of poor black laborers and farmers had risked their wages and contracts in the 1867 electoral campaign to vote with the Republicans. Responding to the pervasive use of economic coercion during the most recent election, W. H. Gibbs of Wilkinson County suggested that the convention authorize an immediate ordinance to rectify the issue. The motion was referred to Castello's General Provisions Committee, and it produced an ordinance making it illegal to dismiss an employee for voting or to coerce the vote of an employee, which was adopted by the whole. It was a small yet tangible effort to address the needs of their constituents.[10]

The Natchez District delegates took other measures to address impoverishment. Abel Alderson from Jefferson County chaired the Committee on Destitution and suggested a plan to help the thirty to forty thousand people who were "destitute and suffering" in Mississippi. He wanted sheriffs to use poll tax revenues to hire the impoverished for "public works" projects and then to provide food and clothing for the workers. Henry P. Jacobs from Adams County authored a provision, later adopted in the bill of rights, that eliminated imprisonment for debt. Other members of the delegation offered motions to eliminate poll taxes, which fell more heavily on the landless. Following these proposals, the convention delegates settled on authorizing the first legislature to organize a "board of public works." And then, in a measure designed to assist the destitute in rising out of poverty, the constitution limited the sale of "tax-forfeited lands" to "tracts smaller than 160 acres or less." The intent here was to break up plantations and to give small farmers and renters an opportunity to enter the ranks of property holders. The Louisiana constitution went even further, limiting the sale of confiscated property to "ten to fifty acres."[11]

Land reform was not the only issue on which Louisiana delegates were more progressive than their neighbors to the east. The first article of the constitution began, "All men are created free and equal," signaling that this document would depart sharply from the prior frameworks that had reinforced white supremacy. Article 2 of the bill of rights declared that all citizens enjoyed "the same civil, political, and public rights." And it further specified that every person had the right to enjoy access to "places of a public character . . . without distinction or discrimination on account of race or color."[12]

The broad, affirmative language owed, in part, to the fact that a majority of Louisiana's delegates were persons of color. By contrast, only 17 percent of Mississippi delegates were of African descent; the smaller share of black delegates resulted in more tepid affirmations of civil rights and political equality. The Mississippi constitution did, however, ban the appropriation of public monies for racist organizations, and it prohibited racial discrimination on public transportation (the latter provision authored by H. P. Jacobs). Another controversial measure addressed the racial composition of the public schools. Support for integrated schools was lukewarm, but black delegates adamantly opposed separate schools. As a compromise, Castello authored an amendment that allowed school districts to establish more than one school, which was a tacit acknowledgement of the possibility of racially separate schools. Louisiana would have none of this. Its constitution explicitly banned "separate schools."[13]

The new constitutions, although differing in their emphases and details, were radical departures in the history of southern jurisprudence. They eliminated the slavelike proscriptions of the Black Codes and in their place implemented a political structure that affirmed the full citizenship of African Americans. Both Mississippi's and Louisiana's constitutions featured expansive bills of rights, made provisions for the establishment of public schools, provided for universal manhood suffrage while disfranchising former Confederate leaders, and removed some distinctions based on race, color, or previous condition of servitude. Yet the new frameworks for governance were also mindful of economic issues and included measures that reflected the protests and demands of farm laborers, who struggled mightily in the new free labor economy. In practical terms, both constitutions fell short of establishing a society in which freedpeople had the same freedom and access as white people, but the deficiencies of the radical constitutions should not detract from their groundbreaking impact. For the first time, the political framework of the state began to reflect the aspirations of its black citizens. Moreover, each constitution furthered the establishment of local democracy by subjecting most county offices to voter approval. While the Black Codes had forced freedpeople to defer to local white authorities in social and economic affairs, the radical constitutions opened a space for freedpeople to govern their communities and to construct new interpersonal relationships across the color line, based on mutual respect.[14]

Schools, Taxes, and Alcorn University

One of the most pressing grassroots demands on Republican politicians was the creation of a state public school system. O. C. French, a white Republican representative from Adams County, introduced Mississippi's public school law and shepherded it through the legislature, but the challenge of creating a public education system involved more than legal action. In both Mississippi and Louisiana, hundreds of school buildings had to be constructed, thousands of teachers had to be hired, and tens of thousands of children needed books and supplies. Most sites for the construction of schools were donated, although some were large meeting halls ill-suited to classroom instruction or, as Adams County's superintendent of education described it, they were "wretched out buildings." Nevertheless, the scale of growth and improvements was astounding. Once Republicans gained control of the Claiborne County School Board, they committed to building eight "substantial and commodious school houses," primarily for the education of black children. In rural Adams County, seven frame school buildings were constructed in the first year of public school operations. Prior to enactment of the public school law of 1870, Jefferson County had two colored schools and one white school for approximately forty-six hundred educable children. Within two years the number of schools had jumped to seventeen black and fourteen white schools. In a relatively short time, the common schoolhouse had become a regular presence across the landscape of the district: fifty-three schools in Adams County, forty-six in Jefferson, fifty-two in Wilkinson, thirty-four in Claiborne, fifteen in Tensas Parish, and eleven in Concordia.[15]

Despite worries about the costs and white resistance to black education, school construction proceeded better than expected in some quarters. The

Natchez city school board built a large brick building, a new and expanded Union Schoolhouse, to accommodate twelve hundred black pupils. Black school board member William H. Lynch (an ex-slave alderman and the brother of John R. Lynch), described to Governor Alcorn the collective effort in Adams County as producing a "feeling here among all classes towards the Public Schools [that] is all that could be desired." "We have been offered more land without price," he continued, "than we can use for School purposes at present."[16]

To pay for school construction as well as teacher salaries and school supplies, state and local governments substantially increased property tax rates. John R. Lynch later recalled that a higher rate of taxation was the best option for the temporary outlay of funds for school construction, particularly since state governments' poor credit ratings limited their ability to borrow funds and the assessed value on property "was so low." Property taxes in Natchez shot up 63 percent within a year and had nearly quadrupled after four years of Republican governance. Similarly, municipal debt soared by forty thousand dollars, until it was nearly equal to the city's annual revenue. Rural parishes and counties struggled even more to absorb the costs of construction and schooling, but despite the fiscal challenge, local Republican governance educated far more children than the combined efforts of private schools, postwar missionary associations, and the Freedmen's Bureau.[17]

Among local whites, attitudes toward a public school system ranged from mild praise to open hostility. Some argued that the interests of the "whole people" were wrapped up in the success of schools and that county schools were "working well," while others described the tax increases, of which school taxes composed a large share, as "oppressive." Edward King, a northern reporter who toured the South in the mid-1870s, best emphasized this dichotomous framework. He had high praise for Natchez's "excellent system" of public schools, especially the "handsome new schoolhouse, called the 'Union,' built expressly" for black children. But on the next page of his narrative he lamented the "very oppressive" taxes in Natchez, amounting to a 6 percent assessment on each $1,000 of assessed property. Shifting the tax burden from the shoulders of the laboring class to the mostly white property holders evoked considerable protest and resentment, yet local freedpeople blunted the backlash. At one public meeting to protest high property assessments, the "tax paying citizens" became "frustrated by the presence of a large number of non-tax paying Republican colored citizens," reported the Natchez Democrat. News of the impending meeting spread through the plantation districts, and scores of rural black laborers traveled to Natchez to demonstrate support for the Republican board of supervisors, much to the chagrin of one planter whose labor force left for town before dawn, leaving him with no one to haul and gin his cotton.[18]

No less in the rural communities, school construction demanded a collective effort from political leaders and ordinary citizens. In 1873 Tensas Parish boasted fifteen schools and a "larger school fund than almost any other parish" in northeast Louisiana, bragged the local newspaper. The school fund swelled because parish taxes, at the behest of Republican voters, fell heavily on the landholding elite. The parish school board, elected by ordinary voters, authorized the construction of school buildings on plantations and dispensed building contracts to local merchants, usually Republican officeholders. A. J. Bryant, a black school board member and the Tensas Parish sheriff, provided all the bricks and timber for the West Point plantation school, and H. R. Steele, the white school board president and district attorney, supplied the materials for a school on his plantation.[19]

By the mid-1870s, although schools had been established across the Natchez District, worsening economic conditions had depleted many county school funds. With some planters unable to pay their property taxes, sheriffs seized control of their lands, which effectively removed those properties from the tax rolls. The Natchez District's elected leaders, however, responded with an array of measures to provide relief to the schools. To alleviate some of the burdens of school expenses, the Adams County School Board provided free schoolbooks to poor children in 1872. The Mississippi legislature called for congressional assistance in building up the state's Common School Fund in 1874, which was a renewal of an earlier and more ambitious effort championed by Congressman Legrand Perce (a white northerner from Natchez) to provide a steady stream of federal dollars to local schools. The lack of funds limited many rural schools to only a four-month term, and some teachers, paid in warrants, saw their wages depreciate rapidly. As a result, perhaps only a fifth of eligible children attended school on a regular basis.[20]

In addition to the financial problems of the new public school system, elected leaders continued to debate the racial composition of the classrooms. The state of Louisiana authorized integrated schools, but the law was largely ignored at the local level. Although black Mississippians grudgingly accepted a separate school system when the radical constitution was drafted in 1868, many publicly opposed separate schools in their neighborhoods. "While we do not believe such [separate] schools the best for either race," explained the *New National Era* in reference to debates in Mississippi, "they will be infinitely superior to no schools." State legislator John R. Lynch, however, won a small victory for the integrationists by amending the public school bill to ensure that if districts established only one school, it must accept all children, irrespective of race.[21]

At the municipal level, school board member and Natchez alderman William H. Lynch, like his brother, opposed "the establishment or maintenance of a white school." When the white citizens of the village of Kingston in rural Adams County petitioned the county school board in 1872 to hire a white teacher for a white school, Lynch led the effort to block the appointment, thereby preventing the school's opening. A school already existed in the town, taught by a black teacher with black students. Lynch was joined by the other black aldermen in denying the appointment of a white teacher, but only temporarily. Although stymied in their efforts to establish biracial schools, Republican school board members ensured, at least, that both black and white teachers would be paid the same salary.[22]

In some rural communities, the issue of racial separatism was linked with the problem of poverty. The Jefferson County School Board struggled to establish separate schools in one corner of the county where there were too few white children to sustain an all-white school. Even though an integrated classroom offered the best solution, one school board member remarked, "[B]oth race[s] in my district are averse to mixed schools." In Wilkinson County the schools were, in 1872, in a "lamentable state of affairs," with "hardly a suitable school building." White "hatred and hostility" toward black schools and an "apathetic indifference" among white residents toward education in general prevented the establishment of a viable system of public education, reported the county school superintendent.[23]

In addition to the new and proliferating public school system that struggled to get off the ground, the Natchez District also boasted the first public university for African Americans in the region. Alcorn University was located near Rodney in Claiborne County on 235 acres of what was once the campus of Oakland College, a Presbyterian school that closed its doors during the Civil War. At first, most black legislators rejected the idea of a separate university for black students, preferring instead to open the state university in Oxford to students of all races. John R. Lynch and others, however, grew to accept the idea of a separate university once Governor James L. Alcorn committed significant state and federal funds to the new school and selected an all-black board of trustees (four of whom resided in the district). An early champion of the institution was Samuel J. Ireland, a black Republican from Claiborne County who was closely allied to the governor and served as the sergeant at arms in the legislature. Ireland and others had high hopes that the university would bring "*intellectual* freedom; [the] freedom to think" to a region bereft of "*intellectual* food." And there was hope that since "Alcorn University is open to *all students*," wrote a correspondent to the *New National Era*, "the resistless logic of education" would begin to weaken "existing prejudices."[24]

Soon after opening its doors to thirty students and three professors in the spring of 1872, Alcorn University was nearly closed down as the issue of racial separatism resurfaced. Following the successful advancement of a civil rights bill, black legislators in the House voted to abolish the institution and planned to force the University of Mississippi to admit "colored youths." The Alcorn abolition bill, however, failed in the Senate, but not before it exposed divisions over how best to advance freedpeople during Reconstruction. Some legislators feared that any "precedent . . . of separate institutions for the races" would undermine efforts to establish equal treatment, reported Thomas Cardozo, a black leader in Vicksburg. But others contested this view. Many ordinary freedpeople, wrote one Alcorn student, "oppose any attempt to mix schools in this State." "Our poor people have been informed of the establishment, aims, and objects of Alcorn University," continued this student, who was born to enslaved parents, and they "'thank God' for it." While an integrated setting would be the preferred option for the "prominent colored men" in the legislature, the student wrote, it would only jeopardize the education of "the poor needy colored people of Mississippi."[25]

In its early years the university struggled to become an effective institution of higher learning while also meeting the needs of the state's black population. The first two presidents, including former U.S. senator Hiram R. Revels from Natchez, were ineffective administrators. In early 1875 half the students refused to attend classes to protest the legislature's repeal of free scholarships. From the beginning, the state had authorized each county to select one scholar for a scholarship, based on competitive exams administered by local officials. Approximately 60 of the 180 students at Alcorn fully depended on this scholarship to attend classes, and so when the affected students and their supporters protested the new policy, they were able to cripple the fledgling school. By 1876 only fifty students remained enrolled. Nonetheless, the college provided an important service to the district, as rural communities depended on Alcorn and other normal schools to supply them with teachers. (The "Howard Normal School," founded and named after Merrimon Howard, produced black female teachers for schools in Adams, Jefferson, and Claiborne Counties.) Most of Tensas Parish's teachers were "college students" whom the *North Louisiana Journal* described as "young men full of courage and pride." And Alcorn University also trained a generation of young black men who went on to fill various federal clerkships in Washington, D.C.[26]

Schools loomed large in the expectations of ordinary freedpeople. Of all the public policy measures that state and local officeholders were involved in, education always ranked high on the list of priorities. Indeed, Republican Party conventions often singled out local administrators, teachers, and citizens for congratulations and praise for "conduct[ing] the educational interests of the people." Maintaining schools was always a challenge and a source of frustration for citizens and leaders alike. Nevertheless, Republican officials created a publicly supported educational system for all children. The substantive gains in education were all the more astonishing considering the factors limiting institutional growth in a largely rural environment. Even absent the resources of an urban or industrialized environment—such as a diversified economy, financial institutions, and charitable organizations—the Natchez District created a public infrastructure that persisted long after other Reconstruction-era policies had been rolled back.[27]

Civil Rights and Equal Justice

Next to demands for free public schools, the demand for civil rights and an equitable justice system rang loudest among freedpeople in the Natchez District. From the masthead of the *Concordia Eagle*, "Equal Rights to All Men," to the resolution of the 1872 Tensas Parish Republican convention, "impartial justice and equal rights to all," local people insisted on fair treatment in public affairs. The *Natchez New South*, a Republican newspaper, gave voice to this sentiment: "[C]olored people . . . demand political and civil equality," and they expect that "in every part of this great Republic . . . the same civil and political rights accorded to white people should be enjoyed by the colored man." Reflecting the optimism that many African Americans felt, elected leaders believed that racial distinctions were destined to be set aside. After all, in an age when a former slave, John R. Lynch, was running for Congress from the very state where Jefferson Davis, "the great apostle of slavery," once ruled, it seemed possible that social relations could be dramatically and swiftly transformed.[28]

Republican legislatures in Louisiana and Mississippi moved quickly to ensure equal access to public facilities and began the difficult process of altering individual and institutional prejudices. Louisiana's 1869 Civil Rights Act prohibited racial discrimination in public transportation and in places of "public resort." The law, however, depended on individuals, not the state, to sue for enforcement. In practice, then, most individuals were unwilling to shoulder the burden of bringing racist proprietors and business owners to court, and so discriminatory policies persisted. Mississippi's first civil rights law similarly lacked a substantial enforcement mechanism; nevertheless, it attracted broad support, especially from Lynch, a freshman state representative from Adams County at the time. Mississippi legislators returned to the issue of civil rights in 1872 in order to expand protections beyond public transit to all public places, except schools and churches. With stricter enforcement measures, including a maximum fine of $1,000 and imprisonment for up to three years, Mississippi became "the first State in the Union to guarantee, by statutory enactment, full civil as well as political rights to all her citizens, without distinction," gushed Governor Ridgley C. Powers.[29]

While the state legislature was debating civil rights, local black officials in Natchez sought to ensure equal access to public spaces at the local level. The board of aldermen passed a limited anti–racial discrimination ordinance in

1872 after an incident at the Institute Hall. Located in the heart of downtown, the hall was a city-owned building used for public performances. George W. Doyle, a black Natchezian, accompanied by "a colored woman," entered the Institute Hall to view a panorama exhibit, but white visitors reacted with hostility when the black couple entered the building. Many immediately "retired from the Hall," noted the local Democratic paper, and "demand[ed] and receiv[ed] their money at the door, and [left] the exhibition without an audience." Outraged by the mistreatment of the black couple, the Republican aldermen passed an ordinance that prevented the hall from being rented out to groups "where discrimination is to be made on account of race, color or previous condition." Although limited in scope to one building, the municipal law marked the first time that racial discrimination had been banned within a particular space in the city. Local whites reacted with contempt, rightly calling the ordinance "an effort to break down a social distinction." Perhaps to appease white hostility and to nurture acceptance of his administration, Mayor Robert H. Wood (a twenty-eight-year-old freeborn politician who was also president of the county board of supervisors) compromised with the critics and set aside "one tier of seats" for black people, an arrangement that George W. Doyle suggested and that the editor of the antagonistic *Natchez Democrat* found tolerable.[30]

The seating compromise did not settle the question of equal public access, though. At the end of the school year, the all-white classrooms at the adjacent Natchez Institute School held examinations, and the public was invited to attend. In the middle of one class's performance, Rev. Randall Pollard, S. S. Meekins, and "one or two other negroes" entered the room. Quietly, the men took their seats toward the front of the class, but the presence of these black men at a white school before a white audience brought the exercises to a standstill. "The children became indignant," and the teacher immediately dismissed the class. In response, Pollard, Meekins, and the others held an "indignation meeting" that night at the courthouse.[31]

That Pollard and Meekins would challenge customary discrimination at the Institute School was not unusual. Both men were Natchez School Board members and had a responsibility to check on the progress of the city's schoolchildren. Pollard had previously confronted segregation, as a slave preacher for the Wall Street Baptist Church before the war and then as the leader of the Rose Hill Church after emancipation. Meekins was a militia captain and an alderman who cast his vote for the city council's antidiscrimination ordinance. In both instances, at the Institute School and Institute Hall, black officeholders used their official authority to reconfigure the local customs that limited black access to public spaces, yet they stopped short of ensuring complete civic equality, tacitly accepting separate schools and segregated spaces in other parts of the city. Their compromise with white critics suggests that black officeholders took a measured approach to social change and hoped to use the institute buildings as models for a shared relational space within the city.[32]

In general, the day-to-day struggles of most African Americans in the Natchez District did not concern issues of equal access to public spaces for the simple reason that the largely rural environment offered few places where access would be a problem. In town markets and at other commercial establishments, black and white people moved about freely, as they had before the Civil War, but they did so with new meaning after black political mobilization. While few freedpeople challenged exclusionary private organizations such as fraternal orders and private establishments like hotels and restaurants, many spaces and buildings in the Natchez District no longer carried the presumption of racial differentiation. "The two races got along well together," boasted Congressman Lynch in recounting life before white supremacist violence devastated the region. A northern reporter had a similar impression of Natchez, noting that the black population "seems to live on terms of amity with the white half." The *Natchez Democrat* in 1873, surprisingly, supported limited equal access, calling on "every steamboat and railroad . . . to furnish . . . accommodations" to black patrons "equal in every respect to those furnished to white people paying the same rate of fare." It is in the altered assumptions about access that the impact of civil rights legislation is most evident, because, as David Young found out, discriminatory practices still persisted. Young—an ex-slave, thirty-six-year-old state representative from Concordia Parish—was prevented by the captain of the steamboat *Robert E. Lee* from renting for himself and his wife a stateroom that was commonly rented to white passengers.[33]

While equal access was more of a tangible concern for black politicians and those of modest means, the issue carried enormous symbolic importance, as it was a prism through which citizenship, education, economic opportunity, and political rights were understood. Perhaps the strongest advocate for civil rights in the Natchez District was John R. Lynch. Throughout his major speeches, and later in his writings, Lynch, whose humble origins as an ex-slave were well known, consistently pushed for the "protection of human rights" by the federal government. He was a leader in the effort to pass the Civil Rights Act of 1875. "I am anxious," he proclaimed from the floor of the House of Representatives in 1876, "to see the day come when the rights and privileges of all classes of citizens will be recognized and universally acquiesced in from one end of the country to the other." For Lynch and many like-minded freedpeople in the Natchez District, their sense of community had expanded since the days of bondage to encompass a broad range of people, especially African Americans in all parts of the nation. Thus, for Lynch, the "outrages having been committed upon innocent colored people" that peppered local newspaper columns provoked anguish and inspired him to demand equal civil and political rights for citizens far removed from his home district.[34]

But Lynch was also aware that the ideal of "perfect toleration of . . . all classes" was not just a policy problem. The real hurdle in settling the so-called southern question was to bring about a radical change in "public sentiment," he proclaimed in a speech before Congress. In this sense, civil rights legislation could only assist the larger struggle of reframing the racist assumptions of white southerners, and this struggle, according to Lynch, would be waged in numerous personal encounters across the color line.[35]

His faith in the power of personal transformation had been emboldened during his tenure in the Mississippi legislature. His peers had elevated him to the role of Speaker of the House at the age of twenty-four, and he had overseen a contentious statewide redistricting process. Yet just before he was to leave for Congress, he was presented with a gold watch and chain in recognition of his services, for which "every member — Republicans and *Democrats* — contributed towards it." Although he was the leader of black Republicans, Lynch proudly recalled that he had gained the respect of his white colleagues and his political opponents. Perhaps only the son of a white overseer and slave mother, a field slave and favorite of an elite planter, could envision racial harmony when most others saw discord and violence. While his friendly relationships with white Democrats did not stem the tide of "organized terrorism" that swept the South in the late 1870s, they do suggest an ethic that emanated from the grass roots, one that privileged face-to-face relationships over social proscriptions.[36]

Developing and enforcing the right to a public sphere in which mutual respect dictated public actions fell to the responsibility of the local justice system. One of the first endeavors of the Republican government in Natchez was to bring fairness and representation to law enforcement. In 1869 the city council appointed four new police officers, two of whom were black men, thereby integrating the police force for the first time. The black officers were specifically directed to have "contact with and authority over" the black community. Mayor Wood continued this practice and doubled the size of Natchez's police force, swelling it to at least eighteen officers, most of whom were black. At one point he temporarily hired fifty extra policemen to ensure a free and fair election in 1871. In the countryside, law enforcement was in the hands of constables. While the transition to an integrated constabulary was slower in the parishes and counties of the Natchez District (there was only one black constable in 1870), within a few years most constables were black. At least fifty black constables operated in the Natchez District during the Reconstruction era, most of whom came from a farming background and had minimal education.[37]

Just as freedmen constituted the backbone of urban and rural law enforcement, so too did they fill the ranks of justices of the peace. While judges and district attorneys (who were nearly all white men) adjudicated major civil and criminal offences, the vast majority of legal disputes found hearing before justices of the peace. At least fifty-nine black men served as justices of the peace during Reconstruction in the Natchez District. Justices of the peace had original jurisdiction in civil cases involving less than $150 and criminal cases below the grade of felony; in addition, they were empowered to hold the accused in "felonious and capital cases" for the grand jury and to set bail. Although some black citizens expected favorable treatment before a black justice—such as the disgruntled defendants who called Justice Cornelius Henderson "a tool of the whites" after he gave them "the full measure of the law"—many other ordinary freed persons were awed by the possibility of receiving a fair hearing and "anxious to avail themselves of such a glorious privilege."[38]

During his tenure as justice of the peace in Adams County (1869–70), John R. Lynch sought to "avoid and prevent friction" between the races. To that end, he deferred to patriarchal authority in numerous complaints brought before his court over the maltreatment of servants, privately asking male heads of household to resolve disputes between female "colored servants" and "the white female head of the house." In this way Lynch saved prominent white families from public embarrassment. Lynch himself had avoided public humiliation as an ill-educated justice by accepting the assistance of a white man (probably William T. Martin, the ex-Confederate general and leading Democrat), who schooled him in the preparation of legal documents.[39]

Nonetheless, much of Lynch's term was devoted to rectifying injustices inflicted on the weakest members of the community. He convicted a white male head of household for beating his black female cook and another white man for cursing, abusing, and threatening the life of "an innocent and inoffensive old colored man." In another instance, in 1869 he imprisoned a gang of black and white men for swindling naïve "country negroes" who were traveling to the city of Natchez. Although many of the judgments amounted to no more than imposing five-dollar fines, Lynch zealously prosecuted the law—so much so that the accumulation of fines he imposed in seven months as justice of the peace was larger than that of most other justices "for seven years," reported the *New National Era*. Beyond the numbers, the profound meaning of young Lynch's career as an officeholder registered in other ways. When an ex-slave justice convicted a white man based on the testimony of another former slave, it is little wonder that many local African Americans, as Lynch later recalled, "magnified" the position "far beyond its importance."[40]

The ability of local officials to bring a sense of justice to ordinary residents, as the Lynch examples indicate, depended on close interactions between officeholders and the people. Sheriffs, in particular, relied on neighborhood leaders to extend their power and influence to the far corners of the counties. In Adams County Sheriff William Noonan (a white northerner) called in David Singleton after he was unable to apprehend an accused murderer. Singleton, whom Noonan deputized as a "special constable," was the wealthy former slave of an elite planter and a friend of the Lynch family. Within twenty-four hours, Singleton traveled to Concordia Parish, found the accused man, and returned him to Natchez for incarceration. Nearly a year later, in 1871, Singleton again arrested suspects that other law enforcement officers could not. In this instance, a small group of black laborers was accused of stealing several head of cattle in rural Adams County. The local justice of the peace, Theodore Lumbar, a freedman and a county supervisor, issued an arrest warrant, but the local constable and other officers were turned away by a show of force at the Linwood plantation, where the accused were holed up. The next day a white deputy sheriff backed up by a "*posse comitatus* of citizens" attempted to arrest them, but they were turned back in a gun battle. Later that same day, the sheriff turned to Singleton, who traveled to the plantation in the Kingston district and promptly "returned with several persons in custody."[41]

How was Singleton, a "special constable," able to arrest armed assailants singlehandedly? The first case involved Anderson Thomas, a thirty-five-year-old carpenter of mixed-race descent who was a politically active resident of Natchez and a member of the Good Samaritans benevolent association. He allegedly shot another Good Samaritan at an association meeting. Singleton's close contacts with the black political elite of Natchez and his intimate knowledge of Concordia Parish (his former master, Alfred V. Davis, had extensive properties in Concordia, and Singleton would later operate a merchant-planting partnership in Concordia with black politician David Young) made him uniquely capable of finding Thomas, confronting him on a personal level, and perhaps convincing him that he would be treated fairly. In the incident at Linwood plantation, Singleton's social standing and reputation as a neighborhood leader may have convinced the accused to feel at ease in his custody in a way that they could not with formal law enforcement officers (and white Republicans).[42]

The sense of fair play and community involvement was nowhere better demonstrated than in the jury system. The two great achievements of the Republican Party in Mississippi, according to Jeremiah M. P. Williams (an ex-slave, Baptist preacher, and state senator from Adams County), were the extension of political offices and the "Jurors Box" to freedmen. From the late 1860s and throughout the next decade, black-majority juries reshaped the nature of local justice, to the consternation of Democratic Party leaders. Freedmen appeared on Louisiana juries as early as 1867, but across the river in Mississippi it took another two years before military governor Adelbert Ames abolished color distinctions on juries. Ordinary African Americans as well as politically active freedmen figured prominently in statewide judicial proceedings, such as the Meridian Ku Klux Klan trials. Locally, freedmen made up six out of ten and possibly as many as three out of four members of the 1873 grand jury pool for Adams County, and of the twenty men selected for the grand jury, seven were politically involved black Republicans. Black-majority juries undoubtedly gave freedpeople a substantial influence in the administration of justice; nevertheless, freedmen's juries did not reflexively exonerate black defendants during Reconstruction. To the dismay of State Representative David Young and Sheriff Oren Stewart (both black), a Concordia Parish grand jury of eleven blacks and two whites indicted both officeholders for separate crimes in 1874.[43]

While local- and state-level civil rights legislation did not produce an equal society, the laws gave the notion of equal treatment in public spaces important validation. It was a further recognition of freedpeople's vision for a democratic social order. And with black law enforcement officials committed to equal treatment in the justice system, ordinary freedpeople could feel a little more secure in their homes and lives.

Land, Railroads, and Economic Development

By the early 1870s the agricultural economy had settled into a system in which most African American farmers worked the land as tenants or as croppers working for shares. Freedpeople had successfully resisted the imposition of gang labor and they had compelled planters to negotiate with them in family units or squads, but few had become prosperous, largely a result of the onerous agricultural credit system.

Cash was scarce, land values had declined, and the antebellum cotton factorage system was in shambles; thus farmers turned to merchants to finance the supplies that they would need to put in a crop. Freedpeople offered their crop for the coming year as collateral, negotiating what was known as a crop lien. While the crop lien gave farmers the credit they needed to commence and sustain operations, many freedpeople despised it. For one, it was a deferred payment system that kept freedpeople's wages locked up in the crop, forcing them to purchase food, clothing, and other items on credit throughout the year. For another, more than one party had a claim on the crop. The landowner demanded a share of the crop for rent, and the merchant demanded his share. In years when the weather damaged the crops, such as in 1866 and 1867, a low yield meant that there was little left for wages after the merchant and planter had taken their shares. In addition, there were many disputes over the accounting of the debt and the prices of goods at merchant stores, contributing to the belief among freedpeople that the crop lien was keeping them in poverty.[44]

Although elected Republicans never attempted to substantially reform the agricultural economy, they did undertake some measures to improve the position of the laboring classes, at least on the margins. The Mississippi legislature in 1872 exempted poor laborers (those earning less than $100) from the garnishment of their wages, and they passed a labor lien law, which compelled planters to pay workers' wages before they demanded rent or before they paid landlords or other merchants. The law made it easier for workers to collect their wages through shares and more difficult for landowners to collect their rent. It was a clear expression of Republicans' commitment to "the protection and encouragement of labor," particularly the labor of black men and women in the fields. Yet laborers' lien laws did not fundamentally alter the credit system that left laborers, landowners, and merchants competing for their part of the crop.[45]

The continuing problems with the crop lien, which were exacerbated by declining cotton prices throughout the 1870s, led Sheriff Merrimon Howard from Jefferson County to complain to Mississippi governor Adelbert Ames. Howard, a fifty-two-year-old ex-slave, identified the "abomnible" lien law as the source all the agricultural problems, in that it had a "demoralizing effect on the poor laboring Class of people" and was "impoverishing this whole country." One of the few Natchez District black politicians who directly addressed the problems of "our farming system," Howard called for legislation to create a cash-based economy that would hopefully remove "the poor class of people out of the clutches of the merchant, and the landed aristocracy." The Mississippi legislature responded to Howard's and others' grievances by passing a bill in 1874 to repeal the crop lien law, but Ames, in a gesture to emphasize his moderate views and because an alternative credit system was not forthcoming, vetoed the bill.[46]

Legislators from the Natchez District delegation, however, offered other specific proposals to advance the interests of black laborers. Philander Balch, a white representative from Jefferson County, attempted to help farmworkers by establishing the right of tenants to pasture their stock on the landlord's property. Representative H. P. Jacobs, four years after failing to provide affordable land for ex-slaves with his black land colony, was still at it, proposing homesteads for "old, worn-out, former slaves and veteran soldiers," among other measures. Legrand W. Perce, a white Republican representing the Natchez District in Congress, addressed the issue of agricultural poverty by proposing to set aside two hundred million acres of public land for the settlement of "landless citizen[s]." While these bills failed to become law, they nonetheless reflect the attention that elected representatives paid to the needs and concerns of their constituents.[47]

Legislators had much more leeway in addressing the narrow concerns of particular individuals or groups. Much of this effort may be lumped into the category of constituent services, in which representatives submitted citizen petitions or bills of relief to a legislative body. Often it was the wealthier individuals who were able to bend the ear of Republican officeholders, such as when O. C.

French sought assistance for Cassius Tillman (a white Natchez merchant) or when John R. Lynch sought to help Katherine Minor (a white Unionist planter). But legislators also sponsored legislation to incorporate local businesses and civic organizations. When district legislators obtained the incorporation of the Port Gibson AME Church or the Jacobs Benevolent Association, they did more than secure the legal charter; they helped to establish the legitimacy of these groups and validated the public import of their work. And legislators were quick to seek relief when natural disasters imperiled their communities. In the spring of 1874, the Mississippi River spilled its banks and inundated many communities in the district. Local officials pressed state authorities to provide the destitute citizens with much-needed food, and they were able to pass a law that offered merchants incentives to extend credit to local farmers until their crops were planted.[48]

Black and Republican politicians were reluctant to enact ambitious agricultural reform measures. Despite the widespread popularity of the practices among ordinary freedpeople, the breakup of plantations and the redistribution of land to freedmen attracted little support from political leaders. Politicians' hesitancy stemmed, in part, from their belief in the inevitability of progress. The Claiborne County superintendent of education gushed about the rapid economic changes that he had witnessed in just a few short years. As late as 1870, only "one small tract of land in the county" was owned by a black person, but four years later "ten thousand acres" were owned by black men. So many black households were working for themselves, as either small farmers or renters or on shares, that the two-horse wagon had become a ubiquitous sight on the streets of Port Gibson, whereas a decade earlier it was the planters' large ten-bale wagons that clogged the streets during the harvest season. Others praised the "evidence of prosperity" in the "new roads, saw-mills, [and] more land put into agriculture" and further suggested that "[n]ow is the colored man's golden hour."[49]

With the establishment of schools for black children and the meteoric rise of some black politicians, it seemed as if there was no social problem that could not be fixed, including agricultural poverty. The solution, political leaders of all stripes believed, was not in land redistribution but in economic development. Local politicians supported measures such as swamp reclamation and subsidies for manufacturing, to be sure, but they held that the harbinger of a revitalized economy and widespread prosperity lay in the iron rails steadily expanding across the American landscape. The "gospel of prosperity"—the widespread belief that railroads would bring affluence and fortune—had captured the hearts and minds of black political leaders.[50]

Natchez businessmen were the first in the district to clamor for railroad construction. As far back as the 1830s, a few merchants had pushed for a railroad line to expand trade and commerce, but local officials never became heavily involved in attracting railroad investment, reflecting the view of most Natchezians that the Mississippi River would remain a profitable and persistent transportation link to national and international markets. The Civil War and the indeterminacy of the early Reconstruction years further delayed efforts to build a railroad. By 1870 Natchez merchants and planters recognized that modernity was bypassing them as the growing railroad network reshaped the nation. Already a major railroad traversed the state's interior from New Orleans to Memphis, diverting commerce from communities along the river. The future of the region's economy, then, depended on connecting trunk lines to the major railways that traversed the South.[51]

The economic future also depended on black elected officials marshalling government resources and community support for the endeavor. As early as 1867, in the wake of a disastrous cotton crop, Merrimon Howard, the formerly enslaved carriage driver who was just on the cusp of his remarkable political career, grasped the political and economic implications of the railroad. He, along with other black and white residents of Jefferson County, had petitioned Congress for a large appropriation to build a railroad from Natchez to Decatur, Alabama. For Howard, the proposed railroad was less important for its trade benefits; instead, he envisioned a public works project that would "give food and employement [sic]" to perhaps fifteen thousand men. Moreover, he suggested that the railroad should employ "Colord labor," which he believed would "give strength to the Republican party" and strike "a *death blow* to Democrats" in Mississippi. No action was taken on the petition, but the local discussions ultimately led to a plan to build a rail line through Jefferson County that connected Natchez to Jackson, Mississippi.[52]

The importance of railroads fostered an unlikely alliance in which wealthy whites depended on assistance from ordinary black people. The Democratic elite, including planters and merchants, had the financial contacts and business expertise to launch a railroad company, but they lacked the capital to sustain a multiyear construction project. Northern capitalists were reluctant to invest in a small trunk line, and state aid was largely insufficient or unavailable. The Louisiana legislature endorsed an array of railroad projects, including the Vidalia, Alexandria & Texas Railroad in 1872, but they promised more direct aid than they actually delivered. The Mississippi legislature passed a bill known as the Subsidy Law to grant state aid to railroad construction, but in practice only one railroad project received state funds before the law expired. In general, southern states lacked the resources to support widespread railroad construction, and the volatile political environment did little to assuage nervous northern financiers. Thus railroad promoters turned to county bond measures for financing, and since bond subscriptions needed a two-thirds vote for approval, the entire project rested in the hands of ordinary black voters in the Natchez District. More specifically, the political and economic elite had to convince farmers, farm laborers, and urban workers that a railroad was in their best interests.[53]

The first line proposed after black enfranchisement was the Natchez, Jackson, and Columbus (NJC) Railroad, chartered in 1870. The line began in Natchez and took a northeasterly course through Jefferson and Claiborne Counties and on to the Mississippi state capital in Jackson. The white financial elite of Natchez dominated the railroad's governing board and selected former Confederate general and prominent Democrat William T. Martin to serve as president. But to broaden the appeal of the railroad, the promoters reached out to Republican leaders and black grassroots activists as the bond vote drew closer. Representative O. C. French (a white northern Republican from Adams County) shepherded the incorporation bill through the legislature and added four black Republicans from the Natchez District to the board of directors, one of whom was Merrimon Howard. Republicans reciprocated by inviting the editor of the *Natchez Democrat* to speak about the importance of "the Railroad" to the mostly black delegates at their 1870 county convention. State Representatives John R. Lynch and O. C. French gave similar speeches on the general benefits that would accrue from a rail connection.[54]

Endorsement by local political leaders worked wonders when the railroad bond issue was put before the people of Adams County. Far above the two-thirds vote needed, 98 percent of the voters endorsed a $600,000 subscription bond for the NJC Railroad. The bond enabled construction to begin in Natchez, but the promoters needed to secure more financing to extend the line to Jackson. Henry P. Jacobs, although a vigorous proponent of black landownership, was also a prominent railroad promoter. He began "canvassing . . . among his colored fellow citizens" in the city and encouraged them to purchase subscriptions to the railroad (the first of four railroad ventures that he promoted). While Jacobs tapped into the grassroots networks, French worked the halls of the state legislature on behalf of the railroad. In close contact with President Martin, French proposed legislation to aid the NJC Railroad while Martin ensured that the Democratic newspapers would endorse the measure.[55]

By and large, railroads attracted bipartisan support, but tangible aid was hard to come by. French failed to secure state aid. And then the Natchez railroad ran up against entrenched opposition in Jefferson County, particularly from residents along the Mississippi River. On the western edge of the county, residents in the small town of Rodney, only one-half mile from the river, rebelled against the rail line. Rodney had a few commercial establishments and a small port and thus was strategically located to deal in river freight traffic, particularly freight headed to Fayette, the county seat to the east. The proposed railroad, however, bypassed Rodney and ran through Fayette, which promised to weaken the small town's local economy and increase its residents' tax burden. (The largest tax in Adams County, at nine mills, was the Railroad Tax.) Here the dynamism of black political mobilization worked against Natchez's interests, as Rodney's black voters viewed river commerce, not a railroad, as vital to their future. Sensing a difficult fight, the prorailroad forces enlisted "every man who had a horse that could be 'hammered, borrowed, bartered, sold'" and sent them "off in the remote parts of [Jefferson] county" to drum up support for bond subscription. Rodney's citizens responded by enlisting the aid of local leaders, who berated those voters intending to vote for the railroad. Thanks to the voters in Rodney, "the very 'hot bed' of opposition," the county subscription bond failed in December 1871.[56]

The proponents of the NJC Railroad did not rest easily in defeat. They pushed through a state law to authorize a new bond subscription vote. For the second election, the prorailroad forces marshaled the leading political and economic leaders of Jefferson and Adams Counties in a direct-advocacy campaign to sway the local black populace. Black officeholders from Natchez—State Senator Jeremiah M. P. Williams, Natchez city attorney George F. Bowles, and Representative Henry P. Jacobs—joined black leaders from Jefferson County, such as Merrimon Howard and George Stewart in making speeches for the railroad. Prominent white Republicans such as E. J. Castello and George St. Clair Hussey and prominent white Democrats—William T. Martin, Paul Botto, and John W. Young—shared the speakers' platforms as they promoted the railroad in at least five different mass meetings across the county, including the Grand Railroad Barbecue. Arrayed against the political and economic elite of Jefferson and Adams Counties were the local leaders of Rodney: black state representative James Cessor and white leaders Guy Wilcox and Captain Jones. Of these men, Cessor, a thirty-nine-year-old freeborn saddler, was the most outspoken critic of the proposed railroad; in the words of one prorailroad observer, Cessor "violently opposed" the line to Natchez.[57]

The antirailroad group claimed that the county could ill afford to take on a $250,000 debt at a time when teachers struggled to provide the most basic resources for schoolchildren. While not opposed to a railroad in principle, Samuel J. Ireland, a black colonel in the state militia and an Alcorn University trustee, lamented the "people's poverty." For his part, Cessor eschewed the financial complexities and launched a "bitter tirade against [the] Democracy," linking the railroad directors to the Democratic Party.[58]

In response, advocates for the railroad appealed to local residents' pocketbooks, sense of community, and belief in progress. A committee of leading white and black residents (including Howard and Stewart) resolved that the Natchez to Jackson railroad offered the best opportunity to "improve our pecuniary condition." At a speech in Rodney, Representative Jacobs promised "full wages" for the county's laborers if they took advantage of the opportunity before them. Similarly, Dr. Hussey, a white Union League activist, assured his skeptical audience that the value of both "real and personal property" would increase, which would augment county revenues and provide additional funds for school construction and teacher salaries. Underlying the prorailroad arguments was the belief—best articulated by white Republican D. C. Kearns—that the railroad was the wave of the future, the hallmark of progress and modernity. Likening the local opposition to English Luddites, Kearns challenged the citizens of Rodney to not let "narrow-minded ignorance and selfishness" stand in the way of the region's prosperity. Even Ireland, a critic of the Natchez line, admitted that railroads were "indispensable in this age of civilization and progress."[59]

Nonetheless, the railroad subscription lost again, but this time by less than one hundred votes out of two thousand cast. Despite enormous pressure from elites and arguments about the general welfare of the region, Rodney citizens voted their local interests. A rail line through Fayette would have diverted commerce from the river town, for which a regional economic boost would have meant little locally. Unfortunately for the residents of Rodney, over the next few decades the Mississippi River shifted to the west, leaving Rodney citizens high and dry and without a reason for existence. Today a few buildings remain, but for all intents and purposes Rodney is a ghost town.[60]

There was little question at the time that the railroad would have improved Natchez's and Fayette's economic outlook, and this assumption brought together an unusual cast of characters. For a brief moment, Republicans and Democrats, former slaveholders and freedpeople looked beyond their seemingly intractable differences and found common cause. Few would have predicted after emancipation that an ex-Confederate general and Democratic politician (William T. Martin) would share the stage as an equal with a Republican black sheriff (Merrimon Howard). In fact, the largely white directors of the railroad were so pleased with Howard's advocacy, despite their ultimate failure, that they presented him with a gold watch and chain. In the Jefferson County railroad elections, two visions of community were on display—one focused on narrow fidelity to place and the other based on mutual interests spread across a wide region—in which neither race, class, nor partisanship was an accurate predictor of disagreement.[61]

The Jefferson County setback nearly thwarted the plans of the Natchez, Jackson, and Columbus Railroad. Local representatives tried again to enlist state support in order to lessen the tax burden on Adams County citizens, who were paying between 8.5 and 10 mills on personal property. Eventually Hinds County (where the city of Jackson was located) approved a $225,000 bond, and with the money that Adams County had allocated, the line continued to be built at a slow pace. By the time tracks reached Fayette from Natchez in 1876, the company was nearly bankrupt, but Martin secured a last-minute financing arrangement from Natchez "capitalists" to keep the company afloat until the railroad finally reached Jackson in 1882.[62]

The struggles of the Natchez to Jackson railroad also demonstrate the substantial difficulties involved in locally financed railroad construction—struggles that plagued other railroad boosters. Of the railroads proposed during Reconstruction, only the NJC line was completed. By the time railroad commerce was able to flow out of and into Natchez, nearly fifty years after the idea was first proposed, the railroad was no longer seen as a harbinger of prosperity but merely as a means of economic survival.[63]

In the early 1870s, six other railroad companies were established in the Natchez District. While all of them failed, the composition of the incorporators and their ambition shed light on the fault lines of Reconstruction politics. Like the NJC, the Vidalia, Alexandria and Texas Railroad Company attracted a mix of Adams County elites, such as William T. Martin, Paul Botto (the editor of the *Natchez Democrat*), and S. M. Preston (a former Union army officer and the chairman of the Natchez branch of the Freedmen's Bank), but it also attracted Concordia Parish economic and political elites, such as planter Alfred V. Davis, Republican judge Wade H. Hough, and black state legislators David Young and George Washington. The Vidalia line, across the river from Natchez, attempted to link the district to the growing Southwest. Another biracial and bipartisan rail venture was the Vicksburg to Natchez line, which included among its incorporators William McCary (the black sheriff of Adams County), Hiram R. Revels (the first black U.S. senator and later the president of Alcorn University), and William T. Martin.[64]

Other railroad companies reflected the factional divisions that came to define Republican politics in the 1870s. The Natchez and New Orleans Railroad Company seemed to attract moderate Republicans, while the Natchez to Brookhaven line appealed to more radical politicians. The latter venture attracted some of Adams County's leading black Republicans, such as John R. Lynch, William Lynch, Henry P. Jacobs, John Peck, and Hiram R. Revels. They were joined by a slew of white Republicans and Jefferson County Republicans (including James Cessor) to head the effort to build an east–west trunk line from Natchez. Befitting their radical politics and the powerful offices of the incorporators (John R. Lynch was Speaker of the House at the time), the Natchez-to-Brookhaven incorporators committed the railway to "equal accommodations" for passengers paying the same fare and exempted the company from paying taxes for thirty years. Another Republican institution, the National Freedmen's Savings and Trust Company of Natchez, whose secretary (William McCary) was to become the first black sheriff of Adams County, financed the project. Not to be outdone, Wilkinson County Republicans embarked on their own campaign to establish rail connections. Their sheriff, William H. Noble, a white Republican, secured a $400,000 subscription from the county's majority black voters for the Meridian, Red River, and Texas Railroad; however, powerful interests in Adams County who wanted to locate a river terminal in Natchez, not Wilkinson County, blocked the extension of state aid to the line. This forced the other counties to abandon the project and demonstrated once again how geographical interests could trump a shared political identity and a similar approach to economic development.[65]

The biracial character of these railroad efforts was no mere aberration. Black Republicans and white Democrats found common cause in the economic advancement of their communities. They worked together on other public transportation projects, such as the building of roads and bridges. Particularly in Natchez, biracial endeavors among political opponents militated against the stereotypical assumptions that plagued crossracial cooperation in many other localities. Moreover, the active involvement of black officeholders in a range of railroad promotional pursuits suggests that black leaders were more involved in the economic well-being of their working-class constituents than historians have recognized. With the cotton economy failing to produce much wealth for landholders and even less for landless laborers, the expansion of markets through railroad construction offered the possibility of breaking out of the cycle of debt that was entrenched in much of the Natchez District. Thus Sheriff Merrimon Howard—one of the most vocal critics of the crop lien system and a railroad promoter—reflected the aspirations of most ordinary black residents who advocated for workers' rights yet were also willing to work with capitalists to initiate economic reform. Unfortunately, railroads, once constructed, offered few tangible benefits to farm laborers, but this unforeseen outcome did not mean that black and Republican officeholders did not *believe* that railroads would bring broad economic benefits to the black population.[66]

In the midst of the reconstruction of the nation, a local reconstruction took place, one in which elected Republicans shifted the focus of government away from the slaveholders and secessionists and toward the laboring population of ex-slaves. From the creation of a public school system to railroad development to the establishment of a more equitable justice system, Republican officeholders implemented many of the desires of their voters. By no means were Republican officeholders able to bring to fruition full equality in public spaces or to arrest the scourge of agricultural poverty, yet most African Americans responded positively to their efforts and were generally pleased with the results, as evident in the repeated Republican electoral victories at every level in the district.

Elected officials sought to balance radical policies with the needs of the entire polity and to operate within the constraints of nineteenth-century governance.

Equally important, black officeholders sought to gain standing and legitimacy in the eyes of their political opponents, to shore up their own authority, and to solidify their new status as administrators of power and resources. These two goals inevitably led to tension between political leaders and the grass roots. Cooperation between black Republicans and white Democrats—in railroad construction, for example—offset some of the hostility harbored by Democrats after the enactment of black suffrage. Most black Republicans were not accepted as equals by their political opponents; still, the inroads made by a few, such as John R. Lynch and Merrimon Howard, cut against white resistance to black office holding. That Lynch could be described in private correspondence between white conservative leaders as a wise politician and could be believed capable of bringing about a situation where "the white people will cheerfully cooperate in bringing about a better state of things," suggests his and others' success in making black governance seem legitimate.[67]

And yet legitimacy had its own costs. By effectively governing and implementing modest reforms that tipped the scales of justice closer to equality, black and Republican politicians presented more of a threat to white supremacy than their opponents had assumed. In their effective electoral mobilization and astute policy initiatives, black Republicans demonstrated that they were a political force to be reckoned with. Because black Republicans did not implode, because they did not become corrupted, and because they governed effectually, white supremacists looked beyond the boundaries of law and acceptable political practices to find a means to regain power. Black politicians had mastered electoral politics in the Natchez District; thus it would take more than electoral politics to unseat them.

Natchez-under-the-Hill, Mississippi. An illustration showing the city of Natchez on the bluffs to the left and the Louisiana bottomlands in the distance on the other side of the river. In the foreground is a drayman bringing goods from the steamboat docks up to the city's merchant stores. Edward King, *The Great South* (Hartford, Conn.: American Publishing Company, 1875), 291.

Natchez Courthouse, 1861. After emancipation and the enfranchisement of black men, the courthouse became a common site for public meetings and election rallies. Few of the Confederate volunteers in this picture could have imagined that freedpeople would appropriate this space for their own mobilization efforts. Thomas H. and Joan W. Gandy Photograph Collection, Mss. 3778, Louisiana and Lower Mississippi Valley Collections, LSU Libraries, Baton Rouge, La.

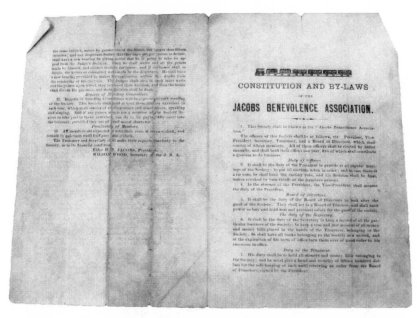

Jacobs Benevolent Association, Constitution and By-Laws. One of the many mutual aid societies that freedpeople created in the wake of emancipation, the Jacobs Benevolent Association was formed in 1867 in Natchez, Mississippi. In their public outreach and institutional structure, such societies served as building blocks in the development of grassroots democracy. The association was founded by Henry P. Jacobs, a Baptist minister who successfully escaped from slavery in the mid-1850s. During Reconstruction, Jacobs was active in Republican politics and was elected to the Mississippi House of Representatives. *The Jacobs Benevolent Society vs. Henry P. Jacobs*, Deed of Indenture, 5 September 1874, Chancery files, #543, Adams County Courthouse, Natchez, Miss.

John R. Lynch. Perhaps the most famous and most influential black politician from the Natchez District, Lynch, who was born into slavery, was a strident advocate of grassroots democracy and also benefited from it, as he was elected to three terms in Congress. The chain attached to his vest is likely the gold watch and chain given to him by the members of the Mississippi House of Representatives in 1873 in recognition of his services as Speaker of the House. Thomas H. and Joan W. Gandy Photograph Collection, Mss. 3778, Louisiana and Lower Mississippi Valley Collections, LSU Libraries, Baton Rouge, La.

Black farmers with cotton bales. The small wagons highlight a significant change in the cotton economy as a result of emancipation and political mobilization. Each wagon represented the product of a household's or a squad's work for the year. These small labor units, which freedpeople pushed for, were a stark change from the gang-labor system that predominated when slavery was legal. In addition, the photograph shows the hybridity of the region, with the interaction of rural and urban residents on the streets of Natchez. Louisiana and Lower Mississippi Valley Collections, LSU Libraries, Baton Rouge, La.

Membership certificate, Knights of Honor of the World. This benevolent organization was created in 1893 by George F. Bowles, an influential black politician in Natchez. The fraternal order spread across the Deep South, and even across the Atlantic Ocean. Unlike early benevolent societies established soon after emancipation, this one excluded women. Such exclusion is a reflection of the diminishment of grassroots democracy and the narrowed space for freedpeople's collective organizing in the wake of electoral violence and disfranchisement. *The Supreme Lodge, Knights of Honor vs. The Supreme Lodge, Knights of Honor of the World, and George F. Bowles,* Adams County Chancery Court, March term, 1898, file #1472, Adams County Courthouse, Natchez, Miss.

FIVE

"True to One Another"

In the summer of 1872, a political struggle reached a fever pitch in Adams County, Mississippi. The setting was the Republican county convention and the purpose was to select a nominee for Congress. The local Democratic newspaper, with a bit of hyperbole, described a cacophonous scene of "fuss and excitement . . . furious recrimination, shaking of clenched fists, continuous hammering with the gavel, and general screeching." Two energetic Republican factions battled on the courthouse floor. Meanwhile, a large audience of local citizens cheered on their allies and shouted down their enemies from the galleries, leading to a feeling that "riotous action" was imminent. One witness put the unruly events to verse and published a doggerel poem in the newspaper. Mimicking Tennyson's "The Charge of the Light Brigade," it read (in part),

> Freedmen to the right of them,
> Freedmen to the left of them,
> Freedmen in front of them
>   *Cussed* and thundered;
> Williams he stormed a spell,
> Boldly shook his fists as well;
> "Now, let me frankly tell,
> Freedmen will break the spell;
>   By which they've been plundered."[1]

The issue that convulsed the proceeding was whether a white radical Republican or a black radical Republican should be nominated. The "spell" that the freedmen broke referred to the successful nomination of the black candidate to Congress—a first in Mississippi history and a rare occurrence during Reconstruction. Although African Americans made up three out of every four residents in Adams County, only a few black men held major public offices at the county and state level in 1872. Thus, according to the poem, entitled "Scrimmage of the Dark Brigade," the black population had been "plundered" of their rightful share of political offices.

But the racial dynamics of this episode are not as clear-cut as they seem. Of the forty-three delegates at the convention, only seven were white, and nearly half of the assembled black delegates supported the white incumbent congressman, Legrand W. Perce. Both Perce and John R. Lynch, the black challenger and the current speaker of the state house of representatives, were experienced officeholders and shared a radical political vision. What then explains this political dispute? What accounts for divisions among black Republican delegates? Who were these delegates, and how did they attain their positions of influence? What enabled Lynch, an ex-slave, to secure the Republican Party nomination and eventually win a seat in the Forty-Third Congress?

Historians often treat factionalism as a problem among party elites, particularly in the conflict between white leaders and aspiring black politicians, and as a result devote little attention to the structural factors that generate political divisions. Some blame black politicians who aspired to higher offices for the factional conflicts that limited the Republican Party's ability to counter a violent and aggressive challenge from the Democrats. If Republicans would have maintained a united front, the thinking goes, then northern support for federal intervention would not have waivered. While Democratic paramilitary organizations are given their due, freedmen's quests for higher office and their related inattention to working-class concerns are treated as contributing factors in the ultimate failure of Reconstruction.[2]

The linkage between factionalism and the fate of Reconstruction, however, tends to obscure the complicated process by which former slaves and freeborn blacks became officeholders. Part of the problem is that historians often treat factionalism as an obstacle that could have been avoided. Perhaps because freedmen voted with such unanimity in the first elections of Radical Reconstruction or because freedpeople shared a common goal in trying to dismantle white supremacist conceptions of citizenship, historians tend to assume that freedmen's solidarity should have persisted. If there was any place where black solidarity was likely to be found, it would be in the Natchez District. The population of the district was overwhelmingly black, Republican, and agrarian. Yet even here, in one of the strongest Republican regions in the country, local partisan leaders could not rest on their laurels; factionalism was ubiquitous.

Intraparty conflicts arose in the Natchez District in part because there was little two-party competition. Personal conflicts and rivalries certainly intensified internal divisions, as well. At the heart of the matter, however, were competing perspectives on office holding. On one side were advocates for broad community representation who believed that local residents should fill public offices. On the other side were those who supported the most qualified or most experienced candidates for office. Generally, rural freedpeople endorsed the former perspective on political representation, while urban black residents and outsiders, especially carpetbaggers, believed that individual merit should be the primary factor in selecting a nominee for political office.

Instead of being seen as a sign of weakness, factional conflicts demonstrate the success of grassroots democracy. When power is diffused and shared among the people, a logical consequence is that many different voices are brought into the public debate, and more often than not these voices disagree. The challenge of democracies, then, is to incorporate a large and varied constituency into a workable framework. Broad representation among various constituencies across the Natchez District did not come easily, but extensive social networks provided neighborhood leaders with the financial backing and communal support necessary to withstand factional eruptions. We can see how political leaders utilized these networks by examining the officeholder bond records, a neglected source for understanding local politics. The nature of these political networks, furthermore, reinforces the point that mid-nineteenth-century people inhabited localized worlds where face-to-face contact governed social intercourse, economic transactions, and political relationships. Just as freedpeople struggled mightily to contest planter power and reconfigure labor relations in a post-emancipation world, they struggled relentlessly to create a democratic society, even as they differed over its implementation.

Officeholders

The Natchez District gave rise to the most powerful Republican operation in the state of Mississippi and one of the most enduring black political movements in the postemancipation South. The district was also one of only four regions in the post-Reconstruction South to elect a black congressman. On the Louisiana side of the district, black Republicans in Concordia and Tensas Parishes dominated local politics, but they had much less statewide power because New Orleans loomed so large in state politics. By contrast, the rural and urban hybridity of the Mississippi counties of the Natchez District, coupled with the more decentralized politics in the state, meant that politicians in Adams, Claiborne, Jefferson, and Wilkinson Counties had considerable statewide power and thus a measure of influence in national politics. It is for this reason that two of the most famous black officeholders in the Reconstruction era came from Natchez. Hiram Revels, a freeborn North Carolinian who served as a chaplain and recruiter for black regiments in the Civil War, moved to Natchez to lead AME Zion Chapel. After an appointment as a city alderman and an elected term in the state senate, he was selected in 1870 by the Mississippi legislature to become the first African American U.S. senator. Another black politician of national renown was John R. Lynch. He was born enslaved in Concordia Parish, served three terms in Congress representing the district's Mississippi River counties, held statewide and national Republican Party positions, and, later in life, wrote an influential memoir of the Reconstruction era.[3]

As important as these men's powerful positions were, they only scratch the surface of the broad-based involvement of black men in governmental and partisan positions. Through an intensive search of local records, I was able to uncover over four hundred African American politicians from the Natchez District who held either public office or party leadership positions in the Reconstruction era. By contrast, the only other previously published tabulation of black lawmakers counted just fifty-nine men from the Natchez District, suggesting that there still is much to be learned about the breadth and depth of nineteenth-century black politics. At the state level, thirty-two black men represented the Natchez District in the Mississippi and Louisiana legislatures between 1868 and 1892 (see table 1). At the county level, ten black men were elected to the office of sheriff. Other elected and appointive positions that black men held include mayor, alderman, postmaster, county supervisor, police juror, coroner, justice of the peace, constable, county treasurer, tax collector, assessor, school board member, and clerk of the court, among others. Black men also held numerous partisan posts, such as delegate to a party convention, member of the Republican executive committee, officer in a local political club, and candidate for office.[4]

At one time or another, African Americans held every state and local political office or position, except for judicial offices. Long denied access to formal education, very few freedmen had the legal training necessary to be judges or district attorneys. Of all the district's black political figures, only George F. Bowles, a freeborn South Carolinian, held a judicial position. He was elected city attorney of Natchez in 1872 and went on to serve in other high-level posts, such as city weigher, school board member, city marshal, chief of police, and, in the late 1880s and early 1890s, state representative.[5]

In many respects Bowles was typical of the black political leaders who served in the higher ranks of county and local government. He was literate and educated, became an officeholder at a young age (twenty-eight), was a landowner (with plantation lands in Louisiana and city lots in Natchez and Vidalia), and joined local social institutions. He was a trustee for the Jacobs Benevolent Society—a Baptist mutual aid association named after Henry P. Jacobs, a local black minister and officeholder—and he founded the Supreme Lodge, Knights of Honor of the World, a black fraternal order. But in other ways, Bowles stood apart from most other black politicians. He was born free in South Carolina, lived in four different states, held public office over the span of twenty-one

TABLE 1. Black State Lawmakers and Sheriffs in the Natchez District

Officeholder	County or Parish	Years
State Senate		
Hiram R. Revels	Adams	1870
Jeremiah M. P. Williams	Adams	1870–74, 1878–80
George W. White	Wilkinson	1874–76
David Young	Concordia	1874–78
A. J. Bryant	Tensas	1876–78
State House of Representatives		
William C. Holland	Tensas	1868–70
David Young	Concordia	1868–74
John R. Lynch	Adams	1870–74
Henry P. Jacobs	Adams	1870–74, 1876–78
Matthew T. Newsome	Claiborne	1870–72
Merrimon Howard	Jefferson	1870–72
H. M. Foley	Wilkinson	1870–74
George W. White	Wilkinson	1870–74
George Washington	Concordia	1872–74, 1878–80
Joseph Smothers	Claiborne	1872–76
Haskin Smith	Claiborne	1872–76
James D. Cessor	Jefferson	1872–78
William Landers	Jefferson	1872–76
J. Ross Stewart	Tensas	1872–78
James Randall	Concordia	1874–76
William Ridgley	Concordia	1874–78
William H. Lynch	Adams	1874–76, 1882–84, 1886–88
Willis Davis	Adams	1874–76
Samuel W. Fitzhugh	Wilkinson	1874–76
Anderson Tolliver	Concordia	1876–80
Robert J. Walker	Tensas	1876–78
Samuel Riley	Wilkinson	1876–78
James W. Shattuck	Wilkinson	1876–78
Solomon Schaifer	Tensas	1878–80
George R. Washington	Adams	1878–80
W. W. Hence	Adams	1880–82
Felix Cory	Adams	1884–86
George F. Bowles	Adams	1888–92
Sheriff		
James Page	Claiborne	1870–71
William McCary	Adams	1871–76
Merrimon Howard	Jefferson	1871–76
James Franklin	Concordia	1872–74

TABLE 1. *Continued*

Officeholder	County or Parish	Years
Andrew J. Bryant	Tensas	1872–76
Oren Stewart	Concordia	1874–76
Thomas Bland	Claiborne	1874–75
Robert H. Wood	Adams	1876–82
John Young	Concordia	1876–78
James Randall	Concordia	1878–80

Source: Justin Behrend, Black Politicians Database, SUNY-Geneseo, http://go.geneseo.edu /BlackPoliticiansDB.

years, was a licensed attorney, and was the editor and publisher of the *Natchez Brotherhood*, a newspaper that ran from 1887 to 1900.[6]

In contrast, minor offices such as justice of the peace, constable, and policeman tended to attract laborers with less formal education and meager personal wealth. Handy Walton and Gabriel Johnson exemplified these second-tier politicians. Walton, a literate black farm laborer without property who was born in Mississippi but lived in Concordia Parish, was twenty-eight when he joined Concordia Parish's Republican executive committee and was later elected justice of the peace, member of the police jury, and school board member in the 1870s. Gabriel Johnson was also born in Mississippi, but he settled in Tensas Parish. Like Walton, he was probably born enslaved, as he was an illiterate and landless farmer. He claimed $140 in personal wealth and served as a delegate to numerous Republican committees and conventions. At the age of twenty-nine in 1872, he was elected justice of the peace of the First Ward.[7]

It is difficult to generalize about how these, and hundreds of other men, rose to leadership positions, as each politician's experience and background was different. Nevertheless, a few patterns are evident that may explain why one farm laborer became a party leader and his neighbor did not. Certainly personal leadership skills helped to advance neighborhood leaders, but so did political connections beyond one's neighborhood. Isham Johnson, a literate farm laborer from Concordia Parish, distinguished himself as a leader when in 1867, at the age of thirty-three, he made a complaint before the local Freedmen's Bureau office on behalf of twenty other freedmen who were discharged from the Forest plantation. His network of contacts extended to Natchez, where, in 1872, he was married by Rev. Adam Jackson, a Republican Party agent and the minister of the region's largest black church. By 1883 Johnson was the Fourth Ward constable in Concordia Parish.[8]

Other leaders, such as Merrimon Howard of Jefferson County and James Page of Claiborne County, rose from community leadership positions to hold powerful county offices. Both Howard and Page lived half their lives as slaves but obtained their freedom in the 1850s. Both were essential in establishing the first black schools in their counties, and both held numerous public offices during Reconstruction, including sheriff and tax collector.[9]

Still others, like John R. Lynch, took advantage of unique opportunities and personal contacts to chart a path to higher office. At the end of the war, Lynch had no discernible skills, was uneducated, and had few prospects that would suggest his rise from slavery to the U.S. Congress. He found employment at a local photography shop, where he met Robert H. Wood, a free black man who, like Lynch, would become a powerful officeholder and with whom he forged a lifelong friendship. Lynch joined a local Republican club in 1867 and distinguished himself as a strong public speaker. In one of his first leadership assignments, the Adams County Republican Party sent young Lynch (age twenty-two) to the state capitol to meet with Mississippi's military governor, Gen. Adelbert Ames, and present a slate of candidates for appointment to county and city offices. Impressed by Lynch's presentation, Ames appointed him to the office of justice of the peace, discarding the local party's candidate, Henry P. Jacobs. But Lynch could not have assumed the office without the timely assistance of two black men who acted as Lynch's bondsmen: William McCary and David Singleton. Both men were landowners and signed his officeholder bond for $1,000 each. It is unclear how Lynch knew McCary, who was a member of a prominent free black family, a barber, and the future sheriff of Adams County, but Lynch was well acquainted with Singleton. Both were former slaves of Alfred V. Davis, one of the wealthiest planters in the South. Lynch worked for a short while in the Dunleith mansion brushing flies from the dining room table while the Davis family ate, and he had known Singleton, Davis's personal body servant, "since boyhood." The two maintained an acquaintance into the Reconstruction years, as they lived next door to each other in Natchez in 1870.[10]

In addition to the widespread presence of African Americans in political office, the Natchez District was notable for the persistence of black office holding, especially in Adams County. John R. Lynch held public office for ten years and was a party leader for twenty-seven years. Similarly, Louis J. Winston, who was born free, served as circuit clerk of Adams County for twenty years, nineteen of them after the end of Reconstruction. Robert H. Wood won election to a variety of offices in the 1870s, such as alderman, justice of the peace, mayor, county supervisor, and sheriff, and from 1880 through 1895 was the Adams County assessor. In other parishes and counties, though rare, a few black men held public office for over a decade. Wesley Dixon, born enslaved in Virginia, worked as a farm laborer, was a minister, and was elected the coroner of Tensas Parish, serving from 1868 until 1890. Thomas Richardson was freed from slavery as a young boy in Claiborne County and grew up to be a licensed attorney, school principal, and postmaster, a position he held off and on for thirty-two years between 1870 and 1911. Samuel W. Fitzhugh, of the Fitzhugh family of Natchez, was also born free, worked as schoolteacher, was elected to one term in the Mississippi legislature during Reconstruction, and later served as a constable in Wilkinson County from 1878 to 1897. Of course, none of these black officeholders could have held office without black and Republican votes. But even after fraud and violence prevented many black men from voting at the polls, the fact that these black politicians still held office suggests that they had attained a degree of legitimacy in the eyes of their white neighbors.[11]

Bond Networks

Of the challenges facing potential officeholders, financial constraints loomed large for black politicians. Mid-nineteenth-century politicians did not need to amass vast fortunes for the marketing of their candidacies like today's politicians, but they were required to post officeholder bonds for most administrative and judicial offices, the sums varying from $500 (for constable) to $75,000 (for tax collector of Adams County). Upon assuming office, an official had to post a bond commensurate with the responsibilities of the position to protect the public in case the official mismanaged funds or stole them. A $500 bond was beyond the reach of most freedpeople, who tended to be landless farmers, and a $75,000 bond ensured that only the wealthiest individuals with the closest connections to the local elite would take office. To put this sum into perspective, the AME Church in Natchez spent one-tenth that amount to purchase downtown property and church buildings, and it took the church six years to pay off its $7,400 debt.[12]

Before assuming office, a politician had to solicit financial support, and he had to maintain that support throughout the entire length of the term. In this way, bondsmen, or sureties, acted as powerful impediments to the rise of independent or radical politicians. Wealthy bondsmen could withdraw their backing at any moment if they felt that their interests were threatened. An example of the perils of maintaining an officeholder bond can be found in the experience of Wilson Wood, a thirty-two-year-old black storekeeper who had previously been a policeman and a justice of the peace. He was elected treasurer of Adams County in 1873, but after his reelection two years later, he could not raise a sufficient bond. The office was then given to the next-highest vote getter, a white Republican who, although he received only 27 percent of the vote, was able to post a sufficient bond and assume the office.[13]

While most black and Republican candidates had little difficulty in attracting freedmen's votes, those same freedmen lacked the wealth and property to endorse an officeholder. So black political leaders turned to affluent men—

wealthy Republicans as well as white elites with Democratic leanings—for financial backing. Yet this support could come at a cost, leaving black politicians beholden to interests at odds with their voters' interests. Most Republican officeholders (white and black) had to reach beyond their political supporters, which often left them, lamented one white sheriff, "entirely at the mercy of some men who have no sympathy politically with us." For this reason, bonds were "a subject in which nearly every officeholder in this County is concerned." The difficulty in obtaining financial backing for public office explains, in part, why white outsiders, who tended to possess greater economic resources, held the top posts in some counties in the Natchez District despite the fact that blacks outnumbered whites by as much as ten to one.[14]

In predominantly rural counties, black leaders depended on wealthy whites to sustain their leadership. Merrimon Howard, a former slave and carriage driver from Jefferson County, relied almost exclusively on white farmers, including his former master, for his bonds as sheriff and tax collector. Similarly, in Tensas Parish, across the river, sureties tended to be white, although the prevalence of wealthy northerners among the planter class ensured that black officeholders did not have to solicit support from former slaveholders. In Wilkinson County, William Noble Jr., a white Mississippi-born planter and sheriff, dominated the local political scene by providing financial support to at least eleven black politicians. White and black sureties supported black officeholders, who tended to be justices of the peace and constables, but the biracialism on black officeholder bonds was not reciprocal. None of the white officeholders in the Wilkinson County bond records claimed a black surety. Not only were black officeholders forced to rely on local whites to hold office, but just as significant, white Republican officeholders were not dependent on freedpeople for their bonds, which limited the extent to which they would act in the interests of working-class voters.[15]

The situation was less bleak in Adams County, where black sureties shouldered substantial portions of the largest bonds and enabled the advancement of an array of radical officeholders, white and black. On Wilson Wood's 1876 treasurer bond, black men pledged 20 percent of the $50,000 bond. Similarly, on William McCary's tax collector bond of 1872, black sureties supplied $18,000 of the $75,000 bond. The important difference here was the sizeable wealth of a few free black families. Before the war, Natchez boasted one of the largest free black communities in Mississippi and included in its ranks an assortment of entrepreneurs, artisans, and small business owners, a few of whom even owned some land. McCary inherited his father's barbering business before he ventured into public office. Likewise, Robert W. Fitzhugh parlayed his family's modest wealth and status as well as his expertise in carpentry and planting into a political career as an alderman, poor farm supervisor, justice of the peace, and postmaster. Robert H. Wood's political career undoubtedly benefited from his father's reputation. In 1870, when the freeborn Wood was elected mayor of Natchez, the first black mayor in Mississippi history, he lived with his white father, Robert W. Wood, a physician who himself had previously been the mayor of Natchez, from 1854 to 1858. Unique family connections gave aspiring black politicians in Natchez a different set of supporters than was typical in the rest of the district and the South in general.[16]

William McCary, the first black sheriff and tax collector in Adams County, benefited from having an established and educated family, but to hold these powerful offices he had to reach out to a wide constituency. The twenty-three sureties on his tax collector's bond ($75,000) reveal the financial burden of the office but also his effort to draw support from many different segments of the county. The bondsmen included merchants, farmers, planters, artisans, carpet-baggers, white Unionists, former Confederates, former slaves, freeborn blacks, and even one black Democrat. A third of the bond came from native-born white southerners, 13 percent from northern-born whites, and another 24 percent from blacks, which was twice as much black support as white Republican officeholders posted. And these black sureties represented the movers and shakers of the local party, such as Speaker of the Mississippi House of Representatives John R. Lynch, former U.S. senator Hiram Revels, Alderman William H. Lynch, Supervisor John Peck, and wealthy farmer David Singleton. It is also possible that the Lynch brothers influenced Patrick H. McGraw, a white druggist and a good friend of their deceased father (a fellow Irishman), to contribute $10,000 to McCary's bond.[17]

The modest yet sizeable wealth of the Natchez black community also allowed black officeholders like McCary to use their bonds to communicate their political leanings and principles. His $20,000 sheriff's bond included only two endorsements, one from a white merchant and the other from a black gun maker, Henry G. Newcomb. Newcomb was an Ohio-born merchant of mixed-race descent and had been an established Natchez storeowner for at least four years before supporting the bond. By allowing a black gunsmith to provide half of his sheriff's bond, the details of which were printed in the local paper, McCary sent a dual message to the county's citizens. He signaled that he would not shirk from his authority to use violence, if necessary, to carry out the duties of the office and that the black community supported his use of force. At the same time, he indicated that he would dispense justice equally by having a white man supply the other half of his bond.[18]

Leading black officeholders also used bonds to build political coalitions and generate a network for their own elevation to higher-level positions. They created a financial base of operations that coincided with their voter-mobilization initiatives to give local politics surprising strength and resiliency. McCary, for his part, extended his influence by pledging money to three other officeholders: a white clerk to the board of supervisors, a black justice of the peace, and a black constable. In Adams County, black men held eleven of twenty county offices in 1872, and on those bonds half included at least one black surety.[19]

Politicians and Landownership

To enter the ranks of the higher-level officeholders and to build a countywide coalition, aspiring political leaders also needed to be landowners. Since land was the only legitimate collateral for bonds, property ownership enabled black officeholders to support other candidates for office through bond endorsements. Land was also a prerequisite for political legitimacy. Landless candidates for countywide or state-level office were greeted with suspicion in some quarters because they did not have a stake in the community. "We do not object to the presence of the negro in the parish jury," stated one white Concordia Parish planter to a northern reporter. "[W]e complain because nine out of ten who sit upon the jury are ignorant and have no property at all." (A Louisiana parish jury was equivalent to a Mississippi county board of supervisors.) For former slaves, the difficulty of landownership (along with illiteracy) probably relegated many talented political leaders to the ranks of lesser offices, such as justice of the peace and constable. However, a few former slaves and landless laborers did become landowners and did rise to higher office, and their political success sheds more light on the importance of social networks in sustaining a new generation of leaders.[20]

With limited means and often facing legal prohibitions against landownership prior to Reconstruction, black people had difficulty acquiring land, but Republican tax policies and friendly officeholders gave aspiring politicians unprecedented opportunities to become property holders. Tax increases on real estate combined with the general scarcity of cash in the postwar era forced many landowners to default on their taxes. In these situations, sheriffs confiscated delinquent properties and auctioned them off at special tax sales. Dozens of planters throughout the Natchez District forfeited their land in the mid-1870s, and, while most were able to later regain possession, some lost their land permanently.[21]

A sympathetic Republican officeholder, then, and a low bid, often gave black politicians their first shot at landownership. James D. Cessor, an up-and-coming black leader from the town of Rodney in Jefferson County, purchased a house and lot at a sheriff's sale in 1869 for the paltry sum of four dollars. Three years later Cessor, who was born free and a saddler by trade, was elected to the state house of representatives, where he served for three terms. In Tensas Parish Solomon Schaifer and Wesley Dixon (both ministers and farm laborers) each gained admission to the ranks of landownership by purchasing city lots through sales brokered by a friendly Republican governing board, and both men subsequently held higher-level county positions: recorder and coroner, respectively. Republican officials had fewer qualms with black landownership than did white property owners, who tended to be former slaveholders, and they gave black bidders a chance to purchase real estate at auction.[22]

John R. Lynch, an ex-slave and Adams County's most powerful black politician, similarly benefited from sheriff's sales. He purchased a small tract of land, two city lots, and a plantation at auction in the early 1870s, but his rise from slave to planter suggests another route by which black leaders acquired land. For Lynch, kin relations were the decisive factor in joining the ranks of major landowners. In his first acquisitions, Lynch joined with his brother, William (also a political activist and officeholder), and together they formed an economic partnership that would endure for over twenty years. The Lynch brothers also benefited from a nonfamily inheritance. They, along with their sister and mother, had befriended a free man of color before the war, who left for them a house and lot in Natchez when he died. With an inheritance, the support of his family, and his own savvy business sense (as a twenty-year-old, he loaned his white employer $500), John R. Lynch purchased his first plot of land from the publisher of the *Natchez Democrat* in 1869, three months before he became the first black officeholder in the Natchez District. This publisher also sold a parcel of land to David Singleton—the earliest recorded land transaction with a freedman. Why a prominent Democrat was willing to sell city lots to former slaves remains a mystery, but Lynch's connections to Singleton, perhaps the wealthiest black man in the district, were fortuitous.[23]

Singleton's wealth originated from a unique relationship with his master, Alfred V. Davis. Unlike most master-slave relationships, this one offered Singleton considerable control over Davis's plantations and allowed him to develop a network of business contacts. Although Singleton never sought public office, he used his affluence to directly support black officeholders (he was a surety, for example, on McCary's tax collector bond and on Lynch's justice of the peace bond), and he used his wealth to form partnerships with other political leaders. He partnered with John R. Lynch's brother, William, in a planting venture. A year later Singleton sold a Vidalia town lot to an ex-slave, a Louisiana legislator named David Young who, within a few years, would control the political operations in Concordia Parish. A few years later Singleton again partnered with Young, this time in a lease contract with laborers on the Worrell plantation, one of four large plantations that the two leased that year. According to the terms of the contract, they supplied their "partners in planting" with rations and implements to make "a crop of Cotton and Corn," but before Singleton and Young received their share of the harvest, the farm laborers were obligated to pay the landowner, A. V. Davis, in "first picked" cotton.[24]

Davis continued to factor into Singleton's business endeavors during Reconstruction and beyond. Singleton first purchased land in Concordia Parish (the lot that he later sold to David Young) from Dr. Robert Carter and Pauline Davis Carter, who was Alfred V. Davis's sister. The Carters moved to Rhode Island and later to Philadelphia after the war, but Pauline Carter continued to divest property, particularly to black politicians and often with her brother acting on her behalf. Between 1870 and 1889 Pauline Carter sold town lots to three black politicians—two state legislators who were also parish school board members and a former sheriff and state legislator—and she sold another plot of land to the Vidalia Black Baptist Church.[25]

The motivations behind these transactions are difficult to determine, yet the connections between Davis and Singleton and between Singleton and black politicians in Adams County and Concordia Parish highlight the importance of personal relationships in economic enterprises and in politics. Singleton might very well have become a major landholder after emancipation regardless, yet his relationship with A. V. Davis undoubtedly facilitated his pursuit of wealth and economic independence, just as the transactions with emerging political figures could not have hurt his business prospects. Comparably, the Lynch brothers and David Young could have relied on white patronage, but Singleton's business and personal relationships gave these men an opportunity to rise from slavery and to assume positions of power without worrying about pleasing white conservative interests, as was the case for black politicians in Jefferson and Wilkinson Counties. Through bond records and land deeds, we can see the importance of financial supporters like David Singleton to the ascendancy of black political power in the Natchez District.[26]

The Rise of Black Politicians in Adams County

Few areas in the postemancipation South were more reliably Republican than the Natchez District. In each election following the introduction of black suffrage, freedmen voted consistently for Republican officeholders at the local, state, and national levels, and they put scores of black men into office. And yet throughout this period of remarkable political success, local partisan organizations struggled to contain internal conflicts between rival politicians and competing factions. Far from the staid image of consistency that the electoral returns suggest, local politics frequently bubbled over in battles between Republicans. By and large political activists warred over partisan nominations and patronage, disputes often fueled by personal rivalries. And although the factional disputes varied from county to county and were shaped by the individuals involved, a few patterns emerge.[27]

Within Republican ranks there was a constant tension between radicals and moderates. Radical factions tended to include a higher percentage of freedmen in their ranks, they strongly endorsed the nomination of blacks to higher-level offices, and they supported radical policies, such as higher property taxes and integrated schools. Moderates, on the other hand, tended to be whiter and include more outsiders, especially white and black northerners. But these were only tendencies; southern-born freedmen joined moderate factions, and northern-born whites allied with radicals.

Black political mobilization had an immediate impact on representation in municipal and county government. Before the war, the ranks of local government were filled with middle-class white men, often from the merchant class. To some extent, that tradition continued when the military governor filled municipal offices in 1867, prior to the first biracial elections. The men appointed to the county board of supervisors and the city board of aldermen were all white, presumably of middle-class status, and somewhat affiliated with the merchant economy. What made them different from their antebellum predecessors was their affiliation with the Republican Party, their loyalty to the Union, and, for many of them, their northern birth. Subsequently, Adelbert Ames, the military governor and future elected governor of Mississippi, appointed three black men to the board of aldermen as replacements, each of whom was freeborn and of mixed-race descent and would go on to hold higher offices.[28]

These small changes paled in comparison to the radical change in the city and county government once these offices were opened to the black electorate. The question of who would fill positions became a major source of political infighting and factionalism. In 1869 the local party split between supporters of Henry P. Jacobs, an Alabama-born ex-slave, Baptist minister, and delegate to the Mississippi constitutional convention, and John R. Lynch, the young justice of the peace. As candidate for the position of state senator, Lynch and his supporters put forward Jeremiah M. P. Williams, an ex-slave Baptist minister, while the Jacobs faction endorsed Jacobs himself. The balloting at the county convention deadlocked when delegate Noah Buchanan, yet another black Baptist minister, refused to support either Williams or Jacobs. The Lynch faction finally broke the impasse by nominating Hiram R. Revels, an AME minister, which met with the approval of Reverend Buchanan. The origins of this factional dispute are not readily apparent; after all, three Baptist ministers held contrasting views and two ended up throwing their support behind a rival denomination's minister. Although Jacobs had little regard for Lynch after the young man was appointed justice of the peace—a position that local Republicans had promised to Jacobs—this dispute does not explain Lynch's adamant opposition to Jacobs or the ongoing factional divisions between Lynch and Jacobs over the next ten years. It was not just personal rivalries that fueled the conflict but also differing political bases. Jacobs allied with white northerners, while Lynch drew support from the free black elite and rural black people.[29]

By 1870, however, locally born African Americans were beginning to make inroads into higher-level county offices and party leadership posts. At the county Republican convention, the delegates overwhelmingly supported Jeremiah M. P. Williams for state senator (filling the seat vacated by Revels, who had recently been advanced to the U.S. Senate) and shot down the candidacy of E. J. Castello. Castello, a white Union army veteran, former constitutional delegate, and current postmaster, had been instrumental in mobilizing new black voters through his Union League activism, but he was suspected of swindling black ex-soldiers out of their military bounties, leading to questions about whether he and other white radicals were more interested in personal gain than in policies that benefited their constituents. Williams, a former slave and local minister, declared at a party caucus that "it was high time the blacks who did the voting should also hold the offices." He denied that he called for a strict color line in local politics, but Williams did admit "that the time had come for the blacks to rely upon themselves more and upon their hitherto white leaders less." The defeat of Castello—known as the "Radical Wheel Horse" for his organizational sophistication—was "very significant," noted the *Natchez Democrat*, because it demonstrated that local black people had harnessed the tools of caucusing and electioneering in order to take control of the political process.[30]

With freedpeople making up more than seven out of ten residents in Adams County, black political activists endeavored to make local offices better reflect the community. As a result, the board of supervisors went from one black member out of five in 1869 to three black members a year later and four black members by 1873, including the president of the board. In Natchez, which had roughly equal numbers of white and black residents, city activists led by John R. Lynch succeeded in electing black men to half of the seats on the board of aldermen, and they propelled Robert H. Wood to the mayor's office—the only elected black mayor in nineteenth-century Mississippi.[31]

With these gains, the growing network of local black politicians set their sights on higher, more powerful offices. In 1871 the black-led locals squared off against the carpetbagger-led faction over the office of sheriff. Against a backdrop of furious politicking, William McCary's black supporters bested the incumbent and carpetbagger favorite, William Noonan, resulting in a black man holding what one historian called "the most important office in the counties, both in responsibilities and in financial returns."[32]

The shift in the makeup of county officeholders can be traced to the organizational structure of the local party, particularly its dependence on rural clubs.

The Adams County Republican Party was arranged in such a way as to give ordinary people a significant voice in political affairs. For every one hundred Republican votes, each precinct club could send one delegate (and an additional delegate for remainders over fifty votes), and it fell to the neighborhood clubs to select these delegates. The power of the rural communities was further reflected in party leadership circles. Six of the seven members of the Adams County Republican executive committee in 1872 were black, and six were either county residents or county officeholders. Across the river in Concordia Parish, the Republican Party was even more dependent on local clubs for the nomination of candidates for office. "Each regularly organized Club of seventy-five members is entitled to two Delegates," reported the *Vidalia Herald*, and clubs with fifty members were permitted one delegate. In this way, freedmen in the hinterlands were empowered to elect a friend, kinsman, or neighbor as a representative of their local community. In Adams County, as in every other county and parish in the Natchez District, the rural delegates outnumbered the city delegates.[33]

The ultimate test of the growing assertiveness of local black politicians came in 1872, when, for the first time, a black candidate sought congressional nomination in the Natchez District. Incumbent Legrand W. Perce, a white, northern-born, former Union military officer, had strong support among other white carpetbaggers. He had distinguished himself in Congress as a determined radical. Even local black leaders considered him "a strong and able man" who "had made a creditable and satisfactory representative." In other words, few Republicans were displeased with his service in office; rather, they questioned his background as a northerner.[34]

Perce's strongest challenger was John R. Lynch. The local Democratic paper considered Lynch to be "probably the best parliamentarian amoung [sic] the Republican members of the House" and "one of the ablest men in his party in the State"—a judgment that was confirmed when he was elected speaker of the Mississippi House of Representatives at the age of twenty-five. But Lynch's political success resulted less from his personal character traits and more from his deep and broad support within the local black community. Like most of his constituents, Lynch was a former slave and had worked as a plantation laborer, but he also drew considerable support from Natchez, where he had lived and worked since the war. Moreover, his experience as a house slave, his mixed racial heritage, and his contacts with leading black families gave him credibility among the black elite. In short, Lynch embodied the experiences and values of most of the Republican constituencies in Adams County, and even more important, he paid close attention to the needs and concerns of rural freedpeople.[35]

Because decision-making power was diffused down to the lower ranks, the congressional nomination was less about Lynch and Perce and more about the direction of the Republican Party and which vision of democracy would be ascendant. One month before the county convention, William J. Davis, a white internal revenue agent in Natchez, sensed a different "disposition" among local freedmen, a desire to "go it alone," and a surge of activism, the origins of which he could not explain: "For instance, last night a *called* meeting of colored *firemen* was converted into a republican mass meeting. A Grant and Wilson Club formed and *all* officers *colored*." At other county conventions in the district, rural black delegates clashed with white carpetbagger leaders over the nomination. A leading white carpetbagger at the Claiborne County Republican convention pushed for a resolution endorsing Perce for Congress, but black delegates, led by Alcorn University treasurer Samuel J. Ireland and supervisor Thomas Bland, blocked the measure and instead instructed the majority-black delegates to vote their consciences. Jefferson County's five delegates, three of whom were black, received similar instructions, which became a tacit endorsement of Lynch.[36]

Not only were most black Republicans willing to pass on Perce, but quite a few Democrats sided with Lynch over Perce. To be sure, many Democrats hoped to exploit divisions within the Republican Party and believed that blacks were incapable of leading a political organization. "The negroes can not 'run the machine' unaided," maintained Richard E. Conner, a white lawyer who dabbled in Democratic politics. He believed that black control of the Republican Party would hasten the time when "the Carpet bag element shall be exterminated root and branch," for then "Southern whites" would be able to sweep back into power. However, other Democrats favored Lynch over Perce because Lynch at least had family and real estate ties to the district, unlike Perce, who was not a resident of the state or a landowner. In fact, he boarded with another white carpetbagger in Natchez. Thus, the *Natchez Democrat* reasoned, "In our judgment, Lynch understands the needs of our District far better than Perce, and will do all he can to advance them wherever party feeling does not get the best of him."[37]

As rare as it was for a black Republican to receive an endorsement from a white supremacist newspaper, the endorsement that really mattered for Lynch was the support of black delegates from the rural precincts. At the Adams County convention, the outnumbered Perce faction used one parliamentary trick after another to try to block Lynch's nomination. In years past these tactics had kept carpetbaggers in power despite their inferior numbers, but since then Lynch and his black campaign managers—William H. Lynch, William McCary, Robert H. Wood, and Robert W. Fitzhugh—had learned the intricacies of partisan meetings and used their own sophisticated procedural maneuvers to move the nomination along. Sensing defeat, the Perce faction stormed out of the county convention to a serenade of jeers and catcalls from the Lynchites, who then broke out in celebration, as their nominee would soon take a seat in the U.S. House of Representatives—the first African American to do so in Mississippi history.[38]

Freedmen broke "the spell" by elevating one of their own to national office, but not all freedmen favored sending Lynch to Congress. The supposedly "white" Perce faction included eighteen black delegates (including Henry P. Jacobs and George F. Bowles, both officeholders and non-natives) and only six white delegates, while Lynch's "freedmen" included three white men. Additionally, the black Perce delegates differed little from the black delegates in the Lynch faction. Both sets of delegates tended to be relatively young men, ranging in age from twenty to forty, from working-class backgrounds. What distinguished the two factions, however, was residency and leadership. Lynch's support came from the rural districts, while Perce drew support from the city and among northerners, both white and black. Although each faction claimed only a few white delegates, the whites in the Perce faction held the top leadership positions.[39]

But why would local black delegates join a faction led by outsiders? One insight into this political phenomenon comes from Cornelius Henderson, a local freedman who was a landowner and served as a justice of the peace and county supervisor. Henderson defended his support of carpetbaggers by arguing that ideally only "intelligent owners of the real estate of the county" should sit on the board of supervisors and that "the intelligent white Republicans [were] the hope of the party in this State." Perhaps many of Perce's black supporters felt the same way—that white northerners with more political experience and more contacts with national party leaders offered the best chance for Republicans to gain legitimacy in Mississippi. It was a reasonable proposition. Given the newness of the party and the history of elite white domination in the South, siding with more experienced whites might have been the safer move. Here, then, was the central conflict in the Lynch vs. Perce factional struggle: would locals or the most "intelligent" best represent the interests of the community? It was a conflict that was repeated in many factional struggles across the Natchez District and the South.[40]

In 1872 in Adams County, the grassroots vision won out. Lynch's nomination to Congress symbolized the ascendancy of local black power. Although factional conflicts continued to roil local politics, by the mid-1870s county, municipal, and legislative offices reflected the population better than at any time in the region's history, and better than they would for at least another one hundred years.

The Healing Art?

Lynch did not celebrate his historic election to Congress for long. A month before he was seated in the House of Representatives, he wrote to Senator Adelbert Ames recommending appointees for six different government jobs.

The specifics of the appointments—revenue officer, collector of customs for the Pearl River district, lighthouse keeper at Pass Christian, route agent for the New Orleans, Mobile and Texas Railroad, Port Gibson postmaster, and cadets at West Point and the Naval Academy—seem fairly inconsequential, yet Lynch's close attention to them highlights the importance that elected officials attached to the dispersal of government jobs. They did so because patronage acted as an adhesive that held competing factions together, provided jobs and contracts for the party's base, and offered much-needed income for officeholders without an independent means of support. Local politicians used patronage to extend their influence to the grass roots, to reward loyal party agents, and to punish dissenters or bolters.[41]

Because of the intimacy of local political circles, officeholders relied on personal relationships to mediate competing claims to government jobs. Lynch based his recommendations to Senator Ames on his *personal* friend[ship]" with the Massachusetts-born former Union army general. "I am not very sure as to his personal friendship for you," Lynch commented on one candidate, and then he directed attention to another because in him "you have not a stronger friend." Although unstated in the correspondence between officeholders, political friendships were forged through "service to the party and the [presidential] administration under which he serves," Lynch later recalled.[42]

After the 1872 city elections in Natchez, Lynch concluded that the Adams County postmaster, E. J. Castello—a white carpetbagger and failed aspirant for the state senate—was not a friend. He had counted on Castello, whom he called "the key to the situation," to work actively for the mainline Republican ticket. To ensure Castello's support, Lynch made a deal with him. He would nominate him for reappointment as postmaster if Castello would "take an active part in the municipal campaign." Instead, Castello broke with Lynch and endorsed a fusionist ticket headed by a moderate white Republican who had endorsed Perce. Knowing that he had betrayed Lynch, Castello wrote directly to Senator Ames the day after the city election and inquired diplomatically about the procedures to seek renomination as postmaster. Lynch, however, would have none of it. He considered the election a "Democratic victory" and Castello's actions to be "unbecoming to his official position." A number of local Republican leaders, all of whom had endorsed Perce over Lynch in the congressional nomination fight, petitioned Ames to renominate Castello, but the senator deferred to Lynch, who made clear his "opposition to the reappointment of Castello." In his place, Lynch nominated his friend and political ally Robert H. Wood, who had just been defeated in the mayoral race. Wood's nomination and Castello's defeat did little to calm the political turmoil in Adams County, but it did send a strong signal that political betrayal would come at a cost.[43]

Just as one controversial political appointment could exacerbate political factionalism, another could mend internal divisions. At the same time that Lynch was putting forward Wood as the new postmaster, he backed Leroy S. Bronn for collector of internal revenue. Bronn, a white northerner who operated a plantation in Adams County, had joined the conservative National Union Republican Party in 1869. The short-lived party had nominated President Grant's brother-in-law, Louis Dent, as governor in an ill-fated attempt to divide Mississippi's Republican Party. But after Dent and his party were soundly defeated, Bronn enacted a "pretty strong . . . political recovery," in Lynch's estimation. Bronn had participated in mainline Republican conventions since 1871 and became a vigorous campaigner for the local and national party tickets. More important, he aligned with the black-led wing of the party in 1872 when most white carpetbaggers supported one of their own. Bronn's loyalty earned him Lynch's "*hearty* approval" and gave Lynch an opportunity to demonstrate that his faction did not draw the color line.[44]

Even though political leaders wielded patronage jobs to cultivate loyalty and punish dissension, practical considerations often drove appeals for appointments. For some Republicans, patronage served as a safety net to protect personal interests and social status in times of hardship. Merrimon Howard, the black sheriff of Jefferson County, petitioned Governor Ames on behalf of State Senator H. B. McClure, a white Mississippian who had neglected his plantation during the 1873 campaign and subsequently faced a dismal cotton harvest. Out of pity and political loyalty, Howard asked Ames to appoint McClure to "some concretive possition [*sic*]," such as chancellor of the district. Black officeholders could be even more dependent on patronage appointments for the salaries, which provided "decent support," noted the *Natchez Democrat* in an article critical of government salaries.[45]

Unlike the Democratic elite of the Natchez District, Republican leaders were not men of independent wealth. Most white Republicans were transplants, and although many tried their hand at cotton planting, relatively few were successful at it. Without deep roots in the community, most carpetbaggers depended on government jobs for their income and livelihood. Thus, for many lower-level or aspiring politicians, patronage jobs became a matter of survival. It was little wonder then that the quest for appointments often took on the characteristics of a "death struggle," as Senator Ames once described it.[46]

After failing to organize a black land colony, George Hitchen, the secretary of Jacobs, Williams, Wood & Company, tried to obtain a federal appointment in Natchez, but competition for patronage jobs was fierce. Hitchen, who himself was born free in Michigan, denounced white outsiders who were seeking the same appointment. In a letter to Senator Charles Sumner of Massachusetts, Hitchen referred to one carpetbagger as an "enemy at heart" and regarding another claimed there was "no fouler, or fithier [sic] mouthed vilifier and Slanderer than he in the South." Frustrated with his failure to convince local power brokers of his loyalty and competence, Hitchen took these slights personally and accused his rivals of intentionally "depriv[ing] me of the Power to Provide for my family." Using his political connections in Washington, he appealed to Sumner and to Freedmen's Bureau commissioner O. O. Howard for jobs. But no amount of flattery or shameless self-promotion could erase the fact that Hitchen had no support where it counted—in local political circles.[47]

George Hitchen's quest for office was only one example of the bitter struggle for patronage jobs that consumed and exasperated political leaders. Although he resisted the undertow at first, Senator Adelbert Ames was pulled into the factional conflict in Natchez and its patronage wars. "I find that Natchez is the worst political hole I ever fell into," Ames confessed to his wife in 1873. "There you have politics, pure and unadulterated by any foreign substance like patriotism or party interests." Natchez's disproportionate share of federal jobs (in relation to the entire Natchez District) attracted a slew of desperate men. Ames tried to rectify the conflict by using "my healing art—patronage—to effect a cure" but found that "the disaffected ones" perpetuated the factionalism in the hopes that more jobs would come their way.[48]

While patronage failed to solve the problem of factionalism, it was instrumental in cultivating grassroots political networks. Mayor Robert H. Wood, for example, doubled the size of Natchez's police force, swelling it to at least eighteen, mostly black, officers. The composition of the police force gave local freedpeople better assurance that they would be dealt with fairly, but Mayor Wood and other Republicans also used policemen to advance their political power. George Morris, the sergeant of the police, was a well-connected political figure: an officer in a Republican club, a delegate to at least two party conventions, and a charter member in a black fire company. Morris's second-in-command, Cpl. Louis J. Winston, was similarly well connected. He was a member of the "Governing Six" who wrested control of the Republican nomination process from the hands of white outsiders. Under Morris and Winston's leadership, Natchez policemen canvassed city neighborhoods for the Republican Party, activities that Democrats and moderate Republicans considered attempts to "bully-rag people." Sheriff William McCary also used his discretionary power to assist members of the black community, including many city police officers. In the summer of 1872, McCary (another member of the "Governing Six") hired twenty bailiffs to help administer the current term of the circuit court in Adams County, all of whom were black and publicly identified as Republicans. As the Jefferson County court made use of only three bailiffs, McCary seemed more interested in advancing the interests of the local Republican Party than in an orderly court.[49]

Bolters and Modocs

While officeholders dispensed patronage jobs to important party leaders as well as to lower-level party agents to reward supporters and to punish detractors, there never were enough government positions to heal the factional conflicts. Moreover, inattention to neighborhood concerns could lead quickly to internal division, resulting in a significant fusionist or bolting challenge to the party hierarchy. The fluid structure of the local Republican Party meant that freedmen-led governments were as vulnerable to insurgent challenges as carpetbagger-led factions.

In Tensas Parish a coalition of white northerners and native-born blacks controlled the local Republican Party during the Reconstruction years, yet a fusionist party of white and black moderates, who aligned with the Democratic Party, decided in 1872 to challenge the parish government. The splintering of parties was in the air. A few months before the fusionists challenged mainline Republicans in Tensas, liberal Republicans had split off from the national party and fused with the national Democratic Party in the 1872 election. Tensas Parish fusionists were led by E. W. Robinson, a black northerner and teacher. They offered a full slate of candidates, but it differed little from the mainline Republican ticket. Both parties put forward black candidates for lesser positions such as justice of the peace and constable, and both parties advanced a mix of black and white candidates for parish offices, often with blacks opposing blacks and whites opposing whites for the same positions. The similarities between the two parties threatened the mainline Republicans' hold on power and prompted them to castigate Robinson and his faction. At the parish convention they passed three resolutions "denounc[ing] the actions of one E. W. Robinson" for the "insult" of forming a competing ticket.[50]

Robinson had moved from Ohio to Louisiana in 1871 to work as a teacher for the children of black farm laborers. Freeborn and educated, he stood out among most Tensas Parish residents, who were nearly all former slaves and farmers by occupation. Not long after arriving, Robinson became involved in partisan politics. He aligned himself with fusionists by joining a senatorial convention of Republican dissenters and entered into a land deal with other leaders of the faction. Republicans attacked him not just for opposing the ticket but also for his outsider status. One resolution at the parish convention claimed that Robinson "force[d] upon our people a ticket composed entirely of strangers and Democrats," which imperiled "our united voices at the ballot box." Outsiders like Robinson faced considerable scrutiny from locals because they had, at best, shallow family and financial roots in the community. The existing white Republican leaders, although northern born like Robinson, by contrast, could claim stronger community connections because they had settled in Tensas in the late 1860s and had purchased vast landholdings. Nonetheless, Robinson had attracted a considerable grassroots following in the town of Waterproof that parish leaders could not ignore.[51]

Robinson's fusionist party divided the newly empowered community of freedpeople and potentially opened the door to white supremacist Democrats, so Tensas Parish Republican leaders addressed the factional threat by absorbing the fusionists into their party after the election. Robinson was given three patronage appointments—deputy sheriff, inspector of weights and measures, and parish school board member—as well as membership on the parish Republican executive committee. By showering Robinson with offices, Republican leaders implicitly acknowledged a serious division among their constituents and hoped that a more inclusive community (with Robinson and his supporters) would enable them to remain in power.[52]

Black dissenters from the Republican Party walked a fine line between criticism and open rebellion. For a few black politicians, moderate politics and support of white Republican leaders led to their ejection from the party. In Claiborne County Matthew T. Newsome—an ex-slave, AME minister, delegate to the 1868 constitutional convention, and state legislator—was "kicked out of the Republican party," presumably for his involvement in a factional dispute. Suspected of aligning with the Democrats, Newsome vigorously defended himself before Senator Ames—the head of the Mississippi Republican Party—hoping to salvage his political career. The appeal, however, failed to arrest his marginalization, and Newsome never again held public office. In a similar vein, Cornelius Henderson never recovered from his perceived association with Democrats. In the early years of Reconstruction, Henderson seemed to be a rising black leader, holding positions as superintendent of the poor, county supervisor, election judge, and justice of the peace. His tenure as justice of the peace, however, rankled "the colored people" in his district, who criticized Henderson for "having sold out to the Democrats, as only a tool of the whites, and as bad a Democrat as any of them." Additionally, some Republicans denounced him for supporting James Alcorn over Ames for the Mississippi Republican governorship. Henderson never held public office again after his public dissent from the party line.[53]

But in their punishment of political dissenters, majority factions had to be careful not to provoke a larger revolt. After a string of nomination victories and after they had taken the reins of municipal and county government, the triumphant radicals of the Lynch faction pushed many of the carpetbaggers out of appointive offices. Stewing over their partisan defeat and the loss of high-salaried positions, the northern-born moderates turned to the Democrats to form a fusionist ticket in Natchez. The origins of the fusionist insurgency dated back to the winter of 1872, only one month after Lynch was elected to Congress, when city Republicans met to nominate candidates for municipal offices. The dynamics of city elections were quite different from those in the rest of the district. Black and white voters were near parity in Natchez, which meant that a mobilized white Democratic vote could come close to winning the election, especially if the Democrats were able to peel off a few Republican voters.

Henry C. Griffin, a white Mississippian, former city clerk, and county school director, led the Republican opposition to Mayor Robert H. Wood's administration. Frustrated with what they perceived to be the financial mismanagement of the city, Griffin and his supporters tried to deny Wood's renomination through the city Republican executive committee, where they held seven of the fourteen seats. But when they failed, the Griffin men turned to the Democratic Party. Local Democratic leaders did not relish the prospect of joining the Griffin-led wing, or the "rascals," as Democratic leader William T. Martin put it; however, they knew that their best "chances of success" lay with the bolters. According to this fusion arrangement, Griffin, a Republican, headed the ticket as the mayoral nominee along with three white Democratic aldermen and one black Republican. Shorn of the carpetbag faction, mainline Republicans nominated Wood and four Republican aldermen, one of whom was white. But with the united support of the Democratic Party and a sizeable faction of Republicans, Griffin unseated Wood as mayor by 187 votes. The fusionist victory ousted the radicals from city government and ushered in a new era of biracial and bipartisan governance that lasted for nearly two decades.[54]

Their triumph over the mainline, black-led Republican Party was not the result of a few white carpetbaggers casting different ballots; rather, the mayoral election of 1872 demonstrated the difficulties of grassroots mobilization. Nearly one-third of the city's Republican vote, according to Lynch, went with the fusionists, suggesting that they had significant black support. Although Republicans continued to hold the mayor's office and a majority on the board of aldermen, the radical faction would never again control city government.[55]

Emboldened by the fusionist victory in the city elections, the carpetbagger-led moderates renewed the factional struggle at the 1873 Adams County Republican convention. The dispute had become so bitter that the Griffin men were now called "Modocs," while Lynch's supporters were referred to as the "Warm Springs Indians." The Modoc Indians of the Pacific Northwest had developed a reputation for treachery when, after a series of battles against the U.S. Army, they offered a false flag of truce and then murdered U.S. officials at a peace conference. Because Modocs had become associated with betrayal in the public mind, the name was a fitting description for the fusionist Republicans in Natchez, at least according to Senator Ames, who described them thusly: "I have from the first looked upon the 'Modocs' as Modocs. They are 'Bolters' naturally, seeking to destroy what they cannot control." Because the Warm Springs Indi-

ans remained loyal to the U.S. government and helped to hunt down the ren-
egade Modocs, this moniker was applied to the Lynch faction for their loyalty to
the mainline Republican Party and their vigorous opposition to the fusionists.[56]

The "Modocs" and "Warm Springers" faced off over the office of sheriff in a
repeat of the 1871 nomination battle. As before, the moderates nominated William Noonan, a white carpetbagger, alderman, and former sheriff (1869–71),
while the radicals put forward the current sheriff, William McCary, a freeborn
Natchez resident. With some hyperbole, the *Natchez Democrat* described the
bitter scene on the convention floor as Republicans vented their frustrations at
nearly four years of internal party divisions: "preacher delegates damned each
other furiously. . . . Parson Smith and [Woodson V.] Howard had called each
other things not fit for ears polite, and Noonan and [Louis J.] Winston had come
together in almost dangerous array, and Wm. Lynch had made as much racket
as usual and been balled to order eleven hundred times or more, and [J. S.]
Montgomery had most indignantly and vociferously repelled the intimation
that he was in the interest of Democrats."[57]

As delegates exchanged disparaging remarks, local residents added their
voice to the cacophony, yelling from the spectator's seats, "'[P]ut him out,' . . .
and crying out 'no' and 'aye' upon questions put" to the floor. When the convention hall was finally quieted, Lynch's Warm Springers, who controlled the
major committees, ruled that the delegates would vote "*viva voce*" for sheriff,
treasurer, and assessor and cast ballots for the rest of the nominees. Warned
that the Modocs had bribed some of the "country delegates" to vote against the
wishes of their rural constituents, Warm Springs leaders pushed for an open
and public vote. Wary of publicly backing the Modocs, the rural black delegates
voted for McCary and other radicals. The victorious Warm Springers captured
each of the major county offices and celebrated their triumph by marching to a
black-owned saloon, "carrying McCary there in a chair," to the festive sounds
of an accompanying band. Less celebratory were the Modocs, whom the local
newspaper concluded were either "politically killed" or "seriously wounded"
in the fallout from the convention. Never again would the moderate Modoc
faction seriously challenge the Republican Party for control of county offices.[58]

The Warm Springers' victory over the Modocs at the 1873 Republican convention effectively put an end to the Republican factional conflicts in Adams
County. The Modocs retained control of city government the following year,
despite efforts by John R. Lynch, Robert W. Fitzhugh, and Robert H. Wood
to find an alternative to the Griffin machine. Their efforts were stifled further
by significant support for Mayor Griffin from the city's blacks. A few months
before the 1874 elections, black militias "on drill or parade" stopped in front of
city hall and "gave three cheers for 'H. C. Griffin, the next Mayor,'" and later a
"caucus" of "sixty-five leading colored men of Natchez" unofficially endorsed

Griffin. But the extent of Modoc power stretched only to the mayor's office and a couple of seats on the board of aldermen; county offices and the congressional seat, retained by Lynch, remained firmly in the radicals' hands.[59]

The 1876 county convention was anticlimactic. Lynch was renominated without any opposition or dissent. Indicative of the settled state of affairs in local Republican politics, rural black supporters were not called on for assistance at the convention. "Scarcely a colored man from the country laid down his hoe," the local paper remarked with chagrin, "or deserted his plow, to swell the crowd of listeners to [hear Lynch's] speech." The diminished black presence at campaign events did not signify a lack of support for the Republican Party, but rather marked the settling of political affairs in Adams County.[60]

Factional conflicts bubbled up across the Natchez District, but only in Natchez were fusionists able to oust the mainline Republican faction. From the most rural and black parishes (Concordia and Tensas) to the most urban and white county (Adams), local political leaders faced continual challenges from within. Even at the high-water mark of Radical Reconstruction, Republican leaders could not rest on their laurels. The nature of a grassroots democracy encouraged dissent, debate, and dialogue, which often bubbled up into formal challenges to the ruling party.[61]

"True to One Another"

In a widely circulated speech in 1871, State Senator Jeremiah M. P. Williams addressed the conflicting themes of factionalism, democracy, and black office holding. He warned of the growing power of the southern Democratic Party and implored his fellow citizens in Natchez to remain "true to one another." His admonition acknowledged the persistent fissures among Republicans and called for a renewed effort to remember the collective bonds that underlay their political power. "We are hated" and "we are outraged and massacred," Williams proclaimed, because "we are black and freedmen" who demand "liberty, the right to vote, to sit on juries, to hold office, and to enjoy the privileges of free education." Although he left the door open to whites by emphasizing "equal rights," the state senator did not envision a color-blind party: "We, the colored people, should not divide or separate politically as long as there is any way proscribed as a race."[62]

The great work that local freedpeople confronted was not just the assurance of their individual rights, but their duty to help protect their brothers and sisters across the South. As black people were being "driven from their homes, insulted, beaten, murdered," they were "seeking refuge in our State," Williams explained. Mississippi would remain "a stronghold" only as long as freedpeople "organize[d] throughout your County," met together "at our firesides," and kept the "churches open." Williams recognized that the essential task of grassroots politics was to create an ethic of mutual obligation that grew out of families and neighborhoods. When "foreign foes or traitorous hands attempt to rob us of our national inheritance," he concluded, "let our hearts and minds be as one; let all Republicans leap from their rests at home to guard the temple of our liberties."[63]

To remain "as one" was one of the more difficult challenges during Reconstruction. An assortment of groups—freedmen and carpetbaggers, blacks and whites, rural residents and city people, radicals and moderates—participated in this unprecedented experiment in postslave democracy. By allowing more voices into the political process, the structure of local Republican parties ensured that remaining united would be all but impossible, but the conflicts also indicate that a grassroots democracy had come into being. Freedmen learned the skills of partisan infighting, found alternative sources for officeholder bonds, developed their own political networks, and then filled local and state offices with local leaders from the community. They battled not only with white supremacist Democrats but also with other Republicans who favored a political hierarchy in which offices were filled by the most qualified or most experienced candidates. At issue, then, in the struggle to win public office was not merely who would wield power but, more importantly, which vision of democracy would be ascendant.

SIX

A Deep Interest in Politics

On Election Day in 1880, Harry "Foote" Smith Jr., a fifty-four-year-old black farmer, took his position at the polling place in Kingston Precinct in rural Adams County, just as he had done in every election "for the last ten years." "I had no official position," he explained to a congressional committee investigating a disputed election. Rather, his job was to distribute Republican ballots to the voters in his neighborhood. He had lived near the town of Kingston for most of his life and had gained the respect of his neighbors in political matters by helping those who were illiterate to verify a legitimate Republican ticket. He was probably born into slavery and worked the same cotton fields sixteen miles outside of Natchez that he had worked before the Civil War. He did not own the land that he farmed but likely contracted with a white landowner for shares of the crop. Little distinguished Harry Smith from his immediate neighbors, except his fervent devotion to the Republican Party. In every election he stood near the polling place, passing out ballots and imploring his friends and neighbors to vote a straight Republican ticket. Harry Smith was one of thousands of ordinary men in the Natchez District who performed similarly unheralded functions for the party and for democracy. Most of these party agents never held office or benefited financially from their partisan labors, but they did express an intense interest in politics, one that has not always been easy to discern.[1]

A few years before Harry Smith testified about his electoral work, another election showcased fervent participation at the grass roots. During the 1876 election in Concordia Parish, groups of black women approached black men waiting in line to vote. The activist women cursed those who were holding fusionist tickets and then forcibly removed the offending ballots and replaced them with mainline Republican tickets. "They said these red tickets [the fusionist ones] were democratic tickets," testified a black cook, "and not to vote them at all; and they jerked the tickets out of the men's hands, and the women would not allow them to vote them at all." Another witness, after describing the intimidation and violence that characterized this contentious election, summed up the events this way: "The women at that poll acted very bad." They were "bad," according to this black election commissioner, not because they had entered the exclusive masculine space of the polling place but because of their particular behavior toward male voters.[2]

Neither the black men nor the black women in Concordia Parish seemed troubled by the female presence at the polls, even though it was unheard of for white women to be there. On occasion, middle-class and elite white women attended political rallies and parades in the mid-nineteenth century, but there is no evidence that party agents addressed them or sought their assistance in electoral mobilization. The working-class black women of Concordia Parish, by contrast, acted as partisans. They drew criticism from their political opponents not for their feminine presence at the polls but because they had disrupted the male prerogative of voting, by "snatch[ing]" tickets out of men's hands. The Concordia Parish election of 1876 raises all sorts of questions about partisanship, gender, and voting, yet one of the commonalities between this episode and the one described by Harry Smith is the intense zeal that many ordinary people devoted to party politics. It is an enthusiasm that has confounded historians.[3]

The reasons for broad political participation in the nineteenth century remain something of a mystery. A scholar recently admitted as much, acknowledging that "we know very little about how or why ordinary men participated in elections." Political historians have focused on the so-called golden age of nineteenth-century democracy—a time of widespread political spectacles and high voter turnouts for white men—to uncover the origins of mass participation. Some describe the era as a period of exceptional interest in party politics, while others question the everyday importance of politics, suggesting that ordinary voters cared more about festivals and frivolity than the candidates, parties, or issues. No matter the perspective, historians of mid-nineteenth-century partisanship have too often focused on individual male voters and neglected the family pressures and communal influences that influenced partisan preferences. Additionally, these scholars have often avoided the political history of African Americans in the Reconstruction era. The anomalies of southern Republicanism after 1868 and the widespread electoral violence that accompanied black male enfranchisement make it difficult to generalize about national patterns. But looked at another way, these irregularities reveal hidden aspects of the practice of everyday politics that help us to better account for the participation of ordinary people in electoral campaigns.[4]

Freedpeople in the Natchez District were highly engaged in electoral politics, and the vast majority identified with and supported the Republican Party. But not all did. A small number of black men joined the Democratic Party, an action that, more often than not, enraged black Republicans. Most historians make only a passing reference to black Democrats, considering them to be either political deviants or pseudoslaves. Despite their small numbers, these Democrats help to bring into sharp relief the boundaries of partisanship and they reveal the choice that freedmen faced at the ballot box. Black Democrats made a calculation that the Democratic community—based on a protective relationship between powerful whites and subordinate blacks—offered a better alternative than the egalitarian-minded Republican community. While this choice might seem odd for freedpeople during Reconstruction, it was not so unusual in the annals of postemancipation societies. A patron-client relationship often followed the master-slave relationship in many Latin American societies. And in the United States, black Democrats were part of a larger continuum of patron-client relations that preceded emancipation and persisted beyond Reconstruction.[5]

As black Republicans and Democrats faced off in political campaigns, social pressure and neighborhood affiliation often determined the outcome of local elections. The centrality of black Democrats and female party agents in certain elections highlights the boundaries of inclusion and exclusion that shaped partisan communities after emancipation. Because casting a ballot was a public act that was scrutinized by community members, voters made their choices in the context of communal pressure. And this pressure from voters, officeholders, and nonvoters helped to fuel the passion and intensity that made Reconstruction-era elections distinctive. Furthermore, by conceptualizing partisan alignment and participation as a competitive public arena in which individuals faced clear choices, this analysis allows for the integration of dissenters and political nonconformists into the overall framework of black politics. In this way we can better understand black male Democrats and black female Republicans as integral to Reconstruction history, rather than an as aberrations that merit brief mention. And we can better understand the vast majority of freedmen, who consistently voted for Republican candidates.

Clubs and Republican Allegiance

At the nexus of parties, politicians, and ordinary people were the numerous neighborhood political clubs that gave the local Republican Party in the Natchez District surprising depth and breadth. Political clubs inherited the organizational framework that the Union Leagues had developed in the late 1860s. But the neighborhood political clubs were different from the Union Leagues in important ways. The Union League relied on outsiders (often white northerners) to instruct freedmen in the political process, whereas clubs were distinctly the creation of local people and neighborhood leaders. Clubs offered a space for neighbors to discuss political issues, organize for partisan events, and select nominees and delegates for party conventions. Yet they also provided an opportunity for ordinary people to feel their latent power. The close physical proximity of club meetings engendered a sense of solidarity. Political clubs, then, were a vital link between leaders and the grass roots in mobilization campaigns and perhaps the space where male voters had their most direct encounter with political ideas and regional issues. It is a bit surprising, then, that historians have paid little attention to partisan clubs during Reconstruction.[6]

In urban environs, clubs were organized by wards, while in the countryside plantation-based clubs were the norm. They met once or twice a month and always before an election. The Republican Party depended on local clubs to elect delegates for party conventions and to advance nominees for public office. Each club was also expected to turn out voters. In their connection to the grass roots and in their ubiquity across the Natchez District, clubs were the foundation of the Republican insurgency that took power and remade the postwar South.[7]

Clubs did not, however, operate independently; instead they were linked to existing social organizations, such as churches, militias, and fire companies. Church leaders often held partisan leadership posts. Alfred Fairfax, a Baptist preacher, was president of a Republican club in Tensas Parish, while Burl Fisher, the secretary for the Pine Street Baptist Church in Natchez, was the vice president of the Robert H. Wood Republican Club. On the grounds of the Pine Ridge Church in Adams County, the French Guards, a black militia named in honor of O. C. French, a white Republican state legislator from Adams County, drilled and paraded. Col. George F. Bowles of the Sixth Militia District, a local Republican activist and perennial officeholder, led a well-armed black militia that frequently drilled in the streets of Natchez in the mid-1870s.[8]

Black fire companies, for their part, appeared to operate as a parallel Republican organization. The top black Republicans in Natchez, men such as William McCary, Robert W. Fitzhugh, William H. Lynch, and Robert H. Wood, were members of the Good Will Fire Company. Of the eleven identifiable officers of the Robert H. Wood Republican Club, more than half were also black firemen. The Deluge No. 1 Fire Company tended to attract more moderate black leaders. Nevertheless, both fire clubs show how associational membership worked hand in hand with electoral mobilization. Together in 1872, the Good Will and Deluge Fire Companies hosted a "grand pic-nic" in Natchez to celebrate Independence Day. The event included a reading of the Declaration of Independence by William McCary, who was simultaneously the Good Will president, the sheriff of Adams County, and the leader of a political club named after him.[9]

In addition to their public performances, clubs and other affiliated partisan organizations subjected policy platforms and potential nominees to intense scrutiny in neighborhood meetings. In one Natchez club meeting, state legislator O. C. French (a white outsider) spoke to city residents, "mostly Republicans," about the elimination of a ferry franchise. French had been attacked in the local press for his complicity in the incident, and he admitted to the assembled club members that "his actions" were "governed more by party motives . . . than a due regard for his constituents." After a few other speeches on the matter from elected officials, Jeremiah M. P. Williams (a Baptist minister and aspiring officeholder) introduced a resolution supporting French and affirming citizen support for "our representatives in the State Legislature." But the club rebelled. They voted down the resolution "with a tremendous outburst of opposition," suggesting that a lucrative franchise for party leaders was less important than a regular transportation link across the Mississippi River.[10]

Local citizens could also voice their displeasure with or their support for public policy at party conventions. Typically, political clubs selected delegates to attend conventions, either directly forwarding representatives or electing delegates to represent a local precinct. The rural nature of the Natchez District combined with the reliance on clubs as the chief political unit meant that the voices of the working class were well represented at party conventions. Farmers or farm laborers made up seven out of ten identifiable delegates at the 1872 and 1873 Tensas Parish Republican conventions. In Concordia Parish, laborers and farmers dominated the ranks of the central partisan organizing body, the Republican parish executive committee, in 1877. The grassroots structure and working-class orientation of Republican Party operations led white Democrats to complain about "colored laborers" who were more interested in "politics and militia business" than their crops.[11]

Party leaders relied on neighborhood clubs not just to fill conventions but also to spread word of upcoming gatherings and events. One Republican newspaper referred to the effort as "laying their wires" and predicted that a "war whoop will soon be sounded" for the campaign ahead. Only "Republican clubs and societies" were aware of an impending meeting at the Natchez courthouse in 1869, but party leaders opened up the proceedings to all residents by ringing the courthouse bell, hoping to attract a wide audience to their message of mutual respect "without distinction of race, color, politics or previous condition." "Bell ringing" and "drum-beating" signaled the beginning of another "Radical meeting" in 1872, which was followed by a "Torch-Light Procession" through Natchez. Party leaders also used flagpoles, decorated with flags and "streamers," to announce partisan gatherings and publicize the party's candidates. When raised, the poles towered over the landscape as a symbolic partisan claim to the territory, and for this reason pole raisings often engendered vigorous confrontations. When Concordia Parish Republicans learned that fusionist party leaders planned to raise a flagpole at the Vidalia courthouse immediately before a

Republican mass meeting, David Young, the parish Republican leader, publicly threatened to throw them "and the flag into the river."[12]

Large gatherings, such as barbecues, processions, and mass meetings, became a staple of partisan organizing because they offered new and unique spaces for freedpeople to rub shoulders with similarly minded people and thereby fostered a sense of partisan identity. These were festive occasions, designed to attract families and households, not just voters, because Republicans recognized that social connections formed the backbone of partisan solidarity. Abundant food and drink, recalled a white Wilkinson County resident, brought "colored laborers together to hear the speakers" at a political rally. Freedpeople expected "plenty of whiskey and as much, as they can get, to eat" at political barbecues, noted a scornful white overseer from a Concordia Parish plantation.[13]

The larger barbecues attracted thousands of people, such as a large gathering in Woodville in 1869. Over four thousand freedpeople, including "a large number of women and children" from Wilkinson and Amite Counties gathered for a procession and meeting, forming one of the largest crowds ever assembled in the town. At noon a parade marched and countermarched through the streets before settling on the grounds of the AME Church for a barbecue. After a few speeches, the "hungry sovereigns" dined on "immense quantities of nicely barbecued beef, mutton and pig," reported the local paper; then they resumed their procession, settled in at the courthouse square, and listened to a few more speeches, at which point the assembly retired to prepare for the evening festivities. Outfitted with "banners, transparencies and torches," the freedpeople marched through the darkened town for the third time that day, stopping at certain points to hear more speeches from local Republican leaders, and finally adjourned "at a late hour."[14]

Parades and mass meetings were integral components of nineteenth-century partisanship because they offered freedpeople a collective experience in which they could feel secure in a shared cause. In addition, they allowed ordinary citizens to encounter their political leaders in intimate settings designed to facilitate interactions between the crowd and the speaker. At another Woodville mass meeting, a black speaker spoke for an hour and a half to a rapt audience of freedpeople, "calling cheer upon cheer from his auditors." All told, local freedpeople listened to at least seven hours of political oratory that day. Summing up another long day of political festivities, the *Woodville Republican* concluded that "all went home feeling that old Wilkinson was safe." Beyond the benefits that such events held for internal mobilization, they sent unmistakable signals to Democrats about the strength and solidarity of black Republicanism.[15]

In addition to barbeques and parades, celebrated politicians helped to attract large crowds at partisan events. In 1872 Lieutenant Governor P. B. S. Pinchback,

Louisiana's highest-ranking black officeholder, spoke to a sizeable gathering in Tensas Parish. "We think there never has been so large an audience composed of both white and black citizens, in our town," noted the *North Louisiana Journal*; "the Republican clubs turned out *en masse* with banners and music." Pinchback's speech was part of a regional campaign swing through the Natchez District. He also spoke at the Black Hawk plantation in Concordia Parish, at a Vidalia "grand barbecue," and at a mass meeting in Natchez. Pinchback encouraged his audience of black laborers and farmers to be subversive when they faced reprisals for voting Republican. He told them "to lie and practice any kind of deception" when their employers inquired about their voting selection.[16]

Democrats were not oblivious to the political advantages of mass meetings. They too used large gatherings to attract black support, but these assemblies also reveal the limits of festivals and frivolity in generating partisan support. In 1876 rural Democratic clubs hosted a "Rally" and "Grand Barbecue" in the Kingston neighborhood, sixteen miles outside of Natchez, and invited "all voters, Democratic and Republican, white and colored" from the surrounding counties to attend. Even so, black turnout was disappointing. "Herculean efforts were made to enlist the negroes on the Democratic side," lamented a white Jefferson County resident; "uniforms were given them, they marched with the white men, were invited to rousing, [*sic*] barbeques with bountiful dinners," yet only "some responded." Despite the attraction of a community feast, a parade, and prominent speakers, most local black people were ill inclined to attend a Democratic gathering. Fancy uniforms and barbecued meat could not overcome the white supremacist ideology that lay at the heart of the Democratic Party.[17]

While Democratic values limited black participation, Republicans' egalitarian-based ideology enhanced turnout at party events. It was not a coincidence that contemporary observers referred to participants at mass meetings in gender-neutral terms or specifically mentioned women's presence. In Woodville "it was not uncommon," recalled one white observer, "to see a thousand negroes on foot and horseback, marching around the public square." In Concordia Parish during the 1876 campaign, Republican candidates and party activists attended mass meetings at eleven different plantations, in addition to frequent gatherings at Vidalia, the parish seat. Almost all of the meetings were held at night, and they ranged from small, secretive gatherings to large meetings of nearly "five hundred men, women, and children," testified a black Republican election commissioner. Although male voters were the primary concern, speakers made a special point to address the women in the audience. In other instances, Republican leaders called on the people, including women and children, to vote as a community. To shame one black Republican who had joined a fusion ticket, State Senator David Young shouted out to his audience, "Now I want a vote from you on the grounds; all of you not in favor of the Jackson ticket give me the signal by raising up [your] hands." All the men, women, and children raised their hands, all except the lone fusionist dissenter.[18]

While Democratic Party gatherings attracted little interest, a bipartisan meeting, often in the form of a joint debate, drew in large numbers of voters and their families. Sometimes the presence of Democrats and Republicans onstage was more complementary than confrontational. At an 1870 barbecue in the Pine Ridge neighborhood of Adams County, Democrat William T. Martin spoke to two thousand county residents about the importance of a local railroad, while freshman state legislator John R. Lynch discussed militias, schools, and the benefits of Radical Republicanism. The all-day event, hosted by a black militia, began with "hacks, buggies, [and] horses" crowding the road from Natchez early in the morning and continued "till a late hour." Following the speeches, "the assembly" gathered at "a very long table . . . covered with several hundred plates" to feast on barbecued meat and other "delicacies." More typical was a Woodville mass meeting in 1869 in which two Republican politicians debated two conservative speakers for three and a half hours. The white Democratic politicians relished the opportunity to speak to a large black audience, but it was a nearly impossible task to reach out to freedpeople while remaining true to the party's ideological assumptions. The local newspaper described the problem that one of the speakers faced: "His speech was addressed to the colored people who were present in large numbers, but with very little effect. The whites present did not like it[;] in fact it was not addressed to them and the colored men present were well enough informed to see through the shallow pretense."[19]

A more fruitful approach to gaining partisan support was through face-to-face politicking, particularly in contentious local elections. But here again, Republican leaders had mastered this strategy and used it to complement their large rallies. In fact, local people expected personal interaction with political candidates. In the lead-up to a crucial railroad vote, Natchez and Fayette politicians went among "small groups of men" discussing the bond measure in the streets of Rodney. Although the officeholders later gave prepared speeches, at least one local observer credited the personal politicking with swaying a significant portion of black voters and called for more of the same. He specifically mentioned that State Senator Jeremiah M. P. Williams, State Representative H. P. Jacobs, "or other intelligent colored Republicans . . . [should] go to the people's houses and talk to them quietly."[20]

Republican success in the Natchez District owed much to the associational web of clubs, social organizations, and political events that brought locals into contact with other like-minded residents. Republican leaders articulated a political vision of egalitarianism, mutual support, and broad participation. And they put those values into practice by organizing local neighborhoods, by reaching out to various constituencies, and by creating events that fostered a sense of participation and enthusiasm. From these hubs of a regional political network, party agents launched their widely successful electoral campaigns.

Black Democrats and Dissent

In the new political world created by universal manhood suffrage, the Democratic Party in the Natchez District faced a nearly impossible task. They needed to reach out to black voters while maintaining a commitment to white supremacy. With so few whites living in the district, Democrats could not hope to win political office without a sizeable number of black votes. The party tried to solve this dilemma by emphasizing patron-client relationships in which black supporters could expect communal protection in return for political deference. It was an alternative to Republicans' egalitarian vision, yet both visions were based in a collectivist politics. Although couching its appeals in the political language of "friendship" and offering freedpeople powerful allies in the white elite, the Democratic Party attracted only a small following among freedpeople. Most former slaves were not tempted by the Democratic Party, but as Reconstruction progressed Democrats expanded their message beyond merely renewing perceived paternalistic ties.

A few black people were drawn to the Democratic Party's promise to bridge the growing postemancipation racial divide. This appeal gained added force in 1872 with the presidential campaign of Horace Greeley. Nominated by liberal Republicans and the Democratic Party, Greeley hoped to attract black votes because of his longtime opposition to slavery and his endorsement of equal rights. Locally, Democrats organized Greeley clubs across the Natchez District, with some electing black officers and others organized exclusively by race. In the city of Natchez, Robinson Crusoe, a thirty-seven-year-old farmer and the second vice president of a Greeley club, declared in the local paper that, as a "colored man," he was voting for Greeley because the New York newspaper editor was a "life-long friend" of black people and because "my old white friends" were willing to endorse Greeley, which "is the best proof that . . . they want to see *our* rights upheld."[21]

In a letter to "My Respected Colored Fellow-citizens," Willis Douglass, a sixty-seven-year-old laborer and vice president of a Greeley club, argued that the Democratic candidate would help avoid the "agitation and strife between the races" that had characterized the previous four years of Republican rule. For Douglass, what mattered in choosing a partisan affiliation was not the policies or platforms but personal interactions. He had been a slave but was fortunate enough to have lived with a "kind and affectionate master" who emancipated him and "all my children." The benevolence of his master taught Douglass that "if the colored man ever needs a friend or helper, he will . . . find him in the Southern white man." He mentioned specifically two embodiments of this patron-client ideal: William T. Martin and William F. Mellen. Both Martin and Mellen were former slaveholders, active Democrats, and practicing attorneys, and both seemed to have meaningful friendships with local black men, including Republicans. In his will, Nelson Fitzhugh, the grocer and AME Church trustee, designated Mellen, whom he called a "friend," as the executor of his estate. On his deathbed, Anthony Hoggatt, a Republican officeholder, signed his will in the presence of Martin, who, at Hoggatt's request, guided his hand in signing the document.[22]

Willis Douglass was only the most articulate of the small but significant group of black men who identified with the Democratic Party out of friendship and loyalty to ex-slaveholders. William Scott, a thirty-eight-year-old black laborer on the Helena plantation in 1876, admitted that he voted Republican during the early Reconstruction-era elections, but he was later drawn to the Democrats when, he explained, "one of my old master's sons with whom I was raised" formed a political club on his plantation. Similarly, Joseph Habbard, a fifty-three-year-old black farmer, switched to the Democrats when "a friend of mine," a white man, became a candidate on a Democratic ticket.[23]

As these testimonies indicate, close relationships across the racial divide on occasion transcended partisan identities. But friendship did not often equate with partisan affiliation because Democrats' vision of racial harmony was predicated on the notion that blacks should be subordinate to whites. Black Democrats formed their own clubs, but most were segregated, unlike the cross-racial Union Leagues and Republican clubs. And while Democrats placed a few freedmen on ballots, there is no indication that black men had a voice in the party or influence in the selection of candidates. On the contrary, the placement of black candidates on Democratic ballots suggested a cynical strategy to split the Republican vote, since they almost always ran against black Republicans. When whites in Wilkinson County praised a conservative black candidate by noting that he "will be guided by the wishes of the white people in whom he confides," they confirmed the belief of most local freedpeople, who interpreted these black candidates as mere "tools" of Democrats who had given up their "independence to think and act" for themselves.[24]

Beyond particular friendships, little seemed to distinguish a black Democrat from a black Republican. Rural black Democrats labored in the fields much like their Republican counterparts, with no discernible difference in landownership. Black democratic leaders tended to be more economically independent yet also dependent on white patronage. Some were skilled artisans, such as carpenters, blacksmiths, and undertakers. One striking difference, at least in Natchez, was that black Democratic leaders tended to be quite a bit older than black Republican activists. Nearly half of those who can be identified in the census records were fifty years of age or older in 1870. Perhaps, like Willis Douglass, they looked back fondly on an earlier era when public strife was muted. These men had, after all, successfully negotiated patron-client relationships with whites before the war, but now those relationships were imperiled by the revolutionary implications of democracy.[25]

Another issue that attracted black men to the Democrats was the lack of material gains during Reconstruction. William Carraway, an elderly black resident of Natchez, switched to the Democrats in 1872 because he found that Republicans had done little to "improve the condition of my colored fellow-citizens." He lamented the low "wages" paid to black farm laborers, which he believed resulted from high taxes on the landowning class. By dividing the "common interest between the laborer and the land-owner," Republicans, he argued, had fostered "strife between the colored and the white men."[26]

In Concordia Parish during the 1876 election, Democrats appealed to black farmers who had grown frustrated with persistent poverty and its effects on the parish community. "They believed," claimed a white overseer and Democratic organizer, "that a change would be the beginning of our prosperity." One disillusioned black farmer switched sides because the black Democratic leader "was a business man." Another became disillusioned with the Republican Party after he lost his deposit of $290 when the Freedman's Savings Bank defaulted in 1874. The bank was a symbol of Republican governance, in that it was created by Republicans to build the savings of African Americans. But the bank could not survive the Panic of 1873, an economic depression that wiped out the savings of many depositors and led to widespread unemployment, particularly in northern cities. The desultory impact of the panic combined with the decline in cotton prices prompted some black farmers to conclude that Republican officeholding had brought "ruin" to the parish, state, and country.[27]

Thomas Dorsey, a farm laborer and president of a black Democratic club on Morgan's plantation, perhaps best expressed the ideological reasons for affiliating with the Democratic Party. He used material impoverishment as a touchstone to articulate an individualist conception of the body politic—a vision that starkly contrasted with Republicans' sense of mutual obligation. "I only thought that as I was a free man," he testified at a congressional hearing, "I could vote for the man I pleased." In conversations with black Republican neighbors, he never claimed that the Democratic Party was best for the community but instead maintained that it offered him the potential for a better life. He voted the Democratic ticket because Democrats promised that he "could lease land much cheaper; and, besides that, they talked about giving the colored people's children education, and as I knowed I had two children, I didn't want them to grow up like wild geese." He continued, "Well, I thought if casting my ticket with the democrats could get this done, as they proposed, I thought I was right

I should help them to do so." To be sure, Republicans also emphasized economic prosperity in their platforms and campaign themes, but for Dorsey, personal, not collective, advancement mattered most in choosing between competing parties.[28]

While individual improvement lay at the heart of the Democratic appeal, Democrats, like their partisan counterparts, strove to create a communal network of support and protection. Identifying with the Democratic Party was a decidedly controversial act for African Americans in the postemancipation South, and many could do so only with the public support of white Democrats. Col. J. Floyd King, a white Democratic organizer and subsequent congressman, gave space and protection to Thomas Dorsey and other black Democratic club members, allowing them to meet on one of the plantations that he managed. In fact, Dorsey and the thirty-five to forty club members all worked on the same plantation (called Morgan's); theirs was the only black Democratic club in Concordia Parish in 1876. Dorsey admitted that he and his fellow club members feared for their lives and that they could not have voted without assurances of protection from white men. One Claiborne County white Democrat admitted, in 1875, that "it was positively dangerous for any negro to pronounce himself a democrat in my county." This Democratic activist acknowledged that white Democrats felt obliged to protect freedpeople who aligned with their party. "If met with personal violence," he explained, black Democrats "expect protection, and would get it." In public speeches, "we pledged ourselves," explained a Concordia Parish white Democrat, "to protect them at the risk of our lives from any injuries which might be inflicted upon them by republican negroes."[29]

To some extent, public declarations of protection seemed to mitigate partisan reprisals. After a group of black men confronted them, Dorsey and a fellow black Democrat said that the group would have killed them on the spot if not for the "white men" who protected them. In another incident in the town of Vidalia, black Republican leader David Young threatened to throw T. P. Jackson—the head of a Democratic-linked, fusionist faction—and other opponents in the river, "and they would have done so," recalled Jackson (the parish court clerk), "but for the protection given them by the Democrats." Yet the protection that whites gave Democratic and fusionist blacks was not absolute. Jackson was reasonably well protected and could freely speak in Vidalia, where most of the white people in the parish lived, but when he visited the rural areas of the parish, where communities were almost entirely black, he was shouted down from speaker platforms and "driven away" from meetings. Fusionist party candidates would not travel to the lower end of the parish, where Republicans' support was greatest and where "the women would get after me with clubs," testified a black candidate on the ticket.[30]

Because partisan affiliation was often associated with neighborhood identity, local politics left little space for individuals to publicly express their personal political beliefs. For this reason, it was rare to find individual black Democrats on plantations. On the one plantation in Concordia Parish that did host a black Democratic club, the one where Thomas Dorsey lived and worked, the principle held, but in reverse: none of the laborers voted the Republican ticket. In Natchez, John Smith, a freeborn shingle maker, complained that he could not "express" his Democratic beliefs "without being called to account by every colored Radical." At a "colored fair," John Fitzhugh, a porter and the secretary of the Greeley Guards, was "attacked, browbeaten and roughly used by several men" who "manifested the intention to intimidate," reported the local paper. Neither Fitzhugh's membership in the Democratic Party or the fact that his brother, Robert W. Fitzhugh, was a Republican alderman was enough to keep him safe from political violence and retribution.[31]

Despite promises of protection, identification with the Democratic Party was especially perilous for black men in certain public settings and during highly charged elections. At an 1872 Republican torchlight parade in Natchez, Frank Pomet, a twenty-four-year-old freedman, was shot as he and his friend, Jack Carraway (a black laborer probably related to William Carraway, the first vice president of the Colored Greeley Club), were walking down the sidewalk as the "McCary Club" passed by. Samuel Weldon, a McCary Club member, black policeman, and brother of Republican officeholder Louis J. Winston, stepped out from the parade and joined the two men for a drink. The three men continued down State Street, took another drink at Zoch's saloon, and then marched "arm in arm" along the parade route. The festive atmosphere came to an abrupt end when Pomet called out, "Hoorah for Greeley!" Weldon then "drew his pistol," pointed it at Pomet's head, and fired. The bullet entered Pomet's right cheek and shattered his jawbone. The shooting was undoubtedly fueled, in part, by alcoholic excess, but intense partisanship also contributed to the altercation. "We understand that both Carraway and Pomet are Greeley men," noted the *Natchez Democrat*, which in and of itself was not enough to raise the ire of black Republicans. Rather, it was the public expression of support for a Democratic candidate at a Republican procession that seemed to set off Weldon and rally Republicans to his defense. After Weldon was charged with violating the peace and dignity of the state, William H. Lynch, a Republican alderman, came to his aid and paid his bail bond.[32]

Even more perilous than publicly identifying with Democrats in the midst of a Republican stronghold was doing so without any networks of support. The case of a white outsider in Concordia Parish illustrates the point. Charles Kelly, who had been working on the Black River near the southern border of the parish, was making his way home to Chicago when he stopped at "a [plantation] church-house to rest himself." He struck up a conversation with some of the freedpeople in the building, and the discussion quickly turned to politics and his political views. "He said he was a democrat," recounted a white Democratic election supervisor, "and intended to vote for Tilden and Hendricks," the Democratic candidates for president and vice president, respectively, in the 1876 election. While many local blacks had their doubts about the leadership of local Republican officeholders, nearly all were staunch supporters of the national Republican ticket. After Kelly announced his partisan affiliation, the black field workers grabbed him and "dragged him out of the church-house, over the levee, and pulled his pants down, and whipped him, and held a pistol to his head," testified a Democratic attorney. Not only was Kelly badly beaten and humiliated, but his attackers escaped punishment. "Names were given," but the sheriff failed to arrest the accused because "the other negroes would secrete them and keep them out of the way."[33]

Without any local attachments, Kelly lacked the protection that a partisan community could provide. Judging from his willingness to stop at a plantation and engage in a conversation with local blacks, Kelly felt safe and not in any particular danger. Perhaps he believed that his whiteness would protect him from harm or that asserting his political views would be inoffensive, since he was not a local voter. Yet in the charged political environment of the 1876 campaign, he entered a community in which partisan belonging, not autonomy, had grown in importance and intensity. Only "personal acquaintance" could overcome racial hostility, noted one white plantation supervisor. "If a white man gets into difficulty with a darkie," he continued, "there is a disposition to crowd the white man."[34]

Public knowledge of one's political affiliation left black Democrats in the heavily Republican Natchez District particularly vulnerable. Because voters cast their ballots openly, neighbors and party agents kept a close tally of the tickets that each voter held. Especially in rural districts, local residents exerted enormous pressure on voters to conform to the political inclinations of the neighborhood. Alex Johnson, a twenty-eight-year-old black farmer from rural Adams County, claimed that he knew "every colored man who would be likely to vote the Democratic ticket" in his neighborhood, which was "not more than four or five." "When there is a campaign," explained Johnson, who served as a Republican U.S. supervisor of elections for his home precinct and later as a constable, "I make myself rather busy trying to find out how people intend to vote." Webster Bowyer, another black farmer and an election inspector, boasted that he knew every black man "in the neighborhood" who had joined a Democratic club. The well-organized Republican clubs registered "every colored man's name" from the precinct and kept tally sheets on each man's voting inclination. "For one of them to vote for a Democrat," recalled a sympathetic white Democrat from Wilkinson County, with notable exaggeration, "was almost to challenge certain death, unless prompt protection was given by the white people." No one was ever killed for affiliating with the Democratic Party in the Natchez District, but the risks for black men who did so could be significant.[35]

Black Women and the Concordia Parish Election of 1876

The 1876 election in Concordia, more than any other in the Natchez District, was one that divided local people; it was the one election in which a Democratic faction came closest to winning power without the use of paramilitary violence. Because the threat to Republican rule was so great and because the stakes were so high, the campaign was one of excess—excess in political rhetoric, intimidation, and mobilization. It was a unique election, particularly regarding the active role that black women played in its outcome. And Concordia Parish was a unique place, in that 93 percent of the population was of African descent (the largest black majority in the nation), and nearly all of these African Americans worked in the cotton fields. But this uniqueness makes the campaign instructive and worth dwelling on. This exaggeration of predominant trends in the Natchez District highlights the boundaries of partisan identity. It also opens a window onto the grassroots passion for politics in the region, helping to illuminate the meaning that ordinary men and women attached to politics.[36]

What also makes this election campaign important is the subsequent congressional investigation into charges of voter fraud and intimidation. The 1876 election was notorious, then and now, for massive levels of political violence that favored Democratic candidates, particularly in South Carolina, Florida, and Louisiana. The Republican-controlled U.S. Senate launched an extensive investigation into the Democratic Party's efforts to secure "home rule" through the barrel of a gun. To counter this effort, the Democratic-controlled U.S. House launched its own investigation into Republican fraud and intimidation in the South, and the events in Concordia Parish were central to Democratic claims of equivalence. The claims were erroneous because no one was killed in the parish for their political beliefs, while hundreds of people in other counties and parishes were killed or assaulted for voting or identifying with the Republican Party. In addition, evidence of electoral fraud never surfaced in Concordia Parish, but there was extensive fraud in the communities that witnessed paramilitary violence, as the next chapter will explain.

This congressional investigation produced the most extensive record of grassroots voting and mobilization in the Natchez District. Three dozen affidavits were recorded and nineteen witnesses answered questions before the House committee, generating testimonies that reflect a wide variety of perspectives, including white and black Democrats, fusionists, Republicans, officeholders, party agents, and ordinary voters. Two important groups, however, did not provide testimonies: black women and mainline Republican leaders (the David Young faction). Whether because they were not asked to participate (as seems likely in the case of the female participants) or because they did not want to endorse a biased investigation, the absence of firsthand accounts from these two perspectives leaves the election picture incomplete. But beyond the limitations of the records and the partisan motivations for these investigations, the testimonies from local residents reveal the social consequences of political dissent as well as the community-wide effort to mobilize Republican votes.[37]

Nearly all black residents identified themselves as loyal Republicans, but as the election neared, a growing number began to express frustration with the local parish government. After nine years of Republican rule, black families still faced persistent poverty, levees were in disrepair, and taxes were higher than small landowners could afford. Schools, one of the great achievements of Reconstruction, also suffered. The buildings were in poor condition, teachers were in short supply, and children attended school only four or five months a year.[38]

The politically frustrated residents directed their ire at David Young, the head of the local Republican Party. Young governed parish affairs like no other black politician in the Natchez District, using his social influence and wealth to bolster his extensive political influence. He was simultaneously a grocery store owner, minister of the leading Baptist church, editor of a local newspaper, a parish school board member, and a state senator. He owned one storehouse, two city lots, and two houses and had joined in a merchant partnership with David Singleton, a wealthy former slave. Under Young's leadership, black Republicans filled most parish offices and dominated local affairs. But his power was not total. In 1876 two brothers, Theodore P. Jackson, the clerk of the parish court, and William Ridgley, a state representative, formed a bolting ticket that nearly unseated Young. The brothers held office as Republicans, but they chafed under Young's leadership.[39]

The division began at a parish Republican convention, quickly escalating from a leadership dispute to a violent confrontation. Jackson introduced a resolution to "re-organize" the Republican executive committee. Young, as the presiding officer, rejected the proposal as immaterial to the proceedings. Jackson then "forced his way to the stand" to make his case personally, reported the *Natchez Democrat*. Young's supporters intercepted Jackson and began to forcibly remove him from the building. Ridgley, Jackson's brother, then rushed to the podium but was stopped by John Young, David Young's brother, who pointed a pistol at him. Jackson became "very much excited" and drew his gun on John Young. In the ensuing tumult, Jackson's gun discharged, "barely missing Senator Young." Ridgley drew his gun and fired "a second shot." Finally, Jackson and Ridgley were restrained, kicked out of the convention hall, and barred from all future parish Republican conventions, effectively ejecting them from the party.[40]

In addition to the vengeful brothers Jackson and Ridgley, David Young faced tough scrutiny from local black residents over his alleged culpability in the wretched condition of the parish schools and his own flirtation with a bipartisan ticket. Two years before, the state government had indicted Young for embezzling $30,000 of school funds. Young, the treasurer of the parish school board at the time, blamed his political enemies for the indictment, and not without reason. Because he had rebuffed his party and endorsed a Democratic congressional candidate in 1874, state Republicans introduced corruption charges in order to punish his "independence." Young had always been a loyal Republican, yet recent events, such as the economic dislocation from the Panic of 1873, the overturning of the Colfax massacre convictions, and the renewed attacks on black governance—most evident in the wide acclaim that a diatribe by James Pike, *The Prostrate State*, received—seem to have led Young to contemplate a cooperative relationship with Democrats. Young had told black voters that popular opinion in the North was beginning to turn against Republican rule in the South and that they needed to align with political moderates to demonstrate their commitment to honest government.[41]

But with his trial for embezzlement looming and sensing a softening of support from the grass roots, Young pulled back from his moderating impulses. He threw his entire machine, "which was large, being head of the church, senator from that district, and so on," behind the mainline Republican Party in 1876, testified a white attorney. Satisfied with his renewed loyalty, state Republican leaders instructed the district attorney to dismiss the indictment. But the damage had been done. After the state's embezzlement charges were set aside, some outraged locals—ten black Republicans and one white man—hired an attorney to review the case against Young and to push for additional indictments. (The missing money may not have been stolen after all but rather devalued from having to sell "free-school warrants" at forty cents on the dollar.) As if the internal revolt was not enough, white paramilitary forces unleashed a wave of political violence across Louisiana and Mississippi during the 1876 election campaign to forcibly expel Republicans from governmental offices. With political assassinations and pitched battles between black and white militias swirling at the edges of his parish, and with growing resentment simmering among locals, David Young confronted a substantial political threat from within—a threat that in previous years could be dismissed as folly but now seemed to herald the demise of grassroots democracy in Concordia Parish.[42]

A few months after the "Vidalia Political Row," in which Jackson and Ridgley violently and unsuccessfully challenged Young's leadership, the two brothers formed a fusionist ticket comprising disgruntled black Republicans, a few black Democrats, and some wealthy white Democrats. To counter the fusionists, Young and his supporters orchestrated a campaign of intimidation to enforce communal solidarity and to denigrate the dissenting opposition. William Ridgley recalled that he was first labeled a Democrat around the time Young was indicted for embezzlement: "[H]e has been telling the colored people in the parish that I was a democrat . . . and he then told them they must always vote for a colored man if he was a republican." Young claimed that the fusionist ticket was really Democratic and argued, his opponents claimed, that "if the democrats succeeded in getting into office the colored people would be enslaved again." At political rallies, Republican speakers recalled the days when "hounds" and "bull-whipp[s]" were used to keep black people in bondage. One black woman, believing that she "would be sold back into slavery," was brought to tears when she saw black men holding Democratic tickets at the polls.[43]

Only eleven years since abolition, slavery had yet to become a distant memory. The pain of enslavement was betrayed in the outpouring of emotions at the polls and political meetings as Republican candidates linked the fusionists to the Democratic Party and the Democrats to slavery. For women, especially, memories of family separation at the slave market, of sexual exploitation, and of brutal punishments may explain why they became intensely interested in the outcome of this election and why they worked to defeat the fusionist ticket.[44]

At the mass meetings preceding the election, Republican leaders made the usual appeals to party and candidate, but what makes this campaign noteworthy is that speakers directly addressed black women in the audience. Women were told to "instruct their husbands to vote against" the fusionist ticket, recalled a black constable. If black men insisted on voting Democratic, "the women [were] advised to quit their husbands," testified an ex-slave landowner. "They told my wife to quit me," the husband of Milly Warfield ruefully noted. At one club meeting, the male leaders told wives to "throw hot water in their husbands' eyes, and . . . that they should shut their doors against them and drive them from their houses." David Young told Peter Hooper, a black justice of the peace, that if he voted the Democratic ticket "his wife must leave him" and "he would be turned out of the society." At another mass meeting, Young addressed the women in the audience and reassured those who left their husbands that "he would take care of them" and help them "to get a divorce," according to multiple witnesses.[45]

Few women took up Senator Young on his offer of male protection, but many women accepted the challenge of keeping black men—their husbands, sons, fathers, and neighbors—from voting with the Democrats. Black farmers who voted for the Republican national ticket signed affidavits swearing that they "often heard colored women . . . say that any colored man who voted the democratic ticket 'ought to be killed.'" The night before the 1876 election, at a Democratic club meeting of black and white men at the Helena plantation, "several colored women came to the room," testified the white club president, "and [they] were so discourteous and so violent that we thought at one time we would be compelled to close the meeting." "The wife of one of the colored men," he continued, "was so obstreperous that she followed her husband clear to the speaker's stand, and it was only with utmost persuasion that we could prevail upon her not to attack her husband in the club-room." Malinda Scott, a thirty-one-year-old laborer, gave her husband so much grief when he publicly identified with the Democrats (she was, in his words, "perfectly unbearable") that he had to threaten "to shoot her" so he could "stay in the house with her." James Foy's wife ran off and left him "for two weeks" after the black justice of the peace endorsed the Democrats. "It has been so of late," concluded a white Democratic club president, "that we cannot ride along the road without some of the women using insulting language to us on account of our political proclivities."[46]

The vociferous actions of black women testify to the threat that the fusionist ticket posed. The Democratic appeal to a black man's sense of independence and to his economic frustration endangered the grassroots solidarity that had propelled Republicans to power. Another measure of the broad appeal of dissenting Republicans and black Democrats can be seen in the overheated rhetoric at Republican rallies. Black and white residents stated that they heard black Republicans calling for black men who voted with the Democrats to have "their heads . . . cut off and their blood drank by the people." In a similar vein, Republican leaders and local blacks said that black men who joined the Democrats should be castrated. The outrageous assertion, repeated in numerous affidavits, unnerved many black men who did not conform to the mainline Republican Party. Although it was likely just hyperbolic political rhetoric, black witnesses testified that at least one black man who expressed sympathy with the Democrats was castrated in Natchez by unknown persons. By linking Democratic affiliation with literal emasculation, black leaders sought to undercut Democrats' masculine appeal. Voting against the Republican ticket would, in essence, strip black men of their manly and communal independence ("voting to put themselves back into slavery"). To make the point more explicit, black women joined in the effort to demonize dissenting black men. Joe Williams, a thirty-seven-year-old black farmer, signed an affidavit attesting that "colored women openly threatened to castrate" him "if he voted the democratic ticket."[47]

The rumors of politically motivated castration and other violent threats challenged a male voter's sense of security, but Republican Party agents also emphasized the communal consequences of voting against the party. As Election Day drew closer, social ostracism became a more common tactic. Joe Williams testified that he had been "forbidden by many colored men to come to their houses." Churches similarly turned against their members who indicated a desire to vote for the fusionist ticket. And congregations rebelled against their clerical leaders. The members of one church threatened to expel their minister "and to burn his church, unless he did desist" from organizing a fusionist club. Andrew Watson, a preacher and field laborer, let it be known that he wanted "a change of government," but in the end he did not vote against the Republicans because "his congregation refused to go to his church." When Eli Johnson, a "prominent republican preacher," decided just before the election to vote against the Republican ticket, an unknown assailant targeted him for retribution, firing shots at him late one night in his front yard. David Young, the head of the parish Republicans, reportedly said that he would force any man "out of church" who organized an anti-Republican party. "The church is the strongest weapon they use," in ensuring a mobilized Republican vote, deduced the white chairman of the Concordia Parish Democratic Party.[48]

But the church was not the only weapon. Republicans threatened "to burn up my place and put me out" for voting Democrat, explained Joe Habit, an ex-slave. He also complained to a congressional committee that three head of his cattle and some sheep were killed as a result of his political views. At one mass meeting held on a plantation, a crowd of field laborers, "aflourishing and aswinging sugar-knives," forced William Ridgley, a black candidate for the state legislature, down from the speaker's platform. At Black Hawk plantation, John Young, David Young's brother, and a few associates armed with "pistols and sugar-knives" prevented Ridgley from speaking. Angry black Republicans threw bricks at Thomas Dorsey, the president of a black Democratic club, and later other men "got a club and hit me alongside the head," he testified. Dorsey's neighbors also threatened to murder "those damn democrat niggers on Morgan's place" on Election Day. Dorsey was quite distressed by these verbal and physical attacks, since they were carried out at the church that he often attended and among his neighbors, whom he believed were "always good friends." But friendship and neighborliness offered little respite for individuals who dared to help advance the interests of the Democratic Party during one of the most tumultuous elections in American history.[49]

Freedpeople did not have to look far to see their fears realized in the region's political struggles. In other parts of the state during the 1876 election campaign, white Democrats whipped, intimidated, and murdered black Republicans. Just across the Mississippi River, white militias massacred black people in two separate instances. The year before in Mississippi the White Leagues had swept through the state, driving Republicans from office and placing Democrats in power. And before that, in 1874, Alabama's government had succumbed to a violent overthrow. In this context, the notion that "they would be put back into slavery" by the Democrats and "driven from their homes" seemed all too likely to freedpeople, even in one of the strongest Republican parishes in the South.[50]

Polling-Place Clashes

If household coercion failed to keep black men in line, if public threats and intimidation did not ensure a unified Republican vote, then party activists took a last stand at the polling places. Casting a ballot was no simple matter during highly contested campaigns, and the public nature of voting meant that the polling place was a vital space for last-minute persuasion and intimidation. Although voting was the sole prerogative of adult males, the men did more than vote on Election Day, and sometimes women intruded on this most masculine of political spaces to assert their interests.[51]

The location of polling places often shaped how the vote would proceed. One benefit of Republican dominance in the Natchez District was that polling places were often set up at sites that were favorable to the local black population. Two of Natchez's four polling places were located at black institutions: the engine house of Good Will Fire Company No. 2 and the AME Zion Church. The other city polling places were set up at prominent civic institutions, such as city hall and the Jefferson Hotel, that were easily identifiable and could accommodate large numbers of people. In the countryside, the lack of buildings limited the options for voting sites; thus they were more likely to be located at privately owned structures, such as plantation houses and stores. In the small town of Rodney in Jefferson County, the ballot box was placed in "an old store on the main street" and sat on the counter. Voters entered from the front of the store and gave their ballots to a "guard" at the door, who then delivered the ticket to the election judge. More inviting to rural black residents were the polling places at a schoolhouse, a space that signified the substantial improvements resulting from Reconstruction and one of the few civic spaces that impoverished black families could claim as their own.[52]

Individuals did not simply walk up to the polls; instead, they gathered together in militaristic style, often organized by clubs, to march there. In some instances, black Republicans came in a "great cavalcade . . . riding about the streets with swords and banners." However they marched, it was "customary" for black voters, testified a black election supervisor, "to assemble at the voting-place at an early hour in the morning," with many often remaining at the polling place throughout the day. In the crowds that developed outside of polling places, party agents distributed tickets, small groups harangued dissenters, men discussed the implications of the election, police officers and marshals scanned the crowds for signs of organized disturbances, and others just enjoyed the day off from work. In 1876 "the courthouse yard and square," recalled a white resident of Woodville, Mississippi, "were crowded with negroes, as was the case at all elections."[53]

To ensure a high voter turnout and a unified vote, party leaders utilized the pressure of club membership to bring men out, and also to provide voters with a sense of security. A lone man stood little chance of resisting concerted pressure from peers and authorities while standing in line waiting to vote, but as a member of a group, the voter was better able to fend off challenges at the doorstep of polling places. For this reason, Republican leaders often brought club members into towns and county seats for mass meetings to inform members of the major political issues and to rally the grass roots for the electoral campaign. On the eve of elections, club members discussed polling-place strategies and received voting instructions from county leaders. Mobilizing voters further ensured that those within the group voted in unison, and it also solved the practical problem of distributing official party ballots to a mostly illiterate population. An illiterate voter had to place his trust in local party agents, for he could not independently authenticate the words on the slips of paper used as party ballots. Thus the very act of voting necessitated a person-to-person intimacy, for which mass meetings, political speeches, and campaign paraphernalia were no substitute.[54]

Each party was responsible for printing and distributing its tickets. Many local newspapers printed the party ticket in their columns, inviting readers to cut out the ballot for use on Election Day. For black voters who could not read or write, this was of little consolation. Party organizers in rural counties faced the added problem of securing a friendly printing press. In many counties, such as Jefferson County, the only printing press was operated by the local newspaper, which was affiliated with the Democratic Party. When Merrimon Howard, the black sheriff and Republican leader in Jefferson County, needed to print his county's and Franklin County's tickets for the 1876 election, he traveled to Natchez, where Republicans operated a press. With tickets in hand, Howard assembled the Republican "central committee," composed of party agents living in the rural districts, at a schoolhouse in the county seat. He passed out the voting tickets "in little packages," instructing the men to keep quiet about the tickets until Election Day and to hand them out at the polls. This tightly controlled distribution of tickets was designed to avoid the circulation of fraudulent ballots and to keep the finite supply of tickets out of the hands of unscrupulous political opponents. The 1871 Jefferson County railroad bond vote was defeated in part because party leaders failed to distribute enough ballots in a timely manner.[55]

In Adams County William H. Lynch, a leading Republican organizer and brother to John R. Lynch, was the primary ticket distributor. In the Kingston district, about sixteen miles outside of Natchez, Lynch personally passed out voting tally sheets and tickets to party agents for the 1880 election. Smith Kinney, a farmer, former slave, and lifelong resident of the community, took the tickets from Lynch and distributed them to his neighbors, telling them "not to let any one touch their tickets until they deposited them in the box." At the same polling place, dozens of outlying black farmers rode up on horses and mules and requested Harry Smith, another ticket distributor. "They would ask me," testified the fifty-four-year-old black farmer who could read but could not write, "'Smith, what is on hand to-day?' And I would answer, 'Gentlemen and friends, remember this is not a day of local affairs.' They would say, 'What ticket have you got?' And I would reply, 'I have the Garfield ticket.' But they would say, 'We don't care so much for the Garfield ticket—we want the [John R.] Lynch ticket.' And I would answer, 'Gentlemen, you don't suppose I would go all the way to Natchez, as long as Lynch was in the field, and leave his ticket behind.'"[56]

Since an election could hinge on the distribution process, party leaders sought out a man "who can influence the people to come his way," noted a Republican Party agent and a former justice of the peace. For Adams County voters, their primary interest was in electing the county's favorite son, John R. Lynch, to another term in Congress—the presidential contest between the Republican candidate, James A. Garfield, and the Democrat nominee, Winfield Scott Hancock, was a secondary concern. Most black men sought out "true and tried Republicans," testified a black farmer and Republican Party agent. In this way, ticket distributors served as vital mediators between partisan leaders and ordinary voters, helping to connect local concerns to national interests.[57]

Despite the presence of trusted party agents, potential voters often struggled to make sense of the voting materials. At the 1872 polls, black Natchezians presented an array of paper slips to election officials for proof of registration. One handed over a receipt from a local merchant; another "presented a Louisiana lease of land as his evidence of citizenship"; still others offered Louisiana registration papers for a Mississippi election. "But," the local newspaper concluded, "every one of them had been provided with the orthodox Grant ticket, and about that not one of them made the slightest mistake."[58]

Yet in other, more contested, elections, deciphering the "orthodox" ballot proved to be a difficult task. "Some of the gentlemen hailed me and said: 'I can't see any difference between these tickets,'" explained Harry Smith, "but I said to them, 'If you want to vote for John R. Lynch you take the ticket that I gave you and Smith Kinney and three or four others here. I know every man I gave tickets to to issue, and you ought to be satisfied that I have only the only ticket, and never had any other.'" Despite these clear instructions, some voters wanted a second or third opinion. "The voters would come to me by dozens for me to personally inspect their tickets," remarked Congressman John R. Lynch, "and see if they were the real republican tickets." At the Kingston polling place, voters approached Abraham Felters, a peace officer and farmer who could read a little but was unable to sign his name. "Is this here Lynch's ticket, for I don't want anything but the Lynch ticket?" voters would ask, and Felters responded, "See, here is Lynch's name on the bottom of the ticket."[59]

EXHIBIT B.—H. B. FOULES.

Republican National Ticket,

For President,

JAMES A. GARFIELD.

——o——

For Vice President,

CHESTER A. ARTHUR.

For Electors for President and Vice President,

HON. WILLIAM R. SPEARS,

HON. R. W. FLOURNOY,

DR. J. M. BYNUM,

HON. J. T. SETTLE,

CAPT. M. K. MISTER, JR.,

DR. R. H. MONTGOMERY,

JUDGE R. H. CUNY,

HON. CHARLES W. CLARKE.

——o——

For Member of the House of Represen tatives from the 6th Congressional District.

JOHN R. LYNCH.

EXHIBIT C.—H. B. FOULES.

Democratic-Conservative

TICKET!

For President,

Winfield Scott Hancock.

For Vice-President,

William H. English.

For Electors for President and Vice-President,

F. G. BARRY,

C. P. NEILSON,

C. B. MITCHELL,

THOMAS SPIGHT,

WILLIAM PRICE,

WILLIAM H. LUSE,

ROBERT N. MILLER,

JOSEPH HIRSH.

For Member of the House of Representatives from the 6th Congressional District.

JAMES R. CHALMERS.

Party tickets from the 1880 election in Adams County. U.S. House, *Testimony in the Contested Election Case of John R. Lynch vs. James R. Chalmers, From the Sixth Congressional District of Mississippi,* 47th Cong., 1st sess., 1881, House Misc. Doc. 12, p. 138.

Ordinary voters were especially concerned about the accuracy of their tickets because the parties used the shape and format of the tickets to sway and confuse voters. Adams County Democrats often printed similarly formatted tickets in the same color as Republican ones to confuse illiterate Republican voters. Seeing a white Democratic supervisor passing out tickets to a group of black men, Harry Smith, the ticket distributor, broke into their ranks, declared, "Beware of false prophets," and began to pass out Republican tickets. To protect black Democratic voters, the Concordia Parish Democratic Party printed white tickets to resemble the yellow Republican tickets, but this created its own confusion. One black man stood at the polls in bewilderment: he held "a yellow [Republican] ticket" in one hand, "around which he had wrapped a remnant of his white [Democratic] ticket," unsure which one to cast. Others had the problem of wanting to vote for a different candidate than one listed on the party ballot. Those who could not write sought out those who could in order to scratch out the printed name and pencil in another. Understandably, party agents deplored the practice for partisan reasons but also because illiterate voters could not verify that the written-in names were the ones they wanted to vote for. "I instructed them," Smith Kinney testified, "not to let any one touch their tickets until they deposited them in the box, and not to have them marked on in any way, not even by a pencil, but to vote them straight as they were."[60]

Confusion at the polls was also the result of organized pressure from party activists who used last-minute coercion to win (or steal) a few more votes. Foul language, alcohol, intense partisanship, and an uncertain outcome combined to produce a highly charged environment at polling places. And male voters expected a combative atmosphere at polling places. Black men at the polls, reported one witness, declared "that any man ought not to grumble about being squeezed and jammed a little while at the polls to put in his vote." At the end of a long day of voting, William J. Davis, a white Republican and treasury agent, described the scene at the 1872 Natchez city election this way: "The Streets are like a perfect *pandemonium*. Drunkards in every direction. Oaths so thick in the air you have to dodge them. Shouting, yelling, shooting fire crackers and worse." As an election official, Davis was charged with counting the ballots, but in attempting to remove the ballot box for counting, he was stopped by "10 Revolvers chucked into my face." A mob rushed to Davis's defense and "bore down" on his assailants. "For a time," he recalled in a letter to Senator Ames, "I stood ballot box clutched in my right [hand,] umbrella in my left hand so thoroughly scared that I suppose my face would have been a good model for a picture of Daniel in the *Lions Den* with the marginal note to the effect that Daniel 'may be recognized' by the blue cotton umbrella under his arm." In this election, moderate Republicans (whom Davis supported), with the help of Democrats, gained the upper hand in city politics and threw out the radical, black-dominated faction led by Mayor Robert H. Wood.[61]

Tensions were also high in the Concordia Parish election of 1876, where an insurgent fusionist party threatened to unseat David Young's political machine. After weeks of vigorous campaigning, numerous threats, and political intimidation, Republican Party agents focused their attention on the polling places—their last stand for beating back the fusionist challenge. It was not surprising, then, that numerous confrontations broke out on Election Day. At Polls Nos. 3 and 4, crowds of Republicans began to form when they noticed groups of black men attempting to vote the fusionist ticket. The crowds soon breached the thirty-foot perimeter of the polling place that was supposed to give voters, as they waited in line, a measure of security. Dozens of people, some with concealed weapons, surged toward the ballot box and "tore down the gallery," forcing the election commissioners to temporarily close Poll No. 3. At Poll No. 5, Democrats had distributed their tickets to black voters the day before the election, but, fatefully, "the names of the justices of the peace and the constables had been left blank," testified a Democratic election commissioner. "When they pulled these tickets out to have these names put on them," recalled a Democratic election commissioner, "they were taken out of their hands and torn up" by black Republicans. Anderson Tolliver, a black justice of the peace and future state legislator, walked up and down the line of voters waiting at Poll No. 6 and told them that they were holding Democratic tickets. He then proceeded to take "them away and gave them Young [or Republican] tickets." At Poll No. 2, 80 David Young supporters clashed with 150 fusionist voters, but the Young men got the upper hand and prevented most of the fusionists from voting the Democratic ticket. One freedman justified his participation in the intimidation by declaring that "he was not going to suffer his people to vote the democratic ticket." At another poll, freedpeople displayed posters, or "printed cuts," of "negroes chased by southern white men with dogs, pistols, &c." These visual images were, a white planter claimed, "calculated to deter colored men from voting the democratic ticket" by implying that Democrats would return black people to slavery.[62]

In the midst of the pushing, shoving, and last-minute politicking were dozens of black women, who converged on the polls in one last attempt to sway the election. Standing along the roadside, women "jeered" at a group of black men from Morgan's plantation (the location of the only black Democratic club in the parish) as they rode into Vidalia to vote the Democratic ticket. Those holding fusionist tickets were told "that if they did not vote the republican ticket they would not have any stock" in the community. "When their husbands came to vote, they came out too," explained Taylor Young, a black farmer and a Republican commissioner (though not related to David Young nor aligned with his faction), "and if their husbands had a Jackson [fusionist] ticket they would snatch it away and give them a Young ticket."[63]

The pressure from freedwomen was extensive. "The election was pretty near all controlled by the women," continued Commissioner Young; "although I was one of the [election] commissioners, I was under the control of a woman." Pressed further by congressional investigators to explain the political influence of local women, he responded, "[W]hen I got talking with any man about the election there would be about fifty or sixty women come around." As a dissenting Republican and a supporter of the fusionist ticket, he had to be mindful of what he said to other voters at the polling place. "I was afraid to express my own free opinion," he confessed. At one mass meeting, "a big crowd" surrounded Bill Smith, a thirty-four-year-old black farmer. When he said that he had voted the Democratic ticket, his presence attracted even greater attention. Then "a woman came around with a hoe and said they were going to kill him," insisted a black witness to the events. Smith fled the scene immediately.[64]

Not only were local black women willing to intrude on the masculine sphere of the polling place, they also acted as other male party agents did, using threats and physical force to ensure that the fusionist ticket would be defeated. They exerted communal pressure in public and private ways that, judging from the outpouring of testimony, clearly had an impact at the ballot box. The extent to which Republican victory owed to the actions of freedwomen at the polls, at political meetings, and in their homes is impossible to determine, but what can be concluded is that these women believed they had a personal stake in the election and a duty to ensure a Republican victory.

Although the fusionists came close to capturing a few local positions, Republicans carried the day. In the race for clerk of the court, the one in which the leader of the fusionists, T. P. Jackson, was a candidate, he lost to the Republican by about four hundred votes, out of twenty-eight hundred cast. In the statewide races it was a different story, as Republicans again trounced the Democratic candidates. Eighty-seven percent of the votes cast from Concordia Parish went for the Republican governor. This was, however, a six-point improvement for the Democratic candidate from the previous election, suggesting that a few dozen (or perhaps a couple hundred) black men voted the straight Democratic ticket.[65]

Frustration with local political leaders in Concordia Parish was widespread, but what may have saved the Republicans were the actions of unenfranchised black women. In their aggressive politicking and in their strong fidelity to the Republican Party, these women seem like anomalies in the larger history of American democracy. White women, by contrast, were never seen at mid-nineteenth-century polling places. Yet politically active black women may be more typical than we have previously acknowledged.[66]

All across the South in the era of Reconstruction, black women acted as party agents, using intimidation and coercion to assist in Republican voter mobilization campaigns. Similarly, black political leaders acknowledged their role and drew on black women's concerted efforts to help win the vote, particularly in elections where black men were swayed by a fusionist ticket or felt coerced to vote a Democratic one. As early as 1868, in the second year that southern black men could vote, freedwomen in Yazoo County, Mississippi, sported Grant and Colfax badges as they worked in the homes of white planters. During the same election season, a northern white missionary described how black women at a polling place "formed a line of one hundred or more, and ran up and down near the line of voters, saying, 'Now Sandy, if you don' vote de radical ticket I won't live wid ye.' 'Now Jack, ef you don' vote for Lincum's men I'll leave ye.'" In Tennessee black women abandoned their labors to join the men at the polls. In Alabama in 1870, black women belonged to a political club and worked to convince black men to not vote Democratic. In 1872 black women in Macon, Georgia, justified their presence at the polls by claiming that it was "part of their religion to keep their husbands and brothers straight in politics." In 1874 black women in a rural district just outside Mobile, Alabama, fearing that "white people wanted to put their children back into slavery," forced black male voters to vote the Republican ticket. Black Republican leaders in Mississippi welcomed black women to political meetings and scoffed at white Democrats who were outraged by the female presence in partisan affairs. John R. Lynch testified that black women would threaten to leave their husbands to prevent them from voting a Democratic ticket. And some of those threats seem to have been realized in Jefferson County, according to a white diarist, who recorded that black Democrats were "persecuted by their own race, their own wives often turning them out of doors." In the Louisiana sugar parishes in 1876, the local Republican Party formed women's auxiliaries to drive black men back to the Republican side. In South Carolina in the same year, women threatened to withhold sex from their men and showed up to the polling places with sticks to emphasize the punishment that black men would receive if they betrayed their women and community. In 1880 a white Mississippi Democrat from Adams County testified that "the female portion" has "a powerful influence" on political issues. In 1883 black women from Danville, Virginia, threatened to leave their husbands for voting Democratic. Thus in at least seven states over the course of fifteen years, black women engaged in partisan activities across the reconstructed South in coordination with local Republican leaders.[67]

The vital role of women in black politics did not escape J. Henri Burch, a freeborn Louisianian and former state legislator. Testifying before a U.S. Senate committee investigating the "Removal of Negroes from the Southern States," Burch spoke at length about the politics of black women:

These women, since reconstruction, have followed their husbands and brothers and all who had a vote, from morning to night, around the parishes demanding that they should vote the Republican ticket, especially if they heard that their husband, or brother, or father, was likely to vote the Democratic ticket. They have been very active since 1868 in all the political movements; they form a large number in all the political assemblages, and they have evidenced a deep interest in all that pertains to politics so far as their husbands and fathers and brothers were concerned; and they have always placed their desire that they should vote the Republican ticket on the ground that it was only through the Republican party and the principles of that party that they could secure homes for themselves and educational advantages for their children, and protection in all rights accorded to them by the Constitution of the nation.

The presence and active participation of women in Republican politics evinced little opposition from black male leaders because their ideological framework did not demand that women should be consigned to private spaces.[68]

Following the logic of grassroots democracy, black women participated in many election campaigns in the Natchez District, reflecting the ethos that gave primacy to a multiplicity of voices in governance. Women, however, did not regularly appear at the polls in close elections between white Democrats and black Republicans or at the extremely violent elections in the late 1870s. Instead, freedwomen intruded on the male sphere of partisan politics when local Republicans were divided. The fusionists of Concordia Parish represented a threat not so much in their numbers as in the way that they challenged the strengths of the grassroots community, namely the household and the church. When neighbor turned against neighbor, ministers turned against congregants, and husbands turned against wives, it may be that women felt a special obligation to hold the community together. They clearly had a vested interest in Republican policies, as Burch suggests. And they may have better recognized—better than black men—the importance of solidarity for a subaltern people.

Ordinary men and women participated in partisan politics and voted (when they were allowed to) in order to advance a particular social vision, to translate political ideologies into practical politics, and because they were pressured by family, friends, and neighbors to vote. Black Republicans valued egalitarian principles—principles that incorporated female voices and actions into the body politic—whereas the Democratic Party offered to its black supporters hierarchy and the individual advancement of males. The existence of black Democrats lays bare the choice that freedpeople faced in the Reconstruction era and highlights the intensity that ordinary voters brought to partisan contests.

Black Democrats evoked particular passion, but not for the usual political reasons. They rarely had enough numbers to challenge the large Republican majorities. Rather, when male farm laborers, draymen, or church leaders forged patron-client relationships with powerful white men and voted their individual interests, they undermined the collective basis of Republican rule. Aligning with Democrats would not just make it more difficult for Republicans to win office, it threatened to silence the voices of freedwomen. There was no role for black women in the Democratic Party.

The partisan conflict also reveals how the memory of slavery was a touch-stone for Reconstruction politics. The political stakes could not have been higher for African Americans during Reconstruction. At a time when the Ku Klux Klan terrorized black communities throughout the South (although not in the Natchez District) and when the Democratic Party's platform called for the rollback of political rights and the economic subordination of black people, election outcomes had a tangible impact on freedpeople's lives. The act of voting was not merely a mechanism to select an officeholder but a weapon to preserve emancipation. Freedpeople understood that their collective freedom was en-sured by a broadly democratic culture. To preserve the democratic society that they had so carefully formed in the years after emancipation, they were willing to pressure male citizens into voting the Republican ticket.

PART THREE

Constricting Democracy

SEVEN

"Organized Terrorism and Armed Violence"

When the members of a rural black church in Jefferson County gathered together for an evening prayer meeting, it is not known what they prayed about or whom they prayed for, but it is likely that their personal safety was at the forefront of their minds. It was Saturday night before the hotly disputed 1876 election, and a few came to the church meeting armed with shotguns and pistols. Their church services had been interrupted before by armed white men, and they anticipated another encounter. As the mostly female congregants were singing, members of a Democratic club rode up and surrounded the church. "You have these night-meetings as prayer-meetings," bellowed the white leader to the black minister, "and then you turn them into political meetings, and we mean to break them up." Upon hearing this, the congregants panicked and began to pour out of the church building, commencing a "terrible firing of guns" that left the captain of the club dead and another member wounded.[1]

Infuriated by the failed attack, the other Democratic clubs in the county scoured the countryside the next day and rounded up about thirty men whom they accused of attending the church meeting. Nearly one hundred Democrats, including many of the leading white men in Jefferson County, participated in the raids and patrolled the ad-hoc prison camp. At the camp they set up a kangaroo court, with the club presidents acting as judges, and condemned the lot of the prisoners to death. They then began to march the prisoners to Fayette, the county seat, for execution, but when the white men stopped at a thicket to unhitch their horses, the black men broke and ran. Some were shot down as they tried to escape, while others were captured and immediately executed. Lewis H. Ingraham, a black student at Alcorn University, was one of the few to get away, fleeing, on the advice of Alcorn president Hiram Revels, across the Mississippi River into Louisiana. But his brother was shot and killed, and his father, wounded, was captured and hanged in the woods. All told, twenty-five to thirty black men were murdered.[2]

The Jefferson County massacre was an exceptional example of the electoral violence that swept over the Natchez District between 1875 and 1878. It was one event among many in which white-line Democrats used excessive force to take over local governments. The attacks targeted the networks within and between black neighborhoods and communities that provided the foundation for Republican power in the region. Among the black men imprisoned in the fields to the east of Fayette were at least two ministers, one of whom was executed. The Democratic clubs also detained two Republican ticket distributors and confiscated their ballots. Two other distributors were murdered, one who was riddled with bullets at his house and another who was captured in Natchez and later lynched in a tree near the church where the massacre had unfolded. County Republican leaders, both black and white, scattered when they learned of the massacre and of the "squads of men out hunting" for them.[3]

The white-line attacks came in a variety of forms due to local contingencies, but they followed a general pattern in the Natchez District. Democratic militias struck first in Claiborne County in 1875, and then followed in the next year with incursions in Wilkinson County and Jefferson County. By 1878, when paramilitary violence visited Tensas and Concordia Parishes, the steadily increasing violence had reached its apogee. Only in Adams County were local citizens able to hold off the invasion of white supremacists, a unique development that will be assessed in the following chapter. The scourge of electoral violence was not new. It had plagued other regions of the South before coming to the Natchez District, as State Senator Jeremiah M. P. Williams reminded Adams County residents in an 1871 speech calling for political solidarity. And so black people in the district, both leaders and ordinary citizens, responded with a variety of tactical and strategic responses to maintain the integrity of their democratic system.

While the goal of the paramilitary insurgency was to oust Republicans from office, the insurgents did so by trying to undermine the vibrant local democracies that were rapidly transforming southern society. In each county or parish in the Natchez District, the white liners' first targets were urban places because Republicans used these public spaces to inform and educate a largely rural constituency about the coming election. The attacks in towns and cities were designed to eliminate the space for political organizing and for biracial politics. From there, the white liners turned to rural neighborhoods and communities. They attacked churches (as in the Jefferson County massacre) to disrupt the associational networks that undergirded black mobilization. They attacked men and women, those who voted and those who identified with Republicans, because they recognized that the system of grassroots governance depended on broad community support. And they attacked polling places because suffrage was the linchpin of democracy—the point at which the multilayered networks converged and expressed the interests of ordinary citizens.[4]

The overwhelming wave of Democratic political violence testifies to both the strength and the limits of local democracies. Congressman John R. Lynch recognized the dynamism of black politics, declaring from the floor of the U.S. House of Representatives in 1876 that the Mississippi Republican Party was "so strong, so powerful . . . that nothing short of organized terrorism and armed violence . . . could crush it out of existence or defeat it at the polls." And that is just what the Democrats did. They could not achieve dominance on their own; rather, Democrats depended on assistance from outsiders—armed bands of white men from counties and parishes surrounding the Natchez District who descended on localities much like foreign invaders. In an environment where face-to-face contact governed political relationships, many white residents were reluctant to harm their black neighbors and sever long-standing social and economic bonds, but outsiders, especially those inflamed by the ideologies of white supremacy, felt no such compunction.[5]

The concerted campaign of political violence exposed a fundamental weakness in grassroots democracies during the Reconstruction era. Local governments were, quite simply, ill-prepared to resist paramilitary violence. The framework of interaction had shifted from one of peace to one of war. In the latter context, factional divisions within the Republican Party had a negligible impact on the course of the violence. Indeed, the marauding bands of armed white Democrats galvanized black Republicans, who voted overwhelmingly against the Democratic Party. Nevertheless, the white liners picked off county governments one at a time, amassing their forces from outside the district and invading at the most opportune moment. Locals lacked the resources (weaponry and transportation) to launch a vigorous military counterattack. Freedpeople instead hoped for state and federal officials to enforce the law and quash illegitimate uses of violence, yet state militias were not called out and only one company of federal troops was deployed to the region and only after the 1876 election. The national appetite for federal intervention in the South had declined and support for equal rights was wavering, and so local freedpeople were left alone to contest the strategic ferocity of the white supremacists. In some counties the Republican Party was eviscerated, while overall the violence narrowed the possibilities for ordinary African Americans to exert their influence on the political process.[6]

Natchez District freedpeople did not sit by passively as white terrorists sought to upend the emancipated society that they had fashioned. They tried an array of violent and nonviolent tactics to stem the tide. While not successful in preserving free and fair elections, their efforts undoubtedly saved the lives of hundreds of local residents. They also spoke out eloquently about the electoral violence. By testifying in multiple congressional investigations into election disputes, freedpeople left an important record of how they were able to withstand the wave of violence. The testimonies were also important political acts in themselves. By voicing the claims of dispossessed citizens, they offered an antithesis to the white-line attacks. In their detailed and measured statements, ordinary black men and women provided a model for how citizens should mediate political disputes. Even in the midst of unparalleled violence, their democratic vision came through.[7]

Establishing the Pattern

All across Mississippi in the summer and fall of 1875, white-line Democratic clubs organized and began to lay the groundwork for a coup d'état. The planned takeover of the state government depended on numerous local campaigns against Republican officeholders and voters. The Natchez District, in which Republicans were strongest, was quiet during this election season, except in Claiborne County.[8]

The troubles in Claiborne began the year before, in 1874, when Ellen Smith (a white woman) married Haskin Smith (a black officeholder). Ellen Smith was the daughter of the proprietors of a Port Gibson hotel. Before the Civil War, Haskin Smith was the slave of Ellen's parents and worked as a waiter in their hotel. After emancipation Haskin became involved in local politics and won election as a justice of the peace in Port Gibson and also as a state representative in the Mississippi House. His marriage to Ellen was not just an interracial marriage, which was uncommon, but a union between a white woman and a black Republican officeholder. It caused quite a stir in the county. William Smith, Ellen's father, who had little trouble with Haskin when he was just a waiter at the hotel, threatened to kill his new son-in-law when he learned that the couple had eloped in Vicksburg. Rising to his defense, local blacks gave notice that retaliation would be swift to anyone who harmed their political leader. When the newlyweds returned to Port Gibson after a short honeymoon, a cadre of armed bodyguards paraded Haskin Smith through the town—a move that may have upset white Democrats even more than the marriage. Not only did local black citizens indicate their support for social equality by protecting the marital union, but their martial display on the streets suggested an increased willingness to publicly assert their power.[9]

Tempers subsided in Port Gibson, but a few months later in the city where the Smiths had eloped and honeymooned tensions boiled over. Vicksburg and the surrounding Warren County were not all that different from the other river counties in the Natchez District, except that they were notorious for the fiscal corruption of some Republican officeholders. In the run-up to the 1874 election, moderate and extremist Democrats debated the proper electoral strategy to overcome large black majorities, but this time the extremists won out. They adopted a white-line platform, eschewing any cooperation with Republican officeholders or black leaders, and publically threatened violent retribution on anyone who voted against them. Local blacks responded by mobilizing their militias and parading through the streets in counter displays of martial solidarity. Nevertheless, the white-line strategy seemed to work. A few hundred black voters stayed home on Election Day, enabling the White Man's Party to secure a small majority. More telling, local law enforcement officials seemed helpless in the midst of armed white militias parading down the streets and armed men publicly threatening to harm those who intended to vote Republican.[10]

Emboldened by their electoral triumph, Vicksburg white liners moved to oust Republicans from county offices. They declared Sheriff Peter Crosby's bond to be invalid, and when he refused to post a new one, a two-hundred-person mob showed up at his office and demanded his resignation. Crosby, a former slave and black veteran of the Union army, quickly complied and then fled to the state capital in Jackson. State officials were outraged by the thuggery and mob rule in Vicksburg, but Governor Adelbert Ames would not commit the state militia nor refer the matter to the courts. Instead, he encouraged Crosby to raise a posse of county residents and take back his office. Crosby rallied black farmers and laborers in the plantation hinterlands and marched to Vicksburg, but the white-line forces, hearing of Crosby's posse, mobilized their own military unit, drawing on whites from the river counties to defend the city. The great fear among the planter class was about to be realized: a general rebellion among the black majority in "its most galling and revolting form," warned a moderate Democrat who feared the implications of racial violence.[11]

The specter of a Haitian-style uprising had long given moderate Democrats the edge in their debates with white-line extremists, but now the prophecy was about to be tested. When the black militias approached the white liners' defensive fortifications they realized that they were outgunned and outmatched. They quickly came to terms and began to withdraw back to the countryside. But as they were leaving the scene, the white liners opened fire on the retreating black posse. Chaos ensued as black men fled and white liners hunted them down, tearing through the neighborhoods in a campaign of slaughter that left at least ninety and perhaps as many as three hundred freedpeople dead. In response, President Grant deployed federal troops to restore order to Vicksburg and to reinstate Crosby, but the damage was revealing. Neither the federal nor the state government could prevent a massacre or the overthrow of a duly elected sheriff. White liners learned that an effective campaign of intimidation and violence could oust local Republican governments and that a massacre would likely prompt the intervention of the U.S. Army.[12]

The troubles in Vicksburg made a deep impression on Claiborne County citizens to the south. "The Vicksburg affair," admitted one of the county's Democratic leaders, "gave a coloring to all these things." In the summer of 1875, the newly formed "White Leagues of Claiborne" announced in a letter to Governor Ames their plan to "get rid" of local white Republicans, or "Scalawags," and they all but begged the governor to send "negro troops" against them because, they boasted, "We have the best rifles and [we are] eager for an opportunity to use them."[13]

Despite the bluster and the recent massacre in Vicksburg, local freedpeople, both women and men, were not cowed by this vigorous campaign of intimidation. They were still in a position of strength and many refused to believe that local white liners, who were their neighbors, would use force. So when white liners began to appear at Republican meetings, black Republicans countered by showing up in overwhelming numbers, and they "completely badgered" and "insulted" their armed opponents. Black female servants warned their white female employers that "they had better behave themselves" because, as a Port Gibson attorney explained, freedpeople were "vastly in the ascendency."[14]

In another instance of local opposition to white-line militancy, black militiamen rallied to the defense of a Republican brass band. The band had spent the weekend in Copiah County to the east, playing before large Republican gatherings, but upon its return a rumor spread through the white community that hundreds of black men were accompanying the band in order to march on and set fire to Port Gibson. White clubs quickly rallied their forces and set off for the county line to intercept the band. Black residents in the plantation districts countered by mobilizing their own militias and then met the brass band near a merchant's store. The black militiamen dug in behind "a little woods" to wait for the advancing white clubs in what seemed to be a replay of the Vicksburg massacre. Instead, a leading white Republican accompanied the white clubs out to the store and mediated the dispute, assuring each side that neither intended to attack the other. The defensive lines were such that if the white liners had charged, the black militiamen would have "nearly cleaned them out," testified the Republican district attorney.[15]

As the election neared, each side attempted to intimidate the other and inflate its own strength with rumors of armed mobilizations. Democrats spread rumors that rural black people were gathering "their shot-guns . . . and young men were loading their guns." Reports of freedpeople marching "into town to destroy the whole town" kept the white liners in a state of frenzy; they organized pickets at the edge of Port Gibson and rushed to the defense at every threatening report. In one instance a band of white men rode up to James Page's house in the middle of the night, demanding to know if he truly intended to lead a black army to burn down Port Gibson. Page, who was the county treasurer and a former sheriff and who had purchased his own freedom in 1857, had long-standing ties to the community and was one of the most respected black men in the region. He responded to the white club with derision: "I do want to fight; I want to fight bad, and if some of you will come up here I will fight you—waking up a man and bringing him out here in his shirt-tail to attend to your damned nonsense!"[16]

That the county could erupt in a violent conflagration still seemed a remote possibility for longtime residents like Page. He had seen violence firsthand when Grant's army swept through the county thirteen years before during the war, but he had subsequently gained the trust of the white populace with his honest business dealings and honorable public service. He knew white club members and black militiamen personally, and he seemed unwilling to accept that this new emancipated society that he had worked so hard to form was being ripped asunder.

Others were beginning to have their doubts. Haskin Smith, the state legislator whose interracial marriage had sown seeds of discord in the county, urged Governor Ames to send "twenty-four guns" from the state militia's arsenal so that the Republican brass band could defend itself from future attacks. And he also suggested that the governor should "organize a militia" in Claiborne County, guaranteeing that leading black Republicans and the rank and file would readily join up. "We are living over a volcano that is liable to burst at any minute," wrote W. D. Sprott, a white Republican and county superintendent of education, in another plea to the governor for help.[17]

Across the state there was growing awareness that this was to be an election like none before it. Many of Mississippi's most influential black leaders were beginning to see that the "death knell" was upon them, so they joined in signing a public letter to warn black voters of "the dangers which so seriously threatens our liberties as American citizens." In the face of inaction from the governor and a lack of interest from the White House, their one hope was that local blacks could resist Democrats' campaign of terrorism. "Let us, with uplifted hands and with one voice," they implored, "swear by Him who led the children of Israel out of the wilderness, that we will save ourselves from the clutches of the Democracy, and that we *will* cast our votes in spite of threats and intimidation."[18]

Recognizing that local neighborhoods and communities could expect little help from state or federal authorities, Democrats turned their attention to suppressing black mobilization. During a Republican procession through downtown Port Gibson, Democrats flashed their weapons and exchanged insults with some of the "two thousand colored voters" in the parade. Once at the barbecue grounds, where dinner and political speeches were scheduled, Republicans found nearly five hundred white men, half on horseback and all outfitted with the most advanced rifles, waiting for them. Republicans were quite specific about the weaponry that the Democrats carried. They were "armed with breech-loading rifles & breech-loading shot-guns," noted a petition from leading black and white Republicans, "with the latest improved Smith & Wesson pistols, of the Russian pattern, loading at the breech, with cartridge-boxes, with bayonets, and any amount of fixed ammunition." Facing the most up-to-date military hardware and an enraged mob, Republican leaders reasoned that it was "better for them to keep the peace at all hazards," so they abandoned their meeting and went home.[19]

Avoiding the provocations of the White League was no easy task, and it did little to impede the Democrats from reaching their larger goal. With White Leaguers riding across the county with impunity, Sheriff Thomas Bland, a freeborn black farmer, turned over his law enforcement responsibilities to a committee of three white Democrats, declaring that he was "unable to keep the peace." Numerous pleas to Governor Ames for troops went unanswered, as did appeals to the federal government for the protection of political and civil rights. On the eve of the election, bands of white men roamed the countryside "hunting influential republicans," harassing Republican voters, and forcing Republican candidates off the ballot.[20]

On Election Day 1875, white-line Democrats amassed at the polls early in the morning. Voting proceeded lightly and without incident until the noon hour, when a procession of nearly four hundred black Republicans approached the Port Gibson polling place. Marching "military-like" but with a large white flag, the unarmed voters strode up to a line of armed white liners. As the two sides faced off, a black man and a white man exchanged words and a scuffle ensued. "Just about that time a pistol was fired," recalled white Republican district attorney E. H. Stiles. The shot broke the long-simmering tension, unleashing the white liners' fury. Fifty white Democrats opened fire on the unarmed black voters, who immediately ran for cover. Six were wounded, and one was killed. Fearful of a counterattack, the Democrats telegraphed Vicksburg and Hazelhurst for reinforcements and then placed a cannon in the middle of the road facing the black section of town. "They cannot vote, for if they come back here there will be another row," lamented the chairman of the Democratic executive committee, who could not control his party's violent members, "and I do not want to see the colored men killed for an election." With no assurances of protection, black Republicans went home, concluding that their lives were worth more than their vote.[21]

It was an impossible situation for black citizens. If they engaged their opponents in an armed clash, they were sure to suffer extensive casualties from their better-armed foes. Just as crucial, entering into combat would undermine the very principle that they held so dear—that political disputes were best mediated through free and fair elections in which every male voter participated on an equal basis. Yet by refusing to go to war against the white liners, they ceded control of the election machinery, and thereby the mechanism used to determine who held power.

Across the county, extremist Democrats pushed aside those calling for restraint and used intimidation and fraud to suppress the Republican vote. At the Bethel and Brandywine Precincts, local Democrats needed help from white liners in neighboring Copiah County and Louisiana to assist in burning Republican ballots and adding Democratic tickets to the ballot boxes. At the Peytona Precinct, black Republicans refused to vote after witnessing white liners drilling in the days leading up to the election and digging a defensive trench near the polling place. At the Grand Gulf Precinct, black voters took a more militant approach. They came to the polls with weapons and in much larger numbers than white Democrats. Instead of an outbreak of violence, a fair election ensued; however, subsequent ballot-box stuffing neutralized the Republican majority. Only at the Rocky Springs Precinct were ballots cast openly and fairly, because there moderate Democrats kept their more violent members under control. Despite the blatant and clumsy voting fraud—Democrats used Port Gibson tickets to stuff Grand Gulf ballot boxes—Republicans never filed a formal complaint to challenge the results because Democrats threatened Republican leaders, such as James Page and Solomon Unger, "with assassination" if they contested the election.[22]

Fraud, intimidation, and violence produced a Democratic victory in Claiborne County for the first time since the enactment of universal manhood suffrage. Across Mississippi, white-line Democrats used similar methods with great effect. Twenty-six counties switched from Republican to Democratic majorities, with none greater than in Yazoo County, where the Republican vote dropped from 2,427 in 1873 to 7 two years later. Whether as a result of local intimidation and fraud or massive violence, the consequence was a new Democratic majority in the state legislature.[23]

Across the Deep South in the states where Republicans still had power, Democrats took notice of the "Mississippi Plan" and the violence that "redeemed" the state. Energized by the Democrats' overwhelming victory, the new legislature moved quickly to oust the governor and lieutenant governor and gain full control of the state government. To further consolidate their power, they passed a new voter registration law that placed Democratic registrars at every election district and empowered these registrars to scrutinize potential voters. The intent was to reduce the black vote and to minimize the subsequent need for violence to ensure that Democrats remained in power.[24]

Strengthened by these new legal powers and emboldened by the absence of federal intervention, white liners set their sights on the remaining Republican counties, particularly those in the Natchez District. The fears of a general black uprising and a Haitian-style race war in which whites would be decimated proved to be unfounded, and so white extremists gained the upper hand in most of the river counties and began to lay the groundwork for the overthrow of local governments. But unlike the 1875 campaign, when there was some caution and some fear of a backlash, Democrats in the subsequent campaigns in 1876 and 1878 pushed harder than ever before, knowing that local Republicans had few friends beyond the district. The result was a war of a different sort, in which, for the first time since the Civil War, skirmishes broke out across the Natchez District, leading to massacres in Wilkinson County, Jefferson County, and Tensas Parish.

The Place and Space of Electoral Violence

The overthrow of Republican rule in Claiborne County fit a pattern that was subsequently refined and extended throughout the Natchez District. White liners used the geography of the district to isolate and weaken county governments and community leaders. In terms of local politics, black leaders traversed the Mississippi River to form networks and alliances, but the river also acted as a barrier to district-wide mobilization. Black people outnumbered whites by nearly ten to one on either bank of the river, yet they were never able to effectively come together as one unit. Ferryboats, of course, could easily negotiate the mighty river, but, in practical terms, it was difficult for ordinary people to stay closely connected to those on the other side. And because the river also served as a political boundary between two states, there were fewer incentives for Louisiana political organizers to coordinate with Mississippi political operatives, despite the fact that the geography and economy of the region brought them all together.

When the white liners attacked, they always came from the interior of the state and moved toward the Mississippi River. Farther away from the riverbanks on the outskirts of the Natchez District, the land changed from bottomland to a hillier topography. The racial demographics of these interior counties were also different, with roughly a one-to-one ratio of blacks to whites in the Louisiana parishes to the west of the district and in the Mississippi counties to the east. It is also worth noting that the counties that bordered the Natchez District all succumbed to political violence and Democratic rule prior to the outbreaks of violence in the district. Thus, when white liners attacked, they pinned freedpeople up against the riverbanks, leaving them few options for escape or retreat and making it more difficult to coordinate a response or counterattack against the invaders. White liners also boosted their military strength in the Natchez District by incorporating experienced marauders from these interior counties. By

1876 the Natchez District was almost entirely surrounded by militaristic bands of white supremacists.[25]

The white liners first targeted the towns and urban spaces in order to concentrate their power, and then they used this terrain as a launching point for attacks at black political strength in rural areas. To gain control of the towns, they turned their attention to white Republican officeholders. White liners explained, sometimes forcefully, that they intended to take control of the government and that an alliance with paramilitary forces would be less disruptive than an open confrontation. One white liner put the matter simply to the leading officeholders of Tensas Parish: they "must get on the Lord's side or they would be killed." The sheriff and parish judge, both white southern Republicans, quickly switched sides and joined the Democrats. This had the effect of giving legitimacy and legal authority to the subsequent scourge of terrorism. In Wilkinson County the Republican sheriff, a former Confederate officer, needed less overt convincing. He made a deal with local white liners that he would call on their assistance to disperse uprisings and they would, in return, "respect his authority" in other matters.[26]

White Republicans were particularly vulnerable in an environment in which the color line was used to distinguish friend from foe. They lived and worked in towns where they were highly visible and had few places to hide. In Claiborne County a "committee" of White Leaguers visited John J. Smith, a state senator, carpetbagger, and former sheriff, and impressed on him the risks of continuing to hold office. The senator was so terribly alarmed that he and his wife immediately fled their home, choosing to wait on the Louisiana side rather than wait on a Claiborne dock for a passing riverboat to take them out of the region. When white liners came looking for J. C. Ellis, a Jefferson County officeholder and native Mississippian, at his home, he escaped only because two black men guided him first through the countryside and then through the "deep woods" to safety in a neighboring county.[27]

With the white Republican leadership either absorbed into the Democratic fold or run out of the county, the larger towns soon became armed encampments populated with paramilitary groups from surrounding counties. In this volatile environment, rumors quickly spread that rural black laborers were mobilizing to march on the major towns. The white liners posted pickets at the outskirts of town, further militarizing the community. In effect, local officials ceded civil authority to the white militias.[28]

The marginalization of white Republican leaders left black leaders more vulnerable. In Wilkinson County, newly formed clubs—referred to as White Men's Clubs, Honest Men's Clubs, and Regulators and loosely affiliated with the Democratic Party—began to target neighborhood leaders. Alfred Black, a former slave, farmer, and local organizer, was nearly lynched by a small group of white men. They tied a noose around his neck, hoisted him into the air, and demanded that he reveal why he was organizing a labor club and whether he intended "to go down to the fight and kill the white people." Black denied the accusations and admitted only to being a member of a club, whereupon the regulators released him with the warning to never vote Republican again. Another group of armed white men hunted down Alexander Branch, an ex-slave, farm laborer, and county supervisor, and told him to resign from office or they would kill him. Branch replied that it was not entirely up to him to decide. After all, he told his tormentors, "if the people are running me, it is not for me to say if the people put me in, I shall have to obtain, and do the best I can." But Branch's commitment to grassroots democracy had its limits, especially in an environment in which the Republican sheriff allowed white paramilitary clubs to run rampant. Branch reasoned that the people's support would not mean much "after I was a dead man," and so he resigned his office.[29]

The Battle of Fort Adams

About six months after Mississippi's infamous 1875 election, black residents in Wilkinson County took a different approach to the paramilitary violence. Instead of avoiding a violent confrontation, they mobilized their militia forces and engaged the invading white liners in what became known as the Battle of Fort Adams. The pitched battle, reminiscent of the skirmishes between companies of Union soldiers and ragtag bands of Confederate guerrillas twelve years before, was the most aggressive opposition to the white-line assault. Wilkinson County freedpeople took the opposite approach from Claiborne County Republicans. They used violence to defend the integrity of their neighborhoods.

In May 1876 the white-line campaign initially followed the usual script. The white Republican sheriff and other prominent Republican officeholders agreed to join the Democrats, and local clubs began to hunt down black political organizers in the rural areas. But then, near the county's southern border with West Feliciana Parish, a white merchant was murdered at his store, either by a black political club or by a white club in blackface. News of the murder quickly crossed the border into West Feliciana and into Amite County to the east, prompting white clubs from those counties to invade Wilkinson County from the interior. At least one black militia in the eastern part of Wilkinson County mobilized in response to the amassed white forces, but the militia was unable to prevent the white mob from rounding up two black neighborhood leaders and lynching them in the woods.[30]

Not long after, rumors of an impending race war began to swirl throughout the county. White forces organized pickets in Woodville, the county seat, to guard against the black militias that they believed "were going to march on the town." Meanwhile, in the densely populated black neighborhoods along the Mississippi River, black militias mobilized to defend their homes from "the whites" who they heard "were killing women and children." Near the river town of Fort Adams, among the bottomlands where they worked the cotton fields both in slavery and in freedom, black residents could see how the events would play out. They knew about the violent election campaigns of the previous year. They also knew that they were boxed into a corner, with white-line forces to the south and east and their backs to the Mississippi River, leaving the northern border with Adams County as their only escape route.[31]

Black militias in Wilkinson County dated back to at least 1869 and were composed of veterans of the Union army. They were armed, experienced, and had superior numbers, yet they were still at a comparative disadvantage in relation to white paramilitary forces. Nearly every freedman owned a gun, usually a shotgun or a pistol, but these weapons were better suited for hunting than for military conflicts. At best, shotguns and "old guns" could be used for a formidable defense, but the weaponry of the white forces clearly overwhelmed the black militias.[32]

As in the other counties and parishes that succumbed to white-line violence, the white clubs, or Regulators, as they were known locally, possessed the latest and most powerful firearms—rifles that could be quickly reloaded and fired with more accuracy and at longer distances than anything the black militias possessed. "These Regulators in our section of the country," explained Emil L. Weber, a white Republican state senator from West Feliciana Parish, "are better armed to-day, all of them, old and young . . . than they were in confederate times, and they are more violent." Additionally, the white forces were mounted and led by former Confederate officers, experienced in battlefield maneuvers. They flooded the region from surrounding counties on horseback, and they commandeered riverboats to transport supplies and to prevent freedpeople from escaping. William T. Martin, a leading Adams County Democrat, prepared to send a force of white Natchezians, outfitted with one hundred "Winchester carbines," on a boat down the Mississippi River to Wilkinson County.[33]

White liners also sensed the strategic implications of the coming confrontation. It was an opportunity to root out the foundation of freedpeople's politics, to "disperse," as one white liner explained, mobilized black communities. Each day more and more armed and mounted white Democrats rode into Woodville looking for a chance to kill black Republicans. According to Hugh M. Foley, a freeborn former state legislator, a force of fifteen hundred armed white men— two-thirds of whom came from outside the county and some from as far away as Baton Rouge—mobilized to attack the black militias in the western half of Wilkinson County. The white forces headed west from Woodville and divided into three companies about three to four miles apart, which then swept into the southwest corner of the county in order to push the black militias north and pin them against a bend in the river known as the Old River Island.[34]

Anticipating an attack, but probably not a three-pronged strike, black militias took up defensive positions at various plantations: along a line of thick briar hedges at one place, at the gin house of another, and at the edge of the quarters of a third. "We came upon a line of battle in an old field," recalled one of the white-line leaders, "which had been formed by some of the negro ex-soldiers, and promptly charged them in columns of four." In each of these skirmishes, the better-armed and better-organized white forces routed the black militias until, after a series of negotiations, the black forces surrendered. About eleven hundred white men then made camp for the night, as an occupying force, in the midst of the black neighborhoods. Between thirty and fifty black men lay dead after the series of military clashes that day.[35]

The next day, black militia forces were conflicted about whether to continue to fight against the white forces or to flee their homes. Some eagerly followed neighborhood leaders such as Mark Klein, a local preacher, who implored local freedmen to muster, for "it was the duty of every colored man to get his gun and fight for his rights." Three to four hundred freedmen assembled at the plantation of John J. Cage (judged to be "a very prominent radical negro" by white liners) and his uncle, but they dispersed once they learned that a white force of over four hundred horsemen was headed their way. They followed others who had already taken flight. Scores of black families fled to the woods or headed north to the relative safety of cities, such as Natchez or Jackson. One of those who fled was Alexander Branch, the county supervisor who was forced to resign from office. With the black leadership class intimidated or run off, Branch reasoned that it was "a fight between the poor people and the rich man now." The only advantage that freedpeople had was their labor: "Their whole capital is in the black men—every dogoned bit of it." Unless the "good [white] gentlemen," he told a senate committee, restrained "those wild men," they would all be "as poor as I am in two years."[36]

Local white residents were divided about the tactics of the paramilitary groups. Some would have liked nothing better than to clear out all of the black residents, but the major landowners were worried that these disturbances would prompt a mass exodus of freedpeople out of the region, leading to economic ruin. On his plantation in western Wilkinson County, William L. Brandon watched with trepidation as his black labor force began to drill in preparation for the attack from the east. When a group of white-line regulators approached secretly, unbeknownst to the hastily organized black militia, Brandon, a former Confederate general, was moved to intervene. He begged the white militia to spare his workers, testified one of the white militia leaders, explaining to them that "there were old negroes in the quarters that had nothing to do with it, and there were women and children there, and it was getting dark and there were a good many men among them that he liked, and [he feared] that a good many innocent ones would be killed." Brandon would undoubtedly benefit from the overthrow of Republican rule and the ouster of laboring men from public office, yet he could not countenance violence against the freedpeople whom he had known for many years. Brandon's stance underscores the importance of outside regulators in the overthrow of local democracy. The outsiders did not see neighbors, workers, or even former slaves; rather, they saw abstractions that threatened their power and racial privilege.[37]

With their backs to the Mississippi River, isolated from black majorities in the surrounding counties, and lacking sufficient weaponry, local freedpeople bravely stood up to the invaders in the most aggressive stand in the Natchez District, but they could not keep the "wild men" at bay. The head of the local Republican Party, Sheriff Noble, instead of defending rural freedpeople, turned against those who had elected him and joined white paramilitary forces in violently suppressing black militias. With Democrats in control of the state, there would be no assistance from the state's militia. Likewise, federal support was not forthcoming. From one former slave's perspective, the condition in Wilkinson County after the white insurrection was "more scarry [sic] than before the war." "I never heard of anybody doing such as they have been doing," he continued, "hanging and shooting them, and going on and catching men and hanging them. I don't know what to think of it." Local neighborhoods had mobilized their militias and had gone to war to defend their emancipated communities from the marauders who wanted to restore white rule. The price of militaristic confrontation was a high one, and the results were little different from those in other counties that confronted paramilitary violence.[38]

Conflicts over Public Space in Jefferson County

Five months later, as the 1876 election campaign began to heat up, Republicans in the Natchez District again faced the dilemma of how to respond to the white-line violence, which seemed certain to reappear. Neither the avoidance strategy in Claiborne County nor the militaristic strategy in Wilkinson County had kept the white liners at bay. In Jefferson County Republican leaders and ordinary black residents tried to find a middle ground between the two approaches. They were still living under the suspicion held by many white people that black people would eventually rise up and slaughter them, so to distance themselves from these scurrilous assumptions, black leaders tried to emphasize the mutual ties of affection across the color line and the shared heritage of American democracy. To accept the violence and engage in it, then, would only reinforce the arguments of the white liners that ordinary black people were unqualified to possess the rights of citizenship. And so freedpeople, in the words of black state representative James B. Cessor, tried "to be a little more magnanimous." But they also made a public stand, choosing to fight nonviolently for rights central to an open democracy: the rights to assemble and speak in public.[39]

While black political leaders struggled to renew and reinforce connections across the partisan divide, white liners went after the leading black officeholder, Merrimon Howard. Similar to the way elite whites in Vicksburg attempted to oust Peter Crosby from office, Jefferson County officials declared Howard's sheriff's bond invalid and required that he make a new one. Howard, a former slave, a founder of black schools in the county, and a loyal Republican, had just won reelection to his third term as sheriff. He enjoyed broad popular support, yet he reluctantly entered the race for a third term only after "my white friends" implored him to remain in office and after Democrats assured him "that no man" would oppose him. But white-line extremists pressured some of Howard's sureties to abandon his bond. He made a new one, but then the board of supervisors raised the bond by $4,000, to a total of $52,000. Howard complied with the new requirement. Subsequently, the new Democratic-majority state legislature passed a law that required all Mississippi sheriffs to post a new bond by August 1876. Exasperated by having to come up with a third bond and learning that local Democrats had pressured one of his longtime bondsmen—"a large merchant"—to withdraw, Howard gave up and let "the office be declared vacant." Thus a combination of pressure on legitimate sureties and new rules forced a popularly (and recently) elected black sheriff out of office just before the pivotal national election of 1876.[40]

Despite the momentum of the white liners, black Republicans were not willing to concede the upcoming election. They resisted the intimidation and proceeded to mobilize as they had done for the last nine years, gathering in urban spaces to prepare for the upcoming election campaign and to celebrate their shared political values. Rural residents became "very enthusiastic" and "commenced flocking to town," testified Howard, in order to learn about the results of the recent Republican national convention and the new party nominees, Rutherford B. Hayes and William A. Wheeler.[41]

Despite the warnings from local Democrats and the recent outbreaks of paramilitary violence in the South, local Republican leaders still did not anticipate an outbreak of violence. There was little history of collective violence in this rural county, neither in the previous elections nor during the Civil War. So like James Page before in Claiborne County, Merrimon Howard initially dismissed the rising threat from white-line clubs. Upon learning that a band of white horsemen were "hunting" for him "all day and night," Howard admitted to a congressional committee investigating Mississippi's electoral violence that he had "treated it as a joke and laughed it off." He ignored the growing hostility because he had developed strong friendships with Democrats and former slaveholders and believed that these friendly relations would prevail. "I want a good report to go out from Jefferson County," pleaded Howard to a crowd of hostile white Democrats, "to show that the white people and colored people here can get along and manage political affairs without any committees from Congress." His faith in local relationships would be sorely put to the test.[42]

Not until a planned pole-raising in the county seat of Fayette did Howard realize that there would be precious little goodwill from his Democratic neighbors. After a parley with a leading Democrat, Howard learned that hundreds of well-armed Democrats from Jefferson and the surrounding counties planned to ambush the Republican gathering and that "there will be bloodshed." Howard sent "men out in all directions," while he personally rode throughout the night "from plantation to plantation" to warn black Republicans to stay at home. Rural blacks heeded Howard's warning and a massacre was averted, but their caution did little to stem the tide of white-line terrorism.[43]

As was becoming clear, more was involved in these urban confrontations than mere control of physical places. The white liners' goal was to marginalize local Republicans and to eliminate the public and discursive space for politics. The implications of this strategy were plain to see for Jefferson County Republicans, so they made one final and risky push to mobilize their members and lay claim to the public spaces. A week and a half before the 1876 election they scheduled a political rally in downtown Fayette, knowing full well that armed Democrats would try to prevent the assembly or attack the participants. To avoid a violent confrontation, Merrimon Howard traveled "to every neighborhood" and instructed the men to leave their weapons at home and instead to bring "their wives and children." Howard hoped that a display of the "educatable children of the county" would make the armed Democrats think twice about attacking the Republican procession. The use of children and women in such a charged and dangerous environment was highly unusual in nineteenth-century politics, but it was not out of the ordinary for freedpeople. Because they had always conceptualized democracy as a broadly participatory movement, women (and children to a lesser extent) had played vital roles in voter mobilization campaigns and public meetings. With the future of their democratic society hanging in the balance, women and their families responded to the call for help at this desperate hour.[44]

To show that they were not intimidated and to demonstrate their own power, approximately three to four thousand men, women, and children gathered on the outskirts of town to march together in one mass procession. They formed into one column with Howard leading the way, followed by the men, and then the women and children in wagons. While they marched, as they had in previous partisan parades, two bands played music to keep the pace. But when they reached the outskirts of town, they found that the street was "completely blockaded" by about two hundred armed white Democrats. In the weeks before the election, white-line military companies from Claiborne, Franklin, and Adams Counties had converged on Jefferson, bolstering the local white-line forces. Farther down the street, another two hundred white men positioned themselves around a cannon in the middle of the road. The black procession halted within twenty feet of the paramilitary forces, close enough for Howard to see the "angry" and "determined" faces of the Democrats.[45]

This confrontation over the little town of Fayette—a county seat with approximately 370 residents—had less to do with control of the narrow streets than with access to public spaces and the legitimacy of black-led governance. Thinking quickly, Howard diverted the Republican procession to another street as the white mob drew closer and then sent them to a black church on the other side of town, where they could set up a "public-speaking stand." Black men encircled the square in front of the church to prevent the Democrats from crashing the meeting. Once secure, Howard sent for John R. Lynch, Mississippi's only black and only Republican congressman, and called for the women so that he could continue the rally. But then Howard, after successfully evading the armed white forces, made a serious mistake. Democratic leaders asked him if they could say a few words, and Howard, after receiving hasty assurances of peace and quiet at the meeting, acceded to the request. After creating a space for Republican assembly in the midst of intense hostility, Howard "made the colored men give way" and allowed about one hundred white Democrats into the inner sanctum of the rally.[46]

Howard's commitment to biracial democracy was such that he could not countenance an exclusively partisan public gathering. Yet that commitment gave white-line Democrats an opening to poison the public sphere and to stifle black political mobilization. Soon after Congressman Lynch began speaking, a white Democrat interrupted him, shouting, "You tell a damned lie." Lynch tried to continue, but each time Democrats "commenced hooting and hallooing." Exasperated by the intransigence of their political opponents, Republican leaders eventually called off the meeting.[47]

A few hundred of the four thousand freedpeople retreated to a railroad depot and eventually listened to a short speech from Lynch, but this small victory paled in comparison to the strategic suppression of grassroots politics by white liners. By controlling the urban places and blunting the voter mobilization rallies, they were able to more freely attack the rural neighborhoods that made up the base of the Republican Party's power in the district. And so one week after the failed mass meeting in Fayette, a small group of armed Democrats surrounded a black church in the countryside, initiating a series of events that culminated in the Jefferson County massacre.[48]

Bulldozing in Tensas

The wave of electoral violence in 1876 that swept over Jefferson County and much of South Carolina, Florida, and Louisiana did not reach Tensas and Concordia Parishes. Local residents voted in free elections and returned large Republican majorities, but they also watched with growing trepidation as Mississippi counties to the east and Louisiana parishes to the west succumbed to Democratic rule in spasmodic outbursts of violence. They knew that nearly thirty black men were killed across the river in Jefferson County for aligning themselves with the Republican Party. They feared Democratic control of Mississippi and Louisiana, and they wondered why the federal government had not intervened. Writing to President-Elect Rutherford B. Hayes, Merrimon Howard expressed the abandonment that many southern African Americans felt: "[I]t is Strang fact that this Goverment *will in vade* any forgen nation for a most trifel in Sult to one of its Citizens a *broad, but* will not protect its *lawal* [loyal] + true freinds at *home*."[49]

By 1878, as another election season was dawning, Tensas Parish residents began to sense that they would be targeted by the "bulldozers" (the term that locals used to describe white-line Democrats). They grew more worried when the leading white Republican officeholders joined the Democrats. Seeing the pattern of white-line suppression begin to take shape right before their eyes, the remaining Republican leaders, all black, made an unusual decision. They gave up trying to organize a Republican campaign and instead worked out an agreement with moderate white Democrats to create a new, Independent ticket, composed almost entirely of white men. It was a testament to how swiftly the political fortunes had shifted that in one of the great Republican strongholds in the South a straight Republican ticket was no longer feasible. Even John R. Lynch recognized the new political reality. He recommended that black people form Independent tickets with "substantial and reliable citizens"—in other words, white property holders—in order to ensure "a fair election and an honest count."[50]

It was a sharp break from the recent political history of the region. Tensas was one of Louisiana's "banner" Republican parishes and provided a functional model for biracial politics in the Deep South. Although black men dominated the ranks of officeholders, white and black public officials had worked together in "perfect harmony and good feeling" during a decade of Republican rule, testified a white planter. But it all changed in the wake of the Mississippi Plan and the rise of the White Leagues.[51]

The one exception on the all-white Independent ticket was Alfred Fairfax, an ex-slave Republican officeholder and the nominee for Congress. Democrats considered Fairfax to be "the great Ajax of the Republican league" and seemed to believe that he was the linchpin of the Independent Party. Fairfax, a thirty-eight-year-old Baptist preacher and farmer, owned ninety-three acres of land and was a member of the parish school board. Quite literally, he stood in the way of an easy conquest of the parish, which made him a prime target for the white liners.[52]

Before black Republican operatives could gather together to organize the campaign for the Independent ticket, the bulldozers raided Fairfax's home. In the dead of night, fifty to one hundred mounted white men rode up swiftly to his house, which was well outside the town of Waterproof, near the levee and about two hundred yards from the river. A handful of white men pushed open the door. When they saw Fairfax reaching for his gun, one bulldozer fired at him. Hearing the gunshots but not being able to see inside the house, the bulldozers fired wildly into the building. One of their own, Capt. John G. Peck, a Catahoula Parish farmer, was gunned down, as was William Singleton, a friend of Fairfax's. Two other of Fairfax's friends were wounded, but Fairfax and his wife escaped unscathed.[53]

Because of the rural surroundings and because most of the attackers were not locals, Fairfax was able to slip away on foot. He made his way the next morning to the planned gathering of black political activists in Tensas Parish. Over the next week, Fairfax traveled throughout the parish along the edges of the fields, across the bayous, and through thickets, at each point relying on friends for shelter and local knowledge of the countryside. Finally, he escaped the parish by riverboat, making his way south to Vidalia, where he was able to find a friendly press to print his side's Independent ballots for the upcoming election.[54]

With Fairfax alive and actively mobilizing black people under the Independent ticket, the bulldozers shifted tactics and began to directly terrorize ordinary black families and households in the parish. Within a few days of the attack at Fairfax's house, at least five hundred armed outsiders descended on Tensas Parish and began to roam through the countryside, even spilling over into neighboring Concordia Parish, all the while hunting for particular neighborhood leaders and other black men. Democratic militias and rifle companies invaded Tensas from at least eight surrounding parishes and counties in the run-up to the election. Although the identities of these men from the interior parishes are mostly unknown, it is likely that they were well versed in paramilitary violence, perhaps even having participated in the Colfax massacre of 1873. Indeed, Captain Peck, the man who was killed while trying to attack Fairfax's home, was selected for his previous bulldozing experience in a neighboring parish. At the very least, they were fully aware of the White League terrorism that plagued the Red River valley and northern Louisiana.[55]

At first black residents responded to the white-line invasion by rising to the defense of their parish and neighborhoods. Hearing of the attack on Fairfax, black clubs from Concordia Parish to the south crossed the border into Tensas and other local blacks gathered together around the town of Waterproof, near Fairfax's home. Meanwhile a sheriff's posse and a company of bulldozers from Franklin Parish headed down to Waterproof from St. Joseph, under the pretext that "the negroes were massed there for bad purposes . . . for committing outrages." The posse, led by former white Republican leaders C. C. Cordill and John W. Register, numbered anywhere from fifty to one hundred men. Two days after the attack on Fairfax's house, an advanced guard came up on the neighborhood where Fairfax lived, known as Bass's place, and took fire from a hundred or so black men arrayed along the levee. Armed mostly with shotguns, the black militia drove off the guard, but their bullets fell short. Paradoxically, the show of force played right into the bulldozers' hands.[56]

Black resistance brought to mind the Haitian insurrectionists who had massacred whites, and so, as one bulldozer put it, to "prevent a scene of slaughter, the like of which would approximate to that of San Domingo," the bulldozers used excessive force against Tensas blacks. When the advanced guard returned with the entire posse, all on horseback, they charged down Bass's Lane through the plantation quarters, firing indiscriminately as black residents fled the bulldozers. About this time, a gin located behind Bass's place went up in flames and consumed seventy bales of cotton. Dick Miller, a black farmer, was detained by the sheriff and blamed for the arson, but instead of incarcerating Miller in the parish jail, the posse lynched him in the swamps. With the election still three weeks off, with outsiders targeting political leaders and ordinary farmers, and with local authorities encouraging the lawlessness, many just hoped to survive the bulldozing scourge.[57]

With the parish Republican leadership in disarray, dozens of small squads composed of former Union soldiers mobilized to protect their families and political leaders. C. E. Ruth, a black justice of the peace and chairman of the Republican convention, encountered one of these squads of about fifteen black men. They "had come to protect" him, they explained. Grateful for the gesture, Ruth took them to a saloon and bought them a quart of whiskey but then told the men to go home. As a magistrate, he could not endorse a vigilante response, no matter how well intentioned. Nonetheless, armed black men frightened white town residents. Waterproof residents sent a letter to the outlying black political clubs, claiming that they had no role in the "Fairfax affair" and pledging to protect the clubs from outsiders if only "they would not molest the town."[58]

As the plea from white residents of Waterproof suggests, many locals were ambivalent and some white people refused to sanction the political terrorism. Almost all of the white candidates on the Independent ticket were planters who were supported by rural farmers and laborers in what came to be known as a "country people's ticket." The supporters of this "independent ticket" decried the influence of all outsiders, carpetbaggers and bulldozers alike. In this sense, the troubles were not merely a "war of races" but also a "white man's fight" over how best to live in a biracial society under democratic governance. Local white men divided between those who aligned with their black neighbors against outsiders and those who welcomed and participated in the havoc instigated by the bulldozers.[59]

Many of the black families that labored on the lands of these Independent whites hoped that the wealth and status of these planters would mitigate the violence. James M. McGill, a planter, former slaveholder, and self-described "Old-line Whig," recalled that he provided sanctuary to a number of his black farm laborers. "Some of the men came and slept in my house, and would not go out of sight of my wife when I was away from the place," McGill explained. "They slept on my gallery, but I did not think there was any danger, and I told them so; but I could not make them think it." Rebecca Ross, a twenty-one-year-old freedwoman who witnessed the attack on Fairfax's house, recalled that she "staid with the white people one part of the time" because she was frightened by the "Franklinites"—the armed white men from Franklin Parish. Other white Independent leaders publically pledged their protection to black Republican leaders and black supporters. "I thought our party ought to have manhood enough," declared a white planter and candidate for justice of the peace, "to protect men who had served us, and we intended to do it."[60]

But even white planters of long standing had difficulty withstanding the bulldozers. Extremist Democrats denounced white members of the Independent ticket as "having drawn the color line"; they questioned their manhood and accused them of leading "the negroes against our friends and neighbors to murder their women and children, to burn, pillage, and destroy." The denunciations were so intense that some white planters could no longer rely on the normal prerogatives that their race and status accorded them. On one plantation, white planters constructed "a barricade of cotton bales" in anticipation of an expected attack from the bulldozers.[61]

The ineffectuality of local planters—who had little in common politically with their laborers except a desire for social peace—was exemplified in a mass meeting on the plantation of Dr. Weatherly, a candidate for coroner. A large crowd of freedpeople gathered to hear black and white speakers for the Independent ticket, but before the meeting could begin bulldozers arrived, armed with Winchester rifles, in a "Buggy Brigade" to prevent any "speech-making."

Weatherly's plantation had been used previously as a site for black celebrations, such as a Fourth of July barbecue. But the presence of the bulldozers unnerved the Independent leaders, who suggested that the meeting be "broken up." Two white women—Mrs. Weatherly and her daughter, Ida—would have none of it. They berated the male political leaders for being cowardly and demanded that they "[h]old a meeting" on their plantation "and if attacked fight," testified one witness. Because of their protestations, the meeting continued, and "quite a number of black people remained," though with a few less speakers.[62]

A remarkable biracial alliance had formed in the midst of unprecedented repression, but this unusual coalition also signified the social chaos unleashed by the bulldozers. The local government had acquiesced to paramilitary Democrats, while state and federal authorities watched from a distance. Local Republican leaders had fled the public scene, and now wealthy male planters cowered before outsiders. For ordinary black residents who labored in the parish's rich cotton fields and did not have the advantages of wealth, status, or powerful friends, their options were limited. Nevertheless, Noah Neely, a twenty-seven-year-old laborer and school board member was appreciative of the planters' "attempt to secure a fair and peaceful election, and to protect the colored people in the exercise of their rights."[63]

One way to secure protection against white-line attacks was by joining the Daylight Club. Organized by the bulldozing wing of the Democratic Party, the club issued certificates of membership and promises of protection. About two hundred freedpeople joined the Democratic club and received "certificates of protection" from Solomon Schaifer, a black Baptist minister and Republican officeholder who switched allegiances during the 1878 campaign. Yet the vast majority of freedpeople spurned the Democrats' offers of protection, including most black leaders.[64]

With few other options, large numbers of freedpeople hid out in the woods, or they fled the parish altogether. It was a dry time of year (October), so whenever the mounted bulldozers took off for one particular plantation or neighborhood, the people could see "the dust curled up from the road . . . over the tops of the trees," recalled one white cotton planter. Seeing the clouds of dust billow up in the distance, black men fled to the woods and swamps that lay behind the cotton fields. Over the two weeks before the election, work in the fields effectively came to a halt as dozens of men (and sometimes women and children) took refuge in the thickly forested regions of the parish, returning to their homes only at night. One black political organizer recalled that the woods were so filled with men that it seemed "as if a lot of sheep was running through the bushes." Constable Duncan C. Smith, a law enforcement officer, slept in the woods at night because, he told a senate committee, the bulldozers "were taking out colored men and hanging and shooting them; and we were afraid it would be our turn next; even women slept in the woods; for if a woman talked too big, they threatened to take her down and whip her." According to one witness, the bulldozers were not satisfied with political intimidation; they terrorized the population by "rob[bing] the poor colored people of their money, watches, wearing apparel, and even the poor and helpless women of their virtue."[65]

In a few short months, the emancipated world that Tensas Parish black residents had fashioned had been nearly upended. White-line invaders ran off their leaders and attacked black people indiscriminately. An untold number of freedpeople were harassed and assaulted, and at least eighteen but probably more than seventy freedpeople were killed during the election campaign of 1878 in Tensas Parish. And unlike in 1875 or in 1876, there was not even a discussion about sending troops to restore order. The Democratic governor of Louisiana, Francis T. Nicholls, endorsed the plan to run off "the leading colored men." And President Hayes did not deviate from his policy of nonintervention in southern elections.[66]

The Last Phase: Voter Fraud

When freedpeople emerged from the woods and other safe havens on Election Day, to the surprise of the white liners, the vast majority of eligible freedmen voted—and they voted for Republican or anti-Democratic candidates. The white-line attacks seriously disrupted mobilization efforts, but, ironically, they somewhat fulfilled the purpose of a mobilization campaign. Everyone in the parish or county had learned of the upcoming election, and everyone knew what each side represented—violence helped to clarify the issues. It is not surprising, then, that black men showed up at the polls in great numbers to vote against the white-line tickets. What was unusual was the small number of white liners who showed up at the polls to threaten black voters. Quite simply, the white liners were spread too thin on Election Day. The hundreds of invaders had to return to their home counties to cast their votes and stuff ballot boxes. Although they ultimately failed to dismantle grassroots black politics, their efforts to control urban spaces and to weaken the Republican leadership had a lasting impact. They left local black citizens with little recourse in contesting the fraudulent election returns.

The majority Republican vote indicates that ordinary black people had rebuffed the intimidation from paramilitary forces. In Tensas, Jefferson, Claiborne, and Concordia, black voters cast ballots for Republican or anti-Democratic tickets, but electoral fraud ultimately discounted vast Republican majorities and gave white-line Democrats control of local government. Wilkinson County was an anomaly to this trend. It was the only locality to post a Republican majority after the paramilitary violence. A few months after the battle of Fort Adams,

Wilkinson County voters went to the polls and, somewhat surprisingly, elected a slate of Republicans. Of course, these Republicans were many of the same white officeholders who sided with the white liners.[67]

Electoral fraud rested on a foundation of white-line violence. The counter-revolutionary insurgency that had paved the way for the Democratic takeover of state governments had severe consequences for the voting process. At every parish polling place, Democratic registrars, appointed by the governor, administered the registration books and counted the votes, increasing the potential for partisan electoral fraud. In Claiborne County in 1876, only professed Democrats were allowed to register to vote without complication. Black Republicans were subjected to an array of trickery, while the few black Democrats were fast-tracked through the registration process. Registrars, using the tactics authorized by the Democratic legislature, asked, "What is your occupation?" and then followed up with, "Where prosecuted?" Thinking that the official referred to "prosecution with a court," some black Republicans answered by referring to "a certain county, before a certain magistrate," when in fact the registrar was only asking where the individual was employed. But the misguided answer was enough for the Democratic registrars to reject the voter application. Such efforts prevented at least five hundred Republicans from registering. On Election Day, Democratic registrars slowed the process of voting to a near standstill and prevented dozens of Republican voters from taking their turn at the ballot box. Then, while voters were waiting in line, a group of Democrats let loose over one hundred "pistol shots" in a coordinated effort to drive black men from the polls. One black man was killed and three others were wounded in the hail of gunfire. Republican postmaster Thomas Richardson, an ex-slave barber, reluctantly turned to the courageous and dedicated Republican voters, much as he had done in 1875, and told them that there was no more point in voting that day: "The same power that makes it necessary to bring guns to the polls will throw out your votes when they are cast, and you had better go home."[68]

In Jefferson County Democrats still had doubts about the effectiveness of their paramilitary tactics, even after they had prevented Republican mass meetings in Fayette and massacred black Republicans in the countryside. Just before the election, leading citizens used economic pressure to influence the vote. They published a resolution in the local newspaper stating that "they will no longer furnish, clothe, feed, hire, or rent to any person who is politically opposed to us, or who will vote against us in the coming election, regardless of race or color." But economic coercion had not worked well in the past and there is little evidence that it made much of a difference in this election. "Political terrorism," reported John R. Lynch to the Senate investigating committee, held sway throughout the county, yet black Republicans crowded the polls. In response, Democrats stole Republican votes. R. H. Truly, the local Democratic newspaper editor, boasted that he possessed keys to all of the county's ballot boxes, and he informed one Republican officeholder that Democratic election officers would "take [Republican votes] out, and substitute democratic votes or tickets" whenever Republicans polled a plurality. In this way, Democrats turned a twelve-hundred-vote Republican majority in 1875 into an eleven-hundred-vote Democratic majority in 1876.[69]

In Tensas Parish, William Coolidge, a black farmer, former member of the police jury, and candidate for justice of the peace on the Independent ticket, mobilized two to three hundred freedmen to march to the polls on Election Day. They came together, as was their routine, to ensure internal solidarity, but this time they also traveled as a large group because they feared an attack from armed bulldozers at the polls. The attacks never came, but Tensas voters faced unprecedented scrutiny at the ballot box. At some polling places, local bulldozers removed Independent tickets from the hands of black voters and replaced them with Democratic tickets. At one precinct, two to three hundred Independent ballots were cast, but only fourteen were counted in the final tally. At others, bulldozers watched carefully how certain black Republican leaders, who had been warned not to vote the Independent ticket, cast their ballots. The night before the election, local bulldozers kidnapped State Senator A. J. Bryant, interrogated him, and vowed to kill him unless he supported the Democratic ticket. Bryant, a thirty-three-year-old minister and landowner, was likely born into slavery and was a loyal Republican, having previously held the offices of sheriff and parish school board member. The next day some of the same bulldozers stood at the polls and watched as Bryant, "afraid they would come after me again," cast a Democratic vote. When Spencer Ross, a sharecropper and leader of a rural political club, reached the polls, he found them crowded with bulldozers, so instead of casting an Independent ticket, he placed a regular Democratic ticket in the box. "I judge if I had voted [the Independent ticket] I would have been killed before I left," he explained.[70]

Intimidation at the polls altered the votes of a few, but most freedmen were able to cast an Independent ballot. Those votes, however, went uncounted. At Poll No. 1, poll watchers recorded 445 votes for the Independents and 15 for the Democrats, yet when the tabulation was released, the Democrats claimed a 50-vote majority. When white Independents demanded a public recount, the Democratic commissioners blithely told them that "they were kings to-day" and there would be no recount. At another poll during the public counting, Independents were surprised to find that Democratic tickets "were on top four inches deep," despite the fact that the last thirty voters had cast Independent tickets. "Then I knew we were beaten," admitted Elisha Warfield, a white planter, former Confederate officer, and candidate on the Independent ticket.[71]

The manipulation of the vote was most evident in Concordia Parish. Although some of the bulldozing from Tensas Parish spilled over into Concordia, local Democrats did not use violent political methods, nor did they nominate an all-white ticket. Instead, they nominated a fusionist ticket of Republicans and Democrats, which included black men for sheriff and coroner as well as white men for the police jury. Two years before, in 1876, a fusionist ticket had nearly captured some local offices, but Republicans, and especially black women at the polls, beat back the challenge. This time the fusionist party had the support of the state Democratic machinery, and Democratic registrars turned away nearly one thousand freedmen from the polls, claiming that they were not on the "poll-list." Black Republicans still voted in overwhelming numbers, but intimidation and fraud undercut their majority. At the Frogmore plantation, a group of armed and mounted men stole the ballot boxes at the end of the day and then burned them in the woods.[72]

For David Young, the head of the Republican Party in Concordia and a candidate for reelection to the state senate, the bulldozing and electoral fraud contributed to a growing disenchantment with the entire political process. Young claimed that he was "fairly elected," and his supporters documented that he won twelve of fourteen polling places. Even the Democratic election commissioners, Young reported, "acknowledged to me and my friends that . . . I was ahead." Despite the evidence of fraud, Young considered it a fruitless enterprise to contest the election results, since Democrats controlled the state legislature. Nor did he have any "confidence in the ability of the [federal] administration to protect the lives of my people down here."[73]

Although state and federal officials did not heed the pleas from freedpeople for help in sustaining their local democracies, it was not for lack of trying. Freedpeople vigorously gave voice to the terrorism in the hopes that some outside authority would come to their rescue. Many of the Wilkinson County residents who fled north to Natchez flooded the offices of the *New South*, a Republican newspaper, demanding that their accounts of depredations be published so that the state and nation would know of the violence and suffering. Their stories, however, would never reach a broader public because the white editor of the *New South* feared that publishing them would "jeopardize my personal safety," adding, "the fact of the matter is, I got tired of hearing so many stories." Direct appeals to President Grant brought attention to the political violence but little else. State Senator Hugh M. Foley demanded that federal soldiers be sent to Wilkinson County so "that we may be protected and saved from personal destruction," but Grant did not send troops to any locality in the Natchez District to ensure a free and fair election. He had become convinced that northern voters had lost their appetite for federal intervention and to send soldiers would only imperil Republicans' chances in the November election.[74]

Some of the stories, however, reached beyond the Natchez District. The journalist and antislavery activist James Redpath produced a series of articles for the *New York Times*, based on firsthand reporting. And, more importantly, dozens of locals testified before congressional committees charged with investigating the extensive electoral violence in Mississippi and Louisiana. Their detailed and impassioned testimonies described the overthrow of local governments and the scourge of terrorism, but this was not enough to prod the federal government to intervene in the South one more time.[75]

Former slaves demonstrated surprising resiliency in overcoming planter rule and establishing a functioning democracy in a postslave society, yet they could not protect themselves from unknown invaders from outside the district. Left unprotected by state and federal authorities, locals could not curb the illegitimate use of force. Once Democrats captured state governments and rewrote the rules for running elections, it became much easier for them to use electoral fraud to drive Republicans from power.

The consequences of the violent usurpation of Republican governments became plainly obvious within a few years. To be sure, the wave of paramilitary violence did not end black political participation or black officeholding. A handful of freedmen continued to hold appointive or elective office in every county and parish in the Natchez District, and freedmen continued to vote after the end of Reconstruction. But the discursive and public space for black politics shrank considerably, making it much more difficult for freedpeople to sustain the political mobilizations that they had leveraged to such great effect after the enactment of universal manhood suffrage. Shorn of a structure to channel broadbased communal mobilizations, freedpeople could not slow the growing power of Democratic Party elites, who proceeded to transform southern society along the lines expressed by the white-line insurgents.[76]

The violent backlash in many ways brings freedpeople's story of emancipation and democracy full circle. Where once Union soldiers from outside the Natchez District had joined with slaves to defeat the Confederate nation and destroy slavery, now a different set of outsiders—white militiamen from the interior counties—joined with local Democrats to weaken grassroots democracy and destroy the Republican Party. Where once an outside military force had tipped the scales of justice toward emancipation, now another military force from beyond the district tipped the scales back toward repression.

EIGHT

Return of Oligarchy

The elections of 1875, 1876, and 1878 marked a sharp break in the history of the Natchez District, and not just for the obvious reasons. The massive electoral violence and massacres that unseated Republicans had no precedent, and they have not been repeated in the decades since. But these elections were pivotal in another way as well. They marked the only time that one county diverged from the rest of the district. Adams County was the only locality to avoid the scourge of white-line attacks. The local Republican Party was not decimated, and the exercise of voting and governance persisted much as it did during Reconstruction. Never before, or since, was one county out of lockstep with the others. While black men went to the polls in massive numbers in Natchez, black families from Tensas and Concordia Parishes abandoned the region for Kansas. While Adams County black officeholders continued to win election and serve unimpeded, their counterparts were murdered (as in Claiborne County) or run out of the state (as in Jefferson County). The juxtaposition of biracial harmony in one county and white supremacist domination in the neighboring counties is one of the most fascinating anomalies in the history of the Natchez District.

What explains the unique history of Adams County in the 1880s? Why was it able to resist the violent trends of the region? The distinctive feature was a viable fusionist compromise between black Republicans and white Democrats. Adams County offered a model for how to meld the interests of white and black residents without resorting to political violence and electoral fraud. The fusionist movement can be thought of as one of the "forgotten alternatives" in the late nineteenth-century South, one that did not predispose a segregated and disfranchised outcome. It offered black Republicans a means to preserve the egalitarian social ethos that undergirded grassroots democracy. On the other side, fusionism appealed to white elites with large commercial and planting interests who feared economic disruption, labor loss, and social chaos. But electoral violence still had an impact on politics and governance in Adams County. The compromise between moderate Republicans and Democrats in city and county government skewed public policies toward the Democrats and gave them important positions despite winning only a small minority of the vote. Ensuring a few more positions for white Democrats seemed to be the price for keeping the violence at bay and for allowing black people to continue to have a voice in governance.[1]

Although somewhat limited in Adams County, electoral violence had a detrimental impact on democracy throughout the Natchez District. To be sure, black politics persisted. Freedmen continued to show up at the polls, and a handful of black politicians remained in office. But local Republican parties effectively ceased operations, and without the party structure to channel their voices and interests, freedpeople lost their most effective mechanism to shape public life. Freedpeople, of course, still shaped public policy and the local economy, most notably in their exodus to Kansas, a response to the terroristic violence of the 1878 election campaign. They continued to mobilize extensively for elections. And they still employed democratic principles in civic and associational organizations. Yet these methods had only limited utility. They could not stop the white liners from fraudulently counting their votes and thus nullifying their electoral majority. They could not stop Democratic legislatures from reversing the policies that had favored freedpeople's rights and aspirations. They found their voices muffled by an electoral system that did not recognize their legitimacy, by a media landscape that stifled Republican views, and by state and federal leaders who ignored pleas from ordinary people to respect and protect their citizenship.

Because of the persistence of black politics and freedpeople's insistence throughout the 1880s that an open and grassroots democracy be restored, exasperated Democratic leaders turned to disfranchisement as the ultimate means to stifle freedpeople's collective power. The enactment of state-level disfranchisement, first in Mississippi and then in Louisiana, was a complete repudiation of the innovative political system that freedpeople had ushered into being after emancipation. It also destroyed Adams County's system of biracial governance. There was no longer any need for white Democrats to pay attention to the interests of the black majority if that majority could not express its choices at the ballot box. The consequence of disfranchisement was not just the elimination of black voices from partisan politics but the return of oligarchic rule. And with their return to political power, elite whites began to implement policies that favored large landowners at the expense of freedpeople.

Another way to measure the deterioration of democracy in the Natchez District is through the shrinking number of sources that document black people's lives. Grassroots democracy provided channels to know what freedpeople were doing, through records of county conventions, public meetings, appeals to sympathetic governors and presidents, legislation and debate from elected representatives, and even through officeholder bonds. In addition, the federal government's interest in helping former slaves establish their freedom and citizenship produced an extensive record of their labor and political struggles. But after white paramilitary forces drove the Republican Party out of the region, the capacity of freedpeople to register their opinions and collective expressions diminished considerably. Democratic newspapers paid far less attention to black residents than Republican papers, which went out of business or were taken over by local Democrats. The federal policy of noninterference in southern elections meant that there were far fewer investigations that recorded the firsthand testimonies of ordinary freedpeople. As the sources become more scarce and fragmented, they unwittingly reveal a more fragmented society. Elections are still one way to measure freedpeople's vision, but in the absence of other records the tabulation of electoral results (in, for instance, polling books) is a blunt tool. In other words, our ability to know what black citizens were doing and thinking was substantially harmed by the white Democrats who undermined grassroots democracy in the Natchez District.

Fusionist Politics in Adams County

Fusionism, of one form or another, had existed in the Natchez District since at least the enfranchisement of black men. Generally it took the form of disgruntled Republican moderates splitting off from the mainline party and linking up with a few Democrats. But a new type of fusionism came into being in 1874 that was not merely the outgrowth of Republican factionalism but the joining of moderate forces from both parties. It originated in Natchez as a nonpartisan People's ticket because the city was the only place in the district in which Democrats had a sizeable following. The People's ticket was not a forerunner of the late nineteenth-century Populist movement but rather a generic name for an independent opposition party. It was composed of blacks and whites, none of whom were prominent Democrats or Republicans, and they based their new party on two principles: "non-partisan municipal government" and the reduction of taxes. The fusionist coalition was initially a rejection of the radical wing of the Republican Party, but over time it also became associated with the rejection of the white-line wing of the Democratic Party.[2]

In a city with a history of biracial political organizing and biracial economic development (through railroads), it was not unusual for a fusionist ticket of this kind to be organized and to gain wide support. In the 1874 city election, the People's candidates swept all of the offices—mayor, aldermen, and school trustees—and won about one third of the black vote. The *Natchez Democrat* considered the election to be a rejection of outside influence or the carpetbag element, noting the "marked manifestation . . . of [a] better feeling between the home people of the two races which constitute the community." A subsequent celebratory torchlight parade seemed to confirm the significance of the fusionist party's victory, as partisan leaders from both races joined the celebration and gave speeches to a large audience of city residents. Speeches were given by William T. Martin (a white Democratic party leader), William Minor Davis (a black People's candidate for school trustee), George F. Bowles (a black Republican moderate), E. J. Castello (a white Republican moderate and former Union League activist), Samuel Ullman (a white People's candidate for school trustee), J. S. Meng (a white Republican parish judge from Concordia Parish), John Peck (a black Republican and chair of the city Republican convention), and Henry C. Griffin (the white mayor on the People's ticket).[3]

In the pivotal election of 1875, the major Republican leaders bolted the mainline ticket and formed a "compromise" ticket with Democrats. Leading the way was Robert H. Wood, the freeborn former mayor and current postmaster. His sights were set on the sheriff's office—occupied by William McCary, a freeborn Republican who was endorsed by the radical wing of the party. Although Wood himself had been endorsed by black radicals when he ran for mayor in 1871, his politics varied over time. He joined a bolting ticket in 1867 in opposition to the Union League–endorsed candidates. Now he endorsed nonpartisan local elections and the selection of "the best men to fill the municipal offices." Perhaps he never was much of a radical and could envision working with white Democrats like his father, who was also a former mayor of Natchez. Or perhaps, sensing the looming conservative backlash against Reconstruction, Wood thought that his best route to political office would be to compromise with moderate Democrats.[4]

Whatever the reason for Wood's embrace of fusionism, it had the desired effect. "The Democratic party . . . allied with the Wood wing in the local canvasses," testified William N. Whitehurst, a white Democratic leader, and defeated the radical candidates for county and state offices. Besides Sheriff McCary, other black radicals, such as William H. Lynch and Willis Davis, lost their seats in the state legislature as moderate Republicans affiliated with the fusionists won office.[5]

Quite unintentionally, however, the fusionists helped John R. Lynch win reelection to Congress. The Republican split brought out "a very heavy vote," Lynch remembered, which gave him more votes than expected and thwarted the plans of "Democratic managers" in other counties to steal the election. Lynch's reelection preserved a radical voice in Congress, but the ascension of fusionists to power marked a readjustment in priorities. True to its fiscally conservative orientation, the new fusionist-dominated board of supervisors immediately cut back on education funding for rural black children by firing seventeen county schoolteachers.[6]

The forging of a bipartisan and biracial political compromise, however, did not prevent intimidation and fraud from plaguing subsequent elections in Adams County. In the same election season in which white liners attacked black Republicans in Wilkinson and Jefferson Counties, white employers in Adams County discharged numerous black men "because they would not promise to vote the democratic ticket," and black draymen who voted for Republicans lost their customer base of white merchants, asserted A. M. Hardy, a white Republican newspaper editor. Crowds of white Democrats disrupted Republican meetings and threatened to kill leading Republicans. As in nearly every other Mississippi county in 1876, white Democratic clubs organized military companies. Armed with the most advanced Winchester rifles and other high-powered weapons, they paraded regularly through Natchez on Saturdays and generally "menace[d] the colored people of the county." In addition, marauding bands of armed white men invaded Adams County on occasion and targeted black residents and Republican leaders. After "50 armed KluKlux" from Jefferson County visited his house one night, a black Republican activist who was active in the presidential campaign fled his home. "The more indiscreet members of the armed Democracy," wrote a Natchez correspondent to the *Chicago Inter-Ocean*, "openly assert that they are in favor of carrying this county if they have to kill every white and fifty colored Republicans to accomplish it."[7]

Despite the bluster, the Democratic opposition never resorted to terrorism in Adams County. In seems that the fusionist compromise gave moderate Democrats influence in local politics and real political power, which had the effect of marginalizing extremists in their party. Just as important, fusionist black leaders established greater legitimacy within the white community by flouting radical Republican leaders. The *Natchez Democrat* proudly noted in the wake of the Wilkinson County troubles that "there is at this time more of a disposition on the part of the colored people to assimilate politically with the whites." For ordinary freedpeople who encountered refugees from political violence on the streets of Natchez, political moderation offered an attractive alternative. The correspondent to the *Inter-Ocean* noted that "this county [Adams] is a paradise compared with the adjoining counties of Wilkinson, Claiborne, and Jefferson." Likewise, influential white leaders feared that an outbreak of bulldozing would degenerate "into the gratification of private piques, personal grudges and private animosities." One white Unionist with Republican sympathies responded to white-line attacks on his plantation by forming a "colored armed guard" to defend his household and laborers. In his autobiography, John R. Lynch credited "the conservative element," referring to white Democratic leaders in Adams County, for "prevent[ing] the adoption of any plan which involved violence and bloodshed." The sentiment was not unusual within the Natchez District, but only in Adams County did this moderate view prevail within Democratic circles. It was a point of pride for many Natchez political leaders, Lynch testified in 1877, that "there was not any material violence" in the county.[8]

Notwithstanding fusionist arrangements and the legitimacy of black office-holders, electoral fraud in 1876 was a serious problem in Adams County, particularly for mainline Republicans. At Kingston Precinct, Republican ballots cast early in the morning disappeared when it came time to make the final count. Democrats had never polled more than nine hundred votes in Adams County, but in this election they increased their vote total by over 80 percent. The fraud in Adams County, however, would have meant little except that most of the other counties in Lynch's congressional district had been plagued by white-line violence. Thus he needed Adams County's large Republican majority to overcome the violence and fraud in other counties. "There has not been a fair election in Mississippi since 1874," protested Lynch to the *Washington Republican*, and he noted that the implications went well beyond officeholding. "Since that time the Democracy have conceived and put in force their infamous shot-gun policy, which has completely and absolutely nullified the rights guaranteed to the colored people by the amendments to the Constitution." By not counting Republican tickets, Democrats were able defeat Lynch and silence one of the most radical voices in the U.S. Congress.[9]

Dispersal and Eradication

While the fusionist arrangement held in Adams County, the "shot-gun policy" of the white liners wreaked havoc across the state. Even after the conclusion of the 1876 election, the violence did not abate. In Claiborne and Jefferson Counties, white liners turned their attention to the remaining Republican leaders. It was not enough to gain control of local and state offices; they intended to eradicate the political leadership of the opposition party.

Claiborne County Democratic leaders targeted James Page and his family. About a month after the 1876 elections, the Claiborne County chancery clerk, a white Democrat, was shot to death, and Harrison Page, James Page's adult son, was blamed for the murder. James Page was born enslaved, yet through his labors as a drayman he was able to purchase his freedom in 1857. After the war he helped to found the first black school in the county and then was elected to the offices of alderman, sheriff, and county treasurer. The evidence against Harrison Page was circumstantial; the Page family ascribed the charges and intimidation, in a plea to Governor J. M. Stone, to "our political opinions."[10]

But it was not just the Pages' long-standing devotion to the Republican Party that placed the family in jeopardy; rather, it was their public opposition to paramilitary violence that threatened their lives and livelihoods. Democrats accused James Page of arming black men and fomenting racial conflict on the day that John R. Lynch visited Port Gibson in October 1876 for a campaign rally. Another alleged organizer of black militiamen, W. D. Sprott, a white Republican and school superintendent, had already fled the county after learning that leading Democrats intended to lynch him. Civil authorities offered Harrison and the other Page brothers no protection from the murdered clerk's family and friends, so the men fled to "the woods" to hide out. Finally responding to the "lawless condition" and "mob-law" in Claiborne County, President Grant, at the bequest of John R. Lynch, ordered a company of federal troops to restore peace and order. The troops had been stationed in Port Gibson during the election violence of 1875 and 1876, but Grant authorized their intervention into local affairs only after the election and only to avert a lynch mob, not to protect citizens in the exercise of their voting rights.[11]

Tensions abated for a short while in Claiborne, but they remained high in Jefferson County following the 1876 election. Democrats targeted the leading Republicans in the county: Merrimon Howard, James D. Cessor, and J. C. Ellis. Howard's career paralleled James Page's in many ways. Like his neighbor to the north, Howard was a former slave who was freed in the 1850s; he was a carriage driver and helped to found the first black school in the county; he also held many offices, including sheriff. But in 1876, shorn of office, Howard nonetheless directly confronted the white liners in a massive procession in Fayette, thereby provoking the ire of leading Democrats. They threatened to kill him, even though he had recently been appointed a special federal marshal. Consequently, Howard fled the county prior to the election. The U.S. marshal for the Southern District of Mississippi, in a report to the U.S. attorney general, described Howard's plight this way: "Howard is a colored man, a staunch Republican, and a leader among his people. Herein is his offending." After the election Howard moved to Washington, D.C., never to return home again. He used his political connections to secure a federal job, but the once-powerful officeholder was now reduced to working as a messenger in the Treasury Department. James D. Cessor, the longtime black Republican legislator, also fled the county, hiding out in Louisiana until the election passed. Like Howard, he eventually left the region and took a federal appointment, moving to Ocean Springs, Mississippi, on the Gulf Coast to work as an internal revenue collector and agent.[12]

With the leading black officeholders driven out of the county, the few remaining white Republican leaders looked to Adams County as a model for restoring a system of open and biracial governance. J. C. Ellis, a white Republican and member of a Unionist family, created a combined ticket of moderate Republicans and Democrats for the 1877 election. It was an effort that acknowledged the shifting political context. No longer could Republicans field their own ticket, but there was still hope that representative government could be reestablished. Indeed, the fusionist ticket attracted wide support from county residents who were repelled by the lawlessness that white-line clubs had spawned. Black men and women were whipped for perceived insults, and a black political activist was lynched outside of Fayette, leading one white planter to confess that he had "lost confidence in this country producing any thing but evil."[13]

Ellis organized a "grand rally" at a rural schoolhouse, hoping to attract black support for what was known as the "independent ticket," but white-line Democrats showed up to the meeting in force, much as they had the previous year to Republican meetings. The armed Democratic clubs prevented every fusionist candidate from speaking, including R. H. Truly, the editor of the local Democratic paper, who the year before had joined the white liners in running Merrimon Howard out of the county. At the rally, a scuffle with a "young hot-headed Democrat" prompted Ellis to flee the county at night, disguised as a laborer. Then the Independent candidate for sheriff, a forty-seven-year-old white planter who considered himself a Democrat, dropped out before the election, but not before lamenting the absence of "free speech and civil liberty" and denouncing "the terrorism of an oligarchy" that had gained control of his county. With the fusionist experiment in Jefferson County smashed and its leaders run off, white-line Democrats were able to use violence to stifle any rival ticket, leaving the black majority voters without a choice at the ballot box.[14]

Meanwhile, in Claiborne County, Harrison Page remained on the loose and the Page family still on the defensive. Despite repeated raids by local authorities, Harrison was able to elude capture, probably because of an extensive kin and political network that alerted him to the presence of the sheriff's men. The Page family lived on the outskirts of Port Gibson in the St. Mary suburb along with many other prominent black families. John N. Byrd, a free black barber and friend of James Page since 1840, first purchased a plot of land in the neighborhood seven years before the Civil War. After emancipation, James Page began to purchase land in this neighborhood—four lots between 1865 and 1869. He sold one lot to his son Isaac, and Harrison purchased his own plot in 1869. In the early 1870s a few other black leaders, including Thomas Richardson, the Port Gibson postmaster, and Nace Bradford, a trustee of the AME Church, also settled in the St. Mary suburb. But it was the Page family that established the most significant presence in the neighborhood, totaling at least thirty-three family members by the late 1870s.[15]

The neighborhood, however, came under a withering attack in November 1878, which devastated the Page family and crippled black politics in the county for decades to come. One morning before dawn, the sheriff of Claiborne County and two deputies visited Harrison Page's house, hoping to arrest him for the chancery clerk murder two years prior. John Sawyer, a neighbor who was staying in the house, saw the law enforcement officers coming and attempted to run away, but one of the deputies fired at him. Hearing the commotion, Harrison appeared and returned fire, killing a deputy and mortally wounding the sheriff. The uninjured deputy fled back to Port Gibson and summoned a posse. "At least 100 men" returned to the St. Mary neighborhood seeking vengeance, Thomas Richardson, the local postmaster and an ex-slave, reported to the Justice Department. The mob murdered three people: Sawyer, "old man [James] Page and a child." And then they set fire to "every house on Pages place" and, according to one newspaper report, proceeded to lay waste to Page's plantation. "Several good dwellings, a cotton-gin, blacksmith-shop, laborers' quarters, etc.," were burnt to the ground. "His horses, mules, cattle and other personal property, of which he had several thousand dollars worth, were stolen or destroyed." The mob then forced all of the Page women and children off the land and sent them across the river "without clothing or money" to the appropriately named town of Hard Times in Tensas Parish, never "to be seen on [the Mississippi] side of the river again." The remaining Page men became fugitives.[16]

The murder of James Page and the dispersal of the Page family marked a rather brutal conclusion to the era of intensive black political mobilization in Claiborne County. News of the Page murders reverberated across the lower Mississippi River valley. From St. Louis to Bay St. Louis on the Gulf Coast, politicians and ordinary freedpeople alike were horrified that a family of such status and reputation could be ruthlessly attacked. Few leaders embodied the radical changes that emancipation unleashed more than James Page. He had purchased his own freedom, forged a communal network of draymen and other black artisans during the Civil War, and established the first black school in the county. He became a landowner and planter and won office as sheriff and county treasurer. Yet the Page family and other leading black families were not oblivious to the dire future that Democratic control portended. They began to sell their properties, and by 1879, all of the politically connected black families had moved out of the St. Mary suburb.[17]

Over a span of three years, Democrats in Claiborne County drove out white Republican leaders, used fraud and intimidation to capture local offices, and finally decimated the county's most prominent black family. Black residents, however, continued to mobilize at subsequent elections—a persistence that national Republican leaders acknowledged by making Thomas Richardson the local postmaster. Richardson, a former slave who became a licensed attorney and who was a secret informant for the Department of Justice during the Page affair, held the position of Port Gibson postmaster from 1870 to 1911, except for one year when he worked for the Ames administration in Mississippi and for the eight years of President Cleveland's Democratic administrations. He was also elected to the Port Gibson city council between 1880 and 1899. Richardson's remarkable continuity in public office highlights the continuing black struggle to establish a grassroots democracy, but one black officeholder was a poor substitute for a system of shared governance and broad diffusion of power.[18]

Exodus

The attacks on the Page family came in the immediate wake of the wave of bulldozing terrorism that afflicted Tensas Parish in the fall of 1878. The murder of perhaps seventy freedpeople and the general trauma that many households faced as they fled to the woods to escape the marauding bands of white liners compounded a desultory social and economic environment that had been worsening in recent years. Cotton, which had garnered high prices in the late 1860s and early 1870s, plummeted in value to prewar levels by 1877, limiting the ability of tenant farmers and sharecroppers to escape rising debt. Democratic-majority legislatures exacerbated the problem by abolishing laborers' claims to wages and instead, with new crop lien laws, giving landowners preference in collecting rent. Many rural families were no closer to landownership in 1879 than they had been a decade earlier. In Concordia Parish, the new Democratic-dominated police jury announced that public schools would not open due to a lack of funds. At a meeting in Tensas Parish a couple of months later, "colored citizens" complained about the "exorbitant prices put on articles of merchandise and produce by our country merchants."[19]

In this context, local black people eagerly embraced rumors that the federal government would provide migrants with land, mules, money, and provisions if they settled in Kansas. Although social and economic hardship contributed to the exodus of thousands from the Natchez District, the primary impetus was the bulldozing and the elimination of ordinary people's voices from governance. Frederick Marshall, a fifty-three-year-old black tenant farmer in Adams County, decided to flee his home when, on Christmas morning before dawn, three or four white men came to murder him. "I had to go some place," he swore in an affidavit, "where I could work without being afraid of my life." And so he settled in Lawrence, Kansas, working as a laborer.[20]

Marshall's experience was similar to that of the Puckett family. Priscilla and Orange Puckett were a young couple in their early twenties, with two young children, who worked as sharecroppers in Tensas Parish. As the 1878 campaign heated up, Orange and his two brothers tried to avoid the election, since "the planters required" that they vote for white-line candidates. "I decided with my two brothers not to vote, [and instead] worked hard, minded my own business, and caused no trouble," explained Puckett. But because they did not vote, and thus did not help the Democratic ticket, bulldozers visited their cabin and "blazed away." Puckett's two brothers were killed, while he "escaped into the nearby woods and hid for fourteen days." He dreaded leaving his fields, but eventually Priscilla convinced him to abandon their home and make for Kansas. The Puckett family settled in Wyandotte County. While safe from bulldozers, their troubles continued. Orange was six months unemployed in 1880 when the census enumerator visited their household.[21]

Because the bulldozing had been most intense on the Louisiana side of the Mississippi River, "Kansas Fever" spread rapidly through the parishes of Concordia and Tensas in the spring of 1879. "The colored people are selling off everything they own," reported an ex-congressman from the area, "and steam-boat landings on the Mississippi are constantly crowded with those fleeing from Democratic hatred and persecution." As scores of laborers and their families uprooted and headed north, the local Democratic newspaper published a slew of disparaging articles on the travails of the migrants in a vain attempt to stem the tide. By April three thousand freedpeople were waiting on the riverbank near Vidalia for a steamboat. "A good many have left Concordia," complained one local planter. He was also frustrated that he could not find any laborers to replace a section of thirty planted acres that had been abandoned by a family that left for Kansas.[22]

Other planters were more alarmed and took unprecedented action to prevent the mass migration. They pressured steamboat operators to prevent black customers from boarding, "even after they tender them the amount of passage money demanded," acknowledged the collector of customs in Natchez in a protest letter to the U.S. attorney general. But black people still boarded steamboats, prompting "white enemies . . . some of whom are mounted and armed, as if we were at war," reported one eyewitness in a letter to President Rutherford B. Hayes, to set up blockades at the river landings, in an effort "to force the negroes back to the places they left."[23]

The sudden and coordinated movement of black families from the bulldozed communities stunned the Democratic elite. They thought that they had finally compelled political deference to white supremacist authority, but instead African Americans registered their disapproval by leaving their homes and restarting their lives in a distant land. As a result, the local cotton economy ground to a halt. By midsummer the crop prospects were "exceedingly unfavorable," grumbled one Concordia planter, because not only had so many black workers left, but those who remained were "demoralized" and "little interested in their work." To attract a stable labor force, some planters reversed their credit policies and eliminated freedpeople's debts for those who chose to stay. In other instances, farmworkers took the initiative. One group in Concordia formed a labor association in order to negotiate with planters for "a uniform system of leasing lands." The labor organizing worked. One year after the migration began, a Concordia Parish planter admitted that he had to offer improved terms to "the system of leasing"; otherwise, he explained, "I would lose the best men on the place."[24]

The exodus provided leverage for farm laborers to improve their position in the cotton economy, but it also gave voters an opportunity to push back against the bulldozers. Fresh off their violence-fueled electoral triumph, Tensas Democrats backpedaled from their strident white-line position. To avoid further labor losses, they supported the modest inclusion of black Republicans in the nomination process for the selection of delegates to the upcoming Louisiana constitutional convention. Partisan committees, authorized by the bulldozers, representing the three major political constituencies (bulldozing Democrats, white Independents, and black Republicans) selected one representative from each group. Rural black voters, however, rejected this contrived formulation and voted for regular Republican candidates—all long-standing Republican officeholders who had opposed the electoral violence. By allowing black Republicans a seat at the table, the bulldozers hoped to mollify the fears of black farm laborers while still maintaining some control over the political process. Instead, freedpeople exploited this opening by reaffirming their commitment to the Republican Party and simultaneously rejecting the legitimacy of the bulldozing regime.[25]

Tensas Democrats made further concessions to black Republicans later when they selected delegates to attend a Vicksburg convention on the Kansas migration. The president of the police jury, a bulldozer named C. C. Cordill, chose seven white men, including one Republican, and seven black men to represent the parish. At the convention the black delegates demanded "fair and free" elections, affirmed black civil and political rights, and called for the elimination of crop lien laws, but the force of these statements was compromised by their failure to endorse the right of workers to move about freely.[26]

The inconclusive response at the Vicksburg convention reflected the mixed message from local black leaders in the district. Alfred Fairfax, whose house was attacked by bulldozers, sparking the bulldozing in Tensas, was one of the few black leaders to join the migration to Kansas. He went on to purchase a two-hundred-acre farm and became the first black man elected to the Kansas legislature. David Young of Concordia took the opposite position. He stood on the levees and implored freedpeople waiting for transit up the river to remain in their homes. Across the river, black delegates from Adams and Claiborne Counties who attended the National Conference of Colored Men endorsed the exodus as a protest, but they did little to help black families from these Mississippi counties move out of the South.[27]

At best, the Kansas migration blunted some of the harsher changes resulting from the campaign of political terrorism in 1878. Some of the darkest fears of freedpeople were allayed when the revised Louisiana Constitution of 1879 preserved universal manhood suffrage. But the intent of the new constitution was to undermine the democracy that freedpeople had crafted in the wake of emancipation. It removed affirmations of "civil, political, and public rights" and gave the governor more appointment powers at the expense of local elections. The impact of bulldozing, however, was most evident in the narrowed space accorded grassroots politics. Black partisanship persisted, yet ordinary laborers and farmers had much less influence. The 1880 Concordia Parish Republican executive committee included only two laborers out of twenty members, yet three years earlier, over half of the members had been laborers or farmers. By 1883 black men still dominated the ranks of the constabulary, but whites held nearly all of the county offices. Black residents outnumbered whites by ten to one, yet the school board was all white and only one black man sat on the police jury.[28]

The political sphere was even more constrained in Tensas Parish. The parish Republican Party continued to operate, but some freedpeople tried an alternative approach by forming a third party. Similar to the fusionist experiment in Natchez, independent white Democrats and black Republicans organized a "People's Party." Black leaders held prominent positions in this new party, but ordinary freedmen were far less represented. E. C. Routh, (aka C. E. Ruth) a former Republican justice of the peace, was party vice president, and Robert J. Walker, a former Republican state representative, was the party secretary. The party principles were somewhat conservative—calling for an "incorruptible judiciary," opposing the state's "onerous indebtedness," and endorsing the right of "every man" to vote and the "impartial distribution of school funds" to both races—reflecting the fusionist political alliance as well as the narrowed range of possibilities in a locality scarred by terrorism.[29]

In spite of its attempt to chart a moderate path, the People's Party had no discernible impact on the next elections. The vast majority of freedpeople remained loyal to the Republican Party, and the bulldozing wing of the Democratic Party had no intention of surrendering its violent grip on local offices. Although some black Republicans had success in this environment, such as Solomon Schaifer, a Baptist minister and former parish recorder who was elected to the state legislature in 1879, on the whole, Democrats continued their war on black assembly and free speech. When Republicans tried to hold a mass rally, as they did in late 1879 at Waterproof, local Democrats harassed the speakers until they finally retreated from the stage. As another election neared, the *North Louisiana Journal* announced that the time had come to restart the bulldozing. "Let every white man assume the individual responsibility," it implored on the eve of the 1880 election, "of seeing that the present condition of affairs in this parish is perpetuated." Although black registered voters outnumbered whites by nearly ten to one, a "commanding general" of the bulldozers was elected to Congress with fifteen hundred votes to spare. Absent local testimony it is impossible to know how such a lopsided election result could have happened, yet the pattern is similar to other elections plagued by white-line fraud and intimidation.[30]

The exodus from the Louisiana river parishes ameliorated some of the harsher policies of the bulldozers and it gave the migrants a chance to start anew in a far less hostile environment, but the exodus did not reverse the decline of grassroots democracy in Tensas or Concordia Parishes. After experiments with fusionist tickets failed, black men continued to register, and the local Republican Party still put up candidates. David Young, once the undisputed Republican powerbroker in Concordia, continued to run for legislative office, but he was never able to dislodge the white supremacists, despite living in a parish where 91 percent of the population was of African descent and overwhelmingly Republican. And thus the ability of ordinary freedpeople to shape policy and channel their grievances was diminished by a lack of representation.[31]

Stabilization and Marginalization

In the midst of an ever-tightening political order that prioritized white supremacy, the remarkable experiment in biracial politics continued in Natchez and Adams County. The People's Party did not last, but the fusionist idea became the primary framework for county and municipal politics from the late 1870s to the early 1890s. Acknowledging the shifting political terrain, John R. Lynch admitted in 1877 to his friend and political ally Senator Blanche K. Bruce, "I don't believe there is a county in the State where the Republicans will make straight-out nominations. In this county (Adams) the indication[s] now are that a fusion ticket will be agreed upon as was done in your county (Bolivar)."[32]

Instead of holding open debates at party conventions, partisan leaders met together privately before an election and divided the public offices between white Democrats and black Republicans, a process sometimes referred to as the "checker-board movement" or the "absorption scheme." Black politicians "with strongly grounded Republican principles," such as Lynch's brother, were "carefully kept off the ticket," reported the *New York Times*, in favor of moderate Republicans. The "County Compromise Ticket" of 1889 listed three black Republicans for county offices (George F. Bowles for state representative, Robert H. Wood for assessor, and Patrick Foley for coroner and ranger) and four white Democrats.[33]

The compromise ticket seemed to be a concession that local black people could tolerate, in contrast to the exclusion of black Republicanism in most parts of the Natchez District. "I am a colored man and a Republican," declared Harry Smith Jr., a ticket distributor and black farmer. "I have never voted any other than a Republican ticket in Presidential or Congressional elections." Although fusionism did not go uncontested, it proved to be a remarkably durable system in Adams County.[34]

Party leaders designated moderate black Republicans for a series of offices under the terms of the fusionist compromise: circuit clerk, tax assessor, coroner and ranger, and one state legislator. Exactly how these individuals were selected is unknown because, unlike the selection of nominees at party conventions of the 1870s in which the public was invited to participate, fusionist candidates were chosen behind closed doors. The positions were often filled by men of mixed-race descent who had been born free. One of the great coups of the Republicans, however, was the election of Louis J. Winston to circuit court clerk in 1876. Winston was the product of a biracial union, the son of Samuel L. Winston, who in 1880 was a Democratic election supervisor, and Francis Augusta, a slave. During Reconstruction he served as a policeman and tax assessor before winning office as circuit clerk at the age of thirty-two. Part of his responsibility was the registration of voters and the examination of poll books. He stood watch over the election process for twenty years, ensuring that black voters, especially, had free and fair access to the ballot. Like Winston, who served as clerk for twenty years, Robert H. Wood also had a long tenure as tax assessor, serving from 1880 to 1895. Also like Winston, Wood was born free and his father was a prominent white Democratic politician. Robert W. Wood, his father, was elected the mayor of Natchez in the late 1850s, the same position that his son held between 1870 and 1872. It is difficult to divine the impact that so many mixed-race Republicans leaders had in Natchez society and politics. The fact that they served for nearly two decades after the white-line violence suggests that they convinced their white neighbors of their legitimacy as politicians and their citizenship as men of color.[35]

Fusionism depended on elite members of black society filling the ranks of the top offices, but it also depended on a full mobilization of black voters. Between 1876 and 1890 an average of thirty-four hundred black men voted in each Adams County election, ensuring that the fusionist compromise would persist. This was not the radical democracy that grassroots activists had pioneered in the early 1870s, since laborers and small farmers were less likely to fill offices and thus their voices were less likely to influence public life. In addition, fusionists had no need for local party conventions, and so ordinary voters and political clubs lost an important venue for registering their influence and opinions. Nevertheless, it was a democratic system that partially incorporated the voices and will of the people. And with it a picture emerges of a society that had learned to avoid the destructiveness of white supremacist politics and that had created a model of biracial and bipartisan cooperation.[36]

In the course of everyday business in Natchez, black leaders abounded in prominent government positions. While Louis J. Winston conducted court and electoral business in the county courthouse, another freeborn black politician presided over the county post office. Robert W. Fitzhugh (of the influential Fitzhugh family) held the federally appointed position for nearly seven years— a patronage position supplied by Congressman John R. Lynch—during which he dutifully delivered the mail to all county residents, white and black alike. He held the post until he died at the age of forty-seven; his replacement was William McCary, another politically connected Republican born free and of mixed-race descent. These were just three of at least twenty-one black men who held local public office in the 1880s and early 1890s. There was also an assortment of policemen and constables, so it was unlikely that residents of Adams County did not encounter a black officeholder in their day-to-day lives between 1876 and 1896. The utter ordinariness of these offices and the lengthy continuity of black officeholding suggests a level of accommodation to biracial bipartisanship among Adams County whites that stands in stark contrast to much of the rest of the Deep South.[37]

Fusionist politics, however, did not sit well with the white liners. Adams County's reputation as a holdout of Republican power provoked mockery from other Mississippi Democrats. The *Fayette Chronicle* wondered why Adams County Democrats had not yet brought down "the decisive blow," considering that the surrounding counties and parishes of Warren, Claiborne, Jefferson, Tensas, and Concordia had already "struck for . . . freedom and white supremacy." "Strike it she must," the paper continued, because "collision between the races is the only argument which has convinced the negro that the white man must rule." Certainly many whites in Adams County were, in the words of a *Natchez Democrat* editorial, "shamed by being called a radical county," but at the same time they took pride in their "reputation for moderation and friendly feeling in both races." Rather than follow the path of political violence that Democrats in other parts of the Deep South had used to great effect, Natchez Democrats instead resorted to electoral fraud to unseat Republicans. Their efforts failed, in large part because John R. Lynch was prepared for this strategy.[38]

Lynch had been fraudulently counted out in 1876, but four years later he anticipated the fraud and sought to build a well-documented case against Democrats' electoral deceptions. The prospects for a Republican victory were daunting, yet Lynch was hopeful because the congressional district, known as the "shoestring" district, included all of the counties in the state bordering the Mississippi River. From the Mississippi Delta in the north to the Natchez District in the south, these were counties with high concentrations of black residents, ranging from 67 to 91 percent of the population. Lynch estimated that Republicans had a majority of fifteen to twenty thousand. But these majorities had been counted out or intimidated in the previous two elections. Lynch knew that some counties were hopelessly corrupt, such as Claiborne County, where Democratic election officials usually replaced Republican votes with Democratic tickets. In these instances, Lynch advised black voters "to remain away from the polls" in order to keep the Democratic vote low. In other counties, such as Jefferson and Adams, Lynch encouraged local activists to mobilize for a high voter turnout to offset anticipated Democratic fraud.[39]

As expected, black voters came out en masse on Election Day, but they were met with delays, obstruction, and fraud. Democratic election inspectors in Natchez slowed the voting process down to a snail's pace as they scrutinized every Republican voter with a series of questions. Old men were asked if they were of voting age or not, and every voter had to explain "where they lived, whose place they lived on, where they were staying, how long they had been staying there, when they had registered," among many more tedious inquiries, testified Charles W. Minor, a twenty-seven-year-old black carpenter and Republican election inspector. The effect was to suppress the vote total, as nearly three hundred black voters were still waiting in line when the polls closed. At the rural Kingston Precinct, Democratic commissioners took the ballot box with them for a lunch break. Lynch later quipped, "[T]hat box stood more in need of being fed than the election officers." At other precincts the votes were thrown out due to unspecified "palpable irregularities."[40]

Republican leaders responded by documenting what they believed to be the true vote and by publicizing their claim of systematic fraud. Prior to the election, local party agents spread the word through the neighborhood clubs that voters should walk up to the polling place with their ticket unfolded and call out "Lynch" upon voting. Republican tally-keepers at the polls then dutifully recorded these shouted votes and later submitted their figures in the contested election case. Armed with documentation of the fraud, Lynch wrote to Republican newspapers in New York City to initiate a nationwide campaign to expose the continuing electoral corruption in the South. Fortunately, Republicans had won majority in the U.S. House in the same election, giving Lynch an opportunity to present his case before the elections committee. After a lengthy investigation, the House reversed the election results of Mississippi's Sixth Congressional District and gave Lynch a seat in the Forty-Seventh Congress.[41]

Once again, Republicans in Washington helped locals preserve a fair system of governance and even provided a glimmer of hope for black Republicanism in the South. But the victory also had a more tangible outcome. It helped to preserve fusionism in Adams County. The 1880 election was the last time that Democrats engaged in systematic fraud to discount Republican votes. Lynch's efforts to extend the example of Adams County fusionism across the state, however, proved to be more difficult. He renewed his repeated plea for southern Republicans to join with the Greenback Party and other independent political movements.[42]

Although Lynch's victory demonstrates the adaptability of freedpeople to the narrowed political possibilities of the post-Reconstruction era, the resilience of black mobilization did not go unnoticed by Republicans' political opponents. Exasperated by Lynch's tenacious campaigning—the *Natchez Democrat* was awed by his ability to "leave no stone unturned to secure the colored vote"— Mississippi's Democratic legislators retaliated by breaking up the shoestring district after the 1880 census. They created a new district that lumped Adams County in with the white-majority counties of southeast Mississippi. As always, the black voters in Adams and Wilkinson counties rallied to Lynch's side, but eleven of the fourteen counties in the new district were majority white, leaving Lynch with only 47 percent of the vote when he went up for reelection in 1882.[43]

John R. Lynch never won elective office again, but neither he nor the black voters who had propelled him to office gave up in their efforts to preserve a grassroots democracy. Before he left Congress, Lynch doled out a number of patronage jobs to friends and supporters. Meanwhile, he continued to organize the Mississippi Republican Party and to find ways around white-line Democrats, speaking to audiences across the country on emancipation, suffrage, and the "race question." Back home in Adams County, black voters could count on a free ballot and a fair count throughout the 1880s. Black associational life continued to flourish, evident in the balls that colored fire companies hosted and in the increasing number of black-led mutual aid associations. When a respectful biracial audience gathered peacefully during the heated 1882 campaign to hear ex-senator Blanche K. Bruce speak on Republicanism, the *Natchez Democrat* bragged that it marked "an epoch in the history of political discussions between opposing parties in the South." But even as a measure of stability settled in, outside interests were already plotting to end Natchez's status as an oasis of biracial fusionism.[44]

Disfranchisement

Although Adams County had created a workable biracial and bipartisan arrangement, a low-grade conflict continued in the other counties in the district. Black citizens registered (though in smaller numbers) and attempted to vote at every election. White-line Democrats responded with intimidation, violence, and fraud, but the persistence of black voters maddened Democrat leaders, leading many to endorse changes in the legal code to permanently eliminate black electoral power. "It is no secret," claimed one leading Mississippi Democrat, "that . . . we have been . . . carrying the elections by *fraud* and violence until the whole machinery for election was about to rot down." Another impetus to the disfranchising efforts came from the revival of the Republican Party. In 1888 Republicans gained control of both houses of Congress and the White House for the first time since 1875, and they began to rally around a federal election bill, which would authorize federal supervisors to monitor congressional elections and would empower federal circuit courts to investigate charges of fraud or intimidation. Lynch's, and others', agitation against the illegal and undemocratic practices of the Democratic Party in the South was beginning to pay off.[45]

To forestall Republican intervention, Mississippi convened a constitutional convention in the summer of 1890 to disfranchise black voters. The intention of the convention was never in doubt. "Let us tell the truth if it bursts the bottom of the Universe," thundered S. S. Calhoon, one of the leaders of the convention movement. "We came here to exclude the negro. Nothing short of this will answer." With near-unanimous support, the convention delegates adopted a poll tax, a literacy test, and stricter registration requirements and extended the list of crimes that would invalidate one's right to vote.[46]

When black and white Mississippians heard of these provisions, along with a new reapportionment scheme, they reacted with skepticism and hostility. Many newspapers catering to white audiences thought that the suffrage restrictions went too far, and they were further aggrieved when the convention delegates broke their promise to submit the constitutional changes to a popular referendum. But the actions of the convention delegates fit a pattern of disdain for the opinions of ordinary people. The election of delegates to the convention was organized with little fanfare or attention, resulting in extremely low turnout across the state. In Natchez only 230 votes were cast among 2,075 eligible voters. Few were more outraged by the usurpation of democracy than Mississippi's black newspapers. The *Natchez Brotherhood*, edited by state legislator George F. Bowles, was aghast. "Disfranchise the negro! Keep him from holding office! In the name of God, where now are the last two amendments to the federal constitution? Will an American congress permit a state to set up an oligarchy by reversing the intents and purposes of the organic law of the land?" Congress's answer seemed to be in the affirmative. The federal elections bill stalled in the face of determined Democratic opposition and reluctant Republican support for black rights. After Mississippi blazed the disfranchising trail, other southern states soon followed. Louisiana's restrictions, implemented in 1898, largely mirrored those of Mississippi's except in their use of the grandfather clause.[47]

The impact of the disfranchising measures on black voting cannot be underestimated. In 1890, before the new constitution was adopted, 80 percent of the black male population in Adams County was registered to vote, totaling 3,204 individuals. Within two years, once the disfranchising measures had gone into effect, black registration dropped by 77 percent. Without black voters to support Republican officeholders, there was no need for a fusionist agreement, and so white Democrats took over all the elected offices.[48]

In addition to eliminating black political power, the disfranchisement provisions also weakened the influence of ordinary white citizens. Lower-class whites faced difficulties in paying the poll tax and demonstrating sufficient literacy (even with the understanding clause as a loophole for illiterate white voters). They also faced fewer choices at the ballot box. Disfranchisement undercut the independent movements that made partisan politics so unpredictable and engaging in the 1880s, leaving only the Democratic Party standing. And increasingly this party was ruled by elites. By 1910 the city of Natchez had stopped holding primary elections, since no one opposed the Democratic Party's candidates. And as a result, few bothered to vote.[49]

With limited access to electoral politics, male black leaders retreated into the associational life that had long buttressed freedpeople's political mobilization. Churches, schools, mutual aid societies, fraternal orders, and businesses flourished and became the primary avenues through which Natchez District black people exerted their power and influence in public life. Black politicians such as Louis J. Winston and the Lynch brothers, perhaps sensing the shifting tides of partisan politics, became more involved in entrepreneurial endeavors in the late 1880s. Winston founded two home loan associations that sought to help black families purchase homes and provide start-up capital for businesses. Similarly, John and William Lynch offered loans to numerous small farmers in Adams County, acting much like bankers to help renters and sharecroppers finance larger land purchases. Rev. Revels A. Adams, the minister of Zion Chapel in Natchez, published a *Cyclopedia of African Methodism in Mississippi* twelve years after the disfranchising constitution was adopted. In this book, Adams, whose father and grandfather were also AME ministers, highlighted middle-class church members—those who ran their own businesses, were college educated, owned substantial real estate, were professionals, or traveled extensively.[50]

These economic undertakings were, in part, an attempt to re-create the Republican network that had so successfully integrated and channeled the interests of ordinary freedpeople. But a home loan association or a church that catered to the urban middle-class was an insufficient substitute. A more ambitious, and somewhat successful, venture was the Knights of Honor of the World (KHW), a black fraternal order created by the lawyer and state legislator George F. Bowles. The intent was to encourage "habits of industry, economy[,] fraternal feeling and christian charity among its members." Founded in 1893 in Natchez, just as the disfranchising provisions were beginning to take effect, the order had grown within five years to include 267 lodges and 5,038 members. Most of the lodges were in Mississippi, Louisiana, and Arkansas, but there were a few lodges in the midwestern and Atlantic coast states and one even in Liberia on the West African coast.[51]

For all of the initial success of the KHW, it was a distinctly different organization from the ones created in the early days of Reconstruction. Although it did not exclude members on the basis of race, in practice the KHW catered only to black men and thus represents a break from the biracial Union Leagues and Republican political clubs. The scope of the KHW was also a departure from that of the partisan communities. Instead of incorporating urban and rural people into a dynamic association that maximized the power of ex-slaves, the KHW was primarily an urban organization that looked inward and an all-male group that excluded women from its meetings.

The result of the dwindling of popular governance was the formation of separate societies within the Natchez District. Black people responded to the bifurcated Jim Crow society by clinging to separate institutions in order to protect their members and better participate in public life. The aim was to establish a refuge from racism and discrimination, and to some extent they were successful. Black institutions and businesses prospered in urban areas as white supremacy seeped further into the culture, excluding black people from many public spaces.

Over time this separate, segregated society became increasingly fractured and notorious. In the 1930s University of Chicago sociologists chose the city of Natchez—once a center of black political power and a vibrant, broad-based community—for an anthropological study of the deep class and race divisions that were then pervasive in the Deep South. The divisions between whites and blacks and within the black community were so persistent that civil rights activists in the 1960s considered the region one of the most intransigent in the South. One of the emblematic regions for plantation slavery in the antebellum era had become one of the archetypes of Jim Crow in the first half of the twentieth century.[52]

Given the historical trajectory of the Natchez District from slavery to segregation, it is often difficult to imagine an interregnum of racial progress and egalitarian-minded politics. Yet the Reconstruction history of the Natchez District reminds us that democracies can take root even in the most trying of circumstances. Opportunities for the creation of a broad-based community that brought rural and urban peoples together in a common cause with a national reach do not come along very often. What is remarkable about the freedpeople in the Natchez vicinity is that they seized this opportunity and radically remade their society. Using their experience of bondage as a counterpoint, they imagined a social system governed by broad civic participation, open access to public life, and an assumption of equality in matters of day-to-day intercourse. Their stunning success in making this social vision a reality led to measurable and tangible improvements in the lives of former slaves. The dozens of public schools that dotted the region exemplified their commitment to using government for broad social uplift and their commitment to shared responsibility through a progressive system of taxation. The mobilization of families and neighborhoods led to better labor terms in the fields and representative governance in the halls of power. Public life was opened to freedpeople; their presence was welcomed at public celebrations and their opinions at public meetings.

Another way to measure the impact of freedpeople's grassroots democracy is through the violent counterreaction to its existence. Once the defeated forces of slavery, secession, and separatism realized how quickly freedpeople were enacting radical policies that were altering long-standing assumptions and practices, they responded with massive violence. The white-line attacks were perhaps the greatest testament to this remarkable experiment in biracial, working-class governance. It was a grassroots democracy that, while decentralized and riven with internal conflicts, proved to be remarkably resistant to economic coercion and racist intimidation. Only an invasion of white supremacists from outside the district followed by state-enacted disfranchisement could bring freedpeople's democracy to its knees.

The defeat of freedpeople's democracy and the subsequent exclusion of black people from the body politic, while tragic, was not all that unusual in comparison with other southern regions and other postemancipation societies. None of the postslave societies in the nineteenth century were able to incorporate former slaves into the body politic as equal citizens, and many still struggle to this day to banish the legacies of bondage. But the remarkable mobilization of freedpeople reminds us that grassroots democracy offered one way out of entrenched inequalities. Freedpeople created a grassroots democracy in which power was shared more equitably and where ordinary people exercised unprecedented influence in governance. They reshaped the political and social order of the Natchez District, upending decades of slaveholder rule, establishing a school system, expanding the body politic, and opening up the public sphere to black residents. The history of former slaves, finally, demonstrates that the roots of egalitarian-based democracy run deep and that these roots are grounded in the historical experiences of African Americans.

NOTES

Introduction. "Wise in Time"

1. Edward King, *The Great South* (Hartford, Conn.: American Publishing Company, 1875), 292–95. On the timing of King's visit to the region, see Edward King, "The Great South," *Scribner's Monthly*, October 1874, 667.

2. *Natchez Democrat*, 19 April 1871, 13 August 1873; *Ouachita Telegraph*, 2 January 1874; *Weekly Louisianian*, 20 February 1875.

3. King, *Great South*, 295. King recorded the unnamed black man's comments in dialect. In this instance, I have adjusted the spelling of certain words to avoid the demeaning intent of King's transcription. The original quote is as follows: "I's done gwine to vote to suit myself. Dave Young nor no udder man ain't gwine to tell me nothin' 'bout my vote."

4. Ibid. W. E. B. Du Bois first pointed out the importance of democracy to Reconstruction history. The original title of his seminal book made the link explicit: *Black Reconstruction of Democracy in America: An Essay toward a History of the Part Which Black Folk Played in the Attempt to Reconstruct Democracy in America, 1860–1880*. See W. E. B. Du Bois, *Black Reconstruction* (New York: Harcourt, Brace and Company, 1935; repr., New York: Atheneum, 1992), ix. For more on the political context of 1874, see Eric Foner, *Reconstruction: America's Unfinished Revolution, 1863–1877* (New York: Harper & Row, 1988), 512–26; Michael W. Fitzgerald, *Splendid Failure: Postwar Reconstruction in the American South* (Chicago: Ivan R. Dee, 2007), 174–84.

5. Historical Census Browser, University of Virginia, Geospatial and Statistical Data Center, 2004, http://fisher.lib.virginia.edu/collections/stats/histcensus/index.html.

6. For more on an earlier generation's scholarship on emancipation and labor, see Willie Lee Rose, *Rehearsal for Reconstruction: The Port Royal Experiment* (Indianapolis: Bobbs-Merrill, 1964); Roger L. Ransom and Richard Sutch, *One Kind of Freedom: The Economic Consequences of Emancipation* (New York: Cambridge University Press, 1977); Leon F. Litwack, *Been in the Storm So Long: The Aftermath of Slavery* (New York: Vintage Books, 1979); Barbara Jeanne Fields, *Slavery and Freedom on the Middle Ground: Maryland during the Nineteenth Century* (New Haven, Conn.: Yale University Press, 1985); Gerald David Jaynes, *Branches without Roots: Genesis of the Black Working Class in the American South, 1862–1882* (New York: Oxford University Press, 1986). For more on freedpeople's labor mobilizations, see Foner, *Reconstruction*; Ira Berlin et al., *Slaves No More: Three Essays on Emancipation and the Civil War* (New York: Cambridge University Press, 1992); Lynda Morgan, *Emancipation in Virginia's Tobacco Belt, 1850–1870* (Athens: University of Georgia Press, 1992); Julie Saville, *The Work of Reconstruction: From*

Slave to Wage Laborer in South Carolina, 1860–1870 (New York: Cambridge University Press, 1994); Leslie A. Schwalm, *A Hard Fight for We: Women's Transition from Slavery to Freedom in South Carolina* (Urbana: University of Illinois Press, 1997); Jeffrey R. Kerr-Ritchie, *Freedpeople in the Tobacco South: Virginia, 1860–1900* (Chapel Hill: University of North Carolina Press, 1999); John C. Rodrigue, *Reconstruction in the Cane Fields: From Slavery to Free Labor in Louisiana's Sugar Parishes, 1862–1880* (Baton Rouge: Louisiana State University Press, 2001); Susan Eva O'Donovan, *Becoming Free in the Cotton South* (Cambridge, Mass.: Harvard University Press, 2007). On the kin and household roots of freedpeople's mobilizations, see Laura F. Edwards, *Gendered Strife and Confusion: The Political Culture of Reconstruction* (Urbana: University of Illinois Press, 1997); Noralee Frankel, *Freedom's Women: Black Women and Families in Civil War Era Mississippi* (Bloomington: Indiana University Press, 1999); Elizabeth Regosin, *Freedom's Promise: Ex-slave Families and Citizenship in the Age of Emancipation* (Charlottesville: University Press of Virginia, 2002); Steven Hahn, *A Nation under Our Feet: Black Political Struggles in the Rural South from Slavery to the Great Migration* (Cambridge, Mass.: Belknap Press of Harvard University Press, 2003); Nancy Bercaw, *Gendered Freedoms: Race, Rights, and the Politics of Household in the Delta, 1861–1875* (Gainesville: University Press of Florida, 2003); Kathleen Ann Clark, *Defining Moments: African American Commemoration and Political Culture in the South, 1863–1913* (Chapel Hill: University of North Carolina Press, 2005). For works that address black electoral participation at the grass roots, see William McKee Evans, *Ballots and Fence Rails: Reconstruction on the Lower Cape Fear* (1966; repr., Athens: University of Georgia Press, 1995); Harold Forsythe, "'But My Friends Are Poor': Ross Hamilton and Freedpeople's Politics in Mecklenburg County, Virginia, 1869–1901," *Virginia Magazine of History and Biography* 105 (1997): 409–38; Donald G. Nieman, "African American Communities, Politics, and Justice: Washington County, Texas, 1865–1890," in *Local Matters: Race, Crime, and Justice in the Nineteenth-Century South*, ed. Christopher Waldrep and Donald G. Nieman eds. (Athens: University of Georgia Press, 2001), 201–24; Michael W. Fitzgerald, *Urban Emancipation: Popular Politics in Reconstruction Mobile, 1860–1890* (Baton Rouge: Louisiana State University Press, 2002); Hahn, *A Nation under Our Feet*; Aaron Astor, *Rebels on the Border: Civil War, Emancipation, and the Reconstruction of Kentucky and Missouri* (Baton Rouge: Louisiana State University Press, 2012). Richard Bensel explored some of these questions; however, he purposefully excluded Reconstruction conflicts from his analysis because of the high levels of violence. While aberrant in comparison with the North, violent southern elections reveal powerful motivations among ordinary freedpeople and whites for partisan and electoral participation. Richard Bensel, "The American Ballot Box: Law, Identity, and the Polling Place in the Mid-Nineteenth Century" *Studies in American Political Development* 17 (Spring 2003): 1–27; Richard Franklin Bensel, *The American Ballot Box in the Mid-Nineteenth Century* (New York: Cambridge University Press, 2004).

7. Much of the scholarship on nineteenth-century politics, focused as it is on parties and institutions, either ignores black politics or subsumes the enfranchisement of African Americans into a continuity argument about the similarities of party politics after the Civil War. These approaches fail to account for one of the largest expansions of the electorate and, conversely, for how parties and institutions violently constricted the body politic. For representative works, see Richard L. McCormick, *The Party Period and Public Policy: American Politics from the Age of Jackson to the Progressive Era* (New York: Oxford University Press, 1986); Joel H. Silbey, *The American Political Nation, 1838–1893* (Stanford, Calif.: Stanford University Press, 1991); Robert H. Wiebe, *Self-Rule: A Cultural*

History of American Democracy (Chicago: University of Chicago Press, 1995); Glenn C. Altschuler and Stuart M. Blumin, *Rude Republic: Americans and Their Politics in the Nineteenth Century* (Princeton, N.J.: Princeton University Press, 2000); Byron E. Shafer and Anthony J. Badger, eds., *Contesting Democracy: Substance and Structure in American Political History, 1775–2000* (Lawrence: University Press of Kansas, 2001); Sean Wilentz, *The Rise of American Democracy: Jefferson to Lincoln* (New York: W. W. Norton, 2005); Charles W. Calhoun, *Conceiving a New Republic: The Republican Party and the Southern Question, 1869–1900* (Lawrence: University Press of Kansas, 2006).

8. Robert A. Dahl, *On Democracy* (New Haven, Conn.: Yale University Press, 1998); Margaret Lavinia Anderson, *Practicing Democracy: Elections and Political Culture in Imperial Germany* (Princeton, N.J.: Princeton University Press, 2000); Mimi Sheller, *Democracy after Slavery: Black Publics and Peasant Radicalism in Haiti and Jamaica* (Gainesville: University Press of Florida, 2000); Sheldon S. Wolin, *Tocqueville between Two Worlds: The Making of a Political and Theoretical Life* (Princeton, N.J.: Princeton University Press, 2001); Charles Tilly, *Democracy* (New York: Cambridge University Press, 2007); Gordon Wood, "The Making of American Democracy," in *The Idea of America: Reflections on the Birth of the United States* (New York: Penguin Press, 2011), 189–212.

9. There is no fixed geographical boundary for the Natchez District in the historical record or in contemporary scholarship. The French, in the eighteenth century, designated the area in southwestern Mississippi along the Mississippi River as the "Natchez District." Unlike historians Michael Wayne and Anthony Kaye, I did not include Warren County and Madison Parish in my study because the city of Vicksburg (in Warren County) represented another major city with its own geographic and political influences. After the war, Vicksburg came to dominate the region to the north, known as the Mississippi Delta (including Madison Parish), whereas Natchez remained the major urban center in the cotton-planting regions south of Warren County. To be sure, Tensas Parish and Claiborne County were within the purview of Vicksburg; however, economic and social ties still drew residents from these localities to Natchez. For more on the geographical and historical importance of the Mississippi River, see Christopher Morris, *The Big Muddy: An Environmental History of the Mississippi and Its Peoples from Hernando de Soto to Hurricane Katrina* (New York: Oxford University Press, 2012). For other conceptualizations of the Natchez District, see Michael Wayne, *Reshaping the Plantation South: The Natchez District, 1860–1880* (Baton Rouge: Louisiana State University Press, 1982); Ronald L. F. Davis, *Good and Faithful Labor: From Slavery to Sharecropping in the Natchez District, 1860–1890* (Westport, Conn.: Greenwood Press, 1982); Anthony E. Kaye, *Joining Places: Slave Neighborhoods in the Old South* (Chapel Hill: University of North Carolina Press, 2007). On the demographics of the Natchez District, see D. Clayton James, *Antebellum Natchez* (Baton Rouge: Louisiana State University Press, 1968), 136–61; Wayne, *Reshaping the Plantation South*, 1, 7–15; Sam Bowers Hilliard, *Atlas of Antebellum Southern Agriculture* (Baton Rouge: Louisiana State University Press, 1984), 8–11, 36–44, 68–71. On elite planters, see William Kauffman Scarborough, *Masters of the Big House: Elite Slaveholders of the Mid-Nineteenth-Century South* (Baton Rouge: Louisiana State University Press, 2003).

10. In 1860 Natchez was larger (6,612 residents) than all of the surrounding cities, including Vicksburg, Jackson, and Baton Rouge. The closest city with a larger population was New Orleans, 150 miles away. During the 1860s Vicksburg grew to become the largest city in the state; however, Natchez remained the second-largest Mississippi city

into the 1880s. See Joseph C. G. Kennedy, *Population of the United States in 1860* (Washington, D.C.: Government Printing Office, 1864), 271. On Natchez and its immediate surroundings, see James, *Antebellum Natchez*; Ronald L. F. Davis, *The Black Experience in Natchez, 1720–1880* (Natchez National Historical Park, Miss.: Eastern National Park & Monument Association, 1994); Winthrop D. Jordan, *Tumult and Silence at Second Creek: An Inquiry into a Civil War Slave Conspiracy*, rev. ed. (Baton Rouge: Louisiana State University Press, 1995). Sixty-four percent of the Natchez District's and nearly 30 percent of Mississippi's free black population lived in Adams County. Historical Census Browser. Approximately 208 free colored people lived in Natchez before the Civil War. By contrast, 2,132 slaves and 4,272 free white people called Natchez their home. See Kennedy, *Population of the United States in 1860*, 272. On the antebellum free black population in Natchez, see William R. Hogan and Edwin A. Davis, eds., *William Johnson's Natchez: The Ante-Bellum Diary of a Free Negro* (Baton Rouge: Louisiana State University Press, 1951); James, *Antebellum Natchez*, 177–81; Davis, *The Black Experience in Natchez*, 47–60; Virginia Meacham Gould, ed., *Chained to the Rock of Adversity: To Be Free, Black and Female in the Old South* (Athens: University of Georgia Press, 1998), 1–38. For more on how urban centers can affect a surrounding rural region, see Randolph Dennis Werner, "Hegemony and Conflict: The Political Economy of a Southern Region, Augusta, Georgia, 1865–1895" (PhD diss., University of Virginia, 1977); William Cronon, *Nature's Metropolis: Chicago and the Great West* (New York: W. W. Norton, 1991).

11. Of the four southern districts that elected a black congressman following Reconstruction, only the Natchez District has yet to receive serious scrutiny in the secondary literature. In addition to Mississippi's Sixth Congressional District, the other districts were Virginia's Fourth, North Carolina's Second, and South Carolina's Seventh. On the other districts, see Jane Dailey, *Before Jim Crow: The Politics of Race in Postemancipation Virginia* (Chapel Hill: University of North Carolina Press, 2000); Eric Anderson, *Race and Politics in North Carolina, 1872–1901: The Black Second* (Baton Rouge: Louisiana State University Press, 1981); Joel Williamson, *After Slavery: The Negro in South Carolina during Reconstruction, 1861–1877* (Chapel Hill: University of North Carolina Press, 1965); Thomas C. Holt, *Black over White: Negro Political Leadership in South Carolina during Reconstruction* (Urbana: University of Illinois Press, 1977); Edward A. Miller Jr., *Gullah Statesman: Robert Smalls from Slavery to Congress, 1839–1915* (Columbia: University of South Carolina Press, 1995). Works that address postemancipation black politics in the Natchez District include Joe Louis Caldwell, "A Social, Economic, and Political Study of Blacks in the Louisiana Delta, 1865–1880" (PhD diss., Tulane University, 1988); and Davis, *The Black Experience in Natchez*. On postemancipation life in the Natchez District, see Wayne, *Reshaping the Plantation South*; Davis, *Good and Faithful Labor*; Aaron D. Anderson, *Builders of a New South: Merchants, Capital, and the Remaking of Natchez, 1865–1914* (Jackson: University Press of Mississippi, 2013). On black life in Mississippi after the Civil War, see Vernon Lane Wharton, *The Negro in Mississippi, 1865–1890* (Chapel Hill: University of North Carolina Press, 1947; repr., New York: Harper & Row, 1965). Biographical information comes from numerous sources that I have compiled in a database on black politicians, Justin Behrend, Black Politicians Database, SUNY-Geneseo, http://go.geneseo.edu/BlackPoliticiansDB (BPDB). My database builds off the information compiled in Steven Hahn's Black Leaders Data Set (see Hahn, *A Nation under Our Feet*, appendix) and was supplemented with Eric Foner's *Freedom's Lawmakers: A Directory of Black Officeholders during Reconstruction* (Baton Rouge: Louisiana State University Press, 1996). I've made my database of black politicians from the Natchez District

available to the public in the hopes that scholars and genealogical researchers might find the information useful and as a step in expanding our knowledge of black political life in the nineteenth century.

12. The voting estimate is based on the white male population of voting age from the Natchez District. Approximately 5,125 white men were eligible to vote in a population of 97,009 in 1860. For further details, see the Historical Census Browser. Select works on white supremacist culture in the nineteenth century include, but are not limited to, John W. Cell, *The Highest Stage of White Supremacy: The Origins of Segregation in South Africa and the American South* (New York: Cambridge University Press, 1982); Joel Williamson, *The Crucible of Race: Black-White Relations in the American South since Emancipation* (New York: Oxford University Press, 1984); George M. Fredrickson, *The Black Image in the White Mind: The Debate on Afro-American Character and Destiny, 1817–1914* (Hanover, N.H.: Wesleyan University Press, 1987); Grace Elizabeth Hale, *Making Whiteness: The Culture of Segregation in the South, 1890–1940* (New York: Vintage, 1998); David Blight, *Race and Reunion: The Civil War in American Memory* (Cambridge, Mass.: Harvard University Press, 2001).

13. For more on Confederate visions for a new republic, see Stephanie McCurry, *Confederate Reckoning: Power and Politics in the Civil War South* (Cambridge, Mass.: Harvard University Press, 2010).

14. On internal community conflicts and political divisions among African Americans during Reconstruction, see Holt, *Black over White*; Armstead L. Robinson, "Beyond the Realm of Social Consensus: New Meanings of Reconstruction for American History," *Journal of American History* 68 (September 1981): 276–97; Elsa Barkley Brown, "Negotiating and Transforming the Public Sphere: African American Political Life in the Transition from Slavery to Freedom," *Public Culture* 7 (1994): 111–50; Fitzgerald, *Urban Emancipation*; Dylan C. Penningroth, *The Claims of Kinfolk: African American Property and Community in the Nineteenth-Century South* (Chapel Hill: University of North Carolina Press, 2003). For more on the paradoxes of democracy, see Charles Tilly, *Trust and Rule* (New York: Cambridge University Press, 2005).

15. Leon Fink, *Workingmen's Democracy: The Knights of Labor and American Politics* (Urbana: University of Illinois Press, 1983); Sean Wilentz, *Chants Democratic: New York City and the Rise of the American Working Class, 1788–1850* (New York: Oxford University Press, 1986); David Montgomery, *Citizen Worker: The Experience of Workers in the United States with Democracy and the Free Market during the Nineteenth Century* (New York: Cambridge University Press, 1993); Mary Ryan, *Civic Wars: Democracy and Public Life in the American City during the Nineteenth Century* (Berkeley: University of California Press, 1998).

16. Profiles of these five individuals, and profiles of hundreds more, can be found in the BPDB.

Chapter One. Into the Arms of Strangers

1. Fanny E. Conner to Lemuel P. Conner, 11 July 1863, Lemuel P. Conner and Family Papers, Louisiana and Lower Mississippi Valley Collections, Louisiana State University (LSU) Libraries, Baton Rouge. Vicksburg fell on 4 July 1863. Union forces occupied Natchez on 13 July 1863. For a fuller account of this process, see Armstead L. Robinson, *Bitter Fruits of Bondage: The Demise of Slavery and the Collapse of the Confederacy, 1861–1865* (Charlottesville: University of Virginia Press, 2005).

2. The slaves likely had seen, or at least heard of, Yankee gunboats, which began to steam past Natchez infrequently after New Orleans fell to federal forces on 28 April 1862. Natchez surrendered to Union gunboats in May 1862, but Union forces did not occupy the city. At the same time, about one thousand Union soldiers temporarily landed in Vidalia, opposite Natchez. See Commandant C. G. Dahlgren to Brig. Gen. Thomas Jordan, 17 May 1862, in *The War of the Rebellion: A Compilation of the Official Records of the Union and Confederate Armies*, 128 vols. (Washington, D.C., 1880–1901), ser. 1, vol. 15, pp. 736–38; Kate Stone, *Brokenburn: The Journal of Kate Stone, 1861–1868*, edited by John Q. Anderson (1955; repr., Baton Rouge: Louisiana State University Press, 1995), 107, 111, 122.

3. For an expansive view of the slave community, see John W. Blassingame, *The Slave Community: Plantation Life in the Antebellum South*, rev. and enlarged ed. (New York: Oxford University Press, 1979); Herbert G. Gutman, *The Black Family in Slavery and Freedom, 1750–1925* (New York: Pantheon Books, 1976). Critics of the notion of a monolithic slave community include Peter Kolchin, "Reevaluating the Antebellum Slave Community: A Comparative Perspective," *Journal of American History* 70 (December 1983): 579–601; Brenda E. Stevenson, *Life in Black and White: Family and Community in the Slave South* (New York: Oxford University Press, 1997); Dylan C. Penningroth, *The Claims of Kinfolk: African American Property and Community in the Nineteenth-Century South* (Chapel Hill: University of North Carolina Press, 2003); Anthony E. Kaye, *Joining Places: Slave Neighborhoods in the Old South* (Chapel Hill: University of North Carolina Press, 2007). For recent studies on how slaves utilized extended networks, see Calvin Schermerhorn, *Money over Mastery, Family over Freedom: Slavery in the Antebellum Upper South* (Baltimore: Johns Hopkins University Press, 2011); Susan Eva O'Donovan, "Universities of Social and Political Change: Slaves in Jail in Antebellum America" in *Buried Lives: Incarcerated in Early America*, ed. Michele Lise Tarter and Richard Bell (Athens: University of Georgia Press, 2012), 124–46.

4. For more on slaves' role in emancipation, see Ira Berlin et al., *Slaves No More: Three Essays on Emancipation and the Civil War* (New York: Cambridge University Press, 1992); Julie Saville, *The Work of Reconstruction: From Slave to Wage Laborer in South Carolina, 1860–1870* (New York: Cambridge University Press, 1994); Leslie A. Schwalm, *A Hard Fight for We: Women's Transition from Slavery to Freedom in South Carolina* (Urbana: University of Illinois Press, 1997); Steven Hahn, *A Nation under Our Feet: Black Political Struggles in the Rural South from Slavery to the Great Migration* (Cambridge, Mass.: Belknap Press of Harvard University Press, 2003), 13–61; Robinson, *Bitter Fruits of Bondage*; Susan Eva O'Donovan, *Becoming Free in the Cotton South* (Cambridge, Mass.: Harvard University Press, 2007).

5. The conceptualization of this chapter has benefited from an engagement with Anthony Kaye's argument on slaves' encounter with new powers during the Civil War, but my argument differs regarding the role of nation-state power. See Kaye, "Slaves, Emancipation, and the Powers of War: Views from the Natchez District of Mississippi," in *The War Was You and Me: Civilians in the American Civil War*, ed. Joan E. Cashin (Princeton, N.J.: Princeton University Press, 2002), 60–84; Kaye, *Joining Places*, 177–207.

6. Drew Gilpin Faust, *The Creation of Confederate Nationalism: Ideology and Identity in the Civil War South* (Baton Rouge: Louisiana State University Press, 1988); Hahn, *A Nation under Our Feet*, 65–68; Stephanie McCurry, *Confederate Reckoning: Power and Politics in the Civil War South* (Cambridge, Mass.: Harvard University Press, 2010).

7. On the role of slaves in passing along information and anticipated rumors of libera-

tion, see Julius Sherrard Scott, "The Common Wind: Currents of Afro-American Communication in the Era of the Haitian Revolution" (PhD diss., Duke University, 1986); Thomas C. Buchanan, *Black Life on the Mississippi: Slaves, Free Blacks, and the Western Steamboat World* (Chapel Hill: University of North Carolina Press, 2004). My analysis of these networks is based on post–Civil War testimony before the Southern Claims Commission (SCC). Authorized by Congress in 1871, the SCC offered loyal citizens compensation for property appropriated by federal forces for legitimate military uses, but to receive compensation claimants had to prove their loyalty to the Union during the war and ownership of the property in question. In the course of this testimony, the SCC files recount experiences of slavery, war, and emancipation in freedpeople's own words—an unparalleled source for understanding their conceptions of community and politics but one not without its problems. Since witnesses gave testimony at least ten years after the events they describe during the Civil War, the claims should not be read uncritically. However, it is important to note that the commissioners presumed that former slaves were loyal to the Union. For an overview of the SCC, see Frank Wysor Klingberg, *The Southern Claims Commission* (Berkeley: University of California Press, 1955).

8. Testimony of George W. Carter and testimony of Richard Dorsey, Richard Dorsey claim, case 4,337, Adams County, Mississippi case files, Settled Case Files for Claims Approved by the Southern Claims Commission, Ser. 732, Southern Claims Commission, Records of the Office of the Third Auditor, Records of the Accounting Officers of the Department of Treasury, Record Group 217, National Archives, Washington, D.C. (cited hereafter as RG 217); testimony of James K. Hyman, James K. Hyman claim, case 14,773, Adams County, Mississippi, Congressional Jurisdiction Case Files, Records of the U.S. Court of Claims, Record Group 123, National Archives, Washington, D.C. (cited hereafter as RG 123); Thomas Turner claim, case 4,329, Adams County, RG 217; Jane Dent claim, case 6,616, Adams County, RG 217; John Smith claim, case 10,801, Adams County, RG 217; David Combs claim, case 20,299, Adams County, RG 217. Each claimant, like Dorsey and Hyman, had to produce at least two witnesses for loyalty and two witnesses for property. But because not all SCC claims have survived and because the claimants often produced only the minimum number of witnesses necessary to make their case, this network should be viewed as a the minimum number of contacts that stitched together the urban black community in Natchez.

9. Testimony of James Page, James Page claim, case 7,353, Claiborne County, RG 217. On Page's network, see the testimonies of Robert Watt, Joseph Bolander, L. Sommers, Elias Unger, Meyer Levy, E. Robbins, W. St. J. E. Parker, A. H. Peck, Henderson Moore, Harry or Henry Hall, Jefferson Copeland, Richard Stamps, William H. Buck, Levin P. Williams, Jackson French, Moses Davenport, William Pinn, and Andrew Gossin in Page's claim, case 7,353, Claiborne County, RG 217; Rosetta L. Newsom claim, case 4,995, Claiborne County, RG 217; Jackson French claim, case 17,047, Claiborne County, RG 217; Moses Davenport claim, case 11,184, Claiborne County, RG 217; William Pinn claim, case 15,294, Claiborne County, Report 7, Office 474, microfiche 2474–2475, Disallowed Claims, Southern Claims Commission, Records of the U.S. House of Representatives, RG 233, National Archives, Washington, D.C. (cited hereafter as RG 233); Andrew Gossin claim, case 15,292, Claiborne County, RG 233. (Some cases in RG 233, such as Gossin's, do not designate a report and office number.) For more on John Byrd, see the testimony of James Page and Rosetta L. Newsom, Rosetta L. Newsom claim, case 4,995, Claiborne County, RG 217. In 1863 the Union army, under Grant's leadership, marched through Claiborne County and confiscated provisions and animals from anyone within their

reach. Biographical information comes from numerous sources that I have compiled in a database, Justin Behrend, Black Politicians Database, SUNY-Geneseo, http://go.geneseo .edu/BlackPoliticiansDB (BPDB).

10. Testimony of George Braxton, Thomas Turner claim, case 4,330, Adams County, RG 217; testimony of William Smoot, Abner Pierce claim, case 22,176, Adams County, RG 217. Alfred V. Davis also owned David Singleton, about whom more will be said later. For now it is enough to emphasize that Singleton was connected to the urban dray network through two draymen, Vincent Brady and Isaac Hughes, who testified on his behalf, thereby establishing a link between the Natchez network and the rural network of carriage drivers.

11. Alfred V. Davis owned 651 slaves in Adams County and Concordia Parish. Francis Surget Jr. owned 456 slaves in Adams County, Wilkinson County, Concordia Parish, and Madison Parish. Gabriel B. Shields owned 444 slaves in Adams County and Concordia Parish. These three nabobs were also related to each other. Davis and Shields married sisters of Francis Surget. William Kauffman Scarborough, *Masters of the Big House: Elite Slaveholders of the Mid-Nineteenth-Century South* (Baton Rouge: Louisiana State University Press, 2003), 12, 467, 469.

12. Testimony of Richard Stamps, Richard Stamps claim, case 5,003, Claiborne County, RG 217.

13. Carriage drivers and draymen were involved in many slave insurrections. See, for example, James Sidbury, *Ploughshares into Swords: Race, Rebellion, and Identity in Gabriel's Virginia, 1730–1810* (Cambridge: Cambridge University Press, 1997).

14. Testimonies of Isaac Hughes and David Singleton, David Singleton claim, case 411, Adams County, RG 123. William Kauffman Scarborough ranks Alfred V. Davis as the nineteenth-largest slaveholder in the South in 1860, owning 651 slaves in Adams County and Concordia Parish. See Scarborough, *Masters of the Big House*, 434. According to the 1860 U.S. Census, Davis possessed a half-million dollars in real estate and $40,000 in personal property. U.S. Bureau of Census, *Eighth Census of the United States: Population, 1860.* "Nabob" refers to a class of about forty slaveholding families distinguished by immense wealth. For more on the Natchez nabobs, see D. Clayton James, *Antebellum Natchez* (Baton Rouge: Louisiana State University Press, 1968), 136–61. It is impossible, of course, to know how much money David Singleton had accumulated, but the census data indicates that he had some entrepreneurial success. After purchasing his and his wife's, daughter's, and son's freedom and moving to Ohio, he claimed, in 1860, $900 in real estate wealth and $100 in personal property. Ten years later he claimed $2,200 in real estate wealth. See U.S. Bureau of Census, *Eighth Census: Population, 1860*; U.S. Bureau of Census, *Ninth Census of the United States: Population, 1870*. For more on schools for black children in Cincinnati, see Wendell P. Dabney, *Cincinnati's Colored Citizens: Historical, Sociological, and Biographical* (Cincinnati: Dabney Publishing Company, 1926), 105–6; Geoffrey J. Giglierano and Deborah A. Overmyer, *The Bicentennial Guide to Greater Cincinnati: A Portrait of Two Hundred Years* (Cincinnati: Cincinnati Historical Society, 1988), 498–99. In Singleton's SCC claim, he noted that he moved his family to Mount Pleasant, Ohio. The Mount Healthy village in Hamilton County just outside of Cincinnati was known to locals as Mt. Pleasant. Singleton's eldest daughter, Mary, age nine, was listed in the 1860 census as attending school.

15. Testimonies of Alex Carter, Isaac Hughes, and David Singleton, David Singleton claim, case 411, Adams County, RG 123.

16. William Ashley Vaughan, "Natchez during the Civil War" (PhD diss., University of Southern Mississippi, 2001), 188–89; testimony of Richard Dorsey, James K. Hyman claim, case 14,773, Adams County, RG 123; testimony of James Hyman, Jane Jones claim, case 19,743, Adams County, Report 7, Office 442, microfiche 2,460, RG 233; testimony of Henry Watkins, Abner Pierce claim, case 22,176, Adams County, RG 217. On the perils of slave runaways, see Kaye, *Joining Places*, 132–36.

17. Testimony of Richard Dorsey, James K. Hyman claim, case 14,773, Adams County, RG 123; testimony of James Hyman, Amanda Jones claim, case 19,850, Adams County, Report 7, Office 439, microfiche 2,459, RG 233; testimony of James Hyman, Jane Jones claim, case 19,743, Adams County, Report 7, Office 442, microfiche 2,460, RG 233; testimony of Richard Dorsey, Jane Jones claim, case 19,743, Adams County, Report 7, Office 442, microfiche 2,460, RG 233; testimony of Richard Stamps, Henderson Moore claim, case 4,992, Claiborne County, RG 217; testimony of James Page, Richard Stamps claim, case 5,003, Claiborne County, RG 217. For other examples of discussing rumors of war in private, see testimony of Andrew Brown, Butler Williams claim, case 19,924, Adams County, Report 9, Office 969, microfiche 3663, RG 233; testimony of Washington Jefferson, Catherine Lucas claim, case 16,373, Adams County, RG 217; testimony of Richard Stamps, Henderson Moore claim, Claiborne County, RG 217. For another example of whispering, see testimony of Henry Farrar, Butler Williams claim, case 19,924, Adams County, Report 9, Office 969, microfiche 3663, RG 233.

18. Testimony of Washington Jefferson, Catherine Lucas claim, case 16,373, Adams County, RG 217; testimony of Lewis Thompson, John Smith claim, case 10,801, Adams County, RG 217; testimony of Clem Hardiman and Lloyd Wigenton, Anthony Lewis claim, case 15,293, Claiborne County, RG 217. For another example of women discussing the implications of war, see the testimony of Charles Smith, Jane Dent claim, case 6,616, Adams County, RG 217.

19. Testimony of John Smith, David Combs claim, case 20,299, Adams County, RG 217; testimony of John Holdman, John Holdman claim, case 19,278, Adams County, RG 217; testimony of Thomas Richardson, Rosetta L. Newsom claim, case 4,995, Claiborne County, RG 217; testimony of Isaac Hughes, David Singleton claim, case 411, Adams County, RG 123; testimony of Jeff Copeland, James Page claim, case 7,353, Claiborne County, RG 217; testimony of Louis J. Winston, Charles Smith claim, case 5,757, Adams County, RG 217; testimony of James Page, Richard Stamps claim, case 5,003, Claiborne County, RG 217; testimony of George Carter, James K. Hyman claim, case 14,773, Adams County, RG 123. For similar statements on the cause of the Civil War, see the testimony of James Page, Rosetta L. Newsom claim, case 4,995, Claiborne County, RG 217; testimony of Joseph Bolander, Richard Stamps claim, case 5,003, Claiborne County, RG 217. For other expressions of Union sympathy, see testimony of James K. Hyman, Richard Dorsey claim, case 4,337, Adams County, RG 217; testimony of Burrel Foley, Burrel Foley claim, case 9,407, Adams County, Report 2, Office 386, microfiche 234, RG 233; testimony of James K. Hyman, James K. Hyman claim, case 14,773, Adams County, RG 123.

20. Testimony of James K. Hyman, Richard Dorsey claim, case 4,337, Adams County, RG 217; testimony of Levin Hooper, Mack and Simon Washington claim, case 8,338, Wilkinson County, RG 123.

21. On the uses of rumor in political struggles, see Steven Hahn, "'Extravagant Expectations' of Freedom: Rumour, Political Struggle, and the Christmas Insurrection Scare of 1865 in the American South," *Past and Present* 157 (November 1997): 122–58. For a fuller

exploration of the slave-insurrection scares in the Natchez District, see Justin Behrend, "Rebellious Talk and Conspiratorial Plots: The Making of a Slave Insurrection in Civil War Natchez," *Journal of Southern History* 77, no. 1 (February 2011): 17–52.

22. How[ell] Hines to Gov. J. J. Pettus, 14 May 1861, Governor Pettus Papers, Mississippi Department of Archives and History (MDAH), Jackson; Susan Sillers Darden Diary, vol. 1, 10 May, 16 May, 18 May 1861, Darden Family Papers, MDAH.

23. For the record, Lincoln never visited Natchez or any part of the Natchez District during the 1860 election campaign or while he was president. The subject of Lincoln frequently came up in the WPA slave narratives because a standard question asked about Lincoln. Thus hundreds of slave narratives discuss perceptions of Lincoln; however, few mention personal encounters with the Republican president. For works that reference these types of Lincoln stories, see B. A. Botkin, ed., *Lay My Burden Down: A Folk History of Slavery* (Chicago: University of Chicago Press, 1945), 16–18; Lawrence W. Levine, *Black Culture and Black Consciousness: Afro-American Folk Thought from Slavery to Freedom* (New York: Oxford University Press, 1977), 88.

24. Davenport was born and raised in Adams County and was owned by Gabriel Shields. Maynard was born in Texas. His master moved "a lot of his slaves," including Maynard, to Natchez once the war began. Tims and his family ran away to Natchez from Jefferson County after federal troops occupied the city. Tims and Maynard moved on from Natchez a few years after the end of the war, while Davenport remained in Adams County for the remainder of his life. Charlie Davenport, interview by Edith Wyatt Moore, in *The American Slave: A Composite Autobiography*, ed. George P. Rawick, vol. 7, *Oklahoma and Mississippi Narratives* (Westport, Conn.: Greenwood Press, 1977), pt. 2, pp. 34–43; Charlie Davenport, interview by Edith Wyatt Moore, in Rawick, *American Slave*, supplement 1, vol. 7, *Mississippi Narratives*, pt. 2, pp. 558–72; Bob Maynard interview, in Rawick, *American Slave*, vol. 7, *Oklahoma and Mississippi Narratives*, pt. 1, pp. 223–26; J. T. Tims, interview by Samuel S. Taylor, in Rawick, *American Slave*, vol. 10, *Arkansas Narratives*, pt. 6, pp. 336–45.

25. Bob Maynard interview, in Rawick, *American Slave*, vol. 7, *Oklahoma and Mississippi Narratives*, pt. 1, p. 225; Charlie Davenport, interview by Edith Wyatt Moore, in Rawick, *American Slave*, vol. 7, *Oklahoma and Mississippi Narratives*, pt. 2, p. 38. Some of Charlie Davenport's extensive testimony appears absurd, the Lincoln story being possibly one example, and yet there are moments in his WPA narrative when Davenport's memory is quite accurate, despite the intervening years. For example, he recalls an incident when "some nigger soldiers [were] plunderin' some houses. Out at Pine Ridge dey kilt a white man named Rogillio." Sure enough, in 1866 four black soldiers were accused of murdering Elias Julien Rogillio, and the body was found along the Pine Ridge road. See Charlie Davenport, interview by Edith Wyatt Moore, in Rawick, *American Slave*, supplement 1, vol. 7, *Mississippi Narratives*, pt. 2, pp. 565–66; State vs. David Diggs, box 17–22, October Term 1866, Circuit Court Case Files, Adams County, Historic Natchez Foundation, Natchez, Miss.

26. J. T. Tims, interview by Samuel S. Taylor, in Rawick, *American Slave*, vol. 10, *Arkansas Narratives*, pt. 6, p. 341; Charlie Davenport, interviewed by Edith Wyatt Moore, in Rawick, *American Slave*, vol. 7, *Oklahoma and Mississippi Narratives*, Pt. 2, p. 38; Bob Maynard interview, in Rawick, *American Slave*, vol. 7, *Oklahoma and Mississippi Narratives*, pt. 1, p. 225.

27. Bob Maynard interview, in Rawick, *American Slave*, vol. 7, *Oklahoma and Mississippi Narratives*, pt. 1, p. 225–26; Charlie Davenport, interview by Edith Wyatt Moore,

in Rawick, *American Slave*, vol. 7, *Oklahoma and Mississippi Narratives*, pt. 2, p. 38. Like Maynard, J. T. Tims vaguely refers to Lincoln entering the home of a slaveholder. Lincoln asked "for work" but was told to wait until after the slaveholder had his dinner. When the slaveholder returned, he found Lincoln "looking over his books." See J. T. Tims, interview by Samuel S. Taylor, in Rawick, *American Slave*, vol. 10, *Arkansas Narratives*, pt. 6, p. 341.

28. For a different interpretation of Lincoln in slaves' imaginations, see Kaye, "Slaves, Emancipation, and the Powers of War," 66. On peasant appeals to a distant ruler, see Daniel Field, *Rebels in the Name of the Tsar* (Boston: Houghton Mifflin, 1976), 1–29; Shahid Amin, "Gandhi as Mahatma: Gorakhpur District, Eastern UP, 1921–2," in *Selected Subaltern Studies*, ed. Ranajit Guha and Gayatri Chakravorty Spivak (New York: Oxford University Press, 1988), 288–342.

29. For more on the planter mind, see Elizabeth Fox-Genovese and Eugene D. Genovese, *The Mind of the Master Class: History and Faith in the Southern Slaveholders' Worldview* (New York: Cambridge University Press, 2005); Elizabeth Fox-Genovese and Eugene D. Genovese, *Slavery in White and Black: Class and Race in the Southern Slaveholders' New World Order* (Cambridge University Press, 2008). On fears that Lincoln's election would lead to slave insurrections, see Charles B. Dew, *Apostles of Disunion: Southern Secession Commissioners and the Causes of the Civil War* (Charlottesville: University Press of Virginia, 2001), 33–34, 40–41, 57, 78, 79–80.

30. Lemuel P. Conner and Family Papers, Document A, in Winthrop D. Jordan, *Tumult and Silence at Second Creek: An Inquiry into a Civil War Slave Conspiracy*, rev. ed. (Baton Rouge: Louisiana State University Press, 1995), 268–84. Conner refers to himself as the president of the committee in Lemuel P. Conner to Leonidas Polk, 12 December 1861, Document T, in Jordan, *Tumult and Silence*, 343–44.

31. Lemuel P. Conner and Family Papers, Document A, in Jordan, *Tumult and Silence*, 268–84; William J. Minor Plantation Diary, 23 September 1861, Document H, in ibid., 317–19.

32. I uncovered twenty-six witnesses in fifty-eight SCC claims that make reference to the hangings in Natchez, and it is because of these claims that my interpretation of the Second Creek slave uprising differs markedly from Winthrop Jordan's account in *Tumult and Silence*.

33. Testimony of Charles Smith, Jane Dent claim, case 6,616, Adams County, RG 217; testimony of George Carter, Richard Dorsey claim, case 4,337, Adams County, RG 217; testimony of James K. Hyman, John Holdman claim, case 19,278, Adams County, RG 217. George Hitchen, a free black man from Michigan who settled in Natchez after the war, claimed that Alexander K. Farrar "helped to Hang 88. of our People." See Hitchen to O. O. Howard, 4 January 1868, Commissioner, Letters Received, m752, roll 53, Records of the Bureau of Refugees, Freedmen, and Abandoned Lands, Record Group 105, National Archives, Washington, D.C. (cited hereafter as BRFAL). Laura S. Haviland investigated the hangings and confirmed 209 executions, listed here by the names of the slave owners: "Frank Susetts [Surget], 26; James Sussets [Surget], 7; Dr. Stanton, 8; Dr. Moseby, 26; widow Albert Dunbar, 48; Mrs. Brady, 12; widow E. Baker, 28; Mrs. Alexander, 16; Dr. George Baldwin, 8; Stephen Odell, 5; G. Grafton, 5; James Brown, 3; Mr. Marshall, 1; Mr. Robinson, 2; Melon Davis, 1; widow Absalom Sharp, 3; Miss Mary Dunbar, 3; Joseph Reynolds, 2; Baker Robinson, 3; Lee Marshall, whipped to death 1; Mrs. Chase, whipped to death 1; a total of 209." Many local residents told her that over 400 had been killed in "this reign of terror," but she could identify only these 209. Laura S. Haviland, *A Woman's*

Life-Work: Labors and Experiences of Laura S. Haviland (Author, 1881; repr., Salem, N.H.: Ayer, 1984), 296–97.

34. Testimony of Richard Dorsey, James K. Hyman claim, case 14,773, Adams County, RG 123; *Natchez Courier*, 27 June 1862; vigilance committee report and resolutions, [not dated], Correspondence and Papers, Undated Personal Correspondence, Alexander K. Farrar Papers, Louisiana and Lower Mississippi Valley Collections, Louisiana State University (LSU) Libraries, Baton Rouge, on microfilm in Kenneth M Stampp, ed., *Records of Ante-Bellum Southern Plantations from the Revolution through the Civil War*, Series I: Selections from LSU, Part 3: The Natchez Area, Reel 7, frames 226–33; Provost Marshal A. K. Farrar to Gov. John J. Pettus, 17 July 1862, Document K, in Jordan, *Tumult and Silence*, 323–24; Haviland, *A Woman's Life-Work*, 297. For more references to Farrar in the SCC records, see testimony of Littleton Barber, Littleton Barber claim, case 5,752, Adams County, RG 217; testimony of James K. Hyman, John Holdman claim, case 19,278, Adams County, RG 217; testimony of George Braxton, Thomas Turner claim, case 4,330, Adams County, RG 217. Gen. Braxton Bragg placed Adams County and Concordia Parish under martial law on 28 April 1862 and appointed A. K. Farrar provost marshal. Vaughan, "Natchez during the Civil War," 83. Farrar owned 322 slaves in 1860. See Scarborough, *Masters of the Big House*, 470.

35. Testimony of George Carter, Richard Dorsey claim, case 4,337, Adams County, RG 217; testimony of Henry Farrar, Butler Williams claim, case 19,924, Adams County, Report 9, Office 969, microfiche 3663, RG 233; testimony of Randall Pollard, John Smith claim, case 10,801, Adams County, RG 217; Maj. N. A. M. Dudley to Bvt. Maj. John Tyler, 15 January 1869, Department of Mississippi, pt. II, ser. 2232, Letters Sent, vol. 49, entry 342, Records of the U.S. Army Continental Commands, 1821–1890, Record Group 393, National Archives, Washington, D.C.; Haviland, *A Woman's Life-Work*, 296.

36. Haviland, *A Woman's Life-Work*, 297. Haviland claims that Dunbar offered $10,000 for one of her slaves and Reynolds $100,000 for two slaves. These figures were many times the average price for slaves, but they may indicate the powerlessness of slaveholders before Confederate authorities. No matter how much was offered, the committee was unwilling to release slaves merely at the behest of their owners.

37. Testimony of Charles Smith, Jane Dent claim, case 6,616, Adams County, RG 217; testimony of Richard Dorsey, Amanda Jones claim, case 19,850, Adams County, Report 7, Office 439, microfiche 2,459, RG 233.

38. J. T. Tims, interview by Samuel S. Taylor, in Rawick, *American Slave*, vol. 10, *Arkansas Narratives*, pt. 6, p. 337; Hahn, *A Nation under Our Feet*, 72.

39. Brig. Gen. Thomas E. G. Ransom to Lt. Col. W. T. Clark, 16 July 1863, in *War of the Rebellion*, ser. 1, vol. 14, pt. 2, p. 681; Jeannie Dean, ed., *Annie Harper's Journal* (Denton, Tex.: Flower Mound Writing Company, 1983), 31; testimony of Abner Pierce, Abner Pierce claim, case 22,176, Adams County, RG 217; Ben Lewis, interview by Edith Wyatt Moore, in Rawick, *American Slave*, supplement. 1, vol. 8, *Mississippi Narratives*, pt. 3, p. 1310; *Natchez Courier*, 25 September 1863. Annie Coulson Harper, the daughter of a clothing merchant, was born in Natchez in 1840. She lived in that city during the early years of the Civil War and later moved to Jefferson County in 1864 when she married William L. Harper. Residing at Secluseval, near Fayette, she wrote a journal, probably in 1879 (as there is a reference to the Kansas exodus), for her daughter Lurline, born in 1873, to explain the tumultuous events of the Civil War era.

40. Dean, *Annie Harper's Journal*, 30; James H. Maury to James J. Maury, 28 Septem-

ber 1863, quoted in John K. Bettersworth, ed., *Mississippi in the Confederacy: As They Saw It* (Baton Rouge: Louisiana State University Press, 1961), 241.

41. Testimony of Jackson French, Solomon Unger, and Estelle Levy, Jackson French claim, case 17,047, Claiborne County, RG 217. Similarly, Nace Bradford, a laborer, helped General Grant find the way to Willow Springs during the Vicksburg campaign. See the testimony of Nace Bradford, Nace Bradford claim, case 15,291, Claiborne County, RG 217. On nominal owners, see Ira Berlin, *Slaves without Masters: The Free Negro in the Antebellum South* (New York: New Press, 1974), 215.

42. Haviland, *A Woman's Life-Work*, 299; Thomas W. Knox, *Camp-Fire and Cotton-Field: Southern Adventure in Time of War* (Philadelphia: Jones Bros., 1865), 328; Dean, *Annie Harper's Journal*, 21; *Natchez Courier*, 20 October 1863. See also Joyce L. Broussard, "Occupied Natchez, Elite Women, and the Feminization of the Civil War," *Journal of Mississippi History* 70, no. 2 (Summer 2008): 179–207.

43. John R. Lynch, *Reminiscences of an Active Life: The Autobiography of John Roy Lynch*, ed. John Hope Franklin (Chicago: University of Chicago Press, 1970), 35–36; Knox, *Camp-Fire and Cotton-Field*, 436–37; Enclosure, Geo. W. Young to Gen. Lorenzo Thomas, 31 March 1864, entry 202A, in Ira Berlin et al., eds., *The Wartime Genesis of Free Labor: The Lower South*, vol. 3, ser. 1 of *Freedom: A Documentary History of Emancipation, 1861–1867* (Cambridge: Cambridge University Press, 1990), 814–17; testimony of Richard Dorsey, Amanda Jones, and Lewis Thompson, Amanda Jones claim, case 19,850, Adams County, Report 7, Office 439, microfiche 2,459, RG 233; testimony of David Combs, David Combs claim, case 20,299, Adams County, RG 217; testimony of Richard Dorsey, Richard Dorsey claim, case 4,337, Adams County, RG 217; testimony of James K. Hyman, James K. Hyman claim, case 14,773, Adams County, RG 123. Many of the claims from black people in the SCC files derive from draymen claiming wagons and mules lost to Confederate attacks while on cotton-hunting expeditions. Most of these claims were rejected because the draymen expected compensation from town merchants, thereby, according to the SCC, negating assertions that they were part of a legitimate military operation. For representative case files, see James K. Hyman claim, case 14,773, Adams County, RG 123; Richard Dorsey claim, case 4,337, Adams County, RG 217.

44. Quoted in Kaye, "Slaves, Emancipation, and the Powers of War," 70; testimony of Tolliver Taylor, William Hardin claim, case 19,537, Adams County, RG 217; Ira Berlin, Joseph P. Reidy, and Leslie S. Rowland, eds., *The Black Military Experience*, ser. 2 of *Freedom: A Documentary History of Emancipation, 1861–1867* (Cambridge: Cambridge University Press, 1982), 656. On the impact of black soldiers, see Berlin et al., *Slaves No More*, 187–233.

45. Ronald L. F. Davis, *The Black Experience in Natchez, 1720–1880* (Natchez National Historical Park, Miss.: Eastern National Park & Monument Association, 1994), 147–57; James E. Yeatman, *A Report on the Condition of the Freedmen of the Mississippi; Presented to the Western Sanitary Commission, December 17, 1863* (St. Louis, 1864), 14. By December 1863 Col. B. G. Farrar, stationed in Natchez, had raised two black regiments. On the strategic significance of black soldiers in the Deep South, see William C. Freehling, *South vs. South: How Anti-Confederate Southerners Shaped the Course of the Civil War* (New York: Oxford University Press, 2001), 85–114.

46. *Natchez Courier*, 25 September 1863; testimony of David Combs, David Combs claim, case 20,299, Adams County, RG 217; testimony of Jane Dent, Jane Dent claim, case 6,616, Adams County, RG 217; Haviland, *A Woman's Life-Work*, 500; testimony of

Richard Dorsey and James K. Hyman, Amanda Jones claim, case 19,850, Adams County, Report 7, Office 439, microfiche 2,459, RG 233; testimony of James Page, James Page claim, case 7,353, Claiborne County, RG 217; testimony of Richard Dorsey, Richard Dorsey claim, case 4,337, Adams County, RG 217; testimony of Washington Jefferson, Catherine Lucas claim, case 16,373, Adams County, RG 217; testimony of Richard Dorsey, Richard Dorsey claim, case 4,337, Adams County, RG 217; testimony of Richard Stamps, Richard Stamps claim, case 5,003, Claiborne County, RG 217. For more on the role of women in the Union military effort, see testimony of Jane Jones, Jane Jones claim, case 19,743, Adams County, Report 7, Office 442, microfiche 2,460, RG 233; testimony of Vinson Brady, Catherine Lucas claim, case 16,373, Adams County, RG 217; testimony of Henderson Moore, Henderson Moore claim, Claiborne County, RG 217; testimony of Richard Stamps, Richard Stamps claim, case 5,003, Claiborne County, RG 217; testimony of Mack Washington, Mack and Simon Washington claim, case 8,338, Wilkinson County, RG 123.

47. Knox, *Camp-Fire and Cotton-Field*, 436. On camp life in federally occupied Mississippi, see Noralee Frankel, *Freedom's Women: Black Women and Families in Civil War Era Mississippi* (Bloomington: Indiana University Press, 1999), 16–23, 32–45.

48. Haviland, *A Woman's Life-Work*, 285–86 (emphasis in original). For more on Fort Pillow and the response of black troops, see Richard L. Fuchs, *The Unerring Fire: The Massacre at Fort Pillow* (Rutherford, N.J.: Fairleigh Dickinson University Press, 1994); Andrew Ward, *River Run Red: The Fort Pillow Massacre in the American Civil War* (New York: Viking, 2005).

49. Testimony of Capt. J. H. Matthews, 10 March 1866, in U.S. Congress, *Report of the Joint Committee on Reconstruction*, 39th Cong., 1st sess., 1866, H. Rep. 30, pt. 3, p. 143 (cited hereafter as *Joint Committee on Reconstruction*); Haviland, *A Woman's Life-Work*, 304 (emphasis in original). The same story is described in A. O. Howell to [unknown recipient], 6 February 1864, American Missionary Association Papers, Mississippi, roll 1, Amistad Research Center, New Orleans, La. (cited hereafter as AMA; all AMA citations in this chapter refer to roll 1).

50. General Ransom estimated that "about 1 able-bodied man to 6 women and children" sought refuge in Natchez. *War of the Rebellion*, ser. 1, vol. 14, pt. 2, p. 681. See also Brig. Gen. Thomas E. G. Ransom to Lt. Col. W. T. Clark, 21 July 1863, #546, box 3, U.S. Army Collection, 1835–1869, LSU. For more on camp life, see Matilda Gresham, *Life of Walter Quintin Gresham, 1832–1895* (Chicago: Rand McNally, 1919), 1:256–57; Davis, *Black Experience in Natchez*, 158–59.

51. Yeatman, *Report on the Condition of the Freedmen*, 13–14; William Henry Elder, *Civil War Diary (1862–1865) of Bishop William Henry Elder, Bishop of Natchez*, ed. Most Reverend R. O. Gerow (Natchez, Miss.[?]: Most Reverend R. O. Gerow, n. d.), 59–60, 62–63; R. O. Gerow, *Cradle Days of St. Mary's at Natchez* (Natchez, Miss.: Hope Haven Press, 1941), 267–68; Dean, *Annie Harper's Journal*, 31; John Eaton, *Grant, Lincoln, and the Freedmen: Reminiscences of the Civil War* (1907; repr., New York: Negro Universities Press, 1969), 162; James Lucas interview, in Rawick, *American Slave*, vol. 7, *Oklahoma and Mississippi Narratives*, pt. 2, p. 96; Haviland, *A Woman's Life-Work*, 285. According to General Grant's orders, camps were to be established at all military posts, and responsibility for their upkeep fell to Union officers. See General Order No. 57, Head-Quarters, Dept. of the Tennessee, Vicksburg, Miss., 11 August 1863, published in the *Natchez Courier*, 18 September 1863. On improved conditions in the camps, see Chaplain Joseph Warren to Col. Samuel Thomas, 10 August 1864, Mississippi Freedmen's Department ("Pre-Bureau Records"), Letters Received, m1914, roll 5, BRFAL. On the indeterminate

status of "contrabands," see Kate Masur, "'A Rare Phenomenon of Philological Vegeta-tion': The Word 'Contraband' and the Meanings of Emancipation in the United States," *Journal of American History*, 93, no.4 (March 2007): 1050–84. For more on the health crisis in contraband camps, see Jim Downs, *Sick from Freedom: African-American Illness and Suffering during the Civil War and Reconstruction* (New York: Oxford University Press, 2012).

52. The order can be found in [An officer stationed in Natchez] to Rev. Geo Whipple, 1 April 1864, AMA (emphasis in original); and in Geo. W. Young to Gen. Lorenzo Thomas, 31 March 1864, entry 202A, in Berlin et al., *Wartime Genesis of Free Labor*, 814–17; General Order No. 57, Head-Quarters, Dept. of the Tennessee, Vicksburg, Miss., 11 August 1863, published in the *Natchez Courier*, 18 September 1863. General Order No. 2, issued February 16, 1864, by Gen. A. A. Ralston, forbade "all contraband negroes . . . from the renting of houses." See Edward McPherson, *The Political History of the United States of America during the Great Rebellion, 1860–1865* (Washington, D.C., 1865; repr., New York: Da Capo Press, 1972), 253. Figures on population during the war are difficult to come by, but a sanitary inspection a couple months after the surrender at Appomattox Court House gives some indication of the swelling of the city's population. It found that 11,255 persons lived in Natchez, including 5,026 blacks, 3,448 whites, and 2,671 soldiers. This was an increase of 41 percent over the 1860 population. Joseph C. G. Kennedy, *Popula-tion of the United States in 1860* (Washington, D.C., 1864), 271; *New York Daily Tribune*, 7 June 1865.

53. Haviland, *A Woman's Life-Work*, 349; S. G. Wright et al. to Gen. Tuttle, 1 April 1864, AMA; S. G. Wright to Rev. Geo. Whipple, 7 April 1864, #71635, AMA; [An officer stationed in Natchez] to Rev. Geo Whipple, 1 April 1864, AMA.

54. S. G. Wright to Rev. Geo. Whipple, 7 April 1864, #71,635, AMA (emphasis in origi-nal); [An officer stationed in Natchez] to Rev. Geo Whipple, 1 April 1864, AMA; Haviland, *A Woman's Life-Work*, 349; Mattie W. Childs to Rev. Whipple, April 1864, AMA; S. G. Wright to Rev. Geo. Whipple, 20 June 1864, AMA; S. G. Wright to Rev. Geo. Whipple, 7 April 1864, #71,630, AMA.

55. [An officer stationed in Natchez] to Rev. Geo. Whipple, 1 April 1864, AMA; S. G. Wright to Rev Geo Whipple, 7 April 1864, #71,630, AMA. See also S. G. Wright to Rev. Geo. Whipple, 7 April 1864, #71,635, AMA.

56. *New York Daily Tribune*, 30 April 1864. The letter was also published in an Iowa newspaper, entry 202B, in Berlin et al., *Wartime Genesis of Free Labor*, 817–19. Not all of the officers agreed with their commander. An assistant surgeon signed on to the mis-sionaries' protest letter, and the superintendent of freedmen appealed up the chain of command for instructions on how to alleviate the suffering induced by the order. See Geo. W. Young to Gen. Lorenzo Thomas, 31 March 1864, entry 202A, in Berlin et al., *Wartime Genesis of Free Labor*, 814–17.

57. S. G. Wright to Rev. Geo. Whipple, 7 April 1864, #71,635, AMA; McPherson, *Political History*, 253; *New York Times*, 17 May 1864; entry 202B, in Berlin et al., *Wartime Genesis of Free Labor*, 817–19; S. G. Wright to Rev. Geo. Whipple, 23 May 1864, AMA. General Tuttle assumed command in Natchez only on March 12. See *New York Times*, 20 March 1864.

58. *Christian Recorder*, 23 July 1864; Special Order No. 31, Col. B. G. Farrar, 18 June 1864, in McPherson, *Political History*, 538; Special Order No. 11, Gen. Mason Brayman, 22 July 1864, in McPherson, *Political History*, 541. Bishop William Henry Elder protested the order but his banishment was short-lived. He was allowed to return to his post less than a month later. For more on the controversy, see Elder, *Civil War Diary*, 76–103.

59. Wilmer Shields to Doctor Mercer, 11 December 1863, and Wilmer Shields to Doctor Mercer, 25 January 1864, folder 8, Wilmer Shields Letters, William Newton Mercer Papers, LSU; Irene Smith to Hon. W. P. Fessenden, 27 October 1864, entry 215, in Berlin et al., *Wartime Genesis of Free Labor*, 853–56; William Tecumseh Sherman, *Memoirs of General W. T. Sherman* (New York: Library of America, 1990), 345–46; testimony of Giles Brooks and testimony of Gabriel Powers, Katherine S. Minor claim, case 7,960, Adams County, RG 217. On Kate Minor and the issue of Union loyalty, see Rebecca M. Dresser, "Kate and John Minor: Confederate Unionists of Natchez," *Journal of Mississippi History* 64 (Fall 2002): 189–216.

60. Gabe Emanuel, interview by Esther de Sola, in Rawick, *American Slave*, supplement 1, vol. 7, *Mississippi Narratives*, pt. 2, pp. 685–86; Amelia Montgomery to Joseph Montgomery, 5 September 1865, Correspondence, Joseph Addison and Family Montgomery Papers, LSU.

61. Michael Wayne, *The Reshaping of Plantation Society: The Natchez District, 1860–1880* (Baton Rouge: Louisiana State University Press, 1983), 7; Ronald L. F. Davis, *Good and Faithful Labor: From Slavery to Sharecropping in the Natchez District, 1860–1890* (Westport, Conn.: Greenwood Press, 1982), 59–73.

62. Brig. Gen. Jas. S. Wadsworth to the Adjutant General, U.S. Army, 16 December 1863, entry 185, in Berlin et al., *Wartime Genesis of Free Labor*, 757–62; W. Burnet to Hon. William P. Mellen, 12 March 1864, entry 199, in ibid., 808–10; James E. Yeatman, *Report to the Western Sanitary Commission in Regard to Leasing Abandoned Plantations, with Rules and Regulations Governing the Same* (St. Louis: Western Sanitary Commission Rooms, 1864), 8.

63. *New York Daily Tribune*, 11 January 1864; *New Orleans Times*, 24 January 1865; Wilmer Shields to Doctor Mercer, 11 December 1863, Mercer Papers, LSU; Col. B. G. Farrar to Capt. T. S. Prescott, 11 December 1864, Benjamin Farrar Papers, LSU; Gresham, *Life of Walter Quintin Gresham*, 1:280.

64. Knox, *Camp-Fire and Cotton-Field*, 424; Col. Saml. Thomas to Brig. Gen. L. Thomas, 15 June 1864, entry 209, in Berlin et al., *Wartime Genesis of Free Labor*, 834–41.

65. Col. Saml. Thomas to Brig. Gen. L. Thomas, 15 June 1864, entry 209, in Berlin et al., *Wartime Genesis of Free Labor*, 834–41; Knox, *Camp-Fire and Cotton-Field*, 448. In a two-week span, military authorities granted hundreds of freedpeople passes to travel beyond the Union lines in Natchez. See Guards and Pickets Passes for Colored Persons, Natchez, Mississippi, 15–31 July 1864, Natchez Trace Slaves and Slavery Collection, Natchez Trace Collection, Center for American History, University of Texas at Austin.

66. Susan Sillers Darden Diary, vol. 2, 4 December 1865, Darden Family Papers, MDAH; Circular issued by Geo. D. Reynolds, Major and Acting Asst. Commissioner, Bureau of Refugees, Freedmen, and Abandoned Lands, Southern Dist. of Miss., in *Natchez Democrat*, 25 November 1865. For more on this insurrectionary scare, see Dan T. Carter, "Anatomy of Fear: The Christmas Day Insurrectionary Scare of 1865," *Journal of Southern History* 42 (August 1976): 345–64; Hahn, "Extravagant Expectations"; Hahn, *A Nation under Our Feet*, 146–59. The sense of just deliverance from a distant yet powerful ruler corresponds with what some scholars refer to as "naïve monarchism." See Field, *Rebels in the Name of the Tsar*, 1–29.

67. *Port Gibson Weekly Standard*, 2 December 1865; J. P. Bardwell to Rev. M. E. Strieby, 20 November 1865, AMA; Wilmer Shields to Doctor Mercer, 19 December 1865, Mercer Papers, LSU; Lt. O. B. Foster to Maj. T. S. Free, 12 December 1865, Mississippi Assistant

Commissioner, m826, Letters Received, roll 30, BRFAL; *Natchez Democrat,* 25 November 1865.

68. *Port Gibson Weekly Standard,* 18 November, 25 November 1865; William T. Martin to Gov. Humphreys, 27 October 1865, in Steven Hahn et al., eds., *Land and Labor, 1865,* ser. 3, vol. 1 of *Freedom: A Documentary History of Emancipation, 1861–1867* (Chapel Hill: University of North Carolina Press, 2008), 823–24; letter from Natchez, *Sterling (Ill.) Gazette,* 16 December 1865; W. T. Martin to Gov. Humphreys, 5 December 1865, Governor Humphreys Papers, Series 779: Correspondence and Papers, MDAH; *Natchez Democrat,* 25 December 1865; testimony of William T. Martin, Katherine S. Minor claim, case 7,960, Adams County, RG 217; W. T. Martin to Maj. Geo. D. Reynolds, 18 November 1865, Governor Humphreys Papers, MDAH; Martin to Humphreys, 27 October 1865, in Hahn et al., *Land and Labor,* 823–24.

69. *Christian Recorder,* 2 December 1865; testimony of W. A. P. Dillingham, *Joint Committee on Reconstruction,* 118.

70. *Natchez Democrat,* 20 November 1865; Petition of We the Colorde peple [to Benjamin G. Humphreys, governor of Mississippi], 3 December 1865, filed as F-41 1865, Registered Letters Received, ser. 2052, MS Asst. Comr., roll 9, BRFAL; testimony of W. A. P. Dillingham, *Joint Committee on Reconstruction,* 118; *Natchez Courier,* 5 October 1865. Another transcription of the petition uses a different sentence break and a different placement of the word "now." The key sentence reads, "we hav [no] [s]uch thought" followed by "now we are free what [would?] we rise for." Hahn et al., *Land and Labor,* 856–58.

71. On Lincoln and the millennial aspects of land redistribution, see Hahn, *A Nation under Our Feet,* 133–37.

72. On freedpeople's complaints to Freedmen's Bureau officers, see Capt. Adam Kemper, Monthly report, 1 January 1866, Miss. Asst. Comr., Letters Received, roll 14, BRFAL.

73. Drew Gilpin Faust, *This Republic of Suffering: Death and the American Civil War* (New York: Alfred A. Knopf, 2008), 226.

Chapter Two. Emancipated Communities

1. For all their problems, the Black Codes did, as Christopher Waldrep has contended, open up the county courts to black people. See Christopher Waldrep, *Roots of Disorder: Race and Criminal Justice in the American South, 1817–80* (Urbana: University of Illinois Press, 1998), 105–19. For more on Presidential Reconstruction and the formation of southern state governments, see Eric Foner, *Reconstruction: America's Unfinished Revolution, 1863–1877* (New York: Harper & Row, 1988), 176–216.

2. U.S. Senate, *Reports of Assistant Commissioners of Freedmen, and Synopsis of Laws on Persons of Color in Late Slave States,* 39th Cong., 2d sess., 1867, S. Exec. Doc. 6, pp. 190–97.

3. Ibid.; William C. Harris, *Presidential Reconstruction in Mississippi* (Baton Rouge: Louisiana State University Press, 1967), 130–39.

4. U.S. Senate, *Reports of Assistant Commissioners,* 181–87; Joe Gray Taylor, *Louisiana Reconstructed, 1863–1877* (Baton Rouge: Louisiana State University Press, 1974), 101.

5. *Christian Recorder,* 23 December 1865; M. Howard to O. O. Howard, 7 April 1866, Commissioner, Letters Received, m752, roll 27, Records of the Bureau of Refugees, Freedmen, and Abandoned Lands, Record Group 105, National Archives, Washington, D.C.

(cited hereafter as BRFAL). On federal efforts to nullify the Black Codes, see "An Act to protect all Persons in the United States in their Civil Rights, and furnish the Means of their Vindication, April 9, 1866," in *The Statutes at Large, Treaties, and Proclamations of the United States of America*, ed. George P. Sanger, (Boston: Little, Brown, 1868), 14:27–30; Harris, *Presidential Reconstruction in Mississippi*, 129, 147; Donald G. Nieman, *To Set the Law in Motion: The Freedmen's Bureau and the Legal Rights of Blacks, 1865–1868* (Millwood, N.Y.: KTO Press, 1979), 77–83.

6. Petition of "We the Colorde peple" to Benjamin G. Humphreys, governor of Mississippi, 3 December 1865, Mississippi Assistant Commissioner, m826, Letters Received, roll 9, BRFAL.

7. Ibid.

8. For more on legal personhood, see Barbara Young Welke, *Law and the Borders of Belonging in the Long Nineteenth-Century United States* (New York: Cambridge University Press, 2010). The scholarship on freedpeople's struggles to define their freedom and to shape communities after emancipation is extensive. Some notable recent works include Steven Hahn, *A Nation under Our Feet: Black Political Struggles in the Rural South from Slavery to the Great Migration* (Cambridge, Mass.: Belknap Press of Harvard University Press, 2003); Dylan C. Penningroth, *The Claims of Kinfolk: African American Property and Community in the Nineteenth-Century South* (Chapel Hill: University of North Carolina Press, 2003); Susan E. O'Donovan, *Becoming Free in the Cotton South* (Cambridge, Mass.: Harvard University Press, 2007); Kate Masur, *An Example for All the Land: Emancipation and the Struggle over Equality in Washington, D.C.* (Chapel Hill: University of North Carolina Press, 2010); John Ernest, *A Nation within a Nation: Organizing African-American Communities Before the Civil War* (Chicago: Ivan R. Dee, 2011); Stephen Kantrowitz, *More than Freedom: Fighting for Black Citizenship in a White Republic, 1829–1889* (New York: Penguin Press, 2012).

9. On "hush harbors" and the private practice of religion, see Albert J. Raboteau, *Slave Religion: The "Invisible Institution" in the Antebellum South* (New York: Oxford University Press, 1978), 212–19. William E. Montgomery describes two churches emerging from emancipation: a formally organized, denominational church attended by free blacks in urban areas and an "invisible" church composed of slave congregations practicing folk religion. See William E. Montgomery, *Under Their Own Vine and Fig Tree: The African-American Church in the South, 1865–1900* (Baton Rouge: Louisiana State University Press, 1993), 36–37.

10. Leon F. Litwack, *Been in the Storm So Long: The Aftermath of Slavery* (New York: Vintage, 1979), 450–71; Montgomery, *Under Their Own Vine*, 254–55; Hahn, *A Nation under Our Feet*, 230–34.

11. On the theological reasons for the racial split in southern churches, see Katharine L. Dvorak, *An African-American Exodus: The Segregation of the Southern Churches* (Brooklyn: Carlson Publishing, 1991), 69–119. Reginald F. Hildebrand discusses the secular and external reasons for the split in *The Times Were Strange and Stirring: Methodist Preachers and the Crisis of Emancipation* (Durham, N.C.: Duke University Press, 1995), 50–72. On the prominence of the Baptist and African Methodist denominations among southern blacks, see Montgomery, *Under Their Own Vine*, 104–5, 107–25.

12. J. H. Bolden (Elder) and four others to Gen. O. O. Howard, 1 July 1865, Miss. Asst. Comr., Letters Received, roll 8, BRFAL. On black Baptists in Natchez, see Randy J. Sparks, *Religion in Mississippi* (Jackson: University Press of Mississippi for the Mississippi Historical Society, 2001), 95; Raboteau, *Slave Religion*, 200; Patrick H. Thompson, *The History of*

Negro Baptists in Mississippi (Jackson, Miss.: R. W. Bailey, 1898), 27–28. Thompson only mentions that the church was deeded to "a free Negro by the name of Marshall." In the 1840, 1850, and 1860 censuses, there was only one free black man with the name of Marshall. He was Harry Marshall, a fifty-six-year-old drayman in 1860, who emancipated his wife and children in the 1830s. This was also the same Harry Marshall who willed his house and lot on Pearl Street to his "good friend and kinswoman Luia Lynch," who was the mother of William H. and John R. Lynch, two of the most influential black politicians in the Natchez District. For more on Marshall, see Harry (Henry) L. Marshall, 23 January 1866, Adams County Wills, book 3, p. 269, Adams County Courthouse(ACCH), Natchez, Miss.; U.S. Bureau of Census, *Eighth Census of the United States: Population, 1860*; U.S. Bureau of Census, *Ninth Census of the United States: Population, 1870*; U.S. Bureau of Census, *Tenth Census of the United States: Population, 1880*.

13. J. H. Bolden (Elder) and four others to Gen. O. O. Howard, 1 July 1865, Miss. Asst. Comr., Letters Received, roll 8, BRFAL; Edward Claton and three others, Deacons from the Wall St. Baptist Church, to A. Johnson, President of the U.S., 3 July 1865, Commissioner, Letters Received, m752, roll 13, BRFAL; Laura S. Haviland, *A Woman's Life-Work: Labors and Experiences of Laura S. Haviland* (Author, 1881; repr., Salem, N.H.: Ayer, 1984), 349–50; Monthly School Report, May 1864, #71,652, American Missionary Association Papers, Mississippi, roll 1, Amistad Research Center, New Orleans, La. (cited hereafter as AMA); S. G. Wright to Geo. Whipple, 9 March 1864, #71,610, AMA, Mississippi, roll 1; S. G. Wright to [unknown recipient], [not dated], #73,249, AMA, Mississippi, roll 3; J. P. Bardwell to Rev. M. E. Strieby, 5 January 1865, #71,719, AMA, Mississippi, roll 1; [unknown author] to Geo. Whipple, 15 June 1864, #71,666, AMA, Mississippi, roll 1; testimony of Randall Pollard, John Smith claim, Case 10,801, Adams County, Mississippi, case files, Settled Case Files for Claims Approved by the Southern Claims Commission, Ser. 732, Southern Claims Commission, Records of the Office of the Third Auditor, Records of the Accounting Officers of the Department of Treasury, Record Group 217, National Archives, Washington, D.C.

14. Thompson, *History of Negro Baptists in Mississippi*, 28, 560. Holley was free in 1860, working as a barber. In 1870 he had fifty dollars' worth of personal property and lived with his wife, Mary, and their newborn infant girl, Mary. U.S. Bureau of Census, *Eighth Census: Population, 1860*; U.S. Bureau of Census, *Ninth Census: Population, 1870*; U.S. Bureau of Census, *Tenth Census: Population, 1880*.

15. Claton and three others to Johnson, 3 July 1865, Comr., Letters Received, roll 13, BRFAL; J. H. Bolden (Elder) and four others to O. O. Howard, 1 July 1865, Miss. Asst. Comr., roll 8, BRFAL; Edward Clayton (Cold) and three other Deacons to Hon. Chief Justice S. P. Chase, 6 July 1865, Miss. Asst. Comr., roll 8, BRFAL. The deacons were Daniel Holley, Edward Claton, Toney Jones, and Henry Johnson. Rev. Boulden's name is listed in register 1 (Comr., Letters Received, roll 1, BRFAL) but not in the letter to which the register refers. Boulden's name does not appear in the letter to Chase either. However, the five men also wrote to Maj. George D. Reynolds, the Freedmen's Bureau agent in charge of the Natchez District. See J. H. Boulden and four others to Maj. G. D. Reynolds, 26 July 1865, Miss. Asst. Comr., roll 8, BRFAL. I was unable to find biographical information on Edward Claton. Daniel Holley was briefly described in note 14 above. Toney Jones may have been the seventy-five-year-old laborer in the 1870 census listed as "Anthony Jones." Henry Johnson was probably the fifty-year-old mulatto woodcutter listed in the 1870 census; however, there were three other black or mulatto laborers listed as Henry Johnson living in Adams County. U.S. Bureau of Census, *Ninth Census: Population, 1870*.

In the Natchez District and other regions under federal occupation, the military appropriated plantation lands for its own use from deserted Confederate property, but by the time the church leaders made their petition, President Johnson had restored all property rights to former Confederates who pledged their loyalty to the Union. See Foner, *Reconstruction*, 183.

16. Endorsement: Howard to Col. Samuel Thomas, 12 August 1865, in Bolden et al. to Howard, 1 July 1865, Miss. Asst. Comr., roll 8, BRFAL; *Natchez Democrat*, 20 August 1866. For a late and unsuccessful plea for "permanent possession of the property," see J. F. Boulden, Elder, to Gen. O. O. Howard, 6 February 1866, Miss. Asst. Comr., roll 13, BRFAL. By contrast, the black members of the Second Presbyterian Church in Natchez had their petition for retention of church property rejected immediately by the bureau. L. Waterson to Maj. Geo. D. Reynolds, 16 February 1866, Miss. Asst. Comr., roll 15, BRFAL.

17. Thompson, *History of Negro Baptists in Mississippi*, 28–29.

18. Ibid., 41–44, 51, 607–8; Eric Foner, ed., *Freedom's Lawmakers: A Directory of Black Officeholders during Reconstruction*, rev. ed. (Baton Rouge: Louisiana State University Press, 1996), 116; U.S. Bureau of Census, *Eighth Census: Population, 1860*; Justin Behrend, Black Politicians Database, SUNY-Geneseo, http://go.geneseo.edu/BlackPoliticiansDB (BPDB). Jacobs testified that he came to Natchez in October 1866, in testimony taken during a Freedmen's Bureau investigation. Testimony of H. P. Jacobs, in "Copy of statement charging *1st Lieut. D. M. White, U. R. C.*, with drunkenness, profanity and want of sympathy with the colored people, and *Capt. E. E. Platt, URC.*, with want of sympathy with colored people, sympathy with secessionists, and with making charges in the collections of claims for negroes," 6 May 1867, Comr., Letters Received, roll 47, BRFAL.

19. Constitution and By-Laws of the Jacobs Benevolence Association, in Jacobs Benevolent Society vs. Henry P. Jacobs, Deed of Indenture, 5 September 1874, Chancery files, #543, ACCH. For more on black benevolent societies, see Peter J. Rachleff, *Black Labor in Richmond, 1865–1890* (1984; repr., Urbana: University of Illinois Press, 1989), 25–32; Kathleen C. Berkeley, "'Colored Ladies Also Contributed': Black Women's Activities from Benevolence to Social Welfare, 1866–1896," in *Black Women in United States History: From Colonial Times through the Nineteenth Century*, ed. Darlene Clark Hine (Brooklyn, N.Y.: Carlson Publishing, 1990), 1:61–83; Elsa Barkley Brown, "Uncle Ned's Children: Negotiating Community and Freedom in Postemancipation Richmond, Virginia" (Ph.D. diss., Kent State University, 1994), 499–519.

20. *Natchez Democrat*, 8 July 1867; *Natchez Tri-Weekly Courier*, 19 May 1869.

21. *Natchez Democrat*, 8 June, 24 June, 8 July 1867; *Natchez Tri-Weekly Courier*, 19 May 1869; *Natchez Democrat*, 9 March, 12 March 1869. The board members were Hiram Littleton and Jackson Minor. Littleton was a plasterer who was also a member of the Robert H. Wood Republican Club and a vice president in the Mississippi Good Will Fire Company No. 2. Minor was a silversmith and a jewelry store owner. For more on Lynch, see John Roy Lynch, *Reminiscences of an Active Life: The Autobiography of John Roy Lynch*, ed. John Hope Franklin (Chicago: University of Chicago Press, 1970).

22. Adams County, Folder: Negro, box 10634, Mississippi Historical Records Survey, Series 447, Works Progress Administration (WPA) Records, Mississippi Department of Archives and History (MDAH), Jackson; *Christian Recorder*, 10 February 1866. For more on the Fitzhugh family, see Rev. Revels A. Adams, *Cyclopedia of African Methodism in Mississippi* (Natchez, Miss.: printed by author, 1902), 146–54; *Christian Recorder*, 23 December 1865; U.S. Bureau of Census, *Ninth Census: Population, 1870*. The AME congrega-

tion purchased the Methodist Episcopal Church property on Union Street for $9,000, with a $3,000 down payment. *Christian Recorder*, 2 June 1866. For more on Fitzhugh and other women like her, see Nik Ribianszky, "'She Appeared to be Mistress of Her Own Actions, Free From the Control of Anyone': Property-Holding Free Women of Color in Natchez, Mississippi, 1779–1865," *Journal of Mississippi History* 67, no. 3 (2005): 217–45.

23. Members of the Daughters of Zion leadership board included Agnes Fitzhugh (president), Mrs. J. Minor (vice president), Mrs. K. Burns (secretary), Miss Harmn (assistant secretary), Hannah Thompson (treasurer), Mrs. K. Pollard (grand marshal), and Mrs. E. Kankins (mother of society). Fitzhugh's, Minor's and Burns's husbands were incorporators of the AME Church in Natchez. *Christian Recorder*, 10 February 1866; Charter of Incorporation of the African Methodist Episcopal Church of Natchez, 8 January 1866, Governor Humphreys Papers, Series 779: Correspondence and Papers, MDAH.

24. *Christian Recorder*, 4 June 1864. On Reverend Tyler, see Clarence E. Walker, *A Rock in a Weary Land: The African Methodist Episcopal Church during the Civil War and Reconstruction* (Baton Rouge: Louisiana State University Press, 1982), 50. On McCary's public reputation, see *Natchez Daily Courier*, 7 November 1861. For more on Methodist churches, see Hildebrand, *The Times Were Strange and Stirring*, 4. Like the Methodists, the Presbyterian Church in antebellum Natchez restricted enslaved members to large galleries within its church building. D. Clayton James, *Antebellum Natchez* (Baton Rouge: Louisiana State University Press, 1968), 251.

25. J. P. Bardwell to Rev. M. E. Strieby, 7 January 1865, #71,722, AMA, Mississippi, roll 1; S. G. Wright to Whipple, 9 March 1864, #71,610, AMA, Mississippi, roll 1; *Christian Recorder*, 6 April 1867. AMA documents spelled Reedy's name as "Ready."

26. Adams, *Cyclopedia of African Methodism*, 77–79; *Christian Recorder*, 25 May 1867.

27. *Christian Recorder*, 25 May 1867. Dr. J. W. C. Pennington led the Zion Chapel in 1865 and in the first months of 1866. He was replaced by Rev. Charles Burch, who later went on to establish a church at Clift Mission. Rev. M. M. Clark followed Burch, and Rev. Hiram Revels followed Clark in late 1868. *Christian Recorder*, 30 December 1865, 30 June 1866, 6 April, 25 May 1867, 7 November 1868.

28. *Christian Recorder*, 30 August 1865, 2 June 1866; *Natchez Democrat*, 2 July 1866, 6 April 1868; First Presbyterian Church to African Methodist Episcopal Church, 14 July 1868, Title Bond, book HH, p. 146, Adams County Land Deeds, ACCH; Charles A.Wickoff to Rev. M. M. Clark and the Board of Trustees Methodist Church (Cold.), 8 September 1868, Miss. Asst. Comr., roll 26, BRFAL; L. Waterson to Geo. D. Reynolds, 16 February 1866, Miss. Asst. Comr., roll 15, BRFAL. The congregation made the final payment on the church building in 1874. See *Natchez Weekly Democrat*, 8 July 1874.

29. Charter of Incorporation of the African Methodist Episcopal Church of Natchez, 8 January 1866, Governor Humphreys Papers, MDAH; *Christian Recorder*, 3 November 1866; U.S. Bureau of Census, *Ninth Census: Population, 1870*; Natchez Good Samaritans, Incorporation Charter, book WW, p. 7, Adams County Land Deeds, ACCH; *Natchez Democrat*, 3 May 1876; Adams County, Folder: Negro, box 10634, WPA Records, MDAH; *Christian Recorder*, 6 April 1867. For more on Stringer, see George A. Sewell and Margaret L. Dwight, *Mississippi Black History Makers* (Jackson: University Press of Mississippi, 1984), 49–51; Foner, *Freedom's Lawmakers*, 206. The original AME trustees were Robert Leeper, Randolph Burns, Nelson Fitzhugh, John Allen, Charles Harris, Hiram Littleton, and Jackson Minor. Fitzhugh had considerable wealth for a "grocer": $3,000 in real estate and $9,000 in personal property. Harris, a drayman, claimed $2,000 in personal

property. Occupational and financial information on these men comes from a variety of sources, including SCC files, the 1860 and 1870 U.S. Census, the *Christian Recorder*, the *Natchez Democrat*, Freedmen's Bureau Bank records, and Adams, *Cyclopedia of African Methodism*.

30. *Natchez Weekly Courier*, 25 June 1866.

31. General aspects of the newspaper are described in Gilbert Anthony Williams, *The "Christian Recorder," Newspaper of the African Methodist Episcopal Church: History of a Forum for Ideas, 1854–1902* (Jefferson, N.C.: McFarland, 1996).

32. *Christian Recorder*, 23 July 1864, 16 December 1865. For more on the varied subjects from the correspondents, see the twenty letters from Natchez published in the *Christian Recorder* between June 1863 and March 1870: 4 June, 23 July 1864, 14 January, 1 July, 29 July, 9 September, 2 December, 16 December, 23 December, 30 December 1865, 6 January, 10 February, 5 May, 2 June, 22 September, 20 October, 3 November 1866, 20 April, 25 May 1867, 11 September 1869.

33. *Natchez Courier*, 7 November 1861; *Natchez Union Courier*, 21 August 1863; *Christian Recorder*, 30 December 1865; BPDB. Catherine McCary's politically active brothers were Charles W., Edward H., John, Louis Winston, Robert W., and Samuel W. For more on the Fitzhugh family, see Nelson Fitzhugh, 4 April 1868, Adams County Wills, book 3, p. 337, ACCH.

34. *Christian Recorder*, 27 January 1866. For more on the *Christian Recorder*, see Montgomery, *Under Their Own Vine*, 136. The *New National Era*, published by Lewis. H. Douglass (Frederick Douglass's son) out of Washington, D.C., between 1870 and 1874, also served as a public forum, particularly for black Republicans across the country. For more on public spheres, see Michael C. Dawson, "A Black Counterpublic?: Economic Earthquakes, Racial Agenda(s), and Black Politics," *Public Culture* 7, no. 1 (Fall 1994): 195–223; Michael C. Dawson, *Black Visions: The Roots of Contemporary African-American Political Ideologies* (Chicago: University of Chicago Press, 2001), 29–33, 53–54; Mary P. Ryan, "Gender and Public Access: Women's Politics in Nineteenth-Century America," in *Habermas and the Public Sphere*, ed. Craig Calhoun (Cambridge, Mass.: MIT Press, 1992), 259–88; Nancy Fraser, "Rethinking the Public Sphere: A Contribution to the Critique of Actually Existing Democracy," in Calhoun, *Habermas and the Public Sphere*, 109–42; Geoff Ely, "Nations, Publics, and Political Cultures: Placing Habermas in the Nineteenth Century," in ibid., 289–339. And, of course, general discussions on the public sphere should begin with Jürgen Habermas, *The Structural Transformation of the Public Sphere: An Inquiry into a Category of Bourgeois Society*, trans. Thomas Burger with the assistance of Frederick Lawrence (Cambridge, Mass.: MIT Press, 1989).

35. *Christian Recorder*, 1 July 1865. A reprint of the article was published in the 14 July 1865 edition of the *New Orleans Tribune*. For more on Murray, see *Christian Recorder*, 29 July 1865; "Obituary Notes: Philip Houston Murray," *Editor and Publisher*, 17, February 1917, 34; Harry Bradshaw Matthews, *African American Journey to Freedom in New York and Related Sites, 1823–1870: Freedom Knows No Color* (Cherry Hill, N.J.: Africana Homestead Legacy Publishers, 2008), 215.

36. *Christian Recorder*, 1 July 1865 (emphasis in original). On the broad support for the Lincoln Monument Fund among black soldiers and freedmen in Natchez, see *New Orleans Tribune*, 11 August 1865.

37. *Christian Recorder*, 1 July 1865 (emphasis in original); Hildebrand, *The Times Were Strange and Stirring*, 69.

38. *Christian Recorder*, 1 July 1865 (emphasis in original); *New York Daily Tribune*, 26 December 1865; *Natchez Democrat*, 8 April 1867. The trustees were Nathan Butler, Abram H. Dixon, Hiram Littleton, and Washington Miller; the ministers, Hugh M. Foley, Adam Jackson, Matthew T. Newsome, and Hiram Revels.

39. *Christian Recorder*, 30 December 1865. On denominational disputes between the AME Church and its rivals (the AME Zion Church, the ME Church, South, the ME Church, North, and the Colored Methodist Church), see Walker, *A Rock in a Weary Land*, 82–107.

40. *Christian Recorder*, 6 January, 20 October 1866.

41. Thompson, *History of Negro Baptists in Mississippi*, 44.

42. Hahn, *A Nation under Our Feet*, 233.

43. *Christian Recorder*, 6 April 1867; Adams, *Cyclopedia of African Methodism*, 19–20; Joe Louis Caldwell, "A Social, Economic, and Political Study of Blacks in the Louisiana Delta, 1865–1880" (Ph.D. diss., Tulane University, 1988), 149–52, 158–60.

44. Lt. J. C. De Gress to Capt. W. H. Sterling, 24 June 1867, Comr., roll 47, BRFAL; *Christian Recorder*, 6 April 1867. See also Michael Wayne, *The Reshaping of Plantation Society: The Natchez District, 1860–1880* (Baton Rouge: Louisiana State University Press, 1983), 138.

45. Edward Henderson to L. O. Parker, 10 September 1867, and Edward Henderson to L. O. Parker, 20 September 1867, Records of the Assistant Commissioner for the State of Louisiana, m1027, Registered Letters and Telegrams Received, roll 16, BRFAL; Whitelaw Reid, *After the War: A Tour of the Southern States, 1865–1866* (1866; repr., New York: Harper & Row, 1965), 519–20. Reid also describes a picture of "Joe Johnson" hanging next to Grant's picture. Joe Johnston (sometimes spelled without the *t*) was a Confederate general mostly known for his retreat before Sherman's army in Georgia. It is possible that the black church members confused Johnston with a Union general, but the placement of Lincoln and Grant's images suggests a basic awareness of national Union figures. Perhaps the Johnson portrait reflected the wishes of the plantation owner, who wanted to remind his black workers that though it might be their church, he still owned the building and the land. Yet if a planter wanted to make a political statement with a Confederate icon, there were many more famous and suitable images than Johnston (e.g., Jefferson Davis, Robert E. Lee, Stonewall Jackson) Another explanation for the portrait is that it might have been not a picture of the Confederate general but a picture of a black merchant sailor named Joe Johnson from early nineteenth century London. See W. Jeffrey Bolster, *Black Jacks: African American Seamen in the Age of Sail* (Cambridge, Mass.: Harvard University Press, 1997), 66–67. For this to be plausible, however, we would have to assume that Reid's audience would think of this Johnson, which seems unlikely given that Joe Johnson the sailor was a rather obscure figure. In the end, I cannot explain the presence of the Johnson image in the black church. For another example of tacked-up pictures of Union officers, see Hannah Rosen, *Terror in the Heart of Freedom: Citizenship, Sexual Violence and the Meaning of Race in the Postemancipation South* (Chapel Hill: University of North Carolina Press, 2009), 69.

46. For a narrower view on the importance of education to freedpeople, see Litwack, *Been in the Storm So Long*, 472–501. For more on the establishment of schools after emancipation, see Robert C. Morris, *Reading, 'Riting, and Reconstruction: The Education of Freedmen in the South, 1861–1870* (Chicago: University of Chicago Press, 1976); Ronald E. Butchart, *Northern Schools, Southern Blacks, and Reconstruction: Freedmen's*

Education, 1862–1875 (Westport, Conn.: Greenwood Press, 1980); Jacqueline Jones, *Soldiers of Light and Love: Northern Teachers and Georgia Blacks, 1865–1873* (Chapel Hill: University of North Carolina Press, 1980); James D. Anderson, *The Education of Blacks in the South, 1860–1935* (Chapel Hill: University of North Carolina Press, 1988); Randy J. Sparks, "'The White People's Arms Are Longer Than Ours': Blacks, Education, and the American Missionary Association in Reconstruction Mississippi," *Journal of Mississippi History* 54, no. 1 (1992): 1–27; Heather Andrea Williams, *Self-Taught: African American Education in Slavery and Freedom* (Chapel Hill: University of North Carolina, 2005); Hilary J. Moss, *Schooling Citizens: The Struggle for African American Education in Antebellum America* (Chicago: University of Chicago Press, 2009); Ronald E. Butchart, *Schooling the Freed People: Teaching, Learning, and the Struggle for Black Freedom, 1861–1876* (Chapel Hill: University of North Carolina Press, 2010).

47. Wm. Thirds to [George] Whipple, 19 November 1863, #71,570, AMA, Mississippi, roll 1; Rev. P. Mixer to S. S. Jocelyn and G. Whipple, 19 January, 1864, #71,579, AMA, Mississippi, roll 1; James E. Yeatman, *A Report on the Condition of the Freedmen of the Mississippi; presented to the Western Sanitary Commission, December 17, 1863* (St. Louis, 1864), 14; *Natchez Weekly Courier*, 10 November 1866, supplement to the 12 November edition; John R. Lynch, "Some Historical Errors of James Ford Rhodes," *Journal of Negro History*, 2, no. 4 (October 1917): 356; J. P. Bardwell to Rev. M. E. Strieby, 5 January 1865, #71,719, AMA, Mississippi, roll 1. Yeatman refers to a "colored girl" named McHughes whose father "was clerk in one of the departments." More than likely, Yeatman was referring to McCary, especially since the description of the "colored girl's" father matches Nelson Fitzhugh, Catherine McCary's father. From the *Courier*, we know that McCary had been teaching since she was fourteen years old. As for Lily Ann Granderson, other sources identify her as Milla Granson, Lila Grandison, and Lillian Granderson, but I think "Lily Ann Granderson" is the most accurate, as it was the name listed on her personal Freedmen's Bank account. See Lily Ann Granderson, account #269,082, Natchez branch, Freedmen's Savings and Trust Company, in *Freedman's Bank Records*, Progeny Software, 1998–2000. On slaves' education, see Williams, *Self-Taught*, 7–29.

48. Haviland, *A Woman's Life-Work*, 300.

49. J. P. Bardwell to Rev. M. E. Strieby, 5 January 1865, #71,719 AMA, Mississippi, roll 1; Haviland, *A Woman's Life-Work*, 300.

50. Haviland, *A Woman's Life-Work*, 300; Bardwell to Strieby, 5 January 1865, #71,719, AMA, Mississippi, roll 1; Jacobs Benevolent Society vs. Henry P. Jacobs, Deed of Indenture, 5 September 1874, Chancery files, #543, ACCH; *Natchez Democrat*, 27 November 1872; U.S. House, *Testimony in the Contested Election Case of John R. Lynch vs. James R. Chalmers, From the Sixth Congressional District of Mississippi*, 47th Cong., 1st sess., 1881, H. Misc. Doc. 12, pt. 3, *Documents*, p. 4; Thompson, *History of Negro Baptists in Mississippi*, 29. Granderson claimed that there was no law prohibiting slaves from teaching other slaves, but the Mississippi Code of 1823 clearly forbade all people of color, slave or free, from teaching slaves "reading or writing, either in the day or night." It is unclear why she was not prosecuted. On legislation related to slave literacy and education, see Williams, *Self-Taught*, 205. The central role of black teachers in black education in the first generation after emancipation is given full expression in Butchart, *Schooling the Freed People*, 17–51.

51. A. O. Howell to [unknown recipient], 6 February 1864, #71,594, AMA, Mississippi, roll 1; P. Mixer to Rev. G. Whipple, 24 June 1864, #71,660, AMA, Mississippi, roll 1; Havi-

land, *A Woman's Life-Work*, 300; Rev. Phineas Mixer to [S. S.] Jocelyn, 25 March 1864, #71,619, AMA, Mississippi, roll 1. In May 1864 two other schools were taught by black teachers, in addition to the nine missionary-run schools.

52. Joe M. Richardson, *Christian Reconstruction: The American Missionary Association and Southern Blacks, 1861–1890* (Athens: University of Georgia Press, 1986).

53. J. P. Bardwell to S. Hunt, 2 November 1866, #72,220, AMA, Mississippi, roll 2; J. P. Bardwell to Geo. Whipple, 2 January 1867, #72,236, AMA, Mississippi, roll 2; Consolidated Report of Freedmens Schools in charge of the AMA for the month of October 1865, Natchez, #71,821, AMA, Mississippi, roll 1; Hattie E. Stryker to J. R. Shipherd, 4 February 1868, #72,262, AMA, Mississippi, roll 2. Of the seven schools in operation immediately after the war, two were regimental schools. They were dissolved in the spring of 1866 when all the black regiments were mustered out of service.

54. Mattie W. Childs to Reverend Whipple, April 1864, #71,639, AMA, Mississippi, roll 1; S. G. Wright to Rev. Henry Coules, 15 March 1864, #71,613, AMA, Mississippi, roll 1; P. Mixer to Rev. G. Whipple, 24 June 1864, #71,660, AMA, Mississippi, roll 1; Monthly Report, November 1865, #71,860, AMA, Mississippi, roll 1. Schooling was available for off-duty soldiers four hours a day, six days a week. See S. G. Wright to Geo. Whipple, 4 January 1865, #71,717, AMA, Mississippi, roll 1.

55. Lynch, *Reminiscences of an Active Life*, 42; *New National Era*, 18 January 1872; *New York Times*, 4 March 1872; Testimony of William T. Martin, *In re John R. Lynch vs. Board of Commissioners of Election*, 9 October 1896, Drawer 432, No. 9, Adams County Circuit Court Case Files, Historic Natchez Foundation, Natchez, Miss.

56. On AMA efforts to limit local black control of schools, see Jones, *Soldiers of Light and Love*, 76; Linda M. Perkins, "The Black Female American Missionary Association Teacher in the South, 1861–1870," in Hine, *Black Women in United States History*, 3:1058; Richardson, *Christian Reconstruction*, 246–49.

57. Blanche Harris to Geo. Whipple, 23 January 1866, Natchez, #71,850, AMA, Mississippi, roll 1; J. P. Bardwell to Geo. Whipple, 20 March 1866, #71,992, AMA, Mississippi, roll 1; J. P. Bardwell to Rev. M. E. Strieby, 5 January 1865, #71,719, AMA, Mississippi, roll 1; S. G. Wright to Geo. Whipple, 12 October 1864, #71,689, AMA, Mississippi, roll 1; *Christian Recorder*, 5 May 1866; J. P. Bardwell to Geo. Whipple, 2 April 1866, #72,029, AMA, Mississippi, roll 1; Palmer Litts to S. G. Wright, 7 March 1866, #71,970, AMA, Mississippi, roll 1.

58. Palmer Litts to S. G. Wright, 25 July 1865, #71,780, AMA, Mississippi, roll 1; S. G. Wright to Geo. Whipple, 28 March 1865, #71,748, AMA, Mississippi, roll 1 (emphasis in original).

59. *Christian Recorder*, 5 May 1866; J. P. Bardwell to Geo. Whipple, 21 May 1866, #72,117, AMA, Mississippi, roll 2; J. P. Bardwell to S. Hunt, 22 June 1866, #72,143, AMA, Mississippi, roll 2; J. P. Bardwell to Geo. Whipple, 2 April 1866, #72,029, AMA, Mississippi, roll 1.

60. J. P. Bardwell to M. E. Strieby, 20 November 1865, #71,842, AMA, Mississippi, roll 1; *Natchez Democrat*, 13 May 1867.

61. J. P. Bardwell to M. E. Strieby, 5 January 1865, #71,719, AMA, Mississippi, roll 1. An emancipation celebration likely became an annual event. *Natchez Democrat*, 8 January 1866.

62. J. P. Bardwell to M. E. Strieby, 20 November 1865, #71,842, AMA, Mississippi, roll 1; Palmer Litts to Samuel Hunt, 15 March 1866, #71,983, AMA, Mississippi, roll 1; Blanche Harris to [unknown recipient], 10 March 1866, #71,971, AMA, Mississippi, roll 1; Maj.

Gen. T. J. Wood to Gen. O. O. Howard, 31 October 1866, Comr., Letters Received, roll 38, BRFAL; Emma M. Stickney to Mr. Hunt, 14 March 1866, #71,980, AMA, Mississippi, roll 1. Likewise, the Freedmen's Bureau used schools in towns and cities as launching points for educational ventures into the hinterlands. See the testimony of Maj. Gen. Lorenzo Thomas, in U.S. Congress, *Report of the Joint Committee on Reconstruction*, 39th Cong., 1st sess., 1866, H. Rep. 30, pt. 4, p. 144 (cited hereafter as *Joint Committee on Reconstruction*).

63. Bvt. Col. N. A. M. Dudley to Mayor Harris, Sheriff, or Mr. Rawlins, 4 November 1868, Department of Mississippi, pt. II, ser. 2232, Letters Sent, vol. 49, entry 266, Records of the United States Army Continental Commands, 1821–1890, Record Group 393, National Archives, Washington, D.C.; testimony of Rev. Joseph E. Roy, *Joint Committee on Reconstruction*, 67; Lt. A. M. Brobst to Insp. Gen. T. L. Fossee, September 1865, Miss. Asst. Comr., Monthly Reports, roll 30, BRFAL; Endorsement by Joseph Warren, Supt. of Education, 9 May 1866, in M. Howard to Gen. O. O. Howard, 7 April 1866, Comr., Letters Received, roll 27, BRFAL; Will H. Bowen to Gen. T. J. Wood, 20 December 1866, Comr., Letters Received, roll 43, BRFAL; Maj. G. D. Reynolds to Lt. Stuart Eldridge, 28 February 1866, Miss. Asst. Comr., Letters Received, roll 16, BRFAL; J. P. Bardwell to Geo. Whipple, 26 March 1866, #71,995, AMA, Mississippi, roll 1.

64. M. Howard to Gen. O. O. Howard, 7 April 1866, Comr., Letters Received, roll 27, BRFAL; Endorsement by Maj. Gen. T. J. Wood, 11 May 1866, in M. Howard to Gen. O. O. Howard, 7 April 1866, Comr., Letters Received, roll 27, BRFAL. For more on Merrimon Howard, see Frank A. Montgomery, *Reminiscences of a Mississippian in Peace and War* (Cincinnati: Robert Clarke Company Press, 1901), 275; BPDB. At a public meeting, the white citizens of Fayette drew up a resolution asking President Johnson to remove the Freedmen's Bureau from Jefferson County. *Natchez Democrat*, 11 December 1865; Maj. T. S. Free to Col. Samuel Thomas, 1 November 1865, Comr., Letters Received, roll 22, BRFAL; Endorsement by Joseph Warren, 9 May 1866, in M. Howard to Gen. O. O. Howard, 7 April 1866, Comr., Letters Received, roll 27, BRFAL.

65. M. Howard to Gen. O. O. Howard, 8 November 1866, Comr., Letters Received, roll 38, BRFAL. Howard made other requests for assistance; see M. Howard to Gen. O. O. Howard, 16 July 1867, and Merryman [Merrimon] Howard to Gen. O. O. Howard, 12 August 1867, Comr., Register of Letters, roll 7, BRFAL. For more on the teacher, see Susan E. Foster, #269,276, *Freedman's Bank Records*, Progeny Software, 1998–2000. On the crop failures of 1866 and 1867, see Roger L. Ransom and Richard Sutch, *One Kind of Freedom: The Economic Consequences of Emancipation*, 2nd ed. (Cambridge: Cambridge University Press, 2001), 64–65. Freedpeople in Natchez also experimented with a system of "direct taxation." See Palmer Litts to W. E. Whiting, 8 September 1865, #71,804, AMA, Mississippi, roll 1; Chaplain Joseph Warren to Lt. Stuart Eldridge, 30 September 1865, Comr., Letters Received, roll 22, BRFAL.

66. H. R. Pease to Bvt. Maj. S. C. Green, 7 July 1868, Miss. Asst. Comr., Letters Received, roll 25, BRFAL. On the size of Port Gibson, see Francis A. Walker, *The Statistics of the Population of the United States, Ninth Census of the United States* (Washington, D.C.: Government Printing Office, 1872), 183. For more on Page, see BPDB.

67. Carrie Clark to Mr. Clark, 8 January 1868; Carrie Clark to Gen. O. O. Howard, 6 February 1868; H. R. Pease to Bvt. Maj. S. C. Green, 7 July 1868, Miss. Asst. Comr., Letters Received, roll 25, BRFAL; W. H. Eldridge to Lt. Merritt Barber, 31 January 1868, Miss. Asst. Comr., Monthly Reports, roll 32, BRFAL; James Page to American Missionary Association, book HH, p. 39, and American Missionary Association to Board of School

Directors, book JJ, p. 373, Claiborne County Land Deeds, Claiborne County Courthouse, Port Gibson, Miss. It is not clear from the Freedmen's Bureau records how Page maintained possession of the property. Superintendent of Education Pease suggested that the "Commanding General would be justified in annulling the sale," but there is no direct evidence of an annulment in the land deeds. We do know that in 1869 Page sold the school property to the AMA and two years later the AMA sold it to the Claiborne County School Board. On the creation of public schools in Mississippi and Louisiana, respectively, see William C. Harris, *The Day of the Carpetbagger: Republican Reconstruction in Mississippi* (Baton Rouge: Louisiana State University Press, 1979), 325–33; Taylor, *Louisiana Reconstructed*, 461–67.

68. Bvt. Maj. Gen. Alvan C. Gillem to Gen. O. O. Howard, 10 April 1867, Comr., Letters Received, roll 43, BRFAL; Wilmer Shields to Doctor Mercer, 1 December 1866, folder 8, Wilmer Shields Letters, William Newton Mercer Papers, Louisiana and Lower Mississippi Valley Collections, Louisiana State University (LSU) Libraries, Baton Rouge; Wilmer Shields to Doctor Mercer, 12 December 1866, folder 8, Mercer Papers, LSU (emphasis in original); Monthly Report of Schools for the Parish of Concordia, Capt. B. B. Brown, 31 July 1866, Records of the Field Offices for the State of Louisiana, m1905, Records Relating to Schools, roll 110, BRFAL. For more on schools set up on plantations, see Capt. B. B. Brown, 10 March 1866, La. Asst. Comr., Register of Letters, roll 5, BRFAL; J. P. Bardwell to Geo. Whipple, 20 March 1866, #71,992, AMA, Mississippi, roll 1; testimony of Gen. Lorenzo Thomas, *Joint Committee on Reconstruction*, 144; *Christian Recorder*, 6 April 1867; Christian Rush, Tri-Monthly Report, 31 October 1867, La. Asst. Comr., Letters Received, roll 19, BRFAL; A. Yzunga del Valle to G. Whipple, 18 August 1868, #45,726, AMA, Louisiana, roll 1.

69. Kate Johnson to Sister [Anna Johnson], 8 December 1872, folder 3, box 1, William T. Johnson and Family Memorial Papers, LSU; Jos. A. Mower to F. D. Sewall, 5 June 1867, and Lt. J. C. De Gress to Capt. W. H. Sterling, 24 June 1867, Comr., Letters Received, roll 47, BRFAL; Monthly Report of Schools for the Parish of Concordia, Capt. B. B. Brown, 31 August 1866, Field Offices La., Records Relating to Schools, roll 110, BRFAL; Edward Henderson to Lt. Jesse M. Lee, 20 November 1867, La. Asst. Comr., Letters Received, roll 16, BRFAL; Monthly Report of Schools for the Parish of Concordia, Christian Rush, 31 December 1867, Field Offices La., Records Relating to Schools, roll 110, BRFAL; Bvt. Maj. Gen. Robt. C. Buchanan to Bvt. Brig. Gen. E. Whittlesey, March 1868, La. Asst. Comr., Reports of Operations and Conditions in Louisiana, roll 27, BRFAL; Tri-Monthly Report, Christian Rush, 30 November 1867, La. Asst. Comr., Letters Received, roll 19, BRFAL. On the constant problem of dilapidated school buildings and chronic rural poverty, see Richardson, *Christian Reconstruction*, 48–49.

70. Ronald L. F. Davis, *Good and Faithful Labor: From Slavery to Sharecropping in the Natchez District, 1860–1890* (Westport, Conn.: Greenwood Press, 1982), 89–115, 190; Nancy Bercaw, *Gendered Freedoms: Race, Rights, and the Politics of Household in the Delta, 1861–1875* (Gainesville: University Press of Florida, 2003), 115–34; René Hayden et al., eds., *Land and Labor, 1866–1867*, ser. 3, vol. 2 of *Freedom: A Documentary History of Emancipation, 1861–1867* (Chapel Hill: University of North Carolina Press, 2013), 369–79.

71. Tri-Monthly Report, Capt. G. H. Dunford, 31 July 1867, La. Asst. Comr., Letters Received, roll 14, BRFAL; Reid, *After the War*, 488; Tri-Monthly Report, Capt. G. H. Dunford, 10 August 1867, La. Asst. Comr., Letters Received, roll 14, BRFAL; Davis, *Good and Faithful Labor*, 104; Copy of Agreement Between Certain Colord persons and Henry S. Metcalf of York Plantation in Adams County Mississippi, 1 January 1868, in Lt. George

Haller to Bvt. Major S. C. Greene, 20 June 1868, Miss. Asst. Comr., Letters Received, roll 23, BRFAL.

72. Edward King, *The Great South* (Hartford, Conn.: American Publishing Company, 1875), 273; Ralph Shlomowitz, "The Squad System on Postbellum Cotton Plantations," in *Toward a New South? Studies in Post–Civil War Southern Communities*, ed. Orville Vernon Burton and Robert C. McGrath Jr. (Westport, Conn.: Greenwood Press, 1982), 272–73; Gerald David Jaynes, *Branches without Roots: Genesis of the Black Working Class in the American South, 1862–1882* (New York: Oxford University Press, 1986), 182–86; Jeannie Dean, ed., *Annie Harper's Journal* (Denton, Tex.: Flower Mound Writing Company, 1983), 37; Capt. B. B. Brown to Capt. W. H. Sterling, 20 February 1867, La. Asst. Comr., Reports of Operations and Conditions in Louisiana, roll 27, BRFAL; testimony of Gen. Lorenzo Thomas, *Joint Committee on Reconstruction*, 144; Agreement with Freedmen, 12 February 1869, Johnson Family Papers, LSU; Wilmer Shields to Doctor Mercer, 13 February 1867, Mercer Papers, LSU. For more on the size and composition of squads, see Jaynes, *Branches without Roots*, 170–73; Hayden et al., *Land and Labor, 1866–1867*, 378–79. Ralph Shlomowitz estimated that squad sizes usually ranged from two to ten members; see "Squad System on Postbellum Cotton Plantations," 266.

73. Tri-Monthly Report, Christian Rush, 10 October 1867, La. Asst. Comr., Letters Received, roll 19, BRFAL; Tri-Monthly Report, Christian Rush, 21 October 1867, La. Asst. Comr., Letters Received, roll 19, BRFAL. For another example in which laborers sent a representative to meet with a Freedmen's Bureau official, see Tri-Monthly Report, G. H. Dunford, 10 August 1867, La. Asst. Comr., Letters Received, roll 14, BRFAL. On Jackson as a Baptist minister, see Caldwell, "Social, Economic, and Political Study," 149–52.

74. Reid, *After the War*, 561; testimony of Gen. Lorenzo Thomas, *Joint Committee on Reconstruction*, 143. For more on planters seeking out and praising ex-soldiers, see Capt. B. B. Brown to Capt. A. F. Hayden, 31 March 1866, La. Asst. Comr., Reports Relating to the Condition of Freedmen and Refugees, roll 28, BRFAL. Of course, many planters also feared black soldiers because they pledged themselves to protect black people and encouraged laborers not to sign one-sided labor contracts. For an example of this fear, see "Mississippi Planter to Three State Legislators," 22 October 1865, in Ira Berlin, Joseph P. Reidy, and Leslie S. Rowland, eds., *The Black Military Experience*, ser. 2 of *Freedom: A Documentary History of Emancipation, 1861–1867* (Cambridge: Cambridge University Press, 1982), 747–49.

75. Capt. Geo. H. Dunford, 20 July 1867, La. Asst. Comr., Letters Received, roll 14, BRFAL; Reid, *After the War*, 547, 550; Davis, *Good and Faithful Labor*, 104–5. For other strikes, see Report of operations and complaints, P. P. Bergevin, 30 November 1868, Miss. Asst. Comr., Reports, roll 33, BRFAL. Similarly, black dockworkers in Natchez went on strike for higher hourly wages, but the strike was defeated because the dockworkers failed to remain unified and halt steamboat traffic. *Natchez Courier*, 9 April 1867, cited in Dorothy Vick Smith, "Black Reconstruction in Mississippi, 1862–1870" (Ph.D. diss., University of Kansas, 1985), 157.

76. Bvt. Maj. Gen. Robt. C. Buchanan to Bvt. Brig. Gen. E. Whittlesey, 31 January 1868, La. Asst. Comr., Reports of Operations and Conditions in Louisiana, roll 27, BRFAL; J. P. Bardwell to Geo. Whipple, 2 April 1866, #72,029, AMA, Mississippi, roll 1. On Litts's status in the Bureau of Refugees, Freedmen, and Abandoned Lands for the Southern District, Mississippi, see Palmer Litts to Rev. Geo. Whipple, 6 March 1866, #71,967, AMA, Mississippi, roll 1. For more on the limitation of squads and the poor crop yields, see Jaynes,

Branches without Roots, 180; Harris, *Presidential Reconstruction in Mississippi*, 171–72, 180–81.

77. Thomas to Gen. O. O. Howard, 15 August 1865, Comr., Letters Received, roll 18, BRFAL; *Natchez Democrat*, 2 April 1866; Davis, *Good and Faithful Labor*, 98; King, *The Great South*, 290.

78. King, *The Great South*, 290; Reid, *After the War*, 564; M. Howard to Gen. O. O. Howard, 7 April 1866, Comr., Letters Received, roll 27, BRFAL; Tri-Monthly Report, Christian Rush, 31 December 1867, La. Asst. Comr., Letters Received, roll 19, BRFAL; Ben Thornton to Lemuel P. Conner, 2 January 1866, folder 47, box 3, Lemuel P. Conner and Family Papers, LSU. For more on the quest for landownership, see Edward Magdol, *A Right to the Land: Essays on the Freedmen's Community* (Westport, Conn.: Greenwood Press, 1977), 139–99; Litwack, *Been in the Storm So Long*, 399–404; Hahn, *A Nation under Our Feet*, 135–43.

79. Maj. Geo. D. Reynolds to Lt. Stuart Eldridge, 2 February 1866, Miss. Asst. Comr., Letters Received, roll 16, BRFAL; Capt. B. B. Brown to Capt. A. F. Hayden, 31 March 1866, and Capt. B. B. Brown, Monthly Report, September 1866, La. Asst. Comr., Reports Relating to the Condition of Freedmen and Refugees, roll 28, BRFAL; testimony of Gen. Lorenzo Thomas, *Joint Committee on Reconstruction*, 144; James T. Organ to William Shorter, 27 November 1866, book O, Conveyance Records, Concordia Parish Courthouse, Vidalia, La. Shorter's leadership position may have derived from his existing leadership role as Baptist minister, or he may have contributed a larger share toward the purchase of the plantation. On his ministerial role, see Caldwell, "Social, Economic, and Political Study," 149–52.

80. Tri-Monthly Report, Christian Rush, 11 November 1867, La. Asst. Comr., Letters Received, roll 19, BRFAL; *Concordia Intelligencer* quoted in *Natchez Democrat*, 18 July 1868. By 1870 the Marengo plantation had appreciated in value by $1,000 to $8,000, and Shorter had accumulated $2,000 in personal property. U.S. Bureau of Census, *Ninth Census: Population, 1870*.

81. Testimony of Gen. Lorenzo Thomas, *Joint Committee on Reconstruction*, 141–43; A. T. Bowie to Bvt. Maj. Gen. Thomas J. Wood, 28 December 1866, Comr., Letters Received, roll 43, BRFAL; Wilmer Shields to Doctor Mercer, 6 October 1869, folder 10, Shields Letters, Mercer Papers, LSU; Reid, *After the War*, 548, 550, 570, 572; J. P. Bardwell to Geo. Whipple, 2 April 1866, #72,029, AMA, Mississippi, roll 1; J. T. Trowbridge, *A Picture of the Desolated States; and the Work of Restoration, 1865–1868* (Hartford, Conn.: L. Stebbins, 1868), 393.

82. William and John J. Lambert to David Singleton, Deed, 21 October 1865, book NN, p. 544, Land Deeds, ACCH; David Singleton to William and John J. Lambert, Mortgage, 21 October 1865, book NN, p. 558, Land Deeds, ACCH; *Christian Recorder*, 3 November 1866; David Singleton and William H. Lynch with Walker Vester et al., Agreement, 11 June 1868, book PP, p. 122, Land Deeds, ACCH; BPDB; *Christian Recorder*, 3 November 1866; Tax assessments, 1870, Adams County Board of Supervisors Minutes, p. 40, ACCH. On the Johnson family operations, see Lease Contract, 14 March 1868, folder 22; Agreement with Freedmen, 12 February 1869, folder 22; Lease Contract, 15 February 1869, folder 22; Lease Contract, 3 February 1870, folder 23; Agreement with Richard Johnson, 9 April 1870, folder 23; Indenture, 20 January 1872, folder 23, in Series II, Legal and Financial Documents, box 1, Johnson Family Papers, LSU; Tax Assessments, 1870, Adams County Board of Supervisors Minutes, p. 44, ACCH. For more on William Johnson, see

Edwin Adams Davis and William Ransom Hogan, *The Barber of Natchez* (Baton Rouge: Louisiana State University Press, 1954); Edwin Adams Davis and William Ransom Hogan, eds., *William Johnson's Natchez: The Ante-Bellum Diary of a Free Negro* (Baton Rouge: Louisiana State University Press, 1993).

83. BPDB.

84. *Christian Recorder*, 5 May 1866. For more on Fitzhugh, see *Christian Recorder*, 3 November 1866; *Natchez Courier*, 12 November 1866.

Chapter Three. New Friends

1. Testimony of Joshua A. Morris, in U.S. Senate, *Testimony Taken by the Joint Select Committee to Inquire into the Condition of Affairs in the Late Insurrectionary States*, 42nd Cong., 2nd sess., 1872, S. Rep 41, vol. 11, p. 318 (cited hereafter as *Late Insurrectionary States*).

2. For studies of black political mobilization that draw attention to modes of production as key explanatory factors, see Michael W. Fitzgerald, *The Union League Movement in the Deep South: Politics and Agricultural Change during Reconstruction* (Baton Rouge: Louisiana State University Press, 1989), 213–33; Julie Saville, *The Work of Reconstruction: From Slave to Wage Laborer in South Carolina, 1860–1870* (New York: Cambridge University Press, 1994); John C. Rodrigue, *Reconstruction in the Cane Fields: From Slavery to Free Labor in Louisiana's Sugar Parishes, 1862–1880* (Baton Rouge: Louisiana State University Press, 2001); John C. Rodrigue, "Labor Militancy and Black Grassroots Political Mobilization in the Louisiana Sugar Region, 1865–1868," *Journal of Southern History* 67 (February 2001): 116–17.

3. *Natchez Democrat*, 22 January, 16 April, 23 April 1866; State vs. David Singleton, box 30–13(12), April term 1866; State vs. Abe Wilkins, box 30–19, April term 1866; State vs. David Singleton, box 21–58 and box 21–56, October term 1866, Adams County Circuit Court Case Files, Historic Natchez Foundation (HNF), Natchez, Miss.; *Natchez Courier*, 23 October 1866.

4. W. T. Martin to Gov. Humphreys, 7 December 1866, Governor Humphreys Papers, Series 779: Correspondence and Papers, Mississippi Department of Archives and History (MDAH), Jackson; State vs. David Singleton, box 30–13(12), April term 1866, Adams County Circuit Court Case Files, HNF. G. H. Lamberton and Samuel L. Winston also posted bonds for Singleton. Winston was the father of Louis J. Winston, one of the most successful black politicians in Natchez, about whom we will learn more later. The following is a list of the Singleton petitioners with the number of slaves that each owned in 1860: A. L. Bingaman (310), A. K. Farrar (322), Alfred V. Davis (651), Wm. Dix (4), Lemuel P. Conner (282), Zebulon York (782), H. B. Shaw (31), Rev. Dr. W. H. Watkins (8), Spencer Wood (7), D. L. Rivers (113), and W. T. Martin (10). U.S. Bureau of Census, *Eighth Census of the United States: Slave Schedules, 1860*; William Kauffman Scarborough, *Masters of the Big House: Elite Slaveholders of the Mid-Nineteenth-Century South* (Baton Rouge: Louisiana State University Press, 2003), 462–72.

5. W. T. Martin to Gov. Humphreys, 7 December 1866; H. B. Shaw to Humphreys, 29 November 1866; Davis to Humphreys, 7 December 1866, Governor Humphreys Papers, MDAH. In his testimony before the SCC, Singleton claimed that he became free in 1854, but there is no mention of are-enslavement. Re-enslavement, quite obviously, would have doomed his claim; however, his testimony does not appear to directly contract the statements made by his white petitioners in 1866. Singleton toed a fine line, but

it didn't work. The scc rejected his claim because they doubted his loyalty and believed that Davis was the likely owner of the property in question. As in 1866, Singleton did not accept rejection lightly and appealed the scc's ruling. After a lengthy and costly appeal before the Court of Claims, Singleton was granted $825 in 1891, one year after he had died. David Singleton claim, case 411, Adams County, Congressional Jurisdiction Case Files, Records of the U.S. Court of Claims, Record Group 123, National Archives, Washington, D.C.

6. Col. Adam L. Bingaman to Humphreys, 27 November 1866; D. L. Rivers to Gov. Humphreys, December 1866, Governor Humphreys Papers, MDAH; Mary E. Hewett, Case No. 755, Probate Records, Adams County Chancery Court, Adams County Courthouse, Natchez, Miss. In testimony before a probate court regarding a debt that Singleton's son owed Mary Hewett's late husband, David Singleton said, "I was pardoned by Gov. Humphreys." Four other freedmen convicted of larceny the same week as Singleton were sentenced to terms of two to three years. *Natchez Courier*, 23 October 1866.

7. Lemuel P. Conner to Gov. Humphreys, 30 November 1866, Governor Humphreys Papers, MDAH; John R. Lynch, *Reminiscences of an Active Life: The Autobiography of John Roy Lynch*, ed. John Hope Franklin (Chicago: University of Chicago Press, 1970), 57. Singleton also endorsed William McCary's bond for Adams County tax collector for $3,000. *Natchez Democrat*, 10 January 1872.

8. *Natchez Weekly Courier*, 12 November 1866; *Christian Recorder*, 20 October 1866. For more on free black barbers in the antebellum South, see Douglas W. Bristol, *Knights of the Razor: Black Barbers in Slavery and Freedom* (Baltimore: Johns Hopkins University Press, 2009), 51, 82–84.

9. *Natchez Weekly Courier*, 12 November 1866; Supplement, *Natchez Weekly Courier*, 12 November 1866; U.S. Bureau of Census, *Eighth Census: Slave Schedules, 1860*. The paper received many letters from "the very best of citizens" that strongly condemned Fitzhugh, but they were not printed. For more on the mob that attacked Fitzhugh, see State vs. William Winston (col'd), box 21–35, and State vs. William Burns (col'd), box 30–93, August term 1866, Adams County Circuit Court Case Files, HNF.

10. *New Orleans Daily Picayune*, 15 September 1864; Supplement, *Natchez Weekly Courier*, 12 November 1866.

11. Samuel W. Fitzhugh served in the Mississippi House of Representatives and as a constable in Wilkinson County. Robert W. Fitzhugh was elected alderman in Natchez; in addition, he held many appointed positions, including postmaster, and a number of partisan positions. Charles W. Fitzhugh served as a Republican delegate to the Mississippi constitutional convention in 1868. Louis Winston Fitzhugh was a constable and election challenger in Adams County. Edward H. Fitzhugh was the secretary of a Republican Club in Natchez, and John Fitzhugh, the only family member to align with the Democrats, served as secretary for a Colored Greeley Club. Justin Behrend, Black Politicians Database, SUNY-Geneseo, http://go.geneseo.edu/BlackPoliticiansDB (cited hereafter as BPDB).

12. Col. Saml. Thomas to Gen. O. O. Howard, 12 April 1866, Commissioner, Letters Received, m752, roll 28, Records of the Bureau of Refugees, Freedmen, and Abandoned Lands, Record Group 105, National Archives, Washington, D.C. (cited hereafter as BRFAL); Maj. T. S. Free to Col. Samuel Thomas, 1 November 1865, Comr., Letters Received, roll 22, BRFAL; Order by the Mississippi Freedmen Bureau's Assistant Commissioner, 31 October 1865, in Steven Hahn et al., eds., *Land and Labor, 1865*, ser. 3, vol. 1 of *Freedom: A Documentary History of Emancipation, 1861–1867* (Chapel Hill: University of

North Carolina Press, 2008), 288–92 (emphasis in original); Circular No. 2, Office of the Assistant Commissioner, Vicksburg, Mississippi, 2 January 1866, reprinted in *Natchez Democrat*, 22 January 1866; Capt. George H. Dunford, Monthly Report, July 1867, Records of the Assistant Commissioner for the State of Louisiana, m1027, Reports, roll 29, BRFAL.

13. G. W. Fisher to Maj. Gen. A. C. Gillem, 2 January 1868, and W. H. Eldridge to Gillem, 24 January 1868, Mississippi Assistant Commissioner, m826, Letters Received, roll 21, BRFAL.

14. Col. N. A. McCaleb to Bvt. Col. Marcus P. Reston, 14 March 1866, Department of Mississippi, pt. II, ser. 2232, Letters Sent, vol. 49, Records of the U.S. Army Continental Commands, 1821–1890, Record Group 393, National Archives, Washington, D.C. (cited hereafter as RG 393); *Natchez Weekly Courier*, 19 March 1866. Brought before a military commission, the black soldiers were acquitted of the murder of Martin Garrity, the white police officer. See *Natchez Democrat*, 30 April 1866. For another version of these events that focuses on the drunkenness and unruliness of the white police officers, see the testimony of Maj. Gen. Lorenzo Thomas, in U.S. Congress, *Report of the Joint Committee on Reconstruction*, 39th Cong., 1st sess., 1866, H. Rep. 30, pt. 4, p. 142 (cited hereafter as *Joint Committee on Reconstruction*). For another instance in which wearing a U.S. military uniform provoked a public confrontation, see Robert Hunley to [?], 17 September 1867, La. Asst. Comr., register of letters, roll 5, BRFAL. For a similar confrontation that took place in Port Gibson, Claiborne County, in which discharged black soldiers were arrested for walking the streets in uniform, see the *Port Gibson Weekly Standard*, 12 May 1866.

15. S. G. Wright to Geo. Whipple, 28 March 1865, #71748, American Missionary Association Papers, Mississippi, roll 1, Amistad Research Center, New Orleans, La.; P. Houston Murray to the editor, *Christian Recorder*, July 1, 1865. In other regions of the South, black people formed political organizations prior to military Reconstruction. See, for example, Susan E. O'Donovan, *Becoming Free in the Cotton South* (Cambridge, Mass.: Harvard University Press, 2007), 213–14, 225–31.

16. Edward McPherson, *A Handbook of Politics for 1868* (Washington, D.C.: Philp and Solomons, 1868), 191–94. For more on the Reconstruction Acts, see Eric Foner, *Reconstruction: America's Unfinished Revolution, 1863–1877* (New York: Harper & Row, 1988), 271–80.

17. For more on the Union League, see Fitzgerald, *Union League Movement in the Deep South*; Steven Hahn, *A Nation under Our Feet: Black Political Struggles in the Rural South from Slavery to the Great Migration* (Cambridge, Mass.: Belknap Press of Harvard University Press, 2003), 177–89. On Reconstruction uncertainties, see Mark Wahlgren Summers, *A Dangerous Stir: Fear, Paranoia, and the Making of Reconstruction* (Chapel Hill: University of North Carolina Press, 2009).

18. *Natchez Courier* quoted in the *New Orleans Daily Picayune*, 9 April 1867; *Natchez Democrat*, 8 April, 15 April, 22 April, 27 May 1867. For an illuminating discussion on how blacks created multiple public spheres and possessed public spaces to make citizenship claims, see Hannah Rosen, *Terror in the Heart of Freedom: Citizenship, Sexual Violence and the Meaning of Race in the Postemancipation South* (Chapel Hill: University of North Carolina Press, 2009), 87–132.

19. *Natchez Democrat*, 15 April, 27 May 1867; BPDB; *Natchez Democrat*, 16 September 1874; testimony of Wilson Wood, in U.S. House, *Testimony in the Contested Election Case of John R. Lynch vs. James R. Chalmers, From the Sixth Congressional District of*

Mississippi, 47th Cong., 1st sess., Misc. Doc. 12, pp. 116–19; Ritual of the Union League of America [1867, 1870], in Walter L. Fleming, ed., *Documentary History of Reconstruction: Political, Military, Social, Religious, Educational & Industrial: 1865 to the Present Time* (Cleveland: Arthur H. Clark, 1907), 2:7–12.

20. *Natchez Weekly Courier*, 19 October 1867; Lynch, *Reminiscences of an Active Life*, 50, 54–57.

21. *Natchez Democrat*, 4 June, 6 August 1868, 21 June 1869, 31 July, 14 August 1872; "Wilkinson County Republican Party Resolutions, January 2, 1869," in U.S. House, *Condition of Affairs in Mississippi, Evidence Taken by the Committee on Reconstruction*, 40th Cong., 3rd sess., 1869, H. Misc. Doc. 53, p. 269; Christian Rush, Tri-Monthly Report, 28 October 1867, La. Asst. Comr., Registered Letters, roll 19, BRFAL; Lt. John W., Hicks to Lt. Nathaniel Burbank, 3 September 1867, La. Asst. Comr., Registered Letters, roll 16, BRFAL.

22. *Natchez Democrat*, 10 June 1867. On slave auctions at the Natchez courthouse, see Ronald L. F. Davis, *The Black Experience in Natchez, 1720–1880* (Natchez National Historical Park, Miss.: Eastern National Park & Monument Association, 1994), 71–74.

23. E. E. Platt to Preston, 31 May 1867, Miss. Asst. Comr., Letters Received, roll 19, BRFAL; "Copy of statement charging 1st Lieut. D. M. White, U. R. C., with drunkenness, profanity and want of sympathy with the colored people, and Capt. E. E. Platt, URC., with want of sympathy with colored people, sympathy with secessionists, and with making charges in the collections of claims for negroes," 6 May 1867, Comr., Letters Received, roll 47, BRFAL. For information on the value of wages and land, see Col. Samuel Thomas to Gen. O. O. Howard, 27 June 1865, Comr., Letters Received, roll 18, BRFAL; *Joint Committee on Reconstruction*, pt. 3, p. 143, and pt. 4, p. 141; Whitelaw Reid, *After the War: A Tour of the Southern States, 1865–1866* (1866; repr., New York: Harper & Row, 1965), 490; George Hitchen to Hon. Charles Sumner, 14 January 1868, Comr., Letters Received, roll 5, BRFAL; F. D. Sewall to Gen. O. O. Howard, 29 January 1868, Comr., Letters Received, roll 55, BRFAL.

24. *Natchez Democrat*, 6 May 1867; Edward Henderson to Capt. J. H. Hastings, 20 June 1867, and Henderson to Hastings, 31 August 1867, La. Asst. Comr., Registered Letters, roll 16, BRFAL; Susan Sillers Darden diary, vol. 2, 22 July 1867, Darden Family Papers, MDAH; Henry W. Warren, *Reminiscences of a Mississippi Carpet-Bagger* (Holden, Mass.: Davis Press, 1914), 35. For similar encounters between freedmen and agents in Claiborne County, see A. S. Alden to Capt. Jas. W. Sunderland, September Report in compliance with circular No. 10, 27 September 1867, Miss. Asst. Comr., Reports, roll 30, BRFAL.

25. *Natchez Democrat*, 8 July 1867. Approximately 5,323 blacks resided in Natchez in 1870. U.S. Bureau of Census, *A Compendium of the Ninth Census* (Washington, D.C.: GPO, 1872), 236.

26. *Natchez Democrat*, 8 July 1867; John Mercer Langston, *A Speech on "Equality Before the Law"* (St. Louis: Democrat Book and Job Printing House, 1866), 21. For more on Langston, see extract of letter from John M. Langston to [Thomas Tullock], 7 July 1867, Robert C. Schenck Papers, roll 6, Rutherford B. Hayes Presidential Center, Fremont, Ohio; John Mercer Langston, *Freedom and Citizenship: Selected Lectures and Addresses of Hon. John Mercer Langston, LL.D.* (Washington, D.C.: Rufus H. Darby, 1883), esp. 99–122; William Cheek and Aimee Lee Cheek, "John Mercer Langston: Principle and Politics," in *Black Leaders of the Nineteenth Century*, ed. Leon F. Litwack and August Meier (Urbana: University of Illinois Press, 1991), 103–26, esp. 117.

27. Tri-Monthly Report, Geo. H. Dunford, 10 August 1867, La. Asst. Comr., Registered Letters, roll 14, BRFAL.

28. *Natchez Democrat*, 23 September 1867; *Natchez Weekly Courier*, 21 September 1867. The delegates to the Republican convention were: E. J. Castello (a white Union League activist and former Union officer, representing Adams County), L. W. Perce (an attorney and former Union officer, representing Adams County), H. P. Jacobs (the black minister of Pine Street Baptist Church, representing Adams County), Charles W. Fitzhugh ("a sprightly and intelligent mulatto from Natchez," representing Wilkinson County), A. Alderson (a native white Mississippian from Jefferson County), Matthew T. Newsome (a black Methodist minister from Claiborne County), and Josh. S. Morris (a former Confederate, representing Claiborne County). Five of the seven (Castello, Jacobs, Fitzhugh, Alderson, and Newsome) were later elected delegates to the Mississippi constitutional convention of 1868.

29. Bvt. Maj. Gen. Alvan C. Gillem to Gen. O. O. Howard, 15 May 1867, Comr., Letters Received, roll 47, BRFAL; Jos. A. Mower to F. D. Sewall, 5 June 1867, Comr., Letters Received, roll 47, BRFAL; Monthly Report, Asst. Comm. to F. D. Sewall, June 1867, La. Asst. Comr., Reports of Operations and Conditions in Louisiana, roll 27, BRFAL; Special Report of Supplies issued to destitute in Sub. Dist. of Natchez, Miss., Capt. E. E. Platt, 24 September 1867, Miss. Asst. Comr., Reports, roll 30, BRFAL. On the collapse of cotton prices that compounded the natural disasters in 1866 and 1867, see Roger L. Ransom and Richard Sutch, *One Kind of Freedom: The Economic Consequences of Emancipation*, 2nd ed. (Cambridge: Cambridge University Press, 2001), 64–65.

30. *New Orleans Republican* reprinted in *New York Times*, 18 August 1867; Edward Henderson to L. O. Parker, 10 September 1867, La. Asst. Comr., Registered Letters, roll 16, BRFAL; Tri-Monthly Reports, Geo. H. Dunford, 20 July, 10 August, 31 August 1867, La. Asst. Comr., Registered Letters, roll 14, BRFAL; Edward Henderson to Capt. J. H. Hastings, 6 August 1867, La. Asst. Comr., Registered Letters, roll 16, BRFAL. On the army worm, see *New York Times*, 20 July, 18 August 1867; Monthly Report, Lt. Col. W. H. Wood, August 1867, La. Asst. Comr., Reports, roll 27, BRFAL; Bvt. Maj. J. A. Mower to Bvt. Brig. Gen. F. D. Sewall, 31 July 1867, Comr., Letters Received, roll 50, BRFAL; Tri-Monthly Report, Geo. H. Dunford, 20 July 1867, La. Asst. Comr., Registered Letters, roll 14, BRFAL. On the cholera outbreak, see Tri-Monthly Report, Geo. H. Dunford, 20 July 1867, La. Asst. Comr., Registered Letters, roll 14, BRFAL; Bvt. Maj. J. A. Mower to Bvt. Brig. Gen. F. D. Sewall, 31 July 1867, Comr., Letters Received, roll 50, BRFAL; Edward Henderson to L. O. Parker, 10 September 1867, La. Asst. Comr., Registered Letters, roll 16, BRFAL; Lt. Col. W. H. Wood to Bvt. Brig. Gen. E. Whittlesey, August 1867, La. Asst. Comr., Reports, roll 27, BRFAL.

31. Narrative Report, [?] to Lt. J. F. Conyingham, August 1867, Miss. Asst. Comr., Reports, roll 30, BRFAL; State vs. Henry Pickney, box 14–66, October term 1868, Adams County Circuit Court Case Files, HNF; P. P. Bergevin, Report of Operations for the Sub District of Woodville, Miss., 31 January 1868, Miss. Asst. Comr., Reports, roll 32, BRFAL; Betty B. Beaumont, *A Business Woman's Journal: A Sequel to "Twelve Years of My Life"* (Philadelphia: T. B. Peterson & Brothers, 1888), 300. On long journeys into town to vote, see Wilmer Shields to Doctor Mercer, 19 June 1867, folder 9, Wilmer Shields Letters, William Newton Mercer Papers, Louisiana and Lower Mississippi Valley Collections, Louisiana State University (LSU) Libraries, Baton Rouge; Edward Henderson to Capt. J. H. Hastings, 20 June 1867, La. Asst. Comr., Registered Letters, roll 16, BRFAL; Tri-Monthly Report, Geo. H. Dunford, 20 July 1867, La. Asst. Comr., Registered Letters, roll 14, BRFAL.

32. Tri-Monthly Report, Geo. H. Dunford, 31 July 1867, La. Asst. Comr., Registered Letters, roll 14, BRFAL; Tri-Monthly Report, Geo. H. Dunford, 20 July 1867, La. Asst.

Comr., Registered Letters, roll 14, BRFAL; Lt. George Haller to Col. H. W. Smith, Narrative Report, August 1867, Miss. Asst. Comr., Reports, roll 30, BRFAL. See also Narrative Report, [?] to Lt. J. F. Conyingham, August 1867, and Record of Complaints, Lt. George Haller, October 1867, Miss. Asst. Comr., Reports, roll 30, BRFAL.

33. Edward Henderson, 20 July 1867, La. Asst. Comr., Records Relating to Murders and Outrages, roll 34, BRFAL; Monthly Report, Geo. H. Dunford, July 1867, La. Asst. Comr., Inspection Reports of Plantations from Subordinate Officers, roll 29, BRFAL.

34. *Weekly Standard*, 24 August 1867; U.S. Bureau of Census, *Compendium of the Ninth Census*, 236. For a similar but less detailed description of a political barbecue, see Wilmer Shields to Doctor Mercer, 6 October 1869, folder 10, Mercer Papers, LSU.

35. Lt. George Haller to Col. H. W. Smith, Narrative Report, August 1867, Miss. Asst. Comr., Reports, roll 30, BRFAL; Haller to Lt. J. F. Cunningham, Report of no. of Plantations visited, 30 September 1867, Miss. Asst. Comr., Reports, roll 30, BRFAL; Capt. James Biddle to Capt. Jas W. Sunderland, 30 September 1867, Miss. Asst. Comr., Reports, roll 30, BRFAL; Edward Henderson to Lt. Jesse M. Lee, 30 September 1867, La. Asst. Comr., Registered Letters, roll 19, BRFAL.

36. Manuscript autobiography, pp. 32–34, folder 2, Private Papers of James Stewart McGehee, vol. 3, James Stewart McGehee Papers, Mss. 2302, 2789, LSU.

37. *Natchez Democrat*, 7 October 1867; Joe Louis Caldwell, "A Social, Economic, and Political Study of Blacks in the Louisiana Delta, 1865–1880" (Ph.D. diss., Tulane University, 1988), 257; Historical Census Browser, University of Virginia, Geospatial and Statistical Data Center, 2004, http://fisher.lib.virginia.edu/collections/stats/histcensus/index .html. Although heavily skewed toward the freedmen, these registration numbers did not diverge substantially from the population figures, but they do suggest that freedpeople were better mobilized. In 1870 whites made up just 20 percent of the residents of the Natchez District. Voter registration figures for 1867 are: Concordia: 2,195 black (91 percent), 199 white (8 percent), 2,394 total; Tensas: 2,413 black (94 percent), 149 white (6 percent), 2,562 total; Wilkinson: 2,274 black (81 percent), 547 white (19 percent), 2,821 total; Adams: 3,210 black (82 percent), 729 white (18 percent), 3,937 total; Jefferson: 1,916 black (78 percent), 541 white (22 percent), 2,457 total; Claiborne: 1,977 black (78 percent), 549 white (22 percent), 2,526 total. For the registration figures reported in the text, I determined the 1870 voting-age population (male citizens twenty-one years age and over) and divided it by the registration figures for 1867. There are anomalies in the results. For example, there were more registered voters in Wilkinson County in 1867 than there were eligible voters in 1870. The shares of the population registered to vote in 1867, by county, are: Adams, 83 percent; Claiborne, 84 percent; Jefferson, 88 percent; Wilkinson, 110 percent; Concordia, 84 percent; Tensas, 77 percent. These percentages correlate with statewide totals. On statewide results, see William C. Harris, *The Day of the Carpetbagger: Republican Reconstruction in Mississippi* (Baton Rouge: Louisiana State University Press, 1979), 76, 84–89; Joe Gray Taylor, *Louisiana Reconstructed, 1863–1877* (Baton Rouge: Louisiana State University Press, 1974), 139; Richard M. Valelly, *The Two Reconstructions: The Struggle for Black Enfranchisement* (Chicago: University of Chicago Press, 2004), 33. Of the 137,561 registered voters in Mississippi in 1867, 79,176 were blacks and 58,385 were whites. Black voters outnumbered white in thirty-four of sixty-one counties. In Louisiana black registered voters totaled 78,230 and among white men the total was over 48,000. The disfranchisement of Confederates had a minimal impact. William C. Harris estimates that fewer than 2,500 ex-Confederates in Mississippi were disqualified from voting. Harris, *Day of the Carpetbagger*, 76–77.

38. Testimony of Maj. Gen. Lorenzo Thomas, *Joint Committee on Reconstruction*, pt. 4, pp. 144, 141; A. Mygatt to O. O. Howard, 4 July 1867, Comr., Letters Received, roll 47, BRFAL. On the tangible benefits derived from military bounties, see Geo. Haller to Maj. S. C. Green, 4 May 1868, Miss. Asst. Comr., Reports, roll 32, BRFAL.

39. *Natchez Weekly Courier*, September 21, 1867; Harris, *Day of the Carpetbagger*, 109; extract of letter from James Lynch to [Thomas Tullock?], 9 July 1867, Schenck Papers, Hayes Presidential Center.

40. Letter to the *Chicago Times* reprinted in the *Natchez Democrat*, 5 August 1867.

41. Edward Henderson to Lt. Col. J. H. Hastings, 20 October 1867, La. Asst. Comr., Registered Letters, roll 16, BRFAL; Edward Henderson to Lt. Jesse M. Lee, 20 November 1867, and Henderson to Lee, 10 December 1867, La. Asst. Comr., Registered Letters, roll 16, BRFAL; Christian Rush to Lee, 30 October 1867, and Tri-Monthly Reports, Christian Rush, 10 October, 30 November 1867, La. Asst. Comr., Registered Letters, roll 19, BRFAL; Henderson to Lee, 31 December 1867, La. Asst. Comr., Registered Letters, roll 16, BRFAL. On the Louisiana vote, see Edward Henderson to Lt. Jesse M. Lee, 30 September 1867, La. Asst. Comr., Registered Letters, roll 19, BRFAL; Taylor, *Louisiana Reconstructed*, 147.

42. Edward Henderson to L. O. Parker, 10 September 1867, La. Asst. Comr., Registered Letters, roll 16, BRFAL.

43. *Natchez Weekly Courier*, 2 November 1867; Harris, *Day of the Carpetbagger*, 80–83. On similar noncooperation in Louisiana, see Taylor, *Louisiana Reconstructed*, 147.

44. *Natchez Weekly Courier*, 12 October 1867; *Natchez Democrat*, 22 April 1867; "Names of speakers and organizers employed or aided by the Union Republican Congressional Committee," 12 September 1867, Schenck Papers, Hayes Presidential Center; *Natchez Democrat*, 17 June, 9 September, 7 October, 18 November 1867; *Natchez Weekly Courier*, 2 November 1867.

45. *Natchez Weekly Courier*, 2 November 1867; *Natchez Democrat*, 1 July 1867. On Castello, see Capt. J. H. Hastings to [?], 24 November 1866, La. Asst. Comr., register of letters, roll 5, BRFAL. Hussey, a Union army surgeon, was stationed at the hospital in the village of Washington as early as August 1865. Parsons, an attorney, does not appear in the public record until the spring of 1867. Jacobs, as we know from the prior chapter, came to Natchez after the war in October 1866. Col. Samuel Thomas to Gen. O. O. Howard, 15 August 1865, Comr., Letters Received, roll 18, BRFAL; *Natchez Democrat*, 8 April 1867.

46. *Natchez Weekly Courier*, 2 November 1867.

47. *Natchez Weekly Courier*, 12 October 1867; *Natchez Democrat*, 9 September 1867.

48. *Natchez Weekly Courier*, 2 November 1867; *Natchez Democrat*, 2 September 1869; U.S. Bureau of Census, *Eighth Census: Slave Schedules, 1860* (Adams County, Mississippi); *Natchez Democrat*, July 8, 1867; U.S. Bureau of Census, *Ninth Census of the United States: Population, 1870* (Adams County, Mississippi); Lynch, *Reminiscences of an Active Life*, 39–40; BPDB. In 1860 Chotard owned 195 slaves in Adams County, Concordia Parish, and Issaquena County.

49. *Natchez Weekly Courier*, 16 November 1867; *Natchez Democrat*, 18 November 1867; Harris, *Day of the Carpetbagger*, 109. At least 2,840 freedmen voted in the election, while only 22 to 32 whites bothered to cast a ballot. The election returns from the two newspapers differ. Seventy-one percent of registered freedmen voted.

50. On election results, see Summary of Elections for Candidates to the State Convention, 1867, E. 403, Department of Arkansas and the 7th Army Corps and the 4th Military District, 1862–1870, Office of Civil Affairs, part I, RG 393.

51. Patrick H. Thompson, *The History of Negro Baptists in Mississippi* (Jackson, Miss.:

R. W. Bailey Printing Co., 1898), 51; *Natchez Weekly Courier*, 21 September 1867; BPDB. Another explanation for Cessor's abstention from the ticket can be found in the *Natchez Democrat*, 23 September 1867: "Jim Cessor, colored, known here as Jim Saucer, was voted out of the Convention on the ground that he was not a true republican."

52. Geo. Haller to Post of Woodville, 17 November 1867, in M. M. Phares to Gen. Gillem, 18 November 1867, Miss. Asst. Comr., Letters Received, roll 22, BRFAL; M. M. Phares to Gen. Gillem, 18 November 1867, Miss. Asst. Comr., Letters Received, roll 22, BRFAL. In the same file, see also H. S. Van Eaton to Gillem, 17 November 1867. From 1820 to 1870, black people substantially outnumbered white people in each of the counties and parishes in the Natchez District. Collectively, the black population as a share of the total varied from 60 percent in 1820 to 82 percent in 1860. In 1870, 80 percent of the population was black. I quantified the percentages of slaves (and blacks) using the Historical Census Browser.

53. H. S. Van Eaton to General Gillem, 24 November 1867, Miss. Asst. Comr., Letters Received, roll 22, BRFAL; York Woodward to M. Barber, 31 December 1867, Miss. Asst. Comr., Letters Received, roll 22, BRFAL. On Hoard's biographical information, see U.S. Bureau of Census, *Ninth Census: Population, 1870*. On Van Eaton's political affiliation, see *Woodville Republican*, 13 November 1869.

54. Capt. James Biddle to Lt. Merritt Barber, 15 November 1867, Miss. Asst. Comr., Reports, roll 30, BRFAL (emphasis in original); J. S. Morris to Gen. Gillem, 16 November 1867, in E. H. Hicks and Thos. Reed, Solicitors, 19 November 1867, Miss. Asst. Comr., Letters Received, roll 21, BRFAL; Biddle to Barber, 9 December 1867, Miss. Asst. Comr., Reports, roll 31, BRFAL.

55. Col. S. M. Preston to Gen. J. F. Farnsworth, 18 January 1866, and S. Manly Preston to L. Thomas, 9 October 1865, Comr., Letters Received, roll 23, BRFAL; S. Manly Preston to L. Thomas, 9 October 1865, Comr., Letters Received, roll 23, BRFAL. Gen. Lorenzo Thomas forwarded Preston's letter to Gen. O. O. Howard, who gave it a "favorable endorsement" and then sent it to Col. Samuel Thomas, assistant commissioner for Mississippi. Col. S. M. Preston to Gen. J. F. Farnsworth, 18 January 1866, Comr., Letters Received, roll 23, BRFAL. By 20 May 1866 every black regiment in Mississippi was mustered out. James Wilford Garner, *Reconstruction in Mississippi* (1901; repr., Baton Rouge: Louisiana State University Press, 1968), 107. On the lack of credit in the postemancipation South, see Gerald David Jaynes, *Branches without Roots: Genesis of the Black Working Class in the American South, 1862–1882* (New York: Oxford University Press, 1986), 30–48. On land associations and black colonies in the postemancipation South, see Edward Magdol, *A Right to the Land: Essays on the Freedmen's Community* (Westport, Conn.: Greenwood Press, 1977), 174–199; Jaynes, 288–295; Hahn, *A Nation Under Our Feet*, 141–42, 167.

56. George Hitchen to Maj. Gen. O. O. Howard, 4 January 1868, Comr., Letters Received, roll 53, BRFAL; Constitution of the Jacobs, Williams, Wood and Co's Land Association, in Gen. F. D. Sewall to O. O. Howard, 29 January 1868, Comr., Letters Received, roll 55, BRFAL; George Hitchen to Hon. Charles Sumner, 14 January 1868, Comr., Letters Received, roll 53, BRFAL; Magdol, *A Right to the Land*, 193–94. Magdol sampled forty of the male subscribers, comparing their names with regimental rosters, Freedmen's Bureau marriage records, and military pension records. He determined that the typical ex-soldier was married and had three children. "G. D. Allen" collected the subscriptions, either in cash or bounty, and gave them to George Hitchen to deposit in a Natchez bank. In Sewall's report, he used the wrong initial for Allen's first name. A prominent

white attorney, Lewis D. Allen allied himself with Republicans in Natchez. By the beginning of 1868, they had amassed $30,000 to $40,000. For more on black soldiers and military bounties, see the Freedmen's Bureau policy on "bounties of colored soldiers," undated, Comr., Unregistered Letters, roll 74, BRFAL; Ira Berlin, Joseph P. Reidy, and Leslie S. Rowland, eds., *The Black Military Experience*, ser. 2 of *Freedom: A Documentary History of Emancipation, 1861–1867*, (Cambridge: Cambridge University Press, 1982), 766; Claude F. Oubre, *Forty Acres and a Mule: The Freedmen's Bureau and Black Land Ownership* (Baton Rouge: Louisiana State University Press, 1978), 164; Donald R. Shaffer, *After the Glory: The Struggles of Black Civil War Veterans* (Lawrence: University Press of Kansas, 2004), 42, 120.

57. Sumner to Howard, 30 January 1868, Comr., Letters Received, roll 55, BRFAL. Four men were listed as residing "on Place." Of the others, the vast majority came from Adams County, but four resided in Jefferson County, and another member may have lived on Greenwood plantation in Claiborne County.

58. "Constitution of the Jacobs, Williams, Wood and Co's Land Association," in Gen. F. D. Sewall to O. O. Howard, 29 January 1868, Comr., Letters Received, roll 55, BRFAL; Hitchen to Sumner, 14 January 1868, Comr., Letters Received, roll 53, BRFAL; A. K. Farrar to Col. James Biddle, 10 February 1868, Comr., Letters Received, roll 54, BRFAL.

59. Thompson, *History of Negro Baptists in Mississippi*, 42; BPDB; Geo. Hitchen to Major Gen Howard, 30 June 1865, Comr., Letters Received, roll 15, BRFAL; F. D. Sewall to Gen. O. O. Howard, 29 January 1868, Comr., Letters Received, roll 55, BRFAL; George Hitchen to Maj. Gen. O. O. Howard, 4 January 1868, Comr., Letters Received, roll 53, BRFAL; Palmer Litts to Geo. Whipple, 22 November 1865, #71,845, American Missionary Association Papers, Mississippi, roll 1, Amistad Research Center, New Orleans; H. R. Pease to Maj. Gen. Gillem, 19 February 1868, in "Endorsements made on letter of Geo. Hitchen," Comr., Letters Received, roll 53, BRFAL; George Hitchen to O. O. Howard, 24 November 1867, Miss. Asst. Comr., Letters Received, roll 22, BRFAL; George Hitchen to Charles Sumner, 20 March 1869, Papers of Charles Sumner, Series I: Letters to Charles Sumner, roll 45, Houghton Library, Harvard University, Cambridge, Mass. The most prominent Wood in Natchez was Robert H. Wood, who became the mayor of Natchez—the only black mayor in Reconstruction Mississippi. Yet there is no direct evidence linking Wood to this land company. Moreover, Wood directly opposed Jacobs in the 1867 election as a candidate on the bolting ticket, making it unlikely that these political opponents would collaborate in such a venture. Lynch, *Reminiscences of an Active Life*, 102–3; Vernon Lane Wharton, *The Negro in Mississippi, 1865–1890* (Chapel Hill: University of North Carolina Press, 1947; repr., New York: Harper & Row, 1965), 167; Sewell and Dwight, *Mississippi Black History Makers* (Jackson: University Press of Mississippi, 1977), 58–59. The general superintendent for the state of Mississippi may have exaggerated a bit when he said that Jacobs had "no education," yet the Baptist minister apparently had no more than a rudimentary education. H. R. Pease to Bvt. Maj. Gen. A. C. Gillem, 19 February 1868, in "Endorsements made on letter of Geo. Hitchen," Comr., Letters Received, roll 53, BRFAL.

60. Hitchen to Sumner, 23 January 1868, in Sumner to Howard, 30 January 1868, Comr., Letters Received, roll 55, BRFAL; George Hitchen to Maj. Gen. O. O. Howard, 4 January 1868, Comr., Letters Received, roll 53, BRFAL; Hitchen to Sumner, 31 January 1868, Comr., Letters Received, roll 55, BRFAL; Farrar to Biddle, 10 February 1868, in Gillem to Howard, Comr., Letters Received, roll 54, BRFAL.

61. George Hitchen to Maj. Gen. O. O. Howard, 4 January 1868, Comr., Letters Received, roll 53, BRFAL; Farrar to Biddle, 10 February 1868, Comr., Letters Received, roll 54,

BRFAL; Hitchen to Sumner, 31 January 1868, in Sumner to Howard, 10 February 1868, Comr., Letters Received, roll 55, BRFAL; Michael Wayne, *The Reshaping of Plantation Society: The Natchez District, 1860–1880* (Baton Rouge: Louisiana State University Press, 1983), 138; Hitchen to Sumner, 23 January 1868, Comr., Letters Received, roll 53, BRFAL. Article 50f the company's constitution stated, "Any member can withdraw from the Company, by paying 25 per cent of his subscription, if done before the first instalment [*sic*] is paid over, afterward, and until the total is paid, ten (10) per cent. But after the whole is paid for, and he had a deed for the same, he may then dispose of it in any other way in which all such property is disposed under the same laws, and wages." Thus each subscriber was promised a deed and title to his portion of the land. "Constitution of the Jacobs, Williams, Wood and Co's Land Association," in Gen. F. D. Sewall to O. O. Howard, 29 January 1868, Comr., Letters Received, roll 55, BRFAL. The planter described the portion of the land along the river as "second bottom, or table land, and considerable of it very fine bottom. . . . It is well watered, and finely timbered." According to historian William Ashley Vaughan, Farrar had the "largest and most valuable" cotton plantation in Adams County, worth $110,000, with $3,000 worth of machinery and farm implements, producing seven hundred bales of cotton on average annually. Vaughan, "Natchez during the Civil War" (Ph.D. diss., University of Southern Mississippi, 2001), 83. According to F. D. Sewall's investigation for the Freedmen's Bureau, tracts of land of one to fifty acres were going for between five and ten dollars an acre, depending on the quality of land and location. He found a nine-hundred-acre plantation selling for $9,000; however, it remains uncertain whether the owners of these tracts of land would be willing to sell to a freedman or a freedmen's land company. By contrast, Jacobs, Williams, and Wood agreed to pay Farrar thirteen dollars an acre for the land along the Homochitto River. F. D. Sewall to Howard, 29 February 1868, Comr., Letters Received, roll 55, BRFAL; Farrar to Biddle, 10 February 1868, Comr., Letters Received, roll 54, BRFAL. Most of the public land in Mississippi was either heavily wooded or swampland. In Louisiana the neglected levee system threatened most public lands with flooding. For more on southern public lands, see Oubre, *Forty Acres and a Mule*, 98, 110–12; Michael L. Lanza, "'One of the Most Appreciated Labors of the Bureau': The Freedmen's Bureau and the Southern Homestead Act," in *The Freedmen's Bureau and Reconstruction: Reconsiderations*, ed. Paul A. Cimbala and Randall M. Miller (New York: Fordham University Press, 1999), 67–92.

62. George Hitchen to Maj. Gen. O. O. Howard, 4 January 1868, Comr., Letters Received, roll 53, BRFAL; testimony of George Braxton, Thomas Turner claim, case 4330, Adams County, Mississippi case files, Settled Case Files for Claims Approved by the Southern Claims Commission, Ser. 732, Southern Claims Commission, Records of the Office of the Third Auditor, Records of the Accounting Officers of the Department of Treasury, Record Group 217, National Archives, Washington, D.C. (cited hereafter as RG 217); Deborah Smith claim, case 14,868, Adams County, Report 3, Office 647, microfiche 728, Disallowed Claims, Southern Claims Commission, Records of the U.S. House of Representatives, Record Group 233, National Archives, Washington, D.C. (cited hereafter as RG 233); John Smith claim, case 10,801, RG 217; Hitchen to Howard, 31 January 1868, Comr., Letters Received, roll 55, BRFAL. For more on the Whitney option, see Hitchen to Sumner, 31 January 1868, in Sumner to Howard, 10 February 1868, Comr., Letters Received, roll 55, BRFAL. For the subscriber list, see Sumner to Howard, 30 January 1868, Comr., Letters Received, roll 55, BRFAL.

63. Farrar to Biddle, 10 February 1868, Comr., Letters Received, roll 54, BRFAL. For more on Farrar, see Wayne, *The Reshaping of Plantation Society*, 35; Michael Wayne,

Death of an Overseer: Reopening a Murder Investigation from the Plantation South (New York: Oxford University Press, 2001), 129–30; Scarborough, *Masters of the Big House*, 142.

64. Farrar to Biddle, 19 February 1868, Comr., Letters Received, roll 54, BRFAL; A. K. Farrar, Mississippi, Case Files of Applications from Former Confederates for Presidential Pardons (Amnesty Papers), 1865–1867, M1003, Records of the Adjutant General's Office, Record Group 94, National Archives, Washington, D.C. See also Confederate Amnesty Papers, Fold3, http://www.fold3.com/title_59/confederate-amnesty-papers/; Hitchen to Sumner, 24 January 1868, Comr., Letters Received, roll 55, BRFAL; George Hitchen to Maj. Gen. O. O. Howard, 4 January 1868, Comr., Letters Received, roll 53, BRFAL. Farrar described "great opposition . . . against me" in Farrar to Biddle, 10 February 1868, Comr., Letters Received, roll 54, BRFAL.

65. Hitchen to Sumner, 23 January 1868, in Sumner to Howard, 30 January 1868, Comr., Letters Received, roll 55, BRFAL; Farrar to Biddle, 19 February 1868, Comr., Letters Received, roll 54, BRFAL; Hitchen to Howard, 14 January 1868, Comr., Letters Received, roll 53, BRFAL.

66. Subscription List in Sumner to Howard, 30 January 1868, Comr., Letters Received, roll 55, BRFAL; Hitchen to Howard, 4 January 1868, Comr., Letters Received, roll 53, BRFAL; Farrar to Biddle, 19 February 1868, Comr., Letters Received, roll 54, BRFAL; Sen. Charles Sumner to Maj. Gen. O. O. Howard, 22 January 1868, Comr., Letters Received, roll 53, BRFAL; Hitchen to Howard, 31 January 1868, Comr., Letters Received, roll 55, BRFAL. In a note to Howard, Sumner wrote, "I enclose another letter from Natchez about the Farrar farm, to which I beg leave to to [*sic*] call your attention. The appeal is most earnest and touching and I trust that something may be speedily done to relieve this distress. I hope too that the seeds which [George Hitchen] desires can be furnished." Sumner to Howard, 30 January 1868, Comr., Letters Received, roll 55, BRFAL.

67. Sewall to Howard, 29 January 1868, Comr., Letters Received, roll 55, BRFAL; Endorsement: H. R. Pease to Bvt. Maj. Gen. A. C. Gillem, 19 February 1868, Comr., Letters Received, roll 53, BRFAL. In his letters to Sumner, Hitchen pleaded for government rations to tide the colony over during the first year. Hitchen to Sumner, 14 January 1868, Comr., Letters Received, roll 53, BRFAL; Hitchen to Sumner, 23 January 1868, Comr., Letters Received, roll 55, BRFAL. The pamphlet, *Homes for the Homeless: What the Republican Party Has Done for the Poor Man*, was printed by the Union Republican Congressional Committee and may have been the one that Jacobs passed around. See *Homes for the Homeless* (Washington, D.C., 1867) in the John Sherman Pamphlet Collection at the Rutherford B. Hayes Presidential Center, Fremont, Ohio. The charges against Hitchen were first raised a few months earlier when he asked the Freedmen's Bureau for a school building. See Hitchen to Howard, 24 November 1867, Miss. Asst. Comr., roll 22, BRFAL. One year earlier, freedpeople from South Carolina attempted to establish a black colony in Florida, but the venture fell to pieces when they learned that the land they had paid for was technically unavailable for homesteading. Not only did the freedpeople lose their investment, but they were left destitute hundreds of miles from home. Lanza, "One of the Most Appreciated Labors," 81–82.

68. Farrar to Biddle, 19 February 1868, Comr., Letters Received, roll 54, BRFAL; Jaynes, *Branches without Roots*, 292.

69. Darden diary, December 30, 1867, Darden Family Papers, MDAH; W. H. Eldridge to Lt. Merritt Barber, 31 January 1868, Miss. Asst. Comr., Reports, roll 32, BRFAL; W. H. Eldridge to Lt. Merritt Barber, 24 February 1868, Miss. Asst. Comr., Reports, roll 32, BRFAL.

70. In Louisiana, state officials were elected on the April ballot.

71. Tri-Monthly Report, Christian Rush, 8 May 1868, La. Asst. Comr., Letters Received, roll 6, BRFAL; Taylor, *Louisiana Reconstructed*, 158–60.

72. *Natchez Democrat*, 11 June, 16 June 1868; E. J. Castello to A. Mygatt, 3 June 1868, Miss. Asst. Comr., Letters Received, roll 23, BRFAL.

73. *Natchez Democrat*, 29 April 1867; U.S. Bureau of Census, *Ninth Census: Population, 1870*; BPDB. For another example of an early biracial Democratic meeting, see *Natchez Democrat*, 22 April 1867.

74. *Natchez Democrat*, 23 July 1866, 14 October, 30 December 1867, 21 May 1868.

75. Testimony of Joshua A. Morris, in *Late Insurrectionary States*, vol. 11, p. 308.

76. George Haller, Record of Complaints in the Month of June 1868, Miss. Asst. Comr., Reports, roll 33, BRFAL; George Haller, Narrative Report, August 1867, Miss. Asst. Comr., Reports, roll 30, BRFAL; Narrative Report, [?] to Lt. J. F. Conyingham, August 1867, Miss. Asst. Comr., Reports, roll 30, BRFAL; George Haller to Bvt. Major S. C. Greene, 20 June 1868, Miss. Asst. Comr., Letters Received, roll 23, BRFAL; George Haller, Record of Complaints in the Month of June 1868, Miss. Asst. Comr., Reports, roll 33, BRFAL; P. P. Bergevin, Report of Operations for June 1868, 30 June 1868, Miss. Asst. Comr., Reports, roll 32, BRFAL; E. J. Castello to A. Mygatt, 3 June 1868, Miss. Asst. Comr., Letters Received, roll 23, BRFAL. For more on complaints in Wilkinson County, see P. P. Bergevin, Report of Operations and Complaints from July 1868, 31 July 1868, Miss. Asst. Comr., Reports, roll 33, BRFAL. In the 1870 census there are two Samuel Andersons listed. Both are listed as farm laborers. But the one living near Woodville was forty-five, married, and had five children. Another Samuel Anderson lived near Fort Adams, was thirty-one years old, married, and had a seven-year-old daughter and $200 worth of personal property.

77. *Natchez Democrat*, 25 June, 12 September 1868. On Democratic appeals to conservative blacks, see Leon F. Litwack, *Been in the Storm So Long: The Aftermath of Slavery* (New York: Vintage Books, 1979), 555.

78. State vs. Thomas Burke, box 14–67, October term 1868, Adams County Circuit Court Case Files, HNF; *Natchez Democrat*, 21 March 1869. Young was charged with stealing in 1869, and in a report on this accusation the *Democrat* reminded its readers that he was the one who spoke in Cotton Square every day the year before on the "beauties of Radicalism." On Young's work on a Concordia Parish cotton plantation, see Tri-Monthly Report, Dunford, 10 August 1867, La. Asst. Comr., roll 14, BRFAL.

79. *Natchez Democrat*, 25 June 1868.

80. *Natchez Democrat*, 23 June, 7 July, 18 July, 7 September, 12 September 1868; Burrel Foley claim, case 9407, Adams County, Report 2, Office 386, microfiche 234, RG 233. For more on Israel Jones, see *Natchez Democrat*, 16 July 1868; Amanda Jones claim, case 19,850, Adams County, Report 7, Office 439, microfiche 2459, RG 233. Very little is known about Anderson Webb, the second vice president. Willis Douglass, the club's secretary, was a sixty-three-year-old laborer who could not read or write.

81. *Natchez Democrat*, 18 July, 25 January 1868.

82. T. P. Sears to General Alvin C. Gillem, 23 November 1867, enclosed in the correspondence from James Biddle to Gillem, 18 December 1867, Miss. Asst. Comr., Letters Received, roll 27, BRFAL.

83. Bvt. Col. N. A. M. Dudley to A. Alderson, 12 June 1868, Entry 66, pp. 205–6, Department of Mississippi, pt. II, E. 2232, Letters Sent, vol. 49, RG 393; Beaumont, *A Business Woman's Journal*, 300; George Haller to S. C. Greene, 20 June 1868, Miss. Asst. Comr., Letters Received, roll 23, BRFAL (my emphasis). See also Darden diary, 19 June 1868, Darden Family Papers, MDAH.

84. *Natchez Democrat*, 10 June 1867, 4 June 1868; E. J. Castello to A. Mygatt, 3 June 1868, Miss. Asst. Comr., Letters Received, roll 23, BRFAL; George Haller to S. C. Greene, 20 June 1868, Miss. Asst. Comr., Letters Received, roll 23, BRFAL; P. P. Bergevin, Report of operations for June 1868, 30 June 1868, Miss. Asst. Comr., Reports, roll 32, BRFAL; *Natchez Democrat*, 5 August 1867. For a similar mass meeting that women and children attended, see *Woodville Republican*, 27 November 1869.

85. *Journal of the Proceedings of the Constitutional Convention of the State of Mississippi, 1868* (Jackson, Miss.: E. Stafford, 1871), 732–33; Harris, *Day of the Carpetbagger*, 144–48.

86. Harris, *Day of the Carpetbagger*, 194–96; Beaumont, *A Business Woman's Journal*, 301–2; *Natchez Democrat*, 14 May 1868. For a persuasive argument that fraud was the likely cause of the constitution's defeat, see Lawrence N. Powell, "Correcting for Fraud: A Quantitative Reassessment of the Mississippi Ratification Election of 1868," *Journal of Southern History* 55 (November 1989): 633–58. Some blacks objected to any restrictions of suffrage rights and voted against the constitution. On black objections to the disfranchising clause, see Lynch, *Reminiscences of an Active Life*, 50–51. For more on planter opposition to Klan violence, see Michael W. Fitzgerald, "Extralegal Violence and the Planter Class: The Ku Klux Klan in the Alabama Black Belt during Reconstruction" in *Local Matters: Race, Crime, and Justice in the Nineteenth-Century South*, ed. Christopher Waldrep and Donald G. Nieman (Athens: University of Georgia Press, 2001), 155–71.

87. Darden diary, 13 July 1867, Darden Family Papers, MDAH; *Natchez Democrat*, 2 December 1867.

88. *New York Times*, 16 July 1868; *Natchez Democrat*, 11 July, 18 July 1868; Subscription List in Sumner to Howard, 30 January 1868, Comr., Letters Received, roll 55, BRFAL; *Natchez Democrat*, 16 July, 18 July 1868. For evidence that many publicly identified black Democrats voted the Republican ticket, see *New York Times*, 7 July 1868. For election results, see *Natchez Democrat*, 7 July 1868. Adams County returned a Republican majority of 2,104; Claiborne County, 1,046; Jefferson County, 1,021; and Wilkinson County, 1,556. Jones's widow, Amanda, filed a claim with the SCC that was disallowed. Of the six witnesses (all black) who testified on Amanda's behalf, three had at least nominal connections to the Republican Party (S. S. Meekins, George W. Carter, and Lewis Thompson), one (Richard Sullivan) sided with an anti-Republican Party (the Conservative Reform Party), and the remaining two witnesses (Richard Dorsey and James K. Hyman) had no public connection to any partisan organization. This witness list suggests that Israel Jones had wide respect in Natchez and that his political views in 1868 did not poison his friendships with black Republicans in the early 1870s. See Amanda Jones claim, case 19,850, Adams County, Report 7, Office 439, microfiche 2459, RG 233.

89. *Natchez Democrat*, 30 June, 7 July, 18 July, 21 July 1868.

90. George Haller discounted this reason in Haller, Report for the Month of July 1868, Miss. Asst. Comr., Reports, roll 33, BRFAL.

91. *Natchez Democrat*, 21 July, 28 July, 1 August, and 12 October 1868; George Haller, Report for the Month of July 1868, Miss. Asst. Comr., Reports, roll 33, BRFAL; N. A. M. Dudley to Saml. C. Greene, 22 July 1868, Dist. of Natchez, Letters Sent, E. 125, pp. 234–35, RG 393; N. A. M. Dudley to John Tyler, 26 December 1868, Dist. of Natchez, Letters Sent, E. 310, pp. 334–35, RG 393. Hewett was a leading organizer of the Constitutional Union Party in Adams County in 1867, a forerunner of the local Democratic Party in 1868, and later he gave speeches to the Colored Democratic Club during the 1872 presidential campaign. *Natchez Democrat*, 30 December 1867, 28 August 1872. Hewett was convicted of

"conspiracy to assault with the intent to outrage and injure" (*Natchez Democrat*, 12 October 1868) and sentenced to a year in the state penitentiary, but he escaped custody before he could be sentenced. He then attempted to murder George C. McKee, a Republican candidate for Congress from northern Mississippi. On this latter charge, see Dudley to Maj. John Tyler, 26 December 1868, E. 310, pp. 334–35, and Dudley to Gov. Warmouth, 7 January 1869, District of Natchez, ser. 2232, Letters Sent, E. 331, pp. 344–45, RG 393; "Reward," in "Documentary Evidence," in U.S. House, *Condition of Affairs in Mississippi*, 267. Cotton was arrested for his involvement in the attack; see *Natchez Democrat*, 23 July 1868; Maj. N. A. M. Dudley to AAA Gen. Saml. C. Greene, 30 July 1868, Dist. of Natchez, Letters Sent, E. 131, pp. 238–39, RG 393. On Cotton's political affiliation, see *Natchez Democrat*, 7 July 1868, 2 September, 16 September 1869. Stewart was still teaching at a rural colored school as late as 1875. Register of Teacher and Teacher Pay Certificates, Adams County, 1873–1890, HNF.

92. A. K. Long to Saml. C. Greene, Report of operations for the month of August 1868, Miss. Asst. Comr., Reports, roll 33, BRFAL; P. P. Bergevin, Report of operations and complaints for month of September 1868, 30 September 1868, Miss. Asst. Comr., Reports, roll 33, BRFAL; Maj. Gen. Edward Hatch to Maj. Gen. O. O. Howard, Monthly Report, October 1868, La. Asst. Comr., Reports of Operations, roll 27, BRFAL; U.S. House, *Use of the Army in Certain Southern States*, 44th Cong., 2nd sess., 1877, H. Exec. Doc. 30, pp. 220–21; Henry Brown Richardson to Parents, 30 November 1868, Henry Richardson Brown and Family Papers, LSU.

93. Harris, *Day of the Carpetbagger*, 206–15, 257; Foner, *Reconstruction*, 340–45. In Concordia, 1,554 votes were cast for Grant, but only 201 for Seymour. In Tensas, 1,018 went for Grant and just 383 for Seymour. Papers in the Case of Sypher vs. St. Martin, 41st Cong., 1st Sess., 1869, H. Misc. Doc. 13, pt. 2, p. 24. On the 1868 presidential election in Louisiana, see *Report of the Joint Committee of the General Assembly of Louisiana on the Conduct of the Late Elections and the Condition of Peace and Order in the State, Session of 1869* (New Orleans: A. L. Lee, 1869); Taylor, *Louisiana Reconstructed*, 161–73.

94. *The Party of Freedom and Its Candidates: The Duty of the Colored Voter* (Washington, D.C., 1868), John Sherman Pamphlet Collection, Rutherford B. Hayes Presidential Center, Fremont, Ohio.

95. *New-Orleans Times*, quoted in the *New York Times*, 3 January 1869. See also *Report of the Commissioner of Agriculture for the Year 1868* (Washington, D.C.: Government Printing Office, 1869), 22–24; William C. Harris, *Presidential Reconstruction in Mississippi* (Baton Rouge: Louisiana State University Press, 1967), 181–82.

Chapter Four. "A New Machinery of Government"

1. *Natchez Democrat*, 26 June 1872; U.S. Bureau of Census, *Eighth Census of the United States: Population, 1860*; U.S. Bureau of Census, *Ninth Census of the United States: Population, 1870*.

2. *Natchez Democrat*, 26 June 1872.

3. For more on the inattention to the policy making of black politicians, see August Meier, "Afterword: New Perspectives on the Nature of Black Political Leadership during Reconstruction," in *Southern Black Leaders of the Reconstruction Era*, ed. Howard N. Rabinowitz (Urbana: University of Illinois Press, 1982), 393–406. On the failure of Republican officeholders, see Howard N. Rabinowitz, *Race Relations in the Urban South, 1865–1890* (New York: Oxford University Press, 1978); Meier, "Afterword," 402; Michael

Perman, *Pursuit of Unity: A Political History of the American South* (Chapel Hill: University of North Carolina Press, 2009), 128–29. Thomas C. Holt, for example, takes black legislators to task for failing to address the material circumstances of the black working class. Holt, *Black over White: Negro Political Leadership in South Carolina during Reconstruction* (Urbana: University of Illinois Press, 1977), 152–53. For close studies of policies at the local level, see Eric Anderson, "James O'Hara of North Carolina: Black Leadership and Local Government," in Rabinowitz, *Southern Black Leaders*, 101–25; Peter Rachleff, *Black Labor in the South: Richmond, Virginia, 1865–1890* (Philadelphia: Temple University Press, 1984); Christopher Waldrep, *Roots of Disorder: Race and Criminal Justice in the American South, 1817–80* (Urbana: University of Illinois Press, 1998); Kate Masur, *An Example for All the Land: Emancipation and the Struggle over Equality in Washington, D.C.* (Chapel Hill: University of North Carolina Press, 2010).

4. *Natchez Democrat*, 19 April 1871.

5. Quoted in "Affairs in Mississippi," *New National Era*, 20 November 1873.

6. The delegates from Claiborne County were a radical and a moderate, respectively: Matthew T. Newsom (an AME minister born in North Carolina) and Edward H. Stiles (a white Mississippian and former Whig). From Jefferson County, two radicals were elected: Abel Alderson and Orange S. Miles (a white Ohioan and farmer). From Adams County, three radicals were elected: Henry P. Jacobs, E. J. Castello, and Fred Parsons (an ex-Union colonel and lawyer who emigrated from England). From Wilkinson County, two radicals were elected: W. H. Gibbs and Charles W. Fitzhugh (a freeborn Mississippian and AME minister). For more on these delegates, see Richard L. Hume and Jerry B. Gough, *Blacks, Carpetbaggers, and Scalawags: The Constitutional Conventions of Radical Reconstruction* (Baton Rouge: Louisiana State University Press, 2008), appendix C, 308–406.

7. From Tensas Parish, two white conservative northerners were elected: Hiram Steele (a planter who was born in Canada but later served as a Union army captain) and Abram Gould (a planter and an ex-Union captain from Connecticut). From Concordia Parish, two white radical northerners were elected: John Harris (a New Yorker who moved to Louisiana to run a plantation) and James Landers (a planter and an ex-Union captain from New Hampshire). On these delegates, see Hume and Gough, *Blacks, Carpetbaggers, and Scalawags*, appendix C, 308–406.

8. *Journal of the Proceedings in the Constitutional Convention of the State of Mississippi, 1868* (Jackson, Miss.: E. Stafford, Printer, 1871), 63–64 (cited hereafter as *Journal of the Mississippi Constitutional Convention*); for other loyalty tests that Castello put forward, see pp. 40, 49. On black activists, see *Christian Recorder*, 1 July 1865.

9. *Journal of the Mississippi Constitutional Convention*, 544; *Constitution Adopted by the State Constitutional Convention of the State of Louisiana, March 7, 1868* (New Orleans, 1868), art. 100 (hereafter cited as Constitution of Louisiana, 1868). Former Confederates in Louisiana also had to admit that "the late rebellion" was "morally and politically wrong." For Mississippi's franchise provisions, see article VII of the 1868 Constitution, or *Journal of the Mississippi Constitutional Convention*, 732–33.

10. For the suffrage provisions, see *Journal of the Mississippi Constitutional Convention*, 266, 347, 720–21; Hume and Gough, *Blacks, Carpetbaggers, and Scalawags*, 86. On Gibbs's motion, see *Journal of the Mississippi Constitutional Convention*, 183; for the ordinance, see p. 352. The punishment for violating this ordinance was the invalidation of the contract, a fine, and disfranchisement for five years.

11. On Alderson's plan, see *Journal of the Mississippi Constitutional Convention*, 85–86,

223–24. The military governor rejected Alderson's proposal. This was not, however, Alderson's only interest in poor relief. He suggested that the delegates petition Congress for assistance in helping "the impoverished and almost destitute people of the State" (16, 30). For Jacobs's provision, see pp. 68, 83, 721; on poll taxes, see pp. 51, 52. The convention later allowed the state legislature to issue a poll tax for the public school fund (324, 363). On the public works, see p. 735. For more on breaking up plantation lands, see p. 739. For Louisiana, see Constitution of Louisiana, 1868, art. 132.

12. Constitution of Louisiana, 1868, art. 1, 2, 13. For previous Louisiana constitutions, see *The Federal and State Constitutions, Colonial Charters, and Other Organic Laws of the States, Territories, and Colonies Now or Heretofore Forming the United States of America*, ed. Francis Newton Thorpe (Washington, D.C.: Government Printing Office, 1909), 3:1380–448. For prior Mississippi constitutions, see Thorpe, *Federal and State Constitutions*, 4:2032–68. On the origin of public rights, see Rebecca J. Scott, "The Atlantic World and the Road to *Plessy v. Ferguson*," *Journal of American History* 94, no. 3 (December 2007): 726–33; Rebecca J. Scott, "Public Rights, Social Equality, and the Conceptual Roots of the *Plessy* Challenge," *Michigan Law Review* 106 (March 2008): 777–804.

13. On the composition of Mississippi delegates, see Hume and Gough, *Blacks, Carpetbaggers, and Scalawags*, 97, 185. On antiracist provisions, see Constitution of Mississippi, 1868, arts. 21, 24; *Journal of the Mississippi Constitutional Convention*, 47, 256. These measures closely divided the delegates and the Natchez District delegation in particular. Ibid., 255, 256; on Castello's amendment, see pp. 324–25. The Natchez District delegation was generally divided on the issue of race in the schools. Stiles consistently voted for segregation in schools (ibid., 316, 317–18, 324–25). For Louisiana's ban on separate schools, see Constitution of Louisiana, 1868, art. 135.

14. For more on the constitutions, see Vernon Lane Wharton, *The Negro in Mississippi, 1865–1890* (Chapel Hill: University of North Carolina Press, 1947; repr., New York: Harper & Row, 1965), 146–51; William C. Harris, *The Day of the Carpetbagger: Republican Reconstruction in Mississippi* (Baton Rouge: Louisiana State University Press, 1979), 132–59; Joe Gray Taylor, *Louisiana Reconstructed, 1863–1877* (Baton Rouge: Louisiana State University Press, 1974), 151–55.

15. On Mississippi's public education law, see *Journal of the House of Representatives of the State of Mississippi*, 1870 session, 352, 402, 447, 455, 463–65, 497, 521, 623, 625 (cited hereafter as *Mississippi House Journal*); *Jackson Weekly Clarion*, 7 April 1870; *Jackson Weekly Pilot*, 11 June 1870; Edward Mayes, *A History of Education in Mississippi*, U.S. Bureau of Education, Circular of Information 2 (Washington, D.C.: GPO, 1899), 282–83; Harris, *Day of the Carpetbagger*, 315–16. On Louisiana's law, see *The Revised Statute Laws of the State of Louisiana, from the Organization of the Territory to the Year 1869, Inclusive* (New Orleans, 1870), 241–63; Taylor, *Louisiana Reconstructed*, 461–65. On Adams County's schools, see *Mississippi House Journal*, 1872 session, 195. On Claiborne County's schools, see *Natchez Democrat*, 9 November 1870. On Jefferson County's schools, see *Mississippi House Journal*, 1872 session, 230–31. On the number of schools in the district, see Reports of County Superintendents, *Mississippi House Journal*, 1874 session, 850–51; Reports of County Superintendents, *Mississippi House Journal*, 1873 session, 803–6, 827, 854–56, 918–23; *North Louisiana Journal*, 21 June 1873; *Concordia Eagle*, 2 October 1875.

16. Wm. H. Lynch to James Lusk Alcorn, 1871, Governor Alcorn Papers, Series 786: Correspondence and Papers, Mississippi Department of Archives and History (MDAH), Jackson. On the Union Schoolhouse, see Reports of County Superintendents, *Mississippi House Journal*, 1872 session, appendix, 193–95.

17. John R. Lynch, *The Facts of Reconstruction* (New York: Neale Publishing, 1913; repr., New York: Arno Press and the New York Times, 1968), 34, 51–52, quote on 86. Natchez taxes were 12.5 mills in 1870; the following year they rose to 20 mills. In 1869 city debt totaled $14,203; it rose to $54,133 by 1871, at a time when annual revenues added up to just $61,000. *Natchez Democrat*, 7 October 1874. Adams County taxes in 1874 amounted to 40.25 mills. *Natchez Democrat*, 19 August 1874. A mill is a monetary unit equal to one-thousandth of a dollar. Thus, a twenty-mill rate is equal to a tax of twenty dollars on each thousand dollars in property value.

18. *Natchez Democrat*, 10 July, 24 July 1872; Edward King, *The Great South* (Hartford, Conn.: American Publishing Company, 1875), 293–95; *Natchez Democrat*, 14 December 1870.

19. *North Louisiana Journal*, 21 June 1873, 6 July 1872, 25 October 1873.

20. Harris, *Day of the Carpetbagger*, 333–34; *Mississippi House Journal*, 1873 session, 38–39, 1633; *Laws of the State of Mississippi, . . . 1874* (Jackson, Miss.: Pilot, 1874), 20–21, 121–22, 122–23; *Laws of the State of Mississippi, . . . 1875* (Jackson, Miss.: Pilot, 1875), 116–17, 155, 168–69; *Jackson Weekly Clarion*, 6 March 1873, 26 January 1876; *Natchez Democrat*, 13 November 1872; *Laws of the State of Mississippi, 1874*, 56–57; Kenneth R. Johnson, "Legrand Winfield Perce: A Mississippi Carpetbagger and the Fight for Federal Aid to Education," *Journal of Mississippi History* 34 (November 1972): 331–56; Reports of County Superintendents, *Mississippi House Journal*, 1873 session, 854–56; Reports of County Superintendents, *Mississippi House Journal*, 1874 session, 832–34. For attendance figures, see Reports of County Superintendents, *Mississippi House Journal*, 1873 session, 923.

21. Taylor, *Louisiana Reconstructed*, 463–64; Harris, *Day of the Carpetbagger*, 150; *New National Era*, 2 June, 16 June, 23 June, 30 June 1870; *Mississippi House Journal*, 1870 session, 500, 501–2.

22. *Natchez Democrat*, 2 October 1872, 13 November 1872, 28 August 1872. The teacher was Hannah G. Foley. She was married to Burrell Foley, a black Democrat. For more on the Foley family, see *Natchez Democrat*, 12 September 1868; Burrell Foley, died 8 May 1880, Wills, book 4, p. 175, Adams County Courthouse, Natchez, Miss.

23. W. W. Wade to Alcorn, 31 January 1871, Governor Alcorn Papers, MDAH; Reports of County Superintendents, *Mississippi House Journal*, 1872 session, appendix, 285–86. See also Reports of County Superintendents, *Mississippi House Journal*, 1873 session, 230–31. Echoing this sentiment, Edward King concluded, after a tour of the Natchez District in the mid-1870s, that "the people of Mississippi, like the people throughout the South, will not hear of mixed schools." See King, *The Great South*, 294.

24. *New National Era*, 7 March 1872, 20 March 1873, 25 January 1872, 6 June 1872 (emphasis in original). For more on Alcorn University, see Harris, *Day of the Carpetbagger*, 347–50.

25. *New National Era*, 4 April 1872, 2 May 1872. For more on Cardozo, see Eric Foner, ed., *Freedom's Lawmakers: A Directory of Black Officeholders during Reconstruction*, rev. ed. (Baton Rouge: Louisiana State University Press, 1996), 40.

26. Harris, *Day of the Carpetbagger*, 349–50; *New National Era*, 7 March 1872, 24 June 1873; M. Howard to Ames, 28 November 1873, folder 148, box 17, Ames Family Papers, Sophia Smith Collection, Smith College, Northampton, Mass.; Governor Adelbert Ames to Frank E. Harris, 4 August 1874; W. H. Furniss to Ames, 27 January 1875; J. F. Boulden to Ames, 20 February 1875; Dr. C. H. Thompson to Ames, 30 November 1875, Governor Ames Papers, Series 803: Correspondence and Papers, MDAH; Ames to M. Howard, 18 August 1874, Governor Ames Papers, Series 802: Letterbooks, MDAH; *Natchez*

Democrat, 17 January 1877; *Jackson Weekly Pilot*, 9 October 1875; *North Louisiana Journal*, 4 January 1874; John R. Lynch, *Reminiscences of an Active Life: The Autobiography of John Roy Lynch*, ed. by John Hope Franklin (Chicago: University of Chicago Press, 1970), 84–85. Representative H. P. Jacobs of Adams County tried to repeal the act that revoked the free scholarships. See *Jackson Weekly Clarion*, 12 January 1876. Alcorn University also reached well beyond the Natchez District for students. See, for example, Alcorn's advertisements in the *New National Era*, 14 May 1874, and in the *Weekly Louisianian*, 30 May, 11 June 1874.

27. *North Louisiana Journal*, 28 September 1872. See also *North Louisiana Journal*, 6 April 1872.

28. *Concordia Eagle*, 2 October 1875; *North Louisiana Journal*, 18 September 1872; *Natchez New South* quoted in the *Weekly Louisianian*, 4 May 1872; *Minneapolis Minnesotian* quoted in the *New National Era*, 7 March 1872. For a similar articulation of equality, see J. Ross Stewart's speech in the *Weekly Louisianian*, 2 November 1872.

29. *Revised Statute Laws of Louisiana* (1870), 93; Roger A. Fischer, *The Segregation Struggle in Louisiana, 1862–77* (Urbana: University of Illinois Press, 1974), 61–87; *Jackson Weekly Clarion*, 31 March, 26 May, 16 June, 30 June 1870; *Jackson Weekly Pilot*, 18 June 1870; *New National Era*, 1 September 1870; Harris, *Day of the Carpetbagger*, 438–46, quote on 446. See also *New National Era*, 4 April 1872, 20 February, 6 March, 22 May, 29 May 1873. The 1872 legislation failed because the bill was stolen in transit between the legislature and the governor's office. See *New National Era*, 25 April 1872. Louisiana also expanded civil rights protections in 1873. See Albert Voorhies, ed., *The Revised Statute Laws of the State of Louisiana* (New Orleans: B. Bloomfield, 1876), 128–29.

30. *Natchez Democrat*, 17 April 1872; Mayor and Aldermen Minutes, 8 April 1872, Natchez City Hall, Natchez, Miss.

31. Mrs. Martin to W. T. Martin, undated, William T. Martin Papers, Natchez Trace Collection, Center for American History, University of Texas at Austin. There is a hint that this confrontation may have taken place at the end of the 1872 school term. Hiram R. Revels referred to an incident, although he did not specify the city or the timing of the event, in a letter to Senator Ames: "[T]he colored members of the board of school directors were not allowed to attend the examination of a white school attended by the children of the most wealthy citizens." H. R. Revels to Ames, 13 November 1872, folder 133, box 15, Ames Family Papers, Smith College.

32. On Pollard and Meekins as school board members, see *Natchez Democrat*, 19 October 1870, 26 January 1873. For more on relational space, see David Harvey, *Cosmopolitanism and the Geographies of Freedom* (New York: Columbia University Press, 2009).

33. Fischer, *The Segregation Struggle in Louisiana*, 61–87; Harris, *Day of the Carpetbagger*, 442, 451–52; Rep. Lynch (Miss.) on Reconstruction and Democratic Rule in Mississippi, *Congressional Record* 4, pt. 6 (12 August 1876): 5540–43; King, *The Great South*, 294; *Natchez Democrat*, 20 February 1873, quoted in Harris, *Day of the Carpetbagger*, 450; Ted Tunnell, *Crucible of Reconstruction: War, Radicalism, and Race in Louisiana, 1862–1877* (Baton Rouge: Louisiana State University Press, 1992), 133–34. On antebellum marketplaces in Adams County, see Terry L. Alford, *Prince among Slaves: The True Story of an African Prince Sold into Slavery in the American South* (New York: Harcourt Brace Jovanovich, 1977; repr., New York: Oxford University Press, 1986), 68–69. Lynch elaborated on the relative racial tolerance in his autobiography: "[C]ordial, friendly, and amicable relations between all classes and parties and both races prevailed everywhere. Fraud, violence, and intimidation at elections were neither suspected nor charged by

anyone, for everyone knew that no occasion existed for such things." Speaking of the period before 1875, Lynch exaggerates the situation in Mississippi, but his comments were closer to reality when applied to the Natchez District. Lynch, *Facts of Reconstruction*, 147. For other instances, see Frederic Trautman, ed., *Travels on the Lower Mississippi, 1879–1880: A Memoir by Ernst von Hesse-Wartegg* (Columbia: University of Missouri Press, 1990), 77. For another example of the limits of state civil rights laws, see *New National Era*, 28 May 1874.

34. Rep. Lynch (Miss.), on H. R. 796, for Protecting All Citizens in Their Civil Rights, *Congressional Record* 3, pt. 2 (3 February 1875): 943–47; *New National Era*, 18 June 1874; Rep. Lynch (Miss.) on Reconstruction, *Congressional Record* 4, pt. 1 (10 February 1876): 1005–7.

35. Rep. Lynch (Miss.) on Reconstruction and Democratic Rule in Mississippi, *Congressional Record* 4, pt. 6 (12 August 1876): 5540–43; Rep. Lynch (Miss.) on the Southern Question, *Congressional Record* 4, pt. 4 (13 June 1876): 3781–84.

36. *New National Era*, 1 May 1873 (emphasis in original); Lynch, *Facts of Reconstruction*, 66.

37. *Natchez Democrat*, 21 April 1869, 7 October 1874, 6 December 1871. On the duties of constables, see *Revised Statute Laws of Louisiana* (1870), 124–26; *The Revised Code of the Statute Laws of the State of Mississippi* (Jackson, Miss.: Alcorn & Fisher, 1871), 71–72. Biographical information comes from numerous sources that I have compiled in a database, Justin Behrend, Black Politicians Database, SUNY-Geneseo, http://go.geneseo .edu/BlackPoliticiansDB (BPDB). Samuel W. Fitzhugh served as constable in Wilkinson County from 1870 to 1871. He then served one term in the state house of representatives before returning to the office of constable between 1878 and 1897. He was also a member of the free black Fitzhugh family from Natchez.

38. *Revised Code of Mississippi* (1871), 257–70; *Natchez Democrat*, June [1873], filed in the William N. Whitehurst Papers, MDAH; Lynch, *Reminiscences of an Active Life*, 60–61. On black justices of the peace, see BPDB. Local documentation (bond records and newspaper coverage) is lacking for Claiborne and Jefferson Counties, so there were probably many more black justices of the peace. I was able to identify nineteen justices of the peace from Concordia, ten from Tensas, fifteen from Adams, one from Claiborne, four from Jefferson, and ten from Wilkinson.

39. Lynch, *Reminiscences of an Active Life*, 60–62. Lynch did not name the "white man" who helped him; however, Martin's testimony at Lynch's suffrage contest in 1896 suggests a personal relationship, if not friendship, between the former slave and the former slaveholder. Martin swore that he had "known John R. Lynch for over forty years" and that after the war Lynch "frequently consulted me about his reading, as he was educating himself, [and] was a justice of the peace of Adams County for several years." On the "white man" in Lynch's autobiography, we know that he had "considerable experience" in legal matters, and there were few in Natchez who had as much legal experience as William T. Martin. In re John R. Lynch vs. Board of Commissioners of Election, 9 October 1896, drawer 432, no. 9, Adams County Circuit Court Case Files, Historic Natchez Foundation (HNF), Natchez, Miss.

40. Lynch, *Reminiscences of an Active Life*, 61–63; *Natchez Democrat*, 31 May 1869; *New National Era*, 1 May 1873.

41. *Natchez Democrat*, 7 December 1870, 18 October 1871. For more on how ordinary people shaped the law and its enforcement, see Laura F. Edwards, *The People and Their*

Peace: Legal Culture and the Transformation of Inequality in the Post-Revolutionary South (Chapel Hill: University of North Carolina Press, 2009).

42. *Natchez Democrat*, 30 November 1870. Thomas was bailed out by leading white Republicans and later was elected a delegate to two county Republican conventions. See *Natchez Democrat*, 7 December 1870, 28 August 1872, 13 August 1873. From the brief description of the incident at the Good Samaritans' meeting, Thomas could have claimed self-defense in the shooting. The outcome of Thomas's trial is unclear. If he did serve any time it was a short sentence; two years later he served as a delegate at the Adams County Republican convention.

43. J. M. P. Williams to Ames, 19 February 1873, folder 140, box 16, Ames Family Papers, Smith College; *Natchez Democrat*, 13 August 1873, 14 October 1874. On black participation in juries, see *Natchez Democrat*, 2 December 1867, 12 July 1869; Harris, *Day of the Carpetbagger*, 56. For one Democratic attorney's frustration with black juries, see William T. Martin to Lemuel Conner, 17 December 1872, Lemuel P. Conner and Family Papers, Louisiana and Lower Mississippi Valley Collections, Louisiana State University Libraries, Baton Rouge. On the Meridian Ku Klux Klan trials, see *Jackson Weekly Clarion*, 22 February 1872. Four of the twelve men on the jury came from the Natchez District: Jackson Minor (Adams), W. V. Howard (Adams), Hiram Littleton (Adams), and A. Poindexter (Claiborne). Howard was a member of the county board of education. Minor and Littleton were leaders in Natchez benevolent associations. I identified the Adams County grand jurors by cross-referencing their names with the 1870 census and my database of black political figures (BPDB). Three of the twenty were white men, and five others did not appear in the census or my database. U.S. Bureau of Census, *Ninth Census: Population, 1870*. For another black-majority jury pool, see State vs. Charles Thomas (cold), box 18–7, August term 1871, Adams County Circuit Court Case Files, HNF. In a close legal study of Warren County during Reconstruction, Christopher Waldrep found that "integrated juries convicted blacks at almost precisely the same rate as earlier all-white juries," and he found little evidence that black juries favored black defendants. Waldrep, *Roots of Disorder*, 129–45.

44. On the problem of the crop lien, see William C. Harris, *Presidential Reconstruction in Mississippi* (Baton Rouge: Louisiana State University Press, 1967), 173–74; Taylor, *Louisiana Reconstructed*, 402–6; Roger L. Ransom and Richard Sutch, *One Kind of Freedom: The Economic Consequences of Emancipation* (Cambridge: Cambridge University Press, 1977), 159–64; Harris, *Day of the Carpetbagger*, 482–85; Ronald L. F. Davis, *Good and Faithful Labor: From Slavery to Sharecropping in the Natchez District, 1860–1890* (Westport, Conn.: Greenwood Press, 1982), 121–51; Michael Wayne, *Reshaping the Plantation South: The Natchez District, 1860–1880* (Baton Rouge: Louisiana State University Press, 1982), 150–96; Gerald D. Jaynes, *Branches without Roots: Genesis of the Black Working Class in the American South, 1862–1882* (New York: Oxford University Press, 1986), 30–48; Harold D. Woodman, *New South, New Law: The Legal Foundations of Credit and Labor Relations in the Postbellum Agricultural South* (Baton Rouge: Louisiana State University Press, 1995); Aaron D. Anderson, *Builders of a New South: Merchants, Capital, and the Remaking of Natchez, 1865–1914* (Jackson: University of Mississippi Press, 2013), 71–111; René Hayden et al., eds., *Land and Labor, 1866–1867*, ser. 3, vol. 2 of *Freedom: A Documentary History of Emancipation, 1861–1867*(Chapel Hill: University of North Carolina Press, 2013), 643–61.

45. *Laws of the State of Mississippi, . . . 1872* (Jackson, Miss.: Kimball, Raymond & Co.,

1872), 13–14, 131–35. On the lack of "producers" legislation during Reconstruction, see Steven Hahn, *A Nation under Our Feet: Black Political Struggles in the Rural South from Slavery to the Great Migration* (Cambridge, Mass.: Belknap Press of Harvard University Press, 2003), 260.

46. M. Howard to Ames, 28 November 1873, folder 148, box 17, Ames Family Papers, Smith College. For more on cotton prices, see Ransom and Sutch, *One Kind of Freedom*, 188–93. For more on the failed repeal of the crop lien law, see Harris, *Day of the Carpetbagger*, 484; Michael Perman, *Road to Redemption: Southern Politics, 1869–1879* (Chapel Hill: University of North Carolina Press, 1984), 147–48; Eric Foner, *Reconstruction: America's Unfinished Revolution, 1863–1877* (New York: Harper & Row, 1988), 542.

47. *Mississippi House Journal*, 1871 session, 70–71; *Jackson Weekly Clarion*, 11 January 1872, 12 January 1876; *Natchez Democrat*, 28 February 1872. Jacobs also was a member of the Committee of Public Lands while a legislator.

48. On bills of relief, see *Mississippi House Journal*, 1870 session, 312; *Mississippi House Journal*, 1871 session, 59, 74, 85. On incorporations, see *Mississippi House Journal*, 1873 session, 1152; *Mississippi House Journal*, 1871 session, 747, 870, 918, 963. Legislators from the Natchez District sponsored the incorporation of at least eight railroads, eight religious bodies, seven fraternal or benevolent associations, twenty-seven businesses, and three fire companies. For the incorporation of other black civic organizations, see *Mississippi House Journal*, 1870 session, 469, 799; *Mississippi House Journal*, 1871 session, 483, 857; *Mississippi House Journal*, 1873 session, 1431; *Mississippi House Journal*, 1874 session, 445. On the 1874 flood, see *Weekly Louisianian*, 2 May 1874; W. H. Noble Jr. to Ames, 1 May 1874; Wm. H. Lynch to Ames, 1 May 1874; W. H. Dunbar and others to Ames, 1 May 1874; Wm. H. Lynch to Ames, 6 June 1874; John R. Lynch and others to Ames, 12 August 1874, Governor Ames Papers, Series 803: Correspondence and Papers, MDAH; *Laws of the State of Mississippi, 1874*, 147–48.

49. Reports of County Superintendents, *Mississippi House Journal*, 1874 session, 850–51; *New National Era*, 26 June 1873; *Natchez Democrat*, 26 April 1871. See also the *Jackson Weekly Pilot*, 15 May 1870. On the lack of political support for land redistribution, see Foner, *Reconstruction*, 236–37, 310–11.

50. *Jackson Weekly Clarion*, 21 April, 28 April 1870, 13 March 1873; *Laws of the State of Mississippi, 1874*, 163–66. On the widespread belief that railroads would bring prosperity, see Mark W. Summers, *Railroads, Reconstruction, and the Gospel of Prosperity: Aid under the Radical Republicans, 1865–1877* (Princeton, N.J.: Princeton University Press, 1984).

51. D. Clayton James, *Antebellum Natchez* (Baton Rouge: Louisiana State University Press, 1968), 190–92, 215. The 1840 tornado ripped through the newly built railroad depot and machine shop in Natchez. Soon after, the railroad went bankrupt.

52. M. Howard to Maj. Gen. O. O. Howard, 16 January 1868, Commissioner, Letters Received, m752, roll 53, Records of the Bureau of Refugees, Freedmen, and Abandoned Lands, Record Group 105, National Archives, Washington, D.C.; *Natchez Courier*, 26 October 1867.

53. Summers, *Railroads, Reconstruction, and the Gospel of Prosperity*, 71–72, 80–82, 185–210. See also Harris, *Day of the Carpetbagger*, 534–37.

54. *Mississippi House Journal*, 1870 session, 123, 636–37, 834; *Natchez Democrat*, 7 December 1870; Harris, *Day of the Carpetbagger*, 541–42. The added men were Merrimon Howard of Jefferson County, James Page and Thomas Richardson of Claiborne County, and Mack Barnes of Adams County. Barnes resided in Claiborne County, although the *Mississippi House Journal* listed him as being from Adams County. Two other white Re-

publicans from the Natchez District were also listed as incorporators: Edward J. Castello of Adams County and Philander Balch, the state representative from Jefferson County. For more details on Martin's prominence in Natchez, see Joyce L. Broussard, "Malvina Matthews: The Murderess Madam of Civil War-Era Natchez," *Journal of Mississippi History* 73 (Spring 2011): 48–51.

55. *Natchez Democrat*, 28 December 1870, 28 June 1871; testimony of O. C. French, U.S. Senate, in *Testimony Taken by the Joint Select Committee to Inquire into the Condition of Affairs in the Late Insurrectionary States*, 42nd Cong., 2nd sess., 1872, S. Rep. 41, vol. 11, pp. 22–23. Only 6 of 1,259 votes were cast against the subscription in a low-turnout election. This can be compared to the vote in 1872 (a more accurate measure of full voting strength), in which 3,783 votes were cast. Roughly 33 percent of the eligible electorate voted in the 1870 election. *Natchez Democrat*, 13 November 1872. For other examples of Jacobs's support for railroad development, see *Jackson Weekly Clarion*, 4 April 1872; *Natchez Democrat*, 31 July 1872; *Laws of the State of Mississippi, 1872*, 234–45, 362–369. For more on French's efforts to promote railroads, see *Jackson Weekly Clarion*, 1 February 1872; *New National Era*, 27 February 1873.

56. *Natchez Democrat*, 13 December 1871. For more on Rodney, see *Natchez Democrat*, 19 June 1872. On Adams County's tax rate, see *Natchez Democrat*, 13 December 1876.

57. *Laws of the State of Mississippi, 1872*, 231–32; *Natchez Democrat*, 5 June, 26 June 1872; Mrs. Martin to W. T. Martin, 15 July [1872], Martin Papers, University of Texas at Austin. Meetings were held at Fayette, Rodney, "the Bend," Dobyn's Store, and Church Hill. Stewart was a schoolteacher who later became a state representative. BPDB.

58. *Natchez Democrat*, 19 June 1872. For other speeches by Cessor, see *Natchez Democrat*, 12 June, 26 June 1872.

59. *Natchez Democrat*, 19 June 1872. At least seven black men, including Merrimon Howard and George Stewart, served on this specially designed railroad committee. All told, thirty-five men represented Jefferson County, except the localities near Rodney, and they passed four resolutions.

60. *Natchez Democrat*, 10 July 1872. Befitting the highly contested nature of this election, a high voter turnout was recorded, especially for a summer election. For November election results, see *Natchez Democrat*, 13 November 1872.

61. *Natchez Democrat*, 24 July 1872.

62. *Mississippi House Journal*, 1873 session, 1294, 1334; *Jackson Weekly Clarion*, 20 February 1873; *Natchez Democrat*, 15 July, 19 August 1874, 13 December 1876, 14 September 1882; *New York Times*, 15 December 1880. For a general history of the railroad, see Harris, *Day of the Carpetbagger*, 542–44.

63. *Natchez Democrat*, 14 September 1882. By 1895 at least three railroads besides the NJC crisscrossed the Natchez District: the Yazoo & Mississippi, the N. O. & N. W. R. W. line out of Vidalia, and a small trunk line between Woodville and Bayou Sara, Louisiana. The only locality without rail access was Tensas Parish. For maps of the rail lines, see Rand McNally and Company, *Atlas of the World* (Chicago: Rand McNally, 1895), available at http://fermi.jhuapl.edu/states/1895/la_1895.jpg and http://fermi.jhuapl .edu/states/1895/ms_1895.jpg; courtesy of the Johns Hopkins University Applied Physics Laboratory.

64. *Natchez Democrat*, 14 February, 8 May, 5 June 1872; *Laws of the State of Mississippi, 1872*, 256–67.

65. *Laws of the State of Mississippi, 1872*, 234–45, 362–69; *Natchez Democrat*, 31 July 1872; Harris, *Day of the Carpetbagger*, 530. Other Republican incorporators on the

Natchez to Brookhaven line included A. H. Foster, M. A. C. Hussey, William Noonan, C. C. Walden, W. J. Davis, George St. Clair Hussey, Merrimon Howard, and James D. Cessor. *Natchez Democrat*, 22 May 1872. On McCary, see the Freedmen's Bank advertisement in the *Natchez Democrat*, 19 October 1870. For early efforts to organize the Meridian company, see *Jackson Weekly Clarion*, 28 April, 7 July 1870.

66. *Natchez Democrat*, 30 September, 14 October 1874; testimony of E. H. Stiles in U.S. Senate, *Report of the Select Committee into the Mississippi Election of 1875*, 44th Cong., 1st sess., 1876, S. Rep. 527, p. 183. For another example of biracial and bipartisan economic development, but with different outcomes and mobilization efforts, see Michael W. Fitzgerald, *Urban Emancipation: Popular Politics in Reconstruction Mobile, 1860–1890* (Baton Rouge: Louisiana State University Press, 2002), 132–62.

67. R. E. Richardson to William Whitehurst, 9 September 1874, Whitehurst Papers, MDAH. Richardson, a physician and planter, worked at Jefferson College as a teacher and possibly its president. Whitehurst served as a judge and commissioner in Adams County before Radical Reconstruction and after.

Chapter Five. "True to One Another"

1. *Natchez Democrat*, 28 August 1872 (emphasis in original).

2. Thomas C. Holt, *Black over White: Negro Political Leadership in South Carolina during Reconstruction* (Urbana: University of Illinois Press, 1977); Eric Foner, *Reconstruction: America's Unfinished Revolution, 1863–1877* (New York: Harper & Row, 1988), 539–41; Michael W. Fitzgerald, *Urban Emancipation: Popular Politics in Reconstruction Mobile, 1860–1890* (Baton Rouge: Louisiana State University Press, 2002); Steven Hahn, *A Nation under Our Feet: Black Political Struggles in the Rural South from Slavery to the Great Migration* (Cambridge, Mass.: Belknap Press of Harvard University Press, 2003), 249, 254; Michael Fitzgerald, *Splendid Failure: Postwar Reconstruction in the American South* (Chicago: Ivan R. Dee, 2007), 119–42. On Republican factionalism, see Lawrence N. Powell, "The Politics of Livelihood: Carpetbaggers in the Deep South," in *Region, Race and Reconstruction: Essays in Honor of C. Vann Woodward*, ed. J. Morgan Kousser and James M. McPherson (New York: Oxford University Press, 1982), 315–47; Foner, *Reconstruction*, 347–49; Richard Nelson Current, *Those Terrible Carpetbaggers: A Reinterpretation* (New York: Oxford University Press, 1988). On Democratic factionalism, see Michael Perman, *The Road to Redemption: Southern Politics, 1869–1879* (Chapel Hill: University of North Carolina Press, 1984). For more on the structural factors that contributed to factionalism, see Michael Les Benedict, *Preserving the Constitution: Essays on Politics and the Constitution in the Reconstruction Era* (New York: Fordham University Press, 2006), 67–89; Lawrence Powell, "Centralization and Its Discontents in Reconstruction Louisiana," *Studies in American Political Development* 20 (Fall 2006): 105–31.

3. The other districts that elected black congressmen after 1876 were South Carolina's First, North Carolina's Second, and Virginia's Fourth. On Revels, see *Jackson Weekly Pilot*, 22 January 1870; Julius E. Thompson, "Hiram Rhodes Revels, 1827–1901: A Reappraisal," *Journal of Negro History* 79, no. 3 (Summer 1994): 297–303. On the constitutional implications of Revels's elevation to the U.S. Senate, see Richard A. Primus, "The Riddle of Hiram Revels," *Harvard Law Review* 119, no. 6 (April 2006): 1680–734. For more on Lynch, see John R. Lynch, *The Facts of Reconstruction* (New York: Neale Publishing, 1913; repr., New York: Arno Press and the New York Times, 1968); John R. Lynch, *Reminiscences of an Active Life: The Autobiography of John Roy Lynch*, ed. John

Hope Franklin (Chicago: University of Chicago Press, 1970); Justin Behrend, "Facts and Memories: John R. Lynch and the Revising of Reconstruction History in the Era of Jim Crow," *Journal of African American History* 97, no. 4 (Fall 2012): 427–48. For recent assessments of Louisiana politics, see Powell, "Centralization and Its Discontents"; James K. Hogue, *Uncivil War: Five New Orleans Street Battles and the Rise and Fall of Radical Reconstruction* (Baton Rouge: Louisiana State University Press, 2006); Justin A. Nystrom, *New Orleans after the Civil War: Race, Politics, and a New Birth of Freedom* (Baltimore: Johns Hopkins University Press, 2010).

4. Justin Behrend, Black Politicians Database, SUNY-Geneseo, http://go.geneseo.edu/ BlackPoliticiansDB, (BPDB); Eric Foner, ed., *Freedom's Lawmakers: A Directory of Black Officeholders during Reconstruction*, rev. ed. (Baton Rouge: Louisiana State University Press, 1996), 249–53. Steven Hahn, in his Black Leaders Data Set, found more than twice as many individuals (3,878) as Foner found in his pioneering work, but, as my research indicates, we still need many more local studies to give a true picture of the breadth and depth of black politics in the Reconstruction era. Hahn describes his data set in *A Nation under Our Feet*, 479–80.

5. BPDB.

6. BPDB. On Bowles's property, see his will in the *Natchez Evening Banner*, 28 December 1899. On his community involvement, see Trustees Baptist Church to S. S. Meekins et al., 5 September 1874, Adams County Land Deeds, book UU, p. 66, Adams County Courthouse (ACCH), Natchez, Miss.; The Supreme Lodge, Knights of Honor vs. The Supreme Lodge, Knights of Honor of the World, and George F. Bowles, case 1472, Chancery files, ACCH.

7. BPDB.

8. BPDB; George H. Dunford, Tri-Monthly Report, 10 August 1867, Records of the Assistant Commissioner for the State of Louisiana, m1027, Registered Letters and Telegrams Received, roll 14, Records of the Bureau of Refugees, Freedmen, and Abandoned Lands, Record Group 105, National Archives, Washington, D.C. (cited hereafter as BRFAL); *Natchez Democrat*, 9 October 1872; *Concordia Eagle*, 12 April 1883.

9. BPDB.

10. BPDB; Lynch, *Reminiscences of an Active Life*, 23–27, 39–40, 55–57; U.S. Bureau of Census, *Ninth Census of the United States: Population, 1870*; testimony of John R. Lynch, David Singleton claim, case 411, Adams County, Congressional Jurisdiction Case Files, Records of the U.S. Court of Claims, Record Group 123, National Archives, Washington, D.C.

11. BPDB. For more on Winston, see Sheryl Lynn Nomelli, "Jim Crow, Louis J. Winston, and the Survival of Black Politicos in Post-Bellum Natchez, Mississippi" (master's thesis, California State University, Northridge, 2004).

12. Solomon Shaifer, Constable, 15 December 1870, Bonds, pp. 127–28, Tensas Parish, Tensas Parish Courthouse (TPCH), St. Joseph, La.; *The Revised Statute Laws of the State of Louisiana, from the Organization of the Territory to the year 1869, Inclusive* (New Orleans, 1870), 77; *Natchez Democrat*, 10 January 1872; First Presbyterian Church to African Methodist Episcopal Church, 14 July 1868, Title Bond, Adams County Land Deeds, book HH, p. 146, ACCH. Aldermen, mayors, state legislators, and members of the board of supervisors and police jury were not required to post a bond. Only a few historians have bothered to analyze bonds or assess the financial obstacles faced by black leaders. Such studies include William McKee Evans, *Ballots and Fence Rails: Reconstruction on the Lower Cape Fear* (Chapel Hill, University of North Carolina Press, 1966; repr.,

Athens: University of Georgia Press, 1995), 164; Christopher Waldrep, "Black Political Leadership: Warren County, Mississippi," in *Local Matters: Race, Crime, and Justice in the Nineteenth-Century South*, ed. Christopher Waldrep and Donald G. Nieman (Athens: University of Georgia Press, 2001), 232; Hahn, *A Nation under Our Feet*, 256–58.

13. State vs. Wilson Wood, box 14–97, October term 1875, Adams County Circuit Court Case Files, Historic Natchez Foundation (HNF), Natchez, Miss. See also State by John J. Smith, agent vs. Wilson Wood et al., box 12–92, April term 1876; State by John J. Smith, agent vs. Wilson Wood et al., box 12–98, April term 1876, No. 40; State by John J. Smith, agent vs. Wilson Wood et al., box 12–99, April term 1876, no. 41, Adams County Circuit Court Case Files, HNF; *Natchez Democrat*, 2 February 1876.

14. Wm. Noonan to Adelbert Ames, January 24, 1870, box 9, Ames Family Papers, Sophia Smith Collection, Smith College, Northampton, Mass. See also John R. Lynch, "Some Historical Errors of James Ford Rhodes," *Journal of Negro History* 2, no. 4 (October 1917): 355. Black population shares for the Natchez District in 1870: Concordia Parish, 93 percent; Tensas Parish, 89 percent; Wilkinson County, 79 percent; Jefferson County, 77 percent; Adams County, 75 percent; Claiborne County, 75 percent. Historical Census Browser, University of Virginia, Geospatial and Statistical Data Center, 2004, http://fisher.lib.virginia.edu/collections/stats/histcensus/index.html.

15. On Howard's bond, see Merriman Howard, Sheriff, 7 December 1874, Old Bonds, Jefferson County, Jefferson County Courthouse, Fayette, Miss. The only black surety that I could identify on any of Howard's bonds was Caleb Collier, an illiterate black farmer who rented the thousand-acre Ashland plantation and contributed to Howard's 1875 sheriff's bond. On Tensas Parish bonds, see A. J. Bryant, Sheriff, 31 December 1872, Bonds, pp. 141–42, TPCH. Bryant's two sureties, Hiram R. Steele and E. L. Whitney, were white carpetbaggers and planters. Although Louisiana Republicans altered state law to allow officeholders, particularly in rural districts, to seek bondsmen outside of parish boundaries, Tensas Parish officeholders filled their bonds with local men. For more on bonds and Louisiana legislation, see *Revised Statute Laws of Louisiana* (1870), 74. On Wilkinson County bonds, see Official Bonds, book 2, Wilkinson County, Wilkinson County Courthouse, Woodville, Miss.

16. State by John J. Smith, agent, vs. Wilson Wood et al., box 12–98, April term 1876, no. 40, Adams County Circuit Court Case Files, HNF; *Natchez Democrat*, 10 January 1872; BPDB; U.S. Bureau of Census, *Ninth Census: Population, 1870*; D. Clayton James, *Antebellum Natchez* (Baton Rouge: Louisiana State University Press, 1968), 96. Unfortunately, Adams County bond books have not survived from the Reconstruction era. There are, however, a couple of books from the 1890s that detail black involvement in posting and supporting bonds. See Official Bonds, 1889–94 and 1895–1906, Adams County, ACCH. To my knowledge, the 1870s bond books from Concordia Parish and Claiborne County have not survived. On the antebellum free black population in Natchez, see William R. Hogan and Edwin A. Davis, eds., *William Johnson's Natchez: The Ante-Bellum Diary of a Free Negro* (Baton Rouge: Louisiana State University Press, 1951); James, *Antebellum Natchez*, 177–81; Ronald L. F. Davis, *The Black Experience in Natchez, 1720–1880* (Natchez National Historical Park, Miss.: Eastern National Park & Monument Association, 1994), 47–60; Virginia Meacham Gould, ed., *Chained to the Rock of Adversity: To Be Free, Black and Female in the Old South* (Athens: University of Georgia Press, 1998), 1–38.

17. *Natchez Democrat*, 10 January 1872; U.S. Bureau of Census, *Ninth Census: Population, 1870*; BPDB. I was unable to identify the birthplace and/or race of four sureties, totaling $22,000 in contributions and 29 percent of the total bond. McCary's sureties

were John Peck (mulatto carpenter), $1,000; Wm. Smoot (black), $500; P. H. McGraw (white druggist), $10,000; L. B. Field (white planter), $10,000; J. W. Young (white farmer and doctor), $3,000; M. Holmes, $5,000; Leroy S. Bronn (white farmer), $1,500; H. C. Griffin (white city clerk), $1,500; P. E. Willman (white builder and carpenter), $10,000; E. J. Castello (white postmaster), $2,500; John R. Lynch (mulatto state legislator), $1,000; Wm. H. Lynch (mulatto alderman), $1,500; F. M. Cooley (white), $1,000; John Smith (mulatto farmer), $3,000; Wm. Huston (white blacksmith), $2,000; David Singleton (black farmer), $3,000; J. N. Ault (white merchant), $1,500; H. R. Revels (black president of Alcorn University), $5,000; Wm. Zoch (white saloon owner), $2,000; L. Heene (white brewer), $5,000; Robert Morman (mulatto farmer), $2,000; Byron Johnson (mulatto barber), $1,000; J. P. Buie (white lawyer), $2,000. On McGraw's relationship to the Lynches, see Lynch, *Reminiscences of an Active Life*, 39. McGraw helped the young John R. Lynch find employment at a photographic shop after the conclusion of the Civil War.

18. *Natchez Democrat*, 10 January 1872. For more on Newcomb, see *Natchez Democrat*, 6 April 1868.

19. At least seven offices had all-white sureties, and one office had all-black support. I was unable to determine the racial makeup for three other bonds. *Natchez Democrat*, 10 January 1872; BPDB.

20. Edward King, *The Great South* (Hartford, Conn.: American Publishing Company, 1875), 296.

21. *The Revised Code of the Statute Laws of the State of Mississippi, . . . 1871* (Jackson, Miss.: Alcorn & Fisher, 1871), 354–59; *Laws of the State of Mississippi, . . . 1872* (Jackson, Miss.: Kimball, Raymond & Co., 1872), 1–7; Michael Wayne, *Reshaping the Plantation South: The Natchez District, 1860–1880* (Baton Rouge: Louisiana State University Press, 1982), 84–86.

22. O. S. Miles to James Cessor, 5 July 1869, book AA, p. 222, Jefferson County Land Deeds, Jefferson County Courthouse, Fayette, Miss.; Police Jury to Solomon Shaifer, 15 December 1871, book G, p. 607; Police Jury to Wesley Dixon, 16 November 1871, book G, p. 603, Tensas Parish Land Deeds, TPCH. Each paid $125 for the lot, and the sales were finalized in late 1871. For another example of a sheriff's sale to a rising black politician, see Sheriff to Lowry Cammack, 12 November, 1869, book G, p. 231, Tensas Parish Land Deeds, TPCH. On Cessor's political experience, see BPDB.

23. On Lynch's landholdings, see James Singleton et al. to John R. Lynch and William H. Lynch, 3 May 1873, Adams County Land Deeds, book SS, p. 435; Anna Holden to John R. and William H. Lynch, 19 June 1873, Adams County Land Deeds, book SS, p. 558; F. J. Arrighi, trustee, to John R. Lynch, 17 April 1875, Adams County Land Deeds, book UU, p. 444; J. H. Veazie et al. to John R. Lynch, 19 May 1875, Adams County Land Deeds, book UU, p. 578, ACCH. Between 1867 and 1916, Lynch was involved in 110 property transactions, and he acquired ownership of or partial interest in at least five plantations. For more on the extent of Lynch's land transactions, see the indexes to the land deeds, both grantor and grantee, at the ACCH. For examples of the Lynch brothers partnership, see John Lambert and wife to John R. and William H. Lynch, 16 January 1869, Adams County Land Deeds, book PP, pp. 298–99; William Noonan to John R. and William H. Lynch, 7 December 1869, Adams County Land Deeds, book PP, p. 634, ACCH. On the inheritance that they Lynch family received, see Harry (Henry) L. Marshall, 23 January 1866, Adams County Wills, book 3, p. 269, ACCH. Marshall willed all of his property to his cousin, Louisa Smith, and upon her death, the house and lot were to go to the Lynches. It is not clear when the Lynches took possession of the house on

Pearl Street. John R. Lynch sold his share of the property to his sister for one dollar in 1883. John R. Lynch to Catherine E. L. Johnson, 2 July 1883, Adams County Land Deeds, book YY, p. 370, ACCH. On Lynch's first property transaction, see John Lambert and wife to John R. and William H. Lynch, 16 January 1869, Adams County Land Deeds, book PP, pp. 298–99, ACCH. For more on the $500 loan, see Nathan H. Black to John Lynch, 4 January 1867, Adams County Land Deeds, book OO, p. 337, ACCH. On the *Natchez Democrat* publisher, see William and John J. Lambert to David Singleton, 21 October 1865, Adams County Land Deeds, book NN, p. 544, ACCH.

24. David Singleton and William H. Lynch with Walker Vester et al., Agreement, 11 June 1868, Adams County Land Deeds, book PP, p. 122, ACCH; David Singleton to David Young, 16 March 1869, Conveyance Records, book O, p. 436; John Martin to Singleton and Young, 23 January 1874, General Mortgages, book R, p. 77, Concordia Parish Courthouse, Vidalia, La.; *Concordia Eagle*, quoted in *Ouachita Telegraph*, 2 January 1874.

25. Robert Carter et al. to David Singleton, 28 January 1868, Conveyance Records, book O, p. 298 (see also Pauline Carter [Mrs.] to David Singleton, 11 January 1878, Conveyance Records, book P, p. 784); Pauline Carter et al. to David Young, 29 August 1870, Conveyance Records, book O, p. 669; Pauline Carter to George Washington, 1 June 1871, Conveyance Records, book P, p. 86; Mrs. Pauline Carter to John Stevenson, George Randall, and others, Trustees of Baptist Church, 9 September 1873, Conveyance Records, book P, p. 281; Mrs. Pauline Carter to James Randall, 21 December 1889, Conveyance Records, book T, p. 193, Concordia Parish Courthouse, Vidalia, La. On the Carters' movements, see Wayne, *Reshaping the Plantation South*, 53.

26. For more on black politics and patron-client relationships, see Harold Forsythe, "'But My Friends Are Poor': Ross Hamilton and Freedpeople's Politics in Mecklenburg County, Virginia, 1869–1901," *Virginia Magazine of History and Biography* 105 (Autumn 1997): 409–38.

27. John R. Lynch's autobiography is a case in point. Peppered throughout the book are stories of nomination contests at the local, state, and federal level, as well as factional disputes with rivals. By contrast, public policy issues warranted only minimal attention. For Lynch, the essence of politics seemed to lie in the formation and consolidation of personal alliances. See Lynch, *Reminiscences of an Active Life*.

28. List of Civil Officers Appointed in Mississippi, 1867–1869, E. 404, Office of Civil Affairs, Department of Arkansas and the Seventh Army Corps and the Fourth Military District, part I, Records of the U.S. Army Continental Commands, 1821–1890, Record Group 393, National Archives, Washington, D.C. (cited hereafter as RG 393). The three were Hiram Revels, the first black U.S. senator; William McCary, the first black sheriff of Adams County; and Robert H. Wood, the first black mayor of Natchez. Revels's appointment came in 1869, while the other two were added a year later. See also *Natchez Democrat*, 3 March 1870. At the time, these boards were referred to as the Board of Police and the Board of Selectmen, respectively. By 1871 they were called the Board of Supervisors and Board of Aldermen," the terms still in current use.

29. Lynch, *Facts of Reconstruction*, 38–43.

30. *Natchez Democrat*, 7 December 1870. On doubts about Union League leaders, see "Copy of statement charging *1st Lieut. D. M. White, U. R. C.,* with drunkenness, profanity and want of sympathy with the colored people, and *Capt. E. E. Platt, URC.,* with want of sympathy with colored people, sympathy with secessionists, and with making charges in the collections of claims for negroes," Comr., Letters Received, m752, roll 47, BRFAL.

31. List of Civil Officers Appointed in Mississippi, 1867–1869, RG 393; *Natchez Demo-*

crat, 12 October 1870, 3 January 1871, 26 January 1873; Vernon Lane Wharton, *The Negro in Mississippi, 1865–1890* (Chapel Hill: University of North Carolina Press, 1947; repr., New York: Harper & Row, 1965), 167. The 1869 board included Washington Ford (white), Richard Rachford (white), W. R. Gilreath (white), J. W. Alexander (white), and Abraham H. Dixon. The members of the 1871 board were J. W. Alexander (white), president, W. R. Gilreath (white), George Johnson, Cornelius Henderson, and Theodore Lumbar. The 1873 board was composed of Robert H. Wood, president, L. S. Bronn (white), Pascal Williams, John Peck, and Randolph Butler. The black aldermen were William McCary, Robert W. Fitzhugh, S. S. Meekins, and William H. Lynch; their white, Republican colleagues were M. A. C. Hussey, C. C. Waldren, L. H. Clapp, and William Noonan.

32. *Natchez Democrat*, 11 October 1871; Wharton, *The Negro in Mississippi*, 169.

33. *Natchez Democrat*, 27 September 1871; Republican Executive Committee Meeting Memo, 23 September 1872, Natchez Archives, History Department, California State University, Northridge; *Vidalia Herald*, 19 August 1870. The 1872 committee included William McCary, chairman, L. S. Bronn, Woodson V. Howard, Pascal Williams, George W. Carter, William H. Lynch, and Wilson Wood. Bronn was the only white member. Bronn, Howard, and Williams lived in rural districts. McCary, Carter, and Lynch lived in Natchez but held county offices: sheriff, county school director, and school board member, respectively. City delegates had more power in Adams County than in the rest of the district, yet they still fell two seats short of the rural delegation, fourteen to sixteen. The two city precincts, Court House and Jefferson Hotel, were allotted seven delegates each. The rural precincts distributed delegates as follows: Washington, five delegates; Kingston and Helm, each three delegates; Pine Ridge and Organ's, each two delegates, and Dead Man's Bend, one delegate. *Natchez Democrat*, 27 September 1871.

34. Lynch, *Reminiscences of an Active Life*, 101. On white carpetbagger support, see William J. Davis to A. Ames, 8 April 1872, folder 125, box 14, Ames Family Papers, Smith College; *Biographical Dictionary of the United States Congress, 1774–1989* (Washington, D.C.: Government Printing Office, 1989), 1631–32. On radical initiatives that Perce sponsored, see *Natchez Democrat*, 28 February, 27 March, 31 July 1872; Kenneth R. Johnson, "Legrand Winfield Perce: A Mississippi Carpetbagger and the Fight for Federal Aid to Education," *Journal of Mississippi History* 34 (November 1972): 331–56.

35. *Natchez Democrat*, 10 January 1872; Lynch, *Reminiscences of an Active Life*, 23–28, 39.

36. William J. Davis to A. Ames, 16 July 1872, folder 125, box 14, Ames Family Papers, Smith College (emphasis in original); *Port Gibson Standard* quoted in *Natchez Democrat*, 21 August 1872; *Fayette Chronicle*, quoted in *Natchez Democrat*, 28 August 1872.

37. R. E. Conner to Lemuel P. Conner, 7 September 1872, folder 59, box 4, Lemuel P. Conner and Family Papers, Louisiana and Lower Mississippi Valley Collections, Louisiana State University (LSU) Libraries, Baton Rouge; *Natchez Democrat*, 28 August, 13 November 1872. On R. E. Conner's politics, see *Natchez Democrat*, 30 December 1867, where Conner is listed as a member of the central executive committee of the Constitutional Union Party.

38. Although sixteen counties made up the congressional district, "it was conceded by all" Republicans, Lynch remembered, "that an Adams County man should be nominated." Lynch, *Reminiscences of an Active Life*, 101. On the county convention, see *Natchez Democrat*, 28 August 1872; Lynch, *Reminiscences of an Active Life*, 101–2.

39. Lynch, *Reminiscences of an Active Life*, 101; *Natchez Democrat*, 28 August 1872. Both factions appear to have had similar educational backgrounds, judging by similar

proportions of literacy, and both sides included artisans and professionals. These generalizations are based on an analysis of the forty-six delegates I was able to identify in the 1870 U.S. Census, out of a total of fifty-nine delegates.

40. *Natchez Democrat*, June [1873], filed in the William N. Whitehurst Papers, Mississippi Department of Archives and History MDAH, Jackson. Henderson's political moderation stems from his support of Alcorn over Ames for governor and his support of a Mississippi-born white Republican for Natchez mayor over Robert H. Wood. Henderson claimed that Wood led a "miserable ring of ignorant financial bunglers." Ibid.

41. John R. Lynch to Ames, 13 February 1873, folder 139, box 16, Ames Family Papers, Smith College.

42. John R. Lynch to Ames, 15 January, 31 January 1873, folder 138, box 16, Ames Family Papers, Smith College (emphasis in original); Lynch, *Reminiscences of an Active Life*, 172. For other examples of patronage requests, see O. S. Miles and P. Balch to Gov. Alcorn, 10 May 1871, Governor Alcorn Papers, Series 786: Correspondence and Papers, MDAH; M. Howard to Gov. Powers, 24 December 1872, Governor Powers Papers, Series 794: Correspondence and Papers, MDAH; Leroy S. Bronn to Gov. Ames, 17 October 1874, Governor Ames Papers, Series 803: Correspondence and Papers, MDAH; John R. Lynch to Ames, 13 February 1873, box 16, folder 139, Ames Family Papers, Smith College; Ames to John R. Lynch, 1 June 1875, Governor Ames Papers, Series 803: Correspondence and Papers, MDAH; John R. Lynch to President Hayes, 17 May 1877, Rutherford B. Hayes Papers, Rutherford B. Hayes Presidential Center, Fremont, Ohio; John R. Lynch to Bruce, 31 July 1877; John R. Lynch to Bruce, 21 September 1877; John R. Lynch to Bruce, 27 October 1877, box 9–2, folder 58, Blanche K. Bruce Papers, Moorland-Spingarn Research Center, Howard University, Washington, D.C. On the relationship between political friendship and patronage, see Gregory P. Downs, *Declarations of Dependence: The Long Reconstruction of Popular Politics in the South, 1861–1908* (Chapel Hill: University of North Carolina Press, 2011).

43. Lynch, *Reminiscences of an Active Life*, 104–6; E. J. Castello to Ames, 24 December 1872, folder 134, box 15; John R. Lynch to Ames, 15 January 1873, folder 137, box 16; John R. Lynch to Ames, 31 January 1873, folder 138, box 16, Ames Family Papers, Smith College. For examples of petitioners on behalf of Castello, see Allison H. Foster to Ames, 27 January 1873, folder 138, box 16; H. P. Jacobs to Ames, 14 February 1873, folder 139, box 16; Wm. Noonan to Ames, 9 March 1873, folder 141, box 16; W. J. Davis to Ames, 15 April 1873, folder 146, box 17, Ames Family Papers, Smith College.

44. John R. Lynch to Ames, 22 February 1873, folder 140, box 16, Ames Family Papers, Smith College (emphasis in original). On Bronn's affiliation with the National Union Republican Party, see *Natchez Democrat*, 2 September 1869, and for more on that party (also known as the "Dent Movement"), see William C. Harris, *The Day of the Carpetbagger: Republican Reconstruction in Mississippi* (Baton Rouge: Louisiana State University Press, 1979), 239–59. Bronn was the only white member of the 1872 county Republican executive committee. See Republican Executive Committee Meeting Memo, 23 September 1872, Natchez Archives, History Department, California State University, Northridge.

45. M. Howard to Ames, 29 November 1873, folder 148, box 17, Ames Family Papers, Smith College; *Natchez Democrat*, 7 October 1874. Wilson Wood's $3,000–$4,000 salary as county treasurer was at least twenty-five times a plantation laborer's annual wages. For more on the salaries of elected officials, see the testimony of William Ridgly in U.S. House, *Select Committee on the Recent Election in the State of Louisiana*, 44th Cong., 2nd sess., 1876, H. Misc. Doc. 34, pp. 223–24.

46. Lynch quoted a statement that Ames had made to him at an earlier meeting. John R. Lynch to Ames, 15 January 1873, folder 137, box 16, Ames Family Papers, Smith College. On the importance of government jobs for carpetbaggers, see Powell, "Politics of Livelihood."

47. George Hitchen to Sumner, 20 March 1869, Papers of Charles Sumner, Series I: Letters to Charles Sumner, roll 45, Houghton Library, Harvard University, Cambridge, Mass.; Geo. W. Hitchen to Howard, 22 May 1869, Comr., Letters Received, roll 62, BRFAL. Sumner was unmoved by Hitchen's overblown fawning: "I have come to consider you my Political Father, Guardian and Protector," and later, "In fact I have well nigh come to the conclusion that I have only two real, lasting friends in the *wide, wide, World*, and those two are Jehovah in Heaven, and Charles Sumner on Earth." George Hitchen to Sumner, 20 March 1869; George Hitchen to Sumner, 24 March 1869, Sumner Papers, Harvard University, roll 45 (emphasis in original).

48. Del to Blanche, 10 September 1873, in *Chronicles from the Nineteenth Century: Family Letters of Blanche Butler and Adelbert Ames*, ed. Blanche Butler Ames (Clinton, Mass.: Colonial Press, 1957), 1:554–56.

49. *Natchez Democrat*, 9 October 1872. On the Natchez police force, see *Natchez Democrat*, 19 April, 29 November 1871, 24 January, 28 August, 27 November 1872, 7 October 1874. On the "Governing Six," see *Natchez Democrat*, 24 January 1872, 16 September 1874. The other members of the "Governing Six" were William H. Lynch, Robert W. Fitzhugh, Robert H. Wood, Wilson Wood, and William McCary. On the use of bailiffs, see *Natchez Democrat*, 31 July, 7 August, 14 August 1872.

50. *North Louisiana Journal*, 28 September, 9 November 1872. In the races for state senator, parish judge, and clerk of the court only whites were candidates; conversely, for the offices of sheriff, recorder, and coroner, blacks from the Republican and fusionist parties vied for the vote.

51. *North Louisiana Journal*, 28 September 1872. On Robinson's alliance with other moderates, see *North Louisiana Journal*, 24 August 1872; C. H. Ross to Alfred Fairfax et al., 25 July 1872, book H, p. 32; E. W. Robinson to John P Harlow, 25 July 1872, book H, p. 93, Tensas Parish Land Deeds, TPCH. Robinson, in combination with Alfred Fairfax (a black minister) and John P. Harlow (a white store clerk), purchased 281.5 acres. However, Robinson immediately sold his share to Harlow. Fairfax and Harlow, like Robinson, were delegates at the senatorial convention. E. L. Whitney and Hiram R. Steele were representative of white Republican leaders with more extensive local ties. Whitney—who held the offices of sheriff, parish judge, tax collector, and state senator—owned $35,000 worth of real estate in 1870, and Steele—a parish judge, district attorney, police juror, and chairman of the parish Republican executive committee—owned $10,000 worth of real estate. U.S. Bureau of Census, *Ninth Census: Population, 1870*. Grassroots support for Robinson was evident at his funeral, which took place two years after his arrival in Tensas Parish. A prisoner whom he was transporting to the St. Joseph jail murdered him in 1873. His funeral procession stretched "nearly a mile" and was "composed of all classes" in the largest funeral in Waterproof's history. *North Louisiana Journal*, 18 October 1873.

52. BPDB. Robinson also became a Waterproof alderman, although it is unclear whether he was elected or appointed.

53. M. T. Newsom to Ames, 1 November 1872, folder 133, box 15, Ames Family Papers, Smith College; History of Reconstruction in Claiborne County, box 10667, Mississippi Historical Records Survey, Series 447, Works Progress Administration Records, MDAH; *Natchez Democrat*, June [1873], filed in the Whitehurst Papers, MDAH; BPDB. The dam-

age was so severe that Newsome had to explicitly distance himself from the Democratic Party, an unnecessary exercise for loyal Republicans: "Democrats . . . are our old enemy," he wrote in a letter to Ames, "and they are the same to day as they were, when Judge [Taney] gave his famous Dred Scott decission [*sic*]. . . . This power the colored people can't afford to trust in their hands." Newsome, however, was restored to his standing in the Claiborne County Republican Party a few years later. In 1875 he was the Republican candidate for coroner and ranger; however, the white-line movement defeated the ticket. *Jackson Weekly Pilot*, 16 October 1875.

54. *Natchez Democrat*, 4 December 1872; William T. Martin to Lemuel Conner, 17 December, 1872, folder 59, box 4, Conner and Family Papers, LSU; John R. Lynch to Ames, 15 January 1873, folder 138, box 16, Ames Family Papers, Smith College. Wood had won election two years earlier by seventy-seven votes. On dissatisfaction with Wood's tenure as mayor, see *Natchez Democrat*, June [1873], filed in the Whitehurst Papers, MDAH.

55. John R. Lynch to Ames, 15 January 1873, folder 137, box 16, Ames Family Papers, Smith College. About a third of black voters cast their ballots for the fusionists two years later. *Natchez Democrat*, 11 November 1874.

56. Adelbert to Blanche, 8 July 1873, in Ames, *Chronicles from the Nineteenth Century*, 1:476. For contemporary reporting on the Modoc War, see *New York Times*, 13 April, 14 May, 4 June 1873. For references to the Modocs and Warm Springers in Natchez, see *Natchez Democrat*, 3 July 1873, 8 July, 15 July, 29 July 1874.

57. *Natchez Democrat*, 13 August 1873. Parson Smith seems to have been a minister, but I found no other information on him. Howard was a black member of the county school board and a member of the county Republican executive committee. Winston was a freeborn mulatto policeman and candidate for tax assessor at the convention. William H. Lynch, a former slave, was the brother of John R. Lynch and a powerful politician in his own right: a Natchez alderman, member of the county school board, member of the county Republican executive committee, and president of the board of poor farm supervisors. James S. Montgomery was a Mississippi-born white Republican moderate. BPDB.

58. *Natchez Democrat*, 13 August 1873. "Killed: Wm. Noonan, H. P. Jacobs, W. W. Hence. Seriously wounded: E. J. Castello, H. C. Griffin, G. F. Bowles, S. S. Meekins, C. C. Walden, L. S. Bronn, and a few more." Two black Modocs lost in the viva voce voting: H. P. Jacobs and W. W. Hence, for treasurer and assessor, respectively. Wilson Wood and Louis J. Winston won the nominations. For state representative, the nominations reflected the competing constituencies within the local party: William H. Lynch (black party leader in Natchez), O. C. French (a white carpetbagger), and Willis Davis (a black rural resident). John Stevenson, a mulatto preacher, was nominated for coroner and apparently ran unopposed.

59. *Natchez Democrat*, 22 July, 29 July, 7 October 1874. On the city Republican convention, see *Natchez Democrat*, 21 October 1874.

60. *Natchez Democrat*, 19 July 1876.

61. A lack of documentation prevents a thorough assessment of political factionalism in the Natchez District. Newspapers are the best source for political struggles; however, only the Natchez newspapers from the Reconstruction era have survived. Furthermore, correspondence with governors tended to be more prevalent in major cities, like Natchez; thus relatively few letters from Concordia, Tensas, Claiborne, Jefferson, and Wilkinson made their way to state capitals.

62. *Natchez Democrat*, 19 April 1871. The speech was printed as a pamphlet, a copy of which was saved in the Ames Family Papers, Smith College.

63. *Natchez Democrat*, 19 April 1871.

Chapter Six. A Deep Interest in Politics

1. Testimony of Harry Smith Jr., in U.S. House, *Testimony in the Contested Election Case of John R. Lynch vs. James R. Chalmers, From the Sixth Congressional District of Mississippi*, 47th Cong., 1st sess., 1881, H. Misc. Doc. 12, pp. 144–45 (cited hereafter as *Lynch vs. Chalmers*); U.S. Bureau of Census, *Ninth Census of the United States: Population, 1870*.

2. Testimony of Stephen Wilkins, in U.S. House, *Select Committee on the Recent Election in the State of Louisiana*, 44th Cong., 2nd sess., 1876, H. Misc. Doc. 34, p. 213 (cited hereafter as *Recent Election*).

3. Testimony of Taylor Young, *Recent Election*, 211–12. Elsa Barkley Brown argues that African Americans considered suffrage to be a collective possession, not just the prerogative of male voters. I don't dispute this point, but I focus instead on the partisan reasons for a broad conceptualization of voting and political participation. See Elsa Barkley Brown, "Negotiating and Transforming the Public Sphere: African American Political Life in the Transition from Slavery to Freedom," *Public Culture* 7 (1994): 111–50; Brown, "To Catch the Vision of Freedom: Reconstructing Southern Black Women's Political History, 1865–1880," in *African American Women and the Vote, 1837–1965*, ed. Ann D. Gordon with Bettye Collier-Thomas, John H. Bracey, Arlene Voski Avakian, and Joyce Avrech Berkman (Amherst: University of Massachusetts Press, 1997), 66–99. See also Leslie A. Schwalm's analysis of black women's quest for citizenship that paralleled and complemented black men's politics in *Emancipation's Diaspora: Race and Reconstruction in the Upper Midwest* (Chapel Hill: University of North Carolina Press, 2009), 175–218. It was more common for women to take an active role in moral reform campaigns and other nonpartisan issues. Notable examples include Ellen Carol DuBois, *Feminism and Suffrage: The Emergence of an Independent Women's Movement in America, 1848–1869* (Ithaca, N.Y.: Cornell University Press, 1978); Mary Ryan, *Women in Public: Between Banners and Ballots, 1825–1880* (Baltimore: Johns Hopkins University Press, 1990); Rosalyn Terborg-Penn, *African American Women in the Struggle for the Vote, 1850–1920* (Bloomington: Indiana University Press, 1998); Martha S. Jones, *All Bound Up Together: The Woman Question in African American Public Culture, 1830–1900* (Chapel Hill: University of North Carolina Press, 2007). In a study of forty-eight mid-nineteenth-century congressional hearings on election disturbances, Richard Bensel found only one instance where a white woman was present at a polling place—before black enfranchisement— and she was there to assist her enfeebled husband to the polls. Bensel, *The American Ballot Box in the Mid-Nineteenth Century* (New York: Cambridge University Press, 2004), 22. For more on white women's participation in partisan gatherings, see Elizabeth R. Varon, *We Mean to Be Counted: White Women & Politics in Antebellum Virginia* (Chapel Hill: University of North Carolina Press, 1998); Christopher J. Olsen, "Respecting 'The Wise Allotment of Our Sphere': White Women and Politics in Mississippi, 1840–1860," *Journal of Women's History* 11, no. 3 (Autumn 1999): 104–26; Alison M. Parker, *Articulating Rights: Nineteenth-Century American Women on Race, Reform, and the State* (DeKalb: Northern Illinois University Press, 2010), 158–62; Jean Harvey Baker, "Public Women and Partisan Politics, 1840–1860," in *A Political Nation: New Directions in Mid-*

Nineteenth-Century American Political History, ed. Gary W. Gallagher and Rachel A. Shelden (Charlottesville: University of Virginia Press, 2012), 64–81.

4. Richard Bensel, "The American Ballot Box: Law, Identity, and the Polling Place in the Mid-Nineteenth Century," *Studies in American Political Development* 17 (Spring 2003): 2. For representative works on nineteenth-century democracy, see Richard L. Mc-Cormick, *The Party Period and Public Policy: American Politics from the Age of Jackson to the Progressive Era* (New York: Oxford University Press, 1986); Joel H. Silbey, *The American Political Nation, 1838–1893* (Stanford, Calif.: Stanford University Press, 1991); Glenn C. Altschuler and Stuart M. Blumin, *Rude Republic: Americans and Their Politics in the Nineteenth Century* (Princeton, N.J.: Princeton University Press, 2000); Byron E. Shafer and Anthony J. Badger, eds., *Contesting Democracy: Substance and Structure in American Political History, 1775–2000* (Lawrence: University Press of Kansas, 2001). For works that stand apart and address the communal nature of politics, see Jean Baker, *Affairs of Party: The Political Culture of Northern Democrats in the Mid-Nineteenth Century* (Ithaca, N.Y.: Cornell University Press, 1983); Paul Bourke and Donald DeBats, *Washington County: Politics and Community in Antebellum America* (Baltimore: Johns Hopkins University Press, 1995).

5. One historian who has examined black Democrats in detail is Edmund L. Drago, in *Hurrah for Hampton!: Black Red Shirts in South Carolina during Reconstruction* (Fayetteville: University of Arkansas Press, 1998). Drago's introductory essay focuses on black Democrats in South Carolina during the 1876 election to counter the perception of the black community as monolithic and to emphasize the long history of black conservatism. His argument, that black people aligned with the Democratic Party because they were conservatives, however, is unconvincing. Sizeable numbers of black men joined Hampton's campaign, but Drago was unable to determine how many were forced or coerced during the exceedingly violent election campaign. For other, passing references to black Democrats, see James E. Sefton, "A Note on the Political Intimidation of Black Men by Other Black Men," *Georgia Historical Quarterly* 52, no. 4 (1968): 443–48; Thomas C. Holt, *Black over White: Negro Political Leadership in South Carolina during Reconstruction* (Urbana: University of Illinois Press, 1977), 211–12; William C. Hine, "Black Politicians in Reconstruction Charleston, South Carolina: A Collective Study," *Journal of Southern History* 49, no. 4 (November 1983): 555–84; Peter Eisenstadt, "Southern Black Conservatism, 1865–1945: An Introduction," in *Black Conservatism: Essays in Intellectual and Political History*, ed. Peter Eisenstadt (New York: Garland Publishing, 1999), 51–80; Steven Hahn, *A Nation under Our Feet: Black Political Struggles in the Rural South from Slavery to the Great Migration* (Cambridge, Mass.: Belknap Press of Harvard University Press, 2003), 226–28. For more on patron-client relationships, see W. E. B. Du Bois, *Souls of Black Folk: Essays and Sketches*, 7th ed. (Chicago: A. C. McClurg, 1907), 152–56; Eric Foner, *Nothing but Freedom: Emancipation and Its Legacy* (Baton Rouge: Louisiana State University Press, 1983), 18–26; Rebecca J. Scott, *Slave Emancipation in Cuba: The Transition to Free Labor, 1860–1899* (1985; repr., Pittsburgh: University of Pittsburgh Press, 2000); Frederick Cooper, Thomas C. Holt, and Rebecca J. Scott, *Beyond Slavery: Explorations of Race, Labor, and Citizenship in Postemancipation Societies* (Chapel Hill: University of North Carolina Press, 2000).

6. For more on space as an important ingredient in political solidarity, see Margaret Kohn, *Radical Space: Building the House of the People* (Ithaca, N.Y.: Cornell University Press, 2003).

7. *Natchez Democrat and Courier*, 8 December, 9 December, 15 December, 16 Decem-

ber, 17 December 1875; testimony of Webster Bowyer, *Lynch vs. Chalmers*, 184; testimony of Thomas Dorsey, *Recent Election*, 166–67; *Vidalia Herald*, 19 August 1870; *Natchez Democrat*, 27 September 1871.

8. *Natchez Democrat*, 5 October, 12 October 1870, 3 July 1873, 15 July, 22 July 1874. Biographical information can be found in Justin Behrend, Black Politicians Database, SUNY-Geneseo, http://go.geneseo.edu/BlackPoliticiansDB (BPDB). Other crossover leaders who held political and associational offices include A. J. Bryant of Tensas, Hugh M. Foley of Wilkinson, and Horace C. Bailey, Nathan Butler, David C. Granderson, and Hiram Littleton of Adams County. In the Mississippi state militia, in which 6,103 black men from the Natchez District were enrolled, 8 black officers were also political leaders. *Journal of the House of Representatives of the State of Mississippi* (Jackson, Miss., 1873), pp. 548–53, Series 1946: House Journals, Mississippi Department of Archives and History (MDAH), Jackson; *Journal of the House of Representatives of the State of Mississippi* (Jackson, Miss., 1874), pp. 688–701, Series 1946, MDAH. The officers were Capt. S. S. Meekins, Capt. John Peck, Col. G. F. Bowles, Lt. Col. Merrimon Howard, Maj. Noah Spillers, Maj. Williams Landers, 2nd Lt. John Johnson, and Capt. Fountain Ballard. For an example of militias taking part in political processions, see *Woodville Republican*, 27 November 1869.

9. *Natchez Democrat*, 3 July, 25 September 1872; BPDB. The leaders of the Deluge Fire Company were listed in the *Natchez Courier*, 23 July 1870, and the *Natchez Democrat*, 20 September 1871. The Good Will Fire Company leaders were listed in the *Natchez Democrat*, 5 April, 19 April 1871, 10 April 1872, and 3 May 1876. All told, forty-one leaders were named, and of those twenty were actively involved in partisan politics. The vast majority of the leaders were artisans (twenty-eight) and most were mulattos (twenty-four). For more on the politics of each fire company, see *Natchez Democrat*, 27 November, 24 December 1872.

10. *Natchez Courier*, 16 July 1870; *Weekly Clarion*, 9 June 1870.

11. *North Louisiana Journal*, 6 April, 28 September 1872, 8 November 1873; *Concordia Eagle*, 3 March 1877; *Natchez Democrat*, 14 December 1870. Thirty-one out of forty-four identifiable Tensas Parish delegates were listed as either "farmer" or "works on farm," according to the 1870 U.S. Census. The Concordia Parish committee was composed of twenty-four members, of whom only the secretary was white. Ten committee members were listed as "laborer" in the census; two were listed as "farmer." I was unable to determine demographic information for six of the men. U.S. Bureau of Census, *Ninth Census: Population, 1870*.

12. *Concordia Eagle*, 2 October 1875; *Natchez Democrat*, 21 June 1869, 31 July 1872; testimony of Merrimon Howard, in U.S. Senate, *Testimony as to Denial of Elective Franchise in Mississippi at the Elections of 1875 and 1876*, 44th Cong., 2nd sess., 1877, Misc. Doc. 45, p. 160 (cited hereafter as *Denial of Elective Franchise*); testimony of T. P. Jackson, *Recent Election*, 227. For more on pole raisings, see the testimonies of Merrimon Howard, J. B. Cessor, and Thomas W. Hunt, *Denial of Elective Franchise*, 159, 165, 252, 904–5.

13. Betty Beaumont, *A Business Woman's Journal: A Sequel to "Twelve Years of My Life"* (Philadelphia: T. B. Peterson and Brothers, 1888), 353; Wilmer Shields to Doctor Mercer, 6 October 1869, folder 10, Wilmer Shields Letters, William Newton Mercer Papers, Louisiana and Lower Mississippi Valley Collections, Louisiana State University Libraries, Baton Rouge.

14. *Woodville Republican*, 27 November 1869. The newspaper estimated that two thousand male voters attended the gathering, making it quite likely that at least twice as

many people were present when women and children are included in the tabulation. For another "political barbecue" that attracted four thousand people to Port Gibson, see *Weekly Standard*, 24 August 1867.

15. *Woodville Republican*, 23 October, 27 November 1869. For more on parades as political acts, see Susan G. Davis, *Parades and Power: Street Theatre in Nineteenth-Century Philadelphia* (Philadelphia: Temple University Press, 1986); Simon P. Newman, *Parades and the Politics of the Street: Festive Culture in the Early American Republic* (Philadelphia: University of Pennsylvania Press, 1997).

16. *North Louisiana Journal*, 12 October 1872; *Natchez Democrat*, 25 September, 9 October 1872. For other occasions when black politicians instructed black voters to lie to their employers about their vote, see *Natchez Democrat*, 18 September 1872.

17. *Natchez Democrat*, 7 October 1876; Jeannie Dean, ed., *Annie Harper's Journal: A Southern Mother's Legacy* (Denton, Tex.: Flower Mound Writing Co., 1983), 43.

18. J. H. Jones, "Reconstruction in Wilkinson County," *Publications of the Mississippi Historical Society* 8 (1904): 158; testimonies of Robert Davis, Taylor Young, and T. P. Jackson, *Recent Election*, 210, 211, 227.

19. *Natchez Democrat*, 12 October 1870; *Woodville Republican*, 13 November 1869. For another example of joint political debates, see *New National Era*, 5 December 1872.

20. *Natchez Democrat*, 19 June 1872.

21. *Natchez Democrat*, 28 August, 14 August 1872 (emphasis in original). For more on black Greeley clubs, see *Natchez Democrat* 31 July, 7 August, 14 August, 21 August, 2 October, 30 October 1872. For more on Greeley's candidacy, see Eric Foner, *Reconstruction: America's Unfinished Revolution, 1863–1877* (New York: Harper & Row, 1988), 502–7.

22. *Natchez Democrat*, 14 August 1872; Nelson Fitzhugh, died 4 April 1868, Wills, book 3, p. 337; Anthony Hoggatt, died 30 January 1903, Wills, book 5, p. 410, Adams County Courthouse, Natchez, Miss.

23. Affidavit of William Scott and Jos. Hubbard [Habbard], in U.S. Senate, *Memorial of Hon. J. E. McDonald, Hon. Lewis V. Bogy, and Hon. John W. Stevenson in Relation to the Counting by the Returning Board of the Vote of the People of Louisiana for the Appointment of Presidential Electors, November 7, 1876*, 44th Cong., 2nd sess., S. Misc. Doc. 14, in *The Miscellaneous Documents of the Senate of the United States for the Second Session of the Forty-Fourth Congress* (Washington, D.C.: GPO, 1877), 282, 283 (cited hereafter as *Counting by the Returning Board*).

24. *Natchez Democrat*, 16 September 1869; *Woodville Republican*, 27 November, 13 November 1869.

25. I identified sixteen black Democratic politicians in my BPDB. Three resided in Concordia Parish, each of whom worked on plantations. The other thirteen hailed from Natchez, but I found demographic information for only nine of them. Befitting an urban environment, the identifiable nine split between laborers and artisans. The Concordia Parish black Democratic political activists were William Davenport, Thomas Dorsey, Louis Hays, and William Richardson. The Adams County black Democratic political activists were Henry Adams, Owen Anderson, William Carraway, William Cotton, Robinson Crusoe, Willis Douglass, John Fitzhugh, Burrell Foley, William Hoggatt, Israel Jones, John Smith, and Anderson Webb.

26. *Natchez Democrat*, August 14, 1872.

27. Testimonies of J. Floyd King and Taylor Young, *Recent Election*, 158, 212; affidavits of Robin Grimes, Edmond Gordon, Daniel Tucker, and Lewis Armstrong, *Counting by the Returning Board*, 278, 279, 281, 285.

28. Testimony of Thomas Dorsey, *Recent Election*, 166, 168.

29. Testimony of J. Floyd King, *Recent Election*, 157–62, 168; testimony of J. D. Vertner, in U.S. Senate, *Report of the Select Committee into the Mississippi Election of 1875*, 44th Cong., 1st sess., 1876, S. Rep. 527, p. 210; testimony of Wade R. Young, *Recent Election*, 155. There were other Democratic clubs with black members in existence, but only one all-black club. On other Democratic clubs, see the testimonies of William Hunter and Wade R. Young, *Recent Election*, 163, 165. For testimony from black club members on Morgan's plantation, see *Counting by the Returning Board*, 278, 279, 281, 282, 287, 288. For another example of a pledge of protection, see *Natchez Democrat*, 18 September 1872.

30. Testimonies of Thomas Dorsey, T. P. Jackson, and William Ridgley, *Recent Election*, 156, 166, 222, 227. Determining William Ridgley's racial identity has been problematic. In congressional testimony, Ridgley was not identified in racial terms. Black witnesses were identified as "colored," but witnesses without racial identification were presumed to be "white." Charles Vincent, in his study of black Louisiana legislators, did not include Ridgley in his list of Concordia state representatives. But the 1870 census and two articles from the *Natchez Democrat* indicated that he was either "black" or "colored." A "William Ridgely" is listed in the 1870 census as a resident of Concordia Parish and is identified as black. In the *Natchez Democrat* (May 10 and 11, 1876), William Ridgley is identified as T. P. Jackson's brother. T. P. Jackson was identified in congressional testimony as "colored," in the census as "black," and in Freedmen's Bank records as "yellow." I should also add that Joe Louis Caldwell, in his detailed study of the Louisiana Delta, identifies Ridgley as "black." *Recent Election*, 220–26; U.S. Bureau of Census, *Ninth Census: Population, 1870*; Charles Vincent, *Black Legislators in Louisiana during Reconstruction* (Baton Rouge: Louisiana State University Press, 1976), 235; Joe Louis Caldwell, "A Social, Economic, and Political Study of Blacks in the Louisiana Delta, 1865–1880" (Ph.D. diss., Tulane University, 1988), 434.

31. *Natchez Democrat*, 7 August, 2 October 1872. John was the only one of Nelson Fitzhugh's six sons to align with the Democratic Party. He worked as a porter and thus was dependent on a white employer, but there is very little to suggest a specific reason for his public affiliation with Democrats.

32. *Natchez Democrat*, 25 September, 2 October 1872. William Zoch, white, was a surety for $2,000 on William McCary's tax collector bond. See *Natchez Democrat*, 10 January 1872.

33. Testimony of Wade R. Young, *Recent Election*, 155, 218. Concordia Parish voters voted for the Republican gubernatorial candidate by a margin of ten to one in 1872 and by nine to one in 1876. See the *Weekly Louisianian*, 16 November 1872; *Recent Election*, appendix. For other testimonies related to the Kelly incident, see testimony of F. S. Shields, *Recent Election*, 194; petition of Wade R. Young, C. A. Pipes, J. George A. Shields, A. W. Metcalfe, Wade H. Hough, Jr., A. N. D. Spencer, and J. [T.] P. Jackson to Hon. J. Madison Wells, chairman, and to the members of the returning-board for the State of Louisiana, *Counting by the Returning Board*, 275–76; affidavit of J.C. Teniday [Ferriday], *Counting by the Returning Board*, 280.

34. Testimony of J. Floyd King, *Recent Election*, 160.

35. Testimonies of Alexander Johnson and Webster Bowyer, *Lynch vs. Chalmers*, 175–77, 182; Jones, "Reconstruction in Wilkinson County," 159. The secret, or Australian, ballot was not adopted widely until later in the century. See Alexander Keyssar, *The Right to Vote: The Contested History of Democracy in the United States* (New York: Basic Books,

2000), 142–43. For more on the implications of rural politics and voting, see Bensel, *American Ballot Box in the Mid-Nineteenth Century*, xiii.

36. Historical Census Browser, University of Virginia, Geospatial and Statistical Data Center, 2004, http://fisher.lib.virginia.edu/collections/stats/histcensus/index.html. In 1870, 9,257 "colored persons" lived in Concordia Parish, which was 92.8 percent of the 9,977 total inhabitants. In 1880 the black population was 91 percent of the total population, 13,594 out of 14,914. I estimated that 77 percent of eligible black men voted in the 1876 election. Packard (the Republican candidate for governor) secured 2,461 votes from Concordia Parish. More than likely, these votes came only from black men. Packard's opponent, Nicholls, received 366 votes. With only 226 eligible white male voters, according to the 1875 census, it is reasonable to assume that all the whites and over one hundred blacks endorsed the Democratic candidate. W. R. Young, a U.S. election supervisor in Concordia, estimated that 150 blacks voted for the Democratic state ticket. *Recent Election*, 154. For more on the numbers, see "Statistics of Registrations and Elections in the State of Louisiana" in the appendix to *Recent Election*.

37. U.S. House, *Select Committee on the Recent Election in the State of Louisiana*, 44th Cong., 2nd sess., 1877, H. Rep. 156; *Recent Election*; *Miscellaneous Documents of the Senate for the Second Session of the Forty-Fourth Congress*, 273–98.

38. Testimony of J. Floyd King, *Recent Election*, 158; testimony of David Young, in U.S. Senate, *Report of the United States Senate Committee to Inquire into Alleged Frauds and Violence in the Elections of 1878*, 45th Cong., 3rd sess., 1879, S. Rep. 855, vol. 1, pp. 371–74 (cited hereafter as *Frauds and Violence in the Elections of 1878*); testimony of F. S. Shields, *Recent Election*, 192.

39. BPDB. Young was a member of the Louisiana state House from 1868 to 1874, and he was a delegate at numerous political conventions. For more on Young's economic and religious interests, see *Natchez Democrat*, 19 April 1871; *Concordia Eagle*, 2 October 1875. On Young's property holdings, see John Martin to Singleton and Young, 23 January 1874, book R, General Mortgages, Concordia Parish Courthouse, Vidalia, La.; John Page to David Young, 2 December 1868, book O; David Singleton to David Young, 16 March 1869, book O; Pauline Carter et al. to David Young, 29 August 1870, book O; Bennett Hitchcock to David Young, 8 March 1871, book O; A. B. Kirby to David Young, 2 December 1871, book P; Alice Williams to David Young, 7 November 1872, book P; Anna E. Adkins to David Young and Oren Stewart, 18 May 1872, book P, Conveyance Records, Concordia Parish Courthouse, Vidalia, La. In the 1874 election, black Republicans were elected to thirteen offices, including state legislator, coroner, all justices of peace, and all constables, and white Republicans were elected to five offices, including parish judge, sheriff, and police jurors. U.S. House, *Contested Election, Spencer vs. Morey, Louisiana*, 44th Cong., 1st sess., H. Misc. Doc. 54, pp. 121–22.

40. There are two differing versions of the "Vidalia Political Row." See *Natchez Democrat*, 10 May, 11 May 1876.

41. *Natchez Democrat*, 21 October 1874; *New Orleans Daily Picayune*, 13 February, 21 February 1875; testimony of Wade R. Young, *Recent Election*, 217; Foner, *Reconstruction*, 512–26; LeeAnna Keith, *The Colfax Massacre: The Untold Story of Black Power, White Terror, and the Death of Reconstruction* (New York: Oxford University Press, 2008), 143–46; Edward King, *The Great South* (Hartford, Conn.: American Publishing Company, 1875), 295. In the 1874 congressional election for Louisiana's Fifth District, William B. Spencer, the Democratic candidate, successfully contested the election, in part by demonstrating fraudulent vote counting in Concordia Parish's Fifth Ward. See U.S. House, *Con-*

tested Election, Spencer vs. Morey, Louisiana, 44th Cong., 1st sess., 1876, H. Rep. 442; U.S. House, Contested Election, H. Misc. Doc. 54. (There is no relation between Wade Young, a white attorney who only moved to Concordia Parish in 1875, and David Young.) David Young's moderating impulses were also in evidence a few months later at the National Press Convention of Colored Journalists. Young questioned whether civil rights issues should be pressed. He took exception to a clause in a report that referred "to the denial of the civil rights of the colored people of the South. He thought enough had been said on that subject and could see no use of keeping the same old whine." Weekly Louisianian, 14 August 1875.

42. Testimonies of Wade R. Young and Judge James G. Leach, Recent Election, 217, 261; Natchez Democrat, 3 January 1877; testimony of David Young, Frauds and Violence in the Elections of 1878, 371–74; testimony of F. S. Shields, Recent Election, 192; Taylor, Louisiana Reconstructed, 486–89. On speculation that David Young might not win election to the state senate in 1874, see Natchez Democrat, 16 September 1874. Endorsed by Governor Kellogg's government, a plea of nolle prosequi was entered in court. The Concordia Parish grand jury, however, exonerated Young of all charges. See Concordia Eagle, 17 April 1875, in Weekly Louisianian, 24 April 1875. A warrant is a written order that instructs a government treasurer to pay the holder. Payment, however, is not guaranteed because it is dependent on the availability of funds. For more on political violence in the Natchez District, see chapter 7.

43. Testimonies of William Ridgley, T. P. Jackson, J. Floyd King, Recent Election, 223, 227, 157–58. The factional conflict between Jackson and Young's faction dated to 1874. See Natchez Democrat, 1 November, 4 November 1874. For other examples of Republicans associating a Democratic victory with a return to slavery, see Counting by the Returning Board, 276, 279, 280, 282, 284, 286, 287.

44. Selected works on the sexual exploitation of female slaves include Deborah Gray White, Ar'n't I a Woman?: Female Slaves in the Plantation South (New York: W. W. Norton, 1985), 78; Elizabeth Fox-Genovese, Within the Plantation Household: Black and White Women of the Old South (Chapel Hill: University of North Carolina Press, 1988), 190, 325–26, 374, 379–80; Thelma Jennings, "'Us Colored Women Had to Go Though a Plenty': Sexual Exploitation of African-American Slave Women," Journal of Women's History 1, no. 3 (Winter 1990): 45–74; Marie Jenkins Schwartz, Born in Bondage: Growing Up Enslaved in the Antebellum South (Cambridge, Mass.: Harvard University Press, 2000) 172–73; Nell Irvin Painter, "Soul Murder and Slavery: Toward a Fully Loaded Cost Accounting," in Southern History across the Color Line (Chapel Hill: University of North Carolina Press, 2002), 15–39; Thavolia Glymph, Out of the House of Bondage: The Transformation of the Plantation Household (New York: Cambridge University Press, 2008), 54–55.

45. Testimonies of Robert Davis and Joe Habit, Recent Election, 210, 215; affidavit of Jos. Hubbard [Habbard], Counting by the Returning Board, 283; affidavit of William Warfield, Counting by the Returning Board, 285; testimonies of J. Floyd King and Robert Davis, Recent Election, 162, 210; affidavit of J. C. Teniday [Ferriday], Counting by the Returning Board, 280. Peter Hooper (referred to in the testimony as "Hoover") joined in the lawsuit against David Young after the state withdrew its indictment, and thus Hooper seemed likely to attract the animus of Young. See the testimony of Judge James G. Leach, Recent Election, 261. For other testimonies of appeals to black women to quit their husbands, see Counting by the Returning Board, 279, 282, 284, 287, 288. For other accounts of women threatening violence, see Counting by the Returning Board, 280, 282, 288. For other state-

ments attesting that Young would take care of the wives, see the affidavits of Milton Ray and Luder [Luther] Howard, *Counting by the Returning Board*, 276, 284.

46. Affidavit of Samuel Walker, *Counting by the Returning Board*, 287; affidavit of J. C. Teniday [Ferriday], ibid., 280; affidavit of William Scott, ibid., 283; affidavit of James Foy, ibid., 294. For other examples of pressure that women exerted, see the affidavits of J. C. Teniday [Ferriday] and Stephen Armstead, ibid., 280, 284; testimony of F. S. Shields, *Recent Election*, 163.

47. Testimony of H. E. Witherspoon and Thomas Dorsey, *Recent Election*, 272, 166–68; affidavit of James Foy, *Counting by the Returning Board*, 294; testimony of William Hunter, *Recent Election*, 163; affidavits of Daniel Tucker, Lewis Hays, Alexander Smart, and Alexander Williams, *Counting by the Returning Board*, 282, 283–84, 287; testimony of J. Floyd King, *Recent Election*, 157; testimony of Charles G. Wade, ibid., 172; affidavit of Alexander Williams, *Counting by the Returning Board*, 287; affidavit of Stephen Armstead, ibid., 284; affidavit of Joe Williams, ibid., 287. For similarly excessive political rhetoric, see the affidavit of William T. Lewis, a white bookkeeper, in which he claimed that a black preacher at a Republican meeting said "that he would cut the head off any colored man that voted the democratic ticket and suck his blood." Ibid., 277.

48. Affidavit of Joe Williams, *Counting by the Returning Board*, 287; testimony of T. P. Jackson, *Recent Election*, 227, 232; testimony of F. S. Shields, ibid., 192–93; affidavit of J. C. Teniday [Ferriday], *Counting by the Returning Board*, 280; affidavit of Jos. Hubbard [Habbard], ibid., 283; testimony of Eli Johnson, *Recent Election*, 255. On the black church as an essential component of political mobilization, see Evelyn Brooks Higginbotham, *Righteous Discontent: The Women's Movement in the Black Baptist Church, 1880–1920* (Cambridge, Mass.: Harvard University Press, 1993), 7.

49. Testimony of Joe Habit, *Recent Election*, 215; testimony of William Ridgley, ibid., 221; testimony of Thomas Dorsey, ibid., 166; affidavit of Thomas Dorsey, *Counting by the Returning Board*, 288. For another example of threats to burn property, see the testimony of Henderson Smith, *Recent Election*, 214. For other examples of violent threats, see the testimonies of Wade R. Young, Joe Habit, Eli Johnson, and H. E. Witherspoon, ibid., 154, 215, 255, 273.

50. Testimony of J. Floyd King, *Recent Election*, 157. For more on the election of 1876, see the bulk of the testimony in *Louisiana in 1876: Report of the Sub-Committee of the Committee on Privileges and Elections of the United States Senate* (Washington, D.C.: GPO, 1877). On the Natchez District massacres, see *Natchez Democrat*, 17 May, 18 May, 19 May, 20 May, 21 May 1876; unpublished manuscript autobiography, box A:3, folder 2, James Stewart McGehee Papers, Louisiana State University Libraries, Baton Rouge; *Denial of Elective Franchise*, 142–44, 174–75, 177–78, 187, 940–45; M. Howard to A. Ames, November 6, 1877 [1876], box 18, folder 153, Ames Family Papers, Sophia Smith Collection, Smith College, Northampton, Mass.

51. For more on the politics of voting, see Bensel, *American Ballot Box in the Mid-Nineteenth Century*.

52. *Natchez Democrat*, 1 November 1874, 7 October 1876; J. B. Deacon, Dist. Atty., ex rel Samuel S. Meekins, William H. Lynch, and M. A. C. Hussey vs. David Williamson, William Burns, J. P. Buie, box 8–2, January term 1874, Adams County Circuit Court Case Files, Historic Natchez Foundation, Natchez, Miss.; testimony of J. B. Cessor, *Denial of Elective Franchise*, 258–59; *Natchez Courier*, 2 November 1867; testimony of Charles W. Minor and Webster Bowyer, *Lynch vs. Chalmers*, 165, 184. The Good Will firehouse was on Commerce Street between Main and State Streets in the Fourth Ward. The AME

church was at the southwest corner of Pine and Jefferson in the Second Ward. City hall was in the Third Ward, and the First Ward polling place was at the corner of Franklin and Canal. On polling places at Tensas and Concordia plantations, see the testimony of V. H. Newell and M. T. Randolph, *Frauds and Violence in the Elections of 1878*, 284, 362–63. On polling places in rural Adams County, see *Natchez Courier*, 2 November 1867; testimony of Louis W. Fitzhugh, *Lynch vs. Chalmers*, 197. On polling places in stores, see testimony of J. B. Cessor, *Denial of Elective Franchise*, 258–59; testimony of Robert Davis, *Recent Election*, 210; testimony of Lennox Scott, *Lynch vs. Chalmers*, 188.

53. *Natchez Democrat*, 3 January 1871; J. T. Vertner to J. Z. George, telegram, 2 November 1875, in U.S. Senate, *Report into the Mississippi Election of 1875*, 409; testimony of J. Floyd King and Taylor Young, *Recent Election*, 158, 211; testimony of Thomas Richardson, *Denial of Elective Franchise*, 200; testimony of Wilson Wood, *Lynch vs. Chalmers*, 118; Jones, "Reconstruction in Wilkinson County," 159. Thomas Quarterman, a white painter and Natchez city clerk, noted an uncharacteristic occurrence at the 1880 election: "white voters crowded at the door before the polls opened," whereas in past elections the early crowd was "principally colored men." See the testimony of Thomas R. Quarterman, *Lynch vs. Chalmers*, 70. For more on marching to the polls, see Julie Saville, *The Work of Reconstruction: From Slave to Wage Laborer in South Carolina, 1860–1870* (New York: Cambridge University Press, 1994), 172–75; Hahn, *A Nation under Our Feet*, 224–25. For more on the culture of polling places, see Christopher J. Olsen, *Political Culture and Secession in Mississippi: Masculinity, Honor, and the Antiparty Tradition* (New York: Oxford University Press, 2000) 121–31; Robert J. Dinkin, ed., *Election Day: A Documentary History* (Westport, Conn.: Greenwood Press, 2002), 62–95; Bensel, *American Ballot Box in the Mid-Nineteenth Century*, 26–85; Kate Kelly, *Election Day: An American Holiday, an American History* (New York: ASJA Press, 2008), 66–141.

54. *Natchez Democrat*, 21 June 1869; testimony of Henry B. Fowles, Webster Bowyer, and Horace C. Bailey, *Lynch vs. Chalmers*, 137, 179, 193–94.

55. Testimony of Merrimon Howard, *Denial of Elective Franchise*, 173; *Natchez Democrat*, 13 December 1871.

56. Testimonies of Henry B. Fowles, Smith Kinney, and Harry Smith Jr., *Lynch vs. Chalmers*, 137, 145.

57. Testimony of George N. Johnson, *Lynch vs. Chalmers*, 157; BPDB; testimony of Horace C. Bailey, *Lynch vs. Chalmers*, 194. Local people gave much more weight to local contests. Referring to the hotly disputed election of 1876 between Hayes and Tilden, Merrimon Howard testified that "the people hardly knew who the presidential candidates were." See the testimony of Merrimon Howard, *Denial of Elective Franchise*, 179.

58. *Natchez Democrat*, 13 November 1872.

59. Testimony of Harry Smith Jr., *Lynch vs. Chalmers*, 146; testimony of John R. Lynch, *Denial of Elective Franchise*, 120; testimony of Abraham Felters, *Lynch vs. Chalmers*, 141. For another instance in which black voters sought to verify their ballots, see *New York Times*, 26 December 1876. Black voters, "sometimes in crowds," also came up to Lynch's brother, William, to verify their tickets. Testimony of William H. Lynch, *Lynch vs. Chalmers*, 148.

60. Dean, *Annie Harper's Journal*, 45; testimony of Harry Smith Jr., *Lynch vs. Chalmers*, 145; testimony of F. S. Shields, *Recent Election*, 193; testimony of Wade R. Young, ibid., 154; testimony of James M. McGill, *Frauds and Violence in the Elections of 1878*, 223; testimony of Smith Kinney, *Lynch vs. Chalmers*, 144.

61. Affidavit of J. C. Teniday [Ferriday], *Counting by the Returning Board*, 280; Wil-

liam J. Davis to Ames, 25 December 1872, folder 134, box 15, Governor Ames Papers, MDAH (emphasis in original). For more on the standard that only a "man of ordinary courage" should vote, see Bensel, *American Ballot Box in the Mid-Nineteenth Century*, 21. For more on Election Day rituals, see Mark Brewin, "Bonfires, Fistfights, and Roaring Cannons: Election Day and the Creation of Social Capital in the City of Philadelphia," in *Social Capital in the City: Community and Civic Life in Philadelphia*, ed. Richardson Dilworth (Philadelphia: Temple University Press, 2006), 40–55.

62. Affidavit of T. E. Sims, Edward Hooper, M. A. Joyce, Rez R. Young, Henry Williams, and Rleas Cook, *Counting by the Returning Board*, 291; testimony of Robert Davis, *Recent Election*, 209–10; testimony of Wade R. Young, ibid., 154, 156; testimony of W. H. Nutt, ibid., 234; affidavit of C. J. Meyer, *Counting by the Returning Board*, 292; affidavit of J. Surgent Shields, George Washington, Hunter Jenkins, Robert Davis, and Beverly Brooks, ibid., 292–93; testimony of H. E. Witherspoon, *Recent Election*, 272; testimony of Henderson Smith, ibid., 214; BPDB; Taylor Young, *Recent Election*, 211; affidavit of Wm. Hunter, L. V. Felters, T. A. Young, and Jordan Young, *Counting by the Returning Board*, 292; affidavit of Alexander Smart, ibid., 284.

63. Testimony of J. Floyd King, *Recent Election*, 158; testimony of H. E. Witherspoon, ibid., 272; testimony of Taylor Young, ibid., 211.

64. Testimony of Taylor Young, *Recent Election*, 211; testimony of Joe Habit, ibid., 215; U.S. Bureau of Census, *Tenth Census of the United States*. For another instance of women violently confronting political dissenters, see the testimony of William Ridgly, *Recent Election*, 222.

65. Testimony of T. P. Jackson, *Recent Election*, 230; ibid., appendix. Jackson testified that his opponent, E. W. Wall, received 1,600 votes, while he gained 1,000 to 1,500. His best guess was about 1,200 votes. In Concordia Parish in 1876, Packard (the Republican candidate for governor) received 2,461 votes, while Nicholls (the Democratic candidate) received 366 votes. Two years earlier in the state treasurer's race, the Republican candidate garnered 2,043 votes to the Democrat's 154.

66. Bensel, "The American Ballot Box," 13.

67. Albert T. Morgan, *Yazoo; or, On the Picket Line of Freedom in the South* (1884; repr., Columbia: University of South Carolina Press, 2000), 230–33; Maria Waterbury, *Seven Years among the Freedmen* (Chicago: T. B. Arnold, 1890), 90–91 (the election in question could also have taken place in Mobile, Alabama; Waterbury wasn't very precise about places and dates); Hahn, *A Nation under Our Feet*, 227–28; *Macon, Georgia, Weekly Telegraph*, October 8, 1872, quoted in Edmund L. Drago, "Militancy and Black Women in Reconstruction Georgia," *Journal of American Culture* 1 (Winter 1978): 841; quoted in Michael W. Fitzgerald, *Urban Emancipation: Popular Politics in Reconstruction Mobile, 1860–1890* (Baton Rouge: Louisiana State University Press, 2002), 211; testimony of J. B. Cessor, *Denial of Elective Franchise*, 255; testimony of John R. Lynch, ibid., 128; Dean, *Annie Harper's Journal*, 44; John C. Rodrigue, *Reconstruction in the Cane Fields: From Slavery to Free Labor in Louisiana's Sugar Parishes, 1862–1880* (Baton Rouge: Louisiana State University Press, 2001), 171; Dorothy Sterling, ed., *We Are Your Sisters: Black Women in the Nineteenth Century* (New York: W.W. Norton, 1984), 370; Foner, *Reconstruction*, 574; Drago, *Hurrah for Hampton!*, 40–43; testimony of W. H. Whitehurst, *Lynch vs. Chalmers*, 65; Brown, "To Catch the Vision of Freedom," 83.

68. Testimony of J. Henri Burch, in U.S. Senate, *Report and Testimony of the Select Committee of the United States Senate to Investigate the Causes of the Removal of the Negroes from the Southern States to the Northern States*, 46th Cong., 2nd sess., 1880, S. Rep.

693, pt. 2, p. 232. For more on Burch, see Eric Foner, ed., *Freedom's Lawmakers: A Directory of Black Officeholders during Reconstruction*, rev. ed. (Baton Rouge: Louisiana State University Press, 1996), 31–32.

Chapter Seven. "Organized Terrorism and Armed Violence"

1. Testimonies of Merrimon Howard and Lewis H. Ingraham, in U.S. Senate, *Testimony as to Denial of Elective Franchise in Mississippi at the Elections of 1875 and 1876*, 44th Cong., 2nd sess., 1877, Misc. Doc. 45, pp. 174–75, 189, 940 (cited hereafter as *Denial of Elective Franchise*).

2. Testimonies of A. M. Hardy, Merrimon Howard, Peter Hurst, and Lewis H. Ingraham, *Denial of Elective Franchise*, 142–47, 174–87, 896–900, 940–50; Susan Sillers Darden Diary, vol. 2, 5–7 November 1876, Darden Family Papers, Mississippi Department of Archives and History (MDAH), Jackson; *New York Times*, 15 November, 16 December 1876; Jeannie Dean, ed., *Annie Harper's Journal: A Southern Mother's Legacy* (Denton, Tex.: Flower Mound Writing Co., 1983), 44.

3. Testimony of Merrimon Howard, *Denial of Elective Franchise*, 176. See also the testimonies of A. M. Hardy, Merrimon Howard, Peter Hurst, and Lewis H. Ingraham, ibid., 144, 178–80, 895–902, 940, 949; Darden Diary, 7 November, 22 December 1876, Darden Family Papers, MDAH; *New York Times*, 16 December 1876. One white Republican, D. C. Kearns, the chancery clerk of Jefferson County, avoided harassment by voting Democrat. See the testimony of Merrimon Howard, *Denial of Elective Franchise*, 700.

4. My interpretation of the role of urban spaces builds off of Margaret Kohn's insight that "atomization is [the] greatest weakness" of poor people mobilizing for political power. "The concentration of bodies," she continues, "is the only available tactic of resistance for those who do not (either literally or metaphorically) carry weapons." Black people in the Natchez District, as we shall see, did carry literal weapons, but their strength lay in their numbers and their ability to act together. See Margaret Kohn, *Radical Space: Building the House of the People* (Ithaca, N.Y.: Cornell University Press, 2003), 43.

5. Rep. Lynch (Miss.) on Reconstruction and Democratic Rule in Mississippi, *Congressional Record* 4, pt. 6 (12 August 1876): 5540. For an illuminating study on the cultural patterns of redemptive suffering that underlay southern electoral violence, see Carole Emberton, *Beyond Redemption: Race, Violence, and the American South after the Civil War* (Chicago: University of Chicago Press, 2013).

6. For arguments that factionalism prevented Republicans from sufficiently responding to Democratic efforts to drive them from power, see Joe Gray Taylor, *Louisiana Reconstructed, 1863–1877* (Baton Rouge: Louisiana State University Press, 1974); Thomas C. Holt, *Black over White: Negro Political Leadership in South Carolina during Reconstruction* (Urbana: University of Illinois Press, 1977); William C. Harris, *The Day of the Carpetbagger: Republican Reconstruction in Mississippi* (Baton Rouge: Louisiana State University Press, 1979); William Gillette, *Retreat from Reconstruction, 1869–1879* (Baton Rouge: Louisiana State University Press, 1979); Otto H. Olsen, ed., *Reconstruction and Redemption in the South* (Baton Rouge: Louisiana State University Press, 1980); George C. Rable, *But There Was No Peace: The Role of Violence in the Politics of Reconstruction* (Athens: University of Georgia Press, 1984); Michael Perman, *The Road to Redemption: Southern Politics, 1869–1879* (Chapel Hill: University of North Carolina Press, 1984); Eric Foner, *Reconstruction: America's Unfinished Revolution, 1863–1877* (New York: Harper & Row, 1988), 512–601; Richard Zuczek, *State of Rebellion: Reconstruction in South Carolina* (Co-

lumbia: University of South Carolina Press, 1996); Edmund Drago, *Hurrah for Hampton!: Black Red Shirts in South Carolina during Reconstruction* (Fayetteville: University of Arkansas Press, 1998). On the role of violence in mobilization campaigns, see J. Morgan Kousser, "The Voting Rights Act and the Two Reconstructions," in *Colorblind Injustice: Minority Voting Rights and the Undoing of the Second Reconstruction*, ed. J. Morgan Kousser (Chapel Hill: University of North Carolina Press, 1999), 23–24.

7. On the importance of giving testimony before federal officials, see Hannah Rosen, *Terror in the Heart of Freedom: Citizenship, Sexual Violence, and the Meaning of Race in the Postemancipation South* (Chapel Hill: University of North Carolina Press, 2009), 222–41.

8. Harris, *Day of the Carpetbagger*, 650–80.

9. *Natchez Democrat*, 8 July 1874; testimonies of E. H. Stiles and J. D. Vertner, in U.S. Senate, *Report of the Select Committee into the Mississippi Election of 1875*, 44th Cong., 1st sess., 1876, S. Rep. 527, pp. 159, 191–92 (cited hereafter as *Mississippi in 1875*). Claiborne County residents were inclined to accept the relationship, since Haskin was raised in the same house as Ellen. E. H. Stiles, a white native of Claiborne County and a Republican legislator, however, qualifies the general acceptance by noting that lower-class whites discussed a violent response to the marriage.

10. Harris, *Day of the Carpetbagger*, 634–37.

11. Quoted in ibid., 640.

12. Ibid., 645–48; Christopher Waldrep, *Roots of Disorder: Race and Criminal Justice in the American South, 1817–80* (Urbana: University of Illinois Press, 1998), 151–69; Steven Hahn, *A Nation under Our Feet: Black Political Struggles in the Rural South from Slavery to the Great Migration* (Cambridge, Mass.: Belknap Press of Harvard University Press, 2003), 297–98.

13. Testimony of J. D. Vertner, *Mississippi in 1875*, 195; E. B. B., I. Mc. M., K. K. K. to A. Ames, June 1875, Governor Ames Papers, Series 803: Correspondence and Papers, MDAH.

14. Testimonies of E. H. Stiles and J. D. Vertner, *Mississippi in 1875*, 163, 193, 195. For other instances of intimidation at Republican meetings, see the testimony of W. D. Sprott, *Denial of Elective Franchise*, 829–31.

15. Testimonies of E. H. Stiles and J. D. Vertner, *Mississippi in 1875*, 164–66, 193–94.

16. Testimony of J. D. Vertner, ibid., 196; James Page quoted in testimony of E. H. Stiles, ibid., 166–67.

17. H. S. Smith to Ames, 3 August 1875, W. D. Sprott to Hon. Adelbert Ames, 6 September 1875, Governor Ames Papers, MDAH.

18. *Jackson Weekly Pilot*, 2 October 1875 (emphasis in original).

19. Testimony of E. H. Stiles, *Mississippi in 1875*, 168; James Page et al. to Hon. A. Ames, [not dated] received November 1, 1875, Governor Ames Papers, MDAH. The display of these weapons communicated Democratic intentions of launching an attack. Bayonets, for example, were used solely for military purposes. For more on these events, see the testimony of W. D. Sprott, *Denial of Elective Franchise*, 831–33.

20. Testimony of E. H. Stiles, *Mississippi in 1875*, 169–72; E. H. Stiles to Ames, 30 October 1875, James Page et al. to Ames, [not dated] received 1 November 1875, Governor Ames Papers, MDAH. On warnings of the "war in Mississippi," see W. W. Dedrick, U.S. Atty., to Geo. H. Williams, Atty. Gen. of the U.S., 13 September 1875, Letters Received, Source Chronological Files, Southern Mississippi District, m970, roll 3, Records of the Department of Justice, Record Group 60, National Archives, Washington, D.C.

21. Testimonies of E. H. Stiles and J. D. Vertner, *Mississippi in 1875*, 172–76, 188, 200–206 (quote on 176).

22. Testimony of E. H. Stiles, ibid., 178–80, 186; Rep. Lynch (Miss.) on Political Affairs, *Congressional Record* 4, pt. 4 (15 June 1876): 3824–25.

23. Harris, *Day of the Carpetbagger*, 650–90; Foner, *Reconstruction*, 559–63.

24. Harris, *Day of the Carpetbagger*, 700–701.

25. Testimonies of D. A. Weber and Emil L. Weber, *Mississippi in 1875*, 1543–79. In the Louisiana parishes of Franklin, Catahoula, and Richland in 1870, nearly 52 percent of the population was black. In Amite, Franklin, Copiah, and Lincoln Counties, blacks made up 51 percent of the total population. Historical Census Browser, University of Virginia, Geospatial and Statistical Data Center, 2004, http://fisher.lib.virginia.edu/collections/stats/histcensus/index.html.

26. Quoted in the testimony of J. Ross Stewart, in U.S. Senate, *Report of the United States Senate Committee to Inquire into Alleged Frauds and Violence in the Elections of 1878*, 45th Cong., 3rd sess., 1879, S. Rep. 855, vol. 1, p. 345 (cited hereafter as *Frauds and Violence in the Elections of 1878*); testimony of James H. Jones, *Mississippi in 1875*, 174–75.

27. Testimony of E. H. Stiles, *Mississippi in 1875*, 167; *New York Times*, 17 September 1877.

28. In Port Gibson, Woodville, Fayette, St. Joseph, and Waterproof, the white liners constructed rudimentary defenses and organized patrols. Testimony of E. H. Stiles, *Mississippi in 1875*, 170–71; testimony of W. H. Noble, ibid., 1598; testimonies of Merrimon Howard and W. D. Sprott, *Denial of Elective Franchise*, 163, 834; testimony of J. R. Loscey, *Frauds and Violence in the Elections of 1878*, 1:265.

29. Testimonies of Alfred Black and Alexander Branch, *Mississippi in 1875*, 1584–88, 1592–93; Justin Behrend, Black Politicians Database SUNY-Geneseo, http://go.geneseo.edu/BlackPoliticiansDB (BPDB). On Black's local leadership, see the testimony of W. H. Noble, *Mississippi in 1875*, 1615. For more on these clubs, see the testimony of Hugh M. Foley, ibid., 1535–36, 1539–40. The extralegal quality of these clubs was evident in their stated intent to capture alleged thieves and to whip them. See the testimonies of William C. Miller, W. H. Noble, and James H. Jones, ibid., 1596, 1611, 1640–41; *Natchez Democrat*, 19 May 1876.

30. Testimony of Emil L. Weber, *Mississippi in 1875*, 1567. The violence that transpired in Wilkinson County took place while the Senate select committee was investigating the 1875 election. The Senate then extended the investigation. See ibid., iv.

31. Testimonies of W. H. Noble and Hugh M. Foley, ibid., 1598, 1538.

32. Testimony of W. H. Noble, ibid., 1617. The first reference to a black militia describes at least four "cavalry companies," including one from Fort Adams, attending a large Republican barbecue. See *Woodville Republican*, 27 November 1869. On black gun ownership, see the testimonies of W. H. Noble and James H. Jones, *Mississippi in 1875*, 1607, 1636.

33. Testimonies of Emil L. Weber and Kenner James, *Mississippi in 1875*, 1570, 1590; Gen. Will. T. Martin to Gov. J. M. Stone, 18 May 1876, Governor Stone correspondence, Series 807: Correspondence and Papers, MDAH. The Regulators had "Winchester rifles" and "Smith & Wesson's improved revolvers." See the testimonies of Hugh M. Foley and Emil L. Weber, *Mississippi in 1875*, 1534, 1573.

34. Testimonies of W. H. Noble and Hugh M. Foley, *Mississippi in 1875*, 1600, 1538; *Natchez Democrat*, 20 May 1876. Hugh M. Foley estimated that there were six to seven hundred white male voters in Wilkinson County. In the most recent election, around

four hundred men cast ballots for the Democratic candidates. Assuming that the vast majority of Democratic voters were white in 1875 and excluding a portion of the eligible voters from paramilitary service due to old age or other infirmities, it seems likely that Wilkinson County could not have mustered a force larger than five hundred white men. Without the outsiders, it would seem impossible for local whites to overthrow black and Republican rule. See the testimony of Hugh M. Foley, *Mississippi in 1875*, 1534; "Election Statistics," ibid., Documentary Evidence, pt. 3, p. 144–45.

35. J. H. Jones, "Reconstruction in Wilkinson County," *Publications of the Mississippi Historical Society* 8 (1904): 172; testimony of Hugh M. Foley, *Mississippi in 1875*, 1535; *New York Times*, 14 November 1876.

36. Testimonies of W. H. Noble, James H. Jones, and Alexander Branch, *Mississippi in 1875*, 1603, 1635–36, 1594; Louis F. Griffin to Gov. J. M. Stone, Martin to Stone, 18 May 1876, Governor Stone correspondence, MDAH. On black families that fled their homes, see testimonies of Hugh M. Foley, Alfred Black, and Alexander Branch, *Mississippi in 1875*, 1537, 1584, 1594; *New York Times*, 14 November 1876.

37. Testimonies of Hugh M. Foley and James H. Jones, *Mississippi in 1875*, 1537, 1634. Certainly, Brandon had an economic interest in keeping his workers alive; however, there is little indication that he endorsed the extremist wing of the Democratic Party. In fact, he joined the protection society headed by Sam Riley, the black state legislator. See the testimony of W. H. Noble, ibid., 1606.

38. Testimony of Peter Crout, ibid., 1629. For more on Noble's complicity, see Jones, "Reconstruction in Wilkinson County," 174–75.

39. Testimony of J. B. Cessor, *Denial of Elective Franchise*, 252. For more on African Americans and the struggle for citizenship, see Evelyn Glenn, *Unequal Freedom: How Race and Gender Shaped American Citizenship and Labor* (Cambridge, Mass.: Harvard University Press, 2002). For more on cultural assumptions about race and manhood that simultaneously legitimized and denigrated black men's armed defense of voting rights, see Emberton, *Beyond Redemption*, 136–67.

40. Testimony of Merrimon Howard, *Denial of Elective Franchise*, 157–58; *New York Times*, 14 October 1876. On Howard's bonds in December 1875 and January 1876, see Merrimon Howard, sheriff and tax collector, Old Bonds, Jefferson County Courthouse, Fayette, Miss. Howard relied on prominent Democrats as sureties: M. Eiseman, Claude Pintard, G. S. Jones, and James McClure. Later the Jefferson County Democratic Party pledged that Democrats could not become a surety on a bond of a non-Democrat. See *Fayette Chronicle*, 14 July 1876, in *Denial of Elective Franchise*, 903–4.

41. Testimony of Merrimon Howard, *Denial of Elective Franchise*, 158.

42. Ibid., 160, 169.

43. *Fayette Chronicle*, 25 August 1876, in *Denial of Elective Franchise*, 904–5; *New York Times*, 14 October 1876; testimony of Merrimon Howard, *Denial of Elective Franchise*, 162.

44. Testimony of Merrimon Howard, *Denial of Elective Franchise*, 165.

45. Ibid., 165–66; M. Howard to Ames, 6 November 1877, folder 153, box 18, Ames Family Papers, Sophia Smith Collection, Smith College, Northampton, Mass. Howard did not mention how many women and children were in the procession, but he did estimate that two thousand men participated. Thus three thousand is a rather conservative estimate.

46. Testimony of Merrimon Howard, *Denial of Elective Franchise*, 167–68. On the size of Fayette, see Department of the Interior, *Statistics of the Population of the United States at the Tenth Census* (Washington, D.C.: GPO, 1881), 196, 198, 233–35, 237.

47. Testimony of Merrimon Howard, *Denial of Elective Franchise*, 167–69. White liners used a similar tactic at a meeting in Port Gibson a week or so prior to this meeting. See the testimony of Thomas Richardson, ibid., 193.

48. Testimony of Merrimon Howard, ibid., 170. See also the testimony of John R. Lynch, ibid., 113–14. The Democrats found the small gathering and, although a fistfight followed, it was broken up quickly.

49. M. Howard to President R. B. Hays, 18 February 1877, Rutherford B. Hayes Papers, Rutherford B. Hayes Presidential Center, Fremont, Ohio (emphasis in original). On the electoral campaigns in Louisiana, see Taylor, *Louisiana Reconstructed*, 486–89; Hahn, *A Nation under Our Feet*, 310–13.

50. *Weekly Louisianian*, 13 October 1877. On the origin of the term "bulldozer" as it relates to political violence, see *New York Times*, 17 November 1876.

51. Testimonies of Elisha Warfield and H. Moses, *Frauds and Violence in the Elections of 1878*, 1:172, 399. On Tensas Parish as one of the top Republican parishes, see the testimony of William Murrell, in U.S. Senate, *Report and Testimony of the Select Committee of the United States Senate to Investigate the Causes of the Removal of the Negroes from the Southern States to the Northern States*, 46th Cong., 2nd sess., 1880, S. Rep. 693, pt. 2, p. 521; *New York Times*, 31 October 1878.

52. Testimony of Duncan Smith, *Frauds and Violence in the Elections of 1878*, 1:235; testimony of Alfred Fairfax, ibid., 2:766, 772; *New York Times*, 20 January, 20 October 1878; BPDB. Fairfax may have acquired his land in 1872 in a combined purchase with E. W. Robinson and John P. Harlow of 281.5 acres. See C. H. Ross to Alfred Fairfax et al., 25 July 1872, book H, p. 32, Tensas Parish, Tensas Parish Courthouse, St. Joseph, La.

53. Testimonies of Arthur Fairfax, Fleming Branch, Daniel Kennedy, Anna Ladd, and Violetta Wallace, *Frauds and Violence in the Elections of 1878*, 1:174–75, 178–80, 184–85, 187–88, 191; testimony of Alfred Fairfax, ibid., 2:766–67; *New York Times*, 9 January, 20 January 1879. One of Fairfax's friends, Fleming Branch, was shot eight times but still escaped.

54. Testimony of H. Moses, *Frauds and Violence in the Elections of 1878*, 1:403; testimony of Alfred Fairfax, ibid., 2:770–71. Most likely, Fairfax had the tickets printed at the offices of the *Concordia Eagle*, which was owned by James P. Ball Jr., a black Republican. The only printing machine in Tensas Parish was operated by the *North Louisiana Journal*, formerly a Republican sheet but in the hands of the bulldozing wing of the Democratic Party by 1878. On the ownership of the *Eagle*, see David Young to James P. Ball Jr., 7 July 1877, Conveyance Records, book P, p. 717, Concordia Parish Courthouse, Vidalia, La.; *Concordia Eagle*, 27 March 1879. On the ownership of the *Journal*, see *North Louisiana Journal* (St. Joseph), 18 January 1879.

55. At the Senate investigation into electoral fraud and violence in the 1878 election, witnesses identified men involved in the Tensas violence from seven surrounding parishes: Franklin, Catahoula, Richland, Concordia, Ouachita, Morehouse, and Washington. See also *New York Times*, 18 October, 23 December 1878. Witnesses also claimed that white men came across the river from Mississippi to intimidate local blacks. Specifically, a company of men from Jefferson County joined in the affray. See Thos. W. Hunt to Luke Lea, U.S. District Attorney, 8 January 1879, Letters Received, Source Chronological Files, Southern Mississippi District, m970, roll 4, Records of the Department of Justice, Record Group 60, National Archives, Washington, D.C. On a connection to the Colfax massacre, see LeeAnna Keith, *The Colfax Massacre: The Untold Story of Black Power, White Terror, and the Death of Reconstruction* (New York: Oxford University Press, 2008), 89.

56. Testimony of J. R. Loscey, *Frauds and Violence in the Elections of 1878*, 1:269. Loscey,

a white store clerk, was impressed into the sheriff's posse. On the clubs and armed bands of black men, see the testimonies of David Young, G. L. Walton, and H. Moses and Governor Nicholls's report on the Tensas Troubles, ibid., 1:371, 376, 400, 600–603; Robert Dabney Calhoun, "A History of Concordia Parish, Louisiana: Sixth Installment: Reconstruction," *Louisiana Historical Quarterly* 16 (April 1933): 325–26.

57. Testimony of L. D. Reeves, *Frauds and Violence in the Elections of 1878*, 1:289. On the attack at Bass's Lane, see the testimonies of Violetta Wallace, J. R. Loscey, T. J. Watson, Abraham Thomas, H. Moses, and Winnie Miller, ibid., 1:193, 264–70, 307–13, 337–39, 400, 468. It should be noted that Alfred Fairfax disputed the accounts of an armed confrontation at Bass's Lane. Instead, he believed that the bulldozers were unprovoked and just shot at any man who ran away. See the testimony of Alfred Fairfax, ibid., 2:774–75. For more on the poor quality of weapons used by blacks, see the testimonies of Col. George Ralston and T. J. Watson, ibid., 1:252, 308. On the murder of Dick Miller, see the testimonies of Duncan C. Smith, L. D. Reeves, T. J. Watson, David Dise, G. L. Walton, H. Moses, Winnie Miller, and Alfred Fairfax, ibid., 1:236, 300, 313, 318, 376, 407, 464–68, 2:469.

58. Testimony of C. E. Ruth and H. Moses, ibid., 1:246–47, 399. See also *New York Times*, 18 October 1878. On armed groups of black men, see the testimonies of James McGill, Duncan Smith, C. E. Ruth, Col. George Ralston, Frank Winston, V. H. Newell, David Dise, H. F. Shaifer, David Young, and G. L. Walton, Governor Nicholls's report, and testimony of Alfred Fairfax, *Frauds and Violence in the Elections of 1878*, 1:209, 210, 225–26, 237, 246, 249–50, 254, 257, 273, 285–86, 318, 329, 370, 376, 602–3, 2:768.

59. Testimonies of Lucien Bland, Robert J. Walker, Col. George Ralston, William D. Rollins, L. D. Reeves and William Coolidge, *Frauds and Violence in the Elections of 1878*, 1:196–97, 200, 255, 262, 306, 455. See also the testimony of James McGill, ibid., 1:215. On the deal to make the Independent ticket, see the testimonies of Lucien Bland, Duncan Smith, Robert J. Walker, A. J. Bryant, J. Ross Stewart, William Coolidge, and Noel N. Neely, ibid., 1:194, 203, 234–35, 239, 242, 333, 342, 455, 482.

60. Testimonies of James M. McGill, Rebecca Ross, and Elisha Warfield, ibid., 1:215, 189, 205; U.S. Bureau of Census, *Ninth Census of the United States: Population, 1870*; U.S. Bureau of Census, *Tenth Census of the United States, 1880*. For more on black laborers who took shelter with planters, see the testimonies of Elisha Warfield and Col. George Ralston, *Frauds and Violence in the Elections of 1878*, 1:172, 252. White leaders of the Independent ticket wrote to the deputy sheriff protesting the arrest warrants for black leaders Robert J. Walker, William Coolidge, and Noah Neely. See the testimony of Lucien Bland, ibid., 1:202.

61. A "Card to the People of Tensas Parish," submitted with the testimony of Lucien Bland, *Frauds and Violence in the Elections of 1878*, 1:200; testimony of Elisha Warfield, ibid., 1:205.

62. Testimonies of J. D. McGill, Lucien Bland, and James M. McGill, ibid., 1:211, 195, 220–21. On prior meetings at the Weatherly plantation, see *North Louisiana Journal*, 6 July 1872. For more on the Weatherly meeting, see the testimonies of Lucien Bland, J. D. McGill, Washington Williams, and C. E. Ruth, *Frauds and Violence in the Elections of 1878*, 1:194–95, 210–11, 233, 245.

63. Letter from "Noah," *Weekly Louisianian*, 14 December 1878. It is likely that the author of this letter was Noah Neely, an ex-slave Republican who rented a farm and held the offices of justice of the peace and parish school board. He tried to organize a fusionist ticket but was chased off by bulldozers. Testimony of Noah H. Neely, *Frauds and Violence*

in the Elections of 1878, 1:481–84; BPDB. For more on the intimidation and violence, see the testimonies of Duncan Smith, Robert J. Walker, C. E. Ruth, William H. Anderson, Spencer Ross, J. Ross Stewart, Elijah Kernall, George Washington, David Young, William Coolidge, Eliza Hill, Henrietta Williams, Solomon Butler, and Robert Buckner, Governor Nicholls's report, and the affidavit of Joseph Lambert, *Frauds and Violence in the Elections of 1878*, 1:236, 237, 239, 244–45, 260, 274–75, 345–46, 355–56, 358–60, 370, 457, 464, 469, 471, 474, 478, 600, 603–4.

64. Testimonies of William H. Anderson, C. E. Ruth, and Washington Williams, *Frauds and Violence in the Elections of 1878*, 1:260, 248, 232; *New York Times*, 23 December 1878. On Schaifer (whose name was spelled at least five other ways), see BPDB.

65. Testimonies of James M. McGill, C. E. Ruth, Washington Williams, and Duncan Smith, *Frauds and Violence in the Elections of 1878*, 1:215, 246, 233, 237; *New York Times*, 23 December 1878. For a layout of the landscape near Waterproof, see Nautical Survey of the Mississippi River, 1878, Chart 53, Historical Map and Chart Collection, Office of Coast Survey, NOAA, http://historicalcharts.noaa.gov/historicals/preview/image/MR53. For more on the edges of plantations, see Christopher Morris, *The Big Muddy: An Environmental History of the Mississippi and Its Peoples from Hernando de Soto to Hurricane Katrina* (New York: Oxford University Press, 2012), 125–39.

66. Testimony of William H. Griffith, *Frauds and Violence in the Elections of 1878*, 1:282–83. On the number of freedpeople killed, see the testimony of William Murrell, in U.S. Senate, *Report and Testimony of the Select Committee of the United States Senate to Investigate the Causes of the Removal of the Negroes from the Southern States to the Northern States*, 46th Cong., 2nd sess., 1880, S. Rep. 693, pt. 2, p. 532. Murrell claimed that as many as 125 were murdered, but he argued that "at the very least calculation, seventy-five" were killed. Other estimates ranged from 40 killed (Coolidge) to 70–80 (Kennedy); see the testimonies of Daniel Kennedy and William Coolidge, *Frauds and Violence in the Elections of 1878*, 1:185, 459. In congressional testimony, eleven executed black men were listed from Tensas Parish: William (Billy) Singleton, Monday Hill, Robert Williams, Dick Miller, Lewis Postlewaite, James Stafford (Starver), Charlie Bethel, William Hunter, Asbury Epps, John Higgins, and Dock Bovay. Seven Concordia men were also named: Commodore Smallwood, Charles Carroll (Curd), Wash Ellis (Hills), Hiram (Hyam or Hyamis) Wilson, Dick (Doc) Smith, Pete Young, and John Robinson.

67. On election results in Claiborne, Jefferson, and Wilkinson Counties, see the table "Vote in Mississippi for 1873, 1875, and 1876," in *Denial of Elective Franchise*, 813. In general, Republican vote totals declined significantly when violence preceded an election. But more indicative of the fraud were the Democratic tallies, which increased substantially, far beyond the natural increase in the white male population of voting age. In addition, there is no evidence that large numbers of black men voted Democratic, whether voluntarily or otherwise. On election results in Tensas and Concordia Parishes, see the testimonies of Col. George Ralston, Lucien Bland, James M. McGill, Elisha Warfield, Thomas A. Johnson, Charles W. Johnson, Charles Lincoln, and David Young, *Frauds and Violence in the Elections of 1878*, 1:170–71, 198, 223, 254, 360–68. In Wilkinson County in 1876, the totals were 1,427 Republican votes to 1,262 Democratic votes. Together they exceed the voting-age population by 121 votes. It could be that the 1870 census figures underestimated the county population or that at least 121 adult men moved to the county between 1870 and 1876; however, an abundance of evidence suggests that the Democratic totals were inflated by fraud and intimidation and the Republican totals suppressed by the same methods.

68. Testimony of Thomas Richardson, *Denial of Elective Franchise*, 191–96. On Democratic registrars in Louisiana, see the testimony of David Young, *Frauds and Violence in the Elections of 1878*, 1:368.

69. *Fayette Chronicle*, 3 November 1876, in *Denial of Elective Franchise*, 906–7; testimonies of John R. Lynch and D. C. Kearns, ibid., 114, 824. For other descriptions of the "terrorism" in Jefferson County, see *New York Times*, 14 October, 26 December 1876. On the election results, see "Vote in Mississippi for 1873, 1875, and 1876," *Denial of Elective Franchise*, 813. Republicans outpolled Democrats 1,922 to 678 in 1875. One year later, Democrats bested Republicans 1,517 to 419. Turnout declined by 25 percent between 1875 and 1876.

70. Testimonies of William Coolidge, Col. George Ralston, A. J. Bryant, and Spencer Ross, *Frauds and Violence in the Elections of 1878*, 1:458, 460, 254, 334–35, 275; *New York Times*, 9 January 1879; BPDB. For another example of intense pressure exerted on a black officeholder, see the testimony of C. E. Ruth, *Frauds and Violence in the Elections of 1878*, 1:245.

71. Testimonies of Lucien Bland and Elisha Warfield, *Frauds and Violence in the Elections of 1878*, 1:198, 170–71. See also the testimony of James M. McGill, ibid., 1:223.

72. Testimonies of Charles W. Johnson, G. L. Walton, Charles Lincoln, David Young, Thomas A. Johnson and M. T. Randolph, ibid., 1:363–66, 375, 366–67, 368, 360, 362–63; *New York Times*, 17 November 1878. On bulldozers in Concordia Parish, see the testimony of George Washington and affidavit of Joseph Lambert, *Frauds and Violence in the Elections of 1878*, 1:358–60, 603–4.

73. Testimony of David Young, *Frauds and Violence in the Elections of 1878*, 1:370–71.

74. Testimony of A. M. Hardy, *Denial of Elective Franchise*, 145; Hugh M. Foley to U. S. Grant, 1 September 1876, in John Y. Simon, ed., *The Papers of Ulysses S. Grant* (Carbondale: Southern Illinois University Press, 1967–2012), 27:321–22n. For more on Grant's decision not to intervene, see John R. Lynch, *The Facts of Reconstruction* (New York: Neale Publishing Company, 1913; repr., New York: Arno Press and the New York Times, 1968), 152–55; Nicholas Lemann, *Redemption: The Last Battle of the Civil War* (New York: Farrar, Straus and Giroux, 2006), 100–134.

75. On Redpath's reporting, see *New York Times*, 2 May, 3 July, 8 July, 27 July, 31 July, 7 August, 14 August, 28 August, 2 September, 5 September, 14 October, 14 November, 17 November, 22 November, 25 November, 26 December 1876, 1 January, 19 June, 5 September 1877, 20 January 1879. For more on Redpath, see John McKivigan, *Forgotten Firebrand: James Redpath and the Making of Nineteenth-Century America* (Ithaca, N.Y.: Cornell University Press, 2008). On testimonies before congressional committees, see, for example, *Mississippi in 1875*, *Denial of Elective Franchise*, and *Frauds and Violence in the Elections of 1878*.

76. The literature on southern African Americans in the post-Reconstruction period is extensive. For exceptional works, see Neil McMillen, *Dark Journey: Black Mississippians in the Age of Jim Crow* (Urbana: University of Illinois Press, 1989); Kevin Gaines, *Uplifting the Race: Black Politics and Culture in the United States since the Turn of the Century* (Chapel Hill: University of North Carolina Press, 1995); Glenda Gilmore, *Gender and Jim Crow: Women and the Politics of White Supremacy in North Carolina, 1896–1920* (Chapel Hill: University of North Carolina Press, 1996); Tera W. Hunter, *To 'Joy My Freedom: Southern Black Women's Lives and Labors after the Civil War* (Cambridge, Mass.: Harvard University Press, 1997); Leon Litwack, *Trouble in Mind: Black Southerners in the Age of Jim Crow* (New York: Alfred A. Knopf, 1998); Jane Dailey, *Before Jim Crow: The*

Politics of Race in Postemancipation Virginia (Chapel Hill: University of North Carolina Press, 2000).

Chapter Eight. Return of Oligarchy

1. C. Vann Woodward, *The Strange Career of Jim Crow*, 3rd rev. ed. (New York: Oxford University Press, 2002), 31–65. For more on biracial political experiments in the late nineteenth-century South, see Eric Anderson, *Race and Politics in North Carolina, 1872–1901: The Black Second* (Baton Rouge: Louisiana State University Press, 1981); Eric Arnesen, *Waterfront Workers of New Orleans: Race, Class, and Politics, 1863–1923* (University of Illinois Press, 1994); David S. Cecelski and Timothy B. Tyson, eds., *Democracy Betrayed: The Wilmington Race Riot of 1898 and Its Legacy* (Chapel Hill: University of North Carolina Press, 1998); Jane Dailey, *Before Jim Crow: The Politics of Race in Postemancipation Virginia* (Chapel Hill: University of North Carolina Press, 2000); Steven Hahn, *A Nation under Our Feet: Black Political Struggles in the Rural South from Slavery to the Great Migration* (Cambridge, Mass.: Belknap Press of Harvard University Press, 2003), 364–411.

2. *Natchez Democrat*, 1 November 1874. The origins of a People's ticket are unclear. In Mississippi the conservative National Union Republican party held a People's Convention in 1869. In local politics a People's Party appeared in Concordia Parish in 1874 and in Tensas Parish in 1879. *Natchez Democrat*, 1 September 1869, 7 October 1874; *North Louisiana Journal* (St. Joseph), 15 March 1879.

3. *Natchez Democrat*, 11 November 1874. The mayor, Henry C. Griffin, and all four of the aldermen were white. The school trustees, however, were equally split between white and black. The *Natchez Democrat* estimated that 245 blacks voted for the People's ticket out of 730 registered black voters. Others to give speeches were: George St. Clair Hussey (a white Republican moderate), Samuel Ullman (a white People's candidate for school trustee), George M. Brown (a white People's candidate for alderman), and A. H. Foster (a white Republican candidate for alderman).

4. *Natchez Democrat*, 21 October 1874. On the compromise ticket, see the testimony of W. H. Whitehurst, Wm. J. Henderson, and Horace C. Bailey, in U.S. House, *Testimony in the Contested Election Case of John R. Lynch vs. James R. Chalmers, from the Sixth Congressional District of Mississippi*, 47th Cong., 1st sess., 1881, H. Misc. Doc. 12, pp. 62, 80–83, 194 (cited hereafter as *Lynch vs. Chalmers*). For more on how "best men" rhetoric undermined the egalitarian principles of black Republicans, see Laura F. Edwards, *Gendered Strife and Confusion: The Political Culture of Reconstruction* (Urbana: University of Illinois Press, 1997), 218–54.

5. Testimony of W. H. Whitehurst, *Lynch vs. Chalmers*, 62. For more on Wood's fusionist campaigning, see *Natchez Democrat*, 23 November 1877. For results of the November 2, 1875, election, see *Natchez Democrat*, Adams County File, Mississippi Department of Archives and History (MDAH), Jackson. The elected fusionists were Henry P. Jacobs (a black outsider who had long opposed the Lynch faction), Fred Parsons (a white northern moderate), and M. A. C. Hussey (a white moderate). Hussey later switched to the Democratic Party. *Natchez Democrat*, 31 January 1877.

6. John R. Lynch, *Reminiscences of an Active Life: The Autobiography of John Roy Lynch*, ed. John Hope Franklin (Chicago: University of Chicago Press, 1970), 168–69; *Natchez Democrat*, 9 January 1876. The Democrats fixed the vote tally so that their candidate, Roderick Seal, would win by 250 votes. But this projection was based on Lynch winning Adams County with a 1,200-vote majority. The high Adams County turnout delayed the

counting until after all the county returns had been published. The final tally gave Lynch a 1,800-vote majority and thus a slim reelection victory.

7. Testimony of A. M. Hardy, in U.S. Senate, *Testimony as to Denial of Elective Franchise in Mississippi at the Elections of 1875 and 1876*, 44th Cong., 2nd sess., 1877, Misc. Doc. 45, pp. 137–40 (cited hereafter as *Denial of Elective Franchise*); L. W. B. Jr. to U.S. Grant, 15 November 1876, in John Y. Simon, ed., *The Papers of Ulysses S. Grant* (Carbondale: Southern Illinois University Press, 1967–2012), 28:28n; *Chicago Inter-Ocean*, 11 October 1876.

8. *Natchez Democrat*, 21 May 1876; *Chicago Inter-Ocean*, 11 October 1876; *Natchez Democrat*, 30 June 1877; A. P. Merrill to Adelbert Ames, 9 October 1875, Governor Ames Papers, MDAH; Lynch, *Reminiscences of an Active Life*, 229; testimony of John R. Lynch, *Denial of Elective Franchise*, 122. Explaining why he might be targeted, Merrill wrote, "The ostensible purpose of the lawless organizations is the seed-cotton buying and selling matter, but the covert and hidden design is political, otherwise why should I be assailed and become the particular object of their vengeance?" President Grant appointed Merrill's son minister to Brussels. See Simon, *Papers of Grant*, 26:185–86n. On Merrill's Unionism, see Michael Wayne, *Reshaping the Plantation South: The Natchez District, 1860–1880* (Baton Rouge: Louisiana State University Press, 1982), 33. For more on conservative opposition to the violence, see *New York Times*, 15 September 1879.

9. Testimony of John R. Lynch, *Denial of Elective Franchise*, 120–21; "Vote in Mississippi for 1873, 1875, and 1876," ibid., 813; *Washington Republican* quoted in *Natchez Democrat*, 27 December 1876. Democrats secured 1,626 votes in 1876, 833 more votes than in 1875. Because the ratification of Mississippi's Reconstruction constitution had been delayed until 1869, the state held state-level elections in odd-numbered years, even though federal elections were held in even-numbered years. To bring the state more in line with the federal system of elections, Mississippi scheduled elections for the Forty-Fifth Congress in 1876, even though it had held elections for the Forty-Fourth Congress just one year prior. Mississippi's congressional delegation was not impaired since Congress did not start its first session until one year after the election. So the Forty-Fourth Congress (1875–76) didn't open until December 6, 1875.

10. *Port Gibson Southern Reville*, 15 December 1876; *Natchez Democrat*, 13 December, 20 December 1876; Joshua Page and others to Stone, 26 December 1876, Governor Stone Papers, Series 807: Correspondence and Papers, MDAH. James Page had at least four grown sons: Harrison, Joshua, Robert, and Isaac.

11. Testimony of W. D. Sprott, *Denial of Elective Franchise*, 835; John R. Lynch to U.S. Grant, 23 December 1876, in Simon, *Papers of Grant*, 27:105. On the Democratic reaction to the gun battles that erupted after Lynch's failed attempt to speak at a Republican mass meeting, see *Jackson Weekly Clarion*, 8 November 1876. On troops stationed in Claiborne County, see *New York Times*, 26 December 1876; William C. Harris, *The Day of the Carpetbagger: Republican Reconstruction in Mississippi* (Baton Rouge: Louisiana State University Press, 1979), 693.

12. J. L. Lake Jr. to Alphonso Taft, Attorney General, 4 January 1877, Letters Received, Source Chronological Files, Southern Mississippi District, m970, roll 3, Records of the Department of Justice, Record Group 60, National Archives, Washington, D.C. (cited hereafter as RG 60); *Philadelphia Inquirer*, 9 March 1877; M. Howard to Ames, 6 November 1877, folder 153, box 18, Ames Family Papers, Sophia Smith Collection, Smith College, Northampton, Mass.; *New York Times*, 16 December 1876; U.S. Bureau of Census, *Tenth Census of the United States: Population, 1880*; *Natchez Democrat*, 9 July 1882. Howard

held his position in the Treasury Department until 1886, when Ethelbert Barksdale, a Democratic congressman and an advocate of bulldozing, objected to his "partisan work in stirring up race strife." Howard was fired despite letters of support sent by two white Democrats, one of whom was Claude Pintard of Natchez. *New York Herald-Tribune*, 29 July 1887. Pintard had endorsed Howard's sheriff bond in 1875 and 1876.

13. *New York Times*, 4 June, 19 June 1877. On the lynching of Dave Ross, see the testimonies of A. M. Hardy and Merrimon Howard, *Denial of Elective Franchise*, 142–44, 178–80; *Natchez Democrat*, 27 December 1876. Ross was one of only two men to escape the white-line mob that massacred twenty-five to thirty men the weekend before the election. Ross also distributed Republican tickets for Merrimon Howard.

14. *New York Times*, 18 September, 19 October 1877; *New York Tribune*, 20 September 1877; *Natchez Democrat*, 23 September 1877. See also *Boston Daily Journal*, 25 September 1877; *New York Times*, 24 October 1877; U.S. Bureau of Census, *Ninth Census of the United States: Population, 1870*; U.S. Bureau of Census, *Tenth Census: Population, 1880*.

15. On John Byrd, see J. B. Thrasher to John N. Bird, 25 April 1854, book BB, p. 335, Claiborne County Land Deeds, Claiborne County Courthouse (CCCH), Port Gibson, Miss.; Rosetta L. Newsom claim, case 4995, Adams County, Mississippi case files, Settled Case Files for Claims Approved by the Southern Claims Commission, ser. 732, Southern Claims Commission, Records of the Office of the Third Auditor, Records of the Accounting Officers of the Department of Treasury, Record Group 217, National Archives, Washington, D. C. Thrasher, a white lawyer born in Kentucky, owned 182 slaves in 1860, but a decade later he was living with Susan Graves, a black woman, and her children. He also partnered with E. H. Stiles, a white Republican, in a law firm. Although far from conclusive, his public cohabitation with a black woman and his acceptance of Republican politics suggest why he might have been willing to sell land to a free black man. On Page's initial sales in the St. Mary neighborhood, see J. S. Mason to James Page, 1 January 1865, book EE, p. 578; John R. Davis to James Page, 1 January 1866, book FF, p. 227; A. Rollins to James Page, 19 April 1867, book FF, p. 433; Jno. B. Winters to James Page et al., 3 April 1869, book HH, p. 222, Claiborne County Land Deeds, CCCH. On Page's sales to his children, see James Page to Isaac Page, 15 November 1867, book GG, p. 155; Stephen Thrasher to Harrison Page, 22 February 1869, book GG, p. 515, Claiborne County Land Deeds, CCCH. On other black leaders who owned property in the St. Mary neighborhood, see W. McD. Sims to Thomas Richardson, 20 April 1872, book KK, p. 20; J. H. Maury to Margaret S. Bradford, 4 May 1872, book KK, p. 45, Claiborne County Land Deeds, CCCH. Margaret was Nace's wife. On the Page family, see T. Richardson to T. W. Hunt, U.S. Marshal, 11 December 1878, Letters Received, roll 4, Dept. of Justice, RG 60.

16. T. Richardson to Thos. W. Hunt, U.S. Marshal, 28 December 1878, Letters Received, roll 4, Dept. of Justice, RG 60; *New York Herald-Tribune*, 18 April 1879. See also T. Richardson to T. W. Hunt, U.S. Marshal, 11 December 1878, Letters Received, roll 4, Dept. of Justice, RG 60. Two months later, two of the Page brothers were captured. See *North Louisiana Journal*, 22 February 1879.

17. On the spread of the news, see the testimony of R. B. Avery, in U.S. Senate, *Report and Testimony of the Select Committee of the United States Senate to Investigate the Causes of the Removal of the Negroes from the Southern States to the Northern States*, 46th Cong., 2nd sess., 1880, S. Rep. 693, pt. 2, p. 284 (cited hereafter as *Removal of the Negroes*); testimony of Charles H. Tandy, ibid., pt. 3, p. 70. On the sales of property, see Saml. Carrick to H. Nelson Jr., 18 March 1876, book TT, p. 534; Irene Page et al. to J. H. and C. B. Gordon, 28 March 1876, book RR, p. 514; Harrison and Lucy Page to Rosalie Unger, 1 May 1876,

book UU, p. 151; James Page to J. H. Gordon et al., 1 January 1877, book UU, p. 280; James Page and Phoebe Page to Herman Simonson, 4 March 1878, book UU, p. 315; Saml. Carrick to J. P. Wilson, 14 May 1878, book UU, p. 359; Isaac Page and wife to H. S. Levy and B. B. Levy, 14 February 1879, book VV, p. 146; Thomas Richardson to Emma J. Dixon, 3 July 1879, book UU, p. 601, Claiborne County Land Deeds, CCCH. Carrick was a county supervisor. The Pages sold their properties to white Republicans: Unger, the Levys, and the Gordons. Also in 1879, the county confiscated James Page's plantation due to delinquent payments and auctioned it off. James Page to B. N. Johnson, 20 October 1879, book VV, p. 113, Claiborne County Land Deeds, CCCH. Phoebe Page, James's wife, had purchased the plantation three years before from John J. Smith, the white Republican state senator who fled the county after Democratic clubs threatened to kill him and his family. For the original purchase, see J. J. Smith to Phoebe Page, 18 March 1876, book RR, p. 434, Claiborne County Land Deeds, CCCH.

18. *New York Times*, 16 July 1890; Rev. Revels A. Adams, *Cyclopedia of African Methodism in Mississippi* (Natchez, Miss., 1902), 172; *Crisis*, October 1911, 228; Justin Behrend, Black Politicians Database, SUNY-Geneseo, http://go.geneseo.edu/BlackPoliticiansDB (BPDB). On Richardson's role as an informant, see his letters to Thomas W. Hunt, a U.S. marshal, in Letters Received, roll 4, Dept. of Justice, RG 60.

19. *North Louisiana Journal*, 24 May 1879. On the revised crop lien laws, see Harold D. Woodman, *New South, New Law: The Legal Foundations of Credit and Labor Relations in the Postbellum Agricultural South* (Baton Rouge: Louisiana State University Press, 1995), 37–39, 47, 55. On the social and economic condition of Tensas Parish, see *North Louisiana Journal*, 12 April 1879; Frederic Trautman, ed., *Travels on the Lower Mississippi, 1879–1880: A Memoir by Ernst von Hesse-Wartegg* (Columbia: University of Missouri Press, 1990), 101–2; William Ivy Hair, *Bourbonism and Agrarian Protest: Louisiana Politics, 1877–1900* (Baton Rouge: Louisiana State University Press, 1969) 45, 51–54; Nell Irvin Painter, *Exodusters: Black Migration to Kansas after Reconstruction* (New York: Knopf, 1977), 56–68; Gilbert C. Fite, *Cotton Fields No More: Southern Agriculture, 1865–1980* (Lexington: University of Kentucky Press, 1984), 6–7, 48. On the closure of public schools, see *Concordia Eagle*, 27 March 1879.

20. Affidavit of Frederick Marshall, *Removal of the Negroes*, 53–54; U.S. Bureau of Census, *Tenth Census: Population, 1880*. For more on the rumors, see *New York Times*, 18 June 1879; Painter, *Exodusters*, 175–77; Hahn, *A Nation under Our Feet*, 331–37. For a similar explanation of the causes of the exodus from the perspective of a black mechanic who traveled through the Natchez District, see C. K. Jenree to President R. B. Hays [*sic*], 16 February 1880, Rutherford B. Hayes Papers, Rutherford B. Hayes Presidential Center, Fremont, Ohio.

21. Trautman, *Travels on the Lower Mississippi*, 102–3; U.S. Bureau of Census, *Tenth Census: Population, 1880*.

22. *New York Times*, 10 March, 27 April 1879; R. E. Conner to Lemuel Conner, 7 May 1879, folder 75, box 6, Lemuel P. Conner and Family Papers, Louisiana and Lower Mississippi Valley Collections, Louisiana State University (LSU) Libraries, Baton Rouge. On anti-exodus articles, see *North Louisiana Journal*, 8 March, 29 March, 12 April, 19 April, 26 April, 3 May, 10 May, 17 May 1879. For more on the political reasons for leaving Louisiana and heading for Kansas, see *New York Times*, 10 March, 20 April 1879; *New York Herald-Tribune*, 18 April 1879. For a similar perspective on the Kansas migration, see Joe Louis Caldwell, "Any Place but Here: Kansas Fever in Northeast Louisiana," in *The African American Experience in Louisiana*, part B, *From the Civil War to Jim Crow*, ed.

Charles Vincent (Lafayette: Center for Louisiana Studies, University of Louisiana at Lafayette, 2000), 418–32.

23. E. J. Castello to Devens, Atty. Gen., 14 May 1879, Letters Received, roll 4, Dept. of Justice, RG 60; Thomas W. Conway to President Hayes, 16 May 1879, Hayes Papers, Hayes Presidential Center. For another account of armed whites turning away black migrants at steamboat landings, see Trautman, *Travels on the Lower Mississippi*, 103.

24. R. E. Conner to Lemuel, 1 July 1879, folder 76, box 6, Conner Family Papers, LSU; Hair, *Bourbonism and Agrarian Protest*, 97; *New Orleans Daily Picayune*, 23 August 1879; R. E. Conner to Lemuel, 18 February 1880, folder 78, box 6, Conner Family Papers, LSU. Conner said that he could not lease "in solidio." It appears that Conner's prior leasing arrangement made each tenant responsible for the whole of the crop. Instead, Conner now contracted with squads and families, shifting the burden of borrowing onto smaller groups and thereby making it more risky for him to lend.

25. *North Louisiana Journal*, 15 March, 22 March 1879. The delegates selected by the bulldozer committee were L. V. Reeves, J. S. Matthews, and A. J. Bryant. Those elected were Wade H. Hough, the senatorial delegate, and H. R. Steele and J. S. Matthews for the representative delegates.

26. *North Louisiana Journal*, 26 April, 10 May 1879; "The Proceedings of a Migration Convention and Congressional Action Respecting the Exodus of 1879," *Journal of Negro History* 4, no. 1. (January 1919): 51–92; Painter, *Exodusters*, 216–20.

27. *Proceedings of the National Conference of Colored Men of the United States, held in the State Capitol at Nashville, Tennessee, May 6, 7, 8 and 9, 1879* (Washington, D. C.: Rufus H. Darby, 1879; repr., Philadelphia: Rhistoric Publications, 1969). John R. Lynch was selected chairman of the convention. Robert W. Fitzhugh and Theo. H. Greene, both from Natchez, and Thomas Richardson, from Port Gibson, attended the conference as delegates. For more on the origin of this meeting, see *New York Times*, 12 February 1879. On Fairfax, see Painter, *Exodusters*, 163. On Young, see Hair, *Bourbonism and Agrarian Protest*, 97.

28. "Constitution of Louisiana, 1879" in *The Federal and State Constitutions, Colonial Charters, and Other Organic Laws of the States, Territories, and Colonies Now or Heretofore Forming the United States of America*, ed. Francis Newton Thorpe (Washington, D.C.: Government Printing Office, 1909), 3:1471–517; Hair, *Bourbonism and Agrarian Protest*, 100–102; *Concordia Eagle*, 3 March 1877, 8 April 1880, 12 April 1883. Of the twenty-four delegates to the 1877 parish convention, I was able to identify ten laborers and two farmers; I could not find any information on five members. Also, all of the members were black except one. Other black officeholders included one member of the Vidalia town council, three justices of the peace (out of eleven), and the town marshal (former sheriff John Young). There were 13,594 black residents and 1,320 white residents in Concordia Parish in 1880. Historical Census Browser, University of Virginia, Geospatial and Statistical Data Center, 2004, http://fisher.lib.virginia.edu/collections/stats/histcensus/index.html.

29. *North Louisiana Journal*, 8 March, 15 March 1879; BPDB. Eight of eleven members of the Republican executive committee were black, and at least three of the black members were farmers. Two were landowners; another was a "house servant." No information could be found for the other two black members, although it is likely that they were farmers or laborers. At least eleven out of twenty-four members of the People's Party executive committee were black. Other planks of the People's Party included endorsing a "reduction of public officers and official fees" and the call for the election of state and parish officials on the same day.

30. *North Louisiana Journal*, 6 December 1879, 30 October, 6 November, 13 November 1880; *New York Times*, 24 November 1879; *New Orleans Louisianian*, 15 November 1879, in *Removal of the Negroes*, 241–42. In addition to Solomon Schaifer, four white Republicans were elected to parish-wide offices in 1879, and black Republicans were elected to three ward-level offices: Wash Nellums and J. J. Hubbard as constables and P. C. Tyler as justice of the peace. On Republican nominations for parish offices, see *North Louisiana Journal*, 8 November 1879. Voter registration figures for Tensas Parish in 1880 were 3,286 blacks and 403 whites. The Democrat, J. Floyd King, received 2,115 votes. His opponent, Lanier, accumulated only 536 votes. The reference to King as a "commanding general" can be found in the testimony of William Murrell, *Removal of the Negroes*, 536.

31. *Natchez Democrat*, 11 January, 22 January, 2 September 1882; Historical Census Browser.

32. John R. Lynch to Bruce, 21 September 1877, folder 58, box 9–2, Blanche K. Bruce Papers, Moorland-Spingarn Research Center, Howard University, Washington, D.C. Other evidence of a fusionist agreement comes from the recollection of an "old-timer" who described a powerful "political ring" composed of black Republicans and white Democrats. Allison Davis, Burleigh B. Gardner, and Mary R. Gardner, *Deep South: A Social Anthropological Study of Caste and Class* (Chicago: University of Chicago, 1941; repr., Los Angeles: Center for Afro-American Studies, University of California, Los Angeles, 1988), 484n, 485n. *Deep South* is a study of Natchez, Mississippi, during the 1930s.

33. *New York Times*, 15 October 1883; W. W. Hence vs. S. H. Lambdin, 12 November 1889, drawer 411, box 6, no. 48, Adams County Circuit Court Case Files, Historic Natchez Foundation (HNF), Natchez, Miss. The ticket was printed for use in the Fourth Supervisor's District; thus candidates for supervisor, justices of the peace, and constable were also listed. Both candidates for constable were black, as was one of the justices of the peace, W. W. Hence, who lost the election and sued his opponent for election fraud.

34. Testimony of Harry Smith Jr., *Lynch vs. Chalmers*, 147.

35. *Natchez Democrat*, 24 September 1882; testimony of Louis J. Winston, In re John R. Lynch vs. Board of Commissioners of Election, 9 October 1896, drawer 432, no. 9, Adams County Circuit Court Case Files, HNF; BPDB. For more on Winston, see Sheryl Lynn Nomelli, "Jim Crow, Louis J. Winston, and the Survival of Black Politicos in Post-Bellum Natchez, Mississippi" (master's thesis, California State University, Northridge, 2004).

36. Adams County Poll Books, 1876–79, 1881–82, 1882–87, 1888–90 (precincts: Beverly, Courthouse, Dead Man's Bend, Jefferson Hotel, Kingston, Palestine, Pine Ridge, and Washington), HNF.

37. *Natchez Democrat*, 19 July 1876; John R. Lynch to Blanche K. Bruce, 21 September 1877, Bruce Papers, Howard University; Robert W. Fitzhugh, died 25 May 1883, Wills, book 4, p. 289, Adams County Courthouse (ACCH), Natchez, Miss.; *New York Times*, 21 October 1883; BPDB. In addition, black men in Adams County held the offices of jailor, school board member, keeper of the poor farm, sheriff, and justice of the peace. On black police officers in Natchez, see Minutes of the Mayor and Alderman, City of Natchez, vols. 19–25, Natchez City Hall, Natchez, Miss. On the racial politics of black postmasters, see *New York Times*, 16 July 1890, in which Thomas Richardson pointedly responds to racist whites in Port Gibson. In a public letter, Richardson wrote, "To all the whites interested in the Port Gibson Post Office, I have simply to say that it would be just as obnoxious for you or your wives to deliver the mail to myself or my wife as it may be for us to deliver mail to you, your wives, or your children, as we are your equals in every respect."

38. *Fayette Chronicle*, quoted in *Weekly Louisianian*, 7 December 1878; *Natchez Democrat*, 27 October, 20 October 1880.

39. *New York Times,* 22 November 1880; Lynch, *Reminiscences of an Active Life,* 182, 224–25. In the intervening election (1878), E. J. Castello, the carpetbagger and former Union League activist, ran on the Republican ticket, but he fared rather poorly, capturing only 17 percent of the vote. Ibid., 209; Stephen Cresswell, *Multiparty Politics in Mississippi, 1877–1902* (Jackson: University Press of Mississippi, 1995), 41. On the racial composition of the "shoestring" district, see Historical Census Browser.

40. Testimony of George N. Johnson and Charles W. Minor, *Lynch vs. Chalmers,* 151, 160; Lynch, *Reminiscences of an Active Life,* 228; *New York Times,* 22 November 1880. For other instances of delay, see the testimonies of Thomas R. Quarterman, Wm. J. Henderson, Clarence G. Johnston, Patrick Foley, and George N. Johnson, *Lynch vs. Chalmers,* 69–71, 73–74, 106–7, 111–12, 151–52. For more on the frauds in the "shoestring" election, see *New York Times,* 27 October, 10 November, 26 November 1880, 8 March, 7 August 1881; *New York Herald-Tribune,* 23 March 1881.

41. Testimony of Smith Kinney, *Lynch vs. Chalmers,* 143; *New York Times,* 22 November 1880; *New York Herald-Tribune,* 23 March 1881. Lynch's long letter prompted the *Times'* editors to denounce the "more outrageous and impudent" frauds of the "White League Democracy." On Lynch's successful contest of the election, see U.S. House, *Contested-Election Case of Lynch vs. Chalmers,* Majority and Minority Report, 47th Cong., 1st sess., 1882, Rep. 931; *New York Times,* 5 April, 29 April, 30 April 1882; *Natchez Democrat,* 30 April 1882.

42. *Boston Daily Advertiser,* 3 October 1877; *New York Times,* 14 September 1883, 7 October 1884.

43. *Natchez Democrat,* 27 August 1882; Lynch, *Reminiscences of an Active Life,* 265–66; Cresswell, *Multiparty Politics in Mississippi,* 74, 80–81. Jefferson and Claiborne were added to the Seventh Congressional District. Of the fourteen counties in the new Sixth District, only two (Adams and Wilkinson) were Republican-majority counties.

44. On patronage jobs, see *Natchez Democrat,* 16 August, 17 August 1882. On Lynch's speeches, see *New Orleans Daily Picayune,* 12 June 1883; *New York Times,* 13 June 1883, 24 April, 23 July, 13 August 1884, 19 June, 22 June 1885, 2 November 1886, 11 February, 22 August 1888, 26 September 1889; *Natchez Democrat,* 13 October, 10 November 1886; Sidney H. Kessler, "The Organization of Negroes in the Knights of Labor," *Journal of Negro History,* 37, no. 3 (July 1952): 274; Richard White, "Civil Rights Agitation: Emancipation Days in Central New York in the 1880s," *Journal of Negro History,* 78, no. 1 (Winter 1993): 16. On black associational life, see *Natchez Democrat,* 8 April, 11 May, 20 May, 26 July, 4 August, 15 August 1882. On Bruce's speech in Natchez, see *Natchez Democrat,* 13 October 1882.

45. Judge J. J. Chrisman quoted in Albert D. Kirwan, *Revolt of the Rednecks: Mississippi Politics, 1876–1925* (Lexington: University of Kentucky Press, 1951), 58 (emphasis in original). On the national Republican resurgence, see Richard E. Welch Jr., "The Federal Elections Bill of 1890: Postscripts and Prelude," *Journal of American History* 52 (December 1965): 511–26; Neil R. McMillen, *Dark Journey: Black Mississippians in the Age of Jim Crow* (Urbana: University of Illinois Press, 1989), 41, 53.

46. Quoted in McMillen, *Dark Journey,* 41.

47. Quoted in William Charles Sallis, "The Color Line in Mississippi Politics, 1865–1915" (Ph.D. diss., University of Kentucky, 1967), 332. On opposition to the suffrage restrictions, see *Natchez Democrat* in the *New York Times,* 11 September 1890; *Natchez Democrat* in the *Jackson Clarion-Ledger,* 19 September 1890; *Jackson Clarion-Ledger,* 3 October, 4 October 1890; William Alexander Mabry, "Disfranchisement of the Negro in Mississippi," *Journal of Southern History* 4 (August 1938): 325; Vernon Lane Wharton,

The Negro in Mississippi, 1865–1890 (Chapel Hill: University of North Carolina Press, 1947), 213–14; James P. Coleman, "The Mississippi Constitution of 1890 and the Final Decade of the Nineteenth Century," in *A History of Mississippi*, ed. Richard Aubrey McLemore (Jackson: University and College Press of Mississippi, 1973), 2:7–8. On election results, see Election Return for Delegates to the Constitutional Convention, 1890, box 453, Adams County Circuit Court Case Files, HNF. For registered voters in Natchez, see the Jefferson Hotel Precinct Poll Book, 1888–90 and Court House Precinct Poll Book, 1889–90, HNF. On Louisiana's 1898 suffrage restrictions, see Thorpe, *Federal and State Constitutions*, 3:1562–67. On Mississippi's disfranchisement provisions, see ibid., 4:2120–21. For more on southern disfranchisement, see Welch, "Federal Elections Bill of 1890"; J. Morgan Kousser, *The Shaping of Southern Politics: Suffrage Restriction and the Establishment of the One-Party South, 1880–1910* (New Haven, Conn.: Yale University Press, 1974); Michael Perman, *Struggle for Mastery: Disfranchisement in the South, 1888–1908* (Chapel Hill: University of North Carolina Press, 2001); R. Volney Riser, *Defying Disfranchisement: Black Voting Rights Activism in the Jim Crow South, 1890–1908* (Baton Rouge: Louisiana State University Press, 2010).

48. Adams County Poll Books, 1888–90, HNF; Historical Census Browser. See also McMillen, *Dark Journey*, table 2.2, for voting-age population in Adams County. For a more extended and detailed analysis of voter registration figures, see Justin J. Behrend, "Losing the Vote: Disfranchisement in Natchez, Mississippi, 1867–1910" (master's thesis, California State University, Northridge, 2000).

49. *Natchez Evening Bulletin*, 6 October 1899; *Natchez Democrat*, 23 September 1910; Perman, *Struggle for Mastery*, 327.

50. Adams, *Cyclopedia of African Methodism in Mississippi*. On Winston's home loan associations, see Louis J. Winston, *Mississippi Co-Operative and Benefit Association* (1891), MDAH; Nomelli, "Jim Crow, Louis J. Winston, and the Survival of Black Politicos," 50–53. On the Lynch brothers' loans, see, for example, Eleanor F. King to J. R. Lynch and W. H. Lynch, 5 January 1884, deed and trust, book YY, p. 580; Eleanor F. King to J. R. Lynch, 9 April 1885, deed, book ZZ, p. 372; John R. Lynch to John L. and Eleanor F. King, 26 December 1893, deed, book 3–K, p. 348, Adams County Land Deeds, ACCH. On the inward turn, especially among black male leaders, toward associational life, see Kevin Gaines, *Uplifting the Race: Black Politics and Culture in the United States since the Turn of the Century* (Chapel Hill: University of North Carolina Press, 1995); Michele Mitchell, *Righteous Propagation: African Americans and the Politics of Racial Destiny after Reconstruction* (Chapel Hill: University of North Carolina Press, 2004), 108–40. In the 1890s Lynch was the president of a Washington, D.C., bank and practiced law in a joint partnership with Robert H. Terrell.

51. *The Supreme Lodge, Knights of Honor vs. The Supreme Lodge, Knights of Honor of the World, and George F. Bowles*, Adams County Chancery Court, March term, 1898, file 1472, ACCH. On the similarities between black fraternal orders and black churches, see John M. Giggie, *After Redemption: Jim Crow and the Transformation of African American Religion in the Delta, 1875–1915* (New York: Oxford University Press, 2008), 59–95.

52. On the anthropological study, see Davis, Gardner, and Gardner, *Deep South*. On civil rights organizing, see Anne Moody, *Coming of Age in Mississippi* (New York: Doubleday, 1968); Jack E. Davis, *Race against Time: Culture and Separation in Natchez since 1930* (Baton Rouge: Louisiana State University Press, 2001). Natchez was considered a Klan stronghold in the 1950s and 1960s.

INDEX

Knights of Honor of the World (Supreme Lodge), 150, 254–55. *See also* Bowles, George F.; mutual aid societies
Ku Klux Klan, 112–13, 121, 137, 203

labor organization: colony, land, 78, 100–106; planter reprisals against, 90–92, 95, 100, 104, 107, 108–9, 111, 244–45, 249; protests, 34, 37, 39, 68–69, 71–74, 106, 245–46, 284n75; squad system, 70–72, 339n24
land: black colony in Adams County, 100–106; church property, 47–48, 52, 276n16, 276n22; claiming property of the disloyal, 47–48; desire for ownership, 89, 102, 109, 120, 184, 244; ownership, black, 16, 101, 139, 150, 153, 155, 157–59, 168, 189, 242, 275n12, 315n51, 337n15; ownership of plantations, 73–75, 243, 311n23, 338n17; plantations, abandoned, 35–36; plantations, claiming, 34–35; plantations, leasing, 74–75; politicians and, 75, 150, 153, 155, 157–59; redistribution of, 37–40, 73, 78, 90, 125, 139; school property, 68; villages of freedpeople, 73
Landers, William, 151, 319n8
Langston, John Mercer, 89
Lewis, Anthony, 19
Lewis, Ben, 26
Lincoln, Abraham, 15, 17, 33, 34; Emancipation Proclamation and, 65–66; portrait of, 59; rumors of, 20–25, 38–39, 266n23, 267n27; and Union League, 85
Lincoln Monument Fund, 55, 278n36
Litts, Palmer, 72
Louisiana: civil rights legislation, 131, 303n29; constitutional convention delegates, 122–23, 125; constitution of 1868, 124–26, 300n9; constitution of 1879, 246–47, constitution of 1898, 253
Lucas, Gideon, 19
Lumbar, Theodore, 136, 313n31
Lynch, James, 94
Lynch, John R., 6, 9; bonds, officeholder, 81, 156, 158, 311n17; candidate for office, 131, 148, 196, 238, 250–52, 335–36n6; on civil rights, 133–34, 303–4n33; club activity, 86; education of, 63; emancipation of, 28; on factionalism, 160–64, 169–72; friendship with politicians, 63, 97, 135, 153, 165–66, 304n39, 312n27; on fusionist politics, 248, 251; land ownership, 158–59, 254, 275n12, 311–12n23; as lawyer and bank president, 342n50a; lecture given by, 50; as officeholder, 128, 129, 133–34, 135, 139, 141, 146, 150, 151, 153, 164–65, 181, 250; on paramilitary violence, 209, 224, 225, 231, 239–40, 241, 252, 339n27, 341n41; partisan leader, 196, 201, 252; railroad promoter, 144; on taxation, 127
Lynch, William H.: bonds, officeholder, 156, 311n17; land ownership, 158–59, 254, 275n12, 311–12n23; officeholder, 127, 128–29, 151, 238, 313n31; partisan leader, 163, 171, 177, 186, 248, 313n33, 315n49, 316n57–58; plantation partnership, 75, 158; railroad promoter, 144

Mably, Keziah, 89–90
Madison Parish, La., 17, 259n9
Marshall, Frederick, 244
Marshall, Harry, 46, 158, 275n12, 311n23
Martin, William T.: attorney for David Singleton, 79–80; militia organizing, 38–39, 219; patron-client, 183; political activity, 108, 119, 170, 195, 238; railroad promoter, 141–44, 181; relationship to John R. Lynch, 63, 135, 304n39; slaveowner, 286n4
Maynard, Bob, 21–22, 266n24
McCary, Catherine A., 54, 60, 65, 82, 280n47
McCary, Robert, 51, 54, 81
McCary, Robert, Jr., 54
McCary, William, 54, 144, 312n8, 313n31; bonds, officeholder, 153, 155–58, 287n7, 310–11n17, 321n32; as partisan leader, 161, 163, 171, 177, 186, 313n33, 315n49; as postmaster, 250; as sheriff, 151, 167, 238
McClure, Henry B., 119, 166

Singleton, David, 9; background of, 17, 80, 264n14, 286n5; as bondsman, 81, 86, 153, 156, 287n7, 311n17; cause of the war, 18; landownership, 75, 158–59; loyal to master class, 79–81, 286n4, 287n6; plantation partnerships, 158–59; as special constable, 136

Sixth Regiment, United States Colored Heavy Artillery, 63, 87. *See also* Union army

slaves: churches, 46–47, 58; communication networks, 15–20, 21–22, 24, 27, 40, 263n8; emancipation, 14, 22, 26, 57; executions of, 21, 24–25, 267n32; family and kin networks, 19; hiring out, 15, 18, 51; impressment, 18; insurrections and rebellion, 20–23; Natchez District, in the, 5; neighborhoods, 14; political consciousness of, 14, 26, 37–40; purchasing freedom, 16, 17; runaways, 1, 13, 22, 24, 25, 26–27, 30, 34, 61; trust, problems of, 16, 18, 25;

Smith, Bill, 200

Smith, Deborah, 19, 103

Smith, Duncan C., 229

Smith, Ellen, 210, 328n9

Smith, H. A., 49

Smith, Harry, Jr., 174–5, 196, 198, 248

Smith, Haskin, 151, 210, 213, 328n9

Smith, John (livery stable owner), 19, 24, 103, 311n17

Smith, John (shingle maker), 186, 320n25

Smith, John, J., 217, 338n17

Smith, William, 210

Smoot, William, 16–17, 311n17

Smothers, Joseph, 151

Southern Claims Commission (scc), 263n7, 269n43, 287n5; network of Natchez draymen, 15–16, 263n8; slave conspiracy, testimony on, 23–24

spaces: churches, 46, 56–59; emancipation and, 27–28; equality and, 131–33; hinterlands during the war, 34–37; parades, 50, 88–90, 186, 223–24; partisan clubs, 176–77, 186; polling places, 194–95, 198–200; public meetings, 85–87, 91, 111, 147, 171, 179,

192; rural and urban, intersection of, 6, 111, 223; segregated, 255; violence and constriction of political space, 208, 216–18, 220, 229–30, 234, 247. *See also* churches; democracy; parades; Republican Party

Sprott, W. D., 213, 241

squads. *See under* labor organization

Stamps, Richard, 17, 19, 29

Steele, Hiram R., 128, 300n7, 310n15, 315n51, 339n25

Stewart, George (black leader in Jefferson County), 142, 307n59

Stewart, George (white teacher in Adams County), 114, 299n91

Stewart, J. Ross, 151

Stewart, Oren, 137, 152

Stiles, E. H., 214, 300n6, 301n13, 328n9, 337n15

St. Joseph, La., 115, 227, 315n51, 329n28. *See also* Tensas Parish, La.

Stratton, Joseph B., 65

Stringer, Thomas W., 53

Stryker, Hattie E., 62

Summit Station, Mississippi, 52

Sumner, Charles, 102, 104–5, 166–67, 296n66, 315n47

Surget, Francis, 16, 264n11, 267n33

Sweet-Home church, 52. *See also* churches

taxation, 55; burden of, 189; progressive system of, 89, 124–25, 127–28, 157–58, 302n17; railroad, 142–43; regressive system of, 108; schools and, 67, 69, 120, 127–28, 282n65. *See also* Republican Party: radical policies

teachers. *See under* freedmen; freedwomen

Tensas Parish, La.: black churches in, 58; cholera in, 90, 95; election results in, 106–7, 247–48, 299n93, 340n30; exodus from, 244–48; factionalism in, 168–69; floods in, 90; labor during the war, 36–37; murders, politically motivated, 115; party convention in, 178; plantations, leasing in, 74–75; poverty in, 69, 72, 95; as Republican stronghold, 225; schools

Tensas Parish, La. (*continued*)
in, 69, 126, 128; slave insurrection
scare in, 20–21; white liner violence
and intimidation in, 225–30, 232. *See
also* Natchez District; St. Joseph, La.;
Waterproof, La.
terrorism: slave insurrection scare and,
23–24; in the South, 134, 172–73, 203;
strategy to undermine democracy,
8, 9; white line, in the Natchez
District, 207–10, 211, 213–15, 217–30,
231–34, 239, 241–45, 336n8. *See also*
Democratic Party; paramilitary
violence
Thomas, Anderson, 136, 305n42
Thomas, Lorenzo, 71, 93–94
Thomas, Samuel, 36–37, 48, 73, 293n55
Thompson, Hannah, 51, 277n23
Thompson, Lewis, 19, 298n88
Thornton, Ben, 73
Tillman, Cassius, 139
Tims, J. T., 21, 25, 266n24, 267n27
Tolliver, Anderson, 151, 199
Trask, E. G., 47, 49
Truly, R. H., 231–32, 242
Turner, Thomas, 16–17, 103
Tuttle, J. M., 33, 271n57
Tyler, Page, 51

Union: allegiance to, 28–29, 59; cause of
Civil War, 17–19, 24
Union army, 16; black soldiers, 28–29,
33, 36, 83–84, 269n45, 288n14; deaths
in Natchez District, 41; emancipation
and, 19, 25, 27; expectation of arrival,
23, 25; health order in Natchez, 31–32;
military bounties, 87, 94, 101, 104–5;
troops in the Natchez District, 26, 29,
32, 115, 211, 241
Union League: attacks on members, 114;
constitutional convention, leaders
as delegates to, 95–98; contrast with
other clubs and fraternal orders,
110, 183, 255; criticism of, 95–97, 110;
fear of reprisal, 77, 113; KKK, fights
against, 112; labor protest, influence
of, 91; meetings of, 56, 84–87, 103, 109,
111; parade, involvement in, 88–89;

political clubs as inheritors of, 176;
political education, role in, 84–88;
rural areas, lesser presence in, 123. *See
also* freedmen; Republican Party
U.S. Congress: disfranchisement,
response to, 252–53; investigations by,
33, 188–89, 251; military bounties, 101,
104; petitions to, 140; Reconstruction
policies, 37, 84, 93, 115, 122, 124;
speeches before, 133–34, 209; testimony
before, 174–75, 188, 209–10, 234. *See
also* Reconstruction Acts, Military
(1867); Republican Party

Van Eaton, Henry S., 99
Vicksburg, Miss., 13, 27, 38, 210–12;
convention on the Kansas migration,
246
Vidalia Herald, 162
Vidalia, La., 1; AME church in, 52; Baptist
church in, 159; black regiments in, 28,
36; political meetings in, 178–80, 185,
189–90; railroad projects in, 140, 144,
307n63; schools in, 61–62; Union army
occupation of, 262n2; voter registration
in, 88; voting in, 199–200. *See also*
Concordia Parish, La.
vigilance committee, 22–24, 38–39
voter registration, 87–89, 92–94, 249. *See
also* voting
voting: act of at polling places, 194–200;
choices that voters faced, 77, 109,
196–98; Reconstruction, to continue,
115–16; suffrage laws, 123–24; white
liner violence, context of, 214–15,
230–34, 251. *See also* democracy;
Democratic Party: disfranchisement,
voter fraud; Republican Party; voter
registration

Walker, Robert J., 151, 247, 332n60
Wall Street Baptist Church, 46–49, 57, 58,
61, 64, 65. *See also* churches
Walton, Handy, 152
Warfield, Elisha, 232
Washington, George, 144, 151
Washington, George R., 151
Washington, John, 87

CPSIA information can be obtained
at www.ICGtesting.com
Printed in the USA
LVOW11s1501310317
529198LV00001B/48/P